THE DEVELOPMENT
OF ARITHMETIC
CONCEPTS AND SKILLS:

CONSTRUCTING ADAPTIVE EXPERTISE

STUDIES IN MATHEMATICAL THINKING AND LEARNING

Alan H. Schoenfeld, Series Editor

THE DEVELOPMENT OF ARITHMETIC CONCEPTS AND SKILLS:

CONSTRUCTING ADAPTIVE EXPERTISE

Edited by

Arthur J. Baroody

University of Illinois
at Urbana-Champaign

Ann Dowker

Oxford University

2003

LAWRENCE ERLBAUM ASSOCIATES, PUBLISHERS
Mahwah, New Jersey   London

Lawrence Erlbaum Associates, Inc., Publishers
10 Industrial Avenue
Mahwah, NJ 07430

Cover design by Kathryn Houghtaling Lacey

Library of Congress Cataloging-in-Publication Data

The development of arithmetic concepts and skills: constructing adaptive expertise / edited by Arthur J. Baroody and Ann Dowker.
     p. cm. – (Studies in mathematical thinking and learning)
   Includes bibliographical references and index.
ISBN 0-8058-3155-X (cl : alk.paper)
ISBN 0-8058-3156-8 (pbk : alk. paper)
    1. Arithmetic–Study and teaching (Elementary)
I. Baroody, Arthur J., 1947-   II. Dowker, Ann.   III. Series.

   QA135.6.D49 2002
   372.7'2044—dc21

                        2002033866

Printed in the United States of America
10   9   8   7   6   5   4   3   2   1

Dedication

We dedicate this book to Herbert P. Ginsburg and Neil O'Connor, two exceptional mentors.

Contents

Foreword

Many educational researchers are interested in how students can be taught subjects so that they develop *adaptive expertise*—the ability to apply meaningfully learned procedures flexibly and creatively. From this perspective, school instruction is successful when students are able to use what they have learned to invent effective procedures for solving *new* problems. Simply being able to complete school exercises quickly and accurately without understanding—what we call *routine expertise*—is not particularly valuable. This is because such competence is extremely limited in that it can be applied effectively only to familiar tasks. Unfortunately, little is known about the process of cultivating adaptive expertise.

Researchers who have studied transfer have almost unanimously concluded that, when solving real-world problems, students seldom aptly apply school-taught procedures that were learned in a short period of time. Similarly, people who have had years of experience solving problems in a given domain may be unable to solve problems outside their experience. Such "experts" can solve familiar types of "problems" quickly and accurately but may not understand why their procedures work. As a result, when these experts are faced with a changed condition or a new problem, they are unable to modify known procedures or invent new ones. This is particularly true for experts in knowledge-lean domains, such as abacus operation, which I studied in detail in the early 1970s. However, even in knowledge-rich domains, some experts' knowledge may consist of narrow, unconnected problem-solving schemas. As a result, these experts may simply classify problems and apply the single-routine solution associated with a particular problem type.

The notion of adaptive experts, which I introduced in Hatano (1982), was a theoretical ideal rather than a model derived from a series of empirical studies. I began by considering the following two questions: What kind of knowledge do flexible and inventive experts construct? And how do they construct it? In other words, I speculated about both the product of adaptive expertise and its acquisition process. Regarding the former, my attention focused on the conceptual knowledge underlying procedures. "Flexibility and adaptability seem to be possible only when there is some corresponding conceptual knowledge to give meaning to each step of the skill and provide criteria for selection among alternatives possibilities for each step within the procedures" (p. 15). I assumed (and still assume) that conceptual knowledge enables experts to construct mental models of the major entities in a content domain, models that can be used in mental simulations. I was very pleased to see that, in their formulation of adaptive expertise in the Preface and chapter 1, the book's editors emphasize the importance of connections among pieces of knowledge, especially between procedural and conceptual knowledge.

I also want to emphasize differences in the learning process between routine expertise and adaptive expertise. Those who are becoming routine experts (i.e., are acquiring knowledge in a conceptual vacuum) often fixate on a single procedure, whether or not it makes sense, and care little about comprehending it. In contrast, those who are constructing adaptive expertise (acquiring meaningful knowledge) often explore a variety of possibilities and try to make sense of their actions. Only the latter acquire the knowledge that can provide the direction and constraints needed to solve novel problems.

I hypothesized that if people ask why a skill works or why each step is needed during its application, such questions can lead them to develop some conceptual knowledge related to that procedure. This is similar to what Donald Schoen (1983) called "reflection-in-action," which characterizes professionals and distinguishes them from technicians. What is common between Schoen's and my formulations is that experts are seldom taught conceptual knowledge in the verbalized form. Instead, they may construct it in the process of solving problems or performing tasks in the domain.

In subsequent work, Kayoko Inagaki and I tried to specify motivational conditions for adaptive expertise—that is, how to nurture this type of expertise. In one such attempt (Hatano & Inagaki, 1992), we proposed the following four conditions for promoting adaptive expertise: (a) encountering novel problems continuously, (b) engaging in interactive dialogue, (c) being freed from urgent external need, and (d) being surrounded by a group that values understanding.

In retrospect, such attempts were too individualistic and needed to be placed in sociocultural contexts. We should have paid greater attention to the nature of the socioculturally organized practice in which participants are learning. For example, when the educational environment is oriented toward solving a fixed class of problems skillfully, participants tend to become experts defined in terms of speed and accuracy (i.e., routine experts). In contrast, when the educational environment requires meeting varied and changing demands, they acquire flexible and adaptive skills (adaptive expertise).

The most critical limitation of the formulation above was that the notion of adaptive expertise was never applied to a variety of subject matter contents. My coauthor and I focused on a single nonacademic example of cooking. This book is an important contribution because its contributors extend our analysis across a range of arithmetic topics, age levels, and contexts. These chapters illustrate that flexibility and inventiveness in mathematics are closely linked to a rich understanding of a topic—to a rich web of connections within a topic (particularly those between procedures and concepts) and to other domains of knowledge. Many of the chapters have clear implications about how to foster adaptive expertise, and several include specific instructional guidelines. I am honored that authors have found the notion of adaptive expertise useful.

—*Giyoo Hatano*
Keio University

References

Hatano, G. (1982). Cognitive consequences of practice in culture specific procedural skills. *The Quarterly Newsletter of the Laboratory of Comparative Human Cognition, 4*, 15–18.

Hatano, G., & Inagaki, K. (1992). Desituating cognition through the construction of conceptual knowledge. In P. Light & G. Butterworth (Eds.), *Context and cognition* (pp. 115–133). Hemel Hempstead, England: Harvester Wheatsheaf.

Schoen, D. (1983). *The reflective practitioner.* New York: Basic Books.

Preface

Educators and other scholars have long debated, often heatedly, how formal instruction can best promote intellectual expertise (see, e.g., Wilson, 2003). From ancient times to the present, the conventional wisdom has been that the best way to promote school-taught arithmetic (and other content) is through direct instruction and drill. For instance, whether the basic "number facts" were presented on a clay tablet (as in Babylonian times and illustrated here) or as a printed table of facts (as is the modern custom), the goal of traditional instruction has been the same—memorize them by rote. Throughout history, critics of traditional schooling have proposed reforms only to be greeted by resistance or even vilification. For instance, in his comedy *The Clouds*, Aristophanes described a debate between a proponent for the "Old Education" (traditional schooling) and a reformer who supports the "New Education" (Socrates' "Think Academy"). The less than objective criticism leveled at the latter is that it would "subvert manly self-control, turn young people into sex-obsessed rebels, and destroy the city" (Nussbaum, 1997, p. 1).

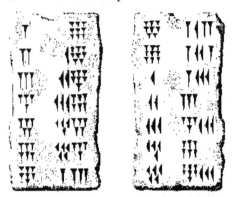

A nine-times table circa 1,800 B.C. (Jacobs, 1982)

More recently, some proponents of reform (e.g., National Council of Teachers of Mathematics, 2000) have recommended, for instance, that teachers encourage children to discover relations and to invent procedures. Critics of this view question why this is important when teachers can simply have students memorize standard and efficient procedures by rote. For example, the columnist Thomas Sowell (a senior fellow at the Hoover Institute, Stanford University) noted, "Only people ignorant of history and too shallow to understand what an enormous task it is to create anything could believe that children can reach any serious understanding of even basic concepts by the faddish methods of 'discovery' and 'creativity' being used in public school classrooms. . . . Most of us will never discover or create anything significant that was not understood" (2000, p. A6).

What is the validity of each of these views? The focus of this book is two related questions that lie at the heart of the current debate about reforming mathematics education: What is the nature of arithmetic expertise? How can instruction best promote it? We have brought together scholars from a variety of specialties, including (cognitive, developmental, educational, and neurological) psychology and (mathematics and special) education to offer theoretical perspectives and much needed empirical evidence about these issues. Both indicate the nature of arithmetic expertise and how to best promote it are far more complex than conventional wisdom and many scholars—both past and present—have suggested.

In the introductory chapter (chapter 1), Baroody traces the history of the debate in the United States about whether computational skills should be memorized by rote or learned in a meaningful manner. He draws three conclusions. The first, in effect, is that children's powerful informal knowledge is typified by what Hatano (1988) called "adaptive expertise" (meaningful procedures that can be flexibly applied to new, as well as familiar, tasks) rather than routine expertise (rotely learned knowledge that can be applied to familiar tasks only). (Adaptive expertise is similar to what Kilpatrick, Swafford, and Findell, 2001, called "computational fluency," which is the ability to use procedures appropriately, efficiently, and flexibly.) The second is that adaptive expertise depends on conceptual understanding (well-connected knowledge) and its integration with procedural knowledge. The third entails providing an explicit definition of what is meant by a *conceptual basis* for a procedural advance, something not done in previous discussions of the relations between conceptual and procedural knowledge (cf. Baroody & Ginsburg, 1986; Carpenter, 1986; Rittle-Johnson & Siegler, 1998).

In chapter 2, Cowan summarizes an analogous historical debate in the United Kingdom between educators who advocate a focus on computational competence and those who advocate a focus on understanding and thinking. (It is worth noting that there are wide cultural and historical variations in the relative emphasis of adaptive expertise and routine expertise. For example, unlike the United States and some other European countries such as France and Italy, the United Kingdom has emphasized cultivating adaptive expertise since the 1960s.) Cowan reviews the research literature in three areas critical to early childhood mathematics instruction: the mastery of single-digit (basic) addition combinations, the development of mental-calculation strategies, and the construction of arithmetic generalizations (principles). As he notes, expertise in all three areas is characterized by flexibility.

In chapter 3, Baroody and Tiilikainen use the conclusions drawn in the introductory chapter to explain why constructivists are not satisfied with more deterministic (associative-learning or information-processing) models of strategy development. The latter do not adequately consider the construction of conceptual knowledge or its integration with procedural knowledge. Baroody and Tiilikainen note, for example, that even preschoolers have conceptual understanding of arithmetic, understanding that permits them to invent their own procedures and adapt them when necessary—albeit not always successfully. They further conclude that the stark contrast between preschoolers' mathematical competence and schoolchildren's mathematical incompetence (found in the United States) is not a paradox when analyzed in terms of Hatano's (1988) constructs of adaptive and routine expertise.

In chapter 4, Baroody, Wilkins, and Tiilikainen summarize an influential model of how arithmetic thinking develops, namely Resnick's (1992) view that this development can be characterized by increasingly general or abstract and, hence, flexible thinking. They then review how the existing research on the development of a key arithmetic concept (namely, additive commutativity, which can be symbolically represented as $a + b = b + a$) is consistent or inconsistent with this model. Baroody et al. conclude by speculating on how knowledge of addition and commutativity progresses from weak schemas (relatively incomplete, context-bound, and unconnected representations) to strong schemas (relatively complete, abstract, and well-connected generalizations)—a development that embodies the construction of adaptive expertise and the acquisition of greater flexibility.

In chapter 5, Seo and Ginsburg describe a long-term case study of a class that explored a key arithmetic symbol, the equals sign. The children's initial interpretation of this symbol was limited and inflexible. Seo and Ginsburg chronicle how context enables and constrains children's understanding of the equal sign. They document the persistence of children's initial understanding of this symbol and how textbooks and teaching practices can reinforce a limited and inflexible view of it. Seo and Ginsburg also describe how teachers can use meaningful and inquiry-based instruction, including cognitive conflict and peer–peer dialogue, to prompt the construction of a broader and more flexible understanding of the equals sign, the adaptive expertise essential for correctly understanding, for instance, algebraic equations later. A key observation they make—one echoed in the chapters by Miura and Okamoto (chapter 8) and Fuson and Burghardt (chapter 10)—is that a crucial role for teachers is helping children to make connections. Seo and Ginsburg also make the important observation that typical testing procedures are well suited for measuring routine expertise but not adaptive expertise. To gauge the latter, more flexible assessment methods, such as the clinical interview, are needed.

In chapter 6, Butterworth, Marschesini, and Girelli present evidence that fostering the mastery of basic multiplication combinations, a key goal of early childhood mathematics instruction, is not simply a matter of providing sufficient practice. Their data indicate that internalizing relational knowledge, namely the commutative property of multiplication, can be an important component in achieving such mastery and may even affect how the basic multiplication combinations are represented in long-term memory. In other words, Butterworth et al.'s results are inconsistent with the traditional view that mastering the basic number combinations is merely a matter of developing routine expertise and are consistent with the view that learning even this basic arithmetic knowledge is a matter of fostering adaptive expertise.

In chapter 7, LeFevre, Smith-Chant, Hiscock, Daley, and Morris summarize additional evidence contradicting the traditional view that mastery of the basic multiplication combinations entails a single process, namely fact retrieval. Their results indicate that even adults flexibly use a variety of strategies to efficiently generate the 100 basic products. A key implication drawn from their results is that researchers need to be more flexible and creative in measuring even knowledge as basic as mastery of the single-digit number combinations.

In chapter 8, Miura and Okamoto discuss how a key sociocultural factor, namely, language, can influence the construction of mathematical understanding and its application. More specifically, because Asian counting-word sequences are highly regular and clearly reflect the grouping-by-ten nature of multidigit numbers and the English counting-word sequence is less so, Asian children can rely more heavily on inducing counting patterns and rules than can English-speaking children. This may give the former an edge in noticing the underlying grouping-by-ten structure of the counting and written number sequence and in constructing thinking (reasoning) strategies for basic addition combinations with sums of more than 10 and their corresponding subtraction combinations. This latter advantage may, in turn, given Asian children an advantage in mental multidigit arithmetic. Put differently, learning to count in an Asian language provides a better basis for acquiring adaptive expertise with numbers that can then be applied to multidigit-number tasks. Miura and Okamoto also discuss how fraction terminology and linguistic conventions can help or hinder mathematical understanding and performance.

In chapter 9, Dowker reviews the evidence on the early development of single- and multidigit computational estimation. She notes that children can use their understanding of numbers and operations on numbers to produce reasonable estimates to arithmetic problems for which they cannot yet calculate an answer. Dowker emphasizes the following point that has often been overlooked by scholars of arithmetic cognition: Children's ability to estimate effectively increases with computational experience and the resulting growth in *general* arithmetic knowledge. She notes further that a child's estimation competence drops off gradually as increasingly larger and less familiar numbers are involved. In other words, when children can draw on their number sense (a rich network of concepts and facts), they flexibly choose appropriate estimation strategies. When they cannot, children resort to using inflexible and ineffective strategies.

In chapters 10 and 11, Fuson and Burghardt and Ambrose, Baek, and Carpenter adduce evidence that suggests critics of mathematics reform who claim most people cannot discover or invent anything significant (such as the columnist Thomas Sowell quoted earlier) underestimate children's mathematical ability. The authors of these chapters detail a variety of children's invented procedures for operating on multidigit written numbers, some of which are as, or more, efficient than the standard algorithms taught in school. They note that discovery and invention can be powerful tools in helping children to achieve genuine mathematical proficiency (cf. Kilpatrick et al., 2001). Specifically, these processes can promote further meaningful learning or *conceptual under-standing*, which can provide a basis of additional adaptive expertise and *com-putational fluency*. Discovery and invention involves children in mathematical inquiry (e.g., provides practice in conjecturing, logical reasoning, and problem solving) and, thus, can foster *strategic mathematical thinking*. Discovering or inventing knowledge for one's self is more likely to promote confidence and *a positive disposition toward learning and using mathematics* than does being spoon-fed mathematical facts and prescriptions. These benefits are reaped even if students "merely" rediscover concepts or reinvent a standard procedure.

Furthermore, Fuson and Burghardt note that conceptual understanding is es-sential for inventing effective strategies and rejecting ineffective ones. In a similar vein, Ambrose et al. describe how not applying conceptual knowledge can limit children's invention of arithmetic strategies and how applying such knowledge can lead them to devise flexible and creative procedures.

The last four chapters touch on the arithmetic learning and knowledge of special populations and what research in this area tells us about the topic in general. In chapter 12, Donlan reviews the evidence regarding the arithmetic development of children with specific language impairments. Consistent with Miura and Okamoto's chapter, he concludes that such impairments can lead to an impoverished mental representation of number and limit the construction of informal arithmetic procedures. However, these deficiencies are neither inevi-table nor total. Indeed, certain aspects of mathematics are surprisingly unim-paired in this population. In brief, the construction of arithmetical adaptive expertise can be facilitated by language in *some* critical ways.

In chapter 13, Jordan, Hanich, and Uberti review research on children with mathematics disabilities in three areas: mastery of basic number combinations, ability to solve word problems, and skill at multidigit calculation. Learning difficulties with these three areas can often be traced back to the failure of schools to promote adaptive expertise. A particularly interesting aspect of this chapter is their review of Huttenlocher and colleagues' research on nonverbal addition and subtraction among preschoolers, competencies that may underlie children's adaptive expertise with informal counting-basic arithmetic solution methods.

In chapter 14, Delazer makes the important point that neuropsychological research has not paid sufficient attention to the role of conceptual knowledge. Her summary and analysis of two influential models in the field and her re-view and analysis of the interesting evidence on the mental-arithmetic per-formance of brain-injured adults reinforce this point. Delazer's review indicates that there is a neuropsychological basis for distinguishing between routine and adaptive expertise.

In chapter 15, Heavey reviews the fascinating evidence regarding arith-metical savants and arrives at the surprising conclusion that their arithmetic proficiencies are not the product of skills learned by rote but the result of a rich (extensive and well-connected) number sense. She also makes the interesting ob-servation that the calculational prowess of arithmetical savants does not exceed those of skilled nonsavant mental calculators and that the skill of both groups is shaped by an early interest in numbers, counting, and mathematical analysis. Like people in general, arithmetic savants use a variety of strategies, many of which are self-invented.

The results of psychological, educational, and clinical studies using a wide variety of arithmetic tasks and populations (including "normally" and atypically developing children, noninjured and brain-injured adults, and savants), then, all point to the conclusion that a key basis for the flexible and creative use of arithmetic procedures (adaptive expertise or computational fluency) is conceptual understanding, knowledge that connects a procedure to a rationale, everyday experiences, analogies, and other skills and concepts. Bisanz and Geary, cognitive psychologists whose work relies more heavily on information-processing theory than constructivism, provide further comment and perspective on chapters 1 to 8 and 9 to 15, respectively. In doing so, they raise additional issues and questions for future research.

This book should be of interest to those who are curious about the nature of arithmetic expertise and those who are interested in promoting it effectively, including:

- researchers whose focus is mathematical cognition or development such as developmental or educational psychologists and neuropsychologists.
- researchers whose focus is mathematics instruction such as mathematics or special educators.
- practitioners, administrators or others interested in improving arithmetic instruction such as teachers, curriculum supervisors, principals, other school administrators, and officials in national and local government education departments.
- graduate students who are preparing for a career in research (in any of the fields noted earlier), teaching, or administration.

—*Arthur J. Baroody*
University of Illinois at Urbana–Champaign

Ann Dowker
Oxford University

References

Baroody, A. J., & Ginsburg, H. P. (1986). The relationship between initial meaningful and mechanical knowledge of arithmetic. In J. Hiebert (Ed.), *Conceptual and procedural knowledge: The case of mathematics* (pp. 75–112). Hillsdale, NJ: Lawrence Erlbaum Associates.

Carpenter, T. P. (1986). Conceptual knowledge as a foundation for procedural knowledge: Implications from research on the initial learning of arithmetic. In J. Hiebert (Ed.), *Conceptual procedural knowledge: The case of mathematics* (pp. 113–132). Hillsdale, NJ: Lawrence Erlbaum Associates.

Hatano, G. (1988). Social and motivational bases for mathematical understanding. In G. B. Saxe & M. Gearhart (Eds.), *Children's mathematics* (pp. 55–70). San Francisco: Jossey-Bass.

Jacobs, H. R. (1982). *Mathematics: A human endeavor* (2nd ed.). San Francisco: Freeman.

Kilpatrick, J., Swafford, J., & Findell, B. (Eds.). (2001). *Adding it up: Helping children learn mathematics.* Washington, DC: National Academy Press.

National Council of Teachers of Mathematics. (2000). *Principles and standards for school mathematics.* Reston, VA: Author.

Nussbaum, M. C. (1997). *Cultivating humanity: A classical defense of reform in liberal education.* Cambridge, MA: Harvard University Press.

Resnick, L. B. (1992). From protoquantities to operators: Building mathematical competence on a foundation on everyday knowledge. In G. Leinhardt, R. Putnam, & R. A. Hattrup (Eds.), *Analysis of arithmetic for mathematics teaching* (pp. 373–425). Hillsdale. NJ: Lawrence Erlbaum Associates.

Rittle-Johnson, B., & Siegler, R. S. (1998). The relation between conceptual and procedural knowledge in learning mathematics: A review of the literature. In C. Donlan (Ed.), *The development of mathematical skills* (pp. 75–110). Hove, East Sussex, England: Psychology Press.

Sowell, T. (January 11, 2000). "Why insist on reinventing wheel?" *The News-Gazette,* p. A6. Champaign–Urbana.

Wilson, S. M. (2003). *California dreaming: Reforming mathematics education.* New Haven: Yale University Press.

CHAPTER 1

THE DEVELOPMENT OF ADAPTIVE EXPERTISE AND FLEXIBILITY: THE INTEGRATION OF CONCEPTUAL AND PROCEDURAL KNOWLEDGE

Arthur J. Baroody
University of Illinois at Urbana–Champaign

In *Hard Times* (Ford & Monod, 1966), Charles Dickens described a teacher by the name of Mr. M'Choakumchild in order to satirize teachers trained to focus on memorizing facts by rote at the expense of all else:

> He . . . had taken the bloom off . . . of mathematics. . . . He went to work . . . looking at all the vessels ranged before him. . . . When from thy boiling store [of facts] thou shalt fill each [vessel] brimful by-and-by, . . . thou . . . kill outright . . . Fancy [imagination, curiosity, creativity] lurking within—or sometimes only maim [it]. (p. 6)

Those interested in improving mathematics instruction have long been concerned about the ineffective, if not harmful, way traditional instruction promotes arithmetic expertise (e.g., Brownell, 1935; Davis, 1984; Erlwanger, 1975; Holt, 1964; Kilpatrick, 1985; Wertheimer, 1945/1959). Consider, for example, two vignettes with dramatically different outcomes.

> **Vignette 1: A Case of Inflexible Mechanical Learning.** Wertheimer (1945/1959) told of a visit he took to a classroom that had just learned how to determine the area of a parallelogram. The students had been taught to measure the length of a parallelogram's base and height and multiply these two values (see Fig. A). After watching them successfully complete several "problems," Wertheimer sought permission from the teacher to ask the class a question. Proud of his students, the teacher readily agreed. Wertheimer stepped to the board, drew a picture similar to the one in Fig. B and asked what its area was. Some students were "obviously taken aback. One pupil [noted]: 'Teacher, we haven't had that yet'" (p. 15). Other students tried to apply the procedure they had been taught but quickly became bewildered. In brief, confronted with a somewhat novel task, the students did not see how their school-taught procedure applied, leaving them utterly helpless.

Figure A:
The school-taught procedure

Figure B:
Wertheimer's variation of the practiced task

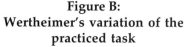
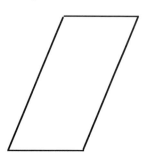

Measured base (*b*): 8 units
Measured height (*h*): 4 units

$A = b \times h = 8 \times 4 = 32$

Vignette 2: A Case of Flexibly Applied Learning. Arianne, a fourth grader, was attempting to divide 901 by 2 in order to solve a problem. Her initial effort (shown in Fig. C) resulted in an answer of 45 with a remainder of 1. Her teacher noticed that she spontaneously revised her answer (shown in Fig. D). Asked why she had changed her answer, Arianne explained that she had checked it. This process was described cryptically in a journal entry the girl recorded later: *I had   answewer of 45R1. I added it together and didn't get 901. So I added a zero and got 900 and added the 1.*

Figure C:
Arianne's Initial Effort

```
     45 R 1
  2 ⟌ 901
     -8
     ‾‾‾
      10
     -10
     ‾‾‾
       1
```

Figure D:
Arianne's Revision

```
     450 R 1
  2 ⟌ 901
     -8
     ‾‾‾
      10
     -10
     ‾‾‾
       1
```

Several months earlier Arianne's class had learned that subtraction could be checked by adding the answer (difference) to the subtracted amount (the subtrahend). If the resulting sum was the same number as the starting amount (minuend), then the answer was presumably correct. The teacher had used small numbers to illustrate the rationale for the procedure (e.g., subtracting 2 from 5 can be undone by adding 2) before demonstrating this checking procedure with multidigit examples like that shown as follows:

$$
\left.
\begin{array}{lrr}
\text{Minuend} & \to & 74 \\
\text{Subtrahend} & \to & \underline{-39} \\
\text{Difference} & \to & 35 \\
& & \underline{+39} \\
& & 74
\end{array}
\right\}
$$

Sum of the difference and the subtrahend matches the minuend

Without further instruction, Arianne applied the principle for checking subtraction to the task of checking her division. Instead of using the inverse operation of multiplication (2 x 45 = 90), she checked her answer informally by using its mathematical equivalent, namely repeated addition of a like term. (Adding 45 + 45 is what she meant by "I added it together and didn't get 901.") After recognizing that 45 could not be the correct solution and adding a 0 to make her answer 450, the girl proceeded to check her new answer in the following manner:

(Note that adding the two 450s undoes the division by 2 and adding on 1 takes into account the remainder of 1.)

$$
\begin{array}{r}
450 \\
\underline{450} \\
900 \\
\underline{1} \\
901
\end{array}
$$

To check whether Arianne really understood the checking procedure for division she had invented, her teacher inquired, "What if we had divided by three?"

Arianne promptly indicated that she would have to add her answer three times.

"Or multiply by three," interjected Alison who had been listening intently to the dialogue.

Note that because these students *understood* the rationale for checking subtraction, they recognized that, in principle, it could be applied to the related, but different, task of checking a division outcome. Moreover, their understanding allowed them the flexibility to adapt their learned procedure so that it could be used in this new context.

Vignette 1 illustrates what Giyoo Hatano (1988) called *"routine expertise,"* knowledge memorized by rote, knowledge that can be used effectively with familiar tasks but not with novel ones, even those that differ only slightly from familiar ones. Vignette 2 illustrates what he called *"adaptive expertise,"* meaningful knowledge that can be applied to unfamiliar tasks as well as familiar ones. In contrast to rote knowledge, which is learned and stored in isolation, meaningful knowledge is learned and stored in relation to other knowledge. That is, it is grasped and represented in connection with other knowledge (Ginsburg, 1977; Hiebert & Carpenter, 1992). If meaningful knowledge is the basis of adaptive expertise (the flexible application of knowledge) and can be characterized as well-connected knowledge (e.g., Ginsburg, 1977;

Hiebert & Carpenter, 1992; Hiebert & Lefevre, 1986), then the construction of well-connected knowledge should be the basis for fostering adaptive expertise or flexibility, as measured by transfer (e.g., understanding new subject matter or inventing a strategy or procedure to solve a novel problem). Analogously, the acquisition of unconnected knowledge should be the basis for promoting routine expertise or inflexibility.

This chapter begins with a historical sketch of the debate about the developmental relations between conceptual and procedural knowledge. Tentative theoretical conclusions about these relations are then outlined. Finally, key implications of these conclusions for current reform efforts are discussed. The aim of this chapter is to provide a general framework for understanding the significance of the chapters that follow and for further explorations of the development of arithmetic concepts, procedures, and adaptive expertise.

Historical Perspective

Researchers interested in the teaching and learning of arithmetic have long distinguished between knowledge memorized by rote and knowledge acquired meaningfully. The former has been equated with computational skill or procedural knowledge; the latter, with understanding or conceptual knowledge. In this section, the early and then the more recent view of this dichotomy are examined.

EARLY VIEWS:
SKILL VERSUS UNDERSTANDING

Resnick and Ford (1981) pointed out that "the relationship between computational skill and conceptual understanding is one of the oldest concerns in the" field of mathematical psychology (p. 246) and that, in the past, the focus was on which was better. In 1935, William A. Brownell outlined three views of arithmetic learning, each of which reflected different assumptions about the importance of computational skill and understanding. After briefly describing these views, we summarize the early skills versus concepts debate.

Three Theories of Arithmetic Learning

In the early 20th century, the following three theories of arithmetic teaching and learning were prominent in the United States: drill, meaning, and incidental-learning theory (Brownell, 1935; cf. Cowan, chap. 2, this volume).

Drill Theory. According to drill theory (Model A in Fig. 1.1), a product of associative theories of learning, instruction should focus on ensuring the (rote) memorization of computational skills (see Cowan, chap. 2, this volume, for a detailed discussion). The basic assumptions of this theory were (a) children must learn to imitate the skills and knowledge of adults, (b) what is learned are associations or bonds between otherwise unrelated stimuli, (c) understand-

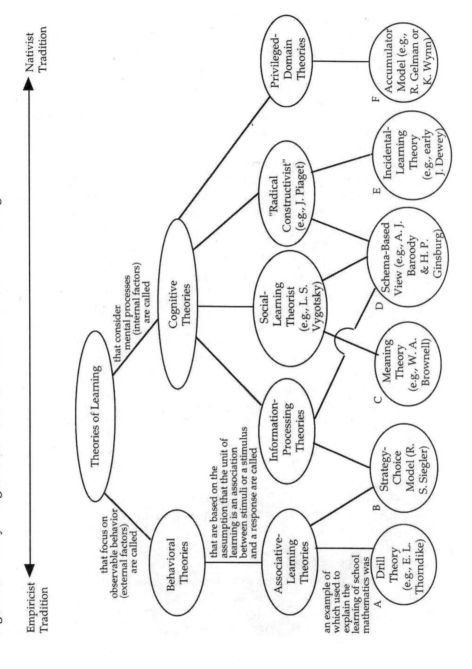

Figure 1.1: The Psychological Roots of Various Theories of Arithmetic Learning

Empiricist
Tradition

Nativist
Tradition

Theories of Learning

that focus on
observable behavior
(external factors)
are called

that consider
mental processes
(internal factors)
are called

Behavioral
Theories

Cognitive
Theories

that are based on the
assumption that the unit of
learning is an association
between stimulus or a stimulus
and a response are called

Associative-
Learning Theories

Information-
Processing
Theories

Social-
Learning
Theorist
(e.g., L. S.
Vygotsky)

"Radical
Constructivist"
(e.g., J. Piaget)

Privileged-
Domain
Theories

an example of
which used to
explain the
learning of school
mathematics was

A Drill
Theory
(e.g., E. L.
Thorndike)

B Strategy-
Choice
Model (R.
S. Siegler)

C Meaning
Theory
(e.g., W. A.
Brownell)

D Schema-Based
View (e.g., A. J.
Baroody
& H. P.
Ginsburg)

E Incidental-
Learning
Theory
(e.g., early
J. Dewey)

F Accumulator
Model (e.g.,
R. Gelman or
K. Wynn)

ing is not necessary for the formation of such bonds, and (d) the most efficient way to accomplish bond formation is through direct instruction and drill. In this view, the learning of single-digit (basic) number combinations such as 5 + 3 = 8 and multidigit renaming procedures such as "carrying" or "borrowing," for example, could be achieved quickly by a well-organized regimen of instruction and practice (Thorndike, 1922). Self-invented procedures by children, such as counting- or reasoning-based computational strategies (e.g., Arianne's procedure for checking division described earlier) were viewed as impediments (see, e.g., Smith, 1921; Wheeler, 1939).

Meaning Theory. Dissatisfaction with traditional mathematics instruction and its theoretical basis (drill theory) led Brownell (1935) to propose meaning theory (Model C in Fig. 1.1). This theory is akin to the social-learning theory of Lev S. Vygotsky (1962) and foreshadowed Hatano's (1988) ideal of adaptive expertise. In Brownell's view, instruction should focus on promoting the meaningful memorization of skills:

> The "meaning" theory conceives arithmetic as a closely knit system of understandable ideas, principles, and processes. According to this theory, the test of learning is not mere mechanical facility in "figuring." The true test is an intelligent grasp upon number relations and the ability to deal with arithmetical situations with proper comprehension of their mathematical as well as their practical significance. (p. 19)

According to meaning theory, teachers must take into three interrelated factors in order to promote the learning of arithmetic with understanding:

• *The complexity of arithmetic learning.* In the traditional drill approach, for instance, instruction on counting and numbers is followed by drill of "number facts." This approach "almost totally neglects the element of meaning and the complexity of the first stage in arithmetic learning" (Brownell, 1935, p. 21). According to meaning theory, children are, at first, expected to engage in "immature" strategies, such as self-invented counting and reasoning strategies (see, e.g., Baroody, 1987b, 1999). These informal methods provide the basis for mature knowledge, including mastery of basic number combinations, understanding of arithmetic principles, and meaningful memorization of multidigit procedures (see also, e.g., Ambrose, Baek, & Carpenter, chap. 11, this volume; Baroody, 1987a; Cowan, chap. 2, this volume; Fuson & Burghardt, chap. 10, this volume).

Brownell (1935) noted that children may initially need to rely on counting-based arithmetic strategies because such strategies may be their only meaningful means of operating on numbers. As soon as they are ready, however, students should be encouraged to use more advanced strategies, such as reasoning (e.g., strategies transforming an unfamiliar problem into a familiar one: $7 + 5 = [7 + 3] + [5 - 3] = 10 + 2 = 12$). Eventually, children come "to a confident knowledge of [a number combination], a knowledge full of meaning because of its frequent verification. By this time, the difficult stages of learning will long since have been passed, and habituation occurs rapidly and easily" (p. 24). Drill may serve to increase the facility and permanence of recall. In sum, "children attain [skill] 'mastery' only after a period during which they deal with [arithmetic] by procedures less advanced (but to them more meaningful) than automatic responses" (Brownell, 1941, p. 96).

• *Pace of instruction.* In the drill approach, children are told or shown, for instance, a "number fact" once or twice and expected to memorize it quickly (within a week), if not almost immediately (a day or so). According to meaning theory, children are not expected to imitate immediately the skill or knowledge of adults. Learning arithmetic—including mastering the basic number combinations and multidigit procedures—is viewed as a slow, protracted process. In the meaning approach, then, time is allowed for children to construct an understanding of arithmetic ideas and to discover and rediscover arithmetic regularities before practice makes the basic number combinations automatic. The result is a more secure knowledge of these combinations, knowledge that is more easily transferred.

• *Emphasis on relations.* According to drill theory, for example, $6 + 5 = 11$ and $7 + 4 = 11$ should not be taught simultaneously because of "associative confusion" or "associative interference." Brownell (1935) argued that addition and subtraction combinations such as $3 + 2 = 5$ or $5 - 3 = 2$ are not facts but *generalizations* and, for teaching purposes, should be treated as such. To help children make such generalizations, teachers need to help them discover a regularity such as $3 + 2 = 5$ many times in many different situations. Furthermore, they should help students see the relations among combinations so that they came to know the basic combinations as a system of knowledge.

Incidental-Learning Theory. Incidental-learning theory (Model E in Fig. 1.1), an analog of Jean Piaget's (radical) constructivist theory, was embodied in John Dewey's early progressive-education movement. This theory was also a reaction to drill theory. According to this view, children should be free to explore the world around them, notice regularities (patterns and relations), and actively construct their own understanding and procedures. In other words, mathematical learning should be the incidental result of satisfying their natural curiosity.

Brownell (1935) concluded that the incidental-learning approach was impractical for three reasons. The first is that "incidental learning, whether through 'units' or through unrestricted experiences, is slow and time-consuming. [A second is that the] arithmetic ability as may be developed in these [unfocused] circumstances is apt to be fragmentary, superficial, and mechanical. [A third is] that teachers generally lacked the expertise to implement such an approach effectively" (pp. 17–18; cf. the more recent analyses by Fuson & Burghardt, chap. 10, this volume; Howe, 1999; Ma, 1999; Seo & Ginsburg, chap. 5, this volume). For these reasons, Brownell advocated direct instruction. Moreover, he felt that interests were socially determined.

Skills Versus Concepts Debate

Proponents of drill theory believed that mathematics instruction should focus on promoting the mastery of basic skills, not on cultivating understanding of mathematical concepts (e.g., Smith, 1921; Thorndike, 1922; Wheeler, 1939). In Hatano's (1988) terms, the aim of instruction was routine, not adaptive, expertise. In contrast, proponents of incidental-learning theory believed the focus of instruction should be fostering conceptual understanding, not on memorizing basic skills.

In advocating meaning theory, Brownell (1935) took a middle course. His meaning approach was a combination of a drill theory and incidental-learning theory. On the one hand, he recommended the judicious use of textbook-based instruction and drill to promote skill mastery. On the other hand, Brownell recognized the value of building on children's experience and discoveries in order to foster conceptual understanding. Put differently, unlike many of his contemporaries, he did not value computational skill over conceptual understanding or vice versa. Brownell appears to have presaged the modern view that both are important—that mathematical competence requires "knowing both what to do and why" (Skemp, 1978, p. 9) and that instruction should focus on promoting adaptive expertise (Hatano, 1988). Although Brownell seems to have favored fostering conceptual knowledge first, he left unclear how it developed and how this development was related to skill development. These issues were taken up in the last two decades of the 20th century.

RECENT VIEWS: SKILL AND UNDERSTANDING

In the early 1980s, Resnick and Ford (1981) called for a cognitive psychology of how computational skills and conceptual understandings of arithmetic are acquired, including the transitions in competence. They further concluded that, whereas past research efforts focused on which was better to promote, future research efforts should focus on how understanding influences learning of computational routine and how skilled computation, in turn, affects conceptual learning. Next, I first outline two modern but different approaches to a cognitive psychology of arithmetic development. I then summarize four perspectives that have emerged from the recent debates about how the developments of mathematical concepts and skills may be related.

Two Modern Views of Arithmetic Development

Geary (1994) noted that currently there are two general theoretical models of arithmetic development: a strategy-choice model (e.g., Siegler, 1986; Model B in Fig. 1.1) and schema-based models (e.g., Baroody & Ginsburg, 1986; Steffe, 1992). Although "both approaches seek to specify the cognitive changes associated with children's arithmetical development" (Geary, 1994, p. 81), each reflects its psychological roots.

Strategy-Choice Model. The strategy-choice model developed by Siegler and his colleagues reflects its roots in associative-learning theory by focusing on children's overt strategies and the practice and reinforcement of arithmetic responses. This model also reflects its origins in information-processing theory with its effort to delineate the internal cognitive mechanisms that govern a child's choice among alternative strategies. See chapters 2 (Cowan) and 3 (Baroody & Tiilikainen) for a detailed discussion and analysis of this model.

A Schema-Based View. One schema-based view (e.g., Baroody & Ginsburg, 1986; Model D in Fig. 1.1) reflects the influence of (a) Piaget's (e.g., 1964) constructivist theory with its focus on the construction of abstract structures (relational knowledge that summarizes information about many particular cases), (b) Vygotsky's (e.g., 1962) social-learning theory with its concern for learning potential or readiness (how much children can benefit from intervention), and (c) information-processing theory with its accounts of the limits of working memory and the drive for cognitive economy.

In chapter 3, Baroody and Tiilikainen compare this schema-based view with the strategy-choice model on three key issues: (a) How do counting-based addition strategies and strategy choice develop? (b) How does mental-arithmetic competence with basic and multidigit combinations evolve? and (c) How are the developments of addition concepts and procedures related? In chapter 4, Baroody, Wilkins, and Tiilikainen extend the discussion of the schema-based view to the development of early arithmetic understanding in general and the concept of additive commutativity in particular.

In chapter 5, Seo and Ginsburg discuss how school instruction can expand a child's conceptual schema for a key formal symbol, namely the equals sign. In chapter 6, Butterworth, Marschesini, and Girelli discuss how conceptual understanding of multplicative commutativity may impact the learning and representation (schemas) of basic number combinations. In chapter 7, LeFevre, Smith-Chant, Hiscock, Daley, and Morris extend the discussion of strategy choice and mental arithmetic to provide a dramatically different view of adult's basic number-combination facility. In chapter 8, Miura and Okamoto explain how language can help shape conceptual schemas of multidigit numbers and fractions (cf. Donlan, chap. 12, this volume). In chapter 9, Dowker considers how conceptual understanding can influence estimation efforts on familiar, somewhat novel, and novel estimation tasks and describes key components of this conceptual knowledge. In chapters 10 and 11, Fuson and Burghardt and Ambrose et al. discuss critical elements of the conceptual schemas underlying nonstandard or standard multidigit procedures and provide insight into the development of these schemas.

In chapters 12 and 13, Donlan and Jordan, Hanich, and Uberti discuss the nonverbal or precounting bases for constructing number and arithmetic schemas and come to different conclusions about the roles of language and instruction (social) factors that may underlie mathematical learning difficulties. In chapter 14, Delazer reflects on the inadequacies of information-processing models that have dominated the field of neuropsychology and takes a step toward a schema-based view by explicitly considering the role of conceptual knowledge in neuropsychological disorders. In chapter 15, Heavey makes the startling conclusion that what underlies the calculational competencies of idiot savants is an intricate web of interconnected number knowledge, not the recall of isolated facts memorized by rote.

The Skills-First Versus Concepts-First Debate and Its Aftermath

In the last quarter of the 20th century, the debate about whether skills or concepts is more important was replaced by a debate about their developmental order. Initially, two polar camps, namely the proponents of the skills-first view and those of the concepts-first view, dominated this debate. In time, two more moderate views were advanced. Summarized next—and discussed further in chapter 3 (Baroody & Tiilikainen) of this volume—are four possible ways skills and concepts can be related.

Possibility 1: Skills First. More behaviorally oriented researchers (e.g., Briars & Siegler, 1984) have proposed that the development of mathematical skills predates and underlies the development of concepts. In this view, arithmetic skills are learned by rote memorization through imitation, practice, and reinforcement. The result is that skill learning is piecemeal. Through applying their skills, children discover arithmetic regularities or concepts. As conceptual knowledge slowly accumulates, it increasingly links together procedural knowledge. A parent or teacher might teach a child, for instance, to count-on from the larger addend (COL; e.g., for 3 + 5: "5, 6, 7, **8**"). Then, by using this procedure to compute sums, the child might discover that both 3 + 5 and 5 + 3 have the same sum and that addend order does not affect the sum (the principle of additive commutativity).

Possibility 2: Concepts First. Some more cognitively oriented researchers (e.g., Briars & Larkin, 1984) have proposed that conceptual knowledge precedes and guides the construction of procedures. For example, Riley, Greeno, and Heller (1983) hypothesized that an understanding of additive commutativity enables children to invent COL. Indeed, more nativist-oriented cognitive psychologists have argued that recent evidence suggests a version of the concepts-first view called the "privileged-domain hypothesis" (e.g., Model F in Fig. 1.1). According to this hypothesis (Geary, 1995; Gelman, 1993; Gelman & Meck, 1992; all cited by Rittle-Johnson & Siegler, 1998; Wynn, 1998), some (mathematical) competencies have been favored by our evolutionary history and, thus, are innate or have an innate basis.

Possibility 3: Iterative Development. One result of a colloquium series at the University of Delaware in the mid 1980s (titled *Conceptual and Procedural Knowledge: The Case of Mathematics*) and its by-product (a book by the same name, edited by James Hiebert, 1986) was an understanding that the developmental relations between concepts and skills are not as straightforward or easily characterized as skills-first or concepts-first proponents suggested.

Baroody and Ginsburg (1986), for instance, proposed an iterative relation between concepts and skills. In this moderate or intermediate perspective, conceptual knowledge can lead to advances in procedural knowledge, the application of which can lead to a conceptual advance, and so forth (see also Baroody, 1992; Fuson, 1988). In this iterative view, children use their conceptual knowledge, for example, to construct a concrete counting-all strategy (CCA; representing each addend with objects and then counting all these objects). Computational experience with this basic strategy can lead to insights that prompt the development of somewhat more advanced strategies. Their use, in turn, can lead to the discovery of additive commutativity, which can prompt the adoption of the advanced strategy COL (e.g., Neches, 1987).

Possibility 4: Simultaneous Development. Another intermediate position proposed by Rittle-Johnson and Siegler (1998) is that procedural and conceptual knowledge develop concurrently. According to this simultaneous-development model, the development of the COL strategy, for instance, is intertwined and inseparable from the development of the additive-commutativity concept.

Tentative Theoretical Conclusions About the Relations Between Conceptual and Procedural Knowledge

Rittle-Johnson and Siegler (1998) noted that existing evidence bears largely on the skills-first and concepts-first views (Possibilities 1 and 2, respectively), because of the difficulties of adequately testing the iterative and simultaneous views (Possibilities 3 and 4, respectively). However, they further concluded, "An iterative relation between procedural and conceptual mastery, seems an especially plausible path of development" (p. 78). Next, I discuss three conclusions drawn by Hiebert and Lefevre (1986) regarding the relations between skills and concepts—conclusions that serve as premises for the iterative (or the simultaneous) view. I then briefly summarize the case for Possibility 3 (and that against Possibilities 1 and 2) in the form of three key guidelines for constructing or evaluating models of arithmetic development.

KEY CONCLUSIONS BY HIEBERT AND LEFEVRE (1986)

Hiebert and Lefevre (1986) defined procedural knowledge (skills) as knowing *how-to* and conceptual knowledge (understanding or concepts) as knowing *why*. Fig. 1.2 summarizes their detailed description of these aspects of mathematical knowledge. On the surface, conceptual and procedural knowledge appear to be clearly distinct. However, Hiebert and Lefevre made the following important points about these two types of knowledge:

1. Whereas conceptual knowledge, by definition, involves interconnected and, hence, meaningful knowledge, procedural knowledge may or may not be connected to other knowledge and, thus, may be meaningful or not.

Figure 1.2: Summary of the Hiebert and Lefevre (1986) Characterizations of Procedural and Conceptual Knowledge

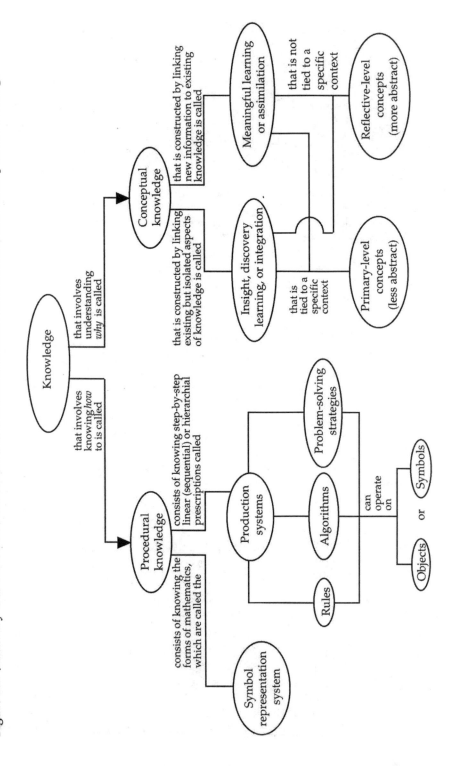

2. The distinction between these two types of knowledge can, in some cases, be fuzzy (see, e.g., Baroody & Ginsburg, 1986).
3. Linking conceptual and procedural knowledge can greatly benefit the acquisition and application of the former, as well as the latter.

THREE ADDITIONAL CONCLUSIONS

In an effort to make sense of what research data are available on the topic, I offer three additional conclusions about the relations between conceptual and procedural knowledge.

1. Conceptual Knowledge Usually Underlies Procedural Innovations

Although children seem to learn many mathematical skills without fully understanding their conceptual basis (e.g., Briars & Siegler, 1984; Fuson, 1988), the skills-first view does not provide an adequate explanation for how they can readily devise or adapt appropriate procedures for various mathematical tasks. (For a detailed critique of this view see, e.g., Gelman and Meck, 1983, 1986, 1992.) Carpenter (1986) rejected the skills-first position:

> It is inappropriate to conclude that conceptual knowledge of some kind is unnecessary for procedural advances. . . . When invention occurs at a procedural level, it often results in errors. . . . If children were simply attempting to increase cognitive economy, they presumably would construct routines that were inappropriate more frequently than they do. (p. 120)

In brief, although Carpenter allowed that rote memorization of computational procedures can occur, he concluded that the learning of procedures, particularly informal ones, has at least some conceptual basis or underpinning (in this volume, see, e.g., Ambrose et al., chap. 11; Fuson & Burghardt, chap. 10).

2. Adaptive Expertise Involves the Integration of Conceptual and Procedural Knowledge

Carpenter (1986) concluded, "There is ample evidence that the development of conceptual knowledge alone does not drive the acquisition of procedures for solving [arithmetic] problems (Baroody & Ginsburg, [1986]; Carpenter & Moser, 1984)" (p. 119). He further noted that the concepts-first "views proposed by Briars and Larkin (1984) and Riley et al. (1983) are overly parsimonious" and that "children's behavior is not as orderly as" they prescribe (p. 119). In particular, such they do not account for systematic differences. For example, although Riley et al. (1983) posited that the same conceptual knowledge underlies children's ability to solve missing-addend problems and counting-on, evidence indicates that they can do the former before the latter (Carpenter & Moser, 1984).

Carpenter (1986) went on to offer a modified concepts-first view that helps account for the variability in children's performance not predicted by concepts-first accounts:

> Advances in children's ability to solve addition and subtraction problems are based on conceptual knowledge, but connections between conceptual and procedural knowledge are established gradually and on a piecemeal basis. Conceptual knowledge is not immediately integrated with all related procedures; rather initially, it is applied locally to individual problems and procedures. (p. 120)

The development of arithmetic adaptive expertise, then, cannot merely be equated with the construction of understanding. It also involves building links between conceptual knowledge and procedural knowledge. Two key implications follow from the hypothesis that the development of arithmetic adaptive expertise can be characterized by the increasing integration of these two types of knowledge:

• *Whereas the distinction between conceptual and procedural knowledge will initially be fuzzy regardless of the nature of instruction, whether the distinction becomes clear later depends heavily on the nature of instruction.* Even with rich instructional experiences, early conceptual development (assimilation and integration) may proceed relatively slowly. Put differently, despite the good intentions of parents, preschool teachers, and others, a child's initial concepts will have relatively few links. Thus, the understanding represented by such "weak schemas" will be relatively isolated, superficial, and inflexible (Baroody & Ginsburg, 1986; Baroody et al., chap. 4, this volume; Mix, Huttenlocher, & Levine, 2002)—not altogether different from procedural knowledge that has few connections to conceptual knowledge.

As development proceeds, the distinction between conceptual and procedural knowledge should remain fuzzy *if* children learn procedures in a meaningful manner. Otherwise, conceptual knowledge (what there is of it) and procedural knowledge may well become distinct. From this perspective, the evidence that indicates arithmetic knowledge has distinct components (in this volume, see, e.g., Delazer, chap. 14; Donlan, chap. 12; Dowker, chap. 9; Heavey, chap. 15; LeFevre et al., chap. 7) is—to some extent—a by-product of pervasive educational practices that promote routine expertise. This conjecture is consistent with Delazer's (chap. 14, this volume) observation that brain-injury reports include cases of intact procedural knowledge and impaired conceptual knowledge but not the reverse. The commonly found pattern of dissociation is what would be expected of patients whose procedural knowledge was not integrated with their conceptual knowledge (who have routine expertise of arithmetic skills). Patients with adaptive expertise might be less prone to exhibit any type of dissociation. Furthermore, key to gauging dissociation is assessing procedures learned meaningful and the conceptual knowledge that *directly* underlies them, not *any* procedural and conceptual knowledge.

• *The integration of conceptual and procedural knowledge should permit greater flexibility in the invention and use of strategies or procedures.* (See, in particular, in this volume, Cowan, chap. 2; Baroody & Tiilikainen, chap. 3; Seo & Ginsburg, chap. 5; Butterworth et al., chap. 6; Dowker, chap. 9; Ambrose et al., chap. 11; Heavey, chap. 15.) Why might more connections yield not only a more complete and deeper understanding but greater flexibility?

Consider the analogy of moving to a new town (Pólya & Szego, 1972). Initially, a newcomer's knowledge of her new hometown is rather incomplete and unconnected. She may know how to get from her house to her workplace and from her house to the grocery store. Unfortunately, if she is at work and needs to go to the grocery store, her only option is to return home, a route that as Frame A of Fig. 1.3 illustrates, can be relatively inefficient. As the person explores her new hometown, she discovers landmarks and streets and can better see how the all fit together. As her knowledge of the town becomes more complete and interconnected, she can find her way around the town more easily. It allows her, for example, to determine the most efficient route from her workplace to the grocery store (see Frame B of Fig. 1.3). Moreover, if this customary path is blocked, the resident's well-connected knowledge gives her the flexibility to determine

Figure 1.3: The Relation Between the Amount of Connected Knowledge and the Degree of Travel Flexibility

Frame A: Sketch of Unconnected Knowledge of New Hometown

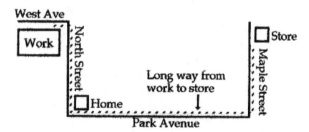

Frame B: Sketch of More Connected Knowledge of a Familiar Hometown

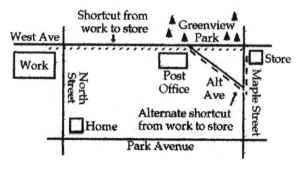

the next-best route. For instance, if the portion of West Street south of Greenview Park is closed for repairs, the well-versed traveler knows that Alt Avenue provides a good alternative route.

3. Conceptual Knowledge Can Play Either a Direct or an Indirect Role in the Invention of Procedures

Like Carpenter's (1986) modified concepts-first view, a schema-based iterative account is grounded on the assumption that development evolves from localized understandings or weak schemas into generalized concepts or strong schemas (Baroody & Ginsburg, 1986; Baroody et al., chap. 4, this volume). Nevertheless, because this account included nonconceptual factors as a mechanism for prompting strategy development or choice, Carpenter rejected it for same reason he dismissed the skills-first view.

However, if a distinction between an *indirect* basis *(conceptual support)* for a procedural advance and a *direct* basis for *(conceptual instigation* of) a procedural advance is made, then the modified concepts-first and the schema-based iterative views can be reconciled. (For example, recognizing that each addend should be represented only once may directly guide a child's effort to invent CCA, but it may only serve as a constraint in the invention of subsequent strategies such as COL.) Unlike the skills-first view, the schema-based iterative account is *not* based on the assumption that procedural innovations motivated by nonconceptual factors occur in a conceptual vacuum. Consider, for example, the argument that the invention of a strategy in which addend order is ignored (e.g., COL) can be motivated by an effort to achieve cognitive economy and, thus, does not require knowledge of commutativity (Baroody, 1987b; Baroody & Gannon, 1984; Baroody & Ginsburg, 1986; Baroody et al., chap. 4, this volume). Such an argument does not exclude an indirect conceptual basis for this innovation. Clearly, children must have at least some conceptual understanding of addition and that disregarding addend order is acceptable, even if they do not necessarily recognize that commuted expressions such as 5 + 3 and 3 + 5 are equivalent.

Two conjectures about the aforementioned distinction seem plausible: (a) A direct role may be the more important of the two. Put differently, conceptual knowledge, rather than nonconceptual factors, may be the primary driving force of self-invented procedures (see, e.g., Fuson & Burghardt, chap. 10, this volume; Heavey, chap. 15, this volume). (b) Nonconceptually motivated (but conceptually supported) procedural advances are probably more prone to be inconsistently applied (generalized), inappropriate (illegal), and less stable (forgotten) than are conceptually motivated ones (again see, e.g., Fuson & Burghardt, chap. 10, this volume). Parenthetically, the former may be misinterpreted as evidence for a conceptual advance (Baroody, 1985) or contribute to the appearance that children use diverse, conceptually motivated strategies.

Educational Implications
for Current Reform Efforts

The psychological debate about the relations between conceptual and procedural has had an impact on the ongoing argument about how to improve mathematics instruction (Ginsburg, Klein, & Starkey, 1998)—sometimes characterized as the "math wars." In order to better understand the math wars and to put it in perspective, two frameworks may be helpful. One is a description of four different instructional approaches. This framework builds on and updates Brownell's (1935) three models of teaching mathematics (discussed in the first section of this chapter). A second is a set of new instructional goals that has emerged from the math wars. In this section, I outline these two frameworks and then use them and the earlier conclusions about the relations between conceptual and procedural knowledge to analyze current efforts to reform mathematics education in the United States.

A SOURCE OF DISAGREEMENT:
DIFFERENT VIEWS OF INSTRUCTION

In this subsection, I first outline different perspectives on mathematics instruction and then discuss how these differences of opinion set off the most recent version of the math wars.

Four Approaches to Mathematics Instruction

Baroody (with Coslick, 1998) identified the following four qualitatively different approaches to teaching mathematics: the skills, conceptual, problem-solving, and investigative approaches. The characteristics of these approaches and how they contrast with each other are summarized in Table 1.1. In this subsection, I describe the parallels between these approaches and Brownell's (1935) three approaches and outline their philosophical and psychological assumptions about teaching and learning mathematics.

The Skills Approach. The skills approach, with its focus on the memorization of basic skills by rote, is analogous to what Brownell (1935) called drill theory. This approach is based on the assumption that mathematical knowledge is simply a collection of socially useful information (facts, rules, formulas, and procedures). Except for the mathematically gifted, children are viewed as uninformed ("empty vessels"), largely helpless, and perhaps incapable of understanding many aspects of school mathematics. The aim of mathematics instruction is to inform them about how to do mathematics. Proponents of the skills approach (e.g., the "back-to-basics" movement) believe that the most efficient way to transmit information is by means of direct instruction and practice—without taking the time to promote understanding about the whys of

Table 1.1: Four Approaches to Mathematics Instruction (Baroody, with Coslick, 1998)

Instructional Approach	Philosophical View			Teaching Style
	Name	Nature of Knowledge	View of Authority	
Skills Approach	Dualism	Right or wrong with no shades of gray: There is *one* correct procedure or answer.	Absolute external authority: As the expert, the teacher is *the* judge of correctness. Procedures or answers that differ from those advocated by the teacher are wrong and not tolerated. Teacher provides definitive feedback (e.g., praise for the correct answer).	Completely authoritarian and extremely teacher centered: Direct instruction (teaching by imposition).
Conceptual Approach	Pluralism	Continuum from right to wrong: There is a choice of possible but not equally valid procedures or answers. Objectively, there is one best possibility.	Tolerant external authority: Teacher accepts diverse procedures and answers but strives for perfection, namely, learning of the best procedure or answer. Teacher provides feedback (e.g., praises all ideas, particularly the conventional one).	Semi-authoritarian and teacher centered: Direct and semi-direct instruction (teaching by "careful" imposition).
Investigative Approach	Instrumentalism	Many right choices: There is a choice of possible procedures or answers and often many are good.	Open internal authority: Teacher or student remains committed to a method or viewpoint as long as it is effective. Teacher responds to incorrect procedures or answers by posing a question, problems, or task that prompts student reflection.	Semi-democratic and student centered: Semi-indirect instruction (guided participatory democracy).
Problem-Solving Approach	Extreme Relativism	No right or wrong: There are many possible, equally valid possibilities.	No external authority: Teacher and each student define his or her own truth. Children evaluate their own conclusions.	Completely democratic and extremely student centered: Indirect instruction (teaching by negotiation).

Table 1.1 continued

	Aim of Instruction	Focus of Instruction	Teacher's/Students' Roles
Skills Approach	Foster routine expertise: the memorization of basic skills (arithmetic and geometric facts, definitions, rules, formulas, and procedures) by rote.	Procedural content (e.g., *how* to add multi-digit numbers).	Teacher serves as a director: an information dispenser (informer) and taskmaster (manager). Because children are viewed as uniformed and helpless, students must be spoon fed knowledge.
Conceptual Approach	Foster adaptive expertise: the meaningful memorization of facts, rules, formulas, and procedures.	Procedural and conceptual content (e.g., *why* you "carry" when adding multi-digit numbers).	Teacher serves as a shepherd: information dispenser (informer) and up-front guide (conductor). Because children are seen as capable of understanding mathematics if helped, they are engaged in quasi-independent activities and discussions.
Investigative Approach	Foster all aspects of mathematical power: positive disposition (e.g., interest, confidence and constructive beliefs about learning and using mathematics), adaptive expertise (understanding of concepts and skills), and mathematical thinking (the capacity to conduct mathematical inquiry including problem solving and reasoning).	Procedural content, conceptual content, and the processes of mathematical inquiry (problem solving, reasoning, conjecturing, representing, and communicating).	Teacher serves as a mentor: activity organizer (instigator) and guide-on-the-side (moderator). Because children have informal knowledge and an inherent need to understand, they are capable of inventing their own solutions and making (at least some) sense of mathematical situations themselves (i.e., students are engaged in semi-independent activities and discussions).
Problem-Solving Approach	Foster mathematical thinking—the ability to conduct mathematical inquiry.	Processes of mathematical inquiry: problem solving, reasoning, conjecturing representing, and communicating.	Teacher serves as a partner: participant, monitor, and devil's advocate. Students engage in relatively independent activities and discussions.

Table 1.1 continued

	Organizing Principle	Methods
Skills Approach	Bottom-up (logically): Sequential instruction from most basic skills to most complex skills such as problem solving.	• Teacher lectures and demonstrates • Textbook based and largely symbolic • Children work in isolation • Practice with an emphasis on written, sterile worksheets • Little or no use of manipulatives or technology
Conceptual Approach	Bottom-up (psychologically): Sequential instruction based on the readiness of students to construct understanding.	• Didactic instruction supplemented by guided discovery learning • Textbook based, but teacher uses, e.g., meaningful analogies and concrete models to explain procedures • Whole-class, small-group, and individual instruction • Children imitate manipulative procedure
Investigative Approach	Top-down (guided): Teacher usually poses a "worthwhile task" (one that is challenging and complex) as way of exploring, learning and practicing basic concepts and skills; teacher may take advantage of teachable moments (e.g., question or problem posed by student).	• Various methods with an emphasis on indirect techniques that involve students in exploring, conjecturing about, and debating ideas (e.g., semi-guided discovery learning) • Projects, problems, everyday situations, science experiments, children's literature, math games, and so forth create a need for learning and practicing math; textbooks serve a supporting role (e.g., a source of worthwhile tasks and resolving disagreements over definitions) • Children often work together in groups • Students encouraged to invent, share, and streamline their own concrete models and, later, written procedures (including the conventional one or equally or more efficient nonconventional ones) • Practice done purposefully • Use of technology is a key aim and central to many learning tasks
Problem-Solving Approach	Top-down (unguided): Class tackles problems of their own choosing, whether or not students have received formal instruction on the content involved.	• Open-ended or unstructured discovery learning • Content instruction done incidentally as needed; little or no use of textbooks • Students encouraged to invent, share and streamline their own concrete models and, later, written procedures

procedures. A teacher directs all aspects of the learning process to ensure efficient inculcation (transmittal and mastery) of basic skills.

In the skills approach, a teacher simply tells children, for instance, that to multiply fractions, the numerator and denominator of the answer is determined by multiplying the two factors' numerators and denominators, respectively. Students then complete numerous computations with the procedure until it is memorized by rote. In brief, because instruction and practice is done without context (a reason) at a largely symbolic (abstract) level, the skills approach is not purposeful (in the sense that instruction builds on students' interests and creates a genuine need to learn and practice mathematics), nor is it typically meaningful. As children seldom are engaged in any real mathematical thinking, the skills approach is almost never inquiry based. (See Jordan et al., chap. 13, this volume, for a discussion of some of the negative consequences of such an approach.) A modern prototype of the skills approach is the Saxon curriculum, which involves well-organized and highly repetitive practice (cf. Thorndike, 1922).

The Conceptual Approach. The conceptual approach, with its focus on the meaningful memorization of skills, is analogous to what Brownell (1935) called meaning theory. This approach is based on the assumption that mathematics is a network of skills and concepts. Children are viewed as capable of understanding mathematics if told or showed why procedures work. The aim of mathematics instruction is to help them learn needed facts, rules, formulas, and procedures in a meaningful way (i.e., with comprehension). A teacher shepherds children toward understanding and mastery of skills.

In the conceptual approach (as typically implemented), symbolic procedures, such as multiplying fractions, are illustrated by a concrete model in the form of a textbook picture or an actual teacher demonstration. Children may even be encouraged to imitate an illustrated model themselves with manipulatives. Thus, although instruction and practice is often without context or purpose, an effort is made to promote meaningful learning. Sometimes students may also be involved in highly guided discovery-learning activities, which provides some experience with the processes of mathematical inquiry. Examples of such an approach are the following textbook series: Glencoe/McGraw Hill's *Mathematics: Applications and Connections* (1999) and Scott Foresman's *California Mathematics* (2001).

The Problem-Solving Approach. The problem-solving approach, with its focus on the development of mathematical thinking (reasoning and problem solving), is analogous to what Brownell (1935) called the incidental-learning approach. Philosophically, this radical approach is at the opposite end of the spectrum from the skills approach. (This is why it is placed at the bottom of Table 1.1.) This approach is based on the assumption that mathematics is, at heart, a way of thinking, a process of inquiry, or a search for patterns in order to solve problems. Children are viewed, on the one hand, as using immature thinking and possessing incomplete knowledge and, on the other hand, as naturally curious creatures who can and must actively construct their own under standing of mathematics. The aim of mathematics instruction is to immerse mathematical novices in mathematical inquiry (solving what are to them real and challenging problems), so that they can develop more mature ways of thinking and incidentally discover and construct more complete mathematical knowledge. A teacher participates in the inquiry as a relatively wise partner who pushes the process along but does not entirely, or even largely, set the agenda or control the inquiry.

In a problem-solving approach, learning content, such as the formal procedure for multiplying fractions, is secondary to developing children's thinking processes. The open-school movement (e.g., Silberman, 1973) or Piagetian curricula (e.g., Furth & Wachs, 1974; Neill, 1960) in the recent past embodied the ideals of such an approach.

The Investigative Approach. The investigative approach, with its focus on meaningful memorization of skills and the development of mathematical thinking, can be thought of as a composite of Brownell's (1935) meaning and incidental-learning theories (i.e., as the union of the conceptual and problem-solving approaches). Like the conceptual approach, mathematics is viewed as a network of skills and concepts. It is also, like the problem-solving approach, viewed as a process of inquiry. Unlike the conceptual approach and similar to the problem-solving approach, children are viewed as capable of actively constructing this understanding. Unlike the problem-solving approach, children's active construction of understanding is mediated, guided, and prompted by the teacher—most often through planned activities, but occasionally by taking advantage of unplanned "learning moments." Like the conceptual approach, an aim of mathematics instruction is to help students learn needed facts, rules, formulas, and procedures in a meaningful fashion. Like the problem-solving approach, students are regularly engaged in mathematical inquiry (to develop problem-solving, reasoning, representing, and communicating competencies). In the investigative approach, a teacher mentors children, guiding their meaningful construction of procedures and concepts and the development of mathematical thinking. Thus, unlike either the skills or the conceptual approach and like the problem-solving approach, a teacher indirectly incites doubt, curiosity, or cognitive conflict by posing worthwhile tasks and by creating a social environment that encourages questioning, inquiry, and reflection (see e.g., Ambrose et al., chap. 11, this volume; Baroody, with Coslick, 1998; Hatano, 1988; Miura & Okamoto, chap. 8, this volume; Seo & Ginsburg, chap. 5, this volume).

In the investigative approach, an instructor uses indirect means to help students construct knowledge. For example, a teacher might guide children to reinvent a procedure, such as the algorithm for multiplying fractions. The first step might be finding or inventing a worthwhile task that creates a genuine need for using the procedure (e.g., adjusting a recipe with fractional measures by fractional amounts, determining the area of a wall space or plot that involves a fractional length and width, or determining the theoretical probability of two independent events in an effort to solve a problem). The teacher might then encourage children to invent their own procedures for solving the problem, methods that may well involve using manipulatives or drawings. Students can then be encouraged to represent the problem and their informally determined solution symbolically and to look for shortcuts to their concrete procedures. Typically, students should quickly reinvent the formal procedure for multiplying fractions (cf. Fuson & Burghardt, chap. 10, this volume; see, e.g., Baroody, with Coslick, 1998, for similar examples with a variety of content). In brief, the investigative approach involves purposeful, meaningful, and inquiry-based instruction. A reasonable approximation of this approach is the *Everyday Mathematics* program (Everyday Learning Corporation, 2001). In this elementary-level curriculum, a teacher encourages self-invention of problem solutions by building on children's informal knowledge.

A Reform Effort and a Firestorm of Criticism

In the United States, a number of efforts to reform mathematics instruction were undertaken during the 20th century (see, e.g., Kilpatrick, 1992, 2001; Kline, 1974; Wilson, 2003). Nearly all of them had little lasting impact on the textbooks and the curricula used in the vast majority of classrooms. (See Cowan, chap. 2, this volume, for a review of reform movements in the United Kingdom.) Ginsburg et al. (1998), for example, concluded that, although Brownell's (1935) meaning theory was embraced by mathematics educators at the university level, Thorndike's (1922) associationist view, by and large, won the hearts and minds of practitioners. Outlined next is a brief review of a recent and ongoing effort to reform mathematics instruction and the criticisms it engendered.

The NCTM Standards. In the last two decades of the 20th century, dissatisfaction with the traditional skills approach led the National Council of Teachers of Mathematics (NCTM) to publish a series of standards documents (1989, 1991, 1995, 2000) laying out a new vision of mathematics instruction. Proposed were changes in both the content of school mathematics and, perhaps more important, the way mathematics is taught. Regarding the former, these standards outlined ambitious goals for mathematics instruction, including conceptual understanding and problem-solving and reasoning competence. Regarding methods of instruction, the proposed reforms include making mathematics instruction relevant to children (purposeful), conceptually based (meaningful), and process based (inquiry based). Thus, although the NCTM recommended using a variety of teaching technique, the general approach recommended is most similar to what was described earlier as the "investigative approach." Like previous reform movements, this proposed approach, which is based on (moderate) constructivist and social-learning principles, has been criticized as impractical.

Criticisms of the NCTM Standards. Critics of the NCTM standards often misinterpreted its 1989 document as advocating the problem-solving approach, which is based on a philosophy of radical constructivism. Some common criticisms stemming from this misconception and counterarguments based on the three conclusions regarding the relations between conceptual and procedural knowledge noted earlier are discussed next.

1. *Conceptual knowledge usually underlies procedural innovations.* Geary (1994), for example, noted that a strict constructivist approach to mathematics education focuses almost exclusively on the acquisition of conceptual knowledge and problem solving—at the expense of skill mastery. Such an extreme position is "based, in part, on a failure to realize that mathematics requires the acquisition of *both* procedural skills and conceptual knowledge" (p. 273). Because constructivist-based instruction shortchanges skill mastery, it "is not likely to lead to substantial long-term improvements in the mathematical skills of . . . children" (p. 266).

Although Geary's (1994) criticism may be true of the problem-solving approach advocated by some strict constructivists, it is not true of the investigative approach advocated by moderate constructivists. As outlined in Hiebert (1986) and in this chapter, moderate constructivism is clearly based on recognition that instruction should develop both conceptual and procedural knowledge. In addition to the development of conceptual understanding and the ability to engage in mathematical inquiry (e.g., problem solving), a key aim of the investigative approach is skill mastery. Indeed, by cultivating adaptive expertise, this purposeful and meaningful approach fosters skill mastery far more effectively than the skills approach, which focuses on promoting routine expertise (see, e.g., the evidence adduced by Carpenter, Fennema, Peterson, Chiang, & Loef, 1989; Hiebert & Carpenter, 1992; Rittle-Johnson & Alibali, 1999). In brief, making concept development a central focus of instruction is not incompatible with skill development; indeed, it can be the most effective way to promote skill mastery.

2. *Adaptive expertise involves the integration of conceptual and procedural knowledge.* Geary (1994) suggested that strict constructivists overlook the clear distinction between procedural knowledge and conceptual knowledge and concluded, "that different teaching techniques are needed for children to acquire procedural and conceptual competencies" (p. 273). "Except for basic numerical and arithmetical skills, most children are not likely to be able to develop mathematical procedures solely on the basis of their conceptual knowledge. Instead, some procedures and equations simply need to taught and practiced" (pp. 265–266).

As recent analyses suggest, there is not a serious conflict between developing procedural knowledge and fostering conceptual knowledge (Howe, 1999; Ma, 1999). As noted earlier in this chapter, flexible and adaptive use of procedures requires the integration of procedural knowledge with conceptual knowledge. Put differently, if the aim of instruction is the meaningful learning of skills, the distinction between procedural and conceptual knowledge becomes blurry and less useful. With rare exceptions, there is no real need to teach elementary-level procedures and concepts in a different manner, nor is it desirable. Using the investigative approach, even more advanced arithmetic procedures taught in grades 1–8 can be invented by children, including those for operating on whole numbers (Ambrose et al., chap. 11, this volume; Fuson & Burghardt, chap. 10, this volume), rational numbers (fractions and decimals), or variables (algebraic symbols). See Baroody with Coslick (1998) for examples of, and instructional guidelines for, each.[1] In short, when instruction focuses on adaptive expertise (the integration of procedural and conceptual knowledge), it does not make sense to use different instructional techniques for fostering skill mastery and concept learning.

3. *Conceptual knowledge can play either a direct or an indirect role in the invention of procedures.* Geary (1994) argued that strict constructivists overlook the importance of drill and practice. He pointed out that conceptual knowledge is not sufficient for the development of computational and problem-solving skills and that drill and practice are necessary for the efficient use of such skills. Citing the research by Briars and Siegler (1984), Geary further concluded that mechanistic learning of skills can enable children to induce basic regularities or concepts.

Moderate constructivists do not disagree that practice has an important role in mastering computational and problem-solving skills. They would, however, argue that purposeful practice after meaningful learning is far more likely to be effective than uninteresting drill of meaningless facts and procedures. Furthermore, as noted earlier, children probably do not learn even basic counting, number, and arithmetic competencies, as Briars and Siegler's (1984) skills-first model suggests, but do so in an iterative fashion in which procedural and conceptual knowledge become increasingly intertwined (Baroody, 1992; Baroody & Ginsburg, 1986; Rittle-Johnson & Siegler, 1998). Thus, a focus of practice should be on discovering relations and integrating different aspects of knowledge (fostering adaptive expertise), not merely internalizing isolated facts and procedures (promoting routine expertise). For example, the practice of single- and multidigit number combinations, should focus on discovering relations and automatizing schemas such as the number-after rule for $n + 1/1 + n$ combinations. In brief, practicing procedures that are not conceptually insti-

---

[1] Geary (1994) further argued that constructivist "fail to distinguish between biologically primary and biologically secondary cognitive skills" and, thus, naively propose the same instructional techniques for learning both (p. 264). That is, whereas simple skills (counting, number, and some features of arithmetic) are innately supported and can be easily discovered by children or learned in appropriate everyday social contexts, more complex skills (e.g., solving algebraic word problems) require very different learning conditions. In fact, although the latter require more "groundwork" to ensure readiness, children can and should be taught more complex mathematics in a manner similar to how basic mathematics can and should be taught. For example, students should first be encouraged to use what they know to devise their own informal methods for solving more complex problems involving, for example, rational numbers (e.g., Mack, 1990, 1993; Post, Cramer, Behr, Lesh, & Harel, 1993; Streefland, 1993), ratios and proportions (e.g., Lamon, 1993; van de Brink & Streefland, 1979), or algebra (NCTM, 1992). They can then be encouraged to find shortcuts for concrete models or other informal methods, a process that can lead them to reinvent formal procedures and formulas (see, e.g., Baroody with Coslick, 1998, for details). Indeed, the quadratic equation is the only formula commonly taught in grades K–8 children are unlikely to re-invent and need to memorize by rote.

gated or at least conceptually supported (promoting routine expertise) makes little sense.

A BASIS FOR AGREEMENT:
NEW INSTRUCTIONAL GOALS

Although some critics of the NCTM standards promoted a "back-to-basics" movement—a return to the skills approach—others searched for a middle ground. The National Research Council (NRC) commissioned a committee of 16, which included proponents of the NCTM (1989, 1991, 1992, 1995, 2000) standards and its critics, to search for this middle ground. The resulting NRC report, *Adding It Up: Helping Children Learn Mathematics* (Kilpatrick, Swafford, & Findell, 2001), echoed Brownell's (1935) goal of meaningful mastery of arithmetic knowledge and Hatano's (1988) ideal of adaptive expertise by specifying that the goal of mathematics instruction should be *mathematical proficiency*. Next, I first describe mathematical proficiency and then discuss the implications of this goal for current reform efforts.

Mathematical Proficiency

Four Aspects of Mathematical Proficiency. As conceptualized earlier by Schoenfeld (1985, 1992), mathematical proficiency involves *conceptual understanding, computational fluency, strategic mathematical thinking,* and a *productive disposition*. The characterizations of the four strands of mathematical proficiency in the following are quoted or based on the definitions appearing in Kilpatrick et al. (2001, p. 5):

- *"Conceptual understanding* [entails] comprehension of mathematical concepts, operations, and relations."
- *Computational fluency* involves skill in computing efficiently (quickly and accurately), appropriately, and flexibly.
- *Strategic mathematical thinking* requires the "ability to formulate, represent, and solve mathematical problems" ("strategic competence") and "the capacity for logical thought, reflection, explanation, and justification" ("adaptive reasoning").
- *Productive disposition* [entails] a habitual inclination to see mathematics as sensible, useful, and worthwhile, coupled with a belief in diligence and one's efficacy."

The Need for Fostering the Four Strands in an Intertwined Manner. Rejecting the skills-first and the concepts-first views, Kilpatrick et al. (2001) further concluded that instruction should foster these four strands of mathematical proficiency in a simultaneous or an *intertwined* manner. Next, I briefly explain why their development must be done in an integrated (a simultaneous or, perhaps, an iterative) manner.

Conceptual understanding is necessary for computational fluency and strategic mathematical thinking and important to a productive disposition. Note that the definition of computational proficiency implies adaptive, rather than mere routine, expertise. Although computational efficiently can be achieved without understanding, conceptual understanding can facilitate knowing when it is appropriate to apply a skill and is critical to modifying its application on new tasks or problems.

Conceptual understanding is also necessary in thoughtfully formulating, representing, and solving problems. It can also support adaptive reasoning. For instance, it is easier to reason logically about familiar or comprehensible situations than unfamiliar or incomprehensible ones. It is also much easier to justify in a convincing manner a procedure one understands than one does not.

Finally, other than for the self-deluded, actually understanding mathematics is normally needed to view it as sensible. Furthermore, children who understand mathematics and view it as basically sensible are more likely to keep working at a problem or the topic and to develop self-confidence than those who do not.

IMPLICATIONS FOR ONGOING REFORM EFFORTS

There is wide, though by no means unanimous, agreement that a traditional, content-oriented skills approach does not adequately foster any aspect of mathematical proficiency, including computational fluency. There is also wide agreement that the same is true of a process-oriented, problem-solving approach, particularly in regard to computational fluency. However, there remains a deep division between those who support the NCTM (2000) standards (the content and process-oriented investigative approach) and those who support an alternative approach to reform (the content and somewhat process-oriented conceptual approach). Next, I assess the latter's and then the former's chances of achieving all aspects of mathematical proficiency.

The California Standards

The instructional goals and approach outlined in the *California Public Schools: Kindergarten Through Grade Twelve* (Curriculum Development and Supplemental Materials Commission, 1999), *California Standards* for short, was developed, in part, as a reaction to the perceived shortcomings of the NCTM (1989, 1991, 1995) standards. For instance, some critics have claimed that instruction based on the NCTM (1989, 1991, 1995) standards is "fuzzy math." It is not clear, though, why encouraging students to understand mathematics, use this understanding to invent solution procedures for challenging problems, justify and defend their procedures and solutions, and critically analyze others' procedures and solutions is fuzzy math. In any case, proponents of the *California Standards* argued for a more direct and rigorous approach.

A Moderate, Conceptual Approach. The goals laid out in chapter 1 of the *California Standards* are clearly consistent with those of the goal of achieving mathematical proficiency (conceptual understanding, computational proficiency, strategic mathematical thinking, and a productive disposition). The three-phase instructional model recommended in chapter 4 to achieve these goals appears most akin to the conceptual approach (meaningful learning of skills and concepts). The mathematics content standards and test examples found in chapter 2 are somewhat consistent with the conceptual approach. Specifically, these standards focus on skills with only some references to understanding them and inquiry competencies.

What's Wrong with a Conceptual Approach? A conceptual approach is based on the questionable assumption that an understanding of mathematics can be *imposed* on children. Constructivists have cautioned that merely viewing or even imitating a concrete model will not automatically or effectively help most students to understand an analogous written procedure (e.g., Baroody, 1989; Baroody, with Coslick, 1998; Clements & McMillen, 1996; Fuson & Burghardt, chap. 10, this volume; Miura & Okamoto, chap. 8, this volume; Seo & Ginsburg, chap. 5, this volume). Efforts to impose understanding on students are frequently unsuccessful because the instruction does not build on children's existing knowledge and, thus, does not promote connected knowledge either by assimilation or integration. As Resnick's (1982) study illustrates, children frequently do not spontaneously see how the steps in a concrete model parallel those in a written procedure (Fuson & Burghardt, chap. 10, this volume). Unfortunately, concrete models illustrated in textbooks or by teachers often do not highlight these links (cf. Fuson & Burghardt, chap. 10, this volume). To make matters worse, concrete models for written procedures are often not related explicitly or clearly to meaningful analogies (Baroody, with Coslick, 1998). For example manipulative-based models for fraction multiplication are only loosely linked, if linked at all, to familiar situations such as finding the area of a rectangle. Thus, they may not understand even the concrete manipulative-based model and may simply memorize it by rote, as they would an incomprehensible written procedure (e.g., Baroody, 1989). All too often, then, efforts to impose concrete models on students do not enhance either conceptual understanding or the thoughtful and flexible use of procedures (i.e., computational proficiency).

Moreover, a conceptual approach does little in the way of socializing children in the ways of mathematical inquiry—that is developing process competencies such as problem solving, reasoning, representing, and communicating. Little or no effort is made to encourage students to use conceptual understanding to propose their own informal models, look for patterns, and devise short cuts that lead to efficient symbolic procedures (cf. Kieren, 1992). Though students may engage in some inductive reasoning and conjecture proposing and testing if involved in guided discovery learning activities, such experiences are often so highly structured they do not promote debate and the need to justify procedures or solution. Finally, problem solving in the conceptual approach usually and merely involves applying a teacher-imposed procedure to similar problems examined in class.

The Need for the Investigative Approach

A carefully implemented investigative approach may be the best way to help all students achieve mathematical proficiency. This moderate approach is more likely than other approaches, including the conceptual approach, to foster genuine conceptual understanding. As this understanding underlies the other aspects of mathematical proficiency, the investigative approach is more likely than other approaches to promote computational fluency, strategic mathematical thinking, and a productive disposition. In terms of the focus of this book, the investigative approach may be the best means for fostering integrated knowledge of procedures and concepts or adaptive expertise.

CONCLUSION

Mathematics instruction cannot be significantly improved, as Brownell (1935) argued, by turning away from more complex methods of instruction because teachers are not sufficiently prepared to implement them. In order to develop truly professional teachers who are capable of implementing the investigative approach, pre- and in-service teacher training needs to foster adaptive expertise with mathematics, mathematical psychology, and effective pedagogy (Ball, 1998; Baroody, in press; Baroody, with Coslick, 1998; Campbell & White, 1997; Even & Lappan, 1994). One reason Chinese schools are relatively effective in fostering mathematical achievement is that their teachers have a relatively deep understanding of the mathematics they teach (Ma, 1999). As Lee S. Shulman observed in the foreword of Ma's (1999) book, although Chinese teachers have studied far less mathematics than U.S. teachers, "What they know they know more profoundly, more flexibly, more adaptively" (p. xi). In essence, despite taking fewer mathematics courses in school, Chinese teachers are afforded the opportunity to construct adaptive expertise for the mathematics that they teach. A profound understanding of how children's mathematical learning and thinking develops (e.g., knowing both the supporting and motivating concepts of a procedure) is also necessary to effectively plan a sequence of worthwhile tasks, create cognitive conflict, and otherwise promote the meaningful learning (assimilation and integration) of concepts and procedures (e.g., Baroody, 1987a; Baroody, with Coslick, 1998; Ginsburg, 1977; Ginsburg et al., 1998). A broad understanding of teaching practices is needed to thoughtfully and flexibly devise or adapt worthwhile tasks, orchestrate classroom discourse, and otherwise create the interesting, meaningful, thought-provoking instruction that promotes adaptive expertise and mathematical proficiency (e.g., NCTM, 1991). In brief, unlike some calls for reform that focus exclusively on improving teachers' mathematical (content) knowledge or attracting those with mathematical expertise, implementing the reforms envisioned by the NCTM will require teachers who have a powerful mathematical, psychological, and pedagogical framework. Only with adaptive expertise in all of these areas will teachers be highly effective at fostering the mathematical proficiency of their students, including their mathematical adaptive expertise.

Acknowledgments

Preparation of this chapter was supported, in part, by a grant ("Early Arithmetic Development") from the University of Illinois Research Board, a Faculty Fellowship awarded by the College of Education at the University of Illinois, and a grant from the National Science Foundation, titled "The Developmental Bases of Number and Operation Sense"(BCS-0111829). The opinions expressed in this chapter are the sole responsibility of the author and do not necessarily reflect the position, policy, or endorsement of the National Science Foundation.

Thanks to the participants of the 1998 spring semester C&I 490 PML (Psychology of Mathematical Learning) seminar, namely, Alexis P. Benson, Kenneth W. Benson, Karim Ezzatkhah-Yenggeh, Lucia Flevares, Ju-shan Hsieh, Hsin-mei Liao, Yu-chi Tai, and Akihiko Takahashi for helping to shape and sharpen the author's thinking about the matters discussed in this chapter.

References

Ball, D. L. (1998). Unlearning to teach mathematics. *For the Learning of Mathematics, 8*(1), 40–48.

Baroody, A. J. (1985). Pitfalls in equating informal arithmetic procedures with specific mathematical conceptions. *Journal for Research in Mathematics Education, 16*, 233–236.

Baroody, A. J. (1987a). *Children's mathematical thinking: A developmental framework for preschool, primary, and special education teachers.* New York: Teachers College Press.

Baroody, A. J. (1987b). The development of counting strategies for single-digit addition. *Journal for Research in Mathematics Education, 18*, 141–157.

Baroody, A. J. (1989). One point of view: Manipulatives don't come with guarantees. *Arithmetic Teacher, 37*(2), 4–5.

Baroody, A. J. (1992). The development of preschoolers' counting skills and principles. In J. Bideaud, C. Meljac, & J. P. Fischer (Eds.), *Pathways to number* (pp. 99–126). Hillsdale, NJ: Lawrence Erlbaum Associates.

Baroody, A. J. (1999). The development of basic counting, number, and arithmetic knowledge among children classified as mentally retarded. In L. M. Glidden (Ed.), *International review of research in mental retardation, Vol. 22* (pp. 51–103). New York: Academic Press.

Baroody, A. J. (in press). The role of psychological research in the development of early childhood mathematics standards. In D. Clements, J. Sarama, & A. M. DiBiase (Eds.), *Engaging young children in mathematics: Findings of the national 2000 conference for preschool and kindergarten mathematics education.* Mahwah, NJ: Lawrence Erlbaum Associates.

Baroody, A. J., with Coslick, R. T. (1998). *Fostering children's mathematical power: An investigative approach to K–8 mathematics instruction.* Mahwah, NJ: Lawrence Erlbaum Associates.

Baroody, A. J., & Gannon, K. E. (1984). The development of commutativity principle and economical addition strategies. *Cognition and Instruction, 1*, 321–329.

Baroody, A. J., & Ginsburg, H. P. (1986). The relationship between initial meaningful and mechanical knowledge of arithmetic. In J. Hiebert (Ed.), *Conceptual and procedural knowledge: The case of mathematics* (pp. 75–112). Hillsdale, NJ: Lawrence Erlbaum Associates.

Briars, D. J., & Larkin, J. G. (1984). An integrated model of skills in solving elementary word problems. *Cognition and Instruction, 1*, 245–296.

Briars, D., & Siegler, R. S. (1984). A featural analysis of preschoolers' counting knowledge. *Developmental Psychology, 20*, 607–618.

Brownell, W. A. (1935). Psychological considerations in the learning and the teaching of arithmetic. In D. W. Reeve (Ed.), *The teaching of arithmetic* (Tenth yearbook, National Council of Teachers of Mathematics, pp. 1–50). New York: Bureau of Publications, Teachers College, Columbia University.

Brownell, W. A. (1941). *Arithmetic in grades I and II. A critical summary of new and previously reported research* (Duke University Research Studies in Education No. 6). Durham, NC: Duke University Press.

Campbell, P. F., & White, D. Y. (1997). Project IMPACT: Influencing and supporting teacher change in predominantly minority schools. In E. Fennema & B. S. Nelson (Eds.), *Mathematics teachers in transition* (pp. 309–355). Mahwah, NJ: Lawrence Erlbaum Associates.

Carpenter, T. P. (1986). Conceptual knowledge as a foundation for procedural knowledge: Implications from research on the initial learning of arithmetic. In J. Hiebert (Ed.), *Conceptual procedural knowledge: The case of mathematics* (pp. 113–132). Hillsdale, NJ: Lawrence Erlbaum Associates.

Carpenter, T. P., Fennema, E., Peterson, P. L., Chiang, C. P., & Loef, M. (1989). Using knowledge of children's mathematics thinking in classroom teaching: An experimental study. *American Educational Research Journal, 26*, 499–532.

Carpenter, T. P., & Moser, J. M. (1984). The acquisition of addition and subtraction concepts in grades one through three. *Journal for Research in Mathematics Education, 15*, 179–202.

Clements, D. H., & McMillen, S. (1996). Rethinking "concrete" manipulatives. *Teaching Children Mathematics, 2*(5), 270–279.

Curriculum Development and Supplemental Materials Commission. (1999). *Mathematics framework for California public schools: Kindergarten through grade twelve.* Sacramento, CA: California Department of Education.

Davis, R.B. (1984). *Learning Mathematics: The cognitive science approach to mathematics education.* Norwood, NJ: Ablex.

Dewey, J. (1963). *Experience and education.* New York: Collier.

Erlwanger, M. (1975). Benny's concept of rules and answers in IPI mathematics. *Journal of Children's Mathematical Behavior, 1*, 7–25.

Even, R., & Lappan, G. (1994). Constructing meaningful understanding of mathematics content. In D. B. Aichele & A. F. Coxford (Eds.), *Professional development for teachers of mathematics* (1994 yearbook, pp. 128–143). Reston, VA: National Council of Teachers of Mathematics.

Everyday Learning Corporation. (2001). *Everyday mathematics.* Chicago: Author.

Ford, G., & Monod, S. (Eds.). (1966). *Hardtimes* [authored by Charles Dickens]: *An authoritative text; Backgrounds, sources and contemporary reactions; criticisms.* New York: Norton.

Furth, H. G., & Wachs, H. (1974). *Thinking goes to school: Piaget's theory in practice.* New York: Oxford University Press.

Fuson, K. C. (1988). *Children's counting and concepts of number.* New York: Springer-Verlag.

Geary, D. C. (1994). *Children's mathematical development: Research and practical applications.* Washington, DC: American Psychological Association.

Gelman, R., & Meck, E. (1983). Preschoolers' counting: Principle before skill. *Cognition, 13*, 343–359.

Gelman, R., & Meck, E. (1986). The notion of principle: The case of counting. In J. Hiebert (Ed.), *Conceptual and procedural knowledge: The case of mathematics* (pp. 29–57). Hillsdale, NJ: Lawrence Erlbaum Associates.

Gelman, R., & Meck, E. (1992). Early principles aid early but not later conceptions of number. In J. Bideaud, C. Meljac, & J. P. Fischer (Eds.), *Pathways to number* (pp. 171–189). Hillsdale, NJ: Lawrence Erlbaum Associates.

Ginsburg, H. P. (1977). *Children's arithmetic.* New York: Van Nostrand.

Ginsburg, H. P., Klein, A., & Starkey, P. (1998). The development of children's mathematical knowledge: Connecting research with practice. In I. E. Sigel & K. A. Renninger (Eds.),

Handbook of child psychology: Vol. 4. Child psychology in practice (5th ed., pp. 401–476). New York: Wiley.

Glencoe/McGraw Hill (1999). *Glencoe mathematics—applications and connections.* New York: Author.

Hatano, G. (1988). Social and motivational bases for mathematical understanding. In G. B. Saxe & M. Gearhart (Eds.), *Children's mathematics* (pp. 55–70). San Francisco: Jossey-Bass.

Hiebert, J. (Ed.). (1986). *Conceptual and procedural knowledge: The case of mathematics.* Hillsdale, NJ: Lawrence Erlbaum Associates.

Hiebert, J., & Carpenter, T. P. (1992). Learning and teaching with understanding. In D. Grouws (Ed.), *Handbook of research on mathematics teaching and learning* (pp. 65–97). New York: Macmillan.

Hiebert, J., & Lefevre, P. (1986). Conceptual and procedural knowledge in mathematics: An introductory analysis. In J. Hiebert (Ed.), *Conceptual and procedural knowledge: The case of mathematics* (pp. 1–27). Hillsdale, NJ: Lawrence Erlbaum Associates.

Holt, J. (1964). *How children fail.* New York: Delta.

Howe, R. (1999). Knowing and teaching elementary mathematics. *Journal for Research in Mathematics Education, 30,* 579–589. (Reprinted from *Notices of the American Mathematical Society, 46,* 881–887)

Kieren, T. E. (1992). Rational and fractional numbers as mathematical and personal knowledge: Implications for curriculum and instruction. In G. Leinhardt, R. Putnam, & R. A. Hattrup (Eds.), *Analysis of arithmetic for mathematics teaching* (pp. 323–371). Hillsdale, NJ: Lawrence Erlbaum Associates.

Kilpatrick, J. (1985). Doing mathematics without understanding it: A commentary on Higbee and Kunihira. *Educational Psychologist, 20,* 65–68.

Kilpatrick, J. (1992). A history of research in mathematics education. In D. Grouws (Ed.), *Handbook of research on mathematics teaching and learning* (pp. 3–38). New York: Macmillan.

Kilpatrick, J. (2001). Where's the evidence? *Journal for Research in Mathematics Education, 32,* 421–427.

Kilpatrick, J., Swafford, J., & Findell, B. (Eds.). (2001). *Adding it up: Helping children learn mathematics.* Washington, DC: National Academy Press.

Kline, M. (1974). *Why Johnny can't add.* New York: Vintage.

Lamon, S. J. (1993). Ratio and proportion: Children's cognitive and metacognitive processes. In T. P. Carpenter, E. Fennema, & T. A. Romberg (Eds.), *Rational numbers: An integration of research* (pp. 131–156). Hillsdale, NJ: Lawrence Erlbaum Associates.

Ma, L. (1999). *Knowing and teaching elementary mathematics: Teachers' understanding of fundamental mathematics in China and the United States.* Mahwah, NJ: Lawrence Erlbaum Associates.

Mack, N. K. (1990). Learning fractions with understanding: Building on informal knowledge. *Journal for Research in Mathematics Education, 21,* 16–32.

Mack, N. K. (1993). Learning rational numbers with understanding: The case of informal knowledge. In T. P. Carpenter, E. Fennema, & T. A. Romberg (Eds.), *Rational numbers: An integration of research* (pp. 85–105). Hillsdale, NJ: Lawrence Erlbaum Associates.

Mix, K. S., Huttenlocher, J., & Levine, S. C. (2002). *Math without words: Quantitative development in infancy and early childhood.* New York: Oxford University Press.

National Council of Teachers of Mathematics (1989). *Curriculum and evaluation standards for school mathematics.* Reston, VA: Author.

National Council of Teachers of Mathematics. (1991). *Professional standards for teaching mathematics.* Reston, VA: Author.

National Council of Teachers of Mathematics. (1992). *Algebra for the twenty-first century: Proceedings of the August 1992 conference.* Reston, VA: Author.

National Council of Teachers of Mathematics (1995). *Assessment standards for school mathematics.* Reston, VA: Author.

National Council of Teachers of Mathematics (2000). *Principles and standards for school mathematics: Standards 2000.* Reston, VA: Author.

Neches, R. (1987). Learning through incremental refinement of procedures. In D. Klahr, P. Langley, & R. Neches (Eds.), *Production system models of learning and development* (pp. 163–219). Cambridge, MA: MIT Press.

Neill, A. S. (1960). *Summerhill: A radical approach to child rearing.* New York: Hart.

Piaget, J. (1964). Development and learning. In R. E. Ripple & V. N. Rockcastle (Eds.), *Piaget rediscovered* (pp. 7–20). Ithaca, NY: Cornell University.

Pólya, G., & Szego, G. (1972). *Problems and theorems in analysis I.* (D. Aeppli, Trans.). New York: Springer.

Post, T. R., Cramer, K. A., Behr, M., Lesh, R., & Harel, G. (1993). Curriculum implications of research on the learning, teaching and assessing of rational number concepts. In T. P. Carpenter, E. Fennema, & T. A. Romberg (Eds.), *Rational numbers: An integration of research* (pp. 327–362). Hillsdale, NJ: Lawrence Erlbaum Associates.

Resnick, L. B. (1982). Syntax and semantics in learning to subtract. In T. P. Carpenter, J. M. Moser, & T. A. Romburg (Eds.), *Addition and subtraction: A cognitive perspective* (pp. 136–155). Hillsdale, NJ: Lawrence Erlbaum Associates.

Resnick, L. B., & Ford, W. W. (1981). *The psychology of mathematics for instruction.* Hillsdale, NJ: Lawrence Erlbaum Associates.

Riley, M. S., Greeno, J. G., & Heller, J. I. (1983). Development of children's problem-solving ability in arithmetic. In H. P. Ginsburg (Ed.), *The development of mathematical thinking* (pp. 153–200). New York: Academic Press.

Rittle-Johnson, B., & Alibali, M. W. (1999). Conceptual and procedural knowledge of mathematics: Does one lead to the other? *Journal of Educational Psychology, 91,* 175–189.

Rittle-Johnson, B., & Siegler, R. S. (1998). The relation between conceptual and procedural knowledge in learning mathematics: A review of the literature. In C. Donlan (Ed.), *The development of mathematical skills* (pp. 75–110). Hove, East Sussex, England: Psychology Press.

Scott Foresman and Company (2001). *California mathematics.* Glencoe, IL: Author.

Schoenfeld, A. H. (1985). *Mathematical problem solving.* New York: Academic Press.

Schoenfeld, A. H. (1992). Learning to think mathematically: Problem solving, metacognition, and sense making in mathematics. In D. A. Grouws (Ed.), *Handbook of research on mathematics teaching and learning* (pp. 334–370). New York: Macmillan.

Siegler, R. S. (1986). Unities across domains in children's strategy choices. In M. Perlmutter (Ed.), *Minnesota Symposium of Child Psychology* (Vol. 19, pp. 1–48). Hillsdale, NJ: Lawrence Erlbaum Associates.

Silberman, C. E. (Ed.). (1973). *The open classroom reader.* New York: Vintage.

Skemp, R. R. (1978). Relational understanding and instrumental understanding. *Arithmetic Teacher, 26*(3), 9–15.

Smith, J. H. (1921, June). Arithmetic combinations. *The Elementary School Journal,* 762–770.

Sophian, C. (1998). A developmental perspective on children's counting. In C. Donlan (Ed.), *The development of mathematical skills* (pp. 27–46). Hove, East Sussex, England: Psychology Press.

Steffe, L. P. (1992). Schemes of action and operation involving composite units. *Learning and Individual Differences, 4,* 259–309.

Streefland, L. (1993). Fractions: A realistic approach. In T. P. Carpenter, E. Fennema, & T. A. Romberg (Eds.), *Rational numbers: An integration of research* (pp. 289–325). Hillsdale, NJ: Lawrence Erlbaum Associates.

Thorndike, E. L. (1922). *The psychology of arithmetic.* New York: Macmillan.

van de Brink, J., & Streefland, L. (1979). Young children (6–8) ratio and proportion. *Educational Studies in Mathematics, 10,* 403–420.

Vygotsky, L. S. (1962). *Thought and language.* Cambridge, MA: MIT Press.

Wertheimer, M. (1959). *Productive thinking.* New York: Harper & Row. (Original work published 1945.)

Wheeler, L. R. (1939). A comparative study of the difficulty of the 100 addition combinations. *Journal of Genetic Psychology, 54,* 295–312.

Wilson, S. M. (2003). *California dreaming: Reforming mathematics education.* New Haven: Yale University Press.

Wynn, K. (1998). Numerical competence in infants. In C. Donlan (Ed.), *The development of mathematical skills* (pp. 3–25). Hove, East Sussex, England: Psychology Press.

CHAPTER 2

DOES IT ALL ADD UP? CHANGES IN CHILDREN'S KNOWLEDGE OF ADDITION COMBINATIONS, STRATEGIES, AND PRINCIPLES

Richard Cowan
University of London

Researchers, including psychologists and mathematics educators, and lay people, including school teachers and administrators, hold conflicting beliefs about the nature of arithmetic expertise (e.g., Ginsburg, Klein, & Starkey, 1998). In this chapter, I describe two vastly different views of this expertise and then discuss how three critical components of this expertise (knowledge of addition combinations, strategies, and principles) develop.

Two Views of Arithmetic Expertise

One conception of arithmetic expertise emphasizes the development of calculational competence; another stresses the development of mathematical understanding and thinking. I illustrate the historical development of these views with examples from English education, but—as the chapter by Baroody (chap. 1, this volume) shows—similar developments have taken place in other countries (Becker & Selter, 1996).

COMPETENCE = COMPUTATIONAL SKILL

In the 19th century, English elementary schools for working class children emphasized arithmetic. These children were not expected to continue their education after elementary school, and the goal of instruction was to give them the skills necessary for work. The emphasis on calculation was enshrined in the standards set in the payment-by-results scheme introduced in 1862. This scheme determined how much funding a school received according to the numbers of students and their performance in examinations. These examinations derived from standards set for each year. The standards only covered arithmetic, reading, and writing. The standards in the 1862 code are listed in Table 2.1. The expectations for arithmetic clearly reflect how the curriculum was shaped by anticipated demands of work and everyday life.

Although the payment-by-results system was gradually dismantled after 1890 (Sutherland, 1984) and despite prominent critics, such as Matthew Arnold, who bemoaned the lack of teaching of arithmetic principles (Arnold, cited in Gosden, 1969), reform of the curriculum was slow. The computational aspects of

Table 2.1: Standards for Each Year Group in the Revised Code of 1862 (from Gosden, 1969). Standard I was for 6 year olds

Standard	Arithmetic	Reading	Writing
I	Form . . . from dictation figures up to 20; add and subtract figures up to 10, orally	Narrative in monosyllables	Form . . . from dictation, letters capital and small, manuscript
II	A sum in simple addition or subtraction and the multiplication table	One of the narratives . . . after monosyllables in an elementary reading book	Copy in manuscript character a line of print
III	A sum in any simple rule as far as short division	A short paragraph from an elementary reading book	A sentence from the same paragraph, slowly read . . . then dictated
IV	A sum in compound rules (money)	A short paragraph from a more advanced reading book	A sentence slowly dictated once . . . from the same book
V	A sum in compound rules (common weights and measures)	A few lines of poetry from a reading book used in the first class	A sentence slowly dictated . . . from a reading book used in the first class
VI	A sum in practice or bills of parcels	A short ordinary paragraph in a newspaper	Another short ordinary paragraph in a newspaper, slowly dictated

arithmetic continued to be emphasized. A 1930 primary school syllabus might specify addition and subtraction up to 10 for the first year, up to 99 for the second year, up to 999 for the third year, and up to 10,000 for the fourth year (Schonell & Schonell, 1957). When inspectors noted children were not competent in either oral or written arithmetic, they attributed the deficiencies to defects in teachers or children, not the method.

Some educators came to believe that deficiencies in children's arithmetic were often the result of premature introduction to "number facts" and computation. Schonell and Schonell (1957) asserted that much failure could be avoided if teachers grounded arithmetic in experience before moving on to formal methods of calculation. They claimed that practice of number facts without understanding was of little value and that arithmetic problems should be rooted in familiar experience before written computation was required (cf. Brownell, 1935). They recommended the use of objects and simple story problems derived from everyday situations of school and home.

Working within the traditional conception of arithmetic expertise, educators changed their beliefs about the methods most likely to achieve it. Understanding arithmetic received increasing emphasis. However, by understanding, these reformers—like the proponents of the Social Utility Movement in the United States (see Kilpatrick, 1992)—meant connecting number facts and arithmetic procedures only to situations in everyday life. Developing fast and accurate computational skill continued to be the goal.

COMPETENCE AS MATHEMATICAL UNDERSTANDING AND THINKING

The second conception of arithmetic expertise developed partly from the radical reform of the school curriculum in the 1950s. This was prompted by the gap between university and school mathematics (Kilpatrick, 1992). The secondary curriculum was revised to provide a better preparation for university mathematics. As all students would be expected to progress from primary to secondary school, this led to reform of the primary curriculum. Another influence was the increase in availability of calculating machines that made unaided computational skill less important. Educators saw the traditional conception of instruction as deficient, because it was disconnected from mathematics and led to routine expertise and limited application of skills. In Britain, the aims for primary mathematics became to make children think for themselves, to give them a knowledge and appreciation of mathematics as a creative subject, and to develop facility with number and quantity relations (Schools Council, 1966).

The new conception of arithmetic expertise emphasized mathematical understanding. Like the "New Math" in the United States (see Kline, 1974), teachers were supposed to develop children's ideas of sets as a basis for understanding number. Addition would be understood as the union of two disjoint sets. Instruction would help children discover the various logical properties of number such as closure, identity, commutativity, and associativity and the inverse relation between addition and subtraction. They should construct their own addition tables and refer to them until they had committed them to memory (see also Wynroth, 1986). A number line would help the child understand the relations between addition and subtraction and would link numbers to measurement.

Educators drew on Piaget's research in two ways. First, they used his work to justify the new emphasis on children's activity and experience (Central Advisory Council for Education, England, 1967). Second, they used his work to provide insight into the difficulties children would have in grasping abstract mathematical ideas (Lovell, 1971; Nuffield Mathematics Project, 1967).

More recently, government agencies have reaffirmed the importance of mental arithmetic (Department of Education and Sciences, 1979). This does not, however, represent a retreat to the traditional conception of arithmetic expertise. The report emphasizes the importance of developing an understanding of mathematics through inquiry and experiment. It also stresses the value of children's using related number combinations (e.g., solving 9 + 6 by recalling 10 + 6 = 16 and reasoning 9 is one less than 10). The traditional conception would have emphasized immediate recall of number facts.

CONCLUSIONS

In this brief history of primary education, I have shown how an earlier focus on knowledge of number facts and computational accuracy has given way to a broader conception that emphasizes principles and the use of strategies. Nevertheless, the traditional view of arithmetic expertise, which dominated the early years of English education, continues to influence school practices and textbooks (Ginsburg et al., 1998). Furthermore, it is still the more prevalent view among parents and employers (Ridgway & Passey, 1995).

The Development of Three Key Components of Addition Expertise

I now review the empirical research regarding the development of three key components of addition expertise, beginning with the single-digit (basic) addition combinations.

BASIC ADDITION COMBINATIONS

The aim of the early elementary arithmetic curriculum was to develop efficient (rapid and accurate) mental and written arithmetic. Educators believed that this would depend on knowledge of 100 basic addition "facts" (i.e., the sums of the digits from 0 to 9).

Relative Difficulty of Addition Combinations

Early research efforts focused on determining whether some facts were better known than other facts and why.

Size Effects and Key Exceptions. Early investigators consistently reported that difficulty increased with size of the sum (Clapp, 1924; Knight & Behrens, 1928; Murray, 1939; Wheeler, 1939). Although tie sums, such as 4 + 4 and 7 + 7, also exhibited this size effect, such combinations were, in general, easier than would be expected by their size. Both of these patterns are evident in Table 2.2, which summarizes the relative difficulties of the addition combinations in the Wheeler (1939) and Murray (1939) studies.

Siegler and Robinson (1982) reanalyzed the data of Knight and Behrens (1928). They found that size of the smaller addend (*min*) was as good a predictor of ranked difficulty as overall sum (*sum*) when all sums were included and was an even better predictor than *sum* when tie sums were excluded. The same pattern emerged in a reanalysis of Wheeler's (1939) data. Both *min* and *sum* accounted for similar proportions of the variance across all sums (68% and 67%). When ties were excluded, *min* was a better predictor than *sum* (88% vs. 73%). Although the predictors were correlated with each other, both make independent contributions (with both predictors: 73% for all sums, 88% excluding ties).

As Table 2.2 illustrates, the relative difficulties of sums with 0 as an addend were less consistent. Some researchers found these to be among the easiest combinations to be learned (Knight & Behrens, 1928; Wheeler, 1939). Others reported them as the hardest (Clapp, 1924; Murray, 1939). As Table 2.2 further illustrates, there were also dramatic differences in the rankings of tie sums. These discrepancies are still worth noting, as several modern researchers (e.g., Ashcraft & Fierman, 1982; Lefevre, Sadesky, & Bisanz, 1996) used Wheeler's rankings to account for variation in reaction times on addition combinations.

Factors Affecting the Relative Difficulty of Addition Combinations

Researchers need to exercise great care in interpreting or using difficulty indexes. As early as the 1930s, Schonell (1937) had ruled out constructing a precise order of difficulty because "modern research shows the degree of difficulty in the various number combinations in the four processes differs considerably from pupil to pupil" (p. 11). Almost five decades later, Baroody (1985) cautioned that Wheeler's (1939) rankings cannot be considered a normative order of difficulty applicable for any population, because difficulty indexes can be affected by a variety of factors.

Methodological Differences. One key factor that can affect difficulty rankings is method of data collection. For example, Wheeler's (1939) study was a small-scale study in which exposure to addition combinations was under some control. In contrast, Clapp (1924) and Murray (1939) derived their rank orders from large-scale surveys of children across several schools.

Instructional Differences. Differences in instruction can have a profound effect on the relative difficulty of basic number combinations. For instance, some Scottish schools studied by Murray (1941) did not include items concerning zero

Table 2.2: Rankings of Difficulty of the 100 Addition Facts According
to Type of Sum, Size of Smaller Addend, in Wheeler
(1939) and Murray (1939)

Size of smaller addend	Type of sum					
	Ties			Nonties[a]		
	Wheeler	Murray	n	Wheeler	Murray
0	1	3	18	14.4	90.0
1	9	8	16	29.3	15.9
2	37.5	14	14	52.2	30.1
3	13	18	12	59.1	47.4
4	4	28	10	75.1	55.2
5	37.5	17	8	84.5	67.4
6	59.5	35	6	89.9	71.3
7	46.5	9	4	95.6	80.5
8	75.5	25	2	96.5	76.0
9	55	26	-	-	-

[a] Figures are mean ranks.

Note. 1 = the least difficult; 100 = the most difficult.

in the tables they taught. So it should not be surprising that he found such combinations relatively difficult. (See Miura & Okamoto, chap. 8, this volume, for a discussion of why instruction in Asian countries can make learning $n + 8/8 + n$ and $n + 9/9 + n$ combinations a much less difficult process.)

Amount of Practice. Addition combinations might vary in difficulty because some are more practiced than others. Thorndike (1922) drew attention to the inequalities of practice given to different bonds in elementary textbooks and these inequalities remain in modern textbooks (Ashcraft & Christy, 1995). Contemporary accounts support the role of differences in exposure (but cf. Baroody, 1994) and draw attention to the part that may be played by parents in giving preschool children practice in simple addition (Siegler & Shrager, 1984). A small study of parents of 2- to 4-year-olds found that the most practiced problems were those with 1 or 2 as the addend.

Associative Facilitation or Interference. Another determinant of combination difficulty might be relations with other bonds (Thorndike, 1922). Learning that $1 + 8 = 9$ might be aided by the association between 8 and 9 developed through mastery of the counting sequence (e.g., Siegler & Shrager, 1984). Although the contribution of associations between numbers formed through practice in tasks other than addition can be beneficial, it may also be a source of error. Murray (1941) analyzed the errors made by 417 Scottish primary school pupils on written tests of the 100 number combinations. He attributed several types of error to misleading associations. For $a + n$ combinations, Murray viewed an answer of $n + 1$ (e.g., responding to $6 + 9$ with an answer of 10) as an intrusion from the counting sequence (see also Siegler & Robinson, 1982; Siegler & Shrager, 1984). He considered an answer of $a, a + 10, n, n + 10, a + a,$ or $n + n$ (e.g., responding to $6 + 9$ with answers of 6, 9, 16, 19, 12, or 18, respectively) an intrusion from other addition knowledge. Other errors, such as responding to $a + n$ with an answer of $a \times n$ or $a - n$ (e.g., responding to $6 + 9$ with 54 or 3) may be due to an intrusion from knowledge of other operations. However, an alternative explanation is that such mental-arithmetic errors are the product of estimation efforts, not retrieval (Baroody, 1988, 1989, 1992, 1994; see Baroody & Tiilikainen, chap. 3, this volume, and Dowker, chap. 9, this volume, for a more complete discussion).

Computational Errors. Miscounting might cause difficulties with some addition combinations. Close-miss errors in which the child's answer differs by one from the correct answer, such as responding to $5 + 8$ with 14 could result from covert computation (Baroody, 1985, 1994; Chazal, as described in Brownell & Chazal, 1935) or the recall of the result of a previous miscount (Siegler & Shrager, 1984). Murray (1941) noted several close-miss errors, but he did not discuss their cause.

Views of Addition-Combination Mastery

Chazal's (in Brownell & Chazal, 1935) characterization of close-miss errors and Murray's (1941) reaction to it epitomize the radically different views of addition-combination learning that persist to this day (e.g., Baroody, 1985, vs. Ashcraft, 1985).

Concept-First View. Brownell and his student Chazal believed that fostering meaningful memorization of basic combinations resulted in better retention and transfer than promoting their memorization by rote (Ginsburg et al., 1998). Brownell and Chazal (1935) justified their position in the following manner:

> It all depends upon one's conception of arithmetic ability. If the pupil knows arithmetic when he has a memoriter [memorized-by-heart] mastery

of hundreds of isolated facts, then perhaps he had best learn those facts by brute memorization. If, on the other hand, he knows arithmetic only when he can use intelligently what he has learned, then he had best make use of his intelligence in learning the facts. (p. 26)

In her study (partly described in Brownell & Chazal, 1935), Chazal assessed third-grade children who had been drilled in the addition combinations in first and second grade. She found that their previous instruction had not resulted in mastery. More specifically, the third-graders answered less than half the addition items immediately without hesitation.

Chazal interviewed her participants to determine the bases for their correct and incorrect responses. She found that many responses were the result of counting or other "indirect" solution methods. In Brownell and Chazal's (1935) view, it is understandable that children first use informal methods that make sense to them.

Skills-First View. Murray (1941) was scathing about Chazal's study. In particular, he did not consider characterizing solutions as "counting" or "solved indirectly" as suitable for psychological analysis. Chazal's study may have provoked such hostility, in part, because her results were used to question the conventional wisdom that learning essentially involved forming and strengthening associations by means of direct instruction and drill.

In a similar vein, when Wheeler (1939) suspected that his participants were answering addition items by mental or physical counting, he suggested that children resorted to such "crutches" because they had developed them in learning number ideas. His solution was "it might be more economical first to teach the number combinations, and later develop the number concepts" (p. 311).

The Importance of Combination Mastery

Although mathematical educators' views of arithmetical expertise and the method for achieving mastery have changed (Askew, 1998; Lovell, 1971; Reys, Suydam, Lindquist, & Smith, 1998), the importance of mastery of number combinations remains:

A child may count 4 fingers and then 5 more to solve 4 + 5. This strategy is perfectly acceptable for a while. However, this counting process should not be repeated every time 4 + 5 is given. We want the child to move to counting on from 4, to thinking "4 + 4 = 8, so 4 + 5 is 9" or other strategies. Eventually we want the child to memorize "4 + 5 = 9" for quick recall. (Reys et al., 1998, p. 155)[1]

---

[1] In A. J. Baroody's opinion, there is general agreement that children need to produce the answers to basic number combinations efficiently. However, as children and adults use a variety of strategies to accomplish this feat (see, e.g., LeFevre, Smith-Chant, Hiscock, Daley, & Morris, chap. 7, this volume), it makes sense to expand our notion of basic number-combination mastery beyond recall or retrieval of isolated facts (Baroody, with Coslick, 1998; Baroody & Tiilikainen, chap. 3, this volume).

A child who cannot efficiently produce the sums of the basic combinations is at a disadvantage in multidigit written and oral arithmetic. As standardized mathematical tests continue to emphasize computation (Ridgway, 1987), this may be why knowledge of number combinations is related to mathematics achievement when measured by standardized tests.

Russell and Ginsburg (1984) conducted an examination of concepts and skills in American children. They found a sample of fourth-grade children who had difficulty in mathematics but were otherwise normal in intelligence and free from emotional and physical disadvantages. They compared this sample with fourth and third graders from the same schools whose mathematics achievement was commensurate with their intelligence and age. Knowledge of number combinations was assessed with a sample of 10 single-digit expressions that excluded ties and addends of one or zero. For each item, the child was asked to tell the answer straight away or report if they had to work it out. Children with mathematics difficulties knew fewer combinations than either their peers or third graders. The only other task that discriminated between these children and both normal groups involved story problems.

Knowledge of number combinations is likewise correlated with mathematics achievement in other cultures. Chiu (1996) studied first- and third-grade Taiwanese children. Using a standardized mathematics test, he constructed groups for each grade of children whose performance was either above average, average, or below average. Knowledge of number combinations varied with group. The only children who knew fewer items than the below-average third graders were the below-average first graders. Individual differences in combination mastery among first graders suggest that factors other than schooling might help account for these differences. However, a study of 78 Greek third graders that also found a high correlation between combination knowledge and mathematics achievement yielded no evidence of differences in involvement in numeracy practices in the home (Ganetsou, 1998).

Accounting for Individual Differences

If differences in combination mastery exist among children, even when the amount of practice is controlled, then such differences may be due to one of several cognitive factors.

Working Memory. One key factor may be working memory (Baddeley, 1986; Hitch & McAuley, 1991). Geary (1993) suggested that practice may be ineffective in promoting mastery of sums if children forget the addends by the time they have worked out the answer. This might occur if the storage capacity of children's working memory is small, or if slowly executed or inherently inefficient strategies put exceptional demands on their working memory.

Numerical Regularities. Another factor that may limit children's ability to profit from practice is a failure to identify patterns and relations (see Baroody & Ginsburg, 1986, for a detailed discussion). Myers and Thornton (1977) claimed that children with learning disabilities benefited considerably from instruction that explicitly emphasized relations among number combinations. Some children may be less disposed to detect patterns and relations because their instruction provides few structured opportunities to look for regularities or little encouragement to do so. A child's disposition to look for arithmetic regularities may also be affected by the richness of the existing conceptual knowledge (see, e.g., Baroody & Tiilikainen, chap. 3, this volume).

Summary

In short, we know that some children master number combinations readily whereas others do not and that this is associated with mathematics achievement. Satisfactory explanations of both these results remain to be established, but some explanations of the first suggest a link with strategies. I turn now to consider research on the strategies children use to solve addition problems.

ADDITION STRATEGIES

Two Views of Expertise

The Traditional View. In the traditional view of arithmetic expertise, memorization of the basic addition facts is the basis for competence in both mental and written addition with either single- or multidigit addends. In this view, extending knowledge of the basic "addition facts" to multidigit additions was a matter of establishing systems of cooperating bonds (Thorndike, 1922) or transfer (Schonell & Schonell, 1957). Thus $50 + 30 = 80$ would be allied to $5 + 3 = 8$, and $12 + 2, 22 + 2, 32 + 2$, and so on would be connected to knowledge of $2 + 2$. The basis for such generalizations to larger items, however, was left undefined.

The Modern View. In the modern conception of arithmetical expertise, the aim of education is to develop flexibility in working with number and to encourage thinking about problems rather than the mindless reproduction of a standard method (Askew, 1998; Baroody, with Coslick, 1998). By encouraging children to use known number combinations to derive other items, they will extend their knowledge of combinations and develop confidence in their ability to do mental arithmetic. By encouraging diverse strategic solutions and requiring students to explain these to others, children will realize that there can be more than one way to work things out and that mathematics is about methods as much as it is about right answers.

Studies of adult expert mathematicians and calculating prodigies support the conception of arithmetical expertise as involving flexibility. Such calculation experts do not solve complex arithmetical problems just by relying on number facts and algorithms (Dowker, 1992; Heavey, chap. 15, this volume; Smith, 1988). They use a wealth of strategies, such as decomposing given problems into simpler ones. For example, the square of 251 may be found by recalling that $(a + b)^2 = a^2 + 2ab + b^2$ and substituting 250 and 1 for a and b, yielding $62500 + 500 + 1$ or 63001. Another characteristic of expert performance in mental arithmetic is the development of procedures that are well adapted to the limitations of human memory. This is shown in the common adoption of the left-to-right method of doing addition. For example, to add 56 and 35, first add 50 and 30 (80), note that the addition of units will result in another ten (80 + 10 or 90), and finally, determine the sum's unit digit by adding 6 + 5 (1)—answer 91. This method has an important advantage over the usual right-to-left method taught in school. Less information requires storage during computation. Whether the flexible strategies and adaptive procedures in adult expertise have developmental precursors is one motivation for current research on the development of children's strategies.

Two Research Traditions

Current research builds on two different traditions: the observation and interview approach used by Ilg and Ames (1951) and others, and the chronometric approach pioneered by Groen and Parkman (1972; Parkman, 1972).

Observation and Interview. Ilg and Ames (1951) distinguished several strategies with different but overlapping periods. These are presented in Table 2.3 with the names given them in some more recent studies (Baroody, 1987; Carpenter & Moser, 1982, 1984; Siegler, 1987).

Carpenter and Moser (1982, 1984) elicited children's strategies with story problems involving single-digit addends (e.g., *Wally had 3 pennies. His father gave him 5 more pennies. How many pennies did Wally have altogether?*). Their participants were interviewed each year from first to third grade. In all problems, the first addend was smaller than the second.[2] Overall, children progressed from counting-all to counting-on with increasing use of number-combination facility and infrequent use of decomposition. Use of counting-on from the first addend (COF) did not clearly differ from counting-on from the larger addend (COL), either in onset or frequency (but cf. Baroody, 1987, 1995; Baroody, Wilkins, & Tiilikainen, chap. 4, this volume). Most children used both strategies during an interview and neither strategy was more likely to appear first. Several children reverted to using counting-all for some sums even when they used COL on others.

The evidence that children use a mixture of counting-based strategies is consistent across several studies. This seems paradoxical if one considers the differences in efficiency. Why should children use a less efficient counting strategy once they have learned to use COL? Baroody and Ginsburg (1986) noted that three factors influence strategy choice: semantic structure of problem, cognitive economy, and problem size.

1. *Semantic structure.* The semantic structure of problems may influence strategy choice. Combine problems (e.g., *Peter has 3 apples, and Anne has 7 apples. How many apples do they have altogether?*) may invoke a conception of

---

[2] Note that, for large-addend + small-addend items, COF and COL are indistinguishable, thus, the reason for using small-addend + large-addend items only.

Table 2.3: Strategies for Addition and Their Ages Ranges Identified by Ilg and Ames (1951) and Their Correspondence with Contemporary Studies

Ilg & Ames		Carpenter & Moser (1982, 1984)	Baroody (1987)	Siegler (1987)
Description	Ages (yrs)			
Concrete Counting Strategies				
• Starting with *one* each time, counts fingers or other objects to represent each addend and to determine a sum.	5–7	Counting-all with models	CC	*Sum*
• Shortcuts to the direct modeling strategy	-	-	CCS	-
Abstract Counting Strategies				
• Starts at one	5–7	Counting-all without models	MCAF, MCAL, CAF, CAL	*Sum*
• Starts with smaller number	5–7	Counting-on from first	MCOF, COF	
• Starts with larger number	6–8	Counting-on from larger	MCOL, COL	*Min*
Other Strategies				
• Guesses	5–7	-	Other	Guess
• Just knows	ties, 6–7 nonties, 7-9	Recall, known fact	Automatic	Retrieval
• Breaks down into known combinations	simple, 7 complex, 8	Derived facts	Other	Decomposition

Note. Baroody (1987) identified a wider range of strategies, including what Fuson (1982) called a "counting entities" strategy, which involves counting out objects to represent one addend before the sum count. However, he found these were rarely used (< 2% of trials).

addition as the combining of sets (a binary or part-part-whole view), whereas change problems (e.g., *Pete has 3 apples. Ann gave him 7 more. How many does Pete have now?*) may prompt a conception of addition as a change of an initial quantity (a unary or change-add-to view). The evidence regarding a semantic effect is mixed. Although De Corte and Verschaffel (1987) observed COL use was more common on combine problems and COF on change problems, Carpenter and Moser (1984) reported variability within problems of the same type.

2. *Cognitive economy.* Cognitive economy may influence strategy choice. COL, for example, puts less demand on working memory than does COF (for small-addend + large-addend items at least). However, the amount of mental effort saved varies directly with the difference between addends. For 3 + 4, for example, COL (starting with 4 and counting on 3 more times) requires only slightly less mental labor than does COF (starting with 3 and counting on 4 more times). This minimal reduction in working-memory load may be offset by the effort required to determine the larger of two close numbers. For 3 + 7, on the other hand, COL requires considerably less working memory than does COF, saving mental effort well beyond the relatively small effort to determine the larger of two distant numbers. Baroody and Ginsburg (1986) noted that, in fact, items such as 2 + 3 and 3 + 4 elicited more use of COF than items such as 2 + 5 and 3 + 7.

3. *Problem size.* The relative gain in efficiency may also underlie the effect of problem size. Children who do not use COL with small-addend items may use it when one addend is large (Baroody & Mason, as cited in Baroody & Ginsburg, 1986; Thomas, 1992). As children also show variability in strategy use on the same item, the previous explanation only partially accounts for strategy variation.

Baroody (1987) took into account the following three factors to generate a comprehensive taxonomy of counting-based addition strategies: the number of addends represented concretely, whether an addend was represented by a simultaneous or sequential display of fingers, and whether representation of an addend was done separately from (before) the sum count (totaling process) or integrated with it (required simultaneous keeping-track and totaling processes). He sampled kindergarten children's strategies over 9 months. This revealed variants of the mental counting-all beginning with the first addend strategy (CAF; e.g., for 2 + 5, counting: "1, 2; 3 [is 1 more]; 4 [is 2 more]; 5 [is 3 more]; 6 [is 4 more]; 7 [is 5 more]"). Two more efficient versions of this strategy involve disregarding addend order: (a) With counting-all beginning with larger addend (CAL), a child starts by verbally counting up to the cardinal value of the larger addend and then proceeds to count-on the other addend, while representing it with fingers in order to keep track (to determine when to stop counting). (b) A modified version of CAL (MCAL) is identical to CAL, except that a child raises a finger or puts out a block while counting up to the cardinal value of the first addend.[3] In this study, too, children who used COL continued to use less sophisticated counting strategies.

Chronometric Approach. Although interviews and observations consistently yielded evidence of diverse strategy use, even by the same child, proponents of a chronometric approach have typically characterized children at different ages as predominantly using one or two strategies (cf. Svenson & Sjöberg, 1983). Ashcraft and Fierman (1982), for example, concluded that first graders used a counting strategy to determine sums, whereas fourth graders used retrieval. The chronometric approach seemed a straightforward method for discriminating between a reproductive process such as retrieval of number facts and a reconstructive process such as a mental counting. The long latency for items with large addends was taken to reflect a counting strategy. If latency did not vary with addend size, then the latencies were presumed to reflect retrieval.

A difficulty for this view was that even adults took longer to answer sums with larger addends. Groen & Parkman (1972) suggested adults used a mixture of retrieval and mental counting. They noted that the slope for adult latencies was only about 20 ms per item. This was much shallower than children's, about 400 ms per item, and much faster than the implicit counting rate for adults, estimated at 150 ms per item. If adults were mentally counting to determine sums, then they could do so remarkably fast. The pattern of the adult data was more plausibly explained by crediting them with the use of a mixture of retrieval and mental counting. Mental counting on a few trials (e.g., 5%) would be sufficient to generate the relation between latency and *min*.

Ashcraft and Stazyk (1981) tested this proposition by removing the slowest 5% of adult trials and reanalyzing the data. They found that latency continued to vary with addend size. To eliminate reliable variation in latency with problem size, they had to remove 50% of the data. They argued adults were unlikely to count on so many trials and, therefore, the problem size effect could not just be due to mental counting. Instead, this effect might reflect differences in associative strength. Determinants of associative strength are frequency of exposure and order of acquisition. Sums with smaller addends are solved faster by adults because they are more familiar with them, rather than because they are easier to compute (but cf. Baroody, 1985, 1994; LeFevre et al., chap. 7, this volume). This explanation of the patterns in adult latencies on addition sums resembles the attempts to explain why children found some addition combinations harder to remember.

A New Approach: Computer Modeling

In a crucial article dealing with the discrepancies between the two forms of strategy research, Siegler (1987) showed that children's latency data are bet-

---

[3] Modified versions of CAF, COF, and COL (MCAF, MCOF, and MCOL, respectively) are also possible (see Baroody, 1987, for details).

ter accounted for by separating trials according to reported and observed strategies. This paved the way for studies that combine both approaches. Taking into
account the basic insights from observational studies that children use a variety of strategies to solve addition problems and that even the same child will
solve the same item by using different strategies (Carpenter & Moser, 1982; Fuson, 1982; Renton, 1992; Siegler & Shrager, 1984; cf. Svenson & Sjöberg, 1983),
Siegler developed a series of accounts and computer models of how children
choose among strategies for a particular sum and how they come to use new
strategies (Shrager & Siegler, 1998; Siegler & Jenkins, 1989; Siegler & Robinson, 1982; Siegler & Shipley, 1995; Siegler & Shrager, 1984; Siegler & Stern,
1998).

Siegler's models reflect the adaptive nature of children's strategy use (e.g.,
backup strategies are used on just those problems where retrieval is likely to be
inaccurate). They also yield the patterns of latencies that chronometric studies
detect. The models integrate knowledge about children's strategies. They go
further by suggesting nonintuitive predictions.[4] Finally, the models do not require the assumption that strategy choice and development depend on explicit
conscious knowledge. This may seem strange to educators who assume that
strategies develop from the deliberate application of principles or that children must know what strategy they are using. However, research on children's
use of mnemonic strategies resulted in the view that conscious decision making
played much less of a role than initially assumed (Flavell, 1985).

As each successive computer model builds on the previous one by incorporating additional elements, I describe them in turn (see also Table 3.1 in chap. 3 of
this volume for an overview of these simulations).

Distribution of Associations Model (DOAM). For the first model,
DOAM, Siegler & Shrager (1984) assumed that children would rely on a retrieved answer if it was retrieved within a certain number of attempts and if its
associative strength exceeded a specific confidence criterion. Both the number
of retrieval attempts and the confidence criterion could vary with addition expression and occasion. A number of answers might be associated with a particular item. What determines the associative strength of each of these answers
are prior knowledge and, more important, how frequently it is practiced. Every
time an answer is given for the expression, the associative strength between the
two is strengthened. For example, an incorrect answer associated with 2 + 3
might include 4, either due to the association with the counting list or to previ-

---

[4] For example, Siegler and Shrager's (1984) model provided a nonintuitive prediction
about the correlations between the percent of backup strategy use and (a) the percent of retrieval errors and (b) the percent of backup errors. According to the distribution of associations model, the use of backup strategies and the percent of retrieval errors both are determined by the distribution of associations and, thus, should be highly correlated.
However, the percent of backup errors is determined by the *difficulty* of a backup strategy
and, thus, should not be highly correlated with the percent of backup strategy use. In fact,
the percent of backup strategy use is more highly correlated with the percent of errors on
retrieval use than with the percent of backup errors.

ously deriving 4 through a miscount. Producing correct answers results in greater gains in associative strength because they are reinforced. If no retrieved answer exceeds the confidence criterion, the child uses a backup strategy. The first step is to form an elaborated representation of the expression, either by forming a mental image or using fingers to represent the addends. If combining the associative strength of the answer to the elaborated representation with the previous associative strength exceeds the confidence criterion, the child states the answer. If not, the child determines the sum by counting a representation of the addends, such as a mental image of objects or raised fingers.

Without assuming conscious strategy selection, DOAM yields adaptive strategy choices in that it uses backup strategies on the most difficult problems as children do. The model matches the variation in latency according to item difficulty that children exhibit. Differences in the associative strength of answers contribute to variability in strategy use across items and even for a particular item. Variations in the confidence criterion further contribute to varying strategy use for a particular item. So a child might rely on a retrieved answer for a particular expression one day and not the next if, on the second occasion, the confidence criterion was higher and the answer had insufficient associative strength.

In an evaluation of this model, Siegler and Shipley (1995) pointed out the following four shortcomings: the assumption of retrieval as the default strategy, the lack of specification how children decided among backup strategies, the lack of generalization to other items (including those not practiced), and the absence of knowledge of the relative difficulty of items or usefulness of strategies. Because it focused on preschoolers doing addition sums with addends between 1 and 5, it did not discriminate among counting strategies.

Adaptive Strategy Choice Model (ASCM). The next model ASCM (Siegler & Shipley, 1995) built on DOAM by incorporating components that learned about strategies, as well as the distributions of associations (addition-item database). Specifically, a strategy database was added to DOAM's addition-item database. From computational experience, ASCM learned about the time required to answer an item using a particular strategy (speed data) and the accuracy of the solution (accuracy data), as well as what answer was given for a particular item (answer data). Like DOAM, the answer data modified the addition-item database. Unlike DOAM, the speed and accuracy data modified the following three subcomponents of the strategy database: (a) item-specific data (the strategy's speed and accuracy for the item actually practiced), (b) featural data (the strategy's speed and accuracy for items that share a particular feature with the practiced item, such as having the same addends), and (c) global data (the strategy's speed and accuracy for all addition items). This and other information stored in the strategy database were the basis for future strategy choices. Another subcomponent of the strategy database was a novelty factor, information reflecting the novelty of the strategy. The novelty factor increased the likelihood that a new strategy will be used. As strategies were used, their novelty declined. Backup strategies varied in accuracy with how much counting they involved but generally increased in accuracy and speed with repeated use.

A simulation of this model that introduced the COL strategy after 60 trials per item approximated Siegler and Jenkins' (1989) developmental data (cf. Baroody & Tiilikainen, chap. 3, this volume). After 750 simulation trials, the correlations with children's error frequencies, solution times, and use of retrieval were each greater than .8. This model features extra sources of variability in the use of strategies both within and among the items. Unlike the previous model, the "developmental order" of strategies is not fixed. Retrieval is not always tried first, although with practice it becomes dominant through being the fastest and most accurate strategy. The order of consideration of backup strategies also varies.

ASCM develops in accuracy and strategy use in ways that reflect some aspects of children's development. The model first uses COL more often than the concrete counting-all strategy on items with particularly small addends (e.g., 1 or 2) and later on those with a greater difference in size of addends. The times that it takes to answer items also correspond with chronometric data. At an early phase, the best predictor of latencies is the sum of the addends (*sum*) just as it is for preschoolers, but later the smaller addend (*min*) is the best predictor (Groen & Resnick, 1977). Subsequently the product of the addends provides the best fit as some chronometric studies have found (Geary, Widaman, & Little, 1986; Geary, Widaman, Little, & Cormier, 1987; Miller, Perlmutter, & Keating, 1984). The differences in how much variance each predictor accounts for are small, as all three are highly correlated.

Nevertheless, a previous explanation of why the product of the addends could be the best predictor of latencies on retrieval trials assumed that arithmetical knowledge was represented in a mental "table of number facts." ASCM has no such representation, and yet it yields the same result. This follows from the assumption that solution times on retrieval trials reflect associative strengths that, in turn, reflect the history of mixed use of backup strategies of counting-all and COL. More specifically, Siegler and Shipley (1995) equated associative strength to the inverse proportion of the average of solution times from using the count-all and COL strategies. The result was the simulation yielded a pattern of solution times for which the product of the addends was a better predictor than either *sum* or *min*.

Running ASCM with varying assumptions about the confidence criteria and probability of correct execution of backup strategies yielded the three patterns of performance that Siegler (1988) had observed in groups of students he called good, not-so-good, and perfectionists. Good students were more accurate and more likely to use retrieval than not-so-good students. Perfectionists relied least on retrieval, but when they did they were more accurate than the good students.

DOAM could also simulate such individual differences, but it could not generalize strategies to novel items. ASCM can generalize because it learns about strategies at the level of items with features in common (includes featural data in its strategy database). A test of generalization was conducted by training on a core of just 10 single-digit expressions and then presenting novel ones. With increasing experience on the core items, ASCM became more likely to use COL when confronted with novel ones where this would be the more adaptive choice.

Strategy Choice and Discovery Simulation (SCADS). The most recent model, SCADS, discovers strategies and learns about them (Shrager & Siegler, 1998). It does so through representing each strategy as a sequence of operators rather than just a unit and maintaining a working memory trace of the strategy's execution, rather than just recording speed and accuracy data. A metacognitive system uses the representation of strategy and the memory trace to formulate new strategies based on the detection of redundant sequences of behavior and the identification of more successful orders of executing operators. Putative new strategies are evaluated for their conformity to criteria for a valid addition strategy specified in a goal sketch. This model can account for the discovery of an abbreviated version of concrete counting-all, the shortcut sum (CAF or CAL) strategy, and for COL's dominance over COF. One interesting result of running the simulation is that SCADS discovers COL after about the same amount of practice children in Siegler and Jenkins' (1989) study required (cf. Baroody & Tiilikainen, chap. 3, this volume).

Conclusions. Overall, the evolution of these models represents considerable progress in accounting for the phenomena of children's development of strategies for solving addition combinations. They show how adaptive strategy choice and evolution can result from associative strength rather than conscious decisions. The models provide alternative explanations for results from chronometric and observational studies and suggest counterintuitive predictions that prompt further research questions. Although information-processing models have their critics (see, e.g., Baroody & Tiilikainen, chap. 3, this volume), their principal virtues are that they encourage precise theorizing and provide a clearer basis for evaluating alternative accounts. Unlike early information-processing models, the newest simulations learn.

The Foci of Future Efforts

Future models will need to incorporate a wider range of strategies. Although decomposition (e.g., $9 + 7 = [9 + 1] + [7 - 1] = 10 + 6 = 16$) and the extension to multidigit addition have yet to be modeled, this may be only a matter of time. Future simulation efforts will also need to deal with the following controversial issues: the basis of acquiring new strategies, the predominance of "retrieval" in older children and adults, and the nature of solutions classified as retrieval.

The Basis of Acquiring New Strategies. The Groen and Resnick (1977) study pointed up what has become a common assumption among researchers: Children can discover or invent strategies such as COL for themselves. These researchers selected preschoolers for initial instruction in counting-all and then gave them extended practice in doing small number sums (addends from 1 to 5). By the end of the practice sessions, several participants showed variation in latencies more consistent with use of COL than with use of counting-all. Unfortunately, the training procedures modeled one of the key discoveries needed to invent COL. The experimenter deliberately varied the order of representing the addends, sometimes beginning with the first, and sometimes with the second. This demonstrated that ignoring addend order is permissible.

Although self-invention or -discovery still remains the most plausible explanation for preschoolers' development of the COL strategy (see, e.g., Baroody, 1987, 1995, 1996), other factors—such as observation and imitation or educational environment—may underlie the learning of this strategy or, at least, affect its discovery.

1. *Observation and imitation.* The role of observation of more competent children or adults or even explicit instruction has been largely ignored in these and older children. Parents and teachers, particularly those with the newer conception of arithmetical expertise, may give schoolchildren models of more sophisticated strategy use. Although SCADS models spontaneous strategy invention, both ASCM and SCADS allow for the possibility of instructional influence through the mechanism that adds novelty points to (temporarily) increase associative strength of a new strategy.

2. *Educational environment.* The educational environment in which the child develops may also affect spontaneous strategy development. Several causes for this have been suggested, including experience in doing sums (Neches, 1987), the application of conceptual knowledge (Resnick, 1983), and the discovery of patterns and relations (Baroody, 1995). The SCADS model incorporates Neches' (1987) model of strategy discovery but not other sources. For Baroody (e.g., 1994, 1995), noticing patterns and relations guides the development of strategies and the learning of number combinations. Furthermore, he doubts whether the distribution-of-associations component common to all three of Siegler's models exists. In particular, he questions whether the associative strength for individual answers to problems develops independently from that of related items (e.g., learning 8 is the answer to 6 + 2 is independent of learning that it is the answer to 2 + 6). If number-rule discovery is important in combination learning and strategy development, then a model incorporating such a mechanism should fit the data better than the SCADS model. However, as noted earlier, individual differences may be relevant (e.g., some children may generalize more to unpracticed number combinations, perhaps because their teachers encourage them to look for connections).

Predominance of Retrieval in Experts. ASCM almost exclusively uses retrieval (95% of trials) by the time it had completed 1,250 addition trials. This is consistent with the common view that adults predominantly or exclusively use retrieval. A study by LeFevre et al. (1996) challenges this view. Only 5 of the 16 undergraduates in their sample claimed to use retrieval on more than 80% of trials, and 3 reported using it on less than 50% of trials. Future research will determine how to reconcile the low reported use of retrieval with the predictions of the model.

There are at least three possible explanations for the discrepancy between ASCM's and LeFevre et al.'s (1996) results. One is that many adults do not receive the practice necessary to master addition combinations during their formal schooling. A second is that the circumstances of testing promoted a much higher confidence threshold for retrieved answers. A third is that the relative associative strengths for the correct answers to simple addition items may have declined. The same people might have predominantly used retrieval for these problems when they were younger. One cause of decline might be a lack of continued practice, just as children forget what they learn in school if they subsequently do not use their knowledge. Another might be a increase in strength of competing associations, such as from other arithmetic tables or other numerical associations (e.g., telephone numbers or even addition in different number bases such as in weights or other measures). Incorporating assumptions about decline in associative strength or increasing competing associations in the model would pose no radical difficulties. So the infrequent use of retrieval by some adults does not necessarily mean the ASCM is invalid.

The Nature of Solutions Classified as "Retrieval." Analyses of adult data (e.g., LeFevre et al., 1996; LeFevre et al., chap. 7, this volume) corroborated several points made by Baroody (1985, 1994) and Siegler (1987) about chronometric studies. For example, good fits were obtained using *sum* and *min* as predictors when no account was taken of the differences in reported strategies and variation among individuals. Baroody conjectured that the perils of averaging across strategies apply to adult data as well as to children's data. Consistent with this conjecture, several adults in the LeFevre et al. (1996) study reported using transformations for some combinations or a rule for items with 0 as an addend.

When retrieval trials were separately analyzed for each individual, problem size continued to predict latency. One possibility, discussed by LeFevre et al. (1996), is that their participants overreported retrieval. Two reasons for overreporting retrieval are social desirability and lack of awareness. Adults are expected to know their addition combinations, and thus social desirability might lead them to overstate knowledge as a basis for their answers. Lack of awareness may cause people to report retrieval simply because they are unaware of computing or applying a rule. As Ashcraft (1990) pointed out, the mere absence of conscious awareness of the answering process is no guarantee that an answer is generated by retrieval. Highly practiced routines can become automatized to the point that they can be carried out without conscious awareness (Baroody, 1983, 1984b, 1985, 1994). Thus, practice in using a rule to solve addition problems might also cause someone to know an answer without knowing how they derived it.

Neither self-report nor speed will distinguish automatic retrieval from rapid nonconscious computation or application of a rule. Neuropsychological investigations of brain-injured patients and functional brain imaging of normal subjects might help make this distinction (Baroody, 1985). A pioneering study by Warrington (1982) reported the case of a 61-year-old doctor, DRC, who following a left parietal intracerebral hematoma was unable to solve simple calculations and answered questions such as 5 + 7 as "13 roughly." Adamant that he had previously solved addition and subtraction combinations automatically, DRC answered less than 20% of single-digit addition items immediately. He was generally correct (89%), but slow. His unimpaired performance on verbal memory, retrieval, and comprehension tests implied his difficulty was just with arithmetic. Warrington (1982) concluded from his ability to define arithmetical operations and judge relative magnitude that DRC's difficulty specifically stemmed from failures in accessing number combinations.

Since Warrington's (1982) report, several neuropsychological studies have produced intriguing evidence of dissociations between components of arithmetic (McCloskey, Caramazza, & Basili, 1985; Sokol, McCloskey, & Cohen, 1989). A recent example is a young male chemistry graduate, DA, who showed severe difficulties with arithmetic following a bone marrow transplant (Hittmair-Delazer, Sailer, & Benke, 1995). His ability to do mental arithmetic with one- or two-digit numbers was severely impaired. For example, he was only correct on half of the single-digit addition items involving addends from 2 to 9. (DA never used backup strategies.) However, he showed no impairment on items such as $n \times 0$ or $n \times 1$, and he displayed knowledge of arithmetical principles such as commutativity $(a + b = b + a)$ in both abstract tasks and problems involving specific numbers. He remembered mathematical formulas such as that for the volume of a cone and facts such as the speed of light. DA could also define imaginary numbers. His procedural knowledge for arithmetic was apparently intact, as he could dictate the steps to be done in multidigit arithmetic. Neuropsychological studies can reveal patterns of impairment that suggest the independence of components of arithmetic. However, this has limitations when the goal is to find out the method of operation within a component. Difficulties with single-digit arithmetic may reflect damaged access either to specific stored information, such as tables, or to specific sets of compiled procedures.

With the development of models of number processing that specify both functional components and neuroanatomical circuits (Dehaene, 1992; Dehaene & Cohen, 1995), it may be possible to discriminate retrieval of memorized facts from unconscious computation using ERPs (event-related potentials) or fMRI (functional magnetic resonance imaging). Dehaene and Cohen (1995) mentioned a study in preparation that distinguished simple and complex multiplication in brain activity. They believed this shows how rote retrieval differs from semantic elaboration. For a detailed discussion of the neuropsychological evidence, see Delazer (chap. 14, this volume).

Summary

Overall, research on addition strategies demonstrates that they evolve adaptively as children progress toward increasingly rapid and efficient strategies. Although an earlier generation considered all methods apart from retrieval as crutches and teachers were likely to forbid the use of fingers, we now see these as a necessary part of children's development. From the very beginning of children's learning to solve addition problems, the methods they invent are valid (cf. Baroody & Tiilikainen, chap. 3, this volume). Siegler and Jenkins (1989) proposed that the reason for this is that new strategies are evaluated by a goal sketch. SCADS includes such a mechanism. The origins of knowledge of addition and the development of more conscious knowledge of arithmetical principles are considered next.

ADDITION PRINCIPLES

Addition involves principles of varying scope. A very general and simple principle is that addition makes more. This principle applies both to natural numbers (the positive integers 1, 2, 3, 4, . . .) and to the addition of any extensive quantities (i.e., quantities that represent measures of dimensions such as length, mass, and volume). At an abstract level, properties such as closure, commutativity, and associativity define a number system.

Knowledge of these principles is important because they provide a theory of addition and explain or constrain applications of this operation. That is, it forms an understanding of the structure of numbers and the process of addition, and it provides the criteria for justifying or evaluating the procedures for mental and written addition. The newer approach to teaching arithmetic in the early years emphasizes children's discovery of number properties, while acknowledging that the students' level of understanding of these properties might reflect general characteristics of their thinking (Lovell, 1971). The rationale for this emphasis reflects both reasons for knowing principles.

Psychological research has sought to find out whether simpler versions of these principles underlie children's arithmetic before learning how to compute with written numbers. The general approach has been to examine whether children's performance of addition tasks implies a grasp of these principles. In considering this research, keep in mind children (a) may adopt procedures that respect these principles without understanding them and (b) may know the principles but fail to apply them in particular contexts. Failure to apply a principle is not equivalent to lack of comprehension of a principle, as Greeno, Riley, and Gelman (1984) have pointed out in distinguishing among utilizational, procedural, and conceptual competence.

Addition Makes More

Evidence of Early Competence. With very small collections, even 4-month-old infants apparently expect addition to produce an increase in number (Wynn, 1995). They look longer when addition of one doll to another results in only one doll rather than two (Wynn, 1992).

Starkey (1992) examined preschoolers' understanding of addition and sub-traction using nonverbal responses. Children from 18 months to 5 years first put balls into an opaque box. They watched as balls were then either added or sub-tracted from the initial quantity. They then removed the balls one at a time. The number of times they reached into the box showed their expectation of the resulting quantity. Most 2-year-olds made more reaches after addition and fewer after subtraction. Often, the number of times the child tried to retrieve a ball exactly matched the number of objects. Success diminished as the initial quantity increased. For addition items, accuracy dropped from 55% for $2 + 1$ to 15% for $3 + 1$. Overall, subtraction items were easier than addition items, but performance still declined from 91% for $2 - 1$ to 52% for $3 - 1$.

However, what these studies show remains in dispute (Baroody, 2000; Clearfield & Mix, 1999; Huttenlocher, Jordan, & Levine, 1994; Mix, 1999; Simon, 1997; Sophian, 1998), and discrepant results cast doubt on the reliability of key findings. For example, Starkey, Spelke, and Gelman (1990) found babies would look longer at a visual display with two objects when they heard a se-quence of two sounds. In contrast, the babies studied by Mix, Levine, and Hutten-locher (1997) looked more at a display with a number of objects that differed from the number of sounds they heard. They showed no preference at all when rate and duration varied randomly with numerosity. The difficulties of work-ing with babies are a considerable challenge to experimental ingenuity (Bremner, 1988). Experimenters have to design tasks that will interest them and maintain their interest, using stimuli that are within their perceptual ca-pabilities. Because the only basis for crediting babies with principles is infer-ence from their actions, we cannot distinguish application from comprehension.

Possible Mechanisms Underlying Early Competence. If the compe-tence displayed by infants (Wynn, 1992) and toddlers (Starkey, 1992) derives from the same process, then it cannot depend on verbal-based counting. The limitation of competence to small numerosities makes subitizing a likely candi-date. Subitizing is a process of determining number that even in adults is lim-ited to small numerosities, that is, numbers less than seven. Klahr and Wallace (1976) proposed that subitizing develops as an accurate and reliable process of quantification before counting, and that through subitizing children might learn to discriminate between number-changing and number-irrelevant trans-formations. Starkey and Cooper (1995) obtained clear evidence that even 2-year-olds who cannot count can subitize and their subitizing is not limited to objects arranged in particular canonical forms. This challenges the account of subitizing by Mandler and Shebo (1982).

Gallistel and Gelman (1992) suggested that subitizing derives from an ac-cumulator mechanism, originally proposed by Meck and Church (1983) to ac-count for rats' ability to discriminate number. Wynn (1995) invoked this mecha-nism to account for human infants' arithmetic. However, other evidence sup-ports an object-token view (Pylyshyn & Storm, 1988; Sears & Pylyshyn, 2000;

Trick & Pylyshyn, 1993, 1994) or mental models view (Clearfield & Mix, 1999; Huttenlocher et al., 1994; Mix, 1999; Mix, Huttenlocher, & Levine, 2002).[5]

Evidence Regarding Older Preschoolers. There is evidence that somewhat older preschoolers' competence with nonverbal addition reflects knowledge that "addition makes more" (Huttenlocher et al., 1994; Jordan, Huttenlocher, & Levine, 1992, 1994; Levine, Jordan, & Huttenlocher, 1992; see Jordan, Hanich, & Uberti, chap. 13, this volume for a detailed discussion). Overall, these studies indicate that young children are more successful on a nonverbal addition task than on either verbally presented story problems or on a task involving symbolic expressions. Furthermore, children's errors are more likely to be ordinally appropriate on nonverbal items.

Dowker and Cowan (1998) reported evidence consistent with the view that verbal-based addition develops later than nonverbal addition and—unlike the latter—is dependent on counting skill. They found many children less than 5 years old are usually unsuccessful at verbally predicting the direction of the result for adding one to even small numerosities (a row of two or three objects). Although proficient counters expected addition to result in a number greater than the previously counted starting amount on 60% of the trials, inaccurate counters did so on only 26% of them. The poor performance of the inaccurate counters is consistent with the argument that counting experience or competence is a key basis for children's understanding of how addition affects verbal number. That is, it may be the link between their nonverbal principle that "addition makes more" and verbal representations of addition.

Closure and Additive Composition

Addition of natural numbers has the property of closure because the sum of any set of natural numbers is itself a natural number. The corollary of this is that any natural number, apart from one, is the sum of other natural numbers. Resnick (1983, 1986) proposed that children have an early intuition of this cor-

---

[5] In A. J. Baroody's opinion, it is important to distinguish between nonverbal subitizing that Klahr and Wallace (1976) discussed and verbal subitizing (Baroody, 2000). The former results in a nonverbal mental representation of some kind; the latter, a nonverbal representation associated with a verbal label or counting number. Currently, it is not clear whether nonverbal subitizing is initially an exact or an inexact process or whether it results in a cardinal representation of a collection or a noncardinal representation (a representation of the entire collection). For example, according to both accumulator and object-token accounts, infants can represent small numerosities precisely. According to the former, though, an infant forms a cardinal representation, whereas, according to the latter, the infant uses a perceptual marker for each item in a collection representation. According to the mental models, infants and toddlers may only be able to estimate numerosities of more than 1 or 2; exact representations of even small quantities such as 2, 3, or 4 may not occur until somewhat later. Existing evidence is not sufficient to distinguish among these possibilities. Furthermore, if children do use an estimation process initially, it is not clear whether it is based on perceptual cues, numerosity, or some combination of the two. See Mix (1999), Baroody (2000), and Mix, Huttenlocher, and Levine (2002) for a detailed discussion and review of the aforementioned models.

ollary, additive composition. Knowledge of additive composition is implicit in the use of the decomposition strategy for solving addition sums (e.g., solving 28 + 15 by solving 20 + 8 + 10 + 5). Use of decomposition is uncommon, but this may not result from ignorance of additive composition. We have seen children use a wealth of valid strategies. Use of one does not preclude ability to use others. Renton (1992) attempted to establish what other strategies a child could use by interviewing 40 children between 6 and 10 years of age after they had done some sums and reported their strategies. She explained the strategies by using a video of a puppet modeling the different strategies. Taking sums they had answered correctly using retrieval, COL, or counting-all, she asked them to solve these items using other methods. Almost all showed how to use the counting strategies to solve problems they reported using retrieval on. Many showed they could have used retrieval on sums they used a counting strategy on. In contrast only one child less than 8 years old and a few older children (7 of 20) proved they could use decomposition to solve an item. Additional research is needed to find out whether this reflects a problem in understanding the principle underlying decomposition or in applying it. (For further analyses on this issue, see Baroody et al., chap. 4, this volume.)

Putnam, deBettencourt, and Leinhardt (1990) explored understanding of decomposition by asking children to complete a puppet's explanations of decomposition solutions to basic addition and subtraction combinations. They compared a sample of third graders with a group of children from special education classrooms from third to fifth grade. About half the participants in each group could explain the solutions to addition combinations, but a much lower percentage successfully explained the solutions to subtraction items. Their innovative approach involved participants in comparing legal and illegal solutions using decomposition. This assesses whether children can operationalize a decomposition strategy for a particular combination and, thus, whether they have implicit knowledge of additive composition. Whether such implicit knowledge is developmentally distinct from explicit knowledge of the principle requires investigation.

Apart from the decomposition strategy, two other tasks are suggested to involve knowledge of additive composition. Resnick (1983) proposed it was implicit in children's solution of story problems such as *Joe had some marbles. Then Tom gave him 5 more marbles. Now Joe has 8 marbles. How many marbles did Joe have in the beginning?* Such problems are not solved by most children before second grade, in contrast to the success even kindergarten children have with problems such as *Joe had 3 marbles. Tom gave him 5 more. How many does Joe have now?*

Another method of assessing additive composition is a shopping task requiring the construction of amounts using coins of different denominations (Nunes & Bryant, 1996). This task has been used to study children in several countries and unschooled illiterate adults. In some languages, the composition of multidigit numbers is readily derived from the spoken number words (e.g., in Asian languages such as Chinese and Japanese the spoken equivalent of "twelve" is "ten-two"). To prevent solutions based merely on matching verbal labels to coins, the shopping task includes some problems with 5-unit and   1-unit coins and others featuring 1- and 10-unit coins. A study comparing English- with Chinese-speaking children showed the latter were better at both types of mixed denomination problem but particularly at problems with 1 and 10 unit coins (Lines & Bryant, as cited in Nunes & Bryant, 1996). Performance on the shopping task predicts success in writing multidigit numbers (Nunes, Bryant, Falcão, & Lima, as cited in Nunes & Bryant, 1996).

Although the empirical relations among use of decomposition, solving more difficult story problems, and success on shopping tasks remain unknown, some evidence suggests shopping problems can be solved before the harder story problems. Martins-Mourão and Cowan (1998) tested children in the first 3 years of primary school at three points during the year. No 5-year-old could combine coins of different combinations correctly at the beginning of the year, but about a fifth (12 of 56) could do so by the end of the year. Almost half the 6-year-olds (20 of 43) succeeded by the middle of the year. In contrast, success on the harder story problems was much rarer. However, this difference may reflect differences in children's understanding of the two tasks. Sophian and Vong (1995) used a more elaborate mode of presentation of harder story problems and found even 5-year-olds were successful.

The conceptual relation between the competencies underlying these achievements is harder to assess. One can analyze them as all manifestations of the same underlying scheme. Resnick (1983, 1986) proposed that they all derive from the part-whole schema. However, for the connection to reflect psychological reality, either children must see the relation between them, or they should show transfer from instruction in one component to the others (Rittle-Johnson & Siegler, 1998). As Baroody (1987) pointed out in discussing the relation between strategy use and knowledge of commutativity, one must be careful not to overestimate the orderliness of children's knowledge.

Commutativity

Addition is commutative because the order of the addends is irrelevant to their sum, that is, $a + b = b + a$. Commutativity is implicit in addition strategies that ignore addend order such as MCAL, CAL, and COL. Use of these strategies is considered by some to be one indication that children know commutativity. After I discuss the evidence for this proposal, I then describe two views about the phases of commutativity development.

The Relation With Strategies That Disregard Addend Order. Two studies have attempted to identify the onset of strategies that reverse addend order by repeatedly assessing young children's addition performance over a period (Baroody, 1987; Siegler & Jenkins, 1989). The results of both are consistent with the proposition that it is unlikely that the invention of the COL strategy is always a result of the deliberate application of commutativity.

Baroody (1987) interviewed 17 kindergarten children 13 times in 8 months. At each time, they were given 10 single-digit addition expressions in which the smaller addend was the first addend. These included seven expressions in which the smaller addend was more than 1. When the child used a strategy that started with the larger addend on 3 or more of the 7 sums, Baroody assessed knowledge of commutativity. The commutativity task consisted of four trials, two in which the expressions were commuted (4 + 5, 5 + 4) and two in which they were not (3 + 7, 3 + 4). Children had to judge whether two expressions had the same answer. At the beginning of the study, only 1 of the 17 participants started with the larger addend; by the end of the study, an additional 6 did so. Of these 7, 5 were using COL, one CAL, and the other MCAL. Strategy use was not associated with commutativity performance. As Baroody and Gannon (1984) found, some children reversed addend order when computing sums but showed no understanding of commutativity. Baroody and Gannon also found the opposite pattern.

Siegler and Jenkins (1989) tracked the strategy use of eight children for 11 weeks. Each week, a child had about three sessions that typically involved seven expressions. After the first 7 weeks, they were introduced challenge items with one addend greater than 10, and the other between 1 and 4 (e.g., 2 + 18). In assessing whether the child was using the COL strategy, two criteria were used. To meet the strict criterion, children had to count from the larger addend unambiguously and accurately describe the way they counted. Children met the loose criterion if they counted from the larger addend but failed to describe accurately what they had done, or used an approach that started with the larger addend but involved counting from *one*, such as CAL or MCAL. During the study, six children met both criteria and one met just the loose criterion. All but two of these children met one criterion before the challenge items. On the challenge items, these children used COL on more than 60% of trials. They subsequently maintained this frequency of use on small-addend items. Whether a child was aware of his or her strategy, and so met the strict criterion, also predicted generalization to other combinations. In brief, the need to save labor when tackling computationally challenging items can prompt the discovery of COL or promote its use even with less challenging items.

An explanation consistent with the SCADS model (Shrager & Siegler, 1998) is that strategy invention can occur at an implicit, unconscious level, and representation accessible to consciousness may follow later through processes of representational redescription (Karmiloff-Smith, 1992; Siegler & Stern, 1998). In this model, once sufficient attentional resources are freed, the only newly discovered strategies that could be used are those that are legal. This is because a new strategy has to meet the criteria set by the goal-sketch filters. These stipulate that both addends are represented and that the result of the strategy includes the representations of both addends. These filters both control what strategies children try and provide the basis for evaluating other people's strategies.

Siegler and Crowley (1994) found that 5-year-olds who could not add did not discriminate between an illegal strategy (counting the first addend twice) and legal strategies (concrete counting-all and COL). Presumably, this is because they lack the goal-sketch filters. In contrast, children who could solve some addition problems judged both COL and the count-all strategy to be smarter than the illegal strategy. This was even true of most children who did not use COL themselves when subsequently given addition items. However, neither they nor the COL users could typically give explicit reasons why COL was smart. Simply noting the smartness of the COL strategy was not sufficient to induce them to use it. Adopting this strategy may depend on whether children perceive an advantage over their existing legal strategy. Consistent with this conclusion, Siegler and Crowley found that even COL users did not consistently judge COL to be smarter than counting-all.[6] Future research may determine the relative efficacy of doing sums, observing more advanced strategy use, and discussing strategies in facilitating strategy evolution and awareness.

Two Views About the Phases of Commutativity Development. Although an explicit knowledge of commutativity is not necessary for developing the COL strategy, two accounts propose that young children may have a more rudimentary grasp of commutativity (Baroody & Gannon, 1984; Resnick, 1992). Baroody and Gannon (1984) proposed four levels of understanding of commutativity. In the first (Level 0), children have a unary conception of addition as a change of state, making an initial set larger. They see $4 + 2$ as "four and two more." In contrast, they view $2 + 4$ as " two and four more." In Level 1, protocommutativity, children may disregard addend order to make computation easier but are, nevertheless, unsure whether $2 + 4$ has the same sum as $4 + 2$. In Level 2, pseudocommutativity, children still have the unary conception of addition, but they know that problems with the same addends have the same sum. Finally in Level 3, true commutativity, children have a binary conception of addition as the combination of two sets and a true mathematical understanding of commutativity.

For Resnick (1992), the distinction between unary and binary conceptions of addition is not developmentally significant. More important, unlike Baroody and Gannon (1984), she emphasized nonnumerical, qualitative understandings as providing a more primitive basis for commutativity. She proposed that children begin with protoquantitative schemas that underpin reasoning about relations between unspecified quantities. These schemas incorporate ideas such

---

[6] In A. J. Baroody's opinion, Siegler and Crowley (1994) did not really demonstrate COL but a primitive (semi-indirect-modeling) version of COL, more akin to a concrete counting-all shortcut. This may help to explain why some of their participants, particularly those using more advanced strategies, did not consider "COL" more advanced than counting-all. Even so, Baroody, Tiilikainen, and Tai (2000) found that COL users overall judged genuine COL, a semi-indirect-modeling version of COL (what Fuson, 1982, called a "counting-entities strategy"), and concrete counting-all to be equally smart. (For a detailed discussion, see Baroody and Tiilikainen, chap. 3, this volume.)

as the commutativity and associativity of addition (Resnick & Singer, 1993). Protoquantitative commutativity may be the recognition that two sets are the same if they are composed of the same parts. Addition experience and its integration with counting may lead to a new form of commutativity, the commutativity of measured quantities. At this level, children maintain that two sets of objects are equivalent if they are composed of the same counted quantities (e.g., three boys and four girls is the same number of children as four boys and three girls). Once children think of numbers as entities in their own right, they can recognize the commutativity of numbers and so judge the equivalence of numerical expressions such as $7 + 4$ and $4 + 7$. Finally, a mathematics of operators involves a general grasp of commutativity.

Comparing these accounts suggests that Baroody and Gannon (1984) focused on one type of commutativity, that is, the commutativity at the numbers level in Resnick's (1992) scheme. The more primitive stages they described are more limited versions of this level of thinking rather than commutativity applied to different entities such as unspecified numerosities or counted quantities of objects. In the following part of the review, I consider the evidence for these separate forms of commutativity and the origins of these understandings.

Sophian, Harley, and Martin (1995) investigated protoquantitative commutativity by asking 4- and 5-year-olds to judge the numerical equivalence of sets of toys composed of specified and unspecified numerosities. Two unspecified numerosities were used, a box and a tray, and two specified numerosities, two and three. Following training on the equivalence of these quantities, children were presented with some commuted and unequal trials. They had to judge whether a puppet had the same number of objects as a doll. In a commuted trial, the puppet might have a tray of pink fish and two birds, whereas the doll had two pink fish and a tray of birds. On these trials, the quantities were the same but they referred to different types of animal and used different orders. On unequal trials, the puppet and doll had either the same unspecified numerosity and different specific numerosities (e.g., a box of pink fish and two birds compared with three pink fish and a box of birds) or the same specific numerosities and different unspecified numerosities (e.g., a box of fish and two birds compared with two fish and a tray of birds). Half the age group could see the animals in the boxes and trays; the rest could not. Whether the items were visible did not affect judgment accuracy, indicating success did not depend on counting. More than half the children in each age group (twelve of twenty-one 4-year-olds, fourteen of twenty-two 5-year-olds) judged all the commuted trials and more than half the unequal trials correctly.

Although the success by these young children is clear, what it means is not. First, were the children obliged to reason about unspecified numerosities? Even when the boxes and trays were covered, children might have remembered the specific numbers of objects they contained. A box always contained four objects and a tray seven. Children may have learned this during the training trials when they were uncovered.

Even if this is discounted, the results are not unambiguous because the task used by Sophian et al. (1995) involved both an unspecified and a specified quantity and, thus, did not involve pure qualitative reasoning. In other words, qualitative reasoning about two unspecified quantities might precede qualitative reasoning about a mix of unspecified and specified quantities.

In one study, Cowan and Renton (1996) compared 7- and 9-year-olds' reasoning on three tasks involving unspecified numerosities exclusively, counted quantities, and written items. In a second study, they gave twenty-four 5-year-olds the unspecified-numerosity and counted-quantity tasks. In both studies, participants did not perform significantly better on the unspecified-numerosities task. In brief, the results were not consistent with Resnick's (1992) view that protoquantitative reasoning about commutativity precedes quantitative or numerical reasoning about the principle (see Baroody et al., chap. 4, this volume, for a more complete discussion of this and related issues).

Ioakimidou (1998) tried to find children who lacked familiarity with addition by studying a sample of 58 Greek 3- and 5-year-olds in a day-care center. She introduced addition to them with two situations (one item put into a box and then one more put in the box or "1 + 1" and two items put in a box and then two more or "2 + 2"), each in two contexts. One involved a visible sum (box remained uncovered) and the other, a hidden sum (box covered after items added). In both contexts, numerals were used to identify the collections added. The main addition task consisted of six trials ("1 + 2," "1 + 3," "2 + 1," "2 + 3," "3 + 1," and "3 + 2") presented in random order in the hidden context. The unspecified-numerosity and counted-quantity commutativity tasks each consisted of four commuted and four unequal trials. Success was defined as a correct answer on at least seven trials. Ioakimidou used two criteria for correct judgment on unequal trials. One was Sophian et al.'s (1995) liberal criterion of simply requiring children to judge the amounts to be different. This is the minimal requirement to show that children discriminate between unequal trials and commuted trials. Another was Cowan and Renton's (1996) conservative criterion, which required children to identify the greater quantity. As Table 2.4 shows, the number "passing" was slightly higher with the liberal criterion than with the conservative criterion. With both criteria, though, more passed the unspecified-numerosity commutativity task than the counted-quantity version, but the difference was not reliable. Protoquantitative commutativity, then, did not appear to emerge before quantitative commutativity.

As part of Ioakimidou's (1998) study, children were given Wynn's (1990) give-a-number task. She reasoned that an understanding of counting might determine children's performance with counted quantities but be irrelevant for that on unspecified-numerosities tasks. Although most children were counters rather than grabbers, Table 2.4 shows that some grabbers succeeded on one or both tasks.

Piaget (1964, 1970) also proposed a link between the discovery of commutativity and counting principles. He believed that children could discover the or-

Table 2.4: Success on Unspecified-Numerosity and Counted-Quantity Commutativity Tasks in Relation to Age, Classification on Wynn's (1990) Give-a-Number Task, and Addition in Ioakimidou (1998)

| | n | Unspecified Numerosity | | Counted Quantity | |
		Different	More	Different	More
Age range					
3:4 – 3:11	21	11	6	7	5
4:0 – 4:11	26	23	16	22	15
5:0 – 5:3	11	11	6	9	3
Give a number					
Grabbers	9	5	3	3	3
Counters	49	40	25	35	20
Simple addition					
No success	27	19	11	15	8
Some success	31	26	17	23	15

Note. Criteria for correct judgment of unequal trials are judging that the sets are different, and judging which set has more.

der-irrelevance principle by reflecting on their counting experience. As evidence, he described an anecdote about a mathematician who, as a child, discovered he got the same result by counting and recounting a set of pebbles in different orders and arrangements. This observation, he noted, was "verified many times in small children under seven years of age" (Piaget, 1964, p. 179) and "studied quite thoroughly with many children" (Piaget, 1970, p. 16). Likewise, with three objects arranged in a single row, a child could discover that, whether counted from left to right or from right to left, the result was still three. Similarly, a child might discover additive commutativity by arranging three objects in a row of one and a row of two and noticing that whichever row was counted first the result or sum was still three.

Although some (e.g., Baroody, 1984a) see the order-irrelevance of counting as independent from additive commutativity, Gelman and Gallistel (1978) considered the former, when combined with the child's beliefs and practices concerning addition, could yield a belief in the latter. This might be limited to addition of specific numbers, because children's experience of addition is limited to particular numerosities. This view implies order-irrelevance might precede commutativity.

Ioakimidou (1998) tested understanding of order-irrelevance in counting by asking them to predict the result of recounting a set of items either in the opposite direction to the first count or after an item had been removed. This testing included subtraction trials controls for indiscriminately predicting all recounts to yield the same answer (Cowan, Dowker, Christakis, & Bailey, 1996). Contrary to Gelman and Gallistel's (1978) conjecture, order-irrelevance of counting did not precede additive commutativity with counted quantities. With the more liberal criterion for unequal trials, 37 children either passed both tasks or failed both tasks, and 20 of the other 21 children passed the commutativity counted-quantities task but failed the order-irrelevance task.

The data also challenge the idea that commutativity is derived from determining sums via counting-based strategies (e.g., Baroody, 1987; Baroody & Gannon, 1984). Table 2.4 shows the relation between success on the commutativity tasks and success on the very simple addition problems. Substantial numbers of participants who answered none of these correctly nevertheless passed the commutativity tasks.

Overall, these results suggest that young children may understand commutativity in some form before they understand the irrelevance of order in counting or know how to add at the verbal level. However, the existing evidence is far from conclusive. The validity of the commutativity tasks is questionable and the wrong type of addition may have been assessed. For example the commutativity tasks may be misleading if children succeeded simply by noting whether the addends match but without realizing the sums are the same (Baroody & Gannon, 1984; Rittle-Johnson & Siegler, 1998). This objection is certainly relevant to the counted-quantities version of the commutativity task. Using the more demanding criterion on the unequal trials may help, but it would be more convincing if some way of discriminating between matching of the addends and knowledge of the sum on commuted trials could be devised. Whether the addend-matching objection applies to protoquantitative commutativity is not so clear. As I understand it, protoquantitative commutativity might be either purely qualitative or partly quantitative. Purely qualitative protocommutativity may underpin a child's judgment that he and his mother had the same breakfast because both had juice and cereal, although both the order in which they consumed them and the amounts differed. Partly quantitative protocommutativity might require some rough match in amounts.

Despite Ioakimidou's (1998) results, addition might play a role in the discovery of commutativity. Her addition tasks concerned verbally represented addends. Possibly, nonverbal addition such as shown by Huttenlocher et al. (e.g., 1994) provides the basis for children's expectation that the sum is independent of the addend order.

Finally, the delay between these earlier forms of commutativity and applying commutativity to written problems requires investigation. Studies by Baroody and Gannon (1984) and Dowker (1998) show considerable variation among children. Although some readily judge problems with commuted addends to have the same sum, others are uncertain. Certain beliefs and practices may encourage some children to refrain from using knowledge of commutativity, or even to think that addition of verbal numbers is not commutative. Baroody, Ginsburg, and Waxman (1983) reported that a few children thought that employing a shortcut strategy, such as using the result of a commuted sum, was cheating. The commutativity of addition is not often exploited in tables of addition combinations that some parents may stick on their children's bedroom walls.

Our knowledge of children's grasp of addition principles is still fragmentary. Radically different conceptions can account for the facts. By third grade, many children have insight into some addition principles but the source of this insight remains in dispute. The challenge of producing tests that both do justice to the principles and are suitable for young children is considerable.

Summary

Children develop considerable competence in addition in the early years of elementary school. From an early age, they display adaptive expertise in their development of strategies and show some grasp of principles. Most become able to answer simple number fact problems without conscious calculation.

Researchers have made considerable progress in describing and explaining the components of children's knowledge of addition. Alternative interpretations of developmental phenomena continue to stimulate research by highlighting areas that require investigation and encouraging critical examination of the methods for assessing children's knowledge. Computational modeling complements this by aiming to provide ever more comprehensive models. We are, however, still some way from providing a full account of the development of expertise.

The following four issues in particular need further investigation. (a) How do the components of addition (facts, strategies, and principles) interact? (b) What role does experience play in causing individual variation and atypical development? (c) What roles do cognitive factors play in creating individual differences? (d) What are the bases of atypical development? Although modern mathematics educators assume that instruction in principles will expedite development of number-combination mastery and addition strategies, clear evidence is lacking. Associations between knowledge and skill are inconclusive;

they can be just as plausibly explained by assuming that the development of skill promotes the discovery of principles. Finding that these components can develop independently does not tell us they must or should do so. Intervention studies can contribute by identifying causal links (Rittle-Johnson & Siegler, 1998). We need to find out how children can develop as much as how they do develop.

Differences between children are common to studies of addition combinations, strategies, and principles. The causes of this heterogeneity are uncertain. Few have investigated how such variation might reflect differences in children's experience and what they learn from it. The conceptions of arithmetic expertise embodied in traditional and contemporary methods of instruction should surely affect children's development. If they do not, this would interest mathematics educators and others who attribute weaknesses in children's arithmetic to past or present forms of instruction. Variations in experience before children start school are undoubtedly important. Many of the studies reviewed concern children's knowledge and skills before formal instruction. However, few have attempted to assess what kinds of experience children may receive at home and how this affects development.

Although some have invoked cognitive factors to explain differences among individuals, few have studied them. Cognitive factors such as working memory need further theoretical development, and their measures are poorly understood. Common to many working-memory tasks is the requirement to store digits. The ability to do this may be as much as a consequence of learning number combinations as learning number combinations is a consequence of the ability to remember digits.

Finally, one goal for developmental studies is the identification of typical patterns of development. These typical patterns inform the construction and evaluation of accounts of number development. However, it is easy to overgeneralize from typical patterns and ignore individuals who clearly develop in different ways. By changing the parameters of the model and varying the kinds and amount of experience, Siegler's computational models show the versatility that is needed to account for differences in strategy development and knowledge of number combinations. Perhaps these may be extended to development of principles.

So several questions about number development remain unanswered. This constrains psychologists' authority to comment on pedagogical practice and the use of psychology to underpin mathematics education. Mathematics education continues to be more a matter of faith than of fact.

References

Ashcraft, M. H. (1985). Is it farfetched that some of us remember our arithmetic facts? *Journal for Research in Mathematics Education, 16*, 99–105.

Ashcraft, M. H. (1990). Strategic processing in children's mental arithmetic: A review and proposal. In D. F. Bjorklund (Ed.), *Children's strategies: Contemporary views of cognitive development* (pp. 185–211). Hillsdale, NJ: Lawrence Erlbaum Associates.

Ashcraft, M. H., & Christy, K. S. (1995). The frequency of arithmetic facts in elementary texts: Addition and multiplication in grades 1–6. *Journal for Research in Mathematics Education, 26*, 396–421.

Ashcraft, M. H., & Fierman, B. A. (1982). Mental addition in third, fourth, and sixth grades. *Journal of Experimental Child Psychology, 33*, 216–234.

Ashcraft, M. H., & Stazyk, E. H. (1981). Mental addition: A test of three verification models. *Memory & Cognition, 9*, 185–196.

Askew, M. (1998). *Teaching primary mathematics: A guide for newly qualified and student teachers*. London: Hodder & Stoughton.

Baddeley, A. (1986). *Working memory*. Oxford: Clarendon.

Baroody, A. J. (1983). The development of procedural knowledge: An alternative explanation for chronometric trends of mental arithmetic. *Developmental Review, 3*, 225–230.

Baroody, A. J. (1984a). More precisely defining and measuring the order–irrelevance principle. *Journal of Experimental Child Psychology, 38*, 33–41.

Baroody, A. J. (1984b). A re-examination of mental arithmetic models and data: A reply to Ashcraft. *Developmental Review, 4*, 148–156.

Baroody, A. J. (1985). Mastery of basic number combinations: Internalization of relationships or facts? *Journal for Research in Mathematics Education, 16*, 83–98.

Baroody, A. J. (1987). The development of counting strategies for single-digit addition. *Journal for Research in Mathematics Education, 18*, 141–157.

Baroody, A. J. (1988). Mental-addition development of children classified as mentally handicapped. *Educational Studies in Mathematics, 19*, 369–388.

Baroody, A. J. (1989). Kindergartners' mental addition with single-digit combinations. *Journal for Research in Mathematics Education, 20*, 159–172.

Baroody, A. J. (1992). The development of kindergartners' mental-addition strategies. *Learning and Individual Differences, 4*, 215–235.

Baroody, A. J. (1994). An evaluation of evidence supporting fact-retrieval models. *Learning and Individual Differences, 6*, 1–36.

Baroody, A. J. (1995). The role of the number-after rule in the invention of computational shortcuts. *Cognition and Instruction, 13*, 189–219.

Baroody, A. J. (1996). Self-invented addition strategies by children classified as mentally handicapped. *American Journal on Mental Retardation, 101*, 72–89.

Baroody, A. J. (2000, May). *Number and operations: Key transitions in the numerical and arithmetic development of typical and special children between the ages of 2 and 6 years.* Paper presented at the Conference on Standards for Preschool and Kindergarten Mathematics Education, Arlington, VA.

Baroody, A. J., with Coslick, R. T. (1998). *Fostering children's mathematical power: An investigative approach to teaching K–8 mathematics*. Mahwah, NJ: Lawrence Erlbaum Associates.

Baroody, A. J., & Gannon, K. E. (1984). The development of the commutativity principle and economical addition strategies. *Cognition and Instruction, 1*, 321–339.

Baroody, A. J., & Ginsburg, H. P. (1986). The relationship between initial meaningful and mechanical knowledge of arithmetic. In J. Hiebert (Ed.), *Conceptual and procedural knowledge: The case of mathematics* (pp. 75–112). Hillsdale, NJ: Lawrence Erlbaum Associates.

Baroody, A. J., Ginsburg, H. P., & Waxman, B. (1983). Children's use of mathematical structure. *Journal for Research in Mathematics Education, 14*, 156–168.

Baroody, A. J., Tiilikainen, S. H., & Tai, Y. (2000, October). The application and development of an addition goal sketch. In M. L. Fernández (Ed.), *Proceedings of the twenty-second annual meeting of the North American chapter of the International Group for the Psychology of Mathematics Education* (Vol. 2, pp. 709–714). Columbus, OH: The ERIC Clearinghouse for Science, Mathematics, and Environmental Education.

Becker, J. P., & Selter, C. (1996). Elementary school practices. In A. J. Bishop, K. Clements, C. Keitel, J. Kilpatrick, & C. Laborde (Eds.), *International handbook of mathematics education* (Vol. 4, pp. 511–564). London: Kluwer.

Bremner, J. G. (1988). *Infancy*. Oxford, England: Blackwell.

Brownell, W. A. (1935). Psychological considerations in the learning and the teaching of arithmetic. In D. W. Reeve (Ed.), *The teaching of arithmetic* (Tenth yearbook, National Council of Teachers of Mathematics, pp. 1–50). New York: Bureau of Publications, Teachers' College, Columbia University.

Brownell, W. A., & Chazal, C. B. (1935). The effects of premature drill on third grade arithmetic. *Journal of Educational Research, 29*, 17–28.

Carpenter, T. P., & Moser, J. M. (1982). The development of addition and subtraction problem-solving skills. In T. P. Carpenter, J. M. Moser, & T. A. Romberg (Eds.), *Addition and subtraction: A cognitive perspective* (pp. 9–24). Hillsdale, NJ: Lawrence Erlbaum Associates.

Carpenter, T. P., & Moser, J. M. (1984). The acquisition of addition and subtraction concepts in grades one through three. *Journal for Research in Mathematics Education, 15*, 179–202.

Central Advisory Council for Education (England). (1967). *Children and their primary schools*. London: HMSO.

Chiu, W. H. (1996). *Memory and mathematics: A comparison of first and third grade children in Taiwan*. Unpublished master's thesis, Institute of Education University of London.

Clapp, F. L. (1924). *The number combinations: Their relative difficulty and the frequency of their appearance in textbooks* (Bulletin No. 1 and Study No. 1). Madison: Bureau of Educational Research, University of Wisconsin.

Clearfield, M., & Mix, K. S. (1999). Number versus contour length in infants' discrimination of small visual sets. *Psychological Science, 10*, 408–411.

Cowan, R., Dowker, A., Christakis, A., & Bailey, S. (1996). Even more precisely assessing children's understanding of the order–irrelevance principle. *Journal of Experimental Child Psychology, 62*, 84–101.

Cowan, R., & Renton, M. (1996). Do they know what they are doing? Children's use of economical addition strategies and knowledge of commutativity. *Educational Psychology, 16*, 407–420.

De Corte, E., & Verschaffel, L. (1987). The effect of semantic structure on first graders' solution strategies of elementary addition and subtraction word problems. *Journal for Research in Mathematics Education, 18*, 363–381.

Dehaene, S. (1992). Varieties of numerical abilities. *Cognition, 44*, 1–42.

Dehaene, S., & Cohen, L. (1995). Towards an anatomical and functional model of number processing. *Mathematical Cognition, 1*, 83–120.

Department of Education and Science. (1979). *Mathematics 5–11: A handbook of suggestions*. London: HMSO.

Dowker, A. (1992). Computational estimation strategies of professional mathematicians. *Journal for Research in Mathematics Education, 23*, 45–55.

Dowker, A. (1998). Individual differences in normal arithmetical development. In C. Donlan (Ed.), *The development of mathematical skills* (pp. 275–302). Hove, East Sussex England: Psychology Press.

Dowker, A., & Cowan, R. (1998). *Relation of order–irrelevance to counting skill and knowledge of addition and subtraction*. Manuscript submitted for publication.

Flavell, J. H. (1985). *Cognitive development*. (2nd ed.). Englewood Cliffs, NJ: Prentice Hall.

Fuson, K. C. (1982). An analysis of the counting-on solution procedure in addition. In T. P. Carpenter, J. Moser, & T. Romberg (Eds.), *Addition and subtraction: A cognitive perspective* (pp. 67–81). Hillsdale, NJ: Lawrence Erlbaum Associates.

Gallistel, C. R., & Gelman, R. (1992). Preverbal and verbal counting and computation. *Cognition, 44*, 43–74.

Ganetsou, E. (1998). [The contributions of cognitive and social psychological factors to explaining variation in primary school children's arithmetical ability]. Unpublished raw data.

Geary, D. C. (1993). Mathematical disabilities: Cognitive, neuropsychological and genetic components. *Psychological Bulletin, 114*, 345–362.

Geary, D. C., Widaman, K. F., & Little, T. D. (1986). Cognitive addition and multiplication: Evidence for a single memory network. *Memory & Cognition, 14*, 478–487.

Geary, D. C., Widaman, K. F., Little, T. D., & Cormier, P. (1987). Cognitive addition: Comparison of learning disabled and academically normal elementary school children. *Cognitive Development, 2*, 249–269.

Gelman, R., & Gallistel, C. R. (1978). *The child's understanding of number*. Cambridge, MA: Harvard University Press.

Ginsburg, H. P., Klein, A., & Starkey, P. (1998). The development of children's mathematical thinking: Connecting research with practice. In I. E. Sigel & K. A. Renniger (Eds.), *Handbook of child psychology* (5th ed., Vol. 4, pp. 401–476). New York: Wiley.

Gosden, P. H. J. H. (1969). *How they were taught*. Oxford, England: Blackwell.

Greeno, J. G., Riley, M., & Gelman, R. (1984). Conceptual competence and children's counting. *Cognitive Psychology, 16*, 94–143.

Groen, G. J., & Parkman, J. M. (1972). A chronometric analysis of simple addition. *Psychological Review, 79*, 329–343.

Groen, G., & Resnick, L. B. (1977). Can preschool children invent addition algorithms? *Journal of Educational Psychology, 69*, 645–652.

Hitch, G. J., & McAuley, E. (1991). Working memory in children with specific arithmetical learning difficulties. *British Journal of Psychology, 82*, 375–386.

Hittmair-Delazer, M., Sailer, U., & Benke, T. (1995). Impaired arithmetic facts but intact conceptual knowledge—A single-case study of dyscalculia. *Cortex, 31*, 139–147.

Huttenlocher, J., Jordan, N. C., & Levine, S. C. (1994). A mental model for early arithmetic. *Journal of Experimental Psychology: General, 123*, 284–296.

Ilg, F., & Ames, L. B. (1951). Developmental trends in arithmetic. *Journal of Genetic Psychology, 79*, 3–28.

Ioakimidou, Z. (1998). *Preschoolers' counting and addition: Skills and understanding*. Unpublished master's thesis, Institute of Education University of London.

Jordan, N. C., Huttenlocher, J., & Levine, S. C. (1992). Differential calculation abilities in young children from middle- and low-income families. *Developmental Psychology, 28*, 644–653.

Jordan, N. C., Huttenlocher, J., & Levine, S. C. (1994). Assessing early arithmetic abilities: Effects of verbal and nonverbal response types on the calculation performance of middle- and low-income children. *Learning and Individual Differences, 6*, 413–432.

Karmiloff-Smith, A. (1992). *Beyond modularity: A developmental perspective*. Cambridge, MA: MIT Press.

Kilpatrick, J. (1992). A history of research in mathematics education. In D. Grouws (Ed.), *Handbook of research on mathematics teaching and learning* (pp. 3–38). New York: Macmillan.

Klahr, D., & Wallace, J. G. (1976). *Cognitive development: An information-processing view*. Hillsdale, NJ: Lawrence Erlbaum Associates.

Kline, M. (1974). *Why Johnny can't add*. New York: Vintage.

Knight, F. B., & Behrens, M. S. (1928). *The learning of the 100 addition combinations and the 100 subtraction combinations*. London: Longman Greens.

LeFevre, J., Sadesky, G. S., & Bisanz, J. (1996). Selection of procedures in mental addition: Reassessing the problem-size effect in adults. *Journal of Experimental Psychology: Learning, Memory, and Cognition, 22*, 216–230.

Levine, S. C., Jordan, N. C., & Huttenlocher, J. (1992). Development of calculation abilities in young children. *Journal of Experimental Child Psychology, 53*, 72–103.

Lovell, K. (1971). *The growth of understanding in mathematics: Kindergarten through grade three*. New York: Holt, Rinehart & Winston.

Mandler, G., & Shebo, B. J. (1982). Subitizing: An analysis of its component processes. *Journal of Experimental Psychology: General, 111*, 1–22.

Martins-Mourão, A., & Cowan, R. (1998). The emergence of additive composition of number. *Educational Psychology, 18*, 377–389.

McCloskey, M., Caramazza, A., & Basili, A. (1985). Cognitive mechanisms in number processing and calculation: Evidence from dyscalculia. *Brain and Cognition, 4*, 171–196.

Meck, W. H., & Church, R. M. (1983). A mode control model of counting and timing processes. *Journal of Experimental Psychology: Animal Behavior Processes, 9*, 320–334.

Miller, K., Perlmutter, M., & Keating, D. (1984). Cognitive arithmetic: Comparison of operations. *Journal of Experimental Psychology: Learning, Memory, and Cognition, 10*, 46–60.

Mix, K. S. (1999). Preschoolers' recognition of numerical equivalence: Sequential sets. *Journal of Experimental Child Psychology, 74*, 309–332.

Mix, K. S., Huttenlocher, J., & Levine, S. C. (2002). *Math without words: Quantitative development in infancy and early childhood*. New York: Oxford University Press.

Mix, K. S., Levine, S. C., & Huttenlocher, J. (1997). Numerical abstraction in infants: Another look. *Developmental Psychology, 33*, 423–428.

Murray, J. (1939). The relative difficulty of the basic number facts. In Scottish Council for Research in Education (Ed.), *Studies in arithmetic* (Vol. 1, pp. 79–116). London: University of London Press.

Murray, J. (1941). Types of errors in the basic number facts. In Scottish Council for Research in Education (Ed.), *Studies in arithmetic* (Vol. 2, pp. 103–133). London: University of London Press.

Myers, A. C., & Thornton, C. A. (1977). The learning disabled child—Learning the basic facts. *Arithmetic Teacher, 25*, 45–50.

Neches, R. (1987). Learning through incremental refinement of procedures. In D. Klahr, P. Langley, & R. Neches (Eds.), *Production systems models of learning and development* (pp. 163–219). Cambridge, MA: MIT Press.

Nuffield Mathematics Project. (1967). *I do, and I understand*. London: Chambers & Murray.

Nunes, T., & Bryant, P. (1996). *Children doing mathematics*. Oxford, England: Blackwell.

Parkman, J. M. (1972). Temporal aspects of simple multiplication and comparison. *Journal of Experimental Psychology, 89*, 333–342.

Piaget, J. (1964). Development and learning. *Journal for Research in Science Teaching, 2*, 176–186.

Piaget, J. (1970). *Genetic epistemology*. New York: Columbia Press.

Putnam, R. T., deBettencourt, L. U., & Leinhardt, G. (1990). Understanding of derived-fact strategies in addition and subtraction. *Cognition and Instruction, 7*, 245–285.

Pylyshyn, Z. W., & Storm, R. W. (1988). Tracking multiple independent targets: Evidence for a parallel tracking mechanism. *Spatial Vision, 3*, 179-197.

Renton, M. (1992). *Primary school-children's strategies for addition*. Unpublished doctoral dissertation, University of London Institute of Education.

Resnick, L. B. (1983). A developmental theory of number understanding. In H. P. Ginsburg (Ed.), *The development of mathematical thinking* (pp. 109–151). New York: Academic Press.

Resnick, L. B. (1986). The development of mathematical intuition. In M. Perlmutter (Ed.), *Minnesota symposia on child psychology* (Vol. 19, pp. 159–194). Hillsdale, NJ: Lawrence Erlbaum Associates.

Resnick, L. B. (1992). From protoquantities to operators: Building mathematical competence on a foundation of everyday knowledge. In G. Leinhardt, R. Putnam, & R. A. Hattrup (Eds.), *Analysis of arithmetic for mathematics teaching* (pp. 373–425). Hillsdale, NJ: Lawrence Erlbaum Associates.

Resnick, L. B., & Singer, J. A. (1993). Protoquantitative origins of ratio reasoning. In T. P. Carpenter, E. Fennema, & T. A. Romberg (Eds.), *Rational numbers: An integration of research* (pp. 107–130). Hillsdale, NJ: Lawrence Erlbaum Associates.

Reys, R. E., Suydam, M. N., Lindquist, M. M., & Smith, N. L. (1998). *Helping children learn mathematics*. (5th ed.). Boston: Allyn & Bacon.

Ridgway, J. (1987). *A review of mathematics tests*. Windsor, England: NFER-Nelson.

Ridgway, J., & Passey, D. (1995). When basic mathematics skills predict nothing: Implications for education and training. *Educational Psychology, 15*, 35–44.

Rittle-Johnson, B., & Siegler, R. S. (1998). The relation between conceptual and procedural knowledge in learning mathematics: A review of the literature. In C. Donlan (Ed.), *The development of mathematical skills* (pp. 75–110). Hove, East Sussex England: Psychology Press.

Russell, R. L., & Ginsburg, H. P. (1984). Cognitive analysis of children's mathematical difficulties. *Cognition and Instruction, 1*, 217–244.

Schonell, F. J. (1937). *Diagnosis of individual difficulties in arithmetic*. Edinburgh, Scotland: Oliver & Boyd.

Schonell, F. J., & Schonell, F. E. (1957). *Diagnosis and remedial teaching in arithmetic*. Edinburgh, Scotland: Oliver & Boyd.

Schools Council. (1966). *Curriculum bulletin no. 1 mathematics in primary schools*. (2nd ed.). London: HMSO.

Sears, C. R., & Pylyshyn, Z. (2000). Multiple object tracking and attentional processing. *Canadian Journal of Experimental Psychology, 54*, 1-14.

Shrager, J., & Siegler, R. S. (1998). SCADS: A model of children's strategy choices and strategy discoveries. *Psychological Science, 9*, 405–410.

Siegler, R. S. (1987). The perils of averaging data across strategies: An example from children's addition. *Journal of Experimental Psychology: General, 116*, 250–264.

Siegler, R. S. (1988). Individual differences in strategy choices: Good students, not-so-good students, and perfectionists. *Child Development, 59*, 833–851.

Siegler, R. S., & Crowley, K. (1994). Constraints on learning in nonprivileged domains. *Cognitive Psychology, 27*, 194–226.

Siegler, R. S., & Jenkins, E. (1989). *How children discover new strategies.* Hillsdale, NJ: Lawrence Erlbaum Associates.

Siegler, R. S., & Robinson, M. (1982). The development of numerical understandings. In H. W. Reese & L. P. Lipsitt (Eds.), *Advances in child development and behaviour* (Vol. 16, pp. 241–312). New York: Academic Press.

Siegler, R. S., & Shipley, C. (1995). Variation, selection, and cognitive change. In T. Simon & G. Halford (Eds.), *Developing cognitive competence: New approaches to process modelling* (pp. 31–76). Hillsdale, NJ: Lawrence Erlbaum Associates.

Siegler, R. S., & Shrager, J. (1984). Strategy choices in addition and subtraction: How do children know what to do? In C. Sophian (Ed.), *Origins of cognitive skills* (pp. 229–293). Hillsdale, NJ: Lawrence Erlbaum Associates.

Siegler, R. S., & Stern, E. (1998). Conscious and unconscious strategy discoveries: A microgenetic analysis. *Journal of Experimental Psychology: General, 127*, 377–397.

Simon, T. J. (1997). Reconceptualizing the origins of number knowledge: A "non-numerical" account. *Cognitive Development, 12*, 349–372.

Smith, S. B. (1988). Calculating prodigies. In L. K. Obler & D. Fein (Eds.), *The exceptional brain* (pp. 19–47). New York: Guilford Press.

Sokol, S. M., McCloskey, M., & Cohen, N. J. (1989). Cognitive representations of arithmetic knowledge: Evidence from acquired dyscalculia. In A. F. Bennett & K. M. McConkie (Eds.), *Cognition in individual and social contexts* (pp. 577–591). Amsterdam: Elsevier.

Sophian, C. (1998). A developmental perspective on children's counting. In C. Donlan (Ed.), *The development of mathematical skills* (pp. 27–46). Hove, East Sussex, England: Psychology Press.

Sophian, C., Harley, H., & Martin, C. S. M. (1995). Relational and representational aspects of early number development. *Cognition and Instruction, 13*, 253–268.

Sophian, C., & Vong, K. I. (1995). The parts and wholes of arithmetic story problems: Developing knowledge in the preschool years. *Cognition and Instruction, 13*, 469–477.

Starkey, P. (1992). The early development of numerical reasoning. *Cognition, 43*, 93–126.

Starkey, P., & Cooper, R. G. J. (1995). The development of subitizing in young children. *British Journal of Developmental Psychology, 13*, 399–420.

Starkey, P., Spelke, E. S., & Gelman, R. (1990). Numerical abstraction by human infants. *Cognition, 36*, 97–127.

Sutherland, G. (1984). *Ability, merit and measurement: Mental testing and English education 1880–1940.* Oxford, England: Clarendon.

Svenson, O., & Sjöberg, K. (1983). Evolution of cognitive processes for solving simple additions during the first three school years. *Scandinavian Journal of Psychology, 24*, 117–124.

Thomas, S. M. (1992). *Children's use of addition strategies: A closer look at procedural and conceptual knowledge.* Unpublished doctoral dissertation, City of London Polytechnic.

Thorndike, E. L. (1922). *The psychology of arithmetic.* New York: Macmillan.

Trick, L. M., & Pylyshyn, Z. W. (1993). What enumeration studies can show us about spatial attention: evidence for limited capacity preattentive processing. *Journal of Experimental Psychology: Human Perception & Performance, 19*, 331-51.

Trick, L. M., Pylyshyn, Z. W. (1994). Why are small and large numbers enumerated differently? A limited-capacity preattentive stage in vision. *Psychological Review, 101*, 80-102.

Warrington, E. K. (1982). The fractionation of arithmetical skills: A single case study. *Quarterly Journal of Experimental Psychology, 34A*, 31–51.

Wheeler, L. R. (1939). A comparative study of the difficulty of the 100 addition combinations. *Journal of Genetic Psychology, 54*, 295–312.

Wynn, K. (1990). Children's understanding of counting. *Cognition, 36*, 155–193.

Wynn, K. (1992). Addition and subtraction by human infants. *Nature, 358*, 749–750.

Wynn, K. (1995). Origins of numerical knowledge. *Mathematical Cognition, 1*, 35–60.

Wynroth, L. (1986). *Wynroth math program—The natural numbers sequence.* Ithaca, NY: Wynroth Math Program.

CHAPTER 3

TWO PERSPECTIVES ON ADDITION DEVELOPMENT

Arthur J. Baroody and Sirpa H. Tiilikainen
University of Illinois at Urbana-Champaign

Over the last three decades, researchers have discovered that children, even preschoolers, have surprisingly powerful everyday (informal) arithmetic knowledge (e.g., Carpenter, Hiebert, & Moser, 1983; Fuson, 1982; Ginsburg, 1977; Huttenlocher, Jordan, & Levine, 1994; Mix, Levine, & Huttenlocher, 1999; Starkey & Gelman, 1982). Consider the case of Alexi, who had not yet begun school (formal) instruction on arithmetic. While playing a mathematics card game with his father, the 7-year-old formed the following number sentence:

$$\boxed{6} \quad \boxed{+} \quad \boxed{3} \quad \boxed{=} \quad \boxed{\text{wild card}}.$$

The boy announced that the sum represented by the wild card was eight. Asked how much six and three was, Alexi put out five fingers on his left hand, one on his right hand, and then three more on his right hand. After counting the fingers, he commented quizzically, "Nine? Nine? I thought 4 + 5 was *nine.*"

Alexi apparently understood the symbolic expression 6 + 3 by assimilating it to his informal concept of addition. His initial estimate of "eight" was probably constrained by this conceptual knowledge (namely, addition makes a collection larger) and, thus, was at least in the right direction (larger than either addend). Alexi then used an informal finger-counting procedure to determine the exact (correct) sum: represent the first addend with objects (e.g., fingers), do the same for the second addend, and then count all the objects (a *concrete counting-all* or *CCA strategy*). As no one had shown him such a strategy, he probably used his informal understanding of addition to invent it. The result of his computational effort apparently created cognitive conflict and doubt—the surprising finding that number combinations with different addends, such as 4 + 5 and 6 + 3, can have the same sum. This, in turn, may have prompted him to rethink his assumptions about numbers and arithmetic (i.e., to begin constructing the "different-names-for-a-number" concept). Put differently, application of his procedural knowledge may have helped prompt a conceptual advance.

This vignette bears on a fundamentally important issue in the field of mathematical psychology: What are the relations between conceptual and procdural knowledge of arithmetic? More specifically, what role does conceptual knowledge typically play in children's learning, choice, and use of informal addition strategies? For example, like Alexi, do children typically use pre-existing conceptual knowledge to self-invent the CCA strategy, and what role exactly does conceptual knowledge play in the subsequent improvements of this strategy? How are the conceptual bases for informal counting-based computational procedures formed, and what role does computational experience typically play in prompting conceptual advances? What role does conceptual knowledge play in the development of mental-arithmetic competence? For instance, does it have a key role in the learning *and* mental representation of single-digit (basic) or even multidigit combinations? If arithmetic knowledge is not genetically favored, how can we best account for children's impressive informal expertise?

Two modern theoretical perspectives often provide different answers to such questions regarding arithmetic development (Geary, 1994). In this chapter, we analyze the strategy-choice model (e.g., Siegler, 1986), which is based on associative-learning and information-processing theories, and compare it with a schema-based view (e.g., Baroody & Ginsburg, 1986), which is based on constructivist and social-learning theory. Our evaluation first focuses on children's development and choice of counting-based strategies for determining sums. Second, we analyze how the two perspectives account for the development of mental arithmetic. Third, we examine two perspectives on how the relations between conceptual and procedural knowledge might yield informal arithmetic competence.

The Development of Counting-Based Strategies and Strategy Choice

At any given time during development, an individual child uses a variety of arithmetic strategies, even with the same item (e.g., Baroody, 1984a; Carpenter & Moser, 1982; Fuson, 1982; Siegler, 1987; Siegler & Jenkins, 1989; Siegler & Shrager, 1984; see also Cowan, chap. 2, this volume).[1] Siegler's (e.g., 1986) strategy-choice model represents the most ambitious effort to account for this variation. As Table 3.1 illustrates, this model has, over time, become less mechanistic and more cognitive in nature. In this section, we outline and evaluate the latest version of this model, namely the strategy choice and discovery simulation (SCADS). In doing so, we discuss how a schema-based view accounts for the phenomena simulated incompletely or inaccurately. We end the section with conclusions about the role of computer simulations in developmental research and their relation to verbal models.

---

[1] At least some earlier researchers were aware that children use multiple arithmetic strategies. For instance, Ilg and Ames (1951) implied that children between 5 and 8 years of age used a mix of addition strategies—the composition of which changed with development. Svenson, Hedenborg, and Lingman (1976) and Svenson and Sjöberg (1983) explicitly discussed children's choices among several addition strategies. Like Ilg and Ames, Svenson and Sjöberg's description of the gradual development of these strategies (see, e.g., their Fig. 2) presaged Siegler's discussion of strategy choice (e.g., Siegler & Shrager, 1984) or his wave theory of development (e.g., Siegler, 1996). A few early researchers suggested that even adults might use a variety of arithmetic strategies (Browne, 1906; Groen & Parkman, 1972).

Table 3.1: Evolution of the Strategy-Choice Model

Variation	Key Characteristics
Distribution of associations model or DOAM (e.g., Siegler, 1986; Siegler & Shrager, 1984)	• "Dumb" in the sense that experience (practice) with one arithmetic combination did not generalize to others. • Conceptual and metacognitive input is minimal. • Associative-learning mechanism does not allow the discovery of new strategies.
Adaptive strategy choice model or ASCM (e.g., Siegler & Shipley, 1995)	• Feedback about the use of a strategy with one arithmetic combination can be generalized to other unpracticed items. • Conceptual and metacognitive input is still minimal. • Associative learning mechanism still does not allow the discovery of new strategies.
Strategy choice and discovery simulation or SCADS (e.g., Shrager & Siegler, 1998)	• Feedback about the use of a strategy with one arithmetic combination can be generalized to other unpracticed items. • Competitive negotiation between associative and metacognitive mechanisms can account for the discovery of new strategies.

OUTLINE OF SCADS

The theoretical rationale for SCADS (Crowley, Shrager, & Siegler, 1997) and its operation (Crowley et al., 1997; Shrager & Siegler, 1998) are discussed in turn.

Rationale

Crowley et al. (1997) compared and evaluated associative and metacognitive models of strategy development vis-à-vis Siegler and Jenkins' (1989) evidence on the development of counting-on from the larger addend (COL). See Table 3.2 for a summary of their analysis. They concluded that neither model

Table 3.2: A Comparison of Associative and Metacognitive Models of Problem Solving and Siegler and Jenkins' (1989) Evidence

Model 1: Associative Model (e.g., Karmiloff-Smith, 1992)	Model 2: Metacognitive Model (e.g., J. R. Anderson, 1993)	Evidence (Siegler & Jenkins, 1989)
1A. Discoveries should occur predictably at impasses (when a child does not have an appropriate strategy available). Appropriate strategies are discovered via trial and error, and a repertoire of appropriate strategies develops via associative processes.	1M. Discoveries can occur at impasses but also by insight (noticing something interesting about prior solutions) or via direct instruction.	1E. Discoveries typically did not occur when a child was at an impasse but at various times and on various problems.
2A. Discoveries should not involve insight; generalization is slow and piecemeal.	2M. Discoveries should be accompanied by explicit, metacognitive knowledge about the insight; generalization is immediate and wholesale.	2E. Discoveries are accompanied by varying degrees of insight; generalization is slow and piecemeal (though somewhat accelerated by metacognitive awareness).
3A. Because they are relying on trial and error, children will try both successful and unsuccessful strategies.	3M. Discoveries are restricted to successful strategies because metacognitive awareness allows children to make predictions about the success of new strategies before they commit to trying it.	3E. "Children never discovered illegitimate addition strategies" (Crowley et al., 1997, p. 469).

could entirely or satisfactorily explain these developmental data (Points 1E, 2E, and 3E in Table 3.2). Crowley et al. proposed a new model, where both associative and metacognitive mechanisms are activated simultaneously and compete to produce a problem-solving strategy. They concluded that the (indirect) interaction of these two mechanisms accounts for the following three key features of Siegler and Jenkins' developmental data:

• 1E. *Discoveries occur at various times on various problems*, because when the required insight occurs is not predictable due to individual differences in metacognitive knowledge.

• 2E. *Discoveries are typically generalized slowly, but occur somewhat faster when there is metacognitive awareness*. This is because the metacognitive system only influences (rather than□controls) the associative systemwhich usually plays the greater role in strategy selection (see Fig. 3.1, particularly Step 5).

• 3E. *Children never discover illegal strategies*, because their goal sketch guides their discoveries and constrains their use.

Figure 3.1: Construction of a Goal Sketch and the Discovery and Generalization of a New Strategy (Crowley et al., 1997)

	Event	Associative System	Metacognitive System
1.	Initial learning of CCA strategy (novel task).	Lack of experience → no confident decision → can't compete to control behavior.	Wins control; creates a representation of each step of the strategy.
	↓	↓	↓
2.	Practicing CCA.	Input from experience → creates its own (separate) representation of the strategy → increasingly confident decisions gradually takes more control.	Increasingly relieved of the burden of micromanaging the execution of CCA → increase in monitoring function.
	↓	↓	↓
3.	After at least a moderate amount of experience with CCA.	With the now familiar task, associative mechanism easily wins competition and controls strategy execution.	Monitoring function requires using and reinforcing only the key elements of its strategy representation; other steps fade from memory → a "goal sketch" of the strategy.
	↓	↓	↓
4.	Discovery of new strategy.	Although adding via CCA is now familiar and automatic, the associative system can be influenced by changes in problem-solving goals.	Monitoring leads to an interesting insight (e.g., noticing a redundancy); metacognitive system → increases its bid to control decision making by setting a new goal.
	↓	↓	↓
5.	Use of new strategy.	Typically, the more efficient associative mechanism wins the competition and chooses CCA because of its established track record.	Occasionally, may choose the goal of using the new strategy → more rapid generalization and greater metacognitive insight into the new strategy.

Operation

The operation of SCADS is compared, in part, with the major achievements in the development of counting-based addition strategy as prescribed by schema-based views (see Table 3.3). SCADS begins each run with two strategies: retrieval and CCA (Achievement 1 in Table 3.3). The former is assumed to be a cognitive capability from infancy; the latter is based on the assumption that CCA "is explicitly taught to young children by their parents" (Shrager & Siegler, 1998, p. 409). The simulation also begins with a built-in goal sketch, which means its initial state represents an experienced user of CCA. Crowley et al. (1997) argued that a child who has just learned CCA would not have an additive goal sketch. This aspect of the metacognitive component is constructed from the repeated application of CCA. As a child practices CCA, the metacognitive component is increasingly relieved of the burden of micromanaging the execution of this strategy and increasingly takes on a monitoring function. This monitoring function requires using only the key elements of CCA and, as a result, only these critical elements are reinforced. The other steps (elements) fade from memory leaving a goal sketch of the strategy.

A schematic summary of how SCADS operates to invent new addition strategies is illustrated in Fig. 3.2. The discovery heuristics, the metacognitive component directly involved in creating new strategies, consists of two strategy-change heuristics: "(a) If a redundant sequence of behavior is detected, then delete one of the two [redundant processes]; and (b) if statistics on a strategy's speed and accuracy show greater success when the strategy is executed in a particular order, then create a version of the strategy that always uses that order (as opposed to the initial procedure of arbitrarily choosing which addend to quantify first)" (Shrager & Siegler, 1998, p. 408). These two heuristics enable the SCADS simulation to "invent" increasingly sophisticated strategies in the following ways:

• Application of the first heuristic can result in Insight #1 (the representation of an addend by counting can be done simultaneously with a sum count; Achievement 4 in Table 3.3), and this insight can prompt invention of, for example, abstract counting-all starting with the first addend (CAF).

• Application of the second heuristic, which is analogous to Achievement 5 in Table 3.3, can prompt the invention of, for instance, abstract counting-all starting with the larger addend (CAL).

• Application of the first heuristic can further result in Insight #2: the representation of an addend by counting is redundant with stating its cardinal value (Achievement 6 in Table 3.3), which can prompt the invention of, say, COL.

EVALUATION OF SCADS

In this subsection, we first evaluate the assumptions on which SCADS is based and then the validity of the model.

Table 3.3: Major Achievements in the Development of Informal Counting Strategies for Computing Sums and Illustrative Strategies Using 3 + 5 as an Example

Achievement	Strategy
1. **Direct modeling.** Children's first appropriate, counting-based addition strategy typically involves using objects to model the meaning of a problem—to concretely represent problems and concretely determine a solution.	1. **Concrete counting-all strategy** (CCA)—a counting strategy that involves (a) directly modeling *both* addends and (b) a separate sum count. For example, for 3 + 5, a child might successively count and raise three fingers to concretely represent the starting amount 3, successively count and raise five fingers to concretely represent the added-on amount 5, and then count all eight fingers to determine the sum.
2. **Short-cutting the direct model.** Children take a small, but useful, step by using patterns to short-cut one or more steps in the direct-modeling (CCA) procedure.	2. **Concrete counting-all shortcut strategies** include using finger patterns to represent each addend. For example, for 3 + 5, a child might automatically (simultaneously) raise three fingers on one hand and then do the same with five fingers on the other hand to represent the addends. The child could then determine the sum by counting all the fingers or by recognizing the number of fingers extended.
3. **Embedded-addend concept → semi-indirect modeling.** Children discover that representing *one* of the addends (e.g., by counting) can be embedded in (i.e., done simultaneously with) the sum count (Fuson, 1992). As a result, they no longer have to concretely represent an addend. Nevertheless, semi-indirect modeling still requires two separate (sequential) counts—one to represent the other addend and a second to determine the sum.	3. **Concrete counting of the added-on amount strategies** —counting strategies that involve indirectly modeling the starting amount and directly modeling the added-on amount with objects either sequentially or simultaneously *before* the sum count. For example, for 3 + 5, a child might first extend five fingers to represent the added-on amount, next *verbally* count up to the cardinal value of the starting amount (*one, two, three*), and then continue this count as she pointed, in turn, to each of the previously extended finger (*four, five, six, seven, eight*). Such strategies are particularly useful for sums greater than 10, making it difficult to represent both addends on the fingers of two hands.
4. **Embedded-addends concept + keeping track → indirect modeling.** Children discover that representing *both* addends can be done simultaneously with the sum count. This, in turn, entails inventing a keeping-track process (continuing a verbal count from a number for a specified interval). Relatively abstract counting strategies, strategies that do not require separate representations of either addend prior to the sum count are now possible.	4. **Abstract counting strategies**—counting strategies that involve indirectly modeling both the starting amount and the added-on amount and, thus, require a keeping-track process done in tandem (simultaneously) with a sum count. For 3 + 5, for instance, a child might "*count-all beginning with the first addend*" (CAF).[a] Verbally count out the starting amount ("One, two, three") and then count, "four [is one more], five [is two more], six [is three more], seven [is four more], eight [is five more]." Note that the portion in brackets is the keeping-track process.
5. **Disregarding addend order.** Simultaneously executing sum and keeping-track counts puts a heavy burden on working memory. For small-addend-first items such as 3 + 5, representing the larger addend first can minimize the keeping-track count and, thus, reduce the load on working memory.	5. **Abstract counting strategies that disregard addend order** such as "*counting-all beginning with the larger addend*" (CAL). For 3 + 5, this could take the form of starting with *one*, counting up to the cardinal value of the larger addend ("...two, three, four, five..."), and then continuing the count for three more terms: "six [is one more], seven [is two more], eight [is three more]."
6. **Embedded cardinal-count concept → counting-on.** Children discover that, in the context of computing sums, stating the cardinal value of an addend is equivalent to counting up to this number (Fuson, 1992). This permits starting the sum count with the cardinal value of the addend (counting-on) instead of counting from *one* (counting-all).	6. **Abstract counting strategies that involve counting-on** such as "*counting-on from the larger addend*" (COL). For 3 + 5, for instance, this might take the form of stating the larger addend ("Five") and counting on three more times: "six [is one more], seven [is two more], eight [is three more]."

[a] Siegler (e.g., Shrager and Siegler, 1998) refers to CCA as "*sum*," and to CAF as "*shortcut sum*." Technically, *sum* refers to the abstract CAF strategy, not to CCA. According to Resnick and Ford (1981, p. 76), the *sum* model has a reaction time (RT) equal to the sum of the two addends (RT = $m + n$), which is approximately the RT a CAF strategy requires. CCA requires counting out items to represent each addend and then counting all the items put out, a process that requires a RT equal to *twice* the sum (RT = $[m] + [n] + [m + n] = 2(m + n)$).

Figure 3.2: Summary of SCADS (Shrager & Siegler, 1998)

```
┌──────────────────────────────────────────────────────────────────▼──┐
│   ┌───────────┐   analyzed in    ┌─────────────────────────────────┐ │
│   │  Problem  │───terms of──────▶│ Strategy Database including      │ │
│   └───────────┘                  │ information about answers given  │ │
│                                  │ previously, their speed, and     │ │
│   ┌───────────┐◀─────────────────│ accuracy                         │ │
│   │ Proposed  │                  └─────────────────────────────────┘ │
│   │ strategy  │   analyzed in    ┌ ─ ─ ─ ─ ─ ─ ─ ─ ─ ─ ─ ─ ─ ─ ─ ─ ┐ │
│   └───────────┘───terms of──────▶  Attentional Spotlight, which       │
│ yields                          │ increases attentional resources   │ │
│ feedback                          for poorly learned strategies, and │
│   ┌───────────┐◀─────────────── │ Goal Sketch Filters, which check  │ │
│   │ Approved  │                    the validity of the strategy       │
│   │ strategy, │                  └ ─ ─ ─ ─ ─ ─ ─ ─ ─ ─ ─ ─ ─ ─ ─ ─ ┘ │
│   │ which     │                                    ▲                  │
│   │ operates  │                                    │                  │
│   │ on the    │                                    │                  │
│   │ problem   │                                    │                  │
│   └───────────┘                                    │                  │
│         │ yields                                   │                  │
│         ▼                                          │                  │
│   ┌───────────┐                  ┌ ─ ─ ─ ─ ─ ─ ─ ─ ─ ─ ─ ─ ─ ─ ─ ┐   │
│   │ Traces of │   (if attentional  Discovery Heuristics, which    │   │
│   │ component │   resources allow)│ permit the invention of new        │
│   │ steps in  │   analyzed by      strategy variations            │   │
│   │ working   │──────────────────▶└ ─ ─ ─ ─ ─ ─ ─ ─ ─ ─ ─ ─ ─ ─ ─ ┘   │
│   │ memory    │                                                       │
│   └───────────┘                                                       │
└──────────────────────────────────────────────────────────────────────┘
```

┌ ─ ─ ┐
│   │ indicates the newly added metacognitive components.
└ ─ ─ ┘

Difficulties with SCADS' Underlying Assumptions

SCADS is based on oversimplified and untested assumptions.

Oversimplified Assumptions. The underlying developmental mechanism (e.g., associative learning, detecting redundancy) does not sufficiently take into account children's developing conceptual knowledge. Thus, although metacognition and concepts (in the form of a goal sketch and "insights") play a critical role in the strategy development modeled by SCADS, this model does not adequately embody the three guidelines for a complete and accurate model of arithmetic development outlined in chapter 1 of this volume.

• *Guideline 1. Conceptual knowledge usually underlies procedural innovations.* From constructivist and social-learning perspectives, SCADS does not provide an adequate explanation of how children actively construct understanding in a social context or how their expanding web of conceptual knowledge promotes the development of increasingly advanced arithmetic procedures. SCADS is a skills-first model in the sense that the procedure CCA is assumed to be learned by rote. Siegler (1997) concluded from data gathered on mothers and their 3-year-olds indicate that parents rarely talk about the goals (meaning) of addition, but that their actions implicitly underscore the key elements of CCA. The formation of a goal sketch (described earlier) could be interpreted as a description of how a child learns the critical attributes of an addition concept. This type of concept formation, however, is essentially a mechanical and passive, associative-winnowing process (rather than one that involves active inductive and/or deductive reasoning, whether done implicitly or explicitly).[2] Furthermore, because its only other mechanism for conceptual development is the insight-by-computational-discovery process, the simulation embodies only one of the two processes (noted earlier in Fig. 1.2 of chapter 1) by which conceptual knowledge is constructed and does that in a narrow manner.

The fundamentally important process of meaningful learning or assimilation (Piaget, 1964) is overlooked altogether, as is the related construct, the "zone of proximal development" (Vygotsky, 1962). Thus, SCADS is silent on two key developmental transitions: how verbally based arithmetic competencies build on nonverbal ones, and how written arithmetic competencies build on both of these informal aspects of arithmetic knowledge. (For a discussion of the first transition, see e.g., Baroody, in press; Jordan, Hanich, & Uberti, chap. 13, this volume, and Mix, Huttenlocher, & Levine, 2002. For a discussion of the second transition, see, e.g., Donlan, chap. 12, this volume, and Munn, 1998.) For example, SCADS does not account for why, when presented word problems or symbolic expressions, some children invent CCA, others learn the strategy with minimal adult intervention (one or two demonstrations), and yet others require more intervention or how these differences affect strategy choice and development (cf. Baroody, 1987b, 1989, 1996).[3]

---

[2] Neither Crowley et al. (1997) nor Shrager and Siegler (1998) described how the metacognitive system knows a priori the critical attributes of addition (the key elements of CCA) or learns to recognize them. That is, without prior conceptual knowledge, it is unclear how the metacognitive system distinguishes between the key steps of CCA (which is necessary to monitor the strategy and reinforce these steps) and other steps (which fade from memory through nonuse). More specifically, it is unclear how the six elements of CCA (described in the last full paragraph of p. 471 in Crowley et al., 1997) are translated into the two standards of SCADS's goal sketch (described in the third paragraph of column 2 on p. 408 of Shrager and Siegler, 1998). The troublesome issue of how an addition goal sketch is formed was avoided in the development of SCADS simply by building the two standards into the program so that they were operational from the start.

[3] SCADS does have a mechanism that could be construed as a simulation of adult intervention (Cowan, chap. 2, this volume). To account for why children would use a new strategy when reasonably effective alternatives already exist, the simulation awards novelty points in direct proportion to newness of a strategy. Novelty points temporarily strengthen the relative associative strength of a new strategy, allowing it to be chosen more often than its relatively feeble track record warrants. Siegler and Shipley (1995, p. 56) noted that this simulates "the observation that people (especially children) are often interested in exercising newly acquired cognitive capabilities (Piaget, 1970)." Novelty points could also be thought of as encouragement by parents or teachers to use a novel and more efficient strategy (Cowan, chap. 2, this volume). However, the novelty-point mechanism does not explain how new information is assimilated in terms of extant knowledge or how the issue of developmental readiness affects this process or a child's interest in engaging it.

The process of insight, discovery, or integration occurs only as a result of computational practice and the application of a metacognitive heuristic. Although Resnick and Ford (1981) noted that "reorganization of procedures by the learner in the course of computational practice" may be "a very general phenomenon in mathematics learning" (p. 247), the integration of knowledge necessary for procedural advances can occur in other ways. Consider how a noncomputational activity could promote, for instance, the grouping-by-ten concept that underlies our base-ten numeration system.   A child engaged in translating multidigit numerals into Egyptian hieroglyphics (e.g., $12 = \cap I I$, where the "heel" = 10 and a "staff" = 1) or vice versa might discover that teen numbers are a composite of a group of 10 and units. She might then use this insight to devise an "over-ten" reasoning strategy for teen sums: $9 + 5 \rightarrow$ transfer a unit from the 5 to the 9 to create a group of 10 and 4 units (Baroody, with Coslick, 1998; see Miura & Okamoto, chap. 8, this volume, for a discussion of how the structure of Asian counting terms can facilitate the discovery of this and related reasoning strategies).

Furthermore, noticing redundancies in a procedure is not the only way computational practice may produce insight. Providing an opportunity to see and reflect on patterns and relations is probably a more important contribution of computational practice. For instance, with computational experience, children appear to notice a connection between two previously isolated aspects of mathematical knowledge: addition involving one and their existing counting-based number-after knowledge (Baroody, 1988, 1989, 1992a, 1995). Specifically, they recognize that the sum of an $n + 1$ combination is simply the number after n in the counting sequence (e.g., the sum of $5 + 1$ is the counting number after *five*: *six*). The resulting integration of addition with their already automatic number-after knowledge enables children to construct a more efficient strategy (the number-after rule) for answering $n + 1$ combinations.

In conclusion, SCADS provides a seriously oversimplified account of addition development. It does not seem to allow for assimilation or integration via the discovery of relational knowledge either within or without the context of computation. As a result, it does not account for class-specific reasoning strategies, such as the over-ten "thinking strategy" or the number-after rule for $n + 1$ (or $1 + n$) combinations. Although SCADS's insight-by-computational-discovery process could be said to mimic what Hiebert and Lefevre (1986) called the development of a "primary-level" (less abstract) concept, neither this process or its goal-sketch formation process give children credit for reflective-level (more abstract) concepts.

• *Guideline 2. Adaptive expertise involves the integration of conceptual and procedural knowledge.* It is not clear how competitive-negotiation models, such as the current version of SCADS, account for the increasing *integration* of extant knowledge that results in sudden insights when solving a novel problem or devising more effective strategies for more familiar tasks. For example, once children discover the relation between number-after knowledge and adding one, they frequently generalize it quickly to other combinations, including those they have not practiced (e.g., Baroody, 1995). In a schema-based view, this conceptual insight further connects the concepts of counting and addition *and* their production systems (the rules and data for generating next numbers and the mechanisms for identifying addition problems, in general, and the class of n + 1 combinations, in particular). With practice, the integrated production system that represents the number-after rule for n + 1 combinations can be compiled and become automatic. In this view, then, development involves increasingly cooperative and integrated relations between conceptual knowledge and procedural knowledge.

In contrast, in a competitive-negotiations model, the metacognitive and associative systems are "representationally encapsulated" (i.e., "neither system can directly inspect or modify the contents of the other"), and they can "only interact through the output of independent encoding and decision-making processes" (Crowley et al., 1997, p. 480). In theory, the metacognitive system can monitor the strategy being executed in working memory, but it cannot access (a) the data stored about other problems; (b) the steps of other strategies; or (c) the speed, accuracy, or other information about other strategies stored in the associative component. This limits what the metacognitive component can discover or its capacity to combine the steps from two existing strategies to create a new one, not an uncommon problem-solving technique. For instance, as currently designed, SCADS cannot discover the number-after relation or devise the number-after rule for n + 1 combinations. Siegler (1997) did note that the metacognitive component includes domain-specific knowledge, such as knowledge of strategies. Although this component might be capable of using such knowledge for comparing and integrating the steps of two strategies, presumably it could do so only *before* a goal sketch of each was completed.

• *Guideline 3. Conceptual knowledge can play either a direct role or an indirect role in procedural inventions.* In SCADS, conceptual knowledge (in the form of a goal sketch), for the most part, plays either an indirect role or a semi-direct role in the discovery of new strategies. It indirectly supports procedural advances by monitoring new strategies and rejecting illegal ones. It plays a semi-direct role by changing task goals and temporarily befuddling the associative mechanism. Although competitive-negotiation models could theoretically account for direct conceptual instigation of a procedural advanced, SCADS does not have this capability.

Untested Assumptions. Two basic assumptions of SCADS essentially remain untested.

1. Currently, there is no direct empirical evidence that children store in the associative memory for strategies or that for problems (number combinations) information about the answers, speed, and accuracy of *each* and every computational effort. (Contradictory evidence for this proposition is detailed in the next section on mental-arithmetic development.) It seems plausible that children, particularly those whose attention and working memory is tied up with devising or mastering a new strategy, might not store such data (Geary, 1993). It also plausible that children construct or elaborate on schemas that

summarize key aspects of experience, instead of mechanically building up an associative network that links each strategy to accuracy, speed, or other data.

2. Currently, there is no systematic evidence that a goal sketch develops in the way Crowley et al. (1997) outlined. For example, children who have just learned CCA should not have a goal sketch and—unlike more experienced adders—should not be able to (a) monitor their strategy, (b) reject illegal strategies, or (c) invent and use legal strategies exclusively. Yet, some such children who use illegal strategies sense there is a difficulty. For example, Jonna, described earlier, appeared to monitor her performance and to recognize (after the fact) that something was wrong with her answer and procedure. Brianna had to have CCA demonstrated twice to learn the strategy, yet a week later and without intervening practice, identified CCA and a semi-indirect modeling strategy (Achievement 3) as "smart" and the counting-an-addend-twice error as "not smart." Other CCA novices do invent CCA shortcuts (Achievement 2 in Table 3.3) or even more advanced strategies (e.g., Achievements 3, 4, and 5) immediately after learning CCA, but not illegal strategies (Baroody, 1987b, 1996; Baroody & Gannon, 1984). The case of Felicia described later in Box 3.1 is further evidence that Crowley et al.'s (1997) assumptions about the development of a goal sketch are questionable.

The Validity of SCADS: Incomplete and Inaccurate Modeling of Developmental Phenomena

A serious difficulty with Siegler and colleagues' theoretical and empirical rationale for SCADS (e.g., Crowley et al., 1997) is that they were highly selective in the developmental data analyzed. Specifically, they basically focused on the results of a single study, namely Siegler and Jenkins' (1989) microgenetic study and did not consider contradictory evidence. Compounding this limitation, the study involved a small and select sample, one that may not be representative of typical development.[4] Furthermore, plausible alternative explanations for developmental data were overlooked. Next, we discuss the implications of these difficulties for (a) Crowley et al.'s (1997) conclusions about Siegler and Jenkins' evidence, (b) their contrasts between associative and metacognitive models, (c) accurately modeling key developmental phenomena identified by the model makers themselves, and (d) modeling other key aspects of addition-strategy development.

Difficulties with Crowley et al.'s (1997) Conclusions About Siegler and Jenkins' (1989) Evidence. Crowley et al.'s (1997) characterizations of

---

[4] Siegler and Jenkins (1989) analyzed the data of eight 4- and 5-year-olds drawn from a university-run preschool. These children were, for the most part, above average in computational ability: Unlike the 19 children excluded from the study, 7 of the 8 participants were accurate on at least half of the pretest trials. (Apparently, the 8th participant was given special training to improve her computational skill.) Moreover, the 7 participants who invented COL did so within a relatively short span of time—within 3 months (cf. Baroody, 1984a, 1987b).

the developmental data are incomplete or inaccurate. Specifically, Points 1E, 2E, and 3E summarized in Table 3.2 do not adequately reflect the complexities or richness of extant developmental data.

• *Point 1E: Discoveries occur at various unpredictable times.* Crowley et al. (1997) concluded that the discovery of addition strategies is the product of a metacognitive mechanism, because Siegler and Jenkins (1989) found little uniformity in their participants' discoveries leading to COL. Unfortunately, they overlooked evidence of key regularities in this developmental process. Baroody (1995) found that some children began to disregard addend order (exhibited Achievement 5 in Table 3.3) soon after discovering that the number-after rule also applied to $1 + n$ combinations. That is, the discovery of a general number-after rule appears to be *one* way children recognize they can start with the larger addend. Furthermore, Baroody's (1995) participants typically began counting-on (exhibited Achievement 6 in Table 3.3) soon after discovering the number-after rule for $n + 1$ combinations (see also Bråten, 1996). Apparently, this induced rule provided a conceptual basis or scaffold for counting-on. For example, children seem to reason that if the sum of $5 + 1$ is the number after *five* in the counting sequence, then the sum of $5 + 3$ must be three numbers after *five* in the counting sequence: "six, seven, eight." As might be expected if the number-after rule served as a scaffold for inventing counting-on, the majority of children (6 of 10) first used this strategy (or first extended this strategy beyond $n + 1$ or $1 + n$ combinations) with $n + 2$ or $2 + n$ combinations, which require minimal attention to the keeping-track process.

Still regarding Point 1E, Crowley et al. (1997) may have underestimated the importance of impasses in motivating both conceptually instigated and nonconceptually motivated (but conceptually supported) procedural advances. In other words, an impasse may prompt, for example, the direct conceptual mechanisms described in the previous paragraph, or it may promote procedural advances independently of them. Consider two examples of the latter.

1. The need to keep track (Achievement 4 in Table 3.3) often creates an impasse that may prompt the development of strategies that involve disregarding addend order (Achievement 5 in Table 3.3). For instance, Case began the Baroody and Gannon (1984) study by relying on CAF. When given $3 + 6$, he tried to use this strategy but stopped counting at *three*, and commented, "I'll count to six, I guess." Apparently recognizing (either consciously or nonconsciously) how hard it would be to continue his count for exactly six more counts (". . . three; four *is one more*; five *is two more*; six *is three more*; seven *is four more*; eight *is five more*; nine *is six more*"), he decided to count out the larger addend first: ("one, two, three, four, five, six") and continue for three more counts (seven *is one more*; eight *is two more*; nine *is three more*"). By inventing CAL, he effectively reduced the cognitively demanding keeping-track process (the italicized portions in the preceding examples) from an extremely difficult six steps to a manageable three steps. Case made this labor-saving discovery even though he apparently did not recognize that, for example, $6 + 4$ and $4 + 6$ had the same sums.

2. When presented multidigit or "challenge problems," some children invent counting-on (Achievement 6 in Table 3.3; Baroody, 1984a; Carpenter & Moser, 1982; Siegler & Jenkins, 1989) to save mental effort, not because they detect redundancy (have an "insight") as Crowley et al. (1997) claimed. That is, this process of invention has the effect of eliminating redundancy, without necessarily involving an explicit or implicit reasoning process about what aspects of the abstract counting-all strategy are redundant (cf. Crowley et al., 1997; Shrager & Siegler, 1998). A case in point is illustrated in Box 3.1.

• *Point 2E: The speed of generalization depends on the degree of metacognitive awareness.* Factors other than the degree of metacognitive awareness, however, can affect how quickly a strategy is generalized. Conceptual factors, including whether a procedural advance is motivated by the discovery of a concept such as the principle of commutativity or a child's sensitivity to the semantic structure of a posed problem, may play a role (e.g., Baroody & Ginsburg, 1986; Baroody, Wilkins, & Tiilikainen, chap. 4, this volume; Cowan, chap. 2, this volume).

Box 3.1: The Case of Felicia

Summarized are aspects of a 13-month case study with Felicia (4 years, 9 months at the start of the study). See Baroody (1984a) for details.

Behavioral Evidence	Discussion
1. Felicia consistently used a legal strategy, such as CAF (Achievement 4 in Table 3.3), for single-digit combinations. To save labor, she invented CAL (Achievement 5 in Table 3.3), apparently without understanding the commutative principle.	1. The use and discovery of only legal strategies indicates that the girl has already constructed an addition goal sketch (Crowley et al., 1997).
2. However, when presented with challenge items, she immediately and consistently used either a COL strategy (e.g., 5 + 22: "23, 24, 25, 26, 27") or a COL-like strategy (e.g., 32 + 6: "31, 32, 33, 34, 35, 36, 37, 38").	2. The somewhat novel task creates an impasse and the opportunity for the metacognitive mechanism to seize control. Immediate generalization of the invented strategy to all other challenge items indicates metacognitive awareness.
3. When single-digit combinations were reintroduced, Felicia reverted to using CAF or CAL.	3. Metacognitive awareness should have enabled the girl to generalize her new strategy to easier items.
4. Moreover, when COL was modeled for her with these smaller combinations and she was asked to evaluate the strategy, the girl declared, "You can't do it that way."	4. At the very least, her goal sketch and metacognitive awareness should have allowed Felicia to recognize COL as a "smart" or "somewhat smart" strategy.
5. Events 2 to 4 reoccurred on several more occasions. At the end of the study, Felicia still relied on CAL and still did not use COL with single-digit items.	5. Further evidence inconsistent with Points 1E and 2E in Table 3.2.

As suggested earlier, the degree to which a strategy is generalized may also depend on nonconceptual factors, including the degree of difficulty required by keeping track. For instance, COL may generalize across $n + 1$ combinations first because such combinations require no keeping track; to $n + 2$ combinations second because such combinations involve minimal keeping track; to $n + 3$, $n + 4$, and $n + 5$ combinations next because keeping track is moderately difficult; and so forth (Baroody & Ginsburg, 1986). As the case of Felicia in Box 3.1 illustrates, some children generalize new strategies in some situations because it saves considerable mental labor but not in others because it doesn't. That is, this phenomenon can occur without a "conceptual insight due to a metacognitive analysis," as Crowley et al. (1997) claimed.

• *Point 3E: Children never invent illegal strategies.* This point illustrates the dangers of generalizing from a small, select sample. Our research indicates that children of all abilities, even those who presumably have a goal sketch, do sometimes invent and use illegal counting-based addition strategies. One such strategy (for smaller-addend-first items) is to create a nondistinct representation of the two addends. For $2 + 4$, for instance, Jonna (almost 8 years old and diagnosed as having learning difficulties) represented the first addend by counting, "One, two" (accompanied by raising two fingers). Next, she looked at the expression and represented the second addend by counting, "three, four" (accompanied by raising two fingers). Then the girl determined the sum by counting the four extended fingers. In effect, the "one, two" was used to represent the first addend *and* the first two counts needed to represent the second addend.[5]

However, the fact that some children do invent and use illegal strategies is not in itself inconsistent with the competitive-negotiations model. Crowley et al. (1997, p. 484, fn. 5) noted that, although CCA novices would not have addition goal sketches, they do have counting goal sketches. Thus, "when inventing addition strategies, these children would not be expected to violate counting principles. However, they would be expected to make errors on how they orchestrate the counting procedures." In brief, it follows from the competitive-negotiations model that CCA novices might invent or use illegal strategies but that experienced users of CCA (or more advanced strategies)—children who have had an opportunity to construct an addition goal sketch—should not.

Inconsistent with this hypothesis, Jonna regularly used her illegal strategy (in 9 of 10 sessions and on approximately a fourth of all smaller-addend-first items) over the course of a year. In all but one instance, the child manifested behavior indicating that she was troubled with its result. For example, in the first session after the girl had just been taught the CCA strategy, she used the illegal strategy to arrive at a sum of "three" for $1 + 3$. Knitting her eyebrows, Jonna glanced at the expression and unsuccessfully tried again. According to the competitive-negotiations model (Crowley et al., 1997), not only would she initially not have had the goal sketch necessary to monitor her efforts, trying to

---

[5] Jonna was interviewed by the second author, who was the first to notice and describe her illegal strategy.

implement the new CCA strategy should have consumed all of the attentional resources of the metacognitive component, leaving none for a monitoring effort.

Subsequent analyses have confirmed that Jonna's behavior is not unique to her or even CCA novices. In reexamining Baroody's (1987b) data, we found that 7 of his 17 participants used a strategy that was behaviorally identical to Jonna's strategy at least twice. In all, about half of his participants used at least one incomplete or flawed counting strategy on at least a handful of trials.[6] Jonna's error or other illegal strategies (e.g., counting one past the larger addend) occurred most frequently while children were mastering CCA or trying to invent abstract strategies, which involve keeping track (see Box 3.2 for an illustrative case).

Recently, we have collected additional evidence that even children who apparently have constructed a "goal sketch" sometimes use illegal strategies (Baroody, Tiilikainen, & Tai, 2000). Consider, for instance, the case of Beth. This bright kindergartner was an accomplished user of CCA or its shortcuts (Achievements 1 and 2 in Table 3.3). Consistent with her possessing an addition goal sketch, Beth considered the CCA and a semi-indirect-modeling strategy (Achievement 3 in Table 3.3) as "smart" but Jonna's procedure and representing one addend twice as "not smart." In a subsequent session, Beth devised a strategy that involved a keeping-track process (Achievement 4 in Table 3.3). For example, for 4 + 2, she counted, "one, two, three, four" (as she extended four fingers consecutively) and then "five, six" (as she extended two more fingers consecutively). Yet for 5 + 6 and 3 + 12, she devised a strategy similar to Jonna's. For 5 + 6, for example, Beth counted, "one, two, three, four, five" (while extending five fingers in turn), next counted, "six" (as she extended one more finger), and then announced an answer of "six." In brief, she devised and used an illegal strategy to deal with relatively challenging problems, despite fairly clear evidence of conceptual knowledge of addition.[7] In analyzing addition errors,

---

[6] This does not include addition errors due to a minor slip (e.g., miscounting a collection while determining a sum) or incorrect answers generated by mental ("estimation") strategies, such as responding to 2 + 6 with "seven."

[7] Consider also the case of Allison, a kindergartner in Baroody and Gannon's (1984) study. In Session 1, she relied on CCA, but for 3 + 7, she used the same illegal embedded-addend-representation strategy as Jonna. In the next session a week later, Allison regularly used a legal strategy that involved an embedded addend representation (Achievement 3 in Table 3.3). In other words, unlike Jonna and like Beth, Allison's incorrect invention appeared to be a miscue on the way to inventing a more advanced (efficient) strategy. It seems likely that some children, at least, may temporarily invent an illegal strategy in the course of mastering achievements listed in Table 3.3 other than Achievement 1. As the cases of Beth (described previously) and Aaron (described in Box 3.2) illustrate (see also Hopkins, 1998), initially devising a keeping-track strategy and integrating this component and a concrete counting strategy to create an abstract counting strategy (Achievement 4) may be a particularly error-prone process. For example, for both addition and subtraction, some children appear to start the keeping-track process too soon—by starting with cardinal value of the first addend (e.g., for 5 + 3, counting "5, 6, 7" or, for 6 + 4, counting "6, 7, 8, 9"; see Baroody, 1984b, 1987a, 1994). Clearly, a systematic effort is needed to determine what illegal strategies children invent, when, and why.

Box 3.2: The Case of Aaron

Aaron participated in Baroody's (1987b) 8-month microgenetic study of kindergartners' addition-strategy development.

<u>Behavioral Evidence</u>

1. In Session 1, Aaron could automatically state the sum of $n + 1$ word problems involving 3 and 1 more and 5 and 1 more.

2. On the third problem (4 and 2 more) he used an illegal strategy, namely "count somewhere beyond the larger addend": "1, 2, 3, 4 (pause), 5, 6 (pause), 7, 8."

3. Unable to solve the problem even with blocks, Aaron was taught a CCA procedure. On three subsequent problems, he apparently used a "larger-addend-plus-two" estimation strategy (i.e., he responded to 3 + 2 with "five," 5 + 3 with "seven," and 4 + 3 with "six"). For the latter two problems, he then successfully used CCA to determine a correct sum.

4. In the second session 2 weeks later, he used the same illegal strategy noted in Point 2 to produce an answer of "nine" to the first item 2 + 6 and had to be retaught the CCA strategy.

5. For the remainder of Session 2 and through Session 8 (3.5 months into the study), he relied on CCA almost exclusively and with 93% accuracy. During this time, he used the illegal count-somewhere-beyond-the-larger-addend strategy three more times.

6. During this same period, Aaron made four other aborted efforts to use a keeping-track process. For instance, in Session 4, he tried to compute the sum of 2 + 3 by counting "1, 2, (pause), 3" and commented, "I'm almost there but I ran out of thinking." He then abandoned the effort and fell back on using CCA.

7. Over the next four sessions (Sessions 9 to 12), he devised a keeping-track process and started relying on COL in Session 13.

<u>Discussion</u>

1. Aaron appeared to understand that (a) addition is an incrementing process (incrementing concept) and (b) his number-after knowledge is useful in answering problems involving $n + 1$ (number-after rule).

2. His invented illegal strategy appears to be constrained or even directly motivated by the two concepts listed in Point 1.

3. He also apparently used his knowledge of the two concepts listed in Point 1 to devise a reasonable estimation strategy: For $n + m$ problems, state an answer two (or more) than the larger addend (rather than one more). Note that all the competencies discussed so far developed before he learned CCA.

4. Ditto Point 2.

5. Despite his conceptual understanding (described in Point 1) and self-awareness (as suggested in Point 6), he continued to use an illegal, albeit a sensible, strategy (cf. Point 1E in Table 3.2).

6. Aaron apparently recognized that keeping track was a difficult process and on several occasions sensibly abandoned the effort in favor of a more reliable procedure, CCA ("I have to do it with the blocks").

7. In time, the lad overcame this predictable impasse (cf. Point 1E in Table 3.2).

Figure 3.3: Types of Addition-Strategy Errors

Procedural knowledge

	−	+
+ Conceptual knowledge	errors of strategy (e.g. Jonna's error or starting the keeping track process too early)	errors of execution (e.g., slips in production)
−	severe errors of strategy or inappropriate strategies	errors of execution and misapplication of the strategy

Note that − ⟷ + is a continuum from relatively incomplete knowledge to relatively complete knowledge.

Note also that conceptual knowledge of addition may develop *before* children start inventing counting strategies, even concrete ones.

then, it appears important to consider the degree of procedural knowledge as well as that of conceptual knowledge. Figure 3.3 illustrates a tentative taxonomy that does so.

Difficulties with Crowley et al.'s (1997) Contrasts Between the Associative and the Metacognitive Models. Clearly, neither the associative model (Model 1 in Table 3.2) nor the metacognitive model (Model 2 in the same table) by itself is adequate to account for the addition-development data. Although both associative processes and conceptual processes might operate simultaneously and compete against each other (as suggested by the competitive-negotiations model), another possibility is that children might rely more on one process in some circumstances and the other in different situations. Specifically, Model 1 can be viewed as a description of how children react to extremely novel problem-solving tasks (unassimilable and, thus, meaningless tasks) and the nature of routine expertise; Model 2, as a description of how they react to moderately novel problem-solving tasks (assimilable and, thus, meaningful tasks) and the nature of adaptive expertise. For example, Rittle-Johnson and Alibali (1999) found that children who received procedural (meaningless) instruction did significantly less well than those who received minimal conceptual (meaningful) instruction in identifying an incorrect procedure or devising a correct one for a moderately novel tasks (cf. Points 2A and 2M in Table 3.2).

According to the schema-based iterative view (e.g., Baroody & Ginsburg, 1986), how a child responds to an arithmetic problem-solving task will depend on where he or she is on the continuum between Model 1 (routine expertise mediated by a weak schema) and Model 2 (adaptive expertise mediated by a strong schema). The case of Felicia (described in Box 3.1 earlier) illustrates a child somewhere in the middle of this continuum. Her invention of a COL or COL-like strategy appeared to be an effort to short-cut her count from 1, so that she could focus her efforts on the cognitively demanding keeping-track process. Her invention was probably guided or constrained by her conceptual knowledge but not instigated by it. Because her new strategy was not conceptually motivated, Felicia abandoned the innovation when it was no longer needed and even rejected its validity.

Whether or not Models 1 and 2 are viewed as a continuum, Point 1A should be amended to include *"direct instruction outside a child's zone of proximal development (i.e., meaningless instruction),"* and Point 1M should be amended to read "direct instruction *within a child's zone of proximal development (i.e., meaningful instruction;* Vygotsky, 1962)." Point 2M probably should be amended to read "Discovery *can often* be accompanied by explicit metacognitive knowledge," because some conceptual breakthroughs occur nonconsciously. Point 3M might better be revised to read, "Discoveries *that are conceptually motivated by a strong schema* are restricted to successful strategies."

Inaccurate Modeling of Key Phenomena Identified by the Model Makers Themselves. Shrager and Siegler (1998) noted that the 30 runs of SCADS with 25 combinations involving the addends 1 to 5 demonstrated the seven major phenomena observed by Siegler and Jenkins (1989). Unfortunately, because their characterizations of these major phenomena were largely incomplete or inaccurate, SCADS faithfully simulates only the following two major phenomena of addition development: (a) choosing adaptively among strategies and (b) discoveries followed correct as well as incorrect performance. The other five phenomena modeled by SCADS are listed as follows, along with questions about the validity of this simulation.

1.   The simulation used multiple strategies throughout. We used Shrager and Siegler's (1998) strategy-scoring scheme to reanalyze Baroody's (1987b) data, which had a larger and more representative sample than the Siegler and Jenkins (1989) study. This analysis revealed significant individual differences in strategy choice. At one extreme, one participant relied almost exclusively on CCA (95% of the time a strategy could be identified) throughout the 8-month study. Ten other participants used this strategy at least two thirds of the time

($\overline{\text{M}}$ = 83%; range 69%–92%) and, on average, used it exclusively on just more than one fourth of their testing sessions. Similarly, a reanalysis of Baroody and Gannon's (1984) data found that 11 of 36 kindergartners used the same strategy on all six trials of the first session, and 7 of these participants used the same strategy again on the six trials of the second session a week later. Svenson and Sjöberg (1983), likewise, commented about their 16 participants: "Looking at individual differences one may note that some subjects tend to use very few strategies while others use several" (p. 121). SCADS, then, does not take into account significant individual differences in strategy choice and may overestimate the number of strategies many children actually use.

2.   SCADS discovered COL on all 30 runs and in a time frame ($\overline{\text{M}}$ = 107 trials) comparable to children ($\overline{\text{M}}$ = 95 trials). In fact, 7, not all 8, of Siegler and Jenkins' (1989) participants appeared to invent COL. With Baroody's (1987b) larger and more representative sample of kindergartners, only 6 of 17 invented COL in a comparable number of trials (104–136 trials). One of these children did so on only one trial (1 + 3). The invention of COL is often delayed considerably among children without the opportunity for much informal arithmetic experience, such as low-income inner-city children (Baroody, Berent, & Packman, 1982). SCADS, then, does not take into account the significant individual differences in how long it takes children to invent COL.

3.   SCADS consistently discovered CAF or CAL before COL. Six of 7 of Siegler and Jenkins' (1989) participants invented such strategies before COL. In Baroody's (1987b) study, 3 children used CAL or both CAF and CAL before inventing COL, another child briefly used COF as a transitional strategy from CCA, and yet another child became secretive during the transitional phase. In brief, although CAF and CAL typically serve as a transition between CCA and COL, these strategies are not the only way this transition is made (Baroody, 1987b; Siegler & Jenkins, 1989).

4.   The simulation was slow to generalize discovered strategies. A reanalysis of Baroody's (1987b) data revealed that 3 of the 5 children who invented COL generalized this strategy relatively quickly. For example, one participant invented COF in Session 2 and used this strategy on 4 of 7 trials before inventing COL in Session 3 and using it on 3 trials. From the third to the last (13th) session, COL was used 62% of the time and was the strategy used most often in 9 of these 11 sessions. Similarly, in the Baroody and Gannon (1984) study, several participants generalized counting-on strategies quickly. For example, Margaret, who used CAF or CAL exclusively in Session 1, invented COF and used this strategy exclusively in Session 2. Megan, who otherwise used CAF or COF, invented COL in Session 1. In the next session a week later, she used COL exclusively. It appears, then, that SCADS does not model the significant individual differences in the ability to generalize a new strategy.

5.   SCADS never executed illegal strategies. As illustrated earlier, the same cannot be said of children, even those experienced in using CCA or who otherwise should have a goal sketch.

Limitations of SCADS Regarding Other Important Developmental Phenomena. The operation of SCADS is at odds with or does not account for six key phenomena in the development of informal addition strategies.

1. As the case of Aaron described in Box 3.2 illustrates, children exhibit a variety of conceptually based addition competencies before they learn CCA. Some researchers have claimed that 5-month-old infants can reliably gauge the results of adding one item to a collection of one ("1 + 1") or taking away one item from a collection of two items ("2 – 1") and, thus, have a primitive sense of incrementing and decrementing (e.g., Wynn, 1992). Even if infants use a non-numerical estimation process based on a perceptual cue such as total perimeter (e.g., Clearfield & Mix, 1999; Mix et al., 2002), instead of a relatively exact nonverbal counting process (e.g., Wynn, 1998) or a relatively exact subitizing process (e.g., Sophian, 1998), other evidence indicates that young children can solve nonverbal problems involving small collections before they can solve comparable word problems (e.g., Jordan, Huttenlocher, & Levine, 1992). (For a more detailed discussion, see Donlan, chap. 12, this volume, and Jordan et al., chap. 13, this volume). For instance, two kindergartners (Athenaria, an African-American girl, and Alexander, a Caucasian boy) were largely successful on non-verbal addition items that involved, for example, seeing three items put under a cover and then seeing one more item put under the cover (see Baroody et al., 2000, for additional examples). These same children had not yet learned a CCA strategy and could not solve word problems, such as *Cookie Monster had three cookies and then got one more cookie. How many cookies did Cookie Monster have altogether? How much is three cookies and one more cookie altogether?*

Furthermore, some children (like Aaron described in Box 3.2) give plausible estimates even before they learn CCA. For example, Christina, an African-American kindergartner, used a number-after strategy (indiscriminately) to solve word problems involving three and one more ("Four, because after three comes four"), two and three more ("Three, because after two comes three"), one and four more ("Five, because after four comes five"), and five and two more ("Six, because after five comes six") before she used CCA to compute sums. Her performance indicated that she understood addition involved incrementing and, for the most part, that the sum had to be larger than either addend.

SCADS does not account for the addition competencies preschoolers exhibit before learning CCA. Put differently, this evidence is inconsistent with Shrager and Siegler's (1998) assumption that the starting point of arithmetic development is parental instruction of CCA and that a goal sketch and other discoveries (conceptual knowledge of addition) occur later as a result of applying this and other addition procedures.

2. Like Alexi (described in the vignette at the beginning of the chapter), many—if not most—children invent CCA (Achievement 1 in Table 3.3). This is made possible because, as noted in Point 1, preschoolers begin to construct a concept of addition *before* they devise counting-based strategies for solving word problems or symbolic expressions.

Because SCADS does not first construct a concept of addition (an addition goal sketch), it cannot invent CCA. CCA is built into the initial program, which mimics the assumption noted earlier—that this strategy is learned by rote through direct instruction.[8]

3. Typically, children do not systematically disregard addend order and begin with the larger addend until after they have invented abstract counting strategies☐and keeping track (Achievement 4 in Table 3.3) becomes an issue. Adding on more than three or so can create an impasse (i.e., create a need to minimize the cognitively demanding keeping-track process). SCADS can learn to start with the larger addend anytime during a run. Indeed, in the one run most fully described by Shrager and Siegler (1998), the simulation did so while it was still using CCA. Psychologically, this makes no sense, because there is no advantage in by doing so (i.e., CCA is equally difficult whether children represent the first or the second addend first).

4. Initially, children's addition seems to be order constrained, and they must discover that addend order is irrelevant (Achievement 5 in Table 3.3). A reanalysis of Baroody's (1987b) results indicates that children who use a CCA or CCA shortcut strategy are at least 8 times more likely to respect addend order than not.[9] Moreover, children tend to rely on CAF before inventing strategies that disregard addend order strategies such as CAL or COL (e.g., Baroody, 1984a, 1987b; Baroody & Gannon, 1984; Carpenter & Moser, 1984; Siegler & Jenkins, 1989). Children's addition strategies may be initially order constrained because of their informal "change-add-to" concept of addition (see Baroody et al., chap. 4, this volume, for a detailed discussion). They overcome this constraint in order to save labor or when they discover commutativity,

---

[8] Shrager and Siegler (1998) cited Saxe, Guberman, and Gearhart (1987). However, in this study, only 7 of 78 (less than 10%) of the parent-child dyads engaged in addition-strategy instruction. Furthermore, Baroody (1987b) found that only 3 of 17 (less than one fifth) of the 4- and 5-year-olds from working-class to upper-middle-class families just beginning kindergarten already knew a CCA strategy. There are several reasons why many parents or child-care providers do not teach CCA either directly or indirectly. One is that they may be unaware of children's informal counting strategies. A related reason is that many adults may have a narrow conception of arithmetic instruction as fostering mastering of "arithmetic" facts and, thus, many focus on flashcard drill and the like. Some parents, either because they are naive about young children's mathematical development or because they hold implicit or explicit constructivist beliefs, may simply act as mediators of experience. For example, A. Anderson (1997) found that when parents interacted with their children in the home environment, they created addition opportunities or problems but did not provide direct instruction on how to determine sums. In contrast, Siegler (1997) reported parents do engage in direct instruction of CCA. It is not clear, though, whether these observation were made in home environments or in a laboratory or whether the mothers were explicitly asked to teach their children how to add or given more open-ended instructions. In brief, the ecological validity of Siegler's results is not clear. Although adult modeling of addition strategies may play a role in children's inventions of such strategies (Cowan, chap. 2, this volume), A. Anderson (1993) noted that what is "even more striking is [their] ability . . . to go beyond imitation and formulate their own conclusions" (p. 28).

[9] Some evidence (e.g., Carpenter & Moser, 1982) indicates that children do not always respect addend order when executing CCA (Achievement 1 in Table 3.3). See pages 79–80 of Baroody and Ginsburg (1986) for a detailed explanation of why this might be.

through computational experience or otherwise (Baroody et al., chap. 4, this volume; Cowan, chap. 2, this volume).

Contrary to the evidence discussed in the previous paragraph, the SCADS simulation is based on the assumption that children's addition is initially not order constrained and then becomes so. SCADS executes the initial counting strategy (CCA) without regard to addend order. This implies that children are initially insensitive to addend order and that additive commutativity is psychologically primary, not discovered. At some point during its run, the simulation then employs the second strategy-change heuristic discussed earlier. This implies that children contravene their extant knowledge of additive commutativity to invent strategies that disregard addend order.

5. The type of word problem affects when CAL or COL is invented. De Corte and Verschaffel (1987) found that children were more likely to invent and use informal addition strategies that disregard addend order when solving part-whole problems that do not imply an order constraint than when solving change-add-to problems that do. For a detailed discussion of how proponents of a schema-based view explain this finding, see Baroody et al. (chap. 4, this volume); the finding is not considered in SCADS.

6. As noted earlier, children typically invent counting-on (Achievement 6 in Table 3.3) immediately after discovering the number-after rule for $n + 1$ combinations (Baroody, 1995; Bråten, 1996). In contrast, SCADS (Shrager & Siegler, 1998) discovers counting-on by detecting redundancies.

CONCLUSIONS

Some scholars have argued that computer simulations based on information-processing theory have important advantages over research based on verbal (constructivist and social-learning) theories. Because simulations require explicitly delineating questions, assumptions, and predictions (e.g., Ashcraft, 1987; Klahr & MacWhinney, 1998), they presumably permit more precise and rigorous theorizing and theory testing (Cowan, chap. 2, this volume). Indeed, simulation-based research is sometimes characterized as "hard science" and superior to the "soft science" based on verbal theories (Crowley et al., 1997; Klahr & MacWhinney, 1998). Klahr and MacWhinney (1998) held SCADS up as an example of the promise of the former and went as far to say that "computational modeling . . . appears to be a necessary condition for advancing our understanding of cognitive development" (p. 670).

However, using a computer simulation does not ensure clarity or rigor for a variety of reasons. Listed as follows are five reasons, four of which were originally proposed by Neches (1982, p. 78; quotes shown in italics):

1. *Since programs are rarely presented in full with accompanying documentation, we remain dependent on verbal descriptions of the model, which raises problems in determining whether the program performs as it does for the reasons claimed by the authors.*

2. *Programs frequently involve simplifying assumptions in order to facilitate implementation.*
3. Programs may be based on untested or incorrect assumptions.
4. *Programs can be written to work only for a restricted set of examples—those presented in the write-up of the research*—and, thus, may provide an incomplete picture of development.
5. *The inputs or database for the program can be structured in ways that simplify the task, but which are not necessarily psychologically plausible* or accurate.

De Corte and Verschaffel (1988) concluded, "For all these reasons, the fact that a computer program runs or even that it is consistent with some empirical data, does not guarantee that it is of psychological significance" (p. 51).

Points 2–5 can, in effect, be summarized in the following manner: The validity of a computer simulation such as SCADS depends on the completeness and accuracy of the developmental theory and data used to design it. As the review in this section suggests, the theoretical and empirical basis of SCADS is seriously incomplete and even inaccurate.

• *Simplified assumptions.* Because its underlying developmental mechanisms (e.g., associative learning, detecting redundancies) do not sufficiently take into account conceptual knowledge and development, even this latest and most sophisticated version of the strategy-choice model does not adequately satisfy the three criteria for sound developmental models of addition outlined in the first chapter (Baroody, chap. 1, this volume).

• *Untested and possibly incorrect assumptions.* Although any simulation is bound to be based on oversimplified assumptions and, thus, incomplete, less understandable is why key assumptions underlying the operation of SCADS (e.g., associative learning of incorrect and correct answers) have not been directly tested and empirically verified. Logically, this would be the first step in rigorously constructing a model. After all, if the premises (assumptions of a simulation) of a logical argument (computer program) are not true, then the conclusions (simulation's data and inferences drawn from them) are questionable.

• *Incompleteness of the model.* Some incomplete aspects of SCADS could be remedied in a relatively simple manner by revising the assumptions on which it is based. For example, the presence of a goal sketch at the beginning of a run could be justified by the assumption that children construct knowledge of addition before they learn counting based strategies for computing. Other incomplete aspects of SCADS will be difficult, if not impossible, to rectify. For example, the modification to the model just proposed does not account for why children sometimes use illegal strategies (as the case of Jonna illustrates) or why they have difficulty recognizing the validity of counting-on (as the case of Felicia illustrates).

• *Inaccurate modeling.* SCADS does not model accurately many of the fundamentally important aspects of informal strategy development, including those the model builders (Shrager & Siegler, 1998) chose themselves. That is, even the select phenomena modeled were not accurately represented because contradictory data were not considered or conclusions were based on a small and unrepresentative sample.

In brief, the development of SCADS is a step toward describing "possible relations between rehearsal [practice] and the specific contents of semantic memory, internal decision processes, and other processes," such as working memory—an effort that Bisanz and LeFevre (1990, p. 216) lamented is all too rare. However, as with any computer program, the output (the value of its data and the implications drawn from it) are only as good as the input (the assumption and data used to devise the program). As De Corte and Verschaffel (1988) noted, a computer simulation is a useful research tool "when applied concurrently with other research techniques" (p. 52). Indeed, for the foreseeable future, the latter will continue to contribute far more to the development of the former (and our understanding of arithmetic development) than vice versa. This is because computer simulations such as SCADS do not adequately or faithfully model children's conceptual development and, hence, their adaptive expertise, which is the hallmark of their informal addition development.

The Development of Mental Arithmetic

As was the case with strategy development, the strategy-choice model (e.g., Siegler, 1986, 1987, 1988) and a schema-based view (e.g., Baroody, 1985, 1994; Baroody & Ginsburg, 1986, 1991) feature different roles for conceptual knowledge in the development of mental arithmetic. In this section, we detail how these two perspectives differ in their accounts of mental addition with single-digit addends and multidigit addends.

SINGLE-DIGIT MENTAL ADDITION

General Differences

The strategy-choice model reflects what Bisanz and LeFevre (1990) noted is the pervasive view in developmental psychology—that factual knowledge and procedural or conceptual knowledge are (largely) independent. The schema-based view is based on the assumption that these aspects of knowledge are interdependent.

Strategy-Choice Model. Earlier, Siegler (e.g., 1986, 1987, 1988) essentially attributed all answers generated covertly to a single process, namely, the retrieval strategy, which is governed almost entirely by deterministic associative-learning principles. He allowed that when retrieval efforts are unsuccessful, children sometimes resort to "sophisticated guessing," in which one last retrieval effort is made and the answer is stated regardless of its associative strength. This process involves sophisticated guessing in the sense that it favors choosing answers given relatively frequently in the past (still having associative strengths) over those previously given relatively infrequently (no longer having associative strength). It has nothing to do with using conceptual knowledge to consciously or otherwise devise an educated guess. In a real sense, then, Siegler granted children strategy choice for observable behavior but not for covert behavior (L. Flevares, personal communication, November 1998).

More recently, Siegler (e.g., Siegler & Jenkins, 1989) has allowed for two additional classes of mental-arithmetic strategies: guesses (giving an answer and explaining, "I just guessed it") and heuristics (e.g., for 3 + 5, saying, "You can add two fives and then take away two, so its eight"). Unfortunately, it is not clear that the former includes systematic estimation strategies like those described by Dowker (chap. 9, this volume). Furthermore, his current operational definitions of *retrieval* (giving an answer and explaining, "I just know [remembered] it"), *guess*, and *heuristic* are problematic, because children may not clearly distinguish among these processes. Worse, they may even misrepresent their real strategy as retrieval to avoid disapproval, please adults, or appear smart (see, e.g., the cases of Brittney and Whitney described on pp. 80 and 87, respectively, in Siegler & Jenkins, 1989). That is, these operational definitions may still result in overestimating the frequency of retrieval. Finally, only the retrieval strategy is represented in the computer simulations of the strategy-choice model.

Like other information-processing models of mental arithmetic adduced in the last decade (e.g., Ashcraft, 1992; Campbell, 1995; Zbrodoff & Logan, 1990), even Siegler's (e.g., Siegler & Shipley, 1995) latest simulation SCADS consists of only two overlapping phases: (a) overt informal strategies and (b) covert retrieval. The possibility that covert nonretrieval strategies are used or constitute an intermediate phase is basically overlooked (Baroody, 1994).

Schema-Based View. According to the schema-based view, covert mental-arithmetic processes include a variety of strategies, some of which entail inexact processes (estimation) and others of which involve exact processes (mental computation, mental reasoning, and memory production). All of these processes are tied to children's number sense and, hence, to their conceptual knowledge (at least to some degree). Paralleling Brownell's (1935, 1941) view, mental arithmetic appears to unfold in three overlapping phases: (a) overt counting strategies; (b) covert but nonautomatic counting, rule-based, and reasoning strategies; and (c) covert and efficient memory-production processes (automatic applications of rules, reasoning, fact retrieval, and possibly even counting). The transition between Phases 2 and 3 might involve semiautomatic counting, rule-based, and reasoning strategies.

Premastery Development: The Nature and Development of Mental-Arithmetic Errors

Given the general differences between the strategy-choice model and the schema-based view, it should not be surprising that their accounts of the source of mental-arithmetic errors and how such errors change with development are dramatically different.

Range of Answers in the Earliest Phase of (Verbal-Based) Mental Arithmetic. According to the strategy-choice model, even children's earliest (verbal-based) mental-arithmetic errors are due to faulty fact retrieval. In this view, the initial representation of number combinations includes only minimal associations between each combination and each of numerous possible answers (e.g., Siegler, 1988). Because a novice's distribution of associations for the combination is relatively flat, children with little or no computational experience tend to respond to it with a broad range of answers.

In the schema-based view, children's initial (verbal-based) mental-arithmetic errors are, in the words of Ilg and Ames (1951), "more an error of method than an error of answer" (p. 10). In this view, novices would not "choose" a retrieval strategy because there is no factual knowledge, as such, in long-term memory (LTM) to retrieve. Instead, they typically seize on what they do know about numbers and operations to make an "educated guess" or estimate. Because their web of conceptual, procedural, and factual knowledge regarding counting-based arithmetic is relatively limited or unconnected, children's initial estimation efforts are likely to be uninformed, inaccurate, and inflexible (for further discussion, see Dowker, chap. 9, this volume).

Aside from computer simulation data (see, e.g., Lemaire & Siegler, 1995; Siegler, 1988), the only empirical evidence supporting the claim that children's earliest mental-arithmetic errors are due to faulty retrieval is distribution-of-associations data for addition (Siegler & Robinson, 1982; Siegler & Shrager, 1984) and subtraction (Siegler, 1987) collected with young children. However, these data were pooled over children who were probably at different developmental levels and, thus, using different strategies. Moreover, no effort was made to distinguish between retrieved responses and responses generated by covert nonretrieval strategies (e.g., using a response-time limit), further confounding the two types of responses (Baroody, 1985, 1994).

In fact, analyses of individual data reveal that mental-arithmetic novices (at the counting-based quantities level) typically do not respond with a wide variety or range of answers but with a highly prescribed set and circumscribed range of responses (Baroody, 1988, 1989, 1992a, 1993, 1999a, 1999b; Dowker, chap. 9, this volume). Like written computational bugs (Brown & Burton, 1978; VanLehn, 1983), these easily identifiable error patterns are consistent with the use of relatively inflexible estimation strategies. For example, multiplication novices typically made a single distinctive error per combination (e.g., consistently combined the factors to create a two-digit product as in 3 x 5 = 35, 4 x 7 = 47, 7 x 3 = 73, and 9 x 4 = 94) or a narrow but well-specified set of errors (e.g., consistently used a factor to create a teen product as in 3 x 5 = 13, 4 x 7 = 14, 7 x 3 = 13, and 9 x 4 = 14 or decade as in 3 x 5 = 30, 4 x 7 = 70, 7 x 3 = 20, and 9 x 4 = 50; Baroody, 1993, 1999b).

The Effects of Previous Knowledge. According to the strategy-choice model, existing associations can either facilitate or interfere with the formation of new associations. For instance, because multiplication is related to the operation of addition, extant addition associations create a small advantage for two types of associative interference errors: (a) related-operation errors, answering with the sum of two factors (e.g., 8 x 3 = 11), and (b) addition-like odd-even errors, the tendency to respond to combinations with two odd or even factors with an even number (e.g., 5 x 3 = 12 or 4 x 6 = 20) and to combinations with mixed factors with an odd number (e.g., 8 x 3 = 25).

According to the schema-based view, "interference" errors, like other early mental-multiplication errors, are largely the product of a mechanically ap-plied estimation strategy. More specifically, some multiplication novices might reason that if you don't know what to do, do what you know. Such chil-dren might then mechanically seize on their existing knowledge of addition and inflexibly manufacture answers by adding the factors (e.g., 3 x 5 = 8, 4 x 7 = 11, 7 x 3 = 10, and 9 x 4 = 13).

The evidence for interference errors (e.g., Lemaire & Siegler, 1995; Miller & Paredes, 1990; Siegler, 1987, 1988; Siegler & Robinson, 1982; Siegler & Shrager, 1984), like that for a flat initial distribution of associations, is suspect because data were collapsed over individual participants and precautions to exclude nonretrieved data were not used. Again, individual data analyses indicate that only a few novices account for the vast majority of so-called related-operation and addition-like odd-even errors. For example, Baroody (1999b) found that two thirds of such errors were made by two of the least experienced multipliers, who apparently consistently used a state-a-sum strategy. The em-pirical evidence of an associative interference or facilitating effect for addition (e.g., Siegler & Shrager, 1984) or subtraction (e.g., Siegler, 1987) is equally suspect (Baroody, 1988, 1989, 1992a, 1994, 1999a).

Evolution of Errors. As with children's earliest errors, changes in the nature and frequency of errors is presumed by many information-processing theorists to reflect changes in the mental architecture of the associative network. In the strategy-choice model, this change is brought about by item-specific practice. Specifically, Siegler (1988) noted that a basic assumption of the distribution of associations model (DOAM) "is that people associate what-ever answer they state, whether correct or incorrect, with the [combination] on which they state it" (p. 261). Every time an answer is computed or stated, even if incorrect, a trace is laid down in LTM (e.g., Siegler & Jenkins, 1989). As the number of traces build up in LTM, the bond or association between an answer and a combination is strengthened. The logical consequence of this argument is the error-learning hypothesis: Each computing error made while practicing the basic combinations is remembered and influences the frequency of mental-arithmetic errors made later. For example, Siegler (1988) noted that children frequently make two types of computational errors when using backup (infor-mal) strategies to determine products: *skip-counting errors* (e.g., 8 x 3: "3, 6, 9, 12, 15, 18, 21") and *minor addition errors* (e.g., 3 x 7 = 7 + 7 + 7 = 14 + 7 = 20). Because of the relatively high frequency of these two types of computational errors, the resulting answers gain disproportionate associative strength rela-tive to other incorrect answers and, thus, factor-related and close-miss errors become the most common mental-multiplication errors in older children and adults.

In the schema-based view, stated or computed answers that are incorrect may have little or no lasting effect on LTM. In this view, changes in error patterns stem largely from the development of general arithmetic knowledge. As children construct knowledge about an operation, they can devise more sophisticated estimation strategies for manufacturing answers. For example, once children understand that 8 x 7 represents "eight groups of seven" or "seven added eight times," they can recognize that the sum of the digits is an implausible estimate and that the answer has to be larger than 20. Somewhat more sophisticated children may draw on skip-count knowledge (the associated string 7, 14, 21, 28, 35, 42, 49, 56, 63) to estimate the product. They may further recognize that the product must come from the latter portion of this string and choose from 49, 56, and 63. Highly sophisticated children may recall that 7 x 7 is 49 and estimate that one more seven would be about 55.

Only indirect evidence of a link between children's computational errors and subsequent mental-arithmetic errors has been adduced. For example, in Experiment 3, Siegler (1988) noted that factor-related and close-miss mental-multiplication errors were more frequent than expected by chance alone (and paralleled the relatively high frequency of analogous computational errors by Experiment 1 children). The only direct longitudinal evidence on the error-learning hypothesis indicates that computational errors are not associated with mental-addition error patterns or changes in these patterns (Baroody, 1988). Moreover, other evidence indicates that error patterns change (e.g., the relative frequency of factor-related and close-miss errors increases), even for unpracticed combinations (Baroody, 1989, 1992a, 1993, 1999a, 1999b).

In summary, the existing evidence is consistent with the hypothesis that, as children construct a more complete web of knowledge about an operation, they devise more accurate estimation strategies and use them more flexibly. The existing data are also consistent with the view that older children and even adults continue to use a variety of covert strategies, at least some of which parallel younger children's overt strategies (LeFevre, Smith-Chant, Hiscock, Daley, & Morris, chap. 7, this volume). In other words, the parallel between the computational errors of younger children and the mental-arithmetic errors of older children and adults may not be indirectly linked by a mental representation (the distribution of associations), as proposed by Siegler (e.g., 1988). It is probably due to the use of nonretrieval strategies by young and old alike (see also LeFevre et al., chap. 7, this volume).

The Development and Nature of Mastery

As with the development and nature of mental-arithmetic errors, the strategy-choice model and the schema-based view provide dramatically different pictures about the development and nature of expertise with single-digit combinations.

Strategy-Choice Model. According to the DOAM, the frequency of practicing the correct answer is the key factor in mastering the basic number combinations (e.g., Siegler, 1986, 1987, 1988). In this view, the correct answer to a combination does not begin to accumulate significant associative strength until a child learns how to compute answers with at least some accuracy. With sufficient accurate practice, the correct answer becomes so highly associated with a problem, a child almost always responds with it.

As with the evolution of errors, Siegler's (1988) model does not include a generalization mechanism by which correct responses to one combination affect the distribution of associations for other combinations, including its commuted counterpart. For example, a child might compute the product of 3 x 8 by counting by eight three times and the product of 8 x 3 by counting by three eight times. As a result, each combination would acquire its own distribution of associations, one that would become peaked independent of the others. In brief, the discovery of relations and the construction of conceptual knowledge do not affect how the basic number combinations are internalized or represented in LTM.

Schema-Based View. According to the schema-based view, the representation of basic combinations is not a distinct aspect of LTM but an integral aspect of the structured framework for general arithmetic knowledge (Baroody, 1985; Baroody & Ginsburg, 1986, 1991). Analogous to models of verbal comprehension, this memory network consists of both nodes (factual data) and connections between nodes (relational information). As relations such as multiplicative commutativity are discovered, they are incorporated into the representation of basic combinations and prompt its reorganization (cf. Butterworth, Marschesini, and Girelli, chap. 6, this volume). As relation-based rules and reasoning processes are practiced, they become increasingly automatic. The memory-production process, then, involves both automatic factual and relational knowledge. For many adults, though, certain aspects of their relational knowledge become relatively efficient but not automatic. Thus, even among adults, relatively fast responses can be the result of automatic memory production or semiautomatic backup strategies—both of which can involve relational knowledge.

According to the schema-based view, relational learning and transfer are an integral part of mastering the basic number combinations in two ways:

1. Children notice arithmetic patterns such as when a number is multiplied by zero, the answer is always zero, or when a number is multiplied by one, the answer is always that number.[10] These regularities are summarized as general (algebraic) rules ($n \times 0 = 0$ and $n \times 1 = n$) in LTM (Schemas 2 and 3 in Fig. 3.4), rules that can be applied to previously unpracticed single-digit or multidigit combinations in an increasingly automatic fashion. There is now some evidence for such rules (e.g., Sokol, McCloskey, Cohen, & Aliminosa, 1991) and considerable agreement about their use even by adults (Ashcraft, 1992; Baroody, 1983,

---

[10] Other examples of arithmetic patterns include the $n + 0 = n$ (additive identity) rule, $n - 0 = n$ (subtractive identity) rule, and the "subtraction of number neighbors equals one" rule (e.g., $6 - 5 = 1$ and $7 - 6 = 1$).

Figure 3.4: Possible Schema Underlying Mental Multiplication Performance (cf. Baroody, 1994)[1]

(1)   *If* the operation sign is times, *then* factor order is irrelevant: Focus on the key term regardless of its position (Commutativity Principle).

$$\downarrow$$

(2)   *If zero* and a number are multiplied, *then* the product is zero ($0 \times n$ or $n \times 0 = 0$ Rule).[2]

$$\downarrow$$

(3)   *If one* and a number are multiplied, *then* the product equals the number ($1 \times n$ or $n \times 1 = n$ Rule).

$$\downarrow$$

(4)   If two and a number are multiplied, then the product equals the number added to itself ($2 \times n$ or $n \times 2 = n + n$ [the related addition double]).

$$\downarrow$$

(5)   *If a larger number* is multiplied by itself, *then* access the associative network (Identity Comparison).[3]

$$\downarrow$$

(6)   *If a larger number* is multiplied by a smaller number, *then* access the associative network (Magnitude Comparison).

$$\downarrow$$

(7)   *If a larger number* multiplies a smaller number, *then* transform the factors and access the associative network (Transformation Process).[4]

[1] The schemata form a hierarchical checklist by which an expert evaluates multiplication problems. Schema 1 has priority over the rest. Unlike subtraction where order is constrained, this commutativity schema permits attention to focus on key terms in the following order of importance: zero, one, and large number. Schema 2 has priority over Schema 3 because the answer is always zero—whether or not the problem also includes 1 (0×1 and $1 \times 0 = 0$) and regardless of the position of the zero.

[2] Because multiplication Schema 2 is so similar to addition Schema 2, children and even experts may confuse the two. The problem is compounded because of the similarity of Schema 1 for addition and multiplication.

[3] Making an identity judgment should be easier than determining which term is larger (making a magnitude comparison). Ties often have faster response times than nonties. If further work does not confirm a tie effect, Schema 4 and Schema 5 would be combined: If a number and itself or a smaller number are multiplied, then access the associative network.

[4] Note that schemas will vary according to an individual's instructional history, culture, and so forth. For example, consistent with Schemas 6 and 7 above, Butterworth et al. (chap. 6, this volume) report that Italian children may convert small-factor-first ($m \times N$) combinations into large-factor-first ($N \times m$) combinations. Whereas, LeFevre et al. (chap. 7, this volume) describe research indicating that Chinese experts do the opposite (i.e., convert $N \times m$ combinations into $m \times N$ combinations).

1985, 1994; Campbell, 1987; Cooney, Swanson, & Ladd, 1988; Kaye, 1986; Lemaire & Siegler, 1995).

2. Children notice arithmetic relations, which allow them to exploit existing knowledge. For example, by noticing that multiplication is commutative, they can reduce by almost half their efforts to memorize the basic multiplication combinations (e.g., Folsom, 1975; Trivett, 1980). Knowledge of a commutative relation may be embodied as schemas (Schemas 1 and 7 in Fig. 3.4), one of which serves to convert small-factor-first expressions such as 3 x 8 into large-factor-first expressions such as 8 x 3. This would permit both 3 x 8 and 8 x 3 to be stored in a retrieval network as a single 8 x 3 = 24 association (Baroody, 1985, 1994; Baroody & Ginsburg, 1986, 1991) and help to account for why small-factor-first combinations often take somewhat longer to retrieve than large-factor-first combinations (Campbell & Graham, 1985). A single representation for commuted combinations would also account for the transfer of practice effects to unpracticed but commuted combinations (Baroody, 1999b; Rickard & Bourne, 1996; Rickard Healy, & Bourne, 1994).[11]

Put differently, a key to learning the basic number combinations—like any consequential information—is discovering regularities. A key to representing this knowledge—like any consequential knowledge—is constructing, elaborating on, and connecting mental structures or schemas. This schema-based view of number-combination mastery is dramatically different from the strategy-choice model or the current conventional wisdom in cognitive psychology in a number of ways.

1. Between the time children use informal counting strategies to determine sums and the time they are expected to master basic combinations, students need the opportunity to discover arithmetic patterns and relations and to use these regularities to construct reasoning strategies (e.g., the schemas depicted in Fig. 3.4). As implied earlier, this critical reasoning phase of meaningful learning is not modeled at all by the strategy-choice model or other information-processing models.

2. Initially, the application of the commutativity schemas (Schemas 1 and 7 in Fig. 3.4) would be relatively slow and might even require conscious effort. With practice, though, their application should become automatic. Such a scenario is consistent with Jerman's (1970) finding that children appear to use different strategies for different types of multiplication combinations and that, with age, they continue to use such strategies with greater automaticity. It is

---

[11] Other examples of arithmetic relations that may form the basis for internalizing basic number combinations include the number-after rule for $n + 1$ combinations and the number-before rule for $n - 1$ (i.e., using extant knowledge of the counting sequence, namely number after and before a given number to add or subtract one from it; Baroody, 1988, 1989, 1992a, 1995), the complement principle for subtraction combinations (i.e., using existing knowledge of addition to determine differences as with $9 - 5 = ? \rightarrow 5 + ? = 9 \rightarrow ? = 4$; Baroody, 1983, 1984c, 1985, 1999a; Baroody & Ginsburg, 1986; Baroody, Ginsburg, & Waxman, 1983; Fuson, 1988, 1992; Putnam, deBettencourt, & Leinhardt, 1990). The complement principle for division combination might be yet another possibility (but cf. LeFevre & Morris, 1999).

also consistent with evidence that even adults use a variety of strategies, including automatic memory production and semiautomatic reasoning or computation, to efficiently determine the products of single-digit combinations (Browne, 1906; LeFevre, Bisanz, et al., 1996; LeFevre & Morris, 1999; LeFevre, Sadesky, & Bisanz, 1996; see LeFevre et al., chap. 7, this volume, for a summary of this evidence). As noted earlier, expert knowledge in the strategy-choice model involves a single strategy, the retrieval of isolated facts.

3. The role of practice is more complicated than suggested by conventional wisdom. Although repetitious practice may help children store factual data in LTM as suggested by the strategy-choice model, it can play two other and, perhaps, more critical roles. (a) Practice, particularly when well motivated (e.g., purposeful and interesting) practice, provides children the opportunity to discover arithmetic patterns and relations that form the basis of schemas. Note that encouraging children's efforts to look for, reflect on, and share arithmetic regularities can promote this schema-building process. (b) Practice can help automatize the use of schemas.

4. The mental representation and memory processing of the basic number combinations (the memory-production system) may be more complicated than suggested by the strategy-choice model and other multiple-association models (e.g., Ashcraft, 1992; Campbell, 1995). Such currently popular models are based on the assumption that this system is an autonomous unit in the brain, consisting of a web of data (factual associations). According to the schema-based view, the representation of the basic combinations is (or at least should be) integrated with general arithmetic knowledge. In this view, the representation consists of a web of data and relations (as embodied by schemas such those depicted in Fig. 3.4). The web becomes enriched by adding *both* data and, perhaps, more important, relations (schemas). A key methodological implication of this is that brain-injury and mental-imaging research needs to examine the memory-production system in terms of microprocesses (e.g., specific relations) that may comprise this skill rather than treating "number-fact retrieval" as a unitary process (cf. Delazer, chap. 14, this volume).

5. The process of constructing the mental representation of basic number combinations should not be viewed simply as a passive associative-learning process but as a dynamic one. That is, as with most memory development, it may not merely be a copying process in which the picture of arithmetic facts slowly becomes clearer with practice (repeated memory tracings). Instead, the construction of this mental representation may be similar to that of other consequential mathematical and nonmathematical knowledge. The process of summarizing regularities, elaborating on these summaries, and connecting them to other summaries to form a complex web of knowledge may entail qualitative changes in number-combination knowledge. For example, insight and the integration of existing knowledge might prompt a new perspective, changes in one or more schemas, or changes in the connections among schemas. Although some of these changes may be relatively minor and local, others may entail significant and widespread modifications and reorganization (Baroody, 1985, 1994; Baroody &

Ginsburg, 1991). Butterworth et al. (chap. 6, this volume) adduce the first evidence of such a major reorganization, one apparently prompted by learning the principle of multiplicative commutativity.

MULTIDIGIT MENTAL ADDITION

Next, we briefly examine the differences between information-processing models and constructivist models regarding multidigit arithmetic.

Information-Processing Models

Information-processing models of mental multidigit computation (the conventional wisdom in cognitive psychology) is based on two fundamental assumptions. The first is that there is a clear distinction between the mental processing of single-digit combinations and that of multidigit combinations (e.g., Ashcraft, Donley, Halas, & Vakali, 1992). More specifically, whereas the former involves fact retrieval, the latter involves the application of procedural knowledge (an algorithm). The second assumption is that experts rely largely, if not exclusively, on a particular algorithm: the standard right-left (renaming) algorithm commonly used to do written addition or subtraction. Mental multidigit addition, for instance, involves using fact retrieval to determine the sum of the ones digits; storing in working memory the ones digit of this sum and, if applicable, a carried digit; using fact retrieval to determine the sum of the digits tens and, if applicable, the sum of this sum and the carried digit; and so forth (see Adams & Hitch, 1998, for a more elaborate discussion of this model and the evidence supporting it).

Schema-Based View

The two basic assumptions underlying information-processing models seem questionable. The distinction between the mental processing of single-digit and multidigit addition and subtraction may be less distinct than such models suggest. As with the former, children initially rely on counting procedures to determine the sum or difference of the latter and invent increasingly sophisticated procedures for doing so (Cobb & Wheatley, 1988; Kamii, 1989). As with single-digit addition and subtraction, they discover patterns and relations that allow them to devise rules or reasoning strategies, which can become automatic. For example, children discover that adding single-digit numbers and 10 results in an analogous teen (e.g., $7 + 10$ or $10 + 7 \rightarrow$ *seven* + teen). This may become embodied as the general (algebraic) "teen rule": $n + 10 \rightarrow n$ + teen. Children also discover relations that allow them to exploit their existing knowledge. They may discover, for instance, that adding a given decade and 10 results in an answer that is the decade after the given decade in the counting-by-tens sequence (e.g., $60 + 10$ or $10 + 60 \rightarrow$ decade after 60: 70). This regularity may be embodied as the general "decade + 10 rule" ($X0 + 10 \rightarrow Y0$, where Y is the decade after X), which can become increasingly automatic. In brief, even more so than single-digit combinations, multidigit combinations provide a rich array of patterns and relations for children to discover and to improve computational fluency (see, e.g., Baroody, with Coslick, 1998).

This analysis and the existing empirical evidence indicate that mental-arithmetic expertise is not characterized by the efficient use of a single right-to-left strategy. In fact, whereas less skilled mental calculators rely on this strategy, more skilled mental calculators tend to rely on left-to-right proce-dures (e.g., Hope & Sherrill, 1987; Madell, 1985). Indeed, merchants the world over, including those who are unschooled, rely on the latter because its relative ease (e.g., Ginsburg, Posner, & Russell, 1981; see, e.g., Nunes, 1992, for a review). In brief, as with computational estimation (Dowker, 1992, 1998, chap. 9, this volume), people more proficient in mental computation use a variety patterns, relations, and strategies—including left-right procedures.

CONCLUSIONS

The discussion in this section regarding the development of mental addition is relevant to the theoretical discussion in the previous section regarding the validity of SCADS. It also has important methodological implications.

Theoretical Implications: The Validity of SCADS

Although SCADS and its immediate successor the adaptive strategy choice model (ASCM) provide a better account of strategy choice and development than does DOAM (see Table 3.2), the assumptions about how basic number combinations are represented and how this representation changes are the same in all three models. More specifically, although ASCM "adds information regarding the speed and accuracy with which the answer was generated to the [strategy] database" (Siegler & Shipley, 1995, p. 59), this feedback does not affect the problem database (the distributions of associations). In essence, ASCM corrected, in Siegler and Shipley's (1995) words, "the dumbness" of DOAM in regard to strategy choice but not the retrieval process. That is, the shaping of the distribution of associations (the problem representation) still involves a literal learning process—one that does not involve generalizations. The same is true for SCADS. Shrager and Siegler (1998) noted that this update "maintains all the mechanisms of ASCM but extends it in three ways" (all of which do not affect the distributions of associations).

Unfortunately, DOAM was based on questionable data. At the time, Siegler (e.g., Siegler & Shrager, 1984) operationally defined retrieval as any response given without evidence of overt counting or figuring (regardless of response time). This definition was based on the incorrect assumption that nonretrieval (backup) strategies are usually executed overtly. Because responses generated by covert estimation, computation, and reasoning strategies were scored as retrieved responses, DOAM was designed using data that confounded retrieved and nonretrieved responses. In effect, ASCM and SCADS were built on a foundation (DOAM) that is an incomplete and inaccurate model of mental-addition development. Put differently, they overlay a model in which the mastery of mental arithmetic is treated essentially as routine expertise, not—as evidence suggests—as adaptive expertise (see, e.g., Heavey, chap. 15, this volume). Thus, the nonintuitive insights generated by any of these simulations need to be treated with caution (cf. Donlan, chap. 12, this volume).

Methodological Implications: Scoring in Context

Traditionally, children's responses to an addition task have been scored on a trial-by-trial basis. However, assessing arithmetic knowledge—particularly the mental-arithmetic performance of young children or novices—requires examining performance across trials or even tasks.

Consider one example: children's responses to $n + 1$ combinations. In response to $7 + 1$, for instance, even a quick answer of "eight" cannot be scored as *fact retrieval* (recall of isolated association) with confidence. If the child responded to $7 + 3$ with "eight" also, he or she may merely be using a mechanical and indiscriminate "state the number after the larger addend" estimation strategy. If the child answers $7 + 1$ and other $n + 1$ items efficiently—including those not previously practiced—but avoids stating the number after the larger addend for other combinations, then he or she is either efficiently employing a COL strategy or using a discriminative number-after rule for these combinations. If the child knows $7 + 1$ is eight, does not know many other $n + 1$ combinations, avoids an answer of eight for, say, $7 + 3$, and does not use a COL (or must use it deliberately), *then* it is reasonable to conclude he or she has memorized an isolated fact by rote.

The Developmental Relations
Between Conceptual and Procedural Knowledge

Research over the last three decades has revealed what appears to be a paradox about children's mathematical development. Preschoolers seem to exhibit remarkable mathematical competencies. For example, considerable evidence suggests that infant and toddlers are capable of discriminating among small collections and can even understand simple transformations (addition and subtraction) involving them (see, e.g., Wynn, 1998, for a review, but cf. Baroody, in press; Baroody et al., chap. 4, this volume; Jordan et al., chap. 13, this volume; Mix et al., 2002; Sophian, 1998). In stark contrast, schoolchildren seem to exhibit remarkable mathematical incompetence. For instance, they struggle with the following: all but the simplest word problems (Carpenter, Matthews, Lindquist, & Silver, 1984; Davis, 1992; Kouba, Carpenter, & Swafford, 1989; Schoenfeld, 1982, 1985), memorizing basic number combinations (e.g., Suydam & Weaver, 1975), and fractions and operations on them (e.g., Behr, Harel, Post, & Lesh, 1992).

Proponents of the concept-first possibility have adduced the privileged-domain hypothesis to explain the paradox between mathematical incompetence. According to this hypothesis, evolutionary pressure or natural selection has produced an innate basis for certain mathematical competencies, which are typically learned in the preschool years. This innate basis makes learning such competencies relatively easy. Other mathematical competencies, such as those typically in school, do not have an innate basis, which makes learning them relatively difficult.

Next, we evaluate an alternative explanation to the privileged-domain hypothesis (the modified skills-first possibility), one proposed by proponents of information-processing theory. We then discuss how the apparent paradox can be resolved by examining it from the perspective of the iterative schema-based view.

MODIFIED SKILLS-FIRST POSSIBILITY

In their literature review, Rittle-Johnson and Siegler (1998) concluded that the existing evidence does not support the privileged-domain hypothesis (see also Sophian, 1998) and offered a modified skills-first account.

Principles for Predicting a Developmental Relation Between Conceptual and Procedural Knowledge

The modified skills-first possibility is based on the following four principles for predicting a developmental relation between conceptual and procedural knowledge:

Conceptual knowledge will precede (directly related) procedural knowledge if
1. a procedure is not demonstrated in everyday life or school, or
2. frequent experience with a concept, either in everyday life or school, precedes instruction of a procedure.

Procedural knowledge will precede conceptual knowledge if
3. a procedure is modeled frequently in everyday life or school before conceptual instruction, or
4. a procedure can be induced from an analogous or related procedure.

Arithmetic-Related Evidence Supporting the Four Developmental Principles

Rittle-Johnson and Siegler (1998) claimed that existing empirical evidence indicates that preschoolers' impressive counting competencies can be attributed to frequent exposure of counting skills in everyday life (Principle 3)[12] and that their impressive informal single-digit arithmetic competencies (e.g., the invention of COL) are due to informal conceptual understanding (Principle 1).[13] In contrast, they concluded, schoolchildren typically learn formal multidigit addition and subtraction algorithms by rote because conventional instruction is not conceptually based (Principle 3).

As an example of Principle 1, Rittle-Johnson and Siegler (1998) noted that both Baroody and Gannon (1984) and Cowan and Renton (1996) found that a conceptual understanding of commutativity was positively correlated with, and—more important—usually developed before, COL. As further evidence of this relation and Principle 1, they cited Siegler and Crowley's (1994) study, in which 5-year-olds who themselves had not yet invented COL rated this procedure and their own counting-all procedure as "smart" and an illegal procedure (counting one addend twice) as "not smart." Rittle-Johnson and Siegler concluded, "thus, most kindergarten children seemed to understand [the irrelevance of addend order and] the importance of representing each addend once and only once before they generated the *min* [COL] procedure" (p. 89).

Analysis of the Arithmetic-Related Evidence

Unfortunately, Rittle-Johnson and Siegler's (1998) evidence of conceptual knowledge preceding the invention of COL does not hold up under scrutiny.

Difficulties With the Analysis of Commutativity Data. There are three difficulties with Rittle-Johnson and Siegler's (1998) analysis of the commutativity data (Baroody & Gannon, 1984; Cowan & Renton, 1996): (a) developmental analyses were done incorrectly or inaccurately, (b) contradictory evidence was not considered, and (c) Principle 1 is a premise that may not always be true.

1. Rittle-Johnson and Siegler (1998) observed that, in both the Baroody and Gannon (1984) and the Cowan and Renton (1996) study, "almost half of the kindergartners who did not use [CAL or COL] succeeded on an assessment of understanding of commutativity" and concluded that "children usually understood commutativity before they generated" CAL or COL (p. 89). However, the key to assessing the developmental order of a prerequisite concept and a procedure is comparing concordant data (e.g., children who exhibit conceptual

---

[12] A difficulty with this conclusion is that it is based on evidence that involves verbal counting (Baroody & Gannon, 1984; Briars & Siegler, 1984; Frye, Braisby, Love, Maroudas, & Nicholls, 1989; Fuson, 1988, all cited in Rittle-Johnson & Siegler, 1998). The innate counting principles proposed by, for example, Gelman and Meck (1986, 1992) are presumed to apply to nonverbal counting. The links between these innate principles and verbal-based counting are presumed to be built up gradually during early childhood.

[13] By positing that a CCA procedure is taught to young children by their parents, Shrager and Siegler (1998) seem to suggest on important exception to this general conclusion about early arithmetic competence. Specifically, they seem to imply that Principle 3 is applicable to this domain at least initially. As discussed earlier, this implication appears to be contradicted by the balance of existing evidence.

competence but not procedural competence) with discordant data (namely, those who exhibit procedural competence but not conceptual competence; Darlington, 1974). When analyzed properly, extant data do not clearly show that commutativity develops before strategies that disregard addend order (see Baroody et al., chap. 4, this volume, for details). Furthermore, Baroody and Gannon's frequency of CAL or COL use was based on *predominant* use of such strategies, not *any* use of them. As the latter is more relevant for gauging whether commutativity is a necessary condition for CAL or COL, Rittle-Johnson and Siegler effectively underestimated the frequency of CAL or COL use. In brief, the results of Baroody and Gannon and Cowan and Renton do not support their contention that an understanding of commutativity precedes the invention of strategies that disregard addend order (CAL or COL).

2.   Rittle-Johnson and Siegler (1998) also overlooked evidence (Baroody, 1987b; Baroody & Gannon, 1984) suggesting that children—like Felicia described earlier in Box 3.1—sometimes invent strategies that disregard addend order (including COL or COL-like strategies) for the sake of cognitive economy and without understanding commutativity (see Baroody et al., chap. 4, this volume).

3.   Such evidence suggests that Principle 1 does not always hold. Put differently, Principle 1 is at odds with the iterative-schema-based proposition that, although indirectly supported by concepts, procedural advances can sometimes be motivated by nonconceptual factors. In brief, the development of informal arithmetic strategies is more complicated than Rittle-Johnson and Siegler (1998) suggest.

Problems with the Strategy-Evaluation Data. Rittle-Johnson and Siegler's (1998) conclusion regarding Siegler & Crowley's (1994) evidence also needs to be interpreted cautiously for the following four reasons, the last of which is probably the most important:

1.   A child may intuitively assume that addend order is irrelevant to obtaining the correct answer, but not necessarily understand that combinations with the same addends but in different orders have the same sums. That is, the child may have only an inchoate understanding of commutativity, what Baroody and Gannon (1984) called "protocommutativity" (see Baroody et al., chap. 4, this volume).

2.   The protocommutativity notion and represent-each-addend-only-once "constraint" are supporting concepts, not the conceptual basis that directly motivates COL. The fact that these conceptual supports precede COL is evidence of only a *weak* form of the Principle 1 hypothesis. Demonstrating that the development of a concept of commutativity actually motivates or instigates COL is necessary to collaborate the strong form of this hypothesis.

3.   Siegler and Crowley's (1994) evidence is ambiguous, because the strategy-use task used to identify COL users included items involving 1 (namely 1 + 3 and 6 + 1). Unfortunately, distinguishing between COL and "retrieval" on

such items can be virtually impossible.[14] As a result, a child using COL only on combinations involving one could have been scored as using retrieval on these items and categorized as a non-COL user.

4. Siegler and Crowley's (1994) finding that children who use strategies less advanced than COL view COL as a legal procedure contradicts Baroody's (1984a) observations in the case study of Felicia, described earlier in Box 3.1. The reason for this discrepancy is that the former modeled a conceptually and procedurally less advanced form of counting-on than did the latter. More specifically, Siegler and Crowley demonstrated a *semi-indirect-modeling* procedure, a procedure that did *not* (a) involve an embedded-addends concept and a keeping-track process (Achievement 4 in Table 3.3), (b) clearly disregard addend order (Achievement 5 in Table 3.3), or (c) entail an embedded cardinal-count concept (Achievement 6 in Table 3.3).[15] Fuson and Secada (1986) found that learning a semi-indirect-modeling version of counting-on did not promote the learning of COL. They concluded that the former requires less developed conceptual knowledge of counting and number than does the latter.[16] Thus, Siegler and Crowley's participants who used a CCA strategy or one of its shortcuts (Achievement 1 or 2 in Table 3.3) evaluated a strategy only somewhat more sophisticated than their own; those who used CAF or CAL (Achievement 4 or 5 in Table 3.3) actually assessed a strategy less advanced than their own. In contrast, Felicia (Baroody, 1984a) evaluated and consistently considered as

---

[14] Siegler and Crowley's (1994) participants were scored as using COL if they started counting from the cardinal value of the larger addend (e.g., for 3 + 5: "5, 6, 7, 8") *or from the number after* the cardinal value of the larger addend (e.g., for 3 + 5: "6, 7, 8"; abbreviated COL). They were scored as using retrieval if they simply gave the sum and explained "I just knew [or remembered] it." With items involving 1, a child might use abbreviated COL (e.g., for 6 + 1, simply state *seven*) and inaccurately explain, "I just knew it." The child might misrepresent her strategy, because it did not involve counting in the ordinary sense, this justification was a relatively easy way to satisfy the interviewer, she was already infected with our cultural bias against using counting strategies to add, or she wanted to appear smart (see, e.g., the protocols of Brittany and Whitney reported by Crowley et al., 1997, or Siegler and Jenkins, 1989). Such a child would have been scored as using retrieval, not COL, in Siegler and Crowley's (1994) study.

[15] Siegler and Crowley (1994) modeled 6 + 8 by *first* concretely representing the *smaller* addend (counting out six items), stating the cardinal value of the larger addend ("eight"), and then continuing the counting from this cardinal value as the collection representing the smaller addend was enumerated ("nine, ten, eleven, twelve, thirteen, fourteen—fourteen is the answer"). The approximate reaction time (RT) of such a strategy would be equal to double the value of the smaller addend (RT of m + n when m < n ~ m + m or 2m). With COL, the RT is approximately equal to the smaller addend (RT of m + n when m < n is approximately m). (This is why COL has also been called the minimum addend or "*min* model.") So the strategy modeled by Siegler and Crowley is a relative of COL but not equivalent to it. It is what Fuson (1982) called a "counting-entities strategy" and similar to what Baroody (1987b) identified as a "counting-entities shortcut" (CE3 in his Fig. 1 on p. 142). Beth, described earlier, identified both CCA and the counting entities strategy as "smart" but—like Felicia—viewed COL as "not smart."

[16] The semi-indirect-modeling version of counting-on requires what Fuson, Richards, and Briars (1982) called the "breakable-chain" level and what Steffe, von Glasersfeld, Richards, and Cobb (1983) called the perceptual-units level. In contrast, COL requires what Fuson et al. (1982) called "numerable-chain" level and what Steffe et al. (1983) called "verbal- or abstract-units" level.

invalid COL, a strategy that requires Achievement 6 in Table 3.3 and was conceptually more advanced than her own (CAL, which requires Achievements 4 and 5).[17]

In brief, again the relations between procedural and conceptual knowledge of simple addition may be more complicated than Rittle-Johnson and Siegler (1998) suggest. In other words, like Briars and Larkin's (1984) and Riley, Greeno, and Heller's (1983) concepts-first view discussed earlier, their modified skills-first view may be overly parsimonious.

ITERATIVE VIEW

Rittle-Johnson and Siegler (1998) concluded that at least three factors account for the discrepancy between preschoolers' mathematical competence and schoolchildren's lack of competence: (a) "greater exposure of young to the procedures and concepts they are learning," (b) "less stringent criteria for young children to be classified as competent, and" (c) "greater news worthiness of demonstrations of young children's competence" (p. 108). Their focus on these three factors suggests that they consider them the most critical causes of the paradox. Although these three factors do help to explain the paradox, they may not be its most important causes. As suggested by the historical review in the first section of this chapter, the key factors in this apparent paradox may be the opportunity for preschoolers to (a) construct conceptual knowledge, (b) use it to devise procedures, or (c) otherwise link procedural knowledge to conceptual knowledge. It is the lack of these opportunities that—not surprising—results in schoolchildren's failures to master formal mathematics.

Frequency-of-Exposure Hypothesis

Undoubtedly, preschool children have many opportunities to use and to see others use a relatively small number of counting and arithmetic competencies, whereas schoolchildren often have only a brief exposure to many concepts and

---

[17] The results of a recent study (Baroody et al., 2000) indicated that, consistent with the case of Felicia (Baroody, 1984a), children who have not yet invented COL may have trouble recognizing this strategy as legal. In fact, five of nine non-COL users favored CCA over COL; three rated the former as "very smart" and the latter as "not smart" in both sessions. For example, Brianna, who had to be taught the CCA strategy in Session 2, consistently rated this strategy as "very smart," the semi-indirect-modeling version of counting-on strategy as "kinda' smart," and the COL strategy as "not smart." For one COL demonstration (6 + 8), she explained, "You're wrong. You started [counting the second addend] at nine. You are supposed to start at one." This explanation is consistent with Fuson's (1992) argument that children must recognize that both addends can be represented in a single count ("embedded integration for both addends" or Achievement 4 in Table 3.3) in order to invent an abstract strategy. For the other (7 + 5), she commented, "Maybe we should count out seven blocks [represent the first addend]." This explanation is consistent with Fuson's observation that children must recognize that it is unnecessary to produce the first addend sequence (i.e., "embedded cardinal-count principle, or Achievement 6 in Table 3.3). Beth, who was an accomplished user of CCA or its shortcuts consistently considered the first two strategies as "smart" but COL as "not smart."

procedures. Observation and imitation of counting and simple arithmetic procedures may play some role in their learning. However, learning such procedures is probably not entirely, or even largely, a passive process but a process of active construction. Children's rule-governed counting errors such as ". . . fourteen, *fiveteen*, sixteen . . ." or "twenty-eight, twenty-nine, *twenty-ten* . . ." is a clear sign of active intelligence (e.g., Ginsburg, 1977). Children do not have to be shown simple addition procedures, including CCA, probably because they can use their conceptual understanding of addition to devise the strategy and model addition situations. Moreover, as noted earlier, they can actively adapt (transfer) their counting and arithmetic knowledge to new tasks.

Mathematics educators have long decried the traditional approach to school mathematics of rushing through a textbook (e.g., Baroody, 1987a) or "mile wide and inch deep" curricula (e.g., Davis, 1986; Third International Mathematics and Science Study as reported by the National Center for Education Statistics at http://nces.ed.gov/timss/). Rapidly paced and overly broad instruction—along with other factors such as not building on children's informal knowledge and reliance on highly didactic and highly symbolic instruction—all contribute to the key underlying problem noted earlier, namely children's difficulty in *understanding* school mathematics.

Different-Criteria Hypothesis

Although some proponents of the privileged-domain hypothesis have used questionably liberal criteria to help support their claims (see, e.g., Baroody, 1992b, for a review), Rittle-Johnson and Siegler's (1998) different-criteria explanation is not entirely on target or fair. The key issue is not that preschoolers' are more procedurally skilled than schoolchildren but that they seem to understand (if only implicitly) what they are doing, whereas schoolchildren do not. A key test of understanding (adaptive expertise) is whether a child can exhibit transfer—devise or adapt a strategy when given a new (previously unpracticed) task. Using this criterion, it does appear that preschoolers are more competent at counting and simple arithmetic than are most schoolchildren with school mathematics.

The examples cited by Rittle-Johnson and Siegler (1998) oversimplify the process of comparing the mathematical competence of the two age groups:

> If 3-year-olds count by assigning approximately one number word to each object, or if they use a fairly systematic, albeit nonconventional, number string, they are often credited with being able to count. In contrast, elementary school children who use buggy subtraction procedures, which deviate from the standard algorithm only on the most demanding problems, are not considered to know the multidigit subtraction procedure. (p. 107)

The focus of counting research is frequently on whether children *understand* a counting principle (conceptual knowledge), such as the one-to-one principle, not on whether they can count accurately (procedural knowledge). Thus, if a child makes a counting error, such as losing track of which items have and have not been counted and recounts an item, it is reasonable to conclude that she observed the one-to-one principle. In other words, a mistake by itself does not eliminate the possibility that the child understands the principle. Moreover, when assessing the one-to-one principle, it is irrelevant whether a child uses a conventional or nonconventional number string.

Likewise, the key research issue (at least for some researchers) is whether schoolchildren understand a multidigit subtraction procedure (i.e., whether procedural knowledge and conceptual knowledge are integrated), not simply whether they can execute the procedure accurately (procedural knowledge only). Children who have learned a renaming procedure for three-digit expressions without zeros but who cannot effectively apply their knowledge to three-digit expressions with a zero can accurately be described as not understanding the procedure. Using a buggy procedure such as $0 - n = n$ (e.g., $370 - 195 = 185$) or moving over zero (e.g., $304 - 195 \rightarrow \overset{1\ 1\ 1}{2\,0\,4} - 195 \rightarrow \overset{\text{A}\ 1\ 1}{2\,0\,4} - 195 = 19$) are further symptoms of this lack of understanding.

Newsworthiness Hypothesis

The current focus on preschoolers' mathematical competence is a justifiable reaction to the earlier view that young children are mathematically incompetent (e.g., James, 1890/1950; Piaget, 1965; Thorndike, 1922). However, there is the danger of overreacting—attributing to preschoolers more competence than they actually have (Baroody, in press). It seems a reasonable bet that the truth lies somewhere between the extremes—between the more nativist privileged-domain view and the more empiricist modified skills-first view.

CONCLUSIONS

In conclusion, preschoolers' suprising competence with counting and basic arithmetic may be due to their opportunity to develop adaptive expertise—to gradually construct procedural knowledge by applying conceptual knowledge and vice versa in a socially mediated environment (e.g., Anderson, 1997; Bruner, 1986; Durkin, Shire, Riem, Crowther, & Rutter, 1986; Lave, Murtaugh, & de la Rocha, 1984; Lawler, 1990; Rogoff, 1990; Saxe et al., 1987; Vygotsky, 1962) and connect and integrate these aspects of knowledge. Schoolchildren's unsurprising arithmetic incompetence may be due to their lack of opportunity to do so.

What aspects of preschoolers' informal experiences—unlike the formal instruction of many schoolchildren—foster adaptive expertise? A key difference may be learning in context as opposed to learning without context. Children learn concepts that are taught in context better than the same concepts taught in a disembodied manner (Donaldson, 1978; Hughes, 1986). Ethnomathematic research (e.g., Carraher, Schliemann, & Carraher, 1998; Lave et al., 1984) has shown that informal mathematical learning—unlike much formal school learning—is usually an integral part of everyday life (see Nunes, 1992, for a review). What this means is that the former typically involves using extant understanding to make sense of and solve real problems, whereas the latter typically involves ignoring, or even suppressing, informal knowledge and memorizing the solutions to symbolic and abstract problems by rote. Put differently, preschoolers are typically involved in meaningful, purposeful, and inquiry-based learning, whereas schoolchildren frequently are not.

Social mediation prompting informal learning in context may play a different and more effective role than that prompting traditional formal learning. The former may focus on creating interesting and challenging opportunities to learn (e.g., Anderson, 1997), whereas the latter focuses on getting through a prescribed—and largely uninspiring and mind-deadening-curriculum. Furthermore, in the case of learning in context, social mediation may focus more on the goals of an activity—including reasons for a procedure (how it is connected to everyday experience) and why it works (how it is connected to underlying concepts), whereas, in the case of traditional school instruction, social mediation focuses on trivial goals (e.g., memorizing information by rote to pass a test) or even distracting goals (e.g., getting a good grade). As Sophian (1998) noted:

> To account for children's eventual mastery of what is initially difficult, we do not need so much to posit that they override initial constraints [as suggested in the privileged-domain view] as that they construct new goals that no longer entail those constraints [a process not addressed by the frequency-of-exposure hypothesis]. Those new goals grow in part out of the very activities engendered by the old goals and in part of the child's engagement in new kinds of socially mediated activity [a process not adequately addressed by either the privileged-domain or the frequency-of-exposure hypothesis]. (p. 46)

Acknowledgments

Preparation of this chapter was supported, in part, by a grant titled "Early Arithmetic Development" to the first author by the University of Illinois Research Board, a Faculty Fellowship awarded to the first author by the College of Education at the University of Illinois, and a grant from the National Science Foundation titled "The Developmental Bases of Number and Operation Sense" (BCS-0111829). The opinions expressed are the sole responsibility of the authors and do not necessarily reflect the position, policy, or endorsement of the National Science Foundation.

We wish to thank the other participants of the 1998 spring semester C&I 490 PML (Psychology of Mathematical Learning) seminar, namely, Alexis Benson, Kenneth W. Benson, Karim Ezzatkhah-Yenggeh, Lucia Flevares, Ju-shan Hsieh, Hsin-mei Liao, Yu-chi Tai, and Akihiko Takahashi for helping to shape and sharpen our thinking about the matters discussed in this chapter.

References

Adams, J. W., & Hitch, G. J. (1998). Children's mental arithmetic and working memory. In C. Donlan (Ed.), *The development of mathematical skills* (pp. 153–173). Hove, East Sussex, England: Psychology Press.

Anderson, A. (1993). Wondering—One child's questions and mathematics learning. *Canadian Children, 18*(2), 26–30.

Anderson, A. (1997). Families and mathematics: A study of parent-child interactions. *Journal for Research in Mathematics Education, 28*, 484–511.

Anderson, J. R. (1993). *Rules of the mind.* Hillsdale, NJ: Lawrence Erlbaum Associates.

Ashcraft, M. H. (1987). Children's knowledge of simple arithmetic: A developmental model and simulation. In J. Bisanz, C. J. Brainerd, & R. Kail (Eds.), *Formal methods in developmental psychology* (pp. 302–338). New York: Springer-Verlag.

Ashcraft, M. H. (1992). Cognitive arithmetic: A review of data and theory. *Cognition, 44*, 75–106.

Ashcraft, M. H., Donley, R. D., Halas, M. A., & Vakali, M. (1992). Working memory, automaticity, and problem difficulty. In J. I. D. Campbell (Ed.), *The nature and origins of mathematical skills* (pp. 301–329). Amsterdam: Elsevier.

Baroody, A. J. (1983). The development of procedural knowledge: An alternative explanation for chronometric trends of mental arithmetic. *Developmental Review, 3*, 225–230.

Baroody, A. J. (1984a). The case of Felicia: A young child's strategies for reducing memory demands during mental addition. *Cognition and Instruction, 1*, 109–116.

Baroody, A. J. (1984b). Children's difficulties in subtraction: Some causes and questions. *Journal for Research in Mathematics Education, 15*, 203–213.

Baroody, A. J. (1984c). A re-examination of mental arithmetic models and data: A reply to Ashcraft. *Developmental Review, 4*, 148–156.

Baroody, A. J. (1985). Mastery of the basic number combinations: Internalization of relationships or facts? *Journal of Research in Mathematics Education, 16*, 83–98.

Baroody, A. J. (1987a). *Children's mathematical thinking: A developmental framework for preschool, primary, and special education teachers.* New York: Teachers College Press.

Baroody, A. J. (1987b). The development of counting strategies for single-digit addition. *Journal for Research in Mathematics Education, 18*, 141–157.

Baroody, A. J. (1988). Mental-addition development of children classified as mentally handicapped. *Educational Studies in Mathematics, 19*, 369–388.

Baroody, A. J. (1989). Kindergartners' mental addition with single-digit combinations. *Journal for Research in Mathematics Education, 20*, 159–172.

Baroody, A. J. (1992a). The development of kindergartners' mental-addition strategies. *Learning and Individual Differences, 4*, 215–235.

Baroody, A. J. (1992b). The development of preschoolers' counting skills and principles. In J. Bideaud, C. Meljac, & J. P. Fischer (Eds.), *Pathways to number* (pp. 99–126). Hillsdale, NJ: Lawrence Erlbaum Associates.

Baroody, A. J. (1993). Early mental multiplication performance and the role of relational knowledge in mastering combinations involving two. *Learning and Instruction, 3*, 93–111.

Baroody, A. J. (1994). An evaluation of evidence supporting fact-retrieval models. *Learning and Individual Differences, 6*, 1–36.

Baroody, A. J. (1995). The role of the number-after rule in the invention of computational short cuts. *Cognition and Instruction, 13*, 189–219.

Baroody, A. J. (1996). Self-invented addition strategies by children classified as mentally handicapped. *American Journal on Mental Retardation, 101*, 72–89.

Baroody, A. J. (1999a). Children's relational knowledge of addition and subtraction. *Cognition and Instruction, 17*, 137–175.

Baroody, A. J. (1999b). The roles of estimation and the commutativity principle in the development of third-graders' mental multiplication. *Journal of Experimental Child Psychology, 74*, 157–193.

Baroody, A. J. (in press). The developmental bases for early childhood number and operations standards. To appear in D. Clements, J. Sarama, & A. M. DiBiase (Eds.), *Engaging young children in mathematics: Findings of the national 2000 conference for preschool and kindergarten mathematics education.* Mahwah, NJ: Lawrence Erlbaum Associates.

Baroody, A. J., Berent, R., & Packman, D. (1982). The use of mathematical structure by inner city children. *Focus on Learning Problems in Mathematics, 4*(2), 5–13.

Baroody, A. J., with Coslick, R. T. (1998). *Fostering children's mathematical power: An investigative approach to K–8 mathematics instruction.* Mahwah, NJ: Lawrence Erlbaum Associates.

Baroody, A. J., & Gannon, K. E. (1984). The development of commutativity principle and economical addition strategies. *Cognition and Instruction, 1,* 321–329.

Baroody, A. J., & Ginsburg, H. P. (1986). The relationship between initial meaningful and mechanical knowledge of arithmetic. In J. Hiebert (Ed.), *Conceptual and procedural knowledge: The case of mathematics* (pp. 75–112). Hillsdale, NJ: Lawrence Erlbaum Associates.

Baroody, A. J., & Ginsburg, H. P. (1991). A cognitive approach to assessing the mathematical difficulties of children labeled learning disabled. In H. L. Swanson (Ed.), *Handbook on the assessment of learning disabilities: Theory, research and practice* (pp. 177–277). Austin, TX: Pro-Ed.

Baroody, A. J., Ginsburg, H. P., & Waxman, B. (1983). Children's use of mathematical structure. *Journal for Research in Mathematics Education, 14,* 156–168.

Baroody, A. J., Tiilikainen, S. H., & Tai, Y. (2000, October). The application and development of an addition goal sketch. In M. L. Fernández (Ed.), *Proceedings of the twenty-second annual meeting of the International Group for the Psychology of Mathematics Education, North American Chapter* (Vol. 2, pp. 709–714). Columbus, OH: The Eric Clearinghouse for Science, Mathematics, and Environment Education.

Behr, M. J., Harel, G., Post, T., & Lesh, R. (1992). Rational number, ratio, and proportion. In D. Grouws (Ed.), *Handbook of research on mathematics teaching and learning* (pp. 296–333). New York: Macmillan.

Bisanz, J., & LeFevre, J. (1990). Strategic and nonstrategic processing in the development of mathematical cognition. In D. F. Bjorklund (Ed.), *Children's strategies: Contemporary views of cognitive development* (pp. 213–244). Hillsdale, NJ: Lawrence Erlbaum Associates.

Bråten, I. (1996). Cognitive strategies in mathematics (Report No. 10). Oslo, Norway: Institute for Educational Research, University of Oslo.

Briars, D. J., & Larkin, J. G. (1984). An integrated model of skills in solving elementary word problems. *Cognition and Instruction, 1,* 245–296.

Briars, D., & Siegler, R. S. (1984). A featural analysis of preschoolers' counting knowledge. *Developmental Psychology, 20,* 607–618.

Brown, J. S., & Burton, R. R. (1978). Diagnostic models for procedural bugs in basic mathematical skills. *Cognitive Science, 2,* 155–192.

Browne, C. E. (1906). The psychology of simple arithmetical processes: A study of certain habits of attention and association. *American Journal of Psychology, 17,* 2–37.

Brownell, W. A. (1935). Psychological considerations in the learning and the teaching of arithmetic. In D. W. Reeve (Ed.), *The teaching of arithmetic* (Tenth yearbook, National Council of Teachers of Mathematics, pp. 1–50). New York: Bureau of Publications, Teachers College, Columbia University.

Brownell, W. A. (1941). *Arithmetic in grades I and II. A critical summary of new and previously reported research* (Duke University Research Studies in Education No. 6). Durham, NC: Duke University Press.

Bruner, J. (1986). Play, thought and language. *Prospect, 16,* 77–83.

Campbell, J. I. D. (1987). Network interference and mental multiplication. *Journal of Experimental Psychology: Learning, Memory, and Cognition, 13,* 109–123.

Campbell, J. I. D. (1995). Mechanisms of simple addition and multiplication: A modified network-interference theory. *Mathematical Cognition, 1,* 121–164.

Campbell, J. I. D., & Graham, D. J. (1985). Mental multiplication skill: Structure, process, and acquisition. *Canadian Journal of Psychology, 39,* 338–362.

Carpenter, T., Hiebert, J., & Moser, J. (1983). Problem structure and first grade children's initial solution processes for simple addition and subtraction problems. *Journal for Research in Mathematics Education, 12*, 27–39.

Carpenter, T. P., Matthews, W., Lindquist, M. M., & Silver, E. A. (1984). Achievement in mathematics: Results from the National Assessment. *Elementary School Journal, 84*, 485–495.

Carpenter, T. P., & Moser, J. M. (1982). The development of addition and subtraction problem-solving skills. In T. R. Carpenter, J. M. Moser, & T. A. Romberg (Eds.), *Addition and subtraction: A cognitive perspective* (pp. 9–24). Hillsdale, NJ: Lawrence Erlbaum Associates.

Carpenter, T. P., & Moser, J. M. (1984). The acquisition of addition and subtraction concepts in grades one through three. *Journal for Research in Mathematics Education, 15*, 179–202.

Carraher, T., Schliemann, A., & Carraher, D. (1988). Mathematical concepts in everyday life. In G. Saxe & M. Gearhart (Eds.), *Children's mathematics* (pp. 71–87). San Francisco: Jossey-Bass.

Clearfield, M., & Mix, K. S. (1999). Number versus contour length in infants' discrimination of small visual sets. *Psychological Science, 10*, 408–411.

Cobb, P., & Wheatley, G. (1988). Children's initial understanding of ten. *Focus on Learning Problems in Mathematics, 10*(3), 1–28.

Cooney, J. B., Swanson, H. L., & Ladd, S. F. (1988). Acquisition of mental multiplication skill: Evidence for the transition between counting and retrieval strategies. *Cognition and Instruction, 5*, 323–345.

Cowan, R., & Renton, M. (1996). Do they know what they are doing? Children's use of economical addition strategies and knowledge of commutativity. *Educational Psychology, 16*, 407–420.

Crowley, K., Shrager, J., & Siegler, R. S. (1997). Strategy discovery as a competitive negotiation between metacognitive and associative mechanisms. *Developmental Review, 17*, 462–489.

Darlington, R. B. (1974). *Radicals and squares.* Ithaca, NY: Logan Hill Press.

Davis, R. B. (1986). Conceptual and procedural knowledge in mathematics: A summary analysis. In J. Hiebert (Ed.), *Conceptual and procedural knowledge: The case of mathematics* (pp. 265–300). Hillsdale, NJ: Lawrence Erlbaum Associates.

Davis, R. B. (1992). Reflections on where mathematics education now stands and on where it may be going. In D. A. Grouws (Ed.), *Handbook of research on mathematics teaching and learning* (pp. 724–734). New York: Macmillan.

De Corte, E., & Verschaffel, L. (1987). The effect of semantic structure on first graders' strategies for solving addition and subtraction word problems. *Journal for Research in Mathematics Education, 18*, 363–381.

De Corte, E., & Verschaffel, L. (1988). Computer simulation as a tool in research on problem solving in subject-matter domains. *International Journal of Educational Research, 12* (*Computer simulations as research tools*, M. Rabinowitz, Guest Ed.), 49–69.

Donaldson, M. (1978). *Children's minds.* New York: Norton.

Dowker, A. (1992). Computational estimation strategies of professional mathematicians. *Journal for Research in Mathematics Education, 23*, 45–55.

Dowker, A. (1998). Individual differences in normal arithmetical development. In C. Donlan (Ed.), *The development of mathematical skills* (pp. 275–302). Hove, East Sussex, England: Psychology Press.

Durkin, K., Shire, B., Riem, R., Crowther, R., & Rutter, D. (1986). The social and linguistic context of early number use. *British Journal of Developmental Psychology, 4*, 269–288.

Folsom, M. (1975). Operations on whole numbers. In J. N. Payne (Ed.), *Mathematics learning in early childhood* (37th Yearbook, pp. 162–190). Reston, VA: National Council of Teachers of Mathematics.

Fuson, K. C. (1982). An analysis of the counting-on solution procedure in addition. In T. P. Carpenter, J. Moser, & T. Romberg (Eds.), *Addition and subtraction: A cognitive perspective* (pp. 67–81). Hillsdale, NJ: Lawrence Erlbaum Associates.

Fuson, K. C. (1988). *Children's counting and concepts of number.* New York: Springer-Verlag.

Fuson, K. C. (1992). Research on whole number addition and subtraction. In D. Grouws (Ed.), *Handbook of research on mathematics teaching and learning* (pp. 243–275). New York: Macmillan.

Fuson, K. C., Richards, J. J., & Briars, D. J. (1982). The acquisition and elaboration of the number word sequence. In C. J. Brainerd (Ed.), *Progress in cognitive development: Vol. 1. Children's logical and mathematical cognition* (pp. 33–92). New York: Springer-Verlag.

Fuson, K. C., & Secada, W. G. (1986). Teaching children to add by counting-on with one-handed finger patterns. *Cognition and Instruction, 3,* 229–260.

Geary, D. C. (1993). Mathematical disabilities: Cognitive, neuropsychological and genetic components. *Psychological Bulletin, 114,* 345–362.

Geary, D. C. (1994). *Children's mathematical development: Research and practical applications.* Washington, DC: American Psychological Association.

Gelman, R., & Meck, E. (1986). The notion of principle: The case of counting. In J. Hiebert (Ed.), *Conceptual and procedural knowledge: The case of mathematics* (pp. 29–57). Hillsdale, NJ: Lawrence Erlbaum Associates.

Gelman, R., & Meck, E. (1992). Early principles aid early but not later conceptions of number. In J. Bideaud, C. Meljac, & J. P. Fischer (Eds.), *Pathways to number* (pp. 171–189). Hillsdale, NJ: Lawrence Erlbaum Associates.

Ginsburg, H. P. (1977). *Children's arithmetic.* New York: Van Nostrand.

Ginsburg, H. P., Posner, J. K., & Russell, R. L. (1981). The development of mental addition as a function of schooling. *Journal of Cross-Cultural Psychology, 12,* 163–178.

Groen, G. J., & Parkman, J. M. (1972). A chronometric analysis of simple addition. *Psychological Review, 79,* 329–343.

Hiebert, J., & Lefevre, P. (1986). Conceptual and procedural knowledge in mathematics: An introductory analysis. In J. Hiebert (Ed.), *Conceptual and procedural knowledge: The case of mathematics* (pp. 1–27). Hillsdale, NJ: Lawrence Erlbaum Associates.

Hope, J. A., & Sherrill, J. M. (1987). Characteristics of unskilled and skilled mental calculators. *Journal for Research in Mathematics Education, 18,* 98–111.

Hopkins, S. (1998). *The simple addition performances of learning disabled adolescent students. An explanation of how the moving-on process for developing reliance on retrieval is impeded by pressure.* Unpublished doctoral thesis, Flinders University, South Australia.

Hughes, M. (1986). *Children and number.* New York: Blackwell.

Huttenlocher, J., Jordan, N. C., & Levine, S. C. (1994). A mental model for early arithmetic. *Journal of Experimental Psychology: General, 123,* 284–296.

Ilg, F., & Ames, L. B. (1951). Developmental trends in arithmetic. *The Journal of Genetic Psychology, 79,* 3–28.

James, W. (1950). *The principles of psychology* (Vol. 1). New York: Dover (Original work published 1890).

Jerman, M. (1970). Some strategies for solving simple multiplication combinations. *Journal for Research in Mathematics Education, 1,* 95–128.

Jordan, N. C., Huttenlocher, J., & Levine, S. C. (1992). Differential calculation abilities in young children from middle- and low-income families. *Developmental Psychology, 28,* 644–653.

Kamii, C. (1989). *Young children continue to reinvent arithmetic—2nd grade.* New York: Teachers College Press.

Karmiloff-Smith, A. (1992). *Beyond modularity: A developmental perspective.* Cambridge, MA: MIT Press.

Kaye, D. (1986). The development of mathematical cognition. *Cognitive Development, 1,* 157–170.

Klahr, D., & MacWhinney, B. (1998). Information processing. In W. Damon (Ed.), *Handbook of child psychology: Volume 2, Cognition, perception, and language* (pp. 631–678). New York: Wiley.

Kouba, V. L., Carpenter, T. P., & Swafford, J. O. (1989). Numbers and operations. In M. M. Lindquist (Ed.), *Results from the Fourth Mathematics Assessment of the National Assessment of Educational Progress* (pp. 64–93). Reston, VA: National Council of Teachers of Mathematics.

Lave, J., Murtaugh, M., & de la Rocha, O. (1984). The dialectic of arithmetic in grocery shopping. In B. Rogoff & J. Lave, (Eds.) *Everyday cognition: Its development in social context* (pp. 67–94). Cambridge, MA: Harvard University Press.

Lawler, R. (1990). Constructing knowledge from interactions. *Journal of Mathematical Behavior, 9*, 177–192.

LeFevre, J., Bisanz, J., Daley, K. E., Buffone, L., Greenham, S. L., & Sadesky, G. S. (1996). Multiple routes to solution of single-digit multiplication problems. *Journal of Experimental Psychology: General, 125*, 284–306.

LeFevre, J., & Morris, J. (1999). More on the relation between division and multiplication in simple arithmetic: Evidence for mediation of division via multiplication. *Memory & Cognition, 27*, 803–812.

LeFevre, J., Sadesky, G. S., & Bisanz, J. (1996). Selection of procedures in mental addition: Reassessing the problem size effect in adults. *Journal of Experimental Psychology: Learning, Memory, and Cognition, 22*, 216–230.

Lemaire, P., & Siegler, R. S. (1995). Four aspects of strategic change: Contributions to children's learning of multiplication. *Journal of Experimental Psychology: General, 124*, 83–97.

Madell, R. (1985). Children's natural processes. *Arithmetic Teacher, 32*(7), 20–22.

Miller, K. F., & Paredes, D. R. (1990). Starting to add worse: Effects of learning to multiply on children's addition. *Cognition, 37*, 213–242.

Mix, K. S., Huttenlocher, J., & Levine, S. C. (2002). *Math without words: Quantitative development in infancy and early childhood.* New York: Oxford University Press.

Mix, K. S., Levine, S. C., & Huttenlocher, J. (1999). Early fraction calculation ability. *Developmental Psychology, 35*, 164–174.

Munn, P. (1998). Symbolic function in pre-schoolers. In C. Donlan (Ed.), *The development of mathematical skills* (pp. 47–71) Hove, East Sussex, England: Psychology Press.

National Center for Education Statistics. (retrieved December 6, 2001). *Third International Mathematics and Science Study* (http://necs.ed.gov/timss/). Washington, DC: author.

Neches, P. (1982). Levels of description in the analysis of addition and subtraction word problems. In T. P. Carpenter, J. Moser, & T. A. Romberg (Eds.), *Addition and subtraction: A cognitive perspective* (pp. 25–38). Hillsdale, NJ: Lawrence Erlbaum Associates.

Nunes, T. (1992). Ethnomathematics and everyday cognition. In D. A. Grouws (Ed.), *Handbook of research on mathematics teaching and learning* (pp. 557–574). New York: Macmillan.

Piaget, J. (1964). Development and learning. In R. E. Ripple & V. N. Rockcastle (Eds.), *Piaget rediscovered* (pp. 7–20). Ithaca, NY: Cornell University.

Piaget, J. (1965). *The child's conception of number.* New York: Norton.

Putnam, R. T., deBettencourt, L. U., & Leinhardt, G. (1990). Understanding of derived-fact strategies in addition and subtraction. *Cognition and Instruction, 7*, 245–285.

Resnick, L. B., & Ford, W. W. (1981). *The psychology of mathematics for instruction.* Hillsdale, NJ: Lawrence Erlbaum Associates.

Rickard, T. C., & Bourne, L. E., Jr. (1996). Some tests of an identical elements model of basic arithmetic skills. *Journal of Experimental Psychology: Learning, Memory, and Cognition, 22*, 1281–1295.

Rickard, T. C., Healy, A. F., & Bourne, L. E., Jr. (1994). On the cognitive structure of basic arithmetic skills. Operation, order, and symbol transfer effects. *Journal of Experimental Psychology: Learning, Memory, and Cognition, 20*, 1139–1153.

Riley, M. S., Greeno, J. G., & Heller, J. I. (1983). Development of children's problem-solving ability in arithmetic. In H. P. Ginsburg (Ed.), *The development of mathematical thinking* (pp. 153–200). New York: Academic Press.

Rittle-Johnson, B., & Alibali, M. W. (1999). Conceptual and procedural knowledge of mathematics: Does one lead to the other? *Journal of Educational Psychology, 91*, 175–189.

Rittle-Johnson, B., & Siegler, R. S. (1998). The relation between conceptual and procedural knowledge in learning mathematics: A review of the literature. In C. Donlan (Ed.), *The development of mathematical skills* (pp. 75–110). Hove, East Sussex, England: Psychology Press.

Rogoff, B. (1990). *Apprenticeship in thinking.* Oxford, England: Oxford University Press.

Saxe, G., Guberman, S., & Gearhart, M. (1987). Social processes in early number development. *Monographs of the Society for Research in Child Development, 52* (Serial No. 2).

Schoenfeld, A. H. (1982). Some thoughts on problem-solving research and mathematics education. In F. K. Lester Jr., & J. Garofalo (Eds.), *Mathematical problem solving: Issues in research* (pp. 27–37). Philadelphia: Franklin Institute Press.

Schoenfeld, A. H. (1985). *Mathematical problem solving.* New York: Academic Press.

Shrager, J., & Siegler, R. S. (1998). SCADS: A model of children's strategy choices and strategy discoveries. *Psychological Science, 9,* 405–410.

Siegler, R. S. (1986). Unities across domains in children's strategy choices. In M. Perlmutter (Ed.), *Minnesota Symposium of Child Psychology* (Vol. 19, pp. 1–48). Hillsdale, NJ: Lawrence Erlbaum Associates.

Siegler, R. S. (1987). Strategy choices in subtraction. In J. Slobada & D. Rogers (Eds.), *Cognitive process in mathematics* (pp. 81–106). Oxford, England: Oxford University Press.

Siegler, R. S. (1988). Strategy choice procedures and the development of multiplication skill. *Journal of Experimental Psychology: General, 117,* 258–275.

Siegler, R. S. (1996). *Emerging minds: The process of change in children's thinking.* New York: Oxford University Press.

Siegler, R. S. (1997). Beyond competence—toward development. *Cognitive Development, 12,* 323–332.

Siegler, R. S., & Crowley, K. (1994). Constraints on learning in nonprivileged domains. *Cognitive Psychology, 27,* 194–226.

Siegler, R. S., & Jenkins, E. (1989). *How children discover new strategies.* Hillsdale, NJ: Lawrence Erlbaum Associates.

Siegler, R. S., & Robinson, M. (1982). The development of numerical understanding. In H. W. Reese & L. P. Lipsitt (Eds.), *Advances in child development and behavior* (Vol. I, pp. 241–312). New York: Academic Press.

Siegler, R. S., & Shipley, C. (1995). Variation, selection, and cognitive change. In G. Halford & T. Simon (Eds.), *Developing cognitive competence: New approaches to process modeling* (pp. 31–76). Hillsdale, NJ: Lawrence Erlbaum Associates.

Siegler, R. S., & Shrager, J. (1984). Strategy choice in addition: How do children know what to do? In C. Sophian (Ed.), *Origins of cognitive skills* (pp. 229–293). Hillsdale, NJ: Lawrence Erlbaum Associates.

Sokol, S. M., McCloskey, M., Cohen, N. J., & Aliminosa, D. (1991). Cognitive representations and processes in arithmetic: Inferences from the performance of brain-damaged subjects. *Journal of Experimental Psychology: Learning, Memory, and Cognition, 17,* 355–376.

Sophian, C. (1998). A developmental perspective on children's counting. In C. Donlan (Ed.), *The development of mathematical skills* (pp. 27–46). Hove, East Sussex, England: Psychology Press.

Starkey, P., & Gelman, R. (1982). The development of addition and subtraction abilities prior to formal schooling in arithmetic. In T. P. Carpenter, J. M. Moser, & T. A. Romberg (Eds.), *Addition and subtraction: A cognitive perspective* (pp. 96–116). Hillsdale, NJ: Lawrence Erlbaum Associates.

Steffe, L. P., von Glasersfeld, E., Richards, J., & Cobb, P. (1983). *Children's counting types: Philosophy, theory, and application.* New York: Praeger Scientific.

Suydam, M., & Weaver, J. F. (1975). Research on mathematics learning. In J. N. Payne (Ed.), *Mathematics learning in early childhood* (37th Yearbook, pp. 43–67). Reston, VA: National Council of Teachers of Mathematics.

Svenson, O., Hedenborg, M. L., & Lingman, L. (1976). On children's heuristics for solving simple additions. *Scandinavian Journal of Educational Research, 20,* 161–173.

Svenson, O., & Sjöberg, K. (1983). Evolution of cognitive processes for solving simple additions during the first three school years. *Scandinavian Journal of Psychology, 24,* 117–124.

Thorndike, E. L. (1922). *The psychology of arithmetic.* New York: Macmillan.

Trivett, J. (1980). The multiplication table: To be memorized or mastered? *For the Learning of Mathematics, 1*(1), 21–25.

VanLehn, K. (1983). On the representation of procedures in repair theory. In H. P. Ginsburg (Ed.), *The development of mathematical thinking* (pp. 197–252). New York: Academic Press.

Vygotsky, L. S. (1962). *Thought and language.* Cambridge, MA: MIT Press.

Wynn, K. (1992). Addition and subtraction by human infants. *Nature, 358,* 749–750.

Wynn, K. (1998). Numerical competence in infants. In C. Donlan (Ed.), *The development of mathematical skills* (pp. 3–25). Hove, East Sussex, England: Psychology Press.

Zbrodoff, N. J., & Logan, G. D. (1990). On the relation between production and verification tasks in the psychology of simple arithmetic. *Journal of Experimental Psychology: Learning, Memory, and Cognition, 16,* 83–97.

CHAPTER 4

THE DEVELOPMENT
OF CHILDREN'S UNDERSTANDING
OF ADDITIVE COMMUTATIVITY:
FROM PROTOQUANTITIVE CONCEPT
TO GENERAL CONCEPT?

Arthur J. Baroody
University of Illinois
at Urbana-Champaign

Jesse L. M. Wilkins
Virginia Polytechnic Institute
and State University

Sirpa H. Tiilikainen
University of Illinois
at Urbana-Champaign

In the last quarter of the 20th century, psychologists' view of young children's mathematical competence changed dramatically. According to the conventional wisdom earlier in the century, preschoolers had little mathematical knowledge or ability. For example, the famous learning theorist Edward L. Thorndike (1922) concluded, "It seems probable that little is gained by using any of the child's time for arithmetic before grade 2, though there are many arithmetic facts that they can [memorize by rote] in grade 1" (p. 198). In other words, children before the age of 7 years or so were considered capable of little more than routine expertise in this domain. More recently, researchers have found a wealth of previously unsuspected informal mathematical strengths in young children and, perhaps, even infants (see, e.g., Baroody & Wilkins, 1999; Fuson, 1992; Ginsburg, Klein, & Starkey, 1998; Wynn, 1998; for detailed reviews). These strengths include key arithmetic concepts, arithmetic reasoning, and self-invented addition strategies, all hallmarks of adaptive expertise.

Although young children's mathematical competence is clearly impressive, it is important not to overestimate it. In this chapter, we examine the development of young children's mathematical thinking using a key arithmetic concept, the principle of additive commutativity, as an example. This principle specifies that the order in which addends are added does not affect the sum (e.g., $5 + 3$ or $3 + 5$ equals 8 and so $5 + 3 = 3 + 5$).

Similar to our efforts here, Resnick (1992) used the development of additive commutativity to illustrate a general model of how mathematical thinking develops. Her model has prompted scrutiny of earlier research on children's understanding of additive commutativity and reignited interest in examining this topic. This literature review has three purposes. The first is to point out a common misconception about Resnick's model, namely, the inference that additive commutativity develops independently of computational experience (e.g., Ganetsou & Cowan, 1995; Sophian, Harley, & Martin, 1995), and to evaluate the empirical evidence for this inference. The second aim is to critically analyze the existing evidence for several key tenets of Resnick's model of commutativity development. As we detail, this evidence does not clearly support or refute the model. A third aim, then, is to propose a modification to Resnick's model: a synthesis that appears to reconcile differing claims and evidence about the development of additive commutativity. Our hope is that this literature review will provide direction for future research and help researchers avoid the methodological problems that confound existing research.

Part I:
A Common Misconception
of Resnick's Model

In this part of the review, we summarize Resnick's (1992) model, describe a common misconception about it regarding the role of computational experience, and evaluate the empirical evidence supporting this misconception.

RESNICK'S MODEL

Resnick (1992) proposed that domain-specific mathematical development involved a progression of four qualitatively different types of mathematical thinking. Her description of how mathematical thinking develops provides an explicit and detailed account of the psychological origins of the commutative property of addition.

Four Kinds of Mathematical Thinking

Resnick (1992) proposed that in any given mathematical domain, children begin with concrete thinking and successively add three levels of increasingly abstract thinking.

Level 1: Mathematics of Protoquantities. At this level, children reason about physical materials without reference to specific numerosities—that is, in qualitative, rather than in quantitative, terms. Qualitative reasoning can involve predicting the direction of an answer, whereas, quantitative reasoning may result in determining the exact answer. By using the former, children can recognize that the action of adding items to a collection increases its size and that the action of taking away items from a collection decreases its size.

Level 2: Mathematics of Quantities. At this level, children can reason about numbers that are tied to a particular and meaningful context. For example, they can estimate or determine that adding two more cookies to a collection of three cookies makes five cookies. They may also recognize that removing the two added cookies returns the collection to the original amount of three cookies.

Level 3: Mathematics of Numbers. At this level, children can reason about specific numbers in the abstract (i.e., about the numbers themselves). For instance, a child can draw logical conclusions about the addition of three and two without concrete referents. They may also recognize—without computing or recalling individual sums and differences—that 3 + 2 − 2 will have an outcome of three. That is, they may understand that subtracting the number *two* undoes adding the number *two*.

Level 4: Mathematics of Operators. At this level, children construct general arithmetic principles. That is, they can treat operations on numbers (as well as the numbers) as conceptual entities that can be reasoned about in the abstract (rather than simply be applied). For instance, children can now recognize a general inverse principle—that adding any number can be undone by subtracting that number or vice versa ($a + b - b = a$ or $a - b + b = a$).

Development of Additive Commutativity

According to Resnick (1992), the origins of additive commutativity reach back to the protoquantitative level and stem from children's general understanding of additive composition, which is represented by a part-whole schema. Even before children can reliably quantify physical materials, "they know that a whole quantity can be cut into two or more parts, that the parts can then be recombined to make the whole, and that the order in which parts are combined does not matter in reconstituting the original amount [see the protoquantitative level in Table 4.1]. . . . As children apply their counting skills in situations that earlier were reasoned about only protoquantitatively, . . . the part/whole schema becomes quantified" (p. 408). Now they apply their schema for protoquantitative commutativity to situations involving specific quantified amounts (see the quantitative level in Table 4.1). When children no longer need concrete referents, they can organize knowledge about the commutative relation among specific numbers (see the numerical level in Table 4.1). In time, children finally switch their attention "from actions on particular numbers to more general relations between numbers" (p. 408). At this point, they understand commutativity as a general property of addition (see the operator level in Table 4.1). That is, instead of accepting commutativity for only some pairs of combinations, children now recognize that "addition by combining is always commutative, no matter what pair of numbers is composed" (p. 405).

Table 4.1: Developmental Levels of Commutativity (Resnick, 1992)

Level of Additive Commutativity	Example
Protoquantitative (prenumerical)	apples + oranges = oranges + apples ($Part_1 + Part_2 = Part_2 + Part_1$)
Quantitative (specific numbers in context)	3 apples + 5 apples = 5 apples + 3 apples
Numerical (specific numbers in the abstract)	$3 + 5 = 5 + 3$
Operator (general arithmetic principle)	$a + b = b + a$

THE ROLE OF COMPUTATIONAL EXPERIENCE

Resnick (1992) clearly implied that knowledge of commutativity at the protoquantitative level can be constructed before children devise informal strategies for computing sums but did not specify what role computational fluency plays in the construction of this knowledge at the quantities level. We outline two different accounts regarding the role of computational experience in the development of commutativity—one inconsistent with Resnick's subsequently stated view and the other being her actual view. We then summarize and analyze the evidence for each view.

Theory

The Independent-of-Computational-Experience Conjecture. A common interpretation of Resnick's (1992) model is that, although the application of counting skills is necessary to quantify the part-whole schema, it is not necessary for the construction of commutativity at the quantities level (see, e.g., Cowan & Renton, 1996; Ganetsou & Cowan, 1995; Sophian et al., 1995). More specifically, experience counting collections and, perhaps, minimal application of counting skills to the task of computing sums is needed to prompt quantitative-level mathematical thinking. However, because children assimilate (concrete) addition situations to a quantitative-level part-whole schema, they immediately (or almost immediately) deduce that such situations are commutative. In other words, there is no need for computational experience in order to discover, for example, that 3 apples and 5 apples are equal to 5 apples and 3 apples. In brief, Resnick's 1992 account has reasonably been interpreted by some researchers as an extension of one of her earlier accounts that implied that additive commutativity was deduced from children's understanding of part-whole relation, rather than discovered from computational experience (see "A 'Part-Whole' Account" described in Resnick, 1983, pp. 124–125).[1]

Resnick's Actual View. In fact, Resnick (L. B. Resnick, personal communication, February 21, 1997) actually believes that additive commutativity "is reconstructed at each successive level, using both what the child knows from the previous level and new knowledge (e.g., the experience of counting and computing). . . . For a child to understand [for example] that 3 apples + 6 apples = 6 apples + 3 apples [requires] more than just applying an existing [part-whole] schema. . . . It would involve also noticing . . . that in both cases the sum is 9 apples."

Evidence

The Independent-of-Computational-Experience Conjecture. Ganetsou and Cowan (1995) directly tested the conjecture that knowledge of commutativity at the quantities level develops independently of children's computational experience by testing their participants on both a commutativity and

---

[1] We also shared this misconception of Resnick's (1992) view until we corresponded with her.

an addition task. These researchers found that some children understood commutativity, even though they had difficulty computing sums or were unable to compute sums.

Sophian et al. (1995) tested the "independence" conjecture indirectly. These researchers assumed that, if young children derived commutativity from their computational experience, then they should understand this relation only in the limited context in which they learned it (i.e., with specific values). Sophian et al. gave half of their 3- to 5-year-old participants a task in which addition models involved visible collections (the specific-values or uncovered task) and the other half a task in which addition models each involved an invisible collection (the nonspecific values or covered task). These researchers found that more than half their participants were successful in judging commutativity and that children in the covered condition did as well as those in the uncovered condition. This led Sophian et al. to conclude that the presence of specific values is not necessary to infer commutativity and that relational knowledge (i.e., qualitative reasoning or protoquantitative thinking) seems to be "the starting point of numerical development" (p. 266).

Resnick's Actual View. Baroody and Gannon (1984) found evidence indicating that computational experience does play a role in the discovery of the commutativity beyond the protoquantities level. More specifically, they found that none of the 9 kindergarten participants who had to be taught a strategy for computing sums appeared to have a solid understanding of the relation on two numerical-level commutativity tasks. Furthermore, about one fourth of their participants counted at one time or another in order to establish the equivalence of commuted pairs.

Consider the case of Kate (reported in detail later in Baroody, 1987a). On the commutativity task administered during the first session, the kindergartner immediately recognized that the identical expressions 6 + 1 and 6 + 1 had the same sum and that 2 + 5 and 2 + 10 (expressions that shared only one addend) had different sums. Presented the commuted expressions 2 + 4 and 4 + 2, she did not respond. Pressed for an answer, she paused and then answered, "The same." Then after quickly and correctly responding to the 0 + 2 and 10 + 10 trial and the 3 + 1 and 0 + 1 trial, she responded to 5 + 3 and 3 + 5 with, "I can't tell." Later with 4 + 6 and 6 + 4, she commented, "That's the one I got so much trouble over." In the second session, she responded quickly to all six commuted trials. Asked why she thought 3 + 4 and 4 + 3 were equivalent, Kate noted, "Because the same numbers in different places look like they add up the same." In a third session, Kate was asked to compute the sum of 6 + 4. After the experimenter recorded her calculated answer of 10 next to the written expression 6 + 4, he wrote 4 + 6 directly underneath the first equation and asked if it would produce the same answer as 6 + 4 or something different. Kate immediately indicated the answer would be the same. Asked why, she commented, "I figured it out when I counted when we played the other game" (a reference to the commutativity task administered in the first session).

In addition, Baroody, Berent, and Packman (1982) found that inner-city first graders who used advanced counting-based addition strategies were significantly more likely to exhibit understanding of commutativity than those who used relatively inefficient strategies (and presumably had less informal addition experience). Baroody (1987c), likewise, found that mentally retarded children who had moderate or regular amounts of computational experience were significantly more likely to use commutativity as a computational shortcut than those who had little or no computational experience.

Analysis

The evidence supporting the independent-of-computational-experience conjecture is not compelling for three reasons.

First, Ganetsou and Cowan's (1995) results were confounded by addend size. Whereas children's judgment of commutativity does not seem to be affected significantly by addend size (Baroody, 1987c; Tiilikainen, Baroody, & Wilkins, 1997; Wright, cited in Nunes & Bryant, 1996), their ability to compute sums clearly is (e.g., Baroody, 1984a, 1987a, 1995; Carpenter & Moser, 1982). Eight of the 10 addition-task trials in Ganetsou and Cowan's study involved relatively difficult combinations—combinations in which one or both of the addends were more than five. Children who rely on concrete strategies cannot easily model such combinations with their fingers or use a visual image of a number to aid calculation. Moreover, all the addition-task combinations were of the smaller-addend-first variety, which are more difficult than the larger-addend-first variety for children who use abstract (verbal) counting procedures but who do not yet disregard addend order (e.g., 3 + 8 would require a cognitively demanding eight-step keeping-track process for such children). Given the size of the combinations used on the addition task, it is not surprising that many of Ganetsou and Cowan's 4- and 5-year-olds did not try computing the sums or did so incorrectly. In brief, Ganetsou and Cowan (1995) may have underestimated their participants' overall computational proficiency.

Second, the results of Sophian et al. (1995) are not inconsistent with Resnick's (1992) actual view. More specifically, it does *not* follow from the latter's view that if computational experience is the mechanism by which an understanding of commutativity is extended to the quantities level, then children should understand this relation only in the context of specific values. Indeed, according to Resnick's model, children should do at least as well on the covered task as on the uncovered task because the former requires a lower level of mathematical thinking than the latter. That is, the covered task involves qualitative-reasoning or protoquantities-level thinking, whereas the uncovered task might involve quantitative-reasoning or quantities-level thinking.

Third, the cross-sectional studies by Ganetsou and Cowan (1995) and Sophian et al. (1995) did not explore how their participants extended the commutativity principle to the quantities level. Ganetsou and Cowan did not independently assess computational competence with small collections, and Sophian et al. did not assess children's computational experience at all. It is possible that prior informal experience with adding small collections led participants in both of these studies to discover the commutativity principle. It is also possible that children can quickly generalize this principle to previously noncomputed specific values or to situations involving nonspecific values. Research is needed to determine whether children discover commutativity in the context of adding small quantities and, if so, whether this knowledge transfers quickly.

Moreover, evidence that children discover commutativity at the numerical level via computational experiences (Baroody, 1987a; Baroody & Gannon, 1984) and that computational experience is associated with commutativity performance at this level (Baroody, 1987c; Baroody et al., 1982) is inconsistent with the independent-of-computational-experience conjecture. On the other hand, this evidence is consistent with Resnick's genetic account that computational experience plays a key role in reconstructing an understanding of commutativity at higher levels of mathematical thinking. Nevertheless, additional research to establish that computational experience plays a direct role in the reconstruction of commutativity at the *quantities level* is still needed.

Part II:
Evidence Regarding Resnick's Model

Does convincing evidence for other key aspects of Resnick's (1992) model exist? In this part of the chapter, we review and analyze the evidence on the following three key hypotheses that stem from her model: (a) the tie between additive commutativity and general knowledge of additive composition, (b) task effects on commutativity performance, and (c) the effects of addend size on commutativity performance.

LINK WITH GENERAL KNOWLEDGE
OF ADDITIVE COMPOSITION

Theory

Resnick (1992) suggested that an understanding of commutativity at the protoquantities level is rooted in general knowledge of additive composition and provides an implicit permission to combine collections in any order.

Evidence

Correlation With Other Tasks Involving Additive Composition. To support her contention that commutativity is derived from a general understanding of additive composition, Resnick (1992) described the case of Pitt (7 years, 7 months). This child was adroit at various tasks requiring additive composition, including flexible enumeration (counting and combining different units such as hundreds, tens, and ones) and using a left-to-right decomposition strategy for multidigit mental addition (e.g., $60 + 35 \rightarrow [60 + 30] + 5 = 90 + 5 = 95$). Pitt also used the commutativity property to short-cut the addition of 11 and 45—explaining that it was equal to 45 and 11, for which he had previously determined the sum, because each involved the same numbers. Resnick concluded, "Commutativity . . . was not a special law for Pitt. It derived from the same principle that allowed him to partition addition problems in different ways but still get the same answer" (p. 382).

Strategies That Disregard Addend Order. As evidence of an implicit commutativity permission, Resnick (1992) noted that children as young as kin-

dergarten age invent strategies that disregard addend order: counting-all beginning with the larger addend (CAL) or counting-on from the larger addend (COL;
e.g., Groen & Resnick, 1977). (For 3 + 5, for instance, CAL involves counting "1, 2,
3, 4, 5; 6 [is one more], 7 [is two more], 8 [is three more]—the sum is eight"; COL,
counting "5; 6 [is one more], 7 [is two more], 8 [is three more]—the sum is eight.")
Turner and Bryant's unpublished study (cited in Bryant, 1994) provided even
more direct evidence of a link between knowledge of commutativity and strategies that disregard addend order. They found that all children who used COL
"appeared to understand commutativity, though not vice versa" (p. 19). Likewise, Cowan and Renton (1996; Experiment 2) found that most children who
used a CAL or COL strategy understood commutativity and some who used less
economical strategies understood the principle as well. On the other hand, some
evidence indicates that the use of such strategies does not necessarily guarantee
success on commutativity tasks (Baroody, 1982, 1987b; Baroody & Gannon, 1984;
S. M. Thomas, personal communication, March 10, 1997).

Analysis

Correlation With Other Tasks Involving Additive Composition.
Unfortunately, testimony that a single 7.5-year-old is successful on various
additive-composition tasks, including commutativity, does not establish that
general competence with additive composition and knowledge of commutativity
are developmentally related. It does not even establish that the former develops
prior to or simultaneously with the latter.

Moreover, other evidence appears to contradict Resnick's (1992) hypothesis
that additive commutativity develops simultaneously with or after other aspects
of additive composition. Sophian et al. (1995) found that most of their 3- and 4-
year-old participants seem to understand commutativity (at the quantities
levels), but Sophian (Sophian & McCorgray, 1994; Sophian & Vong, 1995)
concluded that 4-year-old participants did not understand part-whole relations
(at the quantities level). Taken together, the results of these studies seem to
suggest that an understanding of additive commutativity is not derived from a
general understanding of part-whole knowledge. However, one possible explanation for the discrepancy between Sophian's two studies is that two different
samples of children were used.

In brief, direct evidence is needed to compare when children achieve a
quantitative understanding of additive composition and commutativity. Support
for Resnick's (1992) account would require evidence that children invent various
partitioning strategies based on additive composition (e.g., flexible enumeration
and left-right decomposition strategies) before or about the same time they
understand additive commutativity (at least at the quantities level). Evidence
that children understand part-whole relations at least at the protoquantities level
before they understand commutativity at higher levels would provide additional
support for her account.

Strategies That Disregard Addend Order. Although Bryant's (1994)
conclusion "to treat 2 + 5 in the same way as 5 + 2 is surely to demonstrate an
understanding that 5 + 2 and 2 + 5 are equivalent" (p. 19) is intuitively appealing,
it is not clearly supported by existing evidence. Unfortunately, Turner and

Bryant (cited in Bryant, 1994) did not distinguish between counting-all beginning with the first addend (CAF) and CAL procedures (i.e., CAL use was categorized as CAF use). (For 3 + 5, for example, CAF involves counting: "1, 2, 3; 4 [is one more], 5 [is two more], 6 [is three more], 7 [is four more], 8 [is five more]—the sum is eight.") Their scoring system made it especially likely that they overlooked children who disregarded addend order without understanding the commutativity principle (at the quantities or numerical level). CAL users are more likely than COL users to lack this principled understanding, if for no reason other than the former are typically younger and have less computational experience (opportunity to construct this understanding). Clearly, in the future, researchers need to carefully distinguish between children who disregard addend order (who use CAL as well as COL) and those who do not.

Moreover, Cowan and Renton's (1996) data do not provide clear evidence that children who invent CAL or COL also understand commutativity. Some participants, despite the tester's instructions, may have been successful on the latter task because they focused on the sameness of the addends, as opposed to the sameness of the sums (Baroody & Gannon, 1984). Indeed, participants could have been successful on the commutativity task if they simply focused on the colors of the boxes in which the collections were contained, as opposed to the number of items in the boxes. This strategy would have led to a correct response on all three types of trials: two commuted trials (e.g., a red box + a blue box for the tester and a blue box + a red box for a child), the single identity trial (e.g., a red box + a blue box for the tester and a red box + a blue box for the child), and the two nonequal trials (e.g., a red box + a blue box for the tester and a red box + a black box for the child).

More important, if commutativity is a *necessary condition* for the invention of CAL or COL, then the number of children who understand the principle but who do not use these strategies (critical concordant cases) should be significantly greater than the reverse (discordant cases). However, this was not the case.[2]

On the other hand, Cowan and Renton (1996) argued that evidence that some CAL or COL users do not understand commutativity (e.g., Baroody, 1987b; Baroody & Gannon, 1984) is questionable for three reasons. One is that such

---

[2] Concordant cases are those that are consistent with an order-of-acquisition hypothesis. For Cowan and Renton's (1996) hypothesis, this would include the following cells in a 2 x 2 table: Cell A (knows commutativity but does not use CAL or COL: Com+ & CL-), Cell B (Com+ & CL+), and Cell C (Com- & CL-). The critical concordant case is Cell A. This is because even a huge number of entries in Cells B and C would not help in disentangling the developmental relation between the variables. Discordant cases are inconsistent with an order-of-acquisition, which in this case would be Cell D (Com- & CL+).

Overall, Cowan and Renton (1996) reported more discordant cases (24) than critical concordant cases (17). More specifically, in Experiment 1, there were 11 discordant cases as compared with 2 critical concordant cases when a protoquantities-like commutativity task was used. This was statistically significant ($p < .02$, Test for Equality of Partially Overlapping Frequencies or McNemar chi-square) but in the opposite direction of Cowan and Renton's hypothesis. Using quantities-like and numbers-like commutativity tasks, the figures for discordant versus concordant cases were 4 versus 2 and 2 versus 2, respectively. These figures for Experiment 2 were 3 versus 5 and 4 versus 6, respectively. Cowan and Renton dismissed their discordant results as measurement error. This conclusion is equally, or even more, applicable to their concordant results.

results (like their own discordant results) might simply be due to a small sample size (i.e., measurement error). Although discordant cases (e.g., the case of Kate described earlier) are consistently found across studies (Baroody, 1982, 1987b, Baroody & Gannon, 1984; Cowan & Renton, 1996; S. M. Thomas, personal communication, March 10, 1997) and suggest confusion, a need to count, or an inaccurate knowledge about the noneffect of addend order, measurement error cannot be discounted. Clearly, the developmental relation between commutativity and strategies that disregard addend needs to be investigated with a relatively large sample.

A second reason is that Baroody (1987a; Baroody & Gannon, 1984) may have underestimated children's conceptual competence by requiring them to respond quickly on the commutativity task (to ensure answers were the product of principled reasoning, not computing).[3] Although this is a genuine concern, interviews with children, such as the case of Kate described earlier, suggest that

---

[3] Cowan and Renton (1996) argued that imposing a time limit to prevent children from calculating sums on a commutativity task may underestimate competence for five reason. "[a] How long children take to retrieve and apply the commutativity principle is unknown. [b] Others who did count to work out the answer may nevertheless have known about commutativity: They may have thought that not calculating was cheating (Baroody, Ginsburg, & Waxman, 1983). . . . [c] They may be 'perfectionists' " (pp. 4–5). On the symbolic sum-comparison task, [d] children may miscompute the sum of the first combination and not have confidence in their answer, or [e] analogous to findings with conservation or counting tasks, they might interpret a tester's repetition of the original answer and request to answer a commuted combination as a challenge to their original answer.

In regard to Point a, although the process of retrieving and applying the commutativity principle undoubtedly becomes more automatic over time, it seems reasonable to expect that even young children will be able to complete this process within 4 sec (the time limit used by Baroody & Gannon, 1984). Moreover, on one of Baroody and Gannon's (1984) tasks, participants did not have to determine sums but simply judge whether two expressions had the same sum. The rates of success on this task and the one that required computation were identical.

In regard to Point b, Baroody et al. (1983) found that several children continued to use relational knowledge to short-cut computational efforts, despite their professions it was cheating. In regard to Point c, some of Baroody and Gannon's (1984) participants responded, "I don't know." It would seem that perfectionists would prefer to say, "I need to think" or "I have to figure it out," rather than admit ignorance. In regard to Point d, none of Baroody or Gannon's (1984) or Baroody's (1987b) participants who invented a strategy that disregarded addend order but failed the symbolic sum-comparison commutativity task miscomputed the initial sum. Point e is not relevant because children are not being asked to answer again the same combination. Instead, they are responding to a new and ostensibly different combination. Besides, if Point e were true, then performance on identity trials should have been impaired but was not.

Even though there is no direct evidence to support them, Cowan and Renton's (1996) first four points, at least, are legitimate concerns. However, it is not clear they are reason enough to abandon a time limit. If children are given an unlimited amount of time to decide whether two commuted combinations are equal, there is the very real danger they will mentally or surreptitiously compute the sums rather than use relational knowledge to arrive at a reasoned conclusion. In brief, the lack of a time limit is very likely to *overestimate* conceptual competence, particularly if single-digit combinations are used.

at least a few children who invent CAL or COL do not seem to recognize commutativity (at least at an explicit level).

A third reason is that the commutativity tasks used by Baroody (1987a; Baroody & Gannon, 1984) were symbolic or abstract in nature and, thus, may have underestimated a more concrete understanding of commutativity—understanding at the protoquantities or quantities level (cf. Cowan & Renton, 1996; Ganetsou & Cowan, 1995; Sophian et al., 1995). However, Baroody's participants probably did not fail a commutativity task because it was too abstract. In the Baroody and Gannon (1984) study, both the commutativity and the addition-strategy tasks were symbolic. Yet, although a number of participants responded unsuccessfully to the former, they responded appropriately and intelligently to the latter (e.g., spontaneously inventing more sophisticated informal addition strategies).

Consider, for example, the cases of Case and Meg (Baroody & Gannon, 1984). On the addition-strategy task, Case invented a CAL strategy during Session 2, and Meg switched from relying on CAF in Session 1 to COL in Session 2. Both children were not successful on commutativity tasks administered in Sessions 1 and 2. In a follow-up interview, Meg was asked if 4 + 6 would have the same or different answer as 6 + 4. She thought for about 60 sec, appeared to compute the sum, and finally responded correctly.

In the Baroody (1987b) study, children were not tested on symbolic commutativity task until after they had invented a computational strategy that disregarded addend order in response to a symbolic addition-strategy task. In brief, it is unlikely that children could meaningfully interpret the symbolic expressions in the addition-strategy task and spontaneously invent computational shortcuts but fail to understand similar symbolic expressions in a commutativity task.[4] The issue of the relative difficulty of symbolic commutativity tasks is addressed further in the next section.

TASK EFFECTS

Theory

According to Resnick's (1992) model, knowledge of commutativity evolves from a relatively concrete version to a relatively abstract one. It follows from her model that children will first be successful on commutativity tasks that tap protoquantitive reasoning. Later, they should be successful on tasks that involve quantitative reasoning. Even later, children should be successful on tasks that entail numerical reasoning. They should be successful last on commutativity tasks that require operational-level reasoning. A key implication is that the

---

[4] Three other reasons why Baroody and Gannon's (1984) symbolic format was probably not unfamiliar to their participants and the cause of difficulty on the commutativity task are: (a) During a familiarization session, children were introduced to the written format by playing an addition game. This included relating symbolic addition expressions to a change-add-to meaning. (b) Children were first tested on an addition task in which the symbolism was further linked to a verbal explanation. (c) On Commutativity Task 1, children overwhelmingly responded correctly to identical pairs and combinations with different sums—something that is not likely if they did not understand the symbols.

symbolic task used in earlier research (e.g., Baroody & Gannon, 1984) under-estimated children's understanding of commutativity at least at the protoquanti-ties or quantities level.

Evidence

Although Resnick (1992) did not offer evidence on the hypothesis that children are more successful on concrete versions of commutativity tasks than on abstract versions, three recent studies provide relevant data on this issue.

Cowan and Renton (1996; Experiment 1) compared "abstract" (protoquanti-ties), "concrete" (quantities), and "symbolic" (numerical) commutativity tasks. Their protoquantities task was based on Langford's (1981) qualitative-reasoning task. Children were asked, for example, if a blue box and a yellow box had the same number of pins as a yellow box and a blue box. Unlike Langford's task, children were told beforehand that the pins in the blue boxes were equal and those in the yellow boxes were equal. Although this task was used to gauge gen-eral understanding of commutativity, it does entail the qualitative reasoning characteristics of protoquantitative thinking. Cowan and Renton's quantities task was similar to their protoquantities task, except objects were counted out into the boxes in front of a participant and a number card representing the amount in the box was placed next to the box. Their numerical task used symbolic expressions. In Experiment 1 with forty-eight 6- to 9-year-olds, Cowan and Renton found that 38, 44, and 46 children were successful on the protoquantities, quantities, and numerical tasks, respectively.[5] In Experiment 2 with twenty-four 5-year-olds, participants were equally successful on the protoquantities and quantities tasks. Specifically, 8 were successful on both tasks, 5 were successful on the proto-quantities task but not the quantities task, and 5 were successful on the latter but not the former task.

Sophian et al. (1995) tested 3- to 5-year-olds on covered and uncovered commutativity tasks. The covered task involved determining, for example, whether a small box of objects and three objects was the same as three objects and a small box of objects. White tissue paper covered the objects in the box, and it was established beforehand that the same-sized boxes had the same number of objects. This task was intended to gauge thinking at the protoquantities level. The uncovered task was identical to the covered task, except children could see the objects in the box. This task gauged thinking at the quantities level. Sophian et al. found that their participants did equally well on the covered (proto-quantities) and uncovered (quantities) tasks.

Bermejo and Rodriguez (1993) tested three class levels of children (5- to 6-year-olds, 6- to 7-year-olds, and 7- to 8-year-olds) using quantities-level and numerical-level commutativity tasks. Their circles-and-numbers task (e.g., com-paring the combination pairs oooo + 18 and 18 + oooo) could be considered a quantities-level task, because one addend was represented concretely with circles and children were allowed to count the circles. Three symbolic (numerical-level)

---

[5] The figures reported are corrections provided by R. Cowan (personal communica-tion, January 6, 2000) for those reported by Cowan and Renton (1996): 37, 45, and 36, respectively.

tasks were administered: number combinations involving 1 (e.g., 1 + 16 and 16 + 1), number combinations up to 10 (e.g., 3 + 6 and 6 + 3), and number combinations greater than 10 (e.g., 8 + 11 and 11 + 8). Bermejo and Rodriguez reported a significant main effect for task but no significant differences for the pair-wise post-hoc tests between tasks.[6]

Analysis

Currently, three studies have failed to find the task effect suggested by Resnick's (1992) model. However, all three studies were methodologically flawed in that there was no time limit to deter covert computation on the quantities or numerical commutativity tasks. Indeed, in the Sophian et al. (1995) and Bermejo and Rodriguez (1993) studies, participants were allowed to count overtly on these tasks. As a result, knowledge of commutativity on these types of tasks may have been overestimated. Clearly, further research that eliminates the confounding effects of computation is needed to test for task effects.

THE EFFECT OF ADDEND SIZE

Theory

The ability to solve problems regardless of number size is taken as evidence that a child understands a general principle (see, e.g., Fuson, Pergament, Lyons, & Hall, 1985; Gelman, 1982). Resnick (1992) argued that an understanding of additive commutativity is initially context-bound and tied to number size. Only with the advent of Level 4 thinking (the operator level) does an understanding of this relation achieve the status of a general principle.

Evidence

On the one hand, Ginsburg (1977) cited anecdotal evidence of several primary-school children who seemed to understand the commutativity principle with very small combinations, such as 3 + 2 and 2 + 3, but not with somewhat

---

[6] Three methodological problems cloud the results of Bermejo and Rodriguez (1993). (a) The presence of a concrete collection may have aided computational efforts on the circles + numbers task for younger participants. This could help account for why these children performed slightly better on the circles + numbers task than on the task with number combinations involving one. (Although performance on the circles + numbers tasks was marginally better than that on the other two symbolic tasks, it was not enough to register a statistically significant difference on either the post-hoc tests for task effects or interaction effects.) (b) Because the group x task interaction effects were done in a pair-wise fashion (comparing two of the three groups on two of the four tasks), there were 18 pair-wise comparisons. Unfortunately, the Newman–Keuls, the post-hoc test that was used, does not adjust the significance level to take into account multiple tests and, thus, provides a relatively liberal estimate of significance. In brief, the two statistically significant results may have been due to chance alone. (c) The tasks were administered in eight different orders, yet order effects were not checked before collapsing the data across different order presentations.

larger ones, such as 3 + 9 and 9 + 3 (cf. Holt, 1964). On the other hand, Baroody (1982) described the longitudinal case study of a 5-year-old who began using the relation as a computational shortcut with a range of combinations, including larger single-digit ones such as 3 + 9 and 9 + 3. Comparing combinations with sums less than 10 with those with sums of 10 to 20, Baroody (1987c) found that the size of the addends had practically no effect on the performance of children with mental retardation.

Wright (cited in Nunes & Bryant, 1996) presented 5- to 8-year-olds with addition word problems and three types of written expressions: one that faithfully represented the order of the addends in a problem ($a + b$), another with the addends in reverse order ($b + a$), and yet another that was not an accurate representation of the problem (e.g., $a - b$). Participants were asked to play teacher and indicate which expressions were correct and which were wrong. Presumably, children who understood the principle of additive commutativity would indicate that the $a + b$ and $b + a$ expressions were correct and that the $a - b$ expression was incorrect. Wright varied addend size. Small-addend trials included single-digit numbers with sums to 15; large-addend trials included two-digit numbers with sums of at least 50. Performance across addend size did not differ significantly.

Tiilikainen et al. (1997) examined the performance of 24 kindergartners and 24 first graders on commutativity tasks involving addends of three sizes: single digits (3 to 9), teens (13 to 19), and two digits (26 to 59). Although qualitative analysis indicated addend size affected a few children, like the Wright (cited in Nunes & Bryant, 1996) study described in the previous paragraph, there were no statistically significant size effects.

Analysis

Overall, commutativity appears to be understood as a general principle, applicable across a range of problems. Moreover, Baroody's (1982) longitudinal case study evidence suggests that children quickly generalize the relation once it is discovered.

Ginsburg's (1977) discrepant results may be due to the fact that his primary-level children could surreptitiously compute the sums of smaller combinations but not the sums of larger combinations. It is also possible that, when confronted with the larger combinations, his participants did not apply knowledge of commutativity because, for instance, they did not recognize that the commuted pairs shared the same addend. Alternatively, children may cognitively melt down (e.g., guess wildly, become inattentive) when presented with a task involving large, unfamiliar numbers (cf. Dowker, chap. 9, this volume).

Clearly, though, the evidence for a general understanding of the principle is thin. For example, size effects might become evident with a larger sample than used by Wright (cited in Nunes & Bryant, 1996) or Tiilikainen et al. (1997) or with different tasks than were used in these studies. To date, the effects of addend size have been studied at only the numerical level. Might a size effect be more pronounced when children first extend their understanding of commutativity to the quantities level? Will children at this level generalize the concept as quickly as a few seem to have done at the numerical level? Because the concept may be quickly generalized, cross-sectional studies, even those with a relatively large sample, may not be adequate to detect size effects. What may be needed to address this issue is relatively large-scale microgenetic studies. That is, careful and intensive case studies of a number of children over time may be necessary to document transitions in the development of additive commutativity and gauge whether their understanding, at the moment the principle is first recognized at a particular level, is localized or general.

Furthermore, Resnick's (1983) conjecture that commutativity may first be discovered with $n + 1$ and $1 + n$ combinations needs to be evaluated. Are children, in fact, more prone to discover commutativity with such combinations, and does this relational knowledge generalize immediately or remain localized? Addressing these issues will be difficult because mental or surreptitious computing can more easily confound results with $n + 1$ and $1 + n$ combinations. Perhaps one way around this problem is to use a quasi-qualitative-reasoning task (e.g., where a child is asked if a *many + 1 total* is the same as a *1 + many total*, where it has been established that many = many).

Part III:
Tentative Synthesis

Despite the lack of compelling evidence for a developmental link between additive commutativity and general additive composition, task effects, and addend-size effects, Resnick's (1992) four levels of mathematical thinking make sense. These levels of *what* children represent parallel, for example, the stages of humankind's number-concept development suggested by linguistic analysis (e.g., Dantzig, 1930/1954). They are also consistent with the view that early childhood is marked by qualitative changes in the *way* number can be represented (e.g., Huttenlocher, Jordan, & Levine, 1994; Piaget, 1965; see, e.g., Baroody, 2000; Mix, Huttenlocher, & Levine, 2002, for reviews). Summarized in Table 4.2 is our effort to integrate and extend these two perspectives. More specifically, our "integrated view" combines Resnick's levels of concrete to abstract mathematical thinking (column 2 in the table) with Huttenlocher et al.'s (1994) mental models view (column 1 in the table).

Infant habituation experiments (e.g., Starkey & Cooper, 1980) and toddler transformation studies (e.g., Starkey, 1992; Wynn, 1992) appear to demonstrate that preverbal children can accurately represent collections of up to three or four items and to reason about changes to them. (The latter includes recognizing that adding one item to another should result in two items, not one or three items, and that taking away one item from two should result in one item, or even that taking away three items from four should also result in one). For a detailed review of this literature, see Ginsburg et al. (1998) and Wynn (1998).

However, citing methodological difficulties or alternative explanations, some scholars now suggest that the number and arithmetic competence of preverbal children may have been overestimated (for detailed discussions, see Baroody, 2000; Huttenlocher et al., 1994, Jordan, Hanich, & Uberti, chap. 13, this volume; Mix et al., 2002; Sophian, 1998). Some recent evidence indicates that children's initial representation of number is probably nonverbal, may be based on perceptual cues such as contour length (or a perceptional mechanism, such as an object-file), and—regardless of mechanism—may well be inexact. This pre-Transition 1

Table 4.2: An Integration of Two Models of Mathematical Development

Unlike Resnick's (1992) model, the integrated view (IV) accounts for Transition 1 of the mental models view. As a result, unlike Resnick's model, the IV includes five logically plausible sublevels for protoquantitative thinking: Levels 0, 1, 1A, 1B, and 1C (the highlighted portion of column 2. These levels may extend beyond Transitions 1, 2, or even 3.) Unlike Resnick's model, the IV also accounts for Transition 3 and, thus, the possibility that Levels 3 or 4 reasoning could occur before or after children learn a written representation. Furthermore, the relations among Resnick's four levels may not be entirely linear. For example, the development of Level 3 thinking in one domain may prompt lower level thinking within a phase. Unlike the mental models view, the IV accounts for levels of thinking within a phase. For example, between Transitions 2 and 3, there may be as many as four levels (Levels 1C, 2, 3, and 4). Moreover, unlike the mental models view, the IV includes content knowledge such as that highlighted in column 3. Finally, the IV, unlike Resnick's model or the mental models view, includes an explicit distinction between *nonverbal subitizing* (the rapid apprehension of number without counting) and *verbal subitizing* (rapid number apprehension associated with a number word).

Component 1—Mental Models View (Huttenlocher et al., 1994): Changes in the forms of representations (ways concepts are represented)	Component 2—Based Partly on Resnick's (1992) Development of Mathematical Thinking Model: Changes in the representational content (kinds of conceptual entities)	Examples From Children's Understanding of Number Suggested by the Integrated Model
Pre-Transition 1	Level 0: protoquantitative thinking involving qualitative reasoning about nonquantified entities	Objects can be identified and grouped (classified) by physical properties such as color.
	Level 1: protoquantitative thinking involving qualitative reasoning about inexact, nonverbally represented (uncounted but perceptually estimated) quantities	Collections of objects can be classified/identified by relative size such as their approximate area or total perimeter (contour length).
Transition 1: inexact (estimated) nonverbal representation → exact nonverbal-based representation	Level 1A: first transitional subphase to quantitative thinking involving qualitative reasoning about exact nonverbally subitized and represented quantities	The nonverbally subitized collection ••• is more than the nonverbally subitized collection ••. May start to learn number words but not their meaning.
	Level 1B: second transitional subphase to quantitative thinking involving qualitative reasoning about exact nonverbally subitized, and represented quantities (tied only loosely to number words)	The nonverbally subitized collection ••• is *one more than* the nonverbally subitized collection ••. May recognize that numbers can be used to characterize/identify collections but still fuzzy about what, for example, "two" or "three" means.
Transition 2: exact nonverbal representation → exact, verbal-based representation	Level 1C: third transitional subphase to Level 2 thinking involving quantitative reasoning about exact verbally subitized and represented quantities tied to number labels	The verbally subitized collection ••• or "three" is one more than the verbally subitized collection •• or "two." Clarifies the meaning of "two" (and perhaps somewhat later, "three") and so can consistently apply a number term discriminately.
	Level 2: (counting-based) quantitative reasoning about verbally subitized or counted collections (reasoning about numbers tied to a specific context)	The counted collection ••• is more than the counted collection •• ("one, two, three; ...—three"). is one more than ("one, two,—two").
	Level 3: numerical reasoning (reasoning about numbers in the abstract)	*Three is more than two* because it comes after *two* when counting.
	Level 4: abstract reasoning (generalizing about numerical relations)	"The later a number comes in the counting sequence, the larger the quantity it represents."
Transition 3: exact verbal representation → exact written representation	Level 3: numerical reasoning; Level 4: abstract reasoning	

phase (first row below the headings of Table 4.2) is consistent with Piaget's (e.g., 1965; Piaget & Inhelder, 1969) view of number development. He, likewise, concluded that children's earliest understanding of number was nonverbal, tied to perceptual cues or actions, and imprecise. That is, Piaget (1965) argued that number development begins before children acquire language or other conventional knowledge, stems from perceptual or physical actions or reflections on actions, and, thus, at first, is essentially an estimation process. Even the use of an inexact representation of number can provide the conceptual basis for the emergence of Transition 1 (second row of Table 4.2): Posttoddlers' more exact number and arithmetic competencies.

A pre-Transition 1 phase is also consistent with Resnick's (1992) view that mathematical thinking begins with *protoquantitive reasoning*: qualitative reasoning about amounts of physical materials before the development of verbal counting (Level 1 in Table 4.2). At this level, "comparisons of amounts are made and inferences can be drawn about the effects of various changes . . . on amounts; but no *numerical* [italics added] quantification is involved" (p. 403). Exact numerical representations and reasoning (Transition 1) may not develop until between 2 and 3.5 years of age, when children become capable of symbolic representation generally (e.g., Huttenlocher et al., 1994; Mix, 1999). Another important advance in the way children represent number is tied to the development of counting (Transition 2, the third row in Table 4.2), a transition that could serve as the basis for Resnick's quantitative level of first number and then arithmetic development.

There may, in fact, be up to five phases of development (Levels 0, 1, 1A, 1B, and 1C in Table 4.2) before children engage in quantitative thinking about counted collections (Resnick's Level 2), not a single phase (Level 1) as proposed by Resnick (1992). Two of these five phases might exist before Transition 1—a transition Resnick did not explicitly address. Level 0 might involve pure qualitative reasoning (e.g., recognizing that nonquantified wholes can consist of parts). Level 1 might involve qualitative reasoning about inexactly estimated quantities (e.g., that a whole is more than its parts). Two of the five phases might exist after Transition 1 but before Transition 2. Level 1A might involve qualitative reasoning about exact but nonverbally represented quantities (e.g., the parts •• and • together make some larger whole). Level 1B might involve quantitative reasoning about exact but nonverbally represented quantities (e.g., the parts •• and • together make the larger whole •••). The fifth level, Level 1C, may mark the beginning of Transition 2. At this level, children associate number words with subitized quantities (the part •• or "*two*" and the part • or "*one*" together make the larger whole ••• or "*three*"). Transition 2 or the development of written representational competencies (Transition 3, the fourth row in Table 4.2) may provide the basis for numerical or abstract reasoning for number and operations (Baroody, 2000).[7]

---

[7] Irwin (1996) did find evidence that suggests children understood key aspects of a part-whole concept in an uncounted-quantities context (at a protoquantities level) before doing so in a counted-quantities context (at a quantities level). Her participants were even less successful in a context involving verbally stated numbers (at a numerical level). Three problems with Irwin's methodology, however, render her results inconclusive. First, it is not clear that she really measured part-whole understanding at Resnick's (1992) protoquantities level. For example, 4-year-old participants compared an experimenter's three-

Nevertheless, Resnick's (1992) account of the development of additive commutativity seems to be inaccurate about (a) the generality and coherence of the part-whole schema and (b) the completeness of children's early addition concept. In this part, we discuss each of these problems, propose modifications to Resnick's account, and describe how existing data are consistent with our modified account.

GENERALITY AND COHERENCE OF THE PART-WHOLE SCHEMA

Theory

Problem with Resnick's Account. One possible problem with Resnick's (1992) account of commutativity development is that it seems to be inconsistent about the generality and coherence of children's addition knowledge. On the one hand, she seems to assume that much of a child's experience with quantitative situations is represented and governed by a single part-whole schema based on Piaget's (1965) notion of additive composition, which includes such principles as $Part_1 + Part_2 = $ Whole and $Part_1 + Part_2 = Part_2 + Part_1$. She speaks of "the permissions and constraints on number operations that *the* [italics added] additive composition principle embodies" (Resnick, 1992, p. 375). Resnick concluded that invented counting-based and mental-arithmetic procedures are both principle driven—derived from "this simple and primitive permission based on the composite nature of numbers" (p. 377). Thus, in some key respects, part-whole knowledge, even at the protoquantities level, is represented by what

---

item collection with their own three-item collection, which was then subdivided into parts of two and one items. These collections could easily have been nonverbally subitized, verbally subitized, or subvocally or surreptitiously counted. In other words, children could easily have been using any of several exact-number processes (Level 1B, Level 2, or higher in Table 4.2), instead of an inexact process that characterizes Resnick's protoquantitive level (Level 1 in Table 4.2). Second, it is not clear whether she was actually measuring part-whole knowledge or something else with the so-called protoquantities task. Her participants could have been responding correctly to the covariation trials simply by noticing that an item was added or taken away rather than considering the effects on the child's whole relative to the tester's (cf. Brush, 1978). In effect, the children might have been interpreting the task in terms of a change-add-to view of addition, not in terms of part-whole view. Third, the protoquantities-level task was different from the quantities- and numbers-level tasks in several key respects. With the first task, a child could readily see (by nonverbal or verbal subitizing or by subvocal counting) that a collection of items was split evenly between the tester and himself or herself. With the quantities-level task, for example, the child was asked to give the tester a specified number of items, which the latter then hid in one hand. The tester next placed an unspecified number of items in the other hand, which was then operated on in various ways. The participant could, then, not be sure that the collections in the two hands, were, in fact, equal and may not have been thinking in terms of a specific number of items. Furthermore, unlike the so-called protoquantities task, children did not see both parts in the quantities task. In brief, the three tasks varied in ways other than Resnick's (1992) conceptual level.

Anderson (1984) calls a *strong schema*, a relatively broad and logically coherent generalization (see Table 4.3). Children's behavior and predictions are principle driven, if only implicitly or nonconsciously.

On the other hand, Resnick (1992) clearly implied, for instance, that an understanding of commutativity is initially context-bound and becomes increasingly less so with development. Moreover, this understanding at the quantities and numerical levels is tied to number size. "I would hypothesize that a child might accept commutativity for some number pairs (probably the lower ones on which s/he would presumably have had more computational practice) than others (probably the higher ones)" (L. B. Resnick, personal communication, February 21, 1997). Thus, in other respects, Resnick's description of a part-whole schema resembles what Anderson (1984) called a *weak schema*—a generalization narrow in scope (tied to a particular context) and, perhaps, lacking logical coherence (again see Table 4.3). In this sense, behavior and predictions are based on precedent and predictions are individually looked up rather than logically inferred from general principles. In brief, it is not clear how the part-whole schema that embodies additive composition can, in its early stages, be characterized as both a weak and a strong schema.

Table 4.3: Continuum From Weak to Strong Schemas

Weak Schemas	Relatively Weak Schemas	Relatively Strong Schemas	Strong Schemas
Entail generalizations local in scope			Entail generalizations broad in scope
Low standards of internal (logical) consistency			High standards of internal (logical) consistency
Comprehension is precedent driven			Comprehension is principle driven
No logical basis for a priori reasoning; predictions are looked up			Principled (logical) basis for a priori reasoning; predictions are derived
Informal thinking is intuitive, infra-logical, and implicit	Informal thinking is principled but still unsystematic	Informal thinking is principled and systematic	Formal thinking using explicitly defined principles

Proposed Modification. The apparent inconsistency in Resnick's (1992) model can be reconciled by proposing the following three assumptions: (a) Children at the protoquantitative level of addition understand various part-whole relations gleaned from their everyday preschool experiences. (b) Their initial addition schema might better be characterized as a weak schema. (c) A relatively strong addition schema that coherently embodies all of the principles of additive composition evolves slowly in spurts and can be aided by computational experience.

Children at the protoquantities or even the quantities level of addition may not have a clear idea of the effects of order a priori for three reasons. One is that early development is marked by localized knowledge (e.g., Mix et al., 2002). A second is that, even if young children drew on knowledge gleaned from nonquantitative situations (Level 0 in Table 4.2), it would provide an inconsistent basis for drawing conclusions about the noneffects of order. A third reason is that quantity-related experiences at both the protoquantitative and quantitative levels of number provide inconsistent experiences on the relevance or effect of order.

1. *Localized competence.* Early in development, children's knowledge in one domain is likely to be separate from that of other domains (e.g., diSessa, 1983; Mix et al., 2002). The localized knowledge in nonquantitative domains, then, may well be unconnected or, at best, only loosely connected to that in quantitative domains. Thus, inferences about the effects of order in the former may have little or no impact on the structures (weak schemas) underlying the latter.

2. *Inconsistent experiences in nonquantitative domains.* Although children undoubtedly learn from everyday experiences that materials can come apart and that the parts can be reassembled in any order, they also encounter many nonquantitative situations where the parts cannot be recombined in any order to constitute the original whole. Composing, decomposing, and recomposing a Mr. Potato Head, for instance, can produce clearly different outcomes, as when a child exchanges the position of an ear and the eyes. Or if children remove the hub and wheel from the axle of a toy vehicle, they will quickly discover that replacing the hub first is not practical. Or if children remove the arms of a doll and switch the arms when they replace them, the repaired doll will be visibly different from the original doll. A particularly important example of constrained order in everyday life is language. Children early on recognize, at least implicitly, that the sum of the parts composing a sentence is not impervious to order. For example, "The dog ate my meal" has a profoundly different meaning from "My meal ate the dog." One last particularly relevant example is the counting sequence.[8]

---

[8] Nonquantitative part-whole relations may differ from that embodying additive composition in other ways. In some cases, an object can be disassembled and reassembled but the sum of the parts no longer equals the whole. For example, children who break their mother's prized vase are in trouble because, even if all the pieces of the vase are found and glued back together, its appearance and value will never be the same. In yet other situations, once parts are assembled into a whole, they cannot be disassembled. For example, the eggs, flour, sugar, salt, butter, vanilla, milk, and baking powder that form the ingredients of sugar cookies cannot be extracted from the batter or the cooked cookie.

3. *Inconsistent experiences in quantitative domains.* Even among the quantitative (number) schemas that are the basis for addition schemas, order sometimes matters and other times is irrelevant. In yet other situations, order may be a nonissue, one that may not be incorporated into a number schema. In regard to the last point, consider nonverbal subitizing, which would correspond to number development Level 1B in Table 4.2. This process, if accomplished in a single eye fixation, might not involve ordering even at an implicit level. In such cases, pre-2-year-olds might not have the opportunity to recognize that differently ordered processing results in the same outcome.

Even if more than a single fixation is required for nonverbal subitizing, there is no guarantee that the perceptual-processing mechanism will result in a discovery of the order-irrelevance principle that would be stored as part of the cognitive structure for number. For instance, the perceptual-processing mechanism might entail examining a row of three items in a left-to-right direction at one time and a right-to-left direction a second time and record the outcome but not the process. Thus, a child might be able to use nonverbal subitizing to succeed on an equivalence task involving small numbers but not recognize that order is irrelevant in determining numerosity.

Even if the nonverbal numbering processes did lead to discovery of the order-irrelevance principle, there is no guarantee that children would immediately recognize its applicability to the moderately new (somewhat different) task of addition (e.g., the nonverbal addition task used by Huttenlocker et al., 1994). Note that this point and the previous two points regarding nonverbal subitizing also apply to verbal subitizing, which would appear at Level 1C in Table 4.2. (Unlike nonverbal subitizing, verbal subitizing depends on conventional knowledge of number words, such as when a child recognizes ••• or •̇ • as "three" and states so.)

The issue of order might be particularly confusing to children at the quantitative level of number. Learning the counting sequence, for instance, requires learning terms in a particular order. If a parent places blocks named "one," "two," "three" in a sequential order (the whole) and a child playfully rearranges the numbers (the parts) to create a nonstandard sequence, the reaction of the parent may imply that the order of numbers (the parts) clearly matters.

In other quantitative situations, such as counting a collection, the order in which items are counted is irrelevant to determining its cardinal value (as long as the one-to-one principle is not violated). However, even in object-counting situations, particularly while children are mastering the enumeration process, order may not be irrelevant to determining a successful outcome. That is, in an effort to keep track, children may fixate on counting collections in a particular order or be explicitly instructed to do so.

Even if they do not impose such an order on their object-counting activities, children may not recognize, at least explicitly that order is irrelevant to the enumeration of collections. Indeed, research has shown that the order-irrelevance principle (at the level of verbal counting) does not appear to be explicitly understood until relatively late, 4 to 5.5 years of age (e.g., Baroody, 1984b, 1993; Cowan, Dowker, Christakis, & Bailey, 1996). Given young children's uncertain thinking about the effects of order on the outcome of enumeration efforts, it should not be surprising they do not have a clear understanding of the effects of addend order on the outcome of their addition efforts.

Thus, one task confronting children as they construct addition schemas at the protoquantities level and beyond is determining which part-whole relations (including the effects of order) are applicable to addition. Put differently, they must construct addition schemas that embody the part-whole relations governed by the rules of additive composition. Reflecting on computational experiences may enable children to link quantities-level addition schemas to an order-indifferent number or addition schema constructed earlier at the protoquantities level or, perhaps, to construct an order-indifferent addition schema for the first time (cf. Cowan, chap. 2, this volume).

Another task confronting children may be expanding and systematically defining the rules of additive composition. For example, from their everyday experiences, some children may not recognize that a whole can be constituted with different parts and, as a result, may assume that expressions such as 6 + 4 and 9 + 1 have different sums. Computational experience may help these children discover that there are many names for a number (Baroody, with Coslick, 1998).

Computational experiences may also be necessary for children to construct the more complex properties of additive composition, such as a deep understanding of the complementary relation between addition and subtraction. Resnick (1992) conjectured that if children at the protoquantities level recognize that $P_1 + P_2 = W$, then they should also see that $W - P_1 = P_2$ and $W - P_2 = P_1$. This implies that children at this level recognize the logical necessity that taking one part from a whole results in the second part and vice versa and that $W - P_1 = P_2$ and $W - P_2 = P_1$ are related events. However, although young children seem to have both an increase and a decrease schema and have some sense that they counteract each other (e.g., Bisanz & LeFevre, 1990), a relatively precise and logically coherent understanding of these relations may depend on experience with exact and verbally numbered quantities. In other words, children may not recognize that taking one part from a whole necessarily results in the second part and vice versa (that $W - P_1 = P_2$ and $W - P_2 = P_1$ are related events) until they can, for instance, relate 5 – 3 = ? to 3 + ? = 5 and 5 – 2 = ? to 2 + ? = 5 and see that the Parts 2 and 3 can be combined in any order to make the whole five (3 + 2 or 2 + 3 = 5), that removing one part of a whole leaves the other (e.g., 5 – 3 = 2 and 5 – 2 = 3), and that 5 – 3 and 5 – 2, therefore, are related. In brief, the qualitative experiences and reasoning composing the protoquantities level may not be sufficient to construct all the logical relations that compose additive composition. Some may need to be built up from the quantitative experiences and reasoning characteristic of the quantities level or later levels.

Evidence

The modified account is consistent with four findings discussed earlier in the first two parts of this chapter. First, it helps explain why computational experience is associated with commutativity performance beyond the protoquantities level (Baroody, 1987a, 1987c; Baroody et al., 1982; Baroody & Gannon, 1984). Children who are uncertain about the effects of addend order may be particularly impressed by the result of their computational experiences. Once a clear-cut precedent has been established, they can use it to reason conclusively about other untested situations (see, e.g., the case of Kate described earlier).

Second, the modified account is consistent with Sophian's findings that most 4-year-olds understand additive commutativity (Sophian et al., 1995) but not part-whole relations (Sophian & McCorgray, 1994).[9] Because quantity-level schemas are relatively weak and, thus, still local in scope and disconnected, it makes sense that children's early knowledge is compartmentalized, not broad.

---

[9] Positing multiple part-whole schemas that are initially only loosely connected also explains otherwise inconsistent data about children's early subtraction knowledge. A prevalent view is that the construction of a part-whole concept (an understanding that the whole is the sum of its parts) underlies the complement principle (e.g., Briars & Larkin, 1984; Resnick, 1983, 1992; Riley, Greeno, & Heller, 1983). For example, for children to recognize that $8 - 5 = ?$ can be thought of as $5 + ? = 8$, they must understand—at least implicitly—that 8 is a whole that can be decomposed into two parts, one of which is 5 (Resnick, 1992). According to Sophian and McCorgray (1994), however, 5- and 6-year-olds (but not 4-year-olds) can accurately predict the relative size of a starting amount (the whole) in missing-start take-away problems (e.g., a missing starting amount must be larger than what is taken away) and, thus, already understand part-whole relations.

Why then, as research (e.g., Baroody, 1999; Baroody et al., 1982; Baroody et al., 1983) shows, is the complement relation not apparent to or used by many kindergarten and first-grade children? One possibility is that previously used complement tasks were symbolic and, thus, did not connect with children's intuitive understanding of part-whole relations. Consider, though, that the preliminary tasks in the Baroody (1999) study served to connect symbolic representations of subtraction to the participants' intuitive knowledge of subtraction and presumably their underlying knowledge of this operation (part-whole relations). Consider also that the complement task involved explicitly relating symbolic subtraction expressions to their intuitive take-away meaning of subtraction.

An alternative and more plausible explanation is that young children's intuitive understanding of subtraction and part-whole relations are only loosely connected (Baroody, 1999). That is, intuitively understanding that the starting amount of a take-away situation must be larger than either the amount taken away or the resulting amount is important relational knowledge but not necessarily tantamount to a deep understanding of part-whole relations—that a starting amount such as eight can be decomposed into two parts: five (the amount taken away) and three (the difference). Put differently, children's intuitive view of subtraction as take away may only gradually be connected to a more formal part-whole view of the operation, one that is related to addition.

How might children explicitly or implicitly recognize the connection between their intuitive knowledge of subtraction and part-whole relations? The results of Baroody et al. (1983) suggest one possible mechanism. These researchers found that use of the complement principle to short-cut efforts to determine differences was associated with the relative efficiency of determining the sum of related addition combinations. More specifically, if children used advanced addition strategies such as reasoning strategies or recall, they were more likely to use the complement relation than if they used counting strategies to determine sums. Baroody et al. hypothesized that laborious calculation may so occupy working memory that there is insufficient attention to detect relations between addition and subtraction combinations. This might account for the inconsistent recognition of the complement principle's usefulness in both the Baroody et al. and the Baroody (1999) studies. Specifically, children may have recognized that the applicability of addition knowledge with $6 - 3$ and $8 - 4$, but not other subtraction combinations, because they typically memorize the related addition doubles $3 + 3 = 6$ and $4 + 4 = 8$ before other combinations.

Third, the modified account explains why a significant size effect is typically not found (Baroody, 1982, 1987c; Tillikainen et al., 1997). Computational experience with small numbers may help to transform a relatively weak and fluid addition schema into a relatively strong and stable one in fairly short order. That is, an implicit and uncertain understanding of the effects of addend order is replaced with an explicit and clear-cut understanding that addition is order indifferent. Children can then use this principled knowledge to reason a priori about the effects of addend order involving even large and relatively unfamiliar expressions. The fact that they already (intuitively) recognize that some part-whole situations are order indifferent may further hasten this process.

Fourth, the modified account also helps explain the logically inconsistent behavior Baroody and Gannon (1984) called protocommutativity: why some children invent computational strategies that disregard addend order but are unsuccessful on commutativity tasks (see also Baroody, 1982, 1987b). Protocommutativity may arise because children's early and relatively weak schema of addition does not explicitly prohibit switching addend order. However, when asked to make a prediction about the effects of switching addend order, children with little computational experience do not have a precedent that clearly indicates that addend order is irrelevant. As a result, they are cautious or uncertain about making an a priori prediction.[10] This uncertainty can be compounded, as we discuss later, by children's initial informal view of addition.

Analysis

Although there is some evidence to support the contention that Resnick's (1992) model would benefit by allowing for multiple part-whole relations and initially weak addition schemas, clearly there is a need for more research on the topic. For example, evidence is needed to establish that one or a few computational experiences typically lead children to quickly generalize their understanding of commutativity to previously unpracticed combinations, including those involving relatively large and unfamiliar addends.

COMPLETENESS OF CHILDREN'S EARLY ADDITION CONCEPT

Theory

Problem With Resnick's Account. A second possible problem with Resnick's (1992) account is that it is inconsistent with the conventional view that children initially view addition as a unary operation and only later as a binary operation. According to Weaver (1982), a unary operation is an operation on one

---

[10] Wright (cited in Nunes & Bryant, 1996) offered a different explanation for the relative ease of commutativity tasks that involve part-whole problems. She noted that, with such problems, children may recognize that addition simply involves counting all the objects representing the two addends and, thus, that order-irrelevance counting principle is relevant. With change-add-to problems, which involve a transformation, there is not a direct connection between finding a sum and this counting principle. This is a possible alternative or supplemental explanation for the argument that part-whole problems do not imply an order constraint, whereas change-add-to problems do.

number that results in another. Change-add-to problems, such as Problem A, embody this meaning. A binary operation is an operation on two amounts that results in a third. Part-part-whole problems, such as Problem B, embody this meaning.

- **Problem A**: *Asnami had three candies. Her mother gave her two more. Now how many candies does Asnami have?*
- **Problem B**: *Bethann has three fish and two kittens. How many pets does she have altogether?*

Resnick (1992) appears to assume that young children's thinking involves *both* a unary and a binary conception of addition. Referring to the quantities level, for example, she noted: "It is possible to distinguish several kinds of addition. . . . Addition can mean *combining* 4 apples and 3 apples [binary meaning] or increasing by 5 a set of 20 marbles [unary meaning]" (p. 405; see also her discussion of the four kinds of mathematical thinking on pp. 403 and 404). Furthermore, in her Table 7.2 (p. 403), Resnick included both "increase" (unary) and "combine" (binary) operations at the protoquantities level.

However, citing Brush (1978) and Gelman and Gallistel (1978) as evidence, Fuson (1979) and Weaver (1982) hypothesized that a unary view develops before a binary view. In other words, children initially view the problem situations *Brother has five candies and got two more* and *Brother has two candies and got five more* as different. Because they cannot foresee the equivalence of these different situations and because order can affect the outcome in many real-world situations, most children intuitively conclude (predict) that the outcomes of these different situations are different. For most children, then, addition may initially be tied to an order-constrained part-whole schema—one that implies order does matter.

Proposed Modification. Resnick's (1992) model regarding the development of additive commutativity might be more complete if it took into account the incompleteness of children's initial concept of addition. Building on Fuson (1979) and Weaver's (1982) conjecture, Baroody and Gannon (1984) proposed a different four-level model, which suggested that knowledge of commutativity evolves from a schema based on a unary conception to one based on both a unary and a binary conception (see Table 4.4).

Evidence

Positing an initial order-constrained change-add-to addition schema would explain why, despite the advantage of easing computational effort, most children apparently do not use the commutativity permission to disregard addend order for some time after they begin informally computing sums. Children typically construct a CAF strategy before they do a CAL or a COL strategy (e.g., Baroody, 1987b, 1996; Baroody & Gannon, 1984; Ilg & Ames, 1951; Siegler & Jenkins, 1989). Mentally, they can quickly determine the correct sum of an $n + 1$ problem or expression before that of the equivalent $1 + n$ problem or expression (Groen & Parkman, 1972; Siegler & Robinson, 1982; Siegler & Shrager, 1984; Svenson, 1975), because the number-after rule can be more readily applied, for instance, to

---

Table 4.4: Levels of Commutativity Development (Baroody & Gannon, 1984)

Level 0   (unary conception of addition + noncommutativity): Because of a unary view of addition, children may initially not recognize that addition is commutative. They may interpret, for example, 5 + 3 as *five and three more* and 3 + 5 as *three and five more*—as different situations with different outcomes.

Level 1   (unary conception of addition + protocommutativity): Children intuitively disregard addend order because it minimizes computational effort and seems to work. However, when explicitly asked about commutativity, they still invoke their unary conception of addition and respond incorrectly or hesitantly. Children, treat, for example, three and five more as five and three more to save labor but do not necessarily recognize, that it has the same sum as five and three more.

Level 2   (unary conception of addition + pseudocommutativity): Children might discover commutativity before constructing a binary conception of addition. Put differently, a child might recognize that, although five and three more and three and five more are different situations, they have the same outcome. Weaver (1982) called this understanding *pseudocommutativity*, because it is not consistent with the mathematical definition of commutativity.[a]

Level 3   (binary conception of addition + mathematical commutativity supplements a unary conception + pseudocommutativity). Children finally construct a binary view of addition and, along with it, a "true" mathematical understanding of commutativity (e.g., the parts three and five are interchangeable in forming the whole eight). This view coexists with children's (and adults') more informal unary view of addition and pseudocommutativity (Kaput, 1979).

---

[a] Mathematically, the statements 5 + 3 and 3 + 5 are equivalent and interchangeable: 5 + 3 = 3 + 5 or 3 + 5 = 5 + 3. Psychologically, though, 5 + 3 and 3 + 5 can imply different meanings: Five and three more is a different situation than three and five more (Kaput, 1979). Strictly speaking, commutativity is a property of a binary operation, not a unary operation (Weaver, 1982).

---

7 + 1 ("seven and one more") than to 1 + 7 ("one and seven more"; Baroody, 1987a, 1996).

Inconsistent with the unary-concept-first hypothesis, however, Carpenter and Moser (1984) found that most of their participants used both COF and COL strategies and concluded that COF was not a distinct stage before COL. Furthermore, existing evidence does not show that school-age children find change-add-to problems easier to solve than part-part-whole problems (e.g.,

Carpenter & Moser, 1982, 1984; De Corte & Verschaffel, 1987; Ibarra & Lindvall, 1982; Riley & Greeno, 1988; Riley, Greeno, & Heller, 1983).

In any case, it follows from Resnick's (1992) model that if children have a single part-whole schema representing both unary and binary views of addition, then the commutativity permission underlying the invention of strategies that disregard addend order should apply equally to change-add-to and part-part-whole problems. However, De Corte and Verschaffel (1987) found that semantic structure had a significant effect on whether children used COL. More specifically, their participants were more likely to invent COL in response to part-part-whole problems, problems that were less clearly order constrained.

Two studies provide direct evidence on Resnick's (1992) and Baroody and Gannon's (1984) models of commutativity development. Wright (cited in Nunes & Bryant, 1996) tested primary-level children's understanding of commutativity with change-add-to and part-part-whole problems. Wilkins, Baroody, and Tiilikainen (2001) did so with kindergartners. Contrary to Resnick's position, the participants in both studies were not equally successful on the two types of tasks. Contrary to Baroody and Gannon's position, they were more likely to recognize commutativity in the context of part-part-whole problems.

Analysis

The discrepancy in the evidence regarding the unary-concept-first hypothesis might be attributed to task differences. Baroody (1987b, 1996; Baroody & Gannon, 1984) used a symbolic (numerical-level) task, whereas Carpenter and Moser (1984) used word problems (a quantities-level task). For the reasons outlined in footnote 4, though, it seems unlikely that the use of symbolic expressions with Baroody's participants prevented them from accessing their quantitative-level understanding of commutativity. A more plausible explanation for the discrepancy is that Carpenter and Moser's assessment may not have been sufficiently sensitive to detect stages in strategy development. First, they did not distinguish between CAF and CAL, where distinct stages are more likely to occur (Baroody & Ginsburg, 1986). Second, they tested children only twice a year rather than following their development throughout the time of the study. In other words, the testing procedure may have missed the phase where children used COF exclusively. Furthermore, existing research on the relative ease of change-add-to problems that embody a unary concept and part-part-whole problems that embody a binary concept has studied children in the later phase of early childhood, a point in development where they may have already constructed both concepts of addition.

Although there is some evidence to suggest that children construct a unary view of addition before they do a binary view, the existing evidence is far from conclusive. Needed are microgenetic studies that examine children's computational strategies, including CAF and CAL, for both change-add-to and part-part-whole problems (at the quantities level). Also needed is a systematic examination of *preschoolers'* qualitative reasoning on both types of addition problems. Examining qualitative reasoning appears to be a more accurate measure of conceptual understanding than assessing the number of correct computations (Sophian & McCorgray, 1994).

The results of the De Corte and Verschaffel (1987), Wright (cited in Nunes & Bryant, 1996), and Wilkins et al. (2001) studies indicate that Resnick's (1992) model is incomplete. More specifically, these data indicate that either order-constrained (change-add-to) and order-indifferent (part-whole) addition schemas of young children are not entirely integrated or a single schema incorporating both addition concepts is relatively weak (i.e., applied inconsistently). The results of these three studies also indicate that Baroody and Gannon's (1984) model of commutativity development is inaccurate. More specifically, it may be that protocommutativity (Level 1 in Table 4.4) and pseudocommutativity (Level 2 in Table 4.4) concepts do not occur before children construct a binary view of addition.

The model outlined in Table 4.5 reconciles Resnick's (1992) and Baroody and Gannon's (1984) models with each other and with the results of the De Corte and Verschaffel (1987), Wright (cited in Nunes & Bryant, 1996), and Wilkins et al. (2001) studies. Level 0 children initially construct a unary conception of addition and do not understand the principle of additive commutativity. Children may then construct a binary conception of addition that is only loosely connected to their unary conception and view order as a constraint in some situations and as irrelevant in others. For both conceptions of addition, children at Level 1 may have only an implicit understanding of commutativity: use a commutativity permission to disregard addend order but perform unsuccessfully when explicitly asked about commutativity. The participants in the Wilkins et al. study who were unsuccessful on both the change-add-to and part-part-whole versions of the commutativity task may have been at Levels 0 or 1. Like the inconsistent participants in the Wilkins et al. study, Level 2 children explicitly recognize the commutative relation in part-part-whole situations but not in change-add-to situations. At some juncture, children recognize that even commuted unary situations are equivalent, and this insight may help to further connect this conception of addition with their binary view. Such Level 3 children—like the participants in the Wilkins et al. study who responded correctly to both change-add-to and part-part-whole versions of the commutativity task—are consistently successful on a variety of commutativity tasks.

CONCLUSIONS

Although verbal counting-based computational experience does appear to play a key role in the construction of additive commutativity at the quantities level for many children (e.g., Baroody, 1987a, 1987c; Baroody et al., 1982; Baroody & Gannon, 1984), proponents of the independent-of-computational-experience conjecture may be correct in one important sense. Most children probably begin to construct addition schemas involving part-whole relations before they invent such computational strategies to determine the sum of simple addition word problems or symbolic expressions. More important, some children between 2 and 4 years of age may use other noncomputational strategies—albeit ones that involve determining specific values—to construct an order-indifferent addition/part-whole schema at the quantities level. Using a subitizing process or a mental model, a child might mentally add the same two small collections in different orders (e.g., OO + O and then O + OO) and notice that the outcome is

Table 4.5: Proposed Model of Commutativity Development

Level 0:	unary conception + noncommutativity[a]
Level 1:	unary conception + noncommutativity and binary conception + protocommutativity[b]
Level 2:	unary conception + protocommutativity and binary conception + part-whole ("true") commutativity[c]
Level 3	unary conception + change-add-to commutativity ("pseudocommutativity") and binary conception + part-whole ("true") commutativity

---

[a] Alternatively, Level 0 may consist of two sublevels (unary conception and noncommutativity and then unary conception + protocommutativity), or it may consist of a single level of a somewhat different nature (unary conception + protocommutativity). A Level 0 child might be able to understand part-part-whole problems and respond appropriately to them by assimilating such problem situations to their unary (change-add-to) view of addition.

[b] Level 1 may consist of two or three sublevels: (a) unary and binary conception + noncommutativity (Level 1A), (b) unary conception + noncommutativity and binary conception + protocommutativity (Level 1B), and (c) unary and binary conception + protocommutativity (Level 1C).

[c] At least some children might proceed directly from Level 0 to Level 2 or a sublevel of Level 2: unary conception + noncommutativity and binary conception + part-whole ("true") commutativity.

---

the same in each case. Noticing the equivalence of such cases is more likely to occur if the child associates number labels with each combined collection and the outcomes and could elevate an order-indifferent addition/part-whole schema to the quantities level at a relatively early age. This could account for those children who appear to understand commutativity at the quantities level, even before they devise verbal counting-based computational strategies (cf. Cowan & Renton, 1996; Ganetsou & Cowan, 1995; Sophian et al., 1995). In other words, although the invention of verbal counting-based computational strategies greatly increases the chances of advancing children's understanding of commutativity beyond the protoquantities level, there may be other means involving specific value for doing so.

The evidence regarding the main contentions of Resnick's (1992) model of commutativity development is, at best, contradictory. Clearly, there is a need to empirically test whether commutativity develops simultaneously with other aspects of additive composition, whether children perform better on concrete commutativity tasks than on more abstract ones, and whether they should be more successful on commutativity task involving small, familiar numbers than ones involving large unfamiliar numbers.

Finally, existing evidence (e.g., De Corte & Verschaffel, 1987; Wilkins et al., 2001; Wright, cited in Nunes & Bryant, 1996) is consistent with viewing children's early arithmetic development in terms of multiple, loosely connected weak schemas. Although it remains unclear whether a unary concept develops before, simultaneously with, or even after a binary concept, this evidence suggests that these two concepts of addition may not be initially integrated and subject to the same commutativity permission.

Further research is needed to test each level of the model summarized in Table 4.5. Whether children construct a unary view of addition before a part-part-whole view (Level 0) needs to be examined directly. Whether children who do not understand communtativity first disregard addend order when solving part-part-whole problems only (Level 1) also needs direct empirical confirmation. Evidence that they then respond correctly to commutativity questions worded in terms of part-part-whole situations but not change-add-to situations (Level 2) needs to be replicated. Further evidence is also needed to confirm the next level (Level 3), which would represent progress to a strong addition schema and a relatively broad and logically coherent understanding of addition. This integration of a unary concept of addition, binary concept of addition, and the commutativity permission should, theoretically, greatly promote children's flexibility and adaptive expertise with simple addition.

The levels described in Table 4.5 might be sublevels of Resnick's (1992) numerical level (as Cowan, chap. 2, this volume, suggests). Depending on a particular child's experiences, they may also be sublevels of some other level such as the quantitative level, or they might stretch across two or more of her levels. Clearly, further research is needed to sort out how children's understanding of commutativity, in particular, and their mathematical thinking, in general, evolves.

Acknowledgments

Preparation of this chapter was supported, in part, by a grant ("Early Arithmetic Development") from the University of Illinois Research Board, a Faculty Fellowship awarded by the College of Education at the University of Illinois, and a grant from the National Science Foundation, titled "The Developmental Bases of Number and Operation Sense" (BCS-0111829). The opinions expressed are the sole responsibility of the authors and do not necessarily reflect the position, policy, or endorsement of the National Science Foundation.

References

Anderson, R. C. (1984). Some reflections on the acquisition of knowledge. *Educational Researcher, 13*(9), 5–10.

Baroody, A. J. (1982). Are discovering commutativity and more economical addition strategies related? *Problem Solving, 4*(12), 1–2.

Baroody, A. J. (1984a). The case of Felicia: A young child's strategies for reducing memory demands during mental addition. *Cognition and Instruction, 1,* 109–116.

Baroody, A. J. (1984b). More precisely defining and measuring the order–irrelevance principle. *Journal of Experimental Child Psychology, 38*, 33–41.

Baroody, A. J. (1987a). *Children's mathematical thinking: A developmental framework for preschool, primary, and special education teachers.* New York: Teachers College Press.

Baroody, A. J. (1987b). The development of counting strategies for single-digit addition. *Journal for Research in Mathematics Education, 18*, 141–157.

Baroody, A. J. (1987c). Problem size and mentally retarded children's judgment of commutativity. *American Journal of Mental Deficiency, 91*, 439–442.

Baroody, A. J. (1993). The relationship between the order–irrelevance principle and counting skill. *Journal for Research in Mathematics Education, 24*, 415–427.

Baroody, A. J. (1995). The role of the number-after rule in the invention of computational short cuts. *Cognition and Instruction, 13*, 189–219.

Baroody, A. J. (1996). Self-invented addition strategies by children with mental retardation. *American Journal on Mental Retardation, 101*, 72–89.

Baroody, A. J. (1999). Children's relational knowledge of addition and subtraction. *Cognition and Instruction, 17*, 137–175.

Baroody, A. J. (2000, May). *Number and operations: Key transitions in the numerical and arithmetic development of typical and special children between the ages of 2 and 6 years.* Paper presented at the Conference on Standards for Preschool and Kindergarten Mathematics Education sponsored by the National Science Foundation and Exxon Mobil Foundation, Arlington, VA.

Baroody, A. J., Berent, R., & Packman, D. (1982). The use of mathematical structure by inner city children. *Focus on Learning Problems in Mathematics, 4*(2), 5–13.

Baroody, A. J., with Coslick, R. T. (1998). *Fostering children's mathematical power: An investigative approach to K–8 mathematics instruction.* Mahwah, NJ: Lawrence Erlbaum Associates.

Baroody, A. J., & Gannon, K. E. (1984). The development of commutativity principle and economical addition strategies. *Cognition and Instruction, 1*, 321–329.

Baroody, A. J., & Ginsburg, H. P. (1986). The relationship between initial meaningful and mechanical knowledge of arithmetic. In J. Hiebert (Ed.), *Conceptual and procedural knowledge: The case of mathematics* (pp. 75–112). Hillsdale, NJ: Lawrence Erlbaum Associates.

Baroody, A. J., Ginsburg, H. P., & Waxman, B. (1983). Children's use of mathematical structure. *Journal for Research in Mathematics Education, 14*, 156–168.

Baroody, A. J., & Wilkins, J. L. M. (1999). The development of informal counting, number, and arithmetic skills and concepts. In J. Copley (Ed.), *Mathematics in the early years, birth to five* (pp. 48–65). Reston, VA: National Council of Teachers of Mathematics.

Bermejo, V., & Rodriguez, P. (1993). Children's understanding of the commutative law of addition. *Learning and Instruction, 3*, 55–72.

Bisanz, J., & LeFevre, J. (1990). Strategic and nonstrategic processing in the development of mathematical cognition. In D. F. Bjorklund (Ed.), *Children's strategies: Contemporary views of cognitive development* (pp. 213–244). Hillsdale, NJ: Lawrence Erlbaum Associates.

Briars, D. J., & Larkin, J. G. (1984). An integrated model of skills in solving elementary word problems. *Cognition and Instruction, 1*, 245–296.

Brush, L. R. (1978). Preschool children's knowledge of addition and subtraction. *Journal for Research in Mathematics Education, 9*, 44–54.

Bryant, P. (1994). Children and arithmetic. *Journal of Child Psychology and Psychiatry, 36*, 3–32.

Campbell, J. I. D., & Graham, D. J. (1985). Mental multiplication skill: Structure, process, and acquisition. *Canadian Journal of Psychology, 39*, 338–362.

Carpenter, T. P., & Moser, J. M. (1982). The development of addition and subtraction problem-solving skills. In T. P. Carpenter, J. M. Moser, & T. A. Romberg (Eds.), *Addition and subtraction: A cognitive perspective* (pp. 9–24). Hillsdale, NJ: Lawrence Erlbaum Associates.

Carpenter, T. P., & Moser, J. M. (1984). The acquisition of addition and subtraction concepts in grades one through three. *Journal for Research in Mathematics Education, 15,* 179–202.

Cowan, R., Dowker, A., Christakis, A., & Bailey, S. (1996). Even more precisely assessing children's understanding of the order-irrelevance principle. *Journal of Experimental Child Psychology, 62,* 84–101.

Cowan, R., & Renton, M. (1996). Do they know what they are doing? Children's use of economical addition strategies and knowledge of commutativity. *Educational Psychology, 16,* 407–420.

Dantzig, T. (1954). *Number: The language of science.* New York: The Free Press (original work published 1930).

De Corte, E., & Verschaffel, L. (1987). The effect of semantic structure on first graders' strategies for solving addition and subtraction word problems. *Journal for Research in Mathematics Education, 18,* 363–381.

diSessa, A. A. (1983). Phenomenology and the evolution of intuition. In D. Gentner & A. Stevens (Eds.), *Mental models* (pp. 15–33). Hillsdale, NJ: Lawrence Erlbaum Associates.

Fuson, K. C. (1979, November). *Counting solution procedures in addition and subtraction.* Paper presented at the Wingspread Seminar on the Initial Learning of Addition and Subtraction Skills, Racine, WI.

Fuson, K. C. (1992). Research on whole number addition and subtraction. In D. Grouws (Ed.), *Handbook of research on mathematics teaching and learning* (pp. 243–275). New York: Macmillan.

Fuson, K. C., Pergament, G. G., Lyons, B. G., & Hall, J. W. (1985). Children's conformity to the cardinality rule as a function of set size and counting accuracy. *Child Development, 56,* 1429–1436.

Ganetsou, E., & Cowan, R. (1995, September). *The development of commutativity.* Paper presented at the conference on Language and Mathematical Thinking, London.

Gelman, R. (1982). Accessing one-to-one correspondence: Still another paper about conservation. *British Journal of Psychology, 73,* 209–220.

Gelman, R., & Gallistel, C. R. (1978). *The child's understanding of number.* Cambridge, MA: Harvard University Press.

Ginsburg, H. P. (1977). *Children's arithmetic: The learning process.* New York: Van Nostrand.

Ginsburg, H. P., Klein, A., & Starkey, P. (1998). The development of children's mathematical knowledge: Connecting research with practice. In I. E. Sigel & K. A. Renninger (Eds.), *Handbook of child psychology: Vol. 4. Child psychology in practice* (5th ed., pp. 401–476). New York: Wiley.

Groen, G. J., & Parkman, J. M. (1972). A chronometric analysis of simple addition. *Psychological Review, 79,* 329–343.

Groen, G. J., & Resnick, L. B. (1977). Can preschool children invent addition algorithms? *Journal of Educational Psychology, 69,* 645–652.

Holt, J. (1964). *How children fail.* New York: Delta.

Huttenlocher, J., Jordan, N. C., & Levine, S. C. (1994). A mental model for early arithmetic. *Journal of Experimental Psychology: General, 123,* 284–296.

Ibarra, C. G., & Lindvall, C. M. (1982). Factors associated with the ability of kindergarten children to solve simple arithmetic story problems. *Journal of Educational Research, 5,* 149–155.

Ilg, F., & Ames, L. B. (1951). Developmental trends in arithmetic. *The Journal of Genetic Psychology, 79,* 3–28.

Irwin, K. C. (1996). Children's understanding of the principles of covariation and compensation in part-whole relationships. *Journal for Research in Mathematics Education, 27,* 25–40.

Kaput, J. J. (1979). Mathematics learning: Roots of epistemological status. In J. Lochhead & J. Clement (Eds.), *Cognitive process instruction* (pp. 289–304). Philadelphia: Franklin Institute Press.

Langford, P. E. (1981). A longitudinal study of children's understanding of logical laws in arithmetic and Boolean algebra. *Educational Psychology, 1,* 119–140.

Mix, K. (1999). Preschoolers' recognition of numerical equivalence: Sequential sets. *Journal of Experimental Child Psychology, 74,* 309–332.

Mix, K. S., Huttenlocher, J., & Levine, S. C. (2002). *Math without words: Quantitative development in infancy and early childhood.* New York: Oxford University Press.

Nunes, T., & Bryant, P. (1996). *Children doing mathematics.* Oxford, England: Blackwell.

Piaget, J. (1965). *The child's conception of number.* New York: Norton.

Piaget, J., & Inhelder, B. (1969). The gaps in empiricism. In A. Koestler & J. R. Smythies (Eds.), *Beyond reductionism.* Boston: Beacon Press.

Resnick, L. B. (1983). A developmental theory of number understanding. In H. P. Ginsburg (Ed.), *The development of mathematical thinking* (pp. 109–151). New York: Academic Press.

Resnick, L. B. (1992). From protoquantities to operators: Building mathematical competence on a foundation of everyday knowledge. In G. Leinhardt, R. Putnam, & R. A. Hattrup (Eds.), *Analysis of arithmetic for mathematics teaching* (pp. 373–425). Hillsdale, NJ: Lawrence Erlbaum Associates.

Riley, M. S., & Greeno, J. G. (1988). Developmental analysis of understanding language about quantities and of solving problems. *Cognition and Instruction, 5,* 49–101.

Riley, M. S., Greeno, J. G., & Heller, J. I. (1983). Development of children's problem-solving ability in arithmetic. In H. P. Ginsburg (Ed.), *The development of mathematical thinking* (pp. 153–200). New York: Academic Press.

Siegler, R. S., & Jenkins, E. (1989). *How children discover new strategies.* Hilldale, NJ: Lawrence Erlbaum Associates.

Siegler, R. S., & Robinson, M. (1982). The development of numerical understandings. In H. W. Reese & L. P. Lipsitt (Eds.), *Advances in child development and behavior* (Vol. 1, pp. 241–312). New York: Academic Press.

Siegler, R. S., & Shrager, J. (1984). Strategy choice in addition: How do children know what to do? In C. Sophian (Ed.), *Origins of cognitive skills* (pp. 229–293). Hillsdale, NJ: Lawrence Erlbaum Associates.

Sophian, C. (1998). A developmental perspective on children's counting. In C. Donlan (Ed.), *The development of mathematical skills* (pp. 27–46). Hove, East Sussex, England: Psychology Press.

Sophian, C., Harley, H., & Martin, C. S. M. (1995). Relational and representational aspects of early number development. *Cognition and Instruction, 13,* 253–268.

Sophian, C., & McCorgray, P. (1994). Part–whole knowledge and early arithmetic problem solving. *Cognition and Instruction, 12,* 3–33.

Sophian, C., & Vong, K. I. (1995). The parts and wholes of arithmetic story problems: Developing knowledge in the preschool years. *Cognition and Instruction, 13,* 469–477.

Starkey, P. (1992). The early development of numerical reasoning. *Cognition, 43,* 93–126.

Starkey, P., & Cooper, R. G., Jr. (1980). Perception of numbers by human infants. *Science, 210,* 1033–1035.

Svenson, O. (1975). Analysis of time required by children for simple addition. *Acta Psychologica, 39,* 284–302.

Thorndike, E. L. (1922). *The psychology of arithmetic.* New York: Macmillan.

Tiilikainen, S., Baroody, A. J., & Wilkins, J. L. M. (1997, October). The effects of problem size on children's understanding of additive commutativity. In J. A. Dossey (Ed.), *Proceedings of the nineteenth annual meeting of the International Group for the Psychology of Mathematics Education, North American Chapter*. Normal: Illinois State University.

Weaver, J. F. (1982). Interpretations of number operations and symbolic representations of addition and subtraction. In T. P. Carpenter, J. M. Moser, & T. A. Romberg (Eds.), *Addition and subtraction: A cognitive perspective* (pp. 60–66). Hillsdale, NJ: Lawrence Erlbaum Associates.

Wilkins, J. L. M., Baroody, A. J., & Tiilikainen, S. (2001). Kindergartners' understanding of additive commutativity within the contexts of word problems. *Journal of Experimental Child Psychology, 79*, 23–36.

Wynn, K. (1992). Addition and subtraction by human infants. *Nature, 27*, 749–750.

Wynn, K. (1998). Numerical competence in infants. In C. Donlan (Ed.), *The development of mathematical skills* (pp. 1–25). Hove, East Sussex, England: Psychology Press.

CHAPTER 5

"YOU'VE GOT TO CAREFULLY READ THE MATH SENTENCE ... ": CLASSROOM CONTEXT AND CHILDREN'S INTERPRETATIONS OF THE EQUALS SIGN

Kyoung-Hye Seo
University of Wisconsin, Milwaukee

Herbert P. Ginsburg
Teachers College, Columbia University

What does the "equals sign" mean to young children? Mathematically, it has a relational meaning, "the same as." Many curriculum guides define the equals sign in this way, and many teachers assume that young children understand this formal definition of the symbol. However, research has shown that they usually do not interpret the equals sign as indicating an equivalence relation. In this chapter, we report research on the effects of context on children's interpretations of the equals sign and discuss instructional approaches to foster a general and integrated conception of equals. Specifically, we describe the rationale, methods, results, analysis, and implications of a study that involved examining a constructivist approach to teaching a relational or equivalence meaning of the equals sign.

Rationale

Learning Difficulties

Helping children connect a mathematical symbol to an accurate conceptual understanding of its meaning continues to be a serious problem in mathematics education. For many students, doing mathematics is simply an attempt to get correct answers by manipulating symbols. Unfortunately they often misunderstand symbols or even consider them as meaningless marks on paper. A result of mechanically manipulating symbols is incorrect or even absurd answers. Even when students achieve routine expertise and can consistently obtain correct answers, they cannot justify their answers. Another common symptom of not thinking carefully (or at all) about the meaning of the symbols or their manipulations—not connecting symbols with an accurate conceptual understanding—is a lack of flexibility.

Consider, for example, the equals sign. Various researchers have found that children typically view the equals sign as referring to action—as "get the answer," "makes," "adds up to," or "the end is coming up" (e.g., Baroody & Ginsburg, 1983; Behr, Erlwanger, & Nichols, 1980; Ginsburg, 1982, 1996; Hughes, 1986; Kieran, 1981; Van de Walle, 1980). This operator view of the equals sign limits students' flexibility in three important ways: rejection of noncanonical equations, difficulties determining the unknown for such equations, and interference with understanding more advanced mathematics.

Rejection of Noncanonical Equations. Children with an operator view of the equals sign tend to judge the correctness of equations in an inflexible manner. More specifically, they consider the canonical format $a + b = c$ as the only legitimate form. Because children usually cannot make sense of noncanonical equations such as $c = a + b$ (e.g., $7 = 2 + 5$), $a + b = c + d$ (e.g., $3 + 4 = 2 + 5$), or $c = c$ (e.g., $7 = 7$), they view them as incorrect. In the Behr et al. (1980) study, for example, children aged 6 to 12 years were presented with various forms of equations and asked what the equals sign meant. When shown $? = 2 + 5$ and asked if it made sense, most children considered it incorrect (because how can something make or add up to two plus five) and changed it either to "$2 + 5 = ?$" (because two plus five can make or add up to something) or "$? + 2 = 5$" (because some initial amount and two more can make or add up to five.[1] Behr and his colleagues concluded that "we observe in the children's behavior an extreme rigidity about written sentences, an insistence that statements be written in a particular form, and a tendency to perform actions (e.g., add) rather than to reflect, make judgments, and infer meanings" (p. 15).

Difficulties Determining the Unknown in Noncanonical Equations. Weaver (1973) found that children had greater difficulty solving for a missing element in an equation when the sum (or whole) was on the left and the addends (or parts) were on the right (e.g., $? = 3 + 5$, $8 = 3 + ?$, $8 = ? + 5$) than when the opposite was true (e.g., $3 + 5 = ?$, $3 + ? = 8$, $? + 5 = 8$).

Interference With Understanding More Advanced Mathematics. Several researchers have noted that the operator view of the equals sign might continue into high school and college and make it difficult for children to understand mathematical ideas introduced later (e.g., Baroody & Ginsburg, 1983; Behr et al., 1980). Consider, for instance, the learning of arithmetic principles and algebra.

• **An operator view of the equal sign may make it more difficult to discover, understand, remember, or apply arithmetic principles such as the distributive property of multiplication (e.g., $a [b + c] = ab + ac$).** For instance, children who understand that equals means the "same as" can check their work, reject incorrect equations such as $2(3 + 4) = 6 + 4 = 10$, and revise their procedure to produce correct equations such as $2(3 + 4) = 6 + 8 = 14$.[2]

---

[1] Another common symptom of students' operator view of equals is misusing the symbol to indicate the next step in a solution. In finding the value of the expression $5 \times 4 + 7$, for instance, even many college-level students write $5 \times 4 = 20 + 7 = 27$, not recognizing that 5×4 is not the same number as $20 + 7$ or 27.

[2] Not recognizing that $a(b + c) = ab + ac$ or incorrectly concluding that $a(b + c) = ab + c$ appear to be common errors among upper elementary-level students (Hsieh & Baroody, 2000). Students can overcome these errors by applying the relational meaning of equals and the "do-first" rule for parentheses (i.e., do what is inside the parenthesis first. For example, a child could check her proposition that $2(3 + 4) = 6 + 4$ or 10 by simplifying the left side of the equation in the following manner: $2(3 + 4) \rightarrow 2 (7) \rightarrow 14$. The child should readily

• **An operator view may also interfere with discovering, understanding, remembering, or applying key algebraic processes or principles.** Consider the following three examples:

1. *Difficulties writing algebraic expressions or equations.* Kieran (1992) noted that many students have difficulty writing expressions or equations to represent situations described in word problems. "Instead of thoughtfully inter-preting the mathematical meaning of word problems, they deploy a direct-translation approach analogous to a key-word approach for solving arithmetic word problems. In effect, they mechanically translate word problems phrase-by-phrase into algebraic equations—often with disastrous results" (Baroody, with Coslick, 1998, p. 16-13). Consider the following problem:

> *At Ideal University, there are six times as many students as professors. Write an equation to represent this situation using S to indicate the number of students and P to indicate the number of professors.* (Clement, Lochhead, & Monk, 1981, p. 288)

A common response is $6S = P$, an equation that implies a truly remarkable student-to-professor ratio of 1 to 6. For example, if Ideal University had 10,000 students, the equation implies that the University employed 60,000 professors!

A relational view of equals provides the conceptual basis for understanding the balance-beam analogy for equation, an analogy that is most helpful in writing equations (see, e.g., Baroody, with Coslick, 1998; Borenson, 1991). By understanding that the two sides of an equation must balance (must be the same as one another), students can thoughtfully analyze problems such as the one just given, recognize the folly of such answers as $6S = P$ for themselves, and devise a correct equation such as $S = 6P$.

2. *Inability to mobilize informal or previous formal knowledge.* One reason why students develop only routine expertise of algebra is that they do not think to apply their existing mathematical knowledge. An operator view of equals can contribute to this difficulty. For example, if students do not recognize that each side of an equation must be equal, they may be less likely to use an informal try-and-adjust substitution strategy. This informal strategy involves substituting a numerical value, performing the indicated arithmetic, and comparing the outcome(s) (e.g., for $3n + 5 = 23$, substituting 5 for n, determining that $3 \cdot 5 + 5$ is equal to 20, which is not equal to 23). It is useful in evaluating an equation in its own right and for checking the outcome when formal procedures have been used.

3. *Performing the same operation on both sides of an equation.* A relational meaning of the equals sign provides the conceptual rational for balancing equations—that is, performing the same operation on each side of the equation.

---

recognize that $14 \neq 10$. The resulting cognitive conflict could prompt the child to reconsider her initial incorrect effort $[a(b + c) = ab + c]$ and discover the distributive property: As a must be distributed over both b and c, $a(b + c) = ab + ac$ (Hsieh & Baroody, 2000).

If children view the equals sign simply as an operator, this key algebraic manipulation is meaningless and must be memorized by rote. Children who understand the relational meaning of equals can be guided to discover this key algebraic manipulation (see, e.g., Baroody, with Coslick, 1998; Borenson, 1991), can understand it, and better remember and apply it (e.g., Kieran, 1980, 1981).

Reasons for Children's Limited View of the Equals Sign

Why do children tend to view the equals sign as an operator symbol? Baroody and Ginsburg (1983) offered two reasons.

1. Children's Informal Knowledge of Arithmetic. One reason is that they interpret symbols—and formal mathematics generally—in terms of their existing informal arithmetic, which is largely based on actions, particularly the schemes of counting. Children develop counting skills from a very early age and use them to solve practical arithmetic problems even before their entrance into school. For instance, many preschoolers determine the answer of simple addition problems as "If you have three points and get two more points, how many points do you have now?" by direct modeling: counting out three chips, counting out two more, and counting all of the chips. Young children bring this informal "change-add-to view of addition" to school (Baroody, with Coslick, 1998). When formally introduced to written addition, they assimilate the equals sign to their action schemes and interpret it as an operator symbol. For example, children view the written statement $3 + 2 = 5$ as adding three items and two more to get a particular result.

2. The Nature of Typical Mathematics Instruction. Children's tendency to view the equals sign as an operator symbol is reinforced by the way it is taught. In formal instruction, the equals sign is typically introduced in the context of addition and in the $a + b = ?$ format. Children are provided with little, if any, opportunity to see and use the equals sign in nonarithmetic contexts (e.g., 1 inch = 2.54 cm) or in different forms (e.g., $5 + 3 = 9 - ?$).

Questions: Textbooks, Teacher's Presentation, and Context

Various researchers and educators have emphasized teaching the equals sign in a meaningful way in order to promote the development of strong schemas that can support adaptive expertise and flexible use of knowledge (e.g., Baroody, with Coslick, 1998; Baroody & Ginsburg, 1986; Hiebert, 1984; Hiebert & Lefevre, 1986; Wynroth, 1980). However, existing research leaves a number of key questions about such instruction unanswered, particularly in relation to the role of classroom context and the development of mathematical ideas. Our study attempted to address questions about each of three key components of the teaching-learning process: (a) the curriculum as embodied by the textbooks used in a class, (b) the teacher who implements the curriculum, and (c) the children's experiences with equals sign in different contexts.

Issue 1: How Do Textbooks Present the Equals Sign? We addressed the following questions about textbooks: Do current textbooks support the learning of the relational meaning of the equals sign? How well do children's textbooks actually explain the equals sign in terms of equivalence? To what extent do they present noncanonical written expressions, such as $c = a + b$? Answering these questions will help us understand the extent to which textbook explanations and presentation of problems contribute to children's interpretations of equals.

Issue 2: How Did the Teacher Present the Equals Sign? We explored the following questions concerning the teacher's role: What can a teacher do to foster a relational view of the equals sign? Even when the teacher's goal is promoting this formally correct meaning of the equals sign, how does she actually explain this symbol to her students? Does the teacher, in fact, stress equivalence meaning and explain it adequately? How does the teacher's presentation relate to what is actually in the textbook? (As is well known, the intended curriculum is not always the one taught.) What impact does the teacher's explanation seem to have? Information concerning the teacher's instructional practice may also help us understand the development of children's interpretations of equals.

Issue 3: How Did Context Affect the Children's Interpretation of the Equals Sign? We examined the following questions regarding students' interpretations of equals sign in different contexts: Can providing children experience with various equivalence situations promote a relational view of the equals sign? How do children respond when they are exposed to equals sign in various contexts—including those that stress equivalence (e.g., money equivalents, such as 1 dollar = 100 pennies) as well as the traditional context of canonical arithmetic equation such as $2 + 3 = 5$? If exposed to various contexts, do they develop a view that integrates both operator and relational meanings, or do they still tend to view equals largely as an operator? Do children consistently view the equals sign in operator or relation terms across *all* contexts? Information concerning the role of context will help us to establish the generality of children's interpretations of equals and may also point the way toward effective instructional approaches.

Method

Design

To investigate the three issues discussed, we selected one second-grade classroom in which the teacher was attempting to foster a relational view of the equals sign by using the symbol in a variety of mathematical activities (contexts). We examined, in depth, the textbooks and materials used in this classroom, the instructional practices of the teacher, and the children's understanding of the equals sign in a variety of contexts—employing several research methods including critical analysis of materials, participant observations, and clinical interviews.

Participants

A teacher, Ms. March,[3] and 16 of her 29 second graders from a public school in Manhattan (New York City) participated in this study. The participants were randomly selected and represented a variety of social and cultural backgrounds: 8 children were Caucasian, 4 were African American, 2 were Hispanic, and 2 were Asian Americans. Most of them were from the lower middle class. The teacher, who was Caucasian, had 6 years teaching experience, mostly in the primary grades.

Procedure

Issue 1: Textbooks. Our investigation began with the examination of mathematics curriculum materials. Teachers in Ms. March's school had discretion to decide on curriculum materials for instruction, as long as the district curriculum guidelines were followed. Usually, teachers were provided with a number of recommended curriculum materials, some chosen by teachers, others selected by the school administrators. Basically, Ms. March used two textbooks and a variety of supplementary curriculum materials for mathematics instruction. One textbook was *Moving into Math: Core Book* (Irons, 1994), chosen at the school level, and the other was *Bright Start: Integrate Critical Thinking Skills with Math (Level B;* Casolaro, 1994). Ms. March and the children called the former the "core book" or "blue book" (because it has a blue cover) and the latter, the "workbook." They are called "core book" and "workbook" in this report. We examined the contexts as well as the ways in which the equals sign was presented and the teaching and learning activities provided by these two textbooks.

Issue 2: Teacher's Presentation. To investigate how the teacher presented the equals sign, we observed the math classroom twice a week from October to November and January to March. The primary targets of our observation were the lessons that explicitly dealt with the equals sign or in which the equals sign was used. The observations were guided by questions such as how the teacher presented the equals sign, in what contexts she introduced the equals sign, and what kinds of learning activities or tasks she provided. In addition to writing field notes, we also recorded classroom conversation during the mathematics lessons and collected mathematics handouts and homework. Along with the observations, formal and informal interviews were conducted with the teacher during the recess or after class. We asked the teacher questions such as why she provided particular activities or tasks and what she

---

[3] Ms. March is a pseudonym, as are the names of the children.

expected children to learn from such activities. The aim of these interviews was to understand math instruction from the teacher's perspective.

Issue 3: Context. To investigate children's interpretations of the equals sign in different contexts, we conducted clinical interviews with individual children in April. We chose the clinical interview method because it is better for examining adaptive expertise and flexibility than standardized tests, which generally are geared toward assessing routine expertise. The clinical interview typically involves an extended dialogue between adult and child, careful observation of the child's work, and flexible questioning tailored to the individual child's distinctive views and responses. We developed a protocol consisting of a basic question for each of five different equals-sign contexts (described in the next paragraph) and began clinical interviews with this protocol. However, as the interview proceeded, the interviewer adapted preset questions to fit each interview situation. Sometimes new questions were devised during the interview, sometimes questions were expressed in different ways according to the child, or sometimes questions were asked in different order. By flexibly tailoring questions to each child's responses, the interviewer sought to gain an in-depth understanding of each child's interpretation of the equals sign.

The clinical interview involved four sessions. In the first interview session, only the equals sign was presented, and a child was asked what it was and what it meant (no context). After all participants had the first interview, the second interview was conducted. In this session, the equals sign was presented with plus and minus sign (e.g., $2 + 3 = ?$ and $5 - 2 = ?$), and the child was asked what the equals sign in each number sentence meant (canonical context). Then, noncanonical number sentences such as $? = 2 + 3$ and $3 = 3$ were presented, and the child was asked whether they made sense and why (noncanonical context). In the third interview session, the equals sign was presented in a rod equation (familiar in the context of this classroom) "2 white rods = 1 red rod" (equivalent-rods context). The child was told that he or she could use Cuisenaire rods if he or she wanted, and asked whether it made sense and, if it did, what the equals sign meant in that rod equation. In the last interview session, the child was shown "1 dollar = 100 pennies," a problem also familiar in the context of the classroom, and asked if it made sense and what the equals sign meant (money-equivalents context). All interviews were tape-recorded. Each interview session was transcribed and read carefully before the next session in order to prepare interview questions for individual children.

The clinical interview data were analyzed in the following way. First, a key sentence representing the child's response to each of five basic interview questions was extracted from the transcriptions. Second, a table was made that had five columns, each designating one of five basic interview questions, and rows listing each child's name. The key sentence extracted from each child's responses to each interview question was written in the designated cell. Third, children's responses to each interview question were compared with those of their peers, allowing us to analyze possible differences in how children interpreted the equals sign presented *within* each context. Finally, comparisons were made *across* contexts, thus allowing us to examine differences in children's responses to the five different interview questions.

Results

Issue 1: How Do Textbooks Present the Equals Sign?

The core book consists of 30 topics, including the concepts *more than* and *less than*. Sixteen topics dealt with operations (three fourths of which involved addition and subtraction), three topics covered the recognition of written numbers (reading and writing one-, two-, and three-digit numbers), and seven topics involved measurement and geometry.

As is common in many textbooks, the notion of "equals" is first introduced in the context of addition, but in somewhat different form. For example, the core book first shows a "before" picture of a double domino with 4 and 4 dots. Then it shows another picture of a domino, labeled "after," with one more dot added on (4 and 5 dots). Next, children are asked to tell what happened in the "after" picture and to write an addition fact for each domino picture. Right underneath, to provide an example of addition facts for the domino pictures, the core book presents a series of addition problems written in a vertical form such as:

$$\begin{array}{r} 4 \\ + \ \underline{4} \end{array} \qquad \begin{array}{r} 4 \\ + \ \underline{5} \end{array}$$

Then children are asked to "answer each of these addition facts." It seems that the use of "equals" in this context, which is represented as a horizontal line, not by the symbol =, fails to denote the equivalence relation between $a + b$ and c. Rather, it appears to divide the operation of addition into two parts, the process and the product. The process is determining the sum, and the product is the answer obtained. Indeed, the core book tells the children to write the "answer" right below the line called "equals."

It appears that by using double dominos and adding one more dot to doubles, the developers of the core book attempt to help children discover the double plus one thinking strategy (i.e., $4 + 4 = 8$ and so $4 + 5 = 9$). However, the equals sign introduced in this context is likely to reinforce the children's tendency to perform action when they see written number sentences and to interpret "equals" in terms of actions.

Similarly, the "equals" first appears in the workbook in the context of performing an operation. It is interesting that the workbook employs the "function machine" in teaching addition and subtraction. For example, it introduces a function machine called "math contraption" to the children. If a certain number is put "in" the math contraption, it goes into operation; it sometimes adds a certain number to the original number or sometimes subtracts it from the original number; finally a number comes "out" from the math contraption, preceded by the equals sign. The equals sign in this case also calls for a calculation to produce an answer.

Another workbook activity involves asking children to help a monster finish a "sign board." Inside the sign board there are three circles, a plus sign, a minus sign, an equals sign, and a number (for example, O – O + O = 10), and outside of it three numbers, 4, 6, and 8. The task is basically to add and subtract the proper combination of three numbers to get the specified result. Likewise, most children understood the signboard and similar problems in action terms: "The answer is already here, and the problem is how to make 10," said Berry.

In brief, we found in both core book and workbook little effort to promote the relational view of "equals." The context in which "equals" is introduced is exclusively limited to performing operations. The equals sign rarely appears without plus or minus signs. Furthermore, most number sentences are presented in canonical format such as $a + b = c$ or $a - b = c$. Under these circumstances, the equals sign does not seem to convey the idea of equivalence relation. Instead, it is likely to reinforce the children's tendency to interpret "equals" as action.

Issue 2: How Did the Teacher Present the Equals Sign?

Unlike the textbooks, Ms. March introduced the equals sign in contexts other than performing operations, though not all those contexts involved teaching the equals sign per se. In teaching mathematical symbols, Ms. March believed that:

> It's more important, I think, to give them many opportunities to use the symbols in many situations than simply to tell them, let's say, this is the equals sign and what's one side of the equals sign should be the same as what's the other side of the equals sign. Of course, I do need to articulate exactly what it means at some point, like, "the equals sign indicates equivalency," but kids are making up their own things. They need to construct their own understanding. I would never tell them, like, "now put the equals sign there," or something like that. I mean, it's more important to know why you're doing it and to make sense of it.

By providing various concrete situations in which mathematical symbols could be used, the teacher believed that she could help children construct an accurate (relational) understanding of the mathematical symbols. In her mathematics lessons, six different contexts were observed wherein the equals sign was introduced.

Number-Comparison Context. The first context was when she taught the concepts of "greater than" and "less than." She told children to take three cubes and two cubes, and then asked which pile had more. Children told her three cubes. She wrote the numerals 3 and 2 on the board, and > symbol between them. She then said, "We have a sign here that shows us that there's more on one side than the other side. This is called the *greater than* sign." Next, she wrote 6 and 8 right under "3 > 2," and asked which one is less. Children told her 6. "Does someone want to tell how we can show 6 is less than 8?" she asked. Paul came to the board, and put < between 6 and 8. "Great!" she said, "This sign show us that there's less on one side than the other side. And, it is called the *less than* sign." Then, she told children to take 5 cubes and 5 cubes, and asked which pile had more. Children told her they were the same. "Okay, then how can we show they are the same? Does someone want to write it here?" she asked. David came to the board and put the equals sign between the two numbers. "Super!" she said, "This equals sign represents that these two numbers, 5 and 5, are equal. They are the same." Then, she gave homework that asked them to write the appropriate signs between the numbers.

Addition-and-Subtraction Context. The second context was when the operations of addition and subtraction were taught. Ms. March used a problem-based approach to the topic. After posing a problem (e.g., *Some ladybugs have 5 spots, other ladybugs have 3 spots, and yet other ladybugs have 2 spots. The ladybugs April found in her garden had 18 spots altogether. What ladybugs might April have seen?*), she asked the children to figure out how to solve the problem in their groups using whatever math tools they wished. After group work, the class gathered in the meeting area to share and discuss each group's strategy. Then, Ms. March asked the children to return to their tables, draw pictures showing how they solved the problem in their math journals (e.g., draw the ladybugs showing 18 spots), and then write a number sentence that represented their solution (e.g., $5 + 5 + 3 + 3 + 2 = 18$ or $5 + 5 + 5 + 3 = 18$). She stated that in teaching addition and subtraction she placed more focus on how the children made sense of and approached the problems than whether they got the right answers. Also, she encouraged the children to represent their problem-solving strategies in many different forms such as concrete, semi-concrete (or pictorial), and formal written representations. In this context, the meanings of formal symbols children used to represent their problem-solving strategies (i.e., +, –, and =) were not discussed explicitly as in the first context.

Many-Names-for-a-Number Context. The third context was what Ms. March and the children called "renaming the day." In the morning before the day's schedule began, children wrote at least three other names for that day. For instance, if the day was the fifth of October, children wrote other names for 5 such as $1 + 4 = 5$, $2 + 3 = 5$, and $7 – 2 = 5$. Ms. March stated that this "renaming the day" activity had several purposes. It provided children with opportunities to develop basic arithmetic skills, to get used to writing number sentences as well as mathematical symbols, and to understand that a number could have many different names.

Measurement Context. The fourth context was when she taught the basic units of measurement using Cuisenaire rods. She distributed a box filled with Cuisenaire rods to each table, and told children to build whatever they liked. Then, she asked them whether they found something interesting about this math tool. The children's responses were: "It has many different colors."

"It has many different sizes of sticks." "They are different in length." After listening to the children's responses, she asked "how many different colors are there?" She told the children to take out one of each different color from the box, and put them in front of them. "How many do you have now?" she asked. The children said, "Ten." She then told the children to arrange them from the shortest to the largest, and to tell her the colors from the shortest to the largest.

Teacher: What is the difference between the orange and the blue?
Beth: Orange is bigger than blue.
Teacher: Right. The orange is longer than blue. Now, we have to find out what is the point to this color and this length. Does someone want to tell us?
Alice: Use them count. Um, this white is one, and this red is two because it is the same of two whites, and it goes like three, four, like that.
Teacher: Super! The red equals two whites. How about four whites?
Chris: It equals the purple.
Teacher: Super! The purple equals four whites.
Rich: I found it equals two reds, too.

The children explored various relations among the different colors of rods (e.g., 1 orange = 2 yellows = 5 reds = 10 whites). She then asked them which color of rod was equal to 1 cm, 5 cm, and then 10 cm. Introducing the unit of decimeter, she wrote that 1 dm = 10 cm. At the end of the lesson, she gave the children homework that asked the relations among the Cuisenaire rods (e.g., 1 brown rod = ___ purple rods, 1 blue rod = ___ light-green rods, 1 dark-green rod = ___ red rods).

Equivalent-Coins Context. The last context was when she taught the value of different kinds of coins. First, she showed the children five different kinds of coins—penny, nickel, dime, quarter, and silver dollar—and asked them what each of the coins was called. When the children told her the name of each coin, she wrote the first letter of the name of each coin, p, n, d, q, s, on the board instead of writing the full letters. Then, she asked how many pennies were in a nickel, dime, quarter, and silver dollar, and wrote = after the name of the coins and 1 cent, 5 cents, 10 cents, 25 cents, and 100 cents following the children's answers (e.g., 1 n = 5¢, 1 d = 10¢, and so forth). And then, she gave each group a box of coins, and asked them to show 25 cents using two kinds of coins. After a series of activities showing different amounts of money using two kinds of coins, she gave the children homework about the relation among different kinds of coins.

Everyday-Life Context. Children often used the words "same" and "equal" in a variety of everyday classroom contexts. For example, "I gave an equal amount of time to reading and writing," said Kevin when asked about his plan for "Literacy block"; "They're equal," Ann said after measuring the lengths and widths of two windows drawn on the math handout; "We have an equal number of people who have five letters and six letters in their first names," said the teacher. The word "equal" was often used in their everyday speech when they meant the same.

Issue 3: How Did the Context Affect the Children's Interpretation of the Equals Sign?

We saw that in Ms. March's mathematics lessons, the children used the equals sign in contexts other than performing operations. Sometimes the meaning of the equals sign was discussed explicitly, and sometimes it was not. We also saw the children using the words "same" and "equal" to indicate equivalence in everyday speech. How did these children make sense of the "equals sign" presented in various contexts? What meanings did these children construct through their experiences of using "equals" in various contexts?

Interview 1: No Context. We were interested first in exploring how children viewed the equals sign as a "pure" mathematical symbol, apart from any context. When presented only with the equals sign and asked what it was, 14 of the 16 children responded that it was the equals sign. When asked what the equals sign meant, 2 of these children indicated a relational meaning (i.e., responded that it meant "the same as"). The other 12 interpreted it as an operator symbol. More specifically, as the example of Alice below illustrates, 3 children responded, "The answer." As the case of Rich exemplifies, 3 more said, "Adds up to." As Kevin's comment illustrates, another 3 answered, "The total." As the case of Mark exemplifies, 2 children responded, "What it is or becomes."

> Alice: The equals sign gives the whole entire answer. But, you have to think about what's the right answer. That's what the equals sign asks.
>
> Rich: It means like, if you have two and three, what adds up to.
>
> Kevin: It's equals sign, and it asks you how much is the total, the total number.
>
> Mark: It's equals. . . . That's what it is. It means what it is, like, three and two, what it is, five.

The twelfth child responded, "Equals means, like, if you don't have equals, well, it's like how would you make, like forty minus thirty equals ten? It doesn't make sense if you don't have equals." His response seemed more concerned with the format than with the meaning of the equals sign. He seemed to think that if there was a minus sign (or plus sign), there should be an equals sign so that the sum could be written right after the equals sign. It is interesting that 8 of 12 children spontaneously gave examples to explain the meaning of the equals sign, and all their examples involved the operation of addition or subtraction.

The remaining two participants initially described different, but legitimate, uses to the = symbol. Jessica said, "I see two lines," as did Cornell. The interviewer then asked, "Do you want to think about when you can use them?" Cornell said that he could draw it as a bridge built across the river. Indeed, "=" is often used as a sign for bridge, though in mathematics it has other meaning. Jessica responded to the question as follows:

> If I want to add one more line to this line. . . . Oh, I have a better idea. I take away one line, then I can make it as "taking away." I mean, minus sign. And, I add one more line like this (drawing a vertical line with her finger), I can make a plus. Then, I put this line (the vertical line) like this (drawing a horizontal line with her finger), I can make an equals sign.

Jessica was very excited about her new discovery of how this arbitrary symbolism works. What then does the equals sign mean to her? "Your answer should be after these two lines," said Jessica with a big smile.

Interview 2: Canonical Context. When the equals sign was presented in canonical written addition and subtraction number sentences ($a + b = ?$ or $a - b = ?$ form), participants gave the same responses as those they gave in the first interview. Two children who interpreted it as a relational symbol in the first interview again responded that the equals sign meant the same as (e.g., "Two plus three equals five. It means these two, I mean two plus three, is the same as another number, five"; "They're the same, you know, five minus two and three."). Similarly, 13 children who gave an operator interpretation in the first interview again interpreted the equals sign as an operator. In this second interview, Cornell called = "the equals sign" and said, "If you see the equals, you put the number at the end of these two lines. So, the answer is five, two plus three equals five."

However, some children interpreted the equals sign differently when it was presented in a written addition than in a written subtraction. Four children of 13 who viewed the equals sign as an operator responded that it meant different things when the equals sign was with a plus sign and a minus sign. The following is Paul's interpretation of the equals sign.

Paul:	It's like that, that equals, like four plus five, something equals nine. It means like it is nine all together.
Interviewer:	This equals sign means altogether how much it is. That's what you mean?
Paul:	(Nodding his head) Yeah.
Interviewer:	How about this equals sign in here (showing $9 - 4 = 5$)?
Paul:	It means like you take it away. It means like . . . you pretend that it's erase something, like erase four. And there's no four, so five left.
Interviewer:	This equals sign means something is erased?
Paul:	Yeah, but I would say, it means left.

Interviewer:	Okay . . . um . . . I'm wondering. It sounds like these two equals signs are different.
Paul:	Yeah, they look same, but just different ways.
Interviewer:	Different ways? What do you mean by that?
Paul:	Um, like, they have different meanings. This one (pointing to 5 + 4 = 9) means, like, altogether is. And this one (pointing 9 – 4 = 5) means, like, left something.

For Paul, the equals sign has different meanings; when addition is performed, it means "altogether is," and when subtraction is performed, it means "left." Three other children also interpreted it in the same way—the equals sign has different meanings depending on what kind of operation is performed. But the equals sign still has an operator meaning to them although they differentiate it according to its role in addition and subtraction.

Interview 3: Noncanonical Context. In the third interview the child was presented with a number sentence, $? = a + b$, and asked whether it made sense. Three children who interpreted the equals sign as an operator on the first two tasks accepted the $? = a + b$ form because they had seen such number sentences before (e.g., "Yeah, you can write it that way. I saw it before, I guess, in my first grade. I sometimes write that way."). These 3 children accepted the $c = a + b$ form because they were familiar with it, not necessarily because they understood the equivalence relation between $a + b$ and c.

The other 13 of 16 children responded that it did not make sense because it was backward (e.g., "You wrote it backwards."; "It has to be switched around."; "This 3 + 2 is supposed to come first."). These results are consistent with earlier findings that children who interpreted the equals sign as an operator tended to reject the $? = a + b$ form of written addition.

A new, but not entirely surprising finding, is that the 2 children who interpreted the equals sign as a relational symbol in the first and second interview were also found in this group of 13 children. It appears that the understanding of the equals sign as a relational symbol does not necessarily lead to the acceptance of $? = a + b$ format. The acceptance of noncanonical formats seems to be also related to the child's familiarity with such forms of written addition.

When the $a = a$ form was presented, 11 of the 16 children rejected it and changed it to an operational form such as $0 + 3 = 3$. Again, the two children who interpreted the equals sign as a relational symbol belonged to this group of children. Three of 5 children who accepted the $a = a$ form did so because they had seen it before, though they understood the equals sign as an operator. It is interesting that the remaining 2 children argued that the $3 = 3$ made sense because "three is the same as the three." Consider, for instance, the case of Victor.

| Victor: | Yeah, it makes sense. |
| Interviewer: | What does this number sentence tell you? |

Victor:	Three equals three. Three is three, you know. It's the same.
Interviewer:	I see. Then, what does this equals sign mean?
Victor:	It means the same. Like, three is three.
Interviewer:	Okay. Do you remember this number sentence (showing 2 + 3 = 5)? You told me this equals sign meant the answer.
Victor:	Yeah, it means the answer, you know, five.
Interviewer:	Are these two equals signs different?
Victor:	They mean different things. Like, this one (pointing to the equals sign in 2 + 3 = 5) is for answer, and this one (pointing to the equals sign in 3 = 3) is for the same.

Victor made different interpretations of equals according to the context in which it was presented. It means "the same" in 3 = 3, but it means "the answer" in 2 + 3 = 5. David, who also accepted the $a = a$ form, responded in a similar manner:

Yeah, it's different. It looks the same, but actually it's not exactly same. In here three plus five equals something, it's actually eight, anyway, it means the total, so the total amount is eight. But, in here three equals three. It's the same, like three is the same as three.

David and Victor believed that the equals sign had an operator meaning in one context, but a relational meaning in another context. When there is an operator symbol like the plus or minus sign, the equals sign means "the answer" or "the total"; and when there is no operator symbol, it means "the same as."

Interview 4: Equivalent-Rods Context. In the fourth interview, a child was shown an equation representing the relation between two different colors of Cuisenaire rods, "2 white rods = 1 red rod," and asked whether it made sense and, if it did, what the equals sign meant. The child was also told that he or she could use the Cuisenaire rods if he or she wanted. Twelve of 16 children responded that the rod equation told that 2 white rods are the same as 1 red rod, and so the equals sign in that rod equation referred to the equivalence relation between 2 white rods and 1 red rod. For instance, when asked whether the rod equation "2 white rods = 1 red rod" made sense, Paul said, "Yeah. If I don't know what the Cuisenaire rods are, I wouldn't say, like, two white rods equals one red rod, because I wouldn't know what white and red rods look like. But now, I know what the Cuisenaire rods are. So it means, look [picking out two white rods and one red rod from the box] if you put two white rods and red rod, and you put them both together, like this [putting the red rod underneath two white rod]. It [indicating two white rods] equals the size of the red one."

Interviewer:	Great. Then, what does this equals sign mean?
Paul:	It means equal, you know. Two white rods are exactly same as one red rod.

| Interviewer: | I see. But, I remember you told me before that the equals sign meant "altogether is" or "left." |
| Paul: | Oh, yeah, but, this time it means the same. |

Paul has another meaning of the equals sign in addition to "altogether is" and "left." This time he interpreted it as a relational symbol representing the equivalence relation between different colors of rods. Like Paul, most children who viewed the equals sign as an operator in the first and second interviews (when presented with only the equals sign, and with $a + b = ?$ and $a - b = ?$) interpreted it as a relational symbol in this context. They also responded that the equals sign had different meanings depending on the contexts in which it was used.

In contrast, 4 children interpreted the equals sign in "2 white rods = 1 red rod" as an operator symbol, assimilating it into their operator understanding of the equals sign. The following are their responses:

Victor:	The equals sign actually means add up to, like one white rod plus one white rod equals two white rods, but you can say, two white rods equals one red rod.
Cornell:	It tells you one red rod equals two white rods. It's like one white plus one white equals two whites, but you can switch it to one red rod.
Berry:	It's like one plus one equals two. So you see two white rods, it's like one rod plus one rod, it's two rods, then again it's one red rod.
May:	It means what makes two white rods or one red rod. And that is one plus one.

They certainly knew that 2 white rods have the same length as 1 red rod. However, it seemed that their operator understanding of the equals sign led them to look for some operation in that rod equation. They found the $1 + 1 = 2$ operation in the relation between two rods, and interpreted the equals sign as indicating the $1 + 1$ operation.

It is interesting that 2 children, Rich and Beth, constructed a new meaning of the equals sign while being interviewed. In the first interview when presented with the equals sign, Rich responded that "it means, like, if you have two and three, what adds up to." In the second interview when presented with $a + b = ?$ and $a - b = ?$, he likewise responded that the equals sign "means what's the number if you add up to." However, in the fourth interview when asked whether "2 white rods = 1 red rod" made sense, he responded differently.

| Rich: | Yeah, it means, um, if you have two white rods, and they are the same as one red rod. |
| Interviewer: | I see. Then, this equals sign means . . . |

Rich:	It means the same. There two, I mean, two white rods and one red rod are the same.
Interviewer:	Okay. Is this equals sign different from these (showing 3 + 4 = ? and 8 − 5 = ?)? You told me that the equals sign in here meant what was the number if you add up to . . .
Rich:	Yeah, but . . . um, I don't think . . . they are different. (Long pause) Here (pointing to the equals sign in the equation 3 + 4 = ?), three plus four equals something, um, three plus four equals, it equals something, I mean like . . . put . . . um . . . make that equal . . . um . . . I don't know. I got confused. . . . (Long pause) It equals, um, um . . . it makes them equal.
Interviewer:	What do you mean by that? It makes what equal?
Rich:	Um . . . (Long pause) These two (pointing to 3 + 4 and then the question mark in the equation 3 + 4 = ?), three plus four and seven. Yeah, it mean, means, like, this one, three plus four, equals, I mean, is the same as this one, seven. This one (pointing to 8 − 5 = ?) too. The equals sign means eight minus five equals three, means the same.

Unlike other children who defended their inconsistent interpretations of the equals sign by saying that it had different meanings depending on the context, Rich held back when the interviewer challenged his different interpretations. He felt conflict and became confused. The boy strove to resolve the conflict, reflecting on his interpretations. Rich said "equals" when he meant the same; he was sure that "equals" meant the same as in the rod equation "two white rods equals one red rod"; he repeated "three plus four equals something" trying to make sense of the meaning of "equals" in that number sentence. Finally, he found that the equals sign made three plus four and something (i.e., seven) "equals"—the same as. He now found that the equals sign represents the equivalence relation between numbers just as it represents the equivalence relation between two different colors of rods. And he could see the connection between the equals sign used in the written addition and one in 2 white rods = 1 red rod.

So did Beth. In the first and second interviews she responded that the equals sign meant, "what is it add up to." But, in this fourth interview she interpreted it as meaning the same. When asked whether those equals sign were different, Beth said, "Um . . . no, no, it can't be. . . . This (pointing to the equals sign in 2 white rods = 1 red rod) means the same, and, and, this (pointing to the equals sign in 3 + 5 = ?) means, it means three plus five equals something. It equals something, you know. . . . I mean, it equals."

Interviewer:	What do you mean by that? What is it that equals?
Beth:	Three plus five equals eight. Three and five equals eight. I mean . . . three plus five equals, you know, it equals eight. I

> mean ... um ... like ... okay, like, these two numbers (pointing to 3 + 5) equals eight. You see, this part (pointing to 3 + 5), I mean, the left side is the same as the right side of the equals. You understand what I'm saying?

Her intuition that the equals sign cannot have different meanings and the interpretations that she actually made generated the conflict. She seemed to be certain that "equals" meant the same as in the rod equation "2 white rods = 1 red rod." She uttered aloud "three plus five equals eight" laying stress on "equals," and tried to make sense of the "equals" in that rod equation. And she finally did—the equals sign means "the left side is the same as the right side of the equals." By resolving cognitive conflict, Beth as well as Rich had taken the first step toward a general (non-context-bound) and integrated (well-connected) conception of equals.

Interview 5: Money-Equivalent Contexts. In the last interview, a child was shown a rod equation representing the relation between different kinds of coins, 1 dollar = 100 pennies, and asked whether it made sense and, if it did, what the equals sign meant. Thirteen of the 16 children responded that 1 dollar is the same as 100 pennies, and so the equals sign means the same. Of these children, 12 were those who interpreted the equals sign as meaning "the same as" when shown "2 white rods = 1 red rod" in the fourth interview, and one was Victor who had previously responded inconsistently. In this last interview he said that:

> If you have one dollar, it means, like, okay, if you collect the pennies and, and if you have hundred pennies, you can change them to one dollar bill, because one hundred pennies and one dollar are the same. They're the same, but look different, but actually the same. . . .

The other 3 children who interpreted the equals sign as an operator symbol in the fourth interview noted that the equals sign in "1 dollar = 100 pennies" meant "adds up to" or "what makes." For instance, one said, "It's like one plus one plus one plus, like that, and it adds up to hundred pennies, but you can say it's one dollar." Unlike all the others, these 3 children consistently interpreted the equals sign as an operator across all five contexts. The children's overall responses across five different contexts are presented in Fig. 5.1.

Victor's inconsistent interpretations across the five interviews made us wonder how he made his interpretations. Did he have his own way of interpreting the meanings of the equals sign used in different contexts? Or, did he respond to interviewer's questions as his mood dictates? If he has his own way of interpreting the equals sign, what is it? When the interviewer asked why the equals sign had different meanings, Victor said:

Figure 5.1: Children's Interpretations of Equals

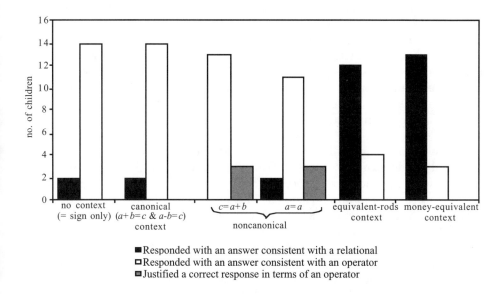

■ Responded with an answer consistent with a relational
□ Responded with an answer consistent with an operator
▣ Justified a correct response in terms of an operator

I mean, it depends on the math sentence you have. Sometimes i t means the answer, I mean, it asks you the answer, but sometimes, i t means add up to. I mean, like, it adds up to something, like, if you put one white and one white together, it adds up to two whites. It's not exactly the answer, it's like, it's just a little different. But, sometimes it means the same, and it's very very different. So you've got to carefully read the math sentence you have, you know.

For Victor, the meaning of the equals sign depended on the math sentence. Most children agreed. When the equals sign is presented in written addition and subtraction, it has an operator meaning such as "the answer," "the total," "add up to," or "what it is." But when it is presented in math sentence such as "2 white rods = 1 red rod" or "1 dollar = 100 pennies," it means the same as. The equals sign has different meanings depending on whether the operation is performed.

Analysis

We first discuss children's interpretations of the equals sign, and then discuss implications of our results for pedagogy.

What Children Know About Equals and Why

The results show that most children in this study constructed context-based multiple meanings of the equals sign. When the equals sign was used in the context of performing operations, they interpreted it as an operator. But they also viewed the equals sign as a relational symbol in the context wherein no arithmetic operation was performed. These children switched between operator and relational meanings of equals depending on the context in which the equals sign was used.

The findings of this study suggest that young children are not limited to the action interpretation of equals as has usually been thought. They do have an everyday notion of equivalence. We noted that in their everyday speech, children used words such as "equal" or "same" to indicate equivalence. And given appropriate experience in a supportive context, most children are capable of an equivalence interpretation of equals. The teacher explicitly used Cuisenaire rods and coins to encourage the idea of equivalence and children seemed to have little difficulty developing a relational view of equals.

However, this relational view of equals was not entirely integrated with the children's informal operator view. Most children retained an operator interpretation and had both a relational and an operator view of equals that were not well connected. They were unable to see how the equals sign in written additions could be interpreted in terms of equivalence. They failed to make connections among equals used in various contexts and instead explicitly stated that equals meant one thing in one context, but another in a different context. They also judged the legitimacy of number sentences in a rigid manner and their judgments were based on experience with specific examples rather than an integrated conception of equals. The performance of these children indicates that their interpretations of equals are tied to a relatively weak schema: Knowledge is context-bound, only loosely connected, and judgments are precedent driven. These children only *appear* to be responding flexibly. That is, their multiple interpretations of equals represent *pseudo-flexibility*. How they interpreted the equals sign was entirely determined by the context.

Why did the children interpret the equals sign in written addition statements as an operator and fail to see that it could be interpreted in terms of equivalence, a tendency that has been noted in many studies? One factor appears to be the nature of instructional experience. First, the teacher seemed to promote an operator meaning of equals in some contexts while emphasizing a relational meaning in other contexts such as Cuisenaire rods and coin activities. In particular, when activities involved addition and subtraction, the teacher as well as mathematics curriculum materials encouraged an operator meaning, providing few opportunities for the children to develop a relational meaning. Both core book and workbook introduced equals exclusively in standard calculation context. And children were asked to write the "answer," "what happened," or "output" of the operation right after the "equals," which thus appeared to represent the results of the operation instead of an idea of equivalence. We note that parents and perhaps the culture at large also tend to see mathematics as getting the right answer as quickly as possible.

Furthermore, an operator approach to equals was promoted in activities that the teacher believed accomplished other purposes. One example involved activities that she saw as encouraging problem solving. In these "problem-solving" activities, however, the children were mainly engaged in finding the answer and writing it down, either after the equals sign or below a line in the vertical format. The teacher also did not explicitly deal with the meaning of equals as she did in Cuisenaire rods or coin activities, and she seldom encouraged the children to use non-canonical forms of number sentences (for example, $18 = 5 + 5 + 3 + 3 + 2$ in the ladybugs problem).

A second example in which the teacher unwittingly encouraged an operator approach involves the morning activity "renaming the date." For the teacher, this activity was aimed at the development of an understanding that a certain number has different names, as well as the development of competence in the arithmetic operation. Children, however, saw this activity as demanding practice in the arithmetic operation. Most children were concerned with "making" or "producing" a certain number (for example, writing 7 on the top and then simply writing $3 + 4$, $2 + 5$, $10 - 3$ without using the equals sign). But the teacher seemed unaware of the children's operator interpretation of equals as they engaged in "renaming the date." If the teacher was concerned with the other names for a number concept, she should have encouraged children to use not only arithmetic equations but also other representations, for instance, $12 =$ ||||||||||, ∩||, X||, *twelve*, or *doce* (see Baroody, with Coslick, 1998).

Unlike standard number sentences, math sentences, such as "2 white rods = 1 red rod" or "1 dollar = 100 pennies," do not seem to promote the use of action schemes (an operator interpretation of equals) for two reasons. One is that these equations do not contain operator symbols like + and −. Children, therefore, may not be prevented from seeing these math sentences as describing a relation. A second is that children may have viewed the task of comparing two different kinds of objects (e.g., white rods and red rods or pennies and dollars) to determine the relation between them as unrelated to computation and, hence, were able to develop a relational meaning for the nonstandard context.

The prevalence of the operator interpretation also seems to be related to children's informal arithmetic, which is largely based on actions, particularly counting actions. For young children, adding is largely combining sets and counting their elements to get a sum. Why should they abandon this notion when they get to school? Why should the presence of an equals sign change their interpretation? At the outset, then, children view written addition as requiring the production of a sum.

The action schemes children bring to school seem to be very powerful, particularly in the context involving numerical format. We often observed that when shown only numbers, the children tended to *do* something, to add or take away. Children employed the action schema with almost any numerical format. This may be related, at least in part, to their tendency to reject $3 = 3$ and change it to a written addition form such as $3 + 0 = 3$. Furthermore, as pointed out above, children's "natural" tendency to operate is reinforced by mathematics curriculum materials, teachers' practices, and perhaps parents and culture at large.

Another reason for the prevalence of the operator view is that, even if young children did accept the equivalence interpretation of the equals sign, they would first have to compute the sum (or remember it) in order to determine whether the equivalence holds true for a particular case. For example, shown $3 + 2 = 5$, the child must first add $3 + 2$ or remember the sum to determine whether it is the same number as 5. In other words, from the point of view of the child, the equals sign may require an operation (or memory of it) even when an equivalence relation is assumed.

And finally, we note that the operational interpretation of the equals sign is, in fact, legitimate from a mathematical point of view. Although it may be interpreted as conveying a relational meaning, the equals sign in written addition problems such as $2 + 3 = 5$ may just as legitimately be considered to have an operator meaning. One view of addition is computational: It involves determining the sum of two numbers, and if this is the case, the $=$ sign truly indicates that one must obtain the correct answer. There is nothing wrong with this interpretation; it is just not the only one possible.

In brief, several factors seem to explain children's strong, almost aggressive, tendency to see the equals sign in written number sentences as indicating the need for an operation. Teachers and curriculum materials encourage this view, albeit sometimes unwittingly; operating is a developmentally "natural" approach to such problems; operating is necessary as a check even if the child accepts the equivalence interpretation; and an operator interpretation is, in fact, legitimate from a mathematical point of view.

A related question is why children fail to generalize number sentences to the notion of equivalence, a notion that they successfully employ in other contexts (coins and Cuisenaire rods). Here, there appear to be two major reasons. One is that the teacher did not encourage transfer. Although she was successful in promoting a relational meaning in some contexts, she provided little opportunity for the children to make connections among the different meanings attached to the different contexts. She did not focus explicitly on how an expression like $3 + 2 = 5$ could be interpreted either in terms of operations or equivalence, or on why one might want to think of $=$ as indicating equivalence in one case (e.g., coins) and the result of an operation in another (e.g., calculation). Instead of actively promoting connections and a deeper understanding of the various meanings of equivalence, the teacher seemed to believe it was sufficient to provide children with a variety of concrete situations in which the conventional mathematical symbols could be used. Unfortunately, she was not aware of the different and unconnected ways in which children interpreted the equals sign in these contexts and of how classroom experience failed to achieve her goals.

Another reason for the lack of transfer is that it may be very hard for young children to entertain two very different interpretations of the same situations *at the same time*. A mathematician may simultaneously understand that the sentence $3 + 2 = 5$ in multiple ways. She may interpret it, for example, as 5 is the same number as $3 + 2$, as $3 + 2$ have been combined to obtain the sum 5, *and* beginning at 3 on the number line and moving forward two increments to reach the number 5. But the child may find it hard enough to understand equivalence by itself or to perform the necessary calculations (or movements on the number line), let alone entertain several of these interpretations simultaneously, especially if the teacher has not made special efforts to help in this endeavor.

So there are many reasons why most children failed to make connections between different conceptions of equals and construct an integrated view of equals. Unlike the majority of participants, however, the performance of several children indicates a general relational view of equals. In particular, the two children who experienced cognitive conflict and resolved it by realizing that equals used in various situations could be thought of as "the same as" show that they had taken the first step toward a general (non-context-bound) and integrated (well-connected) conception of equals. In other words, they had taken the first steps of constructing a strong schema. The construction of an integrated view of equals by these two children seemed to have been largely due to the intervention of the interviewer, not the teacher's instruction. Whereas the teacher did not help children explicitly make connections between the different meanings attached to the different contexts, the clinical interviewer challenged their inconsistent interpretations, induced cognitive conflict, and prompted reflection and integration. Our analysis suggests several implications for pedagogy—for how teachers can help children not only learn different concepts of equals but develop an integrated conception of equals.

Implications for Pedagogy

As implied in the Rationale section earlier, a relational understanding of the equals sign is necessary for fostering adaptive expertise with many aspects of mathematics, including arithmetic principles and algebra. How can instruction cultivate this key concept?

Integration Across Contexts. First, children clearly need to learn the different meanings of the equals sign. For instance, $2 + 3 = 5$ may be interpreted as composing the parts 2 and 3 to form the whole 5, and $5 = 2 + 3$ may be viewed as decomposing the whole 5 into the possible constituents 2 and 3. Similarly, the equation $2 \times 3 = 6$ may be seen as a statement about multiplication and $6 = 3 \times 2$ as a statement about factoring. Although all of such statements may be interpreted as expressing equivalence relations, children need to recognize that there can be multiple context-specific meanings for equations involving the equals sign. They also need to know which interpretation is intended or most sensible in any particular context.

Exposing children to different contexts in which equals is used can be the first step to helping them learn about different meanings of equals. This, of course, is the approach taken by the teacher we observed. And as we have shown, this method is useful but not sufficient. It is likely to result in more flexibility in interpreting the equals sign than shown by children who experience only standard calculation exercises. But at the same time, children exposed to various contexts are unlikely to connect different interpretations and to see how several interpretations might make sense in the same context.

Therefore, in addition to providing exposure to various contexts, teachers should employ several instructional approaches designed to help children integrate different concepts of equals. One approach is using a variety of models, not just the standard change-add-to model of addition. Several writers suggest that models stressing equivalence, like the balance scale, should be employed so that children do not develop only the operator interpretation of equals (e.g., Baroody, 1987; Baroody, with Coslick, 1998; Chatterley & Peck, 1995; Wynroth, 1980). Thus, children learn that a combination such as $3 + 4$ has to be balanced by, and is therefore equivalent to, a sum such as 7. A number statement is correct only if there is balance or equivalence. The balance scale can also illustrate noncanonical equations such as $7 = 3 + 4, 5 + 2 = 3 + 4$, and $7 = 7$.

Nonarithmetic Contexts. Second, introducing the equals sign in non-arithmetic contexts can minimize the tendency to view the equals exclusively as an operator. For example, equals can be first introduced in comparing collections (e.g., $\bullet\!\!\bullet\ = \ \bullet \bullet \bullet$), collections and numbers (e.g., $\bullet \bullet \bullet = 3$), or numbers (e.g., $3 = 3$); see Baroody, 1987; Baroody, with Coslick, 1998; Wynroth, 1980). Also, teachers as well as curriculum materials should expose children more frequently to noncanonical forms of equations so that children become more flexible in writing addition and subtraction sentences and include a relational meaning of equals in the context of performing operations. As we have shown, noncanonical forms are extremely rare in the curriculum materials. Thus, for most children the "$a + b = c$" format becomes *the* method for representing addition. This is even true of some children who viewed the equals sign as a relational symbol. Children's tendency to reject noncanonical forms seemed related, at least in part, to frequency of exposure.

A Different Symbol for the Operator Meaning. Third, using different symbols for different concepts of equals can be also helpful. A mathematical symbol sometimes denotes several ideas, and conversely an idea is sometimes represented by several symbols. The minus sign ($-$), for example, stands for an operation of subtraction and the designation of a number as negative. The equals sign in $2 + 3 = 5$ also can be legitimately interpreted as involving both relational and operator ideas. And conversely, the idea of an equivalence is denoted by "$=$" between numbers, but by "$\equiv$" between sets. Part of the reason for children's difficulty in learning mathematical symbolism may lie in this ambiguity as well as its abstract and arbitrary nature.

One way to help children deal with the multiple meanings of written addition and subtraction is to use different symbols for different ideas. For instance, to stress written addition as an operation, the teacher may write $2 + 3 \rightarrow 5$. To stress written addition as an equivalence relation, the teacher may write $2 + 3 = 5$ and call = "the same number as" (Baroody, 1987; Baroody, with Coslick, 1998; Wynroth, 1980). The use of different symbols, as well as the use of explicit words "the same number as," may clarify for children that different concepts are involved. After a time, the teacher could explain that (for unknown reasons) the symbol $\rightarrow$ is usually not employed in these circumstances and that = is used to indicate both meanings. Or, she may start with children's informal ways of representing the different mathematical ideas and help them gradually bridge their invented symbols to formal symbols.

Teacher Monitoring. Fourth, teachers should be aware of children's qualitatively distinct interpretations of many activities, tasks, and learning situations. We have shown in this study how children's interpretations were different from those of teachers as well as their peers. The teacher in this study believed that children would develop a relational meaning of equals through experiencing it in various contexts. But she was unaware of their different interpretations of activities and learning situations as well as their diverse interpretations of equals. With little or no understanding of children's ideas and interpretations, a teacher is unlikely to provide the assistance necessary to promote the development of their mathematical knowledge. Effective instruction should be built on accurate knowledge of what children know, not on what teachers (and adults) merely think children know.

Using the Clinical Interview to Assess *and* Promote Learning. Finally, we suggest using a form of clinical interviewing as a teaching tool. As we have shown in this study, the clinical interview is an effective means of not only examining process—underlying thinking, understanding, and strategies—but also promoting cognitive conflict and reflection, which foster the construction of more integrated mathematical concepts. Piaget (1987) pointed out that teachers (and other adults) can better help children construct new knowledge by inducing disequilibrium in current cognitive schemes than by directly correcting them. Following the spirit of Piaget's theory, various educators have suggested the use of the clinical interview method in instructional settings (e.g., Ackermann, 1995; Confrey, 1990; Ginsburg, 1997; Ginsburg, Jacobs, & Lopez, 1998; von Glasersfeld, 1987). Using the clinical interview in instructional settings is challenging. Even so, it can be a useful tool for examining the children's understanding, inducing cognitive conflict, and providing them with adequate assistance. In this way, teachers can help their students develop integrated mathematical concepts and adaptive expertise.

References

Ackermann, E. (1995). Construction and transference of meaning through form. In L. P. Steffe & J. Gale (Eds.), *Constructivism in education* (pp. 341–354). Hillsdale, NJ: Lawrence Erlbaum Associates.

Baroody, A. J. (1987). *Children's mathematical thinking: A developmental framework for preschool, primary, and special education teachers.* New York: Teachers College Press.

Baroody, A. J., with Coslick, R. T. (1998). *Fostering children's mathematical power: An investigative approach to K–8 mathematics instruction.* Mahwah, NJ: Lawrence Erlbaum Associates.

Baroody, A. J., & Ginsburg, H. P. (1983). The effects of instruction on children's understanding of the "equals" sign. *The Elementary School Journal, 84,* 199–212.

Baroody, A. J., & Ginsburg, H. P. (1986). The relationship between initial meaningful and mechanical knowledge of arithmetic. In J. Hiebert (Ed.), *Conceptual and procedural knowledge: The case of mathematics* (pp. 75–112). Hillsdale, NJ: Lawrence Erlbaum Associates.

Behr, M., Erlwanger, S., & Nichols, E. (1980). How children view the equals sign. *Mathematics Teaching, 92,* 13–15.

Borenson, H. (1991). *Hands-on equations.* Allentown, PA: Borenson & Associates.

Casolaro, N. (1994). *Bright start: Integrate critical thinking skills with math (level B).* Merrimack, NH: Options.

Chatterley, L. J., & Peck, D. M. (1995). We're crippling our kids with kindness. *Journal of Mathematical Behavior, 14,* 429–436.

Clement, J., Lochhead, J., & Monk, G. (1981). Translation difficulties in learning mathematics. *American Mathematical Monthly, 88,* 286–290.

Confrey, J. (1990). A review of the research on student conception in mathematics, science, and programming. In C. B. Cazden (Ed.), *Review of Research in Education* (Vol. 16, pp. 3–55). Washington, DC: American Educational Research Association.

Ginsburg, H. P. (1982). *Children's arithmetic: How they learn it and how you teach it* (rev. ed.). Austin, TX: Pro-Ed.

Ginsburg, H. P. (1996). Toby's math. In R. J. Sternberg & T. Ben-zeev (Eds.), *In the nature of mathematical thinking* (pp. 175–202). Mahwah, NJ: Lawrence Erlbaum Associates.

Ginsburg, H. P. (1997). *Entering the child's mind: The clinical interview in psychological research and practice.* New York: Cambridge University Press.

Ginsburg, H. P., Jacobs, S. G., & Lopez, L. S. (1998). *Flexible interviewing in the classroom: Learning what children know about math.* Boston, MA: Allyn & Bacon.

Hiebert, J. (1984) Children's mathematics learning: The struggle to link form and understanding. *Elementary School Journal, 84,* 497–513.

Hiebert, J., & Lefevre, P. (1986). Conceptual and procedural knowledge in mathematics: An introductory analysis. In J. Hiebert (Ed.), *Conceptual and procedural knowledge: The case of mathematics* (pp. 1–27). Hillsdale, NJ: Lawrence Erlbaum Associates.

Hsieh, J., & Baroody, A. J. (2000, April). *Children's understanding of the uses of parentheses.* Round table presentation at the annual meeting of the American Educational Research Association, New Orleans, LA.

Hughes, M. (1986). *Children and numbers.* New York: Blackwell.

Irons, C. J. (1994). *Moving into math: Core book.* San Francisco: Mimosa.

Kieran, C. (1980, April). *Constructing meaning for non-trivial equations.* Paper presented at annual meeting of American Educational Research Association, Boston.

Kieran, C. (1981). Concepts associated with the equality symbol. *Educational Studies in Mathematics, 12,* 317–326.

Kieren, T. E. (1992). Rational and fractional numbers as mathematical and personal knowledge: Implications for curriculum and instruction. In G. Leinhardt, R. Putnam, & R. A. Hattrup (Eds.), *Analysis of arithmetic for mathematics teaching* (pp. 323–371). Hillsdale, NJ: Lawrence Erlbaum Associates.

Piaget, J. (1987). Comments on mathematics education. In H. E. Gruber & J. J. Voneche (Eds.), *The essential Piaget: An interpretative guide* (pp. 726–732). New York: Basic Books.

Van de Walle, J. (1980, April). *An investigation of the concept of equality and mathematical symbols held by first, second, and third-grade children: An informal report.* Paper presented at the annual meeting of the National Council of Teachers of Mathematics, Seattle, WA.

von Glasersfeld, E. (1987). Constructivism. In T. Husen & N. Postlethwaite (Eds.), *International encyclopedia of education* (Supplement Vol. 1, pp. 162–163). Oxford: Pergamon.

Weaver, F. (1973). The symmetric property of the equality relation and young children's ability to solve open addition and subtraction sentences. *Journal for Research in Mathematics Education, 4*, 45–46.

Wynroth, L. (1980). *Wynroth math programs—The natural numbers sequence.* Ithaca, NY: Wynroth Math Programs.

CHAPTER 6

BASIC MULTIPLICATION COMBINATIONS: PASSIVE STORAGE OR DYNAMIC REORGANIZATION?

Brian Butterworth, Noemi Marchesini, and Luisa Girelli
Department of Psychology and the Institute of Cognitive Neuroscience,
University College London[1]

The proponents of drill (e.g., Ashcraft, 1985; Thorndike, 1922) and the proponents of meaningful learning (e.g., Baroody, 1985; Brownell, 1935) have long debated how single-digit (basic) number combinations are internalized and mentally represented. The organization of basic number combinations in memory is sometimes regarded as fixed, at least in adults, whether in a tabular array (e.g., Ashcraft & Battaglia, 1978) or in an associative network (e.g., Campbell, 1995). Some scholars, such as Siegler (1988), have proposed an ontogenetic dynamic that gradually shapes the final organization by reducing the relative strength of associative links between an expression and erroneous solutions (e.g., 5, 6, or 7 in the case of 3 + 5), while strengthening the link to the correct answer (8 in the case of 3 + 5). One obvious source of dynamic change is familiarity, in which the more frequently produced or encountered link becomes more strongly represented (e.g., Siegler, 1988). Yet another possible source of dynamic change is the learning of relational knowledge. Such learning may cause a sudden relative strengthening or weakening of links between expressions and their correct solutions. That is, the organization of combinations in memory may be *reorganized* so as to favor some representations of correct basic combinations over others. In this chapter, we describe a study that indicates relational knowledge can be the source of such change.

Rationale

The Case of Additive and Multiplicative Commutativity

Consider addition and multiplication. Both are commutative: 3 + 5 = 5 + 3 and 3 x 5 = 5 x 3. Provided one understands this, one does not need to store both forms of the commuted pair in memory (Baroody, 1985, 1994, 1999; Baroody & Ginsburg, 1991; Rickard & Bourne, 1996; Rickard, Healy, & Bourne, 1994). Thus, one member of the pair may become privileged over (i.e., consistently answered more quickly than) the other. Transformation of the nonprivileged form into the privileged form may help to account for observations that large-number-first

---

[1] Dr. Marchesini also has an appointment in the Department of General Psychology, University of Padua, Italy. Dr. Girelli is now in the Department of Psychology, University of Milano-Bicocca, Italy.

combinations are retrieved faster than small-number-first items (e.g., Campbell & Graham, 1985; Svenson, 1985).

However, we cannot argue for a privileged representation on the basis of economy of storage, because the storage capacity of human memory is not known. Nor can we argue for it on the basis of whether speed of retrieval would be better or worse with one form or two, because any savings in search time might be lost in transforming one form into the other. There is indirect evidence, though, that *learning* is more efficient when only one of a commuted pair is learned. In China and Iceland, children are taught only half of the basic multiplication combinations. In China, for example, they learn 3 x 2 as part of the n x 2 family, and the n x 3 family starts with 3 x 3. Thus, they are never explicitly taught 2 x 3 = 6 (or 0 x 3, 1 x 3, or other 1 x n combinations). There have been many studies demonstrating that Chinese adults are superior to Westerners on multiplication (e.g., LeFevre & Liu, 1997). Needed is direct evidence of a causal link between these two phenomena—that teaching half of the commuted items fosters mastery better than teaching all items.

Where children learn both of the commuted pairs, as in the rote learning of multiplication tables often found in the United States or in most European schools, does this mean that both forms are stored? Even if both are represented in memory, what determines whether there is privileged access to just one of the forms? According to the general learning principles proposed by drill proponents (e.g., Ashcraft, 1985; Thorndike, 1922), the first learned or the more practiced is likely to be the more accessible. This would lead to the prediction that in the United States and the United Kingdom, for instance, 6 x 2 would be privileged over 2 x 6, because the n x 2 family is introduced before and practiced more than the n x 6 family.[2] Evidence that the privileged form is determined by a principle that reflects the meaning of the factors, not by the amount of practice or by priority, would be important support for the meaningful-learning view (Baroody, 1985; Brownell, 1935). This would be particularly true of evidence indicating that the basic number combination can be reorganized in long-term memory (LTM).

Questions Addressed

In this study, we examined whether commuted pairs of basic multiplication combinations require the same response times. If not, is one form privileged? If so, is it the first learned? Does the privileged form change in the course of development?

Overview

Our measure was the time taken to answer each form of the commuted pair problem. That is, will it take longer to retrieve 2 x 6 or 6 x 2? We assume that the

---

[2] This may depend on how U.S. children are taught to interpret multiplication expressions. In programs that build on a "groups-of" meaning, the 2 x n family might well be introduced before the 6 x n family.

form more quickly solved is the one more similar to the stored representation. If they are solved equally quickly we infer that both forms are in memory (or, conceivably, that neither is present).

Although Italian schools foster rote learning of tables, recitation of the tables is the opposite of that in the U.S. and U.K. schools. That is, Italian schoolchildren learn the 2 x *n* family (*due per uno è due* or "two times one is two," *due per due è quattro, due per tre è sei, due per quattro è otto,* and so forth) before the 6 x *n* family. So although these children learn both 2 x 6 and 6 x 2, they are exposed to the former many months, often a year, before the latter. Thus, on the basis of priority of learning and total exposure, 2 x 6 should be privileged over 6 x 2.

However, if children understand the commutative law of multiplication, their mental representation of basic multiplication combinations may reorganize to favor the larger-operand-first (*N* x *m*) items, regardless of the actual chronological order in which children were taught commuted items. (A preference for the *N* x *m* form might also result, in part, from the application of repeated-addition strategies. Such strategies consist of adding the larger operand the number of times indicated by the smaller operand, thus reducing the number of operations to be computed.) A key aim of this study was to check for evidence of a reorganization, as indicated by a switch in which form was answered more quickly.

Method

Participants and Their Previous Multiplication Training

Twenty-eight third graders (mean age = 8 years and 7 months), 31 fourth graders (mean age = 9 years and 5 months), and 30 fifth graders (mean age = 10 years and 6 months) participated in the study. All children were recruited from three classes in a primary school in Northern Italy. None was diagnosed as learning disabled, and they were all introduced to and trained on basic multiplication combinations with the same teaching method.

Multiplication was introduced after children were relatively familiar with addition and subtraction, that is, by the end of the first grade or beginning of the second grade. Multiplication instruction typically began with concrete examples of familiar situations (e.g., dolls and dresses, frame A of Fig. 6.1) and proceeded to more abstract representations such as visualizing arrangement or grouping of objects (frame B of Fig. 6.1) and then grouping of dots (frame C of Fig. 6.1). The use of these different types of representation should help students grasp the meaning of the multiplication itself. It should also help them move from the ability to manipulate and represent quantities of objects to the ability to manipulate and represent numbers as abstract concepts. It is only toward the end of the second grade, beginning of the third grade, that multiplication combinations are introduced starting from the 1 x *n*, 2 x *n*, and 3 x *n* families. At this stage, the commutative law is explicitly taught. The other families are gradually introduced and tested first by repetition of the family sequence (e.g., 2 x 1, 2 x 2, 2 x 3, . . .), then by a single family in random order (e.g., 2 x 4, 2 x 7, 2 x 2, . . .), and finally by all combinations.

Figure 6.1: Three Ways Multiplication Is Illustrated in Italian Primary Schools

A. Familiar Concrete Objects

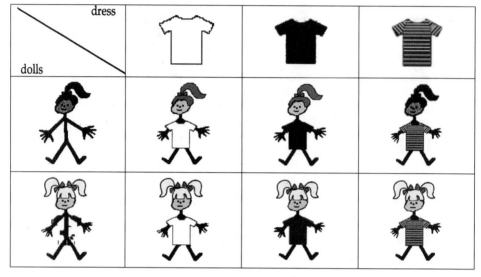

3 dresses x 2 dolls = 6 combinations → 3 x 2 = 6

B. Grouping of Objects

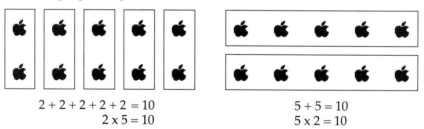

2 + 2 + 2 + 2 + 2 = 10   5 + 5 = 10
2 x 5 = 10   5 x 2 = 10

C. Groupings of Dots

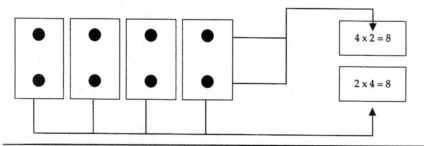

4 x 2 = 8

2 x 4 = 8

Material

Because we wished to assess the effects of the factors of age and grade as well as position of the larger number, we selected just those items that were reasonably familiar to all participants. The results of a pilot study indicated that large items yielded high error rate and were often solved via backup strategies, rather than retrieval from memory. Thus, just the multiplication combinations between 2 x 2 and 6 x 5 were used as stimuli (n = 48). Items were assigned randomly to two different lists, with two constraints: (a) Commuted items were never included in the same list (e.g., 3 x 4 was put in List A, and 4 x 3 in List B), and (b) for half the items on each list the larger operand was first (e.g., 4 x 2) and for the other half it was second (e.g., 2 x 4). The two lists were presented on different days.

Procedure

The testing took place in late January. Each participant was tested individually at school. Stimuli were read aloud to a child, and latencies were hand-timed using a stopwatch from the time the experimenter finished reading the problem until the child began to make a response. Any verbal comment or overt strategies used by the child were recorded, but no attempt was made to distinguish between trials in which participants appeared to retrieve answers from memory and those in which they may have been using another solution strategy. Consecutive trials were separated by an interval of a few seconds. Before the study began, participants were presented with training trials to familiarize them with the task and the experimental setting. Children were asked to do the task the best they could but were told that their performance would not be graded for school in any way.

Results

Within each grade, individuals whose median latency and error rates were below their age group's average were classified as high-skilled participants; all remaining children were classified as low-skilled participants. Following this criterion, the third grade included 13 high-skilled children and 15 low-skilled ones; the fourth grade, 12 high- and 19 low-skilled children; and the fifth grade, 10 high- and 20 low-skilled children.

Because of marked heterogeneity of variance in the data, a reciprocal transformation of reaction times (RTs) and an arcsine transformation of error proportions were performed before the statistical analyses of the results. Harmonic means and error rates for the different sets of problems are reported in Table 6.1.

RTs Analysis

Overall, we found a strong correlation between the magnitude of an item's product (e.g., 20 for 4 x 5) and the median RTs (problem size effect: Spearman

Table 6.1: Harmonic Means of Reaction Times in Seconds (RTs) and Error Rates (ErR) as a Function of Position of the Larger and of Grade Level

	$N \times m$		$m \times N$		Ties	
Grade	RTs	ErR	RTs	ErR	RTs	ErR
Third	3.40	13.5	3.47	13.1	2.15	7.3
Fourth	2.22	9.4	2.50	8.8	1.59	4.8
Fifth	1.90	4.5	2.06	6.1	1.45	0.0

rank correlation $r = 0.479$, $p < .01$; $r = 0.773$, $p < .0001$; $r = 0.764$, $p < .0001$ for third, fourth, and fifth grade, respectively).[3] These findings are in line with previous studies on the development of multiplication skills (e.g., Campbell & Graham, 1985).

Mean-transformed, correct RTs were submitted to a first repeated-measures analysis of variance (ANOVA) with grade (Third, Fourth, and Fifth) and skill (High and Low) as between-subject factors and position of the larger operand (Position of Larger: Left and Right) as a within-subject factor. The main effect of grade ($F[2, 85] = 44.69$, MSE $= .776$, $p < .0001$) was significant. Post-hoc comparisons indicated that each grade differed from the others (Newman–Keuls; all $p < .05$) with means of 3.43 sec, 2.37 sec, and 1.81 sec for Third, Fourth, and Fifth, respectively. It is not surprising that high-skilled participants were significantly faster than low-skilled ones (2.10 sec vs. 2.74 sec; $F[1, 85] = 43.80$, MSE $= .760$, $p < .0001$). It is more critical that the main effect of Position of Larger was significant ($F[1, 85] = 30.63$, MSE $= .049$, $p < .0001$) as well as its interaction with grade ($F[2, 85] = 5.96$, MSE $= .010$, $p < .005$). In fact, $N \times m$ combinations were answered faster than those with the larger operand in Right ($m \times N$ items; 2.34 vs. 2.55), though this effect was significant in Fourth (2.22 vs. 2.50; $F[1, 30] = 36.76$, MSE $= .051$, $p < .0001$) and Fifth only (1.90 vs. 2.06; $F[1, 29] = 13.84$, MSE $= .023$, $p < 001$; Fig. 6.2). No other interactions were significant.

Mean-transformed, correct RTs were then entered in a repeated-measures ANOVA with grade (Third, Fourth, and Fifth) and skill (High and Low) as between-subject factors and min (the smaller of the two operands and position of the larger operand (Left and Right) as within-subject factors. The main effect of grade was significant ($F[2, 85] = 44.28$, MSE $= 2.89$, $p < .0001$); post-hoc

---

[3] These correlations were taken from data on responses to tables from Two through Nine, excluding combinations where both numbers are greater than 5.

Figure 6.2: Mean RTs in Seconds as a Function of the Position of the Larger Operand and Grade Level

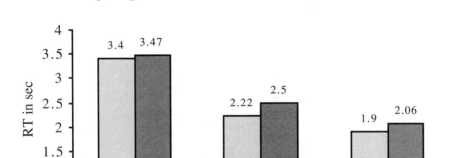

comparison showed that each grade differed from the others (Newman–Keuls; all *ps* < .05). High-skill participants were significantly faster than low-skill participants (*F*[1, 85] = 54.05, MSE = 3.53, *p* < .0001). The *min* factor was significant (*F*[3, 255] = 115.80, MSE = 1.319, *p* < .0001) indicating that overall, RT increased with the size of *min* (with means of 1.92 sec, 2.73 sec, and 3.35 sec for *mins* of Two, Three, and Four, respectively) except for a *min* of Five (2.69 sec). The *min* factor interacted significantly with grade (*F*[6, 255] = 7.89, MSE = .090, *p* < . 0001). In fact, the effect of *min* was greater in older children, though for all subjects the effect was highly significant (all *ps* < .0001; Fig. 6.3).

The main effect of the position of the larger operand was highly significant (*F*[1, 85] = 25.51, MSE = .145, *p* < .0001) as well as its interaction with grade (*F*[2, 85] = 7.99, MSE = .046, *p* < .001), replicating the previous analysis. It is more interesting that there was a significant interaction of *min* x position of larger (*F*[3, 255] = 5.86, MSE = .031, *p* < .005). Decomposition into contrasts revealed that the advantage for items with the larger operand in first position decreases with the size of *min*. In other words, this advantage was highly significant for combinations with *min* of Two (*F*[1, 85] = 31.84, MSE = .197, *p* < .0001) and marginally significant for items with *min* of Three (*F*[1, 85] = 3.63, MSE = .023, *p* = .05), but it was negligible (*F*[1, 85] = 2.87, MSE = .018, *p* = .09) and totally absent (*F*[1, 85] < 1) for *mins* of Four and Five, respectively (see Fig. 6.4).

These results were replicated in a similar by-item ANOVA with *min* (Two, Three, Four, and Five) as between-subjects factor and grade (Third, Fourth, and Fifth) and the position of the larger operand (Left and Right) as within-subjects factors. All main factors were significant: *min* (*F*[3,18] = 11.10, MSE = .286, *p* < .0005), grade (*F*[2, 36] = 180.66, MSE = .434, *p* < .0001), and the position of the larger operand (*F*[1,18] = 22.93, MSE = .027, *p* < .0001). As previously pointed out,

Figure 6.3: Effect of *Min* (the Smaller of the Two Operands) on RT at Different Grade Levels

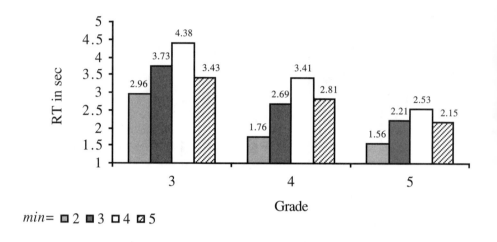

min= ■ 2 ■ 3 □ 4 ▨ 5

Figure 6.4: Mean RT in Seconds as a Function of the Position of the Larger Operand and *Min* (the Smaller Operand)

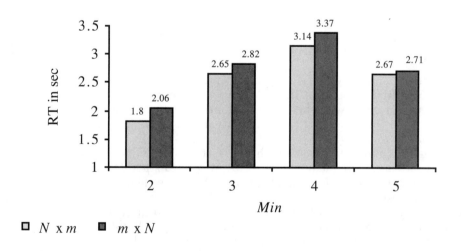

□ *N* x *m*   ■ *m* x *N*

the significant interaction between *min* and grade ($F[6, 36] = 8.51$, MSE = .020, $p <$ .0001) indicated that the relation between latencies and *min* was much steeper for older children than for younger children (Fig. 6.6). Moreover, the effect of the relative order of the operands was again modulated by grade ($F[2, 36] = 7.66$, MSE = .006, $p < .001$) and *min* ($F[3,18] = 6.57$, MSE = .008, $p < .005$).

Error Analysis

Parallel analyses were performed on arcsine-transformed error proportions. A first repeated-measures ANOVA with grade (Third, Fourth, and Fifth) and skill (High and Low) as between-subject factors and the position of the larger operand (Left and Right) as a within-subject factor. The main effect of grade ($F[2, 85] = 11.40$; MSE = .129, $p < .0001$) was significant. Post hoc comparisons indicated that each grade differed significantly form the others (Newman–Keuls; all $ps < .05$) with mean error rates of 13.3%, 9.1%, and 5.3% for Third, Fourth, and Fifth grades, respectively. High-skill participants were significantly more accurate than low-skill participants (3.7% vs. 12.6%; $F[1, 85] = 36.09$; MSE = .407, $p < .0001$). On the other hand, the relative position of the larger operand did not have any effect on the error rate ($F[1, 85] < 1$), nor did it interact with any of the other effects.

A repeated-measures ANOVA with grade (Third, Fourth, and Fifth) and skill (High and Low) as between-subject factors and *min* (Two, Three, Four, and Five) and position of the larger operand (first and second) as within-subject factors. Both main effects of grade $F[2, 85] = 11.37$; MSE = .615, $p < .0001$) and skill ($F[1, 85] = 36.79$, MSE = 1.99, $p < .0001$) were significant, replicating the previous analysis. The *min* factor was significant ($F[3, 255] = 23.53$, MSE = .515, $p < .0001$) as well as its interactions with grade ($F[6, 255] = 3.67$, MSE = .080, $p < .001$) and skill ($F[3, 255] = 11.47$, MSE = .251, $p < .0001$). Although the error rate for all children increased with the magnitude of the *min* and decreased for *min* of Five, this effect for fifth graders was less pronounced, and their error rate was relatively similar across the combinations (Fig. 6.5). Similarly, the effect of *min* was magnified in low-skill participants ($F[3, 153] = 31.05$, MSE = .090, $p < .0001$) compared with high-skill participants ($F[3, 96] = 3.02$, MSE = .026, $p < .05$).

Qualitative Error Analysis

As in previous studies (Campbell & Graham, 1985; McCloskey, Harley, & Sokol, 1991; Siegler, 1988), we classified errors using the following four categories: (a) operand errors (any multiple of one of the operands, such as 5 x 4 = 24), (b) close-miss errors (plus or minus 10% of the correct result, such as 6 x 7 = 38), (c) table errors (answer that belongs to a table different from either operands, such as 3 x 4 = 25), and (d) nontable errors (an answer not included in the any of the tables, such as 3 x 4 = 17). Errors that satisfied more than one of these criteria were assigned to just one category in this order (e.g., 6 x 5 = 31 would have been categorized as a close-miss, not a nontable, error). The distribution of error types is shown in Table 6.2.

Figure 6.5: Mean Error Rates According to Different Grade Levels and
***Min* (Smaller Operand)**

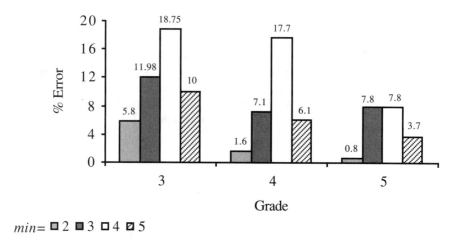

Table 6.2: Percentage of Errors According to Grade Level and Skill

	Type of Errors				
Skill Level	Operand	Close Miss	Table	Nontable	Total
Third grade					
High skill	65.4	15.4	19.2	0	4.2
Low skill	71.3	11.2	11.2	6.3	19.8
Fourth grade					
High skill	84.0	12.0	4.0	0	4.3
Low skill	68.3	22.1	3.8	5.8	11.4
Fifth grade					
High skill	87.5	12.5	0	0	1.6
Low skill	77.5	14.5	6.5	1.5	6.4

The overall error rate decreased with the grade level, but the distribution of error types did not change dramatically across the ages. In fact, for children at all three grade levels, the most frequent errors were operand errors, though the proportions of the other categories seemed to differ across grades. For all grades, close-miss errors were relatively frequent, but the probability of making table errors and nontable errors decreased with age and with experience. High-skill participants were, at any age, more likely than low-skill participants to produce an error that was plausible either in terms of magnitude (i.e., close miss) or in terms of table status (i.e., table vs. nontable numbers).

The corpus of operand errors was further analyzed to disentangle any systematic patterns in the production of incorrect but related answers. In fact, 62.1% of these errors consisted of correct answers for items that not only shared an operand with the target items but were also close in magnitude with respect to the other operand (e.g., 7 x 9 = 56, i.e., the correct response for 7 x 8). This so-called operand-distance effect has been already reported both in non-brain-injured participants (Campbell & Graham, 1985; Miller, Perlmutter, & Keating, 1984) and patients (Sokol, McCloskey, Cohen, & Aliminosa, 1991). Table 6.3 illustrates the relative proportions of operand errors in terms of the operand numerical distance between the target and actual responses. Distance "0" refers to the operand errors corresponding to a multiple of both target operands (e.g., 3 x 6 = 12). It is interesting that the proportion of close-operand errors increases with age as the probability of producing a distant-operand error decreases.

Furthermore, within the errors that could be unambiguously classified, the relative proportion of the operand errors corresponding to a multiple of the smaller or the larger operand as well as of the first or the second operand was analyzed. As the probability of producing a multiple of each operand is equal, a trend in a specific direction may indicate a privileged retrieval format or an

Table 6.3: **Percentage of Operand Errors According to Grade and Distance, Where X is the Distance Between Target and Error Operand (e.g., for 5 x 4 = 24, Error Operand $X \pm 1$ for Target 5)**

		Distance			
Grade	**0**	**$X \pm 1$**	**$1 X \pm 2$**	**$X \pm 3$**	**$X > X \pm 3$**
Third	11.8	55.5	16.8	12.6	3.4
Fourth	18.5	59.8	15.2	4.3	2.2
Fifth	13.4	71.2	9.6	5.4	0.0

order-specific backup strategy (e.g., transforming a multiplication combination into a repeated addition of a particular format).

Third graders were more likely than chance to produce a multiple of the smaller operand (64), χ (1) = 8.32, $p < .01$; they were also more likely than chance to produce a multiple of the first operand (59.4), $\chi = 4.36$, $p < .05$. This pattern was only marginally significant in the fourth graders (First and Smaller, both 60%, $p = .07$). In the fifth grade, the observed operand errors were equally likely to correspond to a multiple of the first or the second factor as well as either the smaller or the larger factor. These results are consistent with the interpretation that younger children who are more familiar with the 2-times and 3-times tables are more likely to produce as errors a multiple of the smaller operand. At the same time, however, they tend to answer the item as it is presented (i.e., by activating the table of the first operand). As skills progress, children seem to be less tied to the item presentation format and the production of operand errors is mainly characterized by the numerical closeness to the correct answers.

Discussion

The overall results indicate that children's performance in simple multiplication changes over the course of skill acquisition both quantitatively and, more critically, qualitatively.

It is clear that children become faster and more accurate with increasing skill levels. From the very beginning, though, both latencies and error profiles are characterized by several standard effects. First, all groups showed a significant item-size effect. In general, RTs increased with the increase of the magnitude of the problem. However, all groups answered items with an operand of 5 more quickly than would be predicted by the numerical size of these combinations. This is an extremely robust effect and has, to date, been attributed to the following rule: Any multiple of 5 may only end in 5 or 0 (Baroody, 1985; Campbell & Graham, 1985). This rule would constrain the number of candidate answers to this set of problems, reducing the chance to produce errors (Campbell & Graham, 1985). Use of this untaught rule so early in the acquisition process suggests that mastery of basic number combinations is not merely a rote learning process but may be facilitated by an appreciation of regularities and principles that govern them (e.g., Brownell, 1935).

The most critical finding, as predicted by our hypothesis, consists of the effect of the relative order of the operands within a given item. In Italian schools, children always learn $m \times N$ combinations (e.g., 2 x 6) before they learn $N \times m$ items (6 x 2). Nevertheless, despite earlier and longer exposure to the $m \times N$ form, children showed a time advantage in answering the $N \times m$ items. However, this effect emerged only *after* the third grade. This evidence parallels that showing children can master practiced combinations *and* their unpracticed commuted counterparts (Baroody, 1999). In brief, it would be surprising if this understanding were not used to organize multiplication knowledge.

A further result seems to favor the hypothesis of a principled reorganization of memory representations. In fact, the order effect did not hold for all items to the same extent but was a function of the size of *min*. Specifically, the relative position of the operands was more critical when the smaller operand was equal to 2 or to 3. These were the items that were learned earliest in school, and it was precisely these that were the most susceptible to reorganization. These results, and in particular the combined effects of the operand order and the magnitude of the problems, may only be considered indicative given the fact that we tested a subset of combinations (i.e., 2 x 2 to 6 x 5). Possibly retesting all single-digit combinations may disclose even more clear-cut results, in particular with regards to the effect of the position of the operands in the most difficult items.

The effects of practice, however, cannot be discounted entirely. Children, in time, minimized the computational effort of their repeated-addition strategies by reorganizing the addends so that they treated m x N items as N x m items and counted N m times. Repeated practice of this shortcut strategy could have contributed to overcoming participants' initial preference for the m x N form. Clearly, further research that controls for this factor is needed.

The qualitative analysis of the errors disclosed further intriguing patterns. From the beginning, operand errors were the most frequent type of errors, but their proportion increased as skills progressed. (These findings are consistent with those of Lemaire & Siegler, 1995, for changes over a 6-month period). It is interesting that within the different groups, the absence of nontable errors characterized the performance of high-skilled children, even within the younger group. Thus, the gradual acquisition and refinement of multiplication skills does not simply involve a faster and more accurate performance. It also entails more plausible errors, both in terms of numerical closeness to the correct product and, in the case of multiples of one of the two factors, numerical relation to an operand (see also Baroody, 1999).

The child learning multiplication facts may not be passive, simply building associative connections between an expression and its answer as a result of practice. Rather, the combinations held in memory may be reorganized in a principled way that takes into account a growing understanding of the operation, including the commutativity principle and, perhaps, other properties of multiplication (e.g., Baroody, 1983, 1984, 1985, 1999).

Acknowledgments

The research was supported by a grant from the Wellcome Trust (045013) to the first author, an ERASMUS E x change studentship to the second author, and EC Human Capital Mobility Fellowship (ERBCHBICT941608) to the third author. We are grateful to the staff and pupils at "Ippolito Nievo" Primary School in Mantua for their participation in this study.

References

Ashcraft, M. H. (1985). Is it farfetched that some of us remember our arithmetic facts? *Journal for Research in Mathematics Education, 16*, 99–105.

Ashcraft, M. H., & Battaglia, J. (1978). Cognitive arithmetic: Evidence for retrieval and decision processes in mental addition. *Journal of Experimental Psychology: Human Learning and Memory, 4*, 527–538.

Baroody, A. J. (1983). The development of procedural knowledge: An alternative explanation for chronometric trends of mental arithmetic. *Developmental Psychology, 3*, 225–230.

Baroody, A. J. (1984). A reexamination of mental arithmetic models and data: A reply to Ashcraft. *Developmental Review, 4*, 148–156.

Baroody, A. J. (1985). Mastery of basic number combinations: Internalization of relationships or facts? *Journal for Research in Mathematical Education, 16*, 83–98.

Baroody, A. J. (1994). An evaluation of the evidence supporting fact-retrieval models. *Learning and Individual Differences, 6*, 1–36.

Baroody, A. J. (1999). The roles of estimation and the commutativity principle in the development of third-graders' mental multiplication. *Journal of Experimental Child Psychology, 74*, 157–193.

Baroody, A. J., & Ginsburg, H. P. (1991). A cognitive approach to assessing the mathematical difficulties of children labeled learning disabled. In H. L. Swanson (Ed.), *Handbook on the assessment of learning disabilities: Theory, research and practice* (pp. 177–227). Austin, TX: Pro-Ed.

Brownell, W. A. (1935). Psychological considerations in the learning and the teaching of arithmetic. In D. W. Reeve (Ed.), *The teaching of arithmetic* (10th yearbook, National Council of Teachers of Mathematics, pp. 1–50). New York: Bureau of Publications, Teachers College, Columbia University.

Campbell, J. I .D. (1995). Mechanisms of simple addition and multiplication: A modified network-interference theory and simulation. *Mathematical Cognition, 1*, 121–164.

Campbell, J. I. D., & Graham D. J. (1985). Mental multiplication skill: Structure, process and acquisition. *Canadian Journal of Psychology, 39*, 338–366.

LeFevre, J., & Liu, J. (1997). The role of experience in numerical skill: Multiplication performance in adults from Canada and China. *Mathematical Cognition, 3*, 31–62.

Lemaire, P., & Siegler, R. S. (1995). Four aspects of strategic change: Contributions to children's learning of multiplication. *Journal of Experimental Psychology: General, 124*, 83–97.

McCloskey, M., Harley, W., & Sokol, S. M. (1991). Models of arithmetic fact retrieval: An evaluation in light of findings from normal and brain-damaged subjects. *Journal of Experimental Psychology: Learning, Memory, and Cognition, 17*, 377–397.

Miller, K., Perlmutter, M., & Keating, D. (1984). Cognitive arithmetic: Comparison of operations. *Journal of Experimental Psychology: Learning, Memory and Cognition, 10*, 46–60.

Rickard, T. C., & Bourne, L. E., Jr. (1996). Some tests of an identical elements model of basic arithmetic skills. *Journal of Experimental Psychology: Learning, Memory, and Cognition, 22*, 1281–1295.

Rickard, T. C., Healy, A. F., & Bourne, L. E., Jr. (1994). On the cognitive structure of basic arithmetic skills. Operation, order, and symbol transfer effects. *Journal of Experimental Psychology: Learning, Memory, and Cognition, 20*, 1139–1153.

Siegler, R. S. (1988). Strategy choice procedures and the development of multiplication skill. *Journal of Experimental Psychology: General, 3*, 258–275.

Sokol, S., McCloskey, M., Cohen N. J., & Aliminosa, D. (1991). Cognitive representations and processes in arithmetic: Interference from the performance of brain-damaged subjects. *Journal of Experimental Psychology: Learning, Memory, and Cognition, 17*, 355–376.

Svenson, O. (1985). Memory retrieval of answers of simple additions as reflected in response latencies. *Acta Psychologica, 59*, 285–304.

Thorndike, E. L. (1922). *The psychology of arithmetic*. New York: Macmillan.

CHAPTER 7

YOUNG ADULTS' STRATEGIC CHOICES IN SIMPLE ARITHMETIC: IMPLICATIONS FOR THE DEVELOPMENT OF MATHEMATICAL REPRESENTATIONS

Jo-Anne LeFevre, Brenda L. Smith-Chant, Karen Hiscock,
Karen E. Daley, and Jason Morris
Carleton University

How do adults produce the answer of a single-digit (simple) number combination such as 3 x 4 or 6 + 9? This question has dominated research on adult mathematical cognition since Ashcraft and Battaglia (1978) proposed experts retrieve answers from memory by activating associative links between combinations and solutions. Nearly all subsequent research on the topic has been based on the assumption adults directly retrieve the answer of a simple combination from some form of mental network (e.g., Ashcraft, 1982, 1987, 1992; Campbell, 1987a, 1987b, 1995; Geary, Widaman, & Little, 1986; LeFevre, Bisanz, & Mrkonjic, 1988; Miller, Perlmutter, & Keating, 1984; Rickard & Bourne, 1996; Stazyk, Ashcraft, & Hamann, 1982; Widaman, Geary, Cormier, & Little, 1989; but cf. Baroody, 1983, 1984, 1985, 1994). In contrast, researchers who examined addition or multiplication performance in children found that they use a mixture of counting procedures, other reconstructive strategies, and retrieved solutions (e.g., Ashcraft, Fierman, & Bartolotta, 1984; Baroody, 1992, 1993, 1995; Cooney & Ladd, 1992; Groen & Parkman, 1972; Jerman, 1970; Siegler, 1988a; Siegler & Shrager, 1984). The development of arithmetic knowledge, therefore, was typically hypothesized to proceed from flexible and adaptive selection from among a variety of procedures by children to the use of a single, efficient, and invariant approach (i.e., direct retrieval) by adults (Ashcraft, 1987; Siegler & Shipley, 1995).

In this chapter, we examine evidence for the view that multiple procedures remain available and are used by adults when generating the answers to basic number combinations. First, we review research in support of the multiple procedure perspective, including (a) similarities between the performance of children and adults, (b) structural analyses of latencies, (c) performance of individuals with brain damage, and (d) adults' self-reports of arithmetic-solution procedures. Second, we address several criticisms of the introspective techniques used to collect information about the use of procedures by providing new data on the validity of self-reports. Finally, we discuss the implications of the multiple-procedure view for other issues in mathematical cognition, including individual differences in performance, cross-cultural effects, and theoretical perspectives on adults' performance. In general, we argue that by extending the notion that multiple-solution procedures for basic arithmetic persist into adulthood, a better understanding can be achieved of how adults maintain flexibility and adaptability in mathematical performance.

Evidence for the Persistence
of Multiple Procedures Among Adults

The view that adults may use more than just memory retrieval to generate answers for simple number combinations was first raised by Browne (1906) and then by Groen and Parkman (1972). In the last 25 years, however, little attention has been given to this possibility (but see Dowker, 1992; Dowker, Flood, Griffiths, Harriss, & Hook, 1996). Solution of single-digit number expressions seemed so simple that many researchers assumed that adults would find it unnecessary to use any other strategy or procedure (e.g., Ashcraft & Battaglia, 1978; Campbell & Graham, 1985; Siegler, 1988a). Next, we discuss four sources of evidence in support of the view that multiple procedures are maintained in the repertoires of adults.

Similarities in the Performance
of Children and Adults

There is ample evidence that children retain and use multiple procedures in a variety of mathematical tasks (e.g., Jerman, 1970), even after they have shown evidence for successful use of an optimally efficient strategy (e.g., Siegler & Stern, 1998). Thus, if adults are assumed to use a single procedure (retrieval) on all simple number combinations, there must be a qualitative reorganization in the way that combinations are processed across development. It is interesting, however, that although adults are faster and more accurate than children, adult performance retains many of the characteristic features that are observed in children's performance. First, adults show advantages for ties (e.g., 3 + 3, 9 x 9) over nonties (e.g., 2 + 4, 9 x 8) on both addition and multiplication combinations (e.g., LeFevre & Liu, 1997; Miller et al., 1984). Second, adults are faster to solve combinations with operands of 5 (e.g., 5 x 4) than comparable combinations that do not involve 5 (e.g., 3 x 7; Campbell & Graham, 1985; LeFevre, Bisanz, et al., 1996). Third, adults show increases in latencies and errors with increases in the size of the operands (the ubiquitous *"problem-size" effect*; e.g., Campbell, 1995; LeFevre, Bisanz, et al., 1996; LeFevre, Sadesky, & Bisanz, 1996; Miller et al., 1984). Effects of ties, 5-operand items, and combination size are generally smaller for adults than for children, but all are extremely persistent and replicable.

Theorists have attributed the effects of ties, 5-operand combinations, and combination size to differential selection of procedures by children. For example, theorists have assumed that ties are solved with retrieval, whereas nonties are solved with a variety of procedures (Siegler & Shrager, 1984). Similarly, in children the advantage for combinations with operands of 5 may reflect the relative ease of using a repeated addition or counting procedure on those combinations as compared with combinations that do not have operands of 5 (Siegler, 1988a; see Butterworth, Marchesini, & Girelli, chap. 6, this volume, for a different explanation).[1] In contrast, the effects of ties, 5-operand combinations, and combination size in adults have been attributed to such experiential and problem-based factors as the differential presentation rates during learning (Ashcraft & Christy, 1995; Geary, 1996), associative confusion (Campbell & Graham, 1985), or the influence of abstract magnitude codes (Campbell, 1995). Only a few researchers have suggested that use of multiple procedures by adults might be a factor in the persistence of these basic effects (Baroody, 1983, 1984, 1985, 1994; LeFevre, Bisanz, et al., 1996; LeFevre, Sadesky, & Bisanz, 1996).

One reason that alternative procedures may persist in a mixture of possible solution approaches is that basic arithmetic is inherently confusing. A small number of symbols (i.e., Arabic digits) are associated with a variety of unrelated answers (Campbell, 1995; Dehaene, 1997). For example, compare the answers for the pair of digits 9 and 3: $9 + 3 = 12$, $9 \times 3 = 27$, $9 - 3 = 6$, and $9 \div 3 = 3$. Within operations, correct answers are often very similar to answers to neighboring combinations (consider $9 \times 6 = 54$ and $7 \times 8 = 56$). Associative interference and confusion effects indicate that experienced adults can easily be misled by plausible answers (e.g., $4 + 4 = 16$; $9 \times 8 = 63$; Campbell, 1987a; Stazyk et al., 1982). Correct retrieval requires extensive practice (Siegler & Shipley, 1995; Zbrodoff, 1995) and remains error-prone for larger numbers (Campbell, 1995; Siegler, 1988a) and for less familiar operations such as division (Campbell, 1997). Hence, in this complex world of confusable symbols, conceptual procedures based on knowledge of the arithmetic operations may serve as useful and necessary alternatives or backup procedures for direct retrieval, especially when an individual is using arithmetic in a context that requires accuracy over speed. For example, we suspect that a great deal of surreptitious counting occurs in real-world calculations, such as when individuals are calculating the amount of time left before their plane leaves or how much to pay the babysitter. The maintenance of alternative or backup procedures by adults would account for at least some of the striking similarities between the performance of children and that of adults.

Structural Analyses

Initially, structural analyses of latencies (and of errors) among children were used to provide support for specific solution procedures. A structural analysis is one in which a feature of the arithmetic combination is used to predict performance. Typical structural variables include the sum of the operands (*sum*), the smaller or minimum operand (*min*), the product of the operands (*product*), and the square of the sum (*sum squared*; see Miller et al., 1984, for further discussion). For example, Groen and Parkman (1972) found that the best predictor of addition latencies for first-grade children was *min* (e.g., 3 in $4 + 3$), consistent with the hypothesis that children solved these combinations by counting-on from the larger addend (i.e., $4 + 3 = 5, 6, 7$). Groen and Parkman then applied the identical structural analysis (i.e., use of the minimum addend to predict latencies) to the data of adults. They found that the *min* model was also a good predictor of adult

---

[1] Even adults process sequences such as "5, 10, 15, 20" more quickly than sequences such as "4, 8, 12, 16" (LeFevre & Bisanz, 1986).

latencies. However, the relatively small increment per count (i.e., approximately 20 ms), compared with the 400 ms increment per count for the children, seemed inconsistent with a model based on internal counting. Based on these structural analyses, Groen and Parkman proposed that adults use direct memory retrieval on most combinations but count on about 5% of combinations. The small increment per counting unit, therefore, represented an averaging between many retrieval trials and a few counting trials.

Subsequently, researchers who applied structural analyses to the data collected from adults rejected the notion that the relation between latencies and the minimum addend reflected a mixture of solution procedures (Ashcraft & Battaglia, 1978; Ashcraft & Stazyk, 1981; Miller et al., 1984). For example, Ashcraft and Battaglia (1978) replicated the results of Groen and Parkman (1972) in that they found that latencies of adults solving simple addition combinations increased as the size of the numbers increased. Ashcraft and Battaglia, however, found that the best predictor of latencies averaged across participants for each combination (i.e., an analysis by items) was *squared sum*, not *min*. They suggested that, because the latency increase with problem size was exponential, rather than linear (see also Ashcraft, 1987; Ashcraft & Stazyk, 1981), adults were using some form of memory-retrieval process to solve addition combinations. Based on these results (and others), various associative models of adults' retrieval processes were proposed in which internal representations of arithmetic knowledge corresponded to structural variables such as *sum squared* or *product* (e.g., Ashcraft, 1987).

Ashcraft and Stazyk (1981) directly tested Groen and Parkman's (1972) prediction that adults use counting on approximately 5% of simple addition combinations. They hypothesized that, if counting was causing the combination-size effect, then deleting the slowest 5% of trials should eliminate the effect. Ashcraft and Stazyk then reanalyzed their data, omitting the slowest 5% of trials, but found that the combination-size effect was still statistically significant. In order to eliminate this effect altogether, they had to omit the slowest 50% of trials. Ashcraft and Stazyk argued that it was implausible that adults used counting on such a large number of trials, and thus rejected the notion that adults used any procedures other than retrieval. They failed to consider the possibility, however, that solution procedures other than counting might be used by adults (Baroody, 1984; LeFevre, Sadesky, & Bisanz, 1996). Unfortunately, most researchers subsequently ignored the notion that adults might use procedures other than retrieval (cf. Baroody, 1983, 1984, 1985, 1994).

Another interpretation of the relations between structural variables and latencies or errors was that the structural measures were indirect indexes of factors such as the frequency of occurrence of combinations during acquisition (Ashcraft, 1992) or associative confusion among related information (Campbell & Graham, 1985). As Ashcraft (1992) noted, however, none of these associative models was entirely satisfactory in explaining the observed features of adult performance. All of these associative models included an explanation for problem size, but none could easily account for the advantages of ties and 5-operand combinations. In contrast, Siegler's (1988a; Siegler & Shrager, 1984) developmental model explained effects of combination size, ties, and 5-operand combinations as a reflection of the experiential history of an individual's solutions. Until recently, however, few attempts were made to use Siegler's model to account for adults' arithmetic performance (cf. Siegler, 1988a; LeFevre, Bisanz, et al., 1996; LeFevre & Liu, 1997; LeFevre, Sadesky, & Bisanz, 1996). Although Siegler (1988a) hypothesized that children use multiple procedures, he assumed that adult performance reflected the associative remnants of children's procedure selection and, hence, that adults used retrieval exclusively.

One reason researchers focused on structural analyses was that the structural predictors were very successful in capturing a large amount of the variability in latencies. Unfortunately, the structural analyses were based on data averaged across participants for each combination (i.e., an item analysis that disregards the variability due to individuals; Lorch & Myers, 1990). For example, Ashcraft and Battalagia (1978) found that the "best" predictor of latencies was *sum squared* and concluded that the best fitting pattern for *all* participants is an exponential increase with combination size. Nevertheless, other structural predictors (such as *min*) typically accounted for almost as much variance as *sum squared* (Baroody, 1984; LeFevre, Sadesky, & Bisanz, 1996; Miller et al., 1984; Mulhern, 1987). The practice of averaging over individuals presumably obscured the possibility that adults' solutions were not as homogenous as had been assumed. Put differently, "adult chronometric data may reflect an averaging over different strategies rather than the use of a single process (cf. Siegler & Robinson, 1982), and this may help to account for inconsistencies within the data of a single subject or sample and the inconsistencies among chronometric studies" (Baroody, 1985, p. 89).

Siegler (1987) explicitly demonstrated that averaging across *procedures*, particularly counting and retrieval strategies, leads to the erroneous conclusion that counting is the best descriptor of performance on all trials. In particular, because counting trials were very slow relative to retrieval trials, they influenced latencies to a degree that was quite out of proportion to their frequency of occurrence (Siegler, 1987). A very similar criticism can be applied to the practice of averaging across individuals. Performance by the slowest individuals can exert a very large influence on the average latency for any particular combination. LeFevre, Sadesky, & Bisanz (1996) analyzed the latencies of adults solving simple addition combinations, calculating the regressions individually for each participant. The amount of variance accounted for by the structural predictor (*product*, in this case) ranged from 0% to 55% across individuals, with a mean of 22%. In contrast, the regression analysis conducted on the same data averaged across individuals (the analysis of items that was equivalent to the analyses used in most of the earlier research) indicated that *product* accounted for 54% of the variance. Clearly, the averaged data presented a very misleading picture of performance for many individuals.

LeFevre, Sadesky, & Bisanz (1996) extended the logic of not collapsing across unlike events by analyzing solution latencies on simple addition items separately for both procedures and participants. They found that the combination-size effect for individuals was very small when only trials on which participants reported retrieving the answer were considered (see also Svenson, 1985). Averaging across participants or procedures and using structural variables to predict latencies led researchers to the incorrect conclusion that there was a strong discontinuity between the performance of children and that of adults on simple arithmetic tasks (cf. Siegler, 1988a).

Neuropsychological Evidence

The view that adults maintain access to multiple procedures is useful in understanding the performance of individuals who have difficulties with mathematics because of acquired brain damage (Dehaene & Cohen, 1995; Kiefer & Dehaene, 1997; McCloskey, 1992). For example, some individuals with left inferior parietal lesions have difficulty solving basic number combinations (McCloskey, Aliminosa, & Sokol, 1991; Warrington, 1982). It is interesting that these deficits in solution processes are often linked to combination size. Specifically, some individuals retained an ability to solve small combinations but not to solve large combinations (Kiefer & Dehaene, 1997; McCloskey, 1992); others lost the ability to solve some families of combinations but could solve others (Hittmair-Delazer, Semenza, & Denes, 1994).

To explain selective impairments related to combination size, Kiefer and Dehaene (1997) hypothesized that individuals with brain damage could lose the ability to perform procedures in arithmetic but retain the ability to retrieve stored facts, and vice versa. This notion is consistent with Sokol, McCloskey, Cohen, and Aliminosa's (1991) observations of two patients suffering from acquired arithmetic deficits. Although able to solve small number combinations, participants P. S. and G. E. lost their ability to solve larger combinations. Further support for the hypothesis that these individuals had lost access to specific forms of procedural knowledge that are distinct from direct associations was supported by the finding that P. S. and G. E. were unable to use the zero rule (i.e., anything multiplied by zero is zero). G. E. also showed severe impairments on n x 1 combinations, which are also often solved with a rule by adults (LeFevre, Bisanz, et al., 1996; LeFevre, Sadesky, & Bisanz, 1996) as well as by children.

Hittmair-Delazer et al. (1994) presented evidence that also supports dissociation between direct retrieval and procedure use. They report the case of B. E., whose specific arithmetic skills were impaired after a cerebral embolism in the left basal ganglia. Although B. E. was unable to retrieve the answers to large multiplication and division combinations, he was able to generate a correct answer 90% of the time using elaborate procedural solutions that demonstrated considerable conceptual understanding of numerical relations. Other researchers have likewise described individuals who could not retrieve the answers to simple number combinations but were able to verbalize or demonstrate alternative (nonretrieval) solutions (McCloskey, Caramazza, & Basili, 1985; Sokol & McCloskey, 1991; Sokol, McCloskey, & Cohen, 1989; Warrington, 1982).

Dehaene and Cohen (1995) suggested that the left inferior parietal region might be involved in the semantic elaboration of information required in order to perform arithmetic strategies. Accordingly, lesions in this area of the brain would not affect direct retrieval because direct retrieval does not involve accessing semantic knowledge. The differential preservation of small and large combinations after brain trauma in this region supports the notion that different combinations may be solved using different cognitive processes. In summary, retrieval and procedural solutions for number combinations appear to satisfy the neuropsychological criteria for a double-dissociation of function, necessary (but not sufficient) support for the view distinct cognitive processes are involved in adults' arithmetic solutions.

Self-Report

A fourth source of evidence supporting the multiple-procedure perspective in adults comes from experimental research in which individuals provide self-reports of their solution procedures, usually on a trial-by-trial basis (Dowker, 1992; Dowker et al., 1996; Geary, Frensch, & Wiley, 1993; Geary & Wiley, 1991; LeFevre, Bisanz, et al., 1996; LeFevre, Sadesky, & Bisanz, 1996; Svenson, 1985). Svenson (1985) asked participants to rate how certain they were (on each trial) that they had used memory retrieval to solve simple addition combinations. She found that the problem-size effect was smallest for those combinations on which the participants were sure that they had used retrieval, and was essentially non-existent if special cases (i.e., ties and combinations with operands of 0, 1, or 10) were excluded from the analyses. These results support the view that averaging across procedures can result in misleading conclusions about the underlying cognitive processes.

In the 1990s, the results of several more studies corroborated Svenson's (1985) findings about the importance of considering selection of solution procedures in simple arithmetic. Geary and Wiley (1991) asked younger and older adults to report how they solved simple addition combinations on each trial. As in the other studies described later, this methodology involves obtaining a retrospective report of the solution procedure on each trial immediately after the participant responds with the answer. Geary and Wiley reported two key findings. (a) Younger adults were more likely to report using procedures other than retrieval on simple addition combinations than were older adults (12% vs. 2%). (b) Latencies on nonretrieval trials were slower than those on retrieval trials, and answers on the former more error-prone than those on the latter. Similar findings were reported for subtraction by Geary et al. (1993), for addition by LeFevre, Sadesky, & Bisanz (1996), and for multiplication by LeFevre, Bisanz, et al. (1996). In all of these studies, performance was closely related to self-reports of procedure use in that responses on "retrieval" trials were fast and accurate, whereas responses on "counting" or "reconstructive" trials were slower and less accurate. Thus, studies in which adults have provided self-reports of their solution procedures support that view that multiple approaches are available when young adults solve simple number combinations.

Summary

Incorporating the notion that some adults make use of nonretrieval procedures to solve basic number combinations into a more general theoretical perspective helps to explain features of their mental arithmetic performance. First, allowing that adults may maintain a mixture of procedures, some of which are found in children, allows for theoretical models that stress the continuity of performance across development (Dowker, 1992; Dowker et al., 1996; Shrager & Siegler, 1998). Second, including aspects of strategy use in adult models helps to illuminate cognitive and neuropsychological models of arithmetic performance. Third, evidence that adult performance parallels that of children, evidence from structural analyses of individual data, evidence of dissociations in adults with brain damage, and introspective evidence from adults solving simple number combinations provide some information about sources of important phenomena such as combination size.

Issues of Validity with
Self-Report Methods

One criticism of the notion that normal adults may maintain and occasionally use procedures other than direct retrieval is that much of the evidence supporting the multiple-procedure perspective is based on introspective techniques, primarily self-reports of solutions among individuals with and without brain damage. To the extent that self-reports are veridical, they provide strong support for the multiple-procedure perspective. However, to the extent that self-reports are incorrect, biased, or influence patterns of performance on arithmetic tasks, they weaken the argument in favor of the multiple-procedure perspective. Hence, it is critical to provide some evidence on the validity of self-reports. Next, we examine the methodological concerns raised by the use of self-reports and present new evidence in favor of their validity.

The substantial body of research showing that children use a variety of solutions to solve simple number combinations is mainly based on observations of overt behavior. Children often count aloud, use their fingers to solve combinations, or use other observable indicators of their solution processes (Lemaire & Siegler, 1995; Siegler & Shrager, 1984). Not all mental activities of interest are expressed as overt behaviors, however, even among children (Baroody, 1999). For example, children report "counting in their heads." Furthermore, because adults rarely show observable evidence of procedure use on simple combinations, researchers must infer mental activities from patterns of behavior. Alternatively, researchers can solicit individuals' self-reports of their mental processes as a direct indication of procedure use.

Russo, Johnson, and Stephens (1989) detailed two specific criticisms of self-report methods. First, introspective techniques may influence how individuals answer combinations. That is performance may be *reactive*. Second, the *veridicality* of self-reports also may be suspect; individuals may be unable to accurately report their mental processes (see Cooney & Ladd, 1992; LeFevre, Bisanz, et al., 1996; Russo et al., 1989; Siegler & Stern, 1998). The latter concern may be a particular problem for solutions of simple number combinations, because adults usually solve such combinations in less than 5 sec. Until recently, there has been little attempt to demonstrate that adults' self-reports of performance on simple combinations are valid reflections of cognitive processing.

Cooney and Ladd (1992) addressed the issue of whether self-reports are reactive and veridical in children. Ten participants in Grade 3 solved single-digit multiplication combinations in each of three report conditions: no reports, concurrent self-reports, or immediately retrospective self-reports. Cooney and Ladd found that performance was reactive in the sense that the children were more accurate in generating answers when they provided self-reports than when they did not, whereas their response latencies in the no-report and retrospective-report conditions were similar. In both the concurrent-report and retrospective-report conditions, children claimed that they used a variety of strategies, but the predominant solution method was direct retrieval. With respect to veridicality, Cooney and Ladd concluded that the reports were probably incomplete. Notably, not all trials reported as memory retrieval were likely pure retrieval because the reaction time profiles were slower on some trials than would be expected theoretically. Furthermore, the participants reported fewer nonretrieval solutions in the retrospective-report condition as compared with the concurrent-report condition.

Despite evidence that self-reports were not completely accurate, Cooney and Ladd (1992) concluded that no substantial distortion of patterns of data appeared to occur across report conditions. They also noted that, because of individual variability in solution procedures, averaging over individuals could be just as misleading as averaging over strategies (e.g., Baroody, 1985; LeFevre, Sadesky, & Bisanz, 1996; Siegler, 1988a). Hence, they suggested that recording information about solution methods is important to understanding patterns of performance. To improve the methodology involved in self-report techniques, they recommended the routine use of a no-report control condition, presumably to help determine baseline levels of performance.

Kirk and Ashcraft (1997) examined the issue of reactivity in adults' self-reports of arithmetic solution strategies. They compared the addition performance of adults in the following four instructional groups ($n = 16$ in each group): (a) a *no-report* condition, (b) a *retrieval-bias* condition in which participants were told that adults normally use retrieval, (c) a *self-report* condition (similar to the instructions used by LeFevre, Sadesky, & Bisanz, 1996), and (d) a *strategy-bias* condition in which the participants were shown examples of procedures and told that many adults use these procedures. Kirk and Ashcraft found that participants performed differently according to the types of instructions given. First, participants reported more use of procedures in the strategy-bias condition (62%) than in the self-report (45%) or retrieval-bias (9%) conditions. Second, reaction times were slower in the strategy-bias condition than in the other three conditions, and the problem-size effect was larger. However, patterns of latencies were similar across the no-report, self-report, and retrieval-bias conditions, with slower latencies in the self-report condition on the largest combinations only (i.e., sums of 15 to 18). Kirk and Ashcraft's results suggest that different instructional biases may influence patterns of performance to some extent, although their findings do not indicate which sort of instructions are most veridical. Even in the retrieval-bias condition, some participants reported using alternative procedures, albeit infrequently. It appears that reports of procedure use can be affected by demand characteristics and by the requirement to verbalize solutions, although patterns of latencies were only reactive under strong strategy-bias instructions.

Clearly, the issues of reactivity and veridicality in self-reports have not yet been fully addressed. In a series of experiments, we compared simple arithmetic performance for groups of individuals who either provided self-reports or did not do so. Our primary objective was to assess the reactivity of self-reports by comparing patterns of performance across groups. In all three experiments, participants produced answers to simple number combinations. In each experiment, one group provided immediate self-reports of solution procedures on a trial-by-trial basis (the self-report group). Another group did not provide self-reports (the no-report group). Neither group was given any examples of potential strategies. The participants in the self-report group were told that (a) people sometimes remembered the answers to these combinations and sometimes solved the combinations in other ways, (b) they should solve the combinations as they usually would, and (c) they would be asked to describe how they solved each combination. Daley and LeFevre (1997) asked participants ($n = 32$) to solve simple subtraction items (e.g., 16 – 9). LeFevre and Morris (1999) asked participants ($n = 32$) to solve simple multiplication and division combinations (in separate blocks). Smith (1996) asked participants ($n = 64$) to solve simple multiplication combinations in two conditions. In one condition, the instructions emphasized speed, and in the other condition, they emphasized accuracy.

Consistent with our earlier work on adults' solution processes, use of retrieval varied across individuals in all three experiments. For participants in the self-report condition, retrieval was reported on 65% of the subtraction trials (Daley & LeFevre, 1997) and on 86% of the multiplication trials (Smith, 1996). LeFevre and Morris (1999) found that participants reported retrieval on 59% of the multiplication trials and reported using a memory-based strategy of visualizing the multiplication table on another 15% of the trials. For division, retrieval was reported on 45% of the trials, and a strategy of recasting the division problem as a multiplication problem (e.g., 48 ÷ 6 = ? as 6 x ? = 48) was reported on another 37% of the trials. Thus, we found that variability in the use of procedures was a persistent phenomenon for a variety of different arithmetic operations.

Reactivity

Performance of the participants in the three experiments is shown in Table 7.1. For the participants in Daley and LeFevre (1997) and in LeFevre and Morris (1999), there were no significant differences in mean latencies on the simple number combinations for self-report versus no-report groups. Smith (1996) found that self-report participants were slower than no-report participants under both accuracy and speed emphases, but this difference is attributable to an uneven distribution of arithmetic skill across the groups, as discussed later. For percent errors, participants in the no-report condition of LeFevre and Morris made significantly more errors than those in the self-report condition (see also Cooney & Ladd, 1992). However, the percentages of invalid trials showed the opposite pattern. Invalid trials are those on which participants made inappropriate vocalizations (e.g., "oh," "umm," or exhale heavily before responding) or fail to respond loudly enough to be detected by the computer. In all three experiments, participants who were required to make self-reports had more invalid trials than participants who did not make them. Thus, requirements to self-report solution procedures on a trial-by-trial basis may have altered the proportion of trials that were invalid versus errors.

Further analyses of these data indicated that it is critical to consider other characteristics of individuals in designs where report requirements are manipulated across groups. The comparisons between report and no-report conditions shown in the upper portion of Table 7.1 are based on the assumption that the participants are equivalent on all relevant characteristics in the two groups, an assumption that is based on the use of random assignment to conditions. However, because we have consistently observed very large individual differences in our studies, we evaluated the validity of this assumption using performance on a separate test of arithmetic fluency (French, Ekstrom, & Price, 1963). In the fluency test, participants answered paper-and-pencil number combinations with instructions to answer quickly. These tasks involved multidigit addition, multiplication, and subtraction operations. The fluency assessment allows comparisons across groups on an equivalent measure.

Table 7.1: Comparison of Arithmetic Fluency, Mean Latencies, Percentage of Errors, and Percentage of Invalid Trials Across Self-Report and No-Report Conditions

	Arithmetic Performance					
	Latency		% Errors		%Invalid	
	SR	NR	SR	NR	SR	NR
			Unadjusted Means			
Daley & LeFevre[a]	1286	1400	7.8	6.9	4.1	2.1
Smith (Accuracy)[b]	1466	1186	7.5	9.7	3.4	2.8
Smith (Speed)[b]	1218	1001	13.3	13.6	4.6	3.0
LeFevre & Morris[c]						
Multiplication	1090	1130	5.5	9.0	5.2	2.0
Division	1235	1238	7.1	12.4	7.0	2.1
			Means Adjusted for Fluency Scores			
Daley & LeFevre[a]	1382	1304	8.2	6.4	4.2	2.0
Smith (Accuracy)[b]	1401	1252	6.7	10.5	3.2	3.0
Smith (Speed)[b]	1170	1050	12.5	14.3	4.4	3.3
LeFevre & Morris[c]						
Multiplication	1097	1122	5.6	8.9	5.2	1.9
Division	1243	1229	7.3	12.2	7.0	2.1

Note. Pairs of numbers in italics are significantly different across report conditions, $ps < .05$.
[a]$n = 16$ per group; subtraction; [b]$n = 32$ per group; multiplication; [c]$n = 16$ per group.

The results of the fluency test were revealing. First, we found strong correlations between arithmetic fluency and latencies on the single-digit number combinations in all of the experiments (correlation coefficients ranging from −.42 in the multiplication condition of LeFevre & Morris, 1999, to −.71 in Daley & LeFevre, 1997, all $ps < .05$; see also LeFevre, Bisanz, et al., 1996). This finding suggests that latencies are strongly influenced by skill independently of experimental manipulations such as the requirement to produce self-reports. Examination of the fluency scores across report groups indicated that only the participants in LeFevre and Morris (1999) were balanced with respect to skill across report groups, with means of 92 ($SD = 22$) and 90 ($SD = 20$) for self-reports and no-reports, respectively.[2] In Smith (1996), the self-report group, by chance, was generally less skilled and had more very low fluency scores than the no-report group with means of 77 ($SD = 20$) and 86 ($SD = 25$), respectively. For the participants in Daley and LeFevre (1997), the converse was apparent, with means of 83 ($SD = 30$) for the self-report group and 68 ($SD = 22$) for the no-report group. Thus, latencies, errors, and percentage of invalid trials from the report and no-report conditions were reanalyzed in analyses of covariance (ANCOVAs) with fluency as the covariant. Three results of these analyses are relevant. First,

---

[2] Across a large number of studies with undergraduate samples, mean performance on the fluency measure is 80 ($SD = 25$).

no differences were found between latencies in self-report and no-report conditions in any of the comparisons (see the lower portion of Table 7.1 for the adjusted means). Second, there was a trend for no-report participants to make more errors than individuals in self-report conditions that was significant for the accuracy condition of Smith (1996) and the multiplication condition of LeFevre and Morris. Third, individuals in the self-report groups of Daley and LeFevre and LeFevre and Morris made more invalid responses than those in the no-report groups, suggesting that this effect was related directly to the demands of providing self-reports.

In each of the three experiments described, more detailed analyses of latencies were completed that included problem size as a variable. For example, Daley and LeFevre (1997) calculated individual regressions for each participant using the minuend as the predictor value and then compared the coefficients across report conditions. Smith (1996) also evaluated combination size using individual regressions, with *product* as the predictor variable. LeFevre and Morris (1999) calculated latencies and errors by problem family and then analyzed combination size by report condition.[3] There were no significant interactions between combination size and report condition in any of these experiments. Smith also found equivalent effects of ties, 5-operand combinations, and interactions between tie or 5-operand status and combination size across report groups. Hence, although participants who provided self-reports responded more cautiously than participants who did not, the similar combination-size effects across groups suggest that self-report requirements did not alter the underlying cognitive processes that determine patterns of latencies.

Veridicality

How accurate are self-reports? This is a difficult issue to address adequately, because at present there is no clear-cut way to verify self-reports. LeFevre, Bisanz, et al. (1996) showed that patterns of multiplication performance were consistent with reports of solution procedures. For example, latencies on counting trials (e.g., solving 3 x 5 as 5, 10, 15) were an approximately linear function of the number of counts required. Analyses of the subtraction data collected by Daley and LeFevre (1997) showed a similar strong relation between number of counts and latencies. Response times were a linear function of the number of counts reported, whereas latencies on the same combinations that were solved with retrieval showed minimal changes as a function of number of counts (see Fig. 7.1).

An alternative approach to assessing validity was used in Daley and LeFevre (1997) and in Smith (1996). In these studies, the participants in both the self-report and no-report groups completed a postexperiment questionnaire about their use of procedures on multiplication, addition, and subtraction combinations. Sample questions from the questionnaire are shown in Table 7.2. For each operation, participants were first asked about their use of memory access to

---

[3] In Smith (1996), the analyses were done with fluency as a covariate, as described above.

Figure 7.1: Latencies on Simple Subtraction Combinations: Counting Trials Versus Retrieval Trials

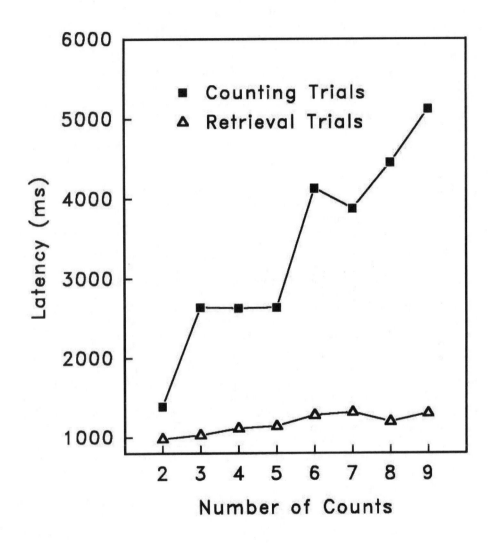

Table 7.2: Sample Questionnaire Items

---

1.   What proportion of the time do you automatically remember the answers to simple multiplication/addition/subtraction problems?

2.   Some people use solutions called derived facts where they use a problem they know to figure out the answer for another problem. For example, on the problem 6 x 7, some people think "6 x 6 = 36, then 36 + 6 = 42." Or, on the problem 9 x 6, some people think "10 x 6 – 6." How often do you use derived fact solutions?

3.   Some people use counting to solve addition problems. For example, for the problem 7 + 2, some people count up "8, 9." How often do you use counting to solve addition problems?

4.   Some people count when they solve subtraction problems. For example, on the problem 13 – 3, some people might count "7, 6, 5." How often do you count to get the answers to subtraction problems?

5.   Overall, please estimate what proportion of the time you solve simple multiplication/ addition/subtraction problems in ways *other than* by automatically remembering the answers?

Note. Participants responded to each question by circling one of the labels on the scale "never, rarely, sometimes, often, or always." Subsequently these responses were coded as 1 through 5, respectively. Thus, a higher "score" reflects greater use of the procedure described in the question. Questions 1 and 5 were the same across operations. Specific examples of questions about particular procedures were tailored to each operation (see Questions 2, 3, and 4). There were a total of 24 questions on the questionnaire.

---

answer simple number combinations.[4] Next, they answered a series of specific questions about various nonretrieval procedures (these depended on the operation), and last, they answered a global question about procedure use for that operation. To ensure that the questionnaire was, valid, we first explored its internal consistency. Second, we compared the questionnaire responses of the self-report and no-report groups, as a measure of the (potential) effects of trial-by-trial reports on questionnaire responses. Finally, we related participants' questionnaire responses to those given on experimental trials. In essence, analyses of the questionnaire data were used to provide cross-validation of the trial-by-trial self-reports.

To evaluate the internal consistency of the questionnaire, the responses to the 24 questions by 111 participants[5] who solved multiplication combinations under self-report requirements were factor analyzed using principal components

---

[4] Division was not included because, at the time the questionnaire was designed, no information was available on the variety of procedures that might be used to solve simple division combinations (cf. LeFevre & Morris, 1999).

[5] These participants included the completed questionnaires for 31 participants in the self-report condition of Smith (1996) plus 80 participants from two unrelated studies. All of these individuals solved multiplication combinations in a self-report condition, completed the fluency test (French et al., 1963), and then completed the questionnaire.

extraction and varimax rotation.[6] Seven factors were extracted that accounted for a total of 65% of the variance in the data. Some of the factors reflected groupings of questions referring to very similar procedures within a given operation, whereas others appeared to capture variability in procedure use that was consistent across operations. First, four questions regarding the use of various forms of repeated addition (e.g., 3 x 2 = 3 + 3) or number series (3 x 5 = 5, 10, 15) clustered together (Factor 1). The three questions about retrieval use factored together (Factor 3), as did the two questions about counting for addition and subtraction combinations (Factor 6). The same is true of the four questions about the use of 0- and 1-operand rules in addition and multiplication (Factor 4) and five questions about use of derived fact strategies on addition and subtraction (Factor 2). Questions regarding the use of multiplication procedures (the general question and the one about use of derived facts) formed a separate cluster (Factor 7). Thus, the questionnaire appeared to be internally consistent in that the patterns of relations across questions made sense, both within and across different operations.

We used the results of the factor analysis to reduce the data from the questionnaire in a meaningful way. Scores based on the seven factors were calculated for each individual who completed the questionnaire in Smith (1996) and Daley and LeFevre (1997) by averaging the ratings for the questions that loaded on each factor. Mean scores across conditions based on these averaged ratings are shown in Table 7.3. A high score on a particular factor, for example, indicates that participants claimed to use those procedures frequently.

Next, we used the questionnaire responses to address the potential reactivity of the self-reports. If either the instructions about procedures or the act of providing self-reports (or both) influenced participants' views of solving simple number combinations, then questionnaire responses may differ across the self-report and no-report groups. For example, self-report participants might claim that they used nonretrieval procedures (reasoning or counting) more frequently than participants in the no-report group. To evaluate whether participants in the self-report and no-report groups differed in their estimates of how frequently they used various procedures, the scores on each of the seven factors were analyzed in a 7(factor) x 2(experiment: multiplication, subtraction) x 2(condition: self-report, no-report) ANOVA, with repeated measures on the first variable. In this analysis, there were no significant effects involving either experiment or report condition ($ps > .4$). Thus, the requirement to provide trial-by-trial reports did not affect the participants' claims about how frequently they used procedures on the questionnaire.

Ratings did vary, however, across the different factors, $F(6, 534) = 63.30$, $p < .001$. Recall that the maximum rating is 5 (i.e., very frequent use of the specified procedure) and a rating of 3 corresponded to "sometimes" used the procedure. Tukey HSD post hoc tests were used to compare the mean ratings across factors. Participants reported using rules on 0- and 1-operand items very frequently ($\chi = 4.3$, Factor 4). Retrieval ($\chi = 3.5$, Factor 3) was used more frequently than any of

---

[6] No attempt was made to find the "best" factor solution by testing different rotations or using alternative extraction methods.

Table 7.3: Responses to Procedure Use Questionnaire: Mean Scores on Each Factor From Two Studies: Smith (1996, Multiplication) and Daley and LeFevre (1997, Subtraction)

Factor Description	Multiplication SR[a] $n = 31$	Multiplication NR[b] $n = 32$	Subtraction SR[a] $n = 16$	Subtraction NR[b] $n = 16$
1 Repeated addition (x)[c]	2.6	2.4	2.2	2.5
2 Derived facts (+, −)	2.8	2.7	2.7	2.7
3 Retrieval (+, −, x)	3.4	3.5	3.6	3.4
4 0 and 1 rules (+, x)	4.3	4.1	4.5	4.6
5 Subtraction procedures	2.7	2.6	3.0	2.6
6 Counting (+, −)	3.0	2.6	2.8	2.6
7 Procedures (x)	2.9	3.0	3.0	3.2

Note. Participants responded to each question by circling one of the labels on the scale "never, rarely, sometimes, often, or always." Subsequently, these responses were coded as 1 through 5, respectively. Thus, a higher value reflects greater use of the procedure described in the question. For factors involving more than one question, ratings were averaged across those questions for each participant to calculate scale scores.
[a]Participants provided self-reports of solution procedures on each arithmetic combination in the experiment.
[b]Participants did not provide reports of solution procedures during the experimental trials.
[c]The operation symbols in parentheses represent the operation(s) that were included in each factor.

the reconstructive procedures. Within the reconstructive procedures, multiplication procedures ($\chi = 3.0$; Factor 7) were reported more frequently than the repeated addition or number series procedures ($\chi = 2.5$; Factor 1). None of the other means differed significantly from one another (χs = 2.7, 2.7, 2.8 for Factors 2, 5, and 6, respectively). The reported frequencies are consistent with the view that retrieval is the most frequently used procedure on combinations that do not involve operands of 0 or 1. However, the moderate level of procedure use reported on the reconstructive procedures indicates that participants are aware of other procedures and that some participants use these procedures at least some of the time.

Third, we used the data from the questionnaire to examine the validity of the self-reports by directly comparing questionnaire responses and trial-by-trial responses. Correlations between the scores for each factor and reported retrieval use were calculated for participants who provided trial-by-trial self-reports (i.e., half of the participants in each of the two studies). As shown in Table 7.4, there were systematic relations between the two forms of self-reports. For multiplication, percentage of retrieval based on trial-by-trial reports of retrieval use was *positively* correlated with reported use of retrieval from the questionnaire and *negatively* correlated with reported use of other multiplication procedures (Factors 1 and 7). Thus, participants who frequently reported retrieval on the experimental trials also reported using retrieval on the questionnaire. For subtraction, the two retrieval measures were also positively correlated and percentage of retrieval was negatively correlated with reported use of subtraction procedures and counting (Factors 5 and 6). Participants who reported nonretrieval procedures on specific problems in the experimental task also claimed to use these procedures on the questionnaire.

To further evaluate the validity of the self-reports on the questionnaire, we calculated correlations between questionnaire responses and performance measure (i.e., latencies, percent errors, and fluency) for all participants. Nonretrieval procedures are slower than retrieval, so individuals who use nonretrieval procedures should be slower and make more errors on the experimental trials than individuals who rely more heavily on retrieval. Furthermore, less skilled individuals typically report less use of retrieval than more skilled individuals, so reported retrieval use should be correlated with the fluency score (LeFevre, Bisanz, et al., 1996; LeFevre, Sadesky, & Bisanz, 1996). These predictions were supported. As shown in Table 7.4, participants who indicated on the questionnaire that they frequently used retrieval had faster latencies, made fewer errors, and had higher fluency scores than participants who used retrieval less frequently. Similarly, use of reconstructive procedures was negatively correlated with fluency and positively correlated with latencies. Thus, performance on both simple and multidigit number combinations is moderately related in plausible ways to selection of procedures.

Table 7.4: Correlations Between Frequency of Procedure Use as Indicated on the Questionnaire and (a) Performance on the Arithmetic Tasks, (b) Trial-by-Trial Reports of Retrieval Use (% Retrieval)

		Arithmetic Performance			% Retrieval	
Factor	Description	Latency[a]	%Errors[a]	Fluency[a]	MULT[b]	SUB[c]
3	Retrieval (+, −, x)	−.34**	−.33**	.35*	.46*	.48[d]
6	Counting (+, −)	.40**	.22*	−.35*	−.43*	−.48[d]
7	Procedures (x)	.29**	.17	−.26*	−.46*	−.30
1	Repeated addition (x)	.26*	.18	−.24*	−.52**	−.18
2	Derived facts (+, −)	.03	.13	−.22*	−.14	−.42
4	0 and 1 rules (+, x)	−.05	−.13	.07	.04	.00
5	Subtraction procedures	−.03	−.05	−.05	−.05	−.66**

[a]All participants with complete questionnaire data from Smith (1996) and Daley and LeFevre (1997); $n = 94$.
[b]Participants from the self-report condition of Smith (1996); $n = 31$.
[c]Participants from the self-report condition of Daley and LeFevre (1997); $n = 16$.
[d]$p = .06$.

* $p < .05$; ** $p < .01$.

In summary, the questionnaire showed reasonable internal validity, and the questionnaire responses did not appear to be affected by the demands to provide trial-by-trial self-reports. With respect to validity, interpretable patterns of relations were found between questionnaire responses and patterns of trial-by-trial reports, and between questionnaire responses and patterns of performance on the experimental trials and on the fluency task. Thus, these analyses suggest that self-reports are meaningful indexes of mental activities.

The modest size of the correlations, however, suggests that adult participants may find it difficult to accurately reflect on their arithmetic solution procedures. This conclusion is consistent with results obtained from children's reports of their solution procedures. Siegler and Stern (1998) found that children sometimes showed evidence of using solution strategies, even when they did not report using those strategies. Cooney and Ladd (1992) found that children underreported the use of strategies when retrospective measures of solution procedures were used, as compared with concurrent reports. As suggested by Cooney and Ladd, the lack of awareness about solution procedures in basic arithmetic probably represents a failure to report all instances of procedure use, rather than deliberate fabrications.

Conclusions

The range of responses on the questionnaire suggest that many adults will admit to using a variety of procedures on simple number combinations, in support of the view that multiple-solution approaches are available. The frequency with which adults use particular solutions, however, may be affected by some kinds of instructional manipulations, especially when solution approaches are specifically stressed (Kirk & Ashcraft, 1997). Other instructional manipulations appear to have little influence on patterns of performance. Smith (1996) found that the main difference in reports of solution procedures across speed versus accuracy instructions was that individuals reported more guessing under speed demands than when accuracy was stressed; the reported use of retrieval did not change. Thus, researchers using self-report methods should try to provide neutral instructions that minimize demand characteristics. Even so, they should be aware that frequencies of solution approaches are relative to contextual factors. Furthermore, patterns of errors and invalid trials in the current studies suggest that individuals who provide self-reports may answer more cautiously than those in no-report conditions. Thus, types or frequencies of errors may also be biased (although self-report instructions are only one factor that may influence error types; LeFevre, 1998).

Cooney and Ladd (1992) suggested that using a no-report control condition was useful in helping to determine baseline performance. However, as seen in the present studies, between-group manipulations of self-reports may be sensitive to the very large individual differences that exist in overall arithmetic skill. Thus, further studies using within-group manipulations of instructions or much larger groups of participants are probably necessary to further evaluate the veridicality and reactivity of self-report methods.

In conclusion, self-report or related protocol techniques are enjoying widespread use across a variety of research domains because they allow for corroboration and extension of important research questions (e.g., Dowker, 1992; Dowker et al., 1996). Hence, it is critical to provide information about the validity of these techniques. In our view, in spite of the limitations of the self-report method, evidence from research that has used this technique provides solid support for the view that adults maintain access to multiple solution procedures.

Implications of the Multiple Procedure Perspective for Understanding Mental Arithmetic

In this section, we consider the implications of the multiple procedure perspective for understanding adult mental arithmetic. This perspective requires a large change in the theoretical orientation of most models of mental arithmetic, but it also helps to account for the large and persistent individual differences that exist in arithmetic performance.

Understanding Individual Differences

One important implication of the view that adults have multiple procedures available relates to the issue of understanding individual differences in simple arithmetic. Siegler (1988b) found that selection of procedures was related to individual differences in arithmetic and spelling performance. He described the following three groups of children: good students, not-so-good students, and perfectionists. The first two groups differed in predictable ways. The good students performed better on addition, subtraction, and spelling tasks than the not-so-good students. The not-so-good students used retrieval as frequently but much less accurately than the good students. In contrast, the perfectionist group performed as accurately as the good students, but used retrieval much less frequently. Siegler attributed these individual differences to the presence of higher confidence criteria among the perfectionists; that is, they were less likely to accept the results of retrieval processing and instead relied more heavily on procedures. This finding suggests that procedure use is not entirely a function of skill and practice (cf. Dowker, 1992; Dowker et al., 1996; Siegler & Shipley, 1995). Instead, some individuals may maintain the availability of procedures. Because nonretrieval procedures tend to be conceptually based, individuals can use these procedures to reconstruct answers if their memory fails or to check retrieved answers in situations that demand accuracy.

Findings such as those reported by Siegler (1988b) suggest that individual variability in arithmetic performance can be better understood if procedure selection is taken into account. To further explore this possibility, we examined the multiplication performance of 48 adults who also completed self-reports on each trial (LeFevre, Smith, & Hiscock, 1997). The participants' reports of procedure use across the 64 multiplication combinations (2 x 2 to 9 x 9) were used to create three procedure groups with 16 individuals per group. *Frequent* procedure users reported nonretrieval solutions on an average of 25% of valid trials, *occasional users* reported nonretrieval solutions on 5% of trials, and *retrievers* reported using memory retrieval on 100% of trials.

Median solution latencies were calculated for each individual and analyzed in 2 (combination size: small, large) x 2 (status: tie, nontie) x 3 (group: frequent, occasional, retriever) ANOVAs, with repeated measures on the first two factors. Small combinations had products of 25 or less, large combinations had products of 27 or greater. Recall that the problem-size effect is typically smaller for ties (e.g., 9 x 9) than for nonties (e.g., 9 x 8). As expected, the effects of combination size, tie status, and the interaction between combination size and tie status were all statistically significant. More important, however, the ties effect depended on group membership. As shown in Fig. 7.2, retrievers did not show an interaction between tie status and combination size. In contrast, the frequent and occasional procedure users showed interactions between tie status and combination size in that the combination-size effect was substantially greater for nonties than for ties. These findings suggest that considering the individual differences in the solution approaches used by adults can advance our understanding of the basic structural effects in arithmetic. In these data, the pattern of interactions between tie status and combination size were consistent with what one might predict based on data from children. Individuals who relied on retrieval did not show differential combination-size effects on tie versus nontie combinations, suggesting that they used equivalent solution procedures across types of combinations. In contrast, individuals who used procedures other than retrieval on a substantial number of combinations showed the "typical" tie by combination size interactions.

Cross-Cultural Research

Incorporating features of procedure use into models of mathematical cognition allows for alternative explanations of adults' basic arithmetic performance that have provided challenges to the existing models of mathematical cognition. For example, cross-cultural research comparing the performance of adults educated in China with that of adults educated in North America indicates that not all adults perform in similar ways. Compared with Canadian- or U.S.-educated individuals, Chinese participants showed smaller combination-size effects (Geary, 1996; LeFevre, 1998; LeFevre & Liu, 1997), smaller advantages for ties over nonties (LeFevre & Liu, 1997), and no significant advantages for combinations with operands of 5 (LeFevre & Liu, 1997). With respect to solution procedures, Chinese participants never reported using procedures other than direct retrieval, with one exception. They reported a strategy of mentally reorganizing combinations into the form "smaller digit" x "larger digit." For example, when presented with 8 x 4, Chinese adults reported that they mentally rearranged the combination as 4 x 8, and then retrieved the answer to 4 x 8 (LeFevre, 1998; LeFevre & Liu, 1997; cf. Baroody, 1984; Butterworth et al., chap. 6, this volume; Svenson, 1985). Consistent with their reports, Chinese participants solved smaller-first combinations (i.e., no reversal required) more quickly than larger-first combinations (i.e., reversal required). North American adults did not report the rearranging strategy and their performance did not show the corresponding pattern observed in the adult Chinese data. Hence, a cultural difference in arithmetic performance is interpretable by considering the selection of procedures across groups of individuals.

Figure 7.2: Latencies on Simple Multiplication Combinations for Ties and for Nonties

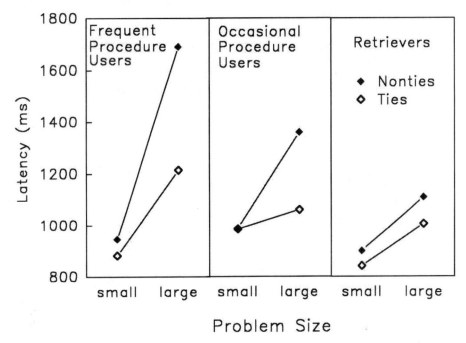

Note. Frequent procedure users reported nonretrieval solutions on an average of 25% of valid trials, *occasional* users reported nonretrieval solutions on an average of 51% of valid trials, and *retrievers* reported using memory retrieval on 100% of valid trials.

Theoretical Considerations

Shrager and Siegler (1998) have recently proposed an "overlapping waves" model of strategy development (see also Svenson & Sjöberg, 1983). They suggest that a variety of strategies are available at any given point, but that the strength (and therefore the use) of these strategies varies with changes in knowledge and experience. As applied to adults, we suggest that this model be extended such that both the availability and the use of different procedures could vary as a function of individual differences and as a function of the situation (see also Dowker et al., 1996). For example, retrieval is clearly the dominant procedure for adults solving simple number combinations, but the extent to which retrieval is used (across groups) can vary with the demands of the task. For some operations, such as subtraction and division, direct retrieval may be used much less frequently than for addition and multiplication (Daley & LeFevre, 1997; Gallant, 1994; LeFevre & Morris, 1999).

Furthermore, when simple arithmetic is embedded in more complex combiations, the selection of procedures is likely to change. For example, Gallant (1994) found that adults reported use of a decomposition strategy 22% of the time when responding to simple items involving "borrowing" (e.g., $16 - 9 = [16 - 6], [10 - 3] = 7$) and 54% when faced with a similar calculation in a more complex context (e.g., $56 - 9 = [56 - 6], [50 - 3] = 47$). Use of the decomposition strategy may be easier than applying the standard (written) algorithm because no borrowing is required. The borrowing procedure appears to place a heavy demand on working memory and is a common source of errors (Ashcraft, Donley, Halas, & Vakali, 1992; Geary et al., 1986; Hitch, 1978). Hence, like children, adults choose from among a variety of solution procedures in flexible and adaptive ways.

Conclusions

In this chapter, we examined evidence in favor of the view that adults maintain and use multiple procedures in their solutions of simple number combinations. Retrieval does appear to dominate adult performance, especially on multiplication and addition combinations, and in arithmetic experiments that emphasize fast solutions across a large number of trials. However, direct retrieval is not the only available solution procedure and selection of procedures among adults depends on a variety of factors. Hence, adults, like children, show evidence of flexible and adaptive cognitive processing on even very simple mathematical tasks. In our view, the multiple-procedure perspective provides a comprehensive framework for understanding the range of arithmetic performance that exists among adults.

Acknowledgments

This research was supported by grants from the Natural Sciences and Engineering Research Council of Canada to Jo-Anne LeFevre.

We thank Brenda Baird and Karen Colton for their assistance with data collection. Chris Herdman and Lauren Meegan provided helpful comments on earlier versions of the manuscript.

References

Ashcraft, M. H. (1982). The development of mental arithmetic: A chronometric approach. *Developmental Review, 2,* 213–236.

Ashcraft, M. H. (1987). Children's knowledge of simple arithmetic: A developmental model and simulation. In J. Bisanz, C. J. Brainerd, & R. Kail (Eds.), *Formal methods in developmental psychology: Progress in cognitive development research* (pp. 302–338). New York: Springer-Verlag.

Ashcraft, M. H. (1992). Cognitive arithmetic: A review of data and theory. *Cognition, 144,* 75–106.

Ashcraft, M. H., & Battaglia, J. (1978). Cognitive arithmetic: Evidence for retrieval and decision processes in mental addition. *Journal of Experimental Psychology: Learning, Memory, and Cognition, 4 ,* 527–538.

Ashcraft, M. H., & Christy, K. S. (1995). The frequency of arithmetic facts in elementary texts: Addition and multiplication in grades 1–6. *Journal for Research in Mathematics Education, 26,* 396–421.

Ashcraft, M. H., Donley, R. D., Halas, M. A., & Vakali, M. (1992). Working memory, automaticity, and problem difficulty. In J. I. D. Campbell (Ed.), *The nature and origin of mathematical skills* (pp. 301–329). Amsterdam: North-Holland.

Ashcraft, M. H., Fierman, B. A., & Bartolotta, R. (1984). The production and verification tasks in mental addition: An empirical comparison. *Developmental* Review, 4, 157–170.

Ashcraft, M. H., & Stazyk, E. H. (1981). Mental addition: A test of three verification models. *Memory & Cognition, 9,* 185–196.

Baroody, A. J. (1983). The development of procedural knowledge: An alternative explanation for chronometric trends of mental arithmetic. *Developmental Review, 3,* 225–230.

Baroody, A. J. (1984). A reexamination of mental arithmetic models and data: A reply to Ashcraft. *Developmental Review, 4,* 148–156.

Baroody, A. J. (1985). Mastery of the basic number combinations: Internalization of relationships or facts? *Journal for Research in Mathematics Education, 16,* 83–98.

Baroody, A. J. (1992). The development of kindergartners' mental-addition strategies. *Learning and Individual Differences, 4,* 215–235.

Baroody, A. J. (1993). Early mental multiplication performance and the role of relational knowledge in mastering combinations involving two. *Learning and Instruction, 3,* 93–111.

Baroody, A. J. (1994). An evaluation of evidence supporting fact-retrieval models. *Learning and Individual Differences, 6,* 1–36.

Baroody, A. J. (1995). The role of the number-after rule in the invention of computational short cuts. *Cognition and Instruction, 13,* 189–219.

Baroody, A. J. (1999). The roles of estimation and the commutativity principle in the development of third-graders' mental multiplication. *Journal of Experimental Child Psychology, 74,* 157–193.

Browne, C. E. (1906). The psychology of simple arithmetical processes: A study of certain habits and associations. *American Journal of Psychology, 17,* 1–37.

Campbell, J. I. D. (1987a). Network interference and mental multiplication. *Journal of Experimental Psychology: Learning, Memory, and Cognition, 13,* 109–123.

Campbell, J. I. D. (1987b). Production, verification, and priming of multiplication facts. *Memory & Cognition, 15,* 349–364.

Campbell, J. I. D. (1995). Mechanisms of simple addition and multiplication: A modified network-interference theory and simulation. *Mathematical Cognition, 1,* 121–164.

Campbell, J. I. D. (1997). On the relation between skilled performance of simple division and multiplication. *Journal of Experimental Psychology: Learning, Memory, and Cognition, 23,* 1140–1159.

Campbell, J. I. D., & Graham, D. J. (1985). Mental multiplication skill: Structure, process, and acquisition. *Canadian Journal of Psychology, 39,* 338–366.

Cooney, J. B., & Ladd, S. F. (1992). The influence of verbal protocol methods on children's mental computation. *Learning and Individual Differences, 4,* 237–257.

Daley, K. E., & LeFevre, J. (1997, June). *Adults' subtraction: A comparison of self-report and no-self-report conditions.* Presented at the annual meeting of the Canadian Society for Brain, Behavior, and Cognitive Science, Winnipeg, Manitoba, Canada.

Dehaene, S. (1997). *The number sense.* New York: Oxford University Press.

Dehaene, S., & Cohen, L. (1995). Toward an anatomical and functional model of number processing. *Mathematical Cognition, 1,* 83–120.

Dowker, A. (1992). Computational estimation strategies of professional mathematicians. *Journal for Research in Mathematics Education, 23,* 45–55.

Dowker, A., Flood, A., Griffiths, H., Harriss, L., & Hook, L. (1996). Estimation strategies of four groups. *Mathematical Cognition, 2,* 113–135.

French, J. W., Ekstrom, R. B., & Price, I. A. (1963). *Kit of reference tests for cognitive factors.* Princeton, NJ: Educational Testing Service.

Gallant, C. (1994). *Adults' strategy selection for simple and complex subtraction problems.* Unpublished honors thesis, Carleton University, Ottawa, Ontario, Canada.

Geary, D. C. (1996). The problem-size effect in mental addition: Developmental and cross-national trends. *Mathematical Cognition, 2,* 63–93.

Geary, D. C., Frensch, P. A., & Wiley, J. G. (1993). Simple and complex mental subtraction: Strategy, choice and speed-of-processing differences in younger and older adults. *Psychology and Aging, 8,* 242–256.

Geary, D. C., Widaman, K. F., & Little, T. D. (1986). Cognitive addition and multiplication: Evidence for a single memory network. *Memory & Cognition, 14,* 478–487.

Geary, D. C., & Wiley, J. G. (1991). Cognitive addition: Strategy choice and speed-of-processing differences in young and elderly adults. *Psychology and Aging, 6,* 474–483.

Groen, G. J., & Parkman, J. M. (1972). A chronometric analysis of simple addition. *Psychological Review, 79,* 329–343.

Hitch, G. J. (1978). The role of short-term working memory in mental arithmetic. *Cognitive Psychology, 10,* 302–323.

Hittmair-Delazer, M., Semenza, C., & Denes, G. (1994). Concepts and facts in calculation. *Brain, 17,* 715–728.

Jerman, M. (1970). Some strategies for solving simple multiplication combinations. *Journal for Research in Mathematics Education, 1,* 95–128.

Kiefer, M., & Dehaene, S. (1997). The time course of parietal activation in single-digit multiplication: Evidence from event-related potentials. *Mathematical Cognition, 3,* 1–30.

Kirk, E. P., & Ashcraft, M. H. (1997, November). *Verbal reports on simple arithmetic: A demanding task.* Presented at the annual meeting of the Psychonomic Society, Washington, DC.

LeFevre, J. (1998). Interactions among encoding, calculation, and production processes in the multiplication performance of Chinese-speaking adults. *Mathematical Cognition, 4,* 47–65.

LeFevre, J., & Bisanz, J. (1986). A cognitive analysis of number-series problems: Sources of individual differences in performance. *Memory & Cognition, 14,* 287–298.

LeFevre, J., Bisanz, J., Daley, K. E., Buffone, L., Greenham, S. L., & Sadesky, G. S. (1996). Multiple routes to solution of single-digit multiplication problems. *Journal of Experimental Psychology: General, 125,* 284–306.

LeFevre, J., Bisanz, J., & Mrkonjic, L. (1988). Cognitive arithmetic: Evidence for obligatory activation of arithmetic facts. *Memory & Cognition, 16,* 45–53.

LeFevre, J., & Liu, J. (1997). The role of experience in numerical skill: Multiplication performance in adults from Canada and China. *Mathematical Cognition, 3,* 31–62.

LeFevre, J., & Morris, J. (1999). More on the relation between division and multiplication in simple arithmetic: Evidence for mediation of division solutions via multiplication. *Memory & Cognition, 27,* 803–812.

LeFevre, J., Sadesky, G. S., & Bisanz, J. (1996). Selection of procedures in mental addition: Reassessing the problem-size effect in adults. *Journal of Experimental Psychology: Learning, Memory, and Cognition, 22,* 216–230.

LeFevre, J., Smith, B. L., & Hiscock, K. (1997). Unpublished data.

Lemaire, P., & Siegler, R. S. (1995). Aspects of strategic change: Contributions to children's learning of multiplication. *Journal of Experimental Psychology: General, 124,* 83–97.

Lorch, R. F., Jr., & Myers, J. L. (1990). Regression analyses of repeated measures data in cognitive research. *Journal of Experimental Psychology: Learning, Memory, and Cognition, 16,* 149–157.

McCloskey, M. (1992). Cognitive mechanisms in numerical processing: Evidence from acquired dyscalculia. *Cognition, 44*, 107–157.

McCloskey, M., Aliminosa, D., & Sokol, S. (1991). Facts, rules, and procedures in normal calculation: Evidence from multiple single-patient studies of impaired arithmetic fact retrieval. *Brain & Cognition, 17*, 154–203.

McCloskey, M., Caramazza, A., & Basili, A. G. (1985). Cognitive mechanisms in number processing and calculation: Evidence from dyscalculia. *Brain & Cognition, 4*, 171–196.

Miller, K. F., Perlmutter, M., & Keating, D. (1984). Cognitive arithmetic: Comparison of operations. *Journal of Experimental Psychology: Learning, Memory, and Cognition, 10*, 46–60.

Mulhern, G. (1987). The development of computational skills in simple mental addition. *Journal of Structural Learning, 9*, 317–328.

Rickard, T. C., & Bourne, L. E., Jr. (1996). Some tests of an identical elements model of basic arithmetic skills. *Journal of Experimental Psychology: Learning, Memory, and Cognition, 22*, 1281–1295.

Russo, J. E., Johnson, E. J., & Stephens, D. L. (1989).The validity of verbal protocols. *Memory & Cognition, 17*, 759–769.

Shrager, J., & Siegler, R. S. (1998). SCADS: A model of children's strategy choices and strategy discovery. *Psychological Science, 9*, 405–410.

Siegler, R. S. (1987). The perils of averaging data over strategies: An example from children's addition. *Journal of Experimental Psychology: General, 116*, 250–264.

Siegler, R. S. (1988a). Strategy choice procedures and the development of multiplication skill. *Journal of Experimental Psychology: General, 117*, 258–275.

Siegler, R. S. (1988b). Individual differences in strategy, choices: Good students, not-so-good students, and perfectionists. *Child Development, 59*, 833–851.

Siegler, R. S., & Robinson, M. (1982). The development of numerical understandings. In H. W. Reese & L. P. Lipsitt (Eds.), *Advances in child development and behavior: Vol. I* (pp. 241–312). New York: Academic Press.

Siegler, R. S., & Shipley, E. (1995). Variation, selection, and cognitive change. In G. Halford & T. Simon (Eds.), *Developing cognitive competence: New approaches to process modeling* (pp. 31–76). Hillsdale, NJ: Lawrence Erlbaum Associates.

Siegler, R. S., & Shrager, J. (1984). Strategy choices in addition and subtraction: How do children know what to do? In C. Sophian (Ed.), *Origins of cognitive skills* (pp. 229–293). Hillsdale, NJ: Lawrence Erlbaum Associates.

Siegler, R. S., & Stern, E. (1998). Conscious and unconscious strategy discoveries: A microgenetic analysis. *Journal of Experimental Psychology: General, 127*, 377–397.

Smith, B. L. (1996). *Effects of instruction on basic multiplication performance: Implications of speeded response and self-report methods.* Unpublished master's thesis, Carleton University, Ottawa, Ontario, Canada.

Sokol, S. M., & McCloskey, M. (1991). Cognitive mechanisms in calculation. In R. J. Sternberg & P. A. Frensch (Eds.), *Complex problem solving: Principles and mechanisms* (pp. 85–116). Hillsdale, NJ: Lawrence Erlbaum Associates.

Sokol, S. M., McCloskey, M., & Cohen, N. (1989). Cognitive representations of arithmetic knowledge: Evidence from acquired dyscalculia. In A. F. Bennett & K. M. McConkey (Eds.), *Cognition in individual and social contexts* (pp. 577–591). Amsterdam: North-Holland.

Sokol, S., McCloskey, M., Cohen, N., & Aliminosa, D. (1991). Cognitive representations and processes in arithmetic: Inferences from the performance of brain-damaged subjects. *Journal of Experimental Psychology: Learning, Memory, and Cognition, 17*, 355–376.

Stazyk, E. H., Ashcraft, M. H., & Hamann, M. S. (1982). A network approach to mental multiplication. *Journal of Experimental Psychology: Learning, Memory, and Cognition, 8*, 320–335.

Svenson, O. (1985). Memory retrieval of answers of simple additions as reflected in response latencies. *Acta Psychologica, 59,* 285–304.

Svenson, O., & Sjöberg, K. (1983). Evolution of cognitive processes for solving simple additions during the first three school years. *Scandinavian Journal of Psychology, 24,* 117–124.

Warrington, E. (1982). The fractionation of arithmetical skills: A single case study. *Quarterly Journal of Experimental Psychology, 34A,* 31–51.

Widaman, K. F., Geary, D. C., Cormier, P., & Little, T. D. (1989). A componental model of mental addition. *Journal of Experimental Psychology: Learning Memory, and Cognition, 15,* 898–919.

Zbrodoff, N. J. (1995). Why is 9 + 7 harder than 2 + 3? Strength and interference as explanations of the problem-size effect. *Memory & Cognition, 23,* 689–700.

CHAPTER 8

LANGUAGE SUPPORTS FOR MATHEMATICS UNDERSTANDING AND PERFORMANCE

Irene T. Miura
San Jose State University

Yukari Okamoto
University of California
Santa Barbara

In this chapter, we review our collaborative efforts with colleagues around the world to examine the influence of language characteristics on children's mathematics understanding and performance. Using cross-national comparisons of numerical language characteristics and children's related mathematical activities, we have attempted to explain the often-reported superior achievement of students from Asian countries (e.g., Lapointe, Mead, & Philips, 1989; McKnight et al., 1987; Stevenson, Lee, & Stigler, 1986; Third International Math and Science Study, 1996) from a language-based perspective. Variations in home and school experiences (CSU Institute for Educational Reform, 1997; Hess, Chang, & McDevitt, 1987; Mordkowitz & Ginsburg, 1987; Stevenson & Stigler, 1992) are typically given as explanations for these achievement differences, and their influence cannot be discounted. However, Asian children demonstrate superior performance on measures of mathematical skills such as verbal counting (Miller, Smith, Zhu, & Zhang, 1995), base-ten understanding (Miura, Okamoto, Kim, Steere, & Fayol, 1993; Song & Ginsburg, 1987), and place-value understanding (Miura et al., 1993) before teaching effectiveness and other school-related factors come into play. We suggest that numerical language characteristics may also be a factor in the superior mathematics performance exhibited by Asian-language speakers (Miura, 1987; Miura & Okamoto, 1989; Miura et al., 1993).

Mathematical activities are inextricably set in cultural contexts with their own tools for thinking and learning, one important tool being the language of mathematics (Rogoff, 1990; Steffe, Cobb, & von Glasersfeld, 1988). Culturally developed tools or symbol systems can influence mental activities without altering basic abilities such as memory or logical reasoning (Nunes, 1992). Nunes (1997) described this facilitation as mediated action; that is, certain tasks are made easier because of tools developed to perform the task, and these differ by cultural group. For example, numeration systems (such as the English-language base-ten system) allow humans to go beyond their natural memory capacities to count large numbers of objects. By contrast, the counting system of the Oksapmin of Papua, New Guinea, using body parts, allows for the enumeration of up to 24 items in some cases and 68 in others (Saxe, 1982). When counting a large number of objects, someone counting in English will be able to outperform someone counting in Oksapmin because the former is using a more efficient counting tool. It is not that the English speaker's memory for digits is necessarily greater than that of the Oksapmin; it is just that the structure of the counting tool is better, thereby making the activity easier to perform.

In our view, the characteristics of different mathematical languages (culturally developed tools for mathematics) may affect performance on certain mathematics tasks (cf. Donlan, chap. 12, this volume; Jordan, Hanich, & Uberti, chap. 13, this volume; Towse & Saxton, 1998). In this chapter, we examine evidence on how the peculiar characteristics of children's languages can affect their understanding of mathematical concepts. Specifically, we describe three examples of language supports for mathematics understanding and performance: (a) the number naming (counting) system, (b) fractions terms, and (c) the use of numeral classifiers. We also discuss children's interpretation of grammatical number (singular and plural) and how this might influence mathematics performance. Although we use the Japanese language for our examples, our comments can be generalized to Chinese and Korean as well.

Number-Naming Systems

The counting system in languages that are rooted in ancient Chinese (among them, Chinese, Japanese, and Korean) are organized so that they are congruent with the traditional base-ten numeration system. In this system, the value of a given digit in a multidigit numeral depends on the face value of the digit (0 through 9) and on its position in the numeral, with the value of each position increasing by powers of 10 from right to left. The spoken numerals in western languages (e.g., *eleven*, *twelve*, and *twenty* in English and *four-twenty* for 80 in French) do not highlight the grouping-by-tens structure of a base-ten numeration system. Also, the order of spoken and written numerals may not agree (e.g., *fourteen* for 14 in English and *three-and-forty* for 43 in German). In Japanese, 11 is read as *ten-one*, 12 as *ten-two*, 14 as *ten-four*, 20 as *two-ten(s)*, 43 as *four-ten(s)-three*, and 80 as *eight-ten(s)*. *Fourteen* and *forty*, which are phonologically similar in English, are differentiated in Japanese; 14 is spoken as *ten-four* and 40 as *four-ten(s)*. Plurals are tacitly understood; thus, the spoken numeral corresponds exactly to the implied quantity represented in the written form (Table 8.1). Furthermore, when character number symbols are used in place of the Arabic numerals, the correspondence between spoken and written numeral is even more precise; for example, the numeral 46 is written in character symbols as four-ten(s)-six.

Effects on Number Representation

Because a Japanese spoken number describes precisely what is represented by the base-ten numeration system (i.e., the syntax and semantics are, as Cobb, 1993, suggests, reflexively related), we surmised that Japanese children's cognitive representation of number might reflect that language organization, whereas English-speaking children's mental representation would not (Miura, 1987).

Table 8.1: Number Names in Four Languages

Number	English	Chinese	Japanese	Korean
1	one	yi	ichi	il
2	two	er	ni	ee
3	three	san	san	sam
4	four	si	shi	sah
5	five	wu	go	oh
6	six	liu	roku	yook
7	seven	qi	shichi	chil
8	eight	ba	hachi	pal
9	nine	jiu	kyu	goo
10	ten	shi	juu	shib
11	eleven	shi-yi	juu-ichi	shib-il
12	twelve	shi-er	juu-ni	shib-ee
13	thirteen	shi-san	juu-san	shib-sam
14	fourteen	shi-si	juu-shi	shib-sah
15	fifteen	shi-wu	juu-go	shib-oh
16	sixteen	shi-liu	juu-roku	shib-yook
17	seventeen	shi-qi	juu-shichi	shib-chil
18	eighteen	shi-ba	juu-hachi	shib-pal
19	nineteen	shi-jiu	juu-kyu	shib-goo
20	twenty	er-shi	ni-juu	ee-shib
21	twenty-one	er-shi-yi	ni-juu-ichi	ee-shib-il
22	twenty-two	er-shi-er	ni-juu-ni	ee-shib-ee
23	twenty-three	er-shi-san	ni-juu-san	ee-shib-sam
30	thirty	san-shi	san-juu	sam-shib
40	forty	si-shi	shi-juu	sah-shib
50	fifty	wu-shi	go-juu	oh-shib
60	sixty	liu-shi	roku-juu	yook-shib
70	seventy	qi-shi	shichi-juu	chil-shib
80	eighty	ba-shi	hachi-juu	pal-shib
90	ninety	jiu-shi	kyu-juu	goo-shib

This is, indeed, what we have found with several Asian and non-Asian-language-speaking groups of children on a behavioral task designed to explore cognitive representation of number. For example, when asked to show the numeral 42 using base-ten blocks (unit blocks and tens blocks, bars that have 10 segments marked on them), U.S., Swedish, and French first graders were most likely initially to represent the numeral using a one-to-one collection (42 unit blocks). Chinese, Japanese, and Korean first graders, on the other hand, represented the numeral with a canonical base-ten representation (4 tens blocks and 2 unit blocks). The Asian-language speakers differed significantly from the non-Asian-language speakers in the kinds of constructions they made. For five numerals (11, 13, 28, 30, and 42), the Asian-language speakers used more canonical base-ten representations than did the non-Asian-language speakers. The Asian-language speakers used fewer one-to-one collection representations than did the others. Place value (i.e., the meaning of tens and ones in a two-digit numeral) appeared to be an integral element of those representations (Miura, Kim, Chang, & Okamoto, 1988; Miura et al., 1993). When asked if they could show the number in a different way (using the blocks), the Asian-language speakers were better able than non-Asian-language speakers to make two different constructions for each number, suggesting greater flexibility in dealing with number quantities.

It is important to note that the children in these studies were in the first half of first grade. They had no prior experience with the base-ten blocks or instruction on using them. The study participants also had not received systematic teaching in place-value concepts. The procedure of constructing numbers using blocks was designed to be a behavioral measure of cognitive representation of number. Thus, children's performance in this endeavor was intended to assess their mental image of number rather than to examine their number-constructing ability. Trial items were single-digit numerals that do not allow for canonical and noncanonical constructions. If these items imposed a possible bias toward making one-to-one collection constructions, the bias seems selectively to have affected only the samples of non-Asian-language speakers. Asian-language speakers overwhelmingly showed an initial preference for making canonical constructions. A second trial assessed children's ability (and flexibility) to deal intellectually with the same number quantity in a different (or novel) way. Overall, Asian-language speakers were better able to make two different constructions than were non-Asian-language speakers.

We have found from our studies that English-speaking U.S. children can be taught to use the blocks to make canonical constructions, but that this does not necessarily indicate a change in their cognitive representation of number. Instead, it appears that children may simply have acquired proficiency in using blocks to construct numbers. Once children receive instruction in using the blocks, they almost always use a canonical construction to represent numbers. However, this does not automatically lead to an understanding of place value. For example, an experienced second grader, when shown a noncanonical construction of 3 ten blocks and 12 unit blocks and asked what number the blocks represented, said, "42." When asked to write 42 on a card, she wrote the numeral, "312." The connection between the concrete construction and the written representation was missing. This lack of transfer from one medium to another has also been found in the work of others (Baroody, 1987; Fuson, 1990). Fuson (1990), for example, instructed children in multidigit addition and subtraction using wooden blocks and then moved to paper and pencil algorithms. When children experienced difficulty in the latter context, she had to remind them to "think wood," presumably evoking a visual memory of the problem-solving procedure using the concrete blocks. Similarly, Baroody (1987) taught first graders Egyptian hieroglyphics, a pictorial base-ten system in which 10 was a unique symbol. Instruction eventually progressed from Egyptian numbers to standard notation. When children encountered difficulty solving a problem in the latter context, they had to be reminded to think of the algorithm in Egyptian numbers. Thus, if the block-construction procedure is to be considered a valid measure of children's cognitive representation of number, the blocks can only be used with children who have not been instructed in their use.

Effects on Counting

In our initial studies of children's cognitive representation of number, we attempted to use U.S. kindergartners. We found that many of the 5-year-olds we tested could not count consistently and accurately from *one* to *fifty*. Therefore, we turned to children in the first half of first grade. By contrast, we found no such difficulties with Korean kindergartners (Miura et al., 1988).

In Miller and Stigler's (1987) study of counting behavior, Chinese-speaking children showed the same pattern of development of counting skills as did U.S. preschoolers. However, the Chinese children made significantly fewer errors in number naming than did U.S. children. The activity of generating number labels poses little problem for Chinese children, and in this aspect of counting, they surpass their U.S. counterparts.

In conclusion, the regularity of the Asian number-naming systems gives children learning those systems an advantage that is clear, particularly when verbal-counting skill is taken as a whole (Miller, 1996). Counting from *one* to *nine* in Japanese, Chinese, and Korean can become automatized quickly, because it is used to count to *ten* and then used again to count from 11 to 19. In addition, children do not have to learn the decade number names, a requirement that often hinders U.S. children's counting. Because counting in the early grades is also a tool for problem solving, it is a skill that can also directly affect this aspect of mathematics performance.

Effects on Place-Value Understanding

We also tested children's place-value understanding and found a positive correlation between the use of canonical constructions to represent numbers and understanding of place-value concepts (the meaning assigned to individual units in a multidigit numeral). On a set of five place-value tasks, Japanese first graders demonstrated significantly greater understanding of place-value concepts than did U.S. children (Miura & Okamoto, 1989). In a comparison with French, Swedish, and U.S. children (Miura et al., 1993), Japanese and Korean speakers showed significantly better understanding of place-value concepts, which we believe may also be related to the organization of the number-naming system. On five tasks involving place-value understanding, all of the Korean and Japanese first graders completed at least one problem correctly; 42% of Japanese children and 54% of the Korean first graders were able to solve all five problems correctly. By contrast, the Swedish, French, and U.S. children in the study performed significantly less well; 50% of the U.S. first graders could not solve any of the problems correctly.

In a study comparing 6-year-old Taiwanese and English children's understanding of additive composition and counting, Lines and Bryant (reported in Nunes & Bryant, 1996) noted that Chinese speakers showed a distinct advantage over English speakers in counting and in combining units of different sizes (in this case 1, 5, and 10). This was particularly true for additive composition involving decades. The authors concluded that the regularity and transparency of the Chinese counting system appeared to facilitate children's learning significantly. This influence seems to result from the linguistic cues provided by the number naming system and from a general understanding of additive composition that is supported by the system.

Effects on Addition and Subtraction Performance

Because counting to *nine* can become quickly automatized (as noted earlier) and because the numbers 11 to 19 are simple composites of the decade term for *ten* and the *one*-to-*nine* sequence, Asian-speaking children need only learn the sums to 10 (instead of 18 as with English-speaking children). For example, 8 + 7 can be thought of as 8 + 2 + 5 or 10 + 5, which can immediately be translated into the spoken answer "ten and five" (e.g., *juu-go* in Japanese). Similarly for subtraction, 15 – 7 can be thought of as 10 – 7 + 5.

In the specific area of addition and subtraction with regrouping (borrowing and carrying), which is taught at the second-grade level in both Japan and the United States, the Japanese number-naming system may have an important effect. In the addition algorithm, 59 + 8 = ?, the numbers in the ones column total 17. English speakers must ask themselves if they can regroup or trade to make a ten. If the answer is, yes, this results in a regrouped 1 ten and 7 ones. The 7 is written in the ones column, and the 1 (which represents 1 ten) is added to the 5 in the tens column. In Japanese, the sum of the numbers in the ones column is spoken as *ten-seven*. Therefore, it is understood that a ten has been formed, and 1 ten belongs in the tens column, eliminating the intermediate assessment step, and keeping the meaning of the individual digits in the solution intact.

Consider the subtraction item 67 – 59 = ? There are at least two possible solution methods for this item after determining that there are not enough units in the ones column to solve the problem without regrouping. For one, 1 ten from the tens column can be traded or regrouped for 10 ones to make the number in the ones column a 17. Then, the solution 8 is determined by subtracting 9 from 17. If the regrouped 17 is spoken as *ten-seven*, a second solution becomes possible: 9 can be subtracted from the 10 to leave a remainder of 1, which is then added to the 7 to equal 8 in the ones column.

U.S. children are taught to solve the subtraction algorithm using the first method, trading, or regrouping (e.g., *Addison-Wesley Mathematics*, 1993). The terms vary by textbook publisher. The second method can be used easily by Japanese children because their number language treats the teen numbers (11 to 19) as 10 + a single-digit number; thus, the two numbers (10 and the single-digit number) can be dealt with separately in the solution process. Whereas English-speaking children must learn the addition and subtraction combinations to 18, Japanese-speaking children do not have to master number combinations beyond 10. (For further discussion of how cultural differences in counting systems impact arithmetic performance, see Butterworth, 1999).

Mathematics Terms: Fractions

The part-whole concept of common fractions may also be easier to understand in Asian languages. In these languages, the concept of fractional parts is embedded in the mathematics terms used for fractions. For example, in Japanese, one third is spoken as *san bun no ichi,* which is literally translated as, "of three parts, one." Thus, unlike the English word, *third,* the Japanese term, *san bun,* directly supports the concept of the whole divided into three parts. In teaching numerical fractions and the concept of one third, U.S. second-grade textbooks (e.g., *Addison-Wesley Mathematics,* 1993) include drawings of geometric figures divided into three parts with one of the parts distinguished from the rest by being shaded. This fraction is defined in the text in the following way:

$$\frac{1 \text{ of the}}{3 \text{ equal parts.}}$$

Although there has been research examining children's informal or intuitive understanding of rational numbers (Hunting & Sharpley, 1988; Kieren, 1988; Mack, 1993), there have been no studies that focus specifically on the influence of language characteristics on children's early conceptualizations of fractions. We wondered if the Japanese and Korean vocabulary of fractions might influence the meaning these children ascribe to numerical fractions, and if this would result in their being able to associate numerical fractions with their corresponding pictorial representations prior to formal instruction (Miura, Okamoto, Vlahovic-Stetic, Kim, & Han, 1999).

First and second graders in Croatia, Korea, and the United States participated in a study with data collection at three separate times: middle of Grade 1, end of Grade 1, and beginning of Grade 2. Different samples of children were used for each data point. Examination of textbooks showed that the children had not had formal instruction in fraction concepts prior to the testing. Children were given eight written fractions (1/3, 2/3, 2/4, 3/4, 2/5, 3/5, and 4/5); each numerical fraction was followed by four geometric figures (circles, squares, or rectangles) with varying portions shaded (pictorial representation choices). In each case, the correct choice was a representation partitioned into a number of equal-sized regions corresponding to the denominator and with a number of shaded regions corresponding to the numerator. The fractions were read aloud by the teacher, and children were asked to draw a circle around the picture in the row that showed the fraction.

There was a developmental difference in children's performance, with Korean children better able at all levels to associate complex numerical fractions with their pictorial representations. The difference was only marginally significant at the middle of Grade 1. However, by the end of the first-grade academic year, Korean children's performance was significantly better than that of the other two groups, and by the beginning of Grade 2, 25 of the Korean children (76% of the total participants) correctly identified all eight fractions. No Korean child gave more than two incorrect responses. Only one second grader in the United States and no child in Croatia were able to identify all eight fractions correctly. The results suggest that the Korean language may influence the meaning these children give to numerical fractions, and that this enables children to associate numerical fractions to their corresponding pictorial representations prior to formal instruction. Whether this early understanding affects subsequent knowledge of rational number concepts is an area that needs further exploration. We continue to examine and extend this research. We have added samples of French- and Croatian-speaking children whose numerical language characteristics are similar to those of English-speaking U.S. children. We have also added a Japanese-speaking sample (Miura et al., 2000).

Linguistic Forms—Numeral Classifiers

Numeral classifiers are used in Japanese and other Asian languages when enumerating (or counting) objects. This linguistic form is a special morpheme that indicates certain semantic features of whatever is being counted (Sanches, 1977). For example, when counting five pencils in Japanese, one cannot use the cardinal number alone. One must say, *go-hon*, where *go* is *five* and *hon* is the numeral classifier for long, thin objects. Which classifier is used depends on the perceptual characteristics of the objects or on distinctions between human and other animal forms (Naganuma & Mori, 1962). This is similar to the situation in English when counting mass nouns, such as water, paper, or cattle. In English, one does not say, "One water, two waters," and so forth; it is necessary to say, "One *drop* of water, two *drops* of water," and so forth. Likewise, instead of one paper, two papers . . . or one cattle, two cattles . . . , counting entails one *piece of* paper, two *pieces of* paper . . . or one *head of* cattle, two *heads of* cattle . . . In brief, the classifier in Asian counts acts like the italicized portion in the previous examples.

Numeral classifiers are a linguistic convention. They may reflect certain cognitive categories, but they not do so consistently. For example, although a pencil and an umbrella (both long, thin objects) share the same classifier in Japanese, a crayon does not. Thus, the acquisition of numeral classifiers seems to be motivated by a search for convention, not by a need to find linguistic forms for categories that children wish to discuss. The forms are a hindrance because they make counting objects in these languages difficult. The pronunciation of the classifiers may change depending on the quantity, and the pronunciation of the number terms is affected by the classifier as well. For example, in Japanese, the numbers one to three are these: *ichi*, *ni*, and *san*. Adding the numeral classifier *pon* (long, thin thing) to these number terms results in the following: *ippon*, *nihon*, and *san bon*. It is the speaker's task to learn which objects require a particular classifier, how the number form changes with the various classifiers, and how the classifiers themselves are altered depending on the numeral used. The verbal complexity that must be dealt with may make the numeral classifier particularly salient.

With respect to mathematics, the numeral classifier may add coherence to the items being enumerated; it may act to integrate the items into a set, rather than treating them as individual items. Numeral classifiers also may serve as placeholders in that they are used anaphorically to denote referents that have already been introduced in the text (Downing, 1986).

The word problem in English,

> *Joe has 6 marbles.*
> *He has 2 more than Tom.*
> *How many does Tom have?*

would be translated into Japanese as,

> *Joe has 6 (ko) marbles,*
> *2 (ko) more than Tom.*
> *How many (ko) does Tom have?*

The numeral classifier, *ko*, is used when counting small, round objects. The problem is understood as "Joe has 6 (small, round thing) marbles, 2 (small, round thing) more than Tom. How many (small, round thing) does Tom have?" In Japanese, nouns, but not the corresponding numeral classifiers, are frequently omitted from numerical phrases once the referent has been established. Thus, the use of the numeral classifier may make problems more concrete; numbers in isolation (as in the phrase "two more than Tom") are not an abstract quantity. The numeral classifier acts as a concept signifier and may also serve to engage children in a stronger visual representation of what the story problem is asking (e.g., removing the ambiguity from the final question). The influence of numeral classifiers on children's solution of arithmetic story problems needs further exploration and is an area of research in which we are currently engaged.

The Lack of Singular and Plural Markers

In English, the responsibility for number information rests with the speaker; that is, the speaker must select the communicative markers necessary to convey number meaning. In Japanese and Korean, this responsibility is shared between the speaker and listener. Listeners must be sensitive to cues provided explicitly by the speaker or by the communicative context in which the information is given. In English, a plural noun may be indicated by the appropriate suffix, by a plural form of the noun, by a plural article or determiner, or by a plural form of the verb used with the noun. In Korean and Japanese, there are no markers to differentiate plural from singular forms of a noun (Matsumoto, 1985; Soga, 1984); there is no method for verbs to agree in number with their noun subjects; there are no articles or other determiners that carry number meaning. In these languages, plurality is conveyed by explicit reference, either by a specific number or terms such as "many" and "all," or implicitly through situational cues. In Korean, a special marker, *dl*, is added to a noun to emphasize plural meaning. This marker is not used systematically to indicate plurality, but only when the speaker wishes to stress the plural meaning already denoted by a number term or the situational context.

In general, the Japanese or Korean listener must attend carefully to cues provided in the sentence or to the situation in which the sentence is presented in order to determine if the meaning implied is singular or plural. For example, *Hito ga iru*, in Japanese, can mean both "There is a person," and "There are people." When number information is important in the communication, the speaker must add the explicit number information or provide situational cues, which are then interpreted by the listener.

We conducted a study in Tokyo, Japan, and Seoul, Korea, with preschool children, fourth graders, eighth graders, and college students to assess sensitivity to contextual cues in determining singular and plural meaning of sentences (Miura, Okamoto, Kim, & Sato, 1998). Participants were provided with sheets of paper on which were drawn 1 item and 12 items, were read a sentence, and were asked to circle the picture that best illustrated the statement. Seven nouns were used: three contexts (neutral, singular, and plural) for each item were presented in counterbalanced order. For example, the item, apple, was presented in three contexts: a neutral context, "There apple"; a singular context, "There apple in lunch box"; and a plural context, "There apple in produce market." For each sentence, participants were asked to choose either the picture of 1 apple or 12 apples.

Japanese preschool children were at-chance in their responses in the neutral condition, but followed the trends of the older Japanese children in the singular and plural context conditions. Korean preschoolers gave responses similar to the older children in only the plural context condition. For older speakers of Korean and Japanese, the assigning of singular or plural meaning appeared to be sensitive to contextual or situational cues provided by the modifying phrase. As might be expected, for the neutral (no modifying phrase) context, the interpretations were less predictable. This sensitivity to context seems to be an early acquisition. Although the preschool children in Korea gave similar responses across the three conditions, fourth-grade children in both nations performed as if they had considered the modifier when making their interpretations. The performance of the fourth graders did not differ from that of the eighth graders and adults in each country.

Typically, number (singular or plural) does not affect understanding in a conversation, and in this study, the test conditions were an artifact imposed by the examiner—therefore, the interpretations were a forced choice. The participants were not accustomed to having to make a singular or plural interpretation, and an interesting finding was that context did not provide unanimous agreement on interpretation. Indeed, in each case of the singular and plural conditions, the opposite interpretation could be made. For example, for "apple in lunch box," it is conceivable that there might be more than one apple in a lunch box. At the same time, for "apple in produce market," there could be just one apple left in the market.

Thus, in the Korean and Japanese languages, when number is important to the meaning conveyed, a specific term (or number) must be used in the statement. This may make numbers particularly salient to Asian-language speakers because they are used only when it is imperative to do so. This may also have a special impact in mathematics education where numbers play a significant role, especially in the elementary school years. At the same time, the need to attend to subtle, contextual cues for meaning might assist the Asian-language speaker to develop other skills such as comprehension monitoring that could affect academic performance broadly.

Summary Comments

In this chapter, we examined language factors that we believe may influence children's mathematics understanding and performance and account, at least in part, for the superior performance of Asian-language speakers on international comparisons of mathematics achievement. In the early school years, these culturally specific characteristics of mathematics languages serve to facilitate mathematics activities in a variety of ways. The Asian number-naming system, which directly reflects the base-ten, place-value rationale for written numbers, is regular and transparent. This may help children to develop a deep understanding of number concepts, including the understanding of place-value concepts, and to facilitate understanding of addition and subtraction with regrouping. Numbers (especially those from 10 to 19, which are particularly difficult in non-Asian languages) are readily generated and their component parts easily understood. When solving problems requiring regrouping, children can deal with ten and the additional units separately in their computations.

The direct effect of specific mathematics terms, such as the spoken fraction words, was also discussed. Asian fraction words themselves may provide support for understanding fraction concepts. Speakers of Asian-languages exhibit an intuitive (or socially acquired) knowledge of numerical fraction concepts prior to school instruction that exceeds that of their non-Asian-language speaking counterparts.

Two additional linguistic characteristics of Asian languages and their possible influence on mathematics understanding and performance were described. First, numeral classifiers, which are perceptual or categorical in nature, must be used when enumerating objects. These numeral classifiers, as part of arithmetic story problems, may diminish ambiguity by making the referent clear, add coherence to items and assign them to a set, and provide a stronger visual representation of what a problem is asking. Second, the lack of plural and singular markers in written and verbal discourse results in numbers being used explicitly when numerosity is important. The use of numbers only when necessary might add a particular salience to numerical information not found for speakers of marked languages. Another consequence is that, in addition to speakers marking number in discourse, listeners must also constantly monitor comprehension in order to know whether they understand what a speaker is saying.

These language characteristics may also provide support for a deep understanding of related mathematics concepts that contributes to the development of what Hatano (1988) has called adaptive expertise. Adaptive experts are those who are able to apply problem-solving skills to new situations. They differ from routine experts, that is, those whose problem-solving skills are limited to problems similar to those they have practiced, in their ability to adapt and extend their knowledge and skills to novel problem situations. Adaptive expertise in a particular domain results from rich conceptual knowledge that is constructed by individuals as they attempt to understand the elements of the problem domain. One important component of that construction process, according to Hatano, is the knowledge that one does not understand. "In order for cognitive incongruity to occur, people must themselves recognize the inadequacy of their comprehension. To do this, they must be able to monitor their own comprehension" (p. 59). Comprehension monitoring that is by necessity an integral part of all Asian-language discourse may provide the cultural context in which children are uniquely motivated to understand and make sense of the concepts, language, and procedures they encounter in school. At the same time, the characteristics of the mathematics language may facilitate mathematics performance and mediate the development of conceptual knowledge in this domain.

References

Addison-Wesley Mathematics: Grade 2. (1993). Menlo Park, CA: Addison-Wesley.

Baroody, A. J. (1987, April). Video tape workshops for teachers: A cognitive perspective on early number development. Paper presented at the annual meeting of the American Educational Research Association, Washington, DC.

Butterworth, B. (1999). The mathematical brain. London: Macmillan.

Cobb, P. (1993, April). Cultural tools and mathematical learning: A case study. Paper presented at the annual meetings of the American Educational Research Association, Atlanta, GA.

CSU Institute for Education Reform. (1997). Lessons in perspective: How culture shapes math instruction in Japan, Germany and the United States. Sacramento, CA: Author.

Downing, P. (1986). Anaphoric use of classifiers in Japanese. In C. Craig (Ed.), Noun classes and categorization: Proceedings of a symposium on categorization and noun classification (pp. 345–375). Amsterdam: Benjamins.

Fuson, K. C. (1990). Conceptual structures for multiunit numbers: Implications for learning and teaching multidigit addition, subtraction, and place value. Cognition and Instruction, 7, 343–403.

Hatano, G. (1988). Social and motivational bases for mathematical understanding. In G. B. Saxe & M. Gearhart (Eds.), Children's mathematics (pp. 55–70). San Francisco: Jossey-Bass.

Hess, R. D., Chang, C.-M., & McDevitt, T. M. (1987). Cultural variations in family beliefs about children's performance in mathematics: Comparisons among People's Republic of China, Chinese-American, and Caucasian-American families. *Journal of Educational Psychology, 79,* 179–188.

Hunting, R. P., & Sharpley, C. F. (1988). Fraction knowledge in preschool children. *Journal for Research in Mathematics Education, 19,* 175–180.

Kieren, T. E. (1988). Personal knowledge of rational numbers: Its intuitive and formal development. In J. Hiebert & M. Behr (Eds.), *Number concepts and operations in the middle grades* (pp. 162–181). Reston, VA: Author.

LaPointe, A. E., Mead, N. A., & Philips, G. W. (1989). *A world of differences* (Rep. No. 19-CAEP-01). Princeton, NJ: Educational Testing Service.

Mack, N. K. (1993). Learning rational numbers with understanding: The case of informal knowledge. In T. P. Carpenter, E. Fennema, & T. A. Romberg (Eds.), *Rational numbers: An integration of research* (pp. 85–106). Hillsdale, NJ: Lawrence Erlbaum Associates.

Mathematics achievement in the middle school years: IEA's Third International Math and Science Study. (1996). Chestnut Hill, MA: TIMSS International Study Center.

Matsumoto, K. (1985). A study of tense and aspect in Japanese (Doctoral dissertation, University of Southern California, 1981). *Dissertation Abstracts, 46,* 966-A.

McKnight, C. C., Crosswhite, F. J., Dossey, J. A., Kifer, E., Swafford, J. O., Travers, K. J., & Cooney, T. J. (1987). *The underachieving curriculum: Assessing U.S. school mathematics from an international perspective.* Champaign, IL: Stipes.

Miller, K. F. (1996). Origins of quantitative competence. In R. Gelman & T. K.-F. Au (Eds.), *Perceptual and cognitive development* (pp. 213–241). San Diego, CA: Academic Press.

Miller, K. F., Smith, C. M., Zhu, J., & Zhang, H. (1995). Preschool origins of cross-national differences in mathematical competence: The role of number-naming systems. *Psychological Science, 6,* 56–60.

Miller, K. F., & Stigler, J. W. (1987). Counting in Chinese: Cultural variation in a cognitive skill. *Cognitive Development, 2,* 279–305.

Miura, I. T. (1987). Mathematics achievement as a function of language. *Journal of Educational Psychology, 79,* 79–82.

Miura, I. T., Kim, C. C., Chang, C.-M., & Okamoto, Y. (1988). Effects of language characteristics on children's cognitive representation of number: Cross-national comparisons. *Child Development, 59,* 1445–1450.

Miura, I. T., & Okamoto, Y. (1989). Comparisons of U.S. and Japanese first graders' cognitive representation of number and understanding of place value. *Journal of Educational Psychology, 81,* 109–113.

Miura, I. T., Okamoto, Y., Kim, C. C., & Sato, S. (1998, July). *Contextual influences on determining singular and plural meaning in Japanese and Korean.* Paper presented at the biennial meetings of the International Society for the Study of Behavioral Development, Berne, Switzerland.

Miura, I. T., Okamoto, Y., Kim, C. C., Steere, M., & Fayol, M. (1993). First graders' cognitive representation of number and understanding of place value: Cross-national comparisons—France, Japan, Korea, Sweden, and the United States. *Journal of Educational Psychology, 85,* 24–30.

Miura, I. T., Okamoto, Y., Kim, C. C., Vlahovic-Stetic, V., Han, J. H., Lemaire, P., & Hatano, G. (2000, July). *The development of numerical fraction understanding: Cross-national comparisons.* Paper presented at the biennial meeting of the International Society for the Study of Behavioral Development, Beijing, China.

Miura, I. T., Okamoto, Y., Vlahovic-Stetic, V., Kim, C. C., & Han, J. H. (1999). Language supports for children's numerical fractions: Understanding of cross-national comparisons. *Journal of Experimental Child Psychology, 74,* 356–365.

Mordkowitz, E. R., & Ginsburg, H. P. (1987). Early academic socialization of successful Asian American college students. *Quarterly Newsletter of the Laboratory for Comparative Human Cognition, 9,* 85–91.

Naganuma, N., & Mori, K. (1962). *Practical Japanese.* Tokyo: Tokyo School of the Japanese Language.

Nunes, T. (1992). Cognitive invariants and cultural variation in mathematical concepts. *International Journal of Behavioral Development, 15,* 433–453.

Nunes, T. (1997). Systems of signs and mathematical reasoning. In T. Nunes & P. Bryant (Eds.), *Learning and teaching mathematics: An international perspective* (pp. 28–44). Hove, East Sussex, England: Psychology Press.

Nunes, T., & Bryant, P. (1996). *Children doing mathematics.* Oxford, England: Blackwell.

Rogoff, B. (1990). *Apprenticeship in thinking. Cognitive development in social context.* New York: Oxford University Press.

Sanches, M. (1977). Language acquisition and language change: Japanese numeral classifiers. In B. G. Blount & M. Sanches (Eds.), *Sociocultural dimensions of language change* (pp. 51–62). New York: Academic Press.

Saxe, G. B. (1982). Developing forms of arithmetic operations among the Oksapmin of Papua New Guinea. *Developmental Psychology, 18,* 583–594.

Soga, M. (1984). Tense and aspect in modern colloquial Japanese. *Papers in Linguistics, 17*(2), 223–233.

Song, M.-J., & Ginsburg, H. P. (1987). The development of informal and formal mathematics thinking in Korean and U.S. children. *Child Development, 58,* 1286–1296.

Steffe, L. P., Cobb, P., & von Glasersfeld, E. (1988). *Construction of arithmetical meanings and strategies.* New York: Springer-Verlag.

Stevenson, H. W., & Stigler, J. W. (1992). *The learning gap.* New York: Summit.

Stevenson, H. A., Lee, S.-Y., & Stigler, J. W. (1986). Mathematics achievement of Chinese, Japanese, and American children. *Science, 231,* 593–699.

Towse, J., & Saxton, M. (1998). Mathematics across national boundaries: Cultural and linguistic perspectives on numerical competence. In C. Donlan (Ed.), *The development of mathematical skills* (pp. 129–150). Hove, East Sussex, England: Psychology Press.

CHAPTER 9

YOUNG CHILDREN'S ESTIMATES FOR ADDITION: THE ZONE OF PARTIAL KNOWLEDGE AND UNDERSTANDING

Ann Dowker
University of Oxford

In recent years, arithmetic estimation has attracted increasing attention from both educators (e.g., Levine, 1982; Paull, 1972; Reys, Rybolt, Bestgen, & Wyatt, 1982; Rubenstein, 1985; Sowder, 1992) and cognitive psychologists (e.g., Dehaene and Cohen, 1991; Dehaene, Spelke, Pinel, Stanescu, & Tsivkin, 1999; Warrington, 1982). In this chapter, I first review the literature in an effort to delineate key issues about the development of expertise with computational estimation. I next summarize a recent study on the topic and then discuss its findings in light of the general issues identified in the literature review.

Literature Review

Interest in estimation by both educational and cognitive researchers has led to attempts to determine the course of its development. Most of the research in the area, with a few exceptions (Baroody, 1989, 1992; Sowder & Wheeler, 1989), has dealt with children over 10 years old (e.g., Edwards, 1984; LeFevre, Greenham, & Waheed, 1993; Reys et al., 1982; Rubenstein, 1985) or with adults (Dowker, 1992; Dowker, Flood, Griffiths, Harriss, & Hook, 1996; Levine, 1982). This means that estimation has usually been studied after it is at least partially established, rather than charting its emergence. The major exception to this tendency has been Baroody's (1989, 1992) research into the addition estimates of kindergarten (approximately 5-year-old) children. He found that their responses to unknown addition sums often involved neither random responding nor unsuccessful attempts to recall learned facts, but primitive estimation strategies that reflected incomplete arithmetic knowledge. The most common of these strategies were stating an addend, adding 1 to an addend, and (somewhat less often) adding 10 to an addend. The latter two strategies were seen as qualitatively more advanced than the first and as reflecting the knowledge that addition involves incrementing.

The issues of the emergence and developmental course of estimation depend rather crucially on how estimation is operationally defined. There is, in fact, no single definition, and the term can be and is used in senses ranging from the use of certain specific approximate calculation strategies, to any guess as to a numerical quantity. It is here defined simply as giving an approximate answer to an arithmetic item (i.e., without precise calculation).

Educational Aspects of Estimation

Prior to 1980, there were only a few scattered efforts to study the nature and educational importance of estimation (e.g., Dickey, 1934; Faulk, 1962; Reeve, 1936; Sauble, 1955). Since 1980, estimation has received increased attention from educationists and educational policy makers in Britain (Cockcroft, 1982; Department of Education and Science and the Welsh Office, 1989) and in the United States (Sowder, 1987). This increasing emphasis stems in part from the practical importance of estimation. Cockcroft (1982), for example, stated that "ability to estimate is important not only in many kinds of employment but in the ordinary activities of adult life."

Estimation experience has also been proposed to have a beneficial effect on other arithmetic abilities, by playing a role in developing awareness of, and resourcefulness with, number relations. In an early study, Sauble (1955) pointed out that "mental computation and estimation . . . stimulate the development of more mature understandings of basic principles and number relations. . . . Pupils who succeed . . . in estimating do not always employ standardized prescribed thought patterns. Instead, these pupils develop ingenuity and resourcefulness in dealing with numbers" (p. 38).

Slater (1990) suggested that school instruction in estimation reflects neither its importance nor its nature: "In many everyday situations estimations are used more than exact computations, yet school teaching does not reflect this" (pp. 10–11). When estimation is encouraged, it tends to take the form of asking children to estimate the answer to an arithmetic problem, before doing the exact calculation (e.g., Baroody, with Coslick, 1998; Slater, 1990). In practice, children tend to respond to such requests by calculating first and then rounding their answer to a multiple of 10. Such instruction may fail to convey to children the purposes of estimation, which is rarely used when one can and intends to get an exact answer.

There has been considerable historical and cultural variation as to when estimation is formally introduced. Younger primary school children (5- to 9-year-olds) in Britain have, until recently, had significant formal experience with measurement estimation and numerosity estimation but had much less experience with arithmetic estimation. Recently, the government has recommended that British schools place increased emphasis on mental calculation, and one consequence is that children from Year 3 (approximately age 7) are expected to learn to check the results of calculations by using rounding strategies. It is as yet too soon to know the effects of this recommendation.

Some studies have looked more directly at the effects of mathematics educational practices on estimation. Forrester and Pike (1998) have studied the social and linguistic contexts of the mathematics classrooms in which students learn to estimate and the ways in which children acquire the language of approximation and estimation. These studies have emphasized estimation involving measurement rather than computation, and as discussed later, there appear to be important differences between computational and measurement estimation.

Educational practices vary between cultures and countries, and some studies have compared estimation by children in different countries. For example, Reys et al. (1991) found that Japanese fifth- and eighth-grade pupils were better at mental calculation than their American counterparts, but that "their tendency to use pencil-and-paper procedures mentally often interfered with the estimation process" (p. 55).

The Cognitive Aspects of Estimation

The Componential Nature of Estimation. Educational researchers have drawn a sharp distinction between arithmetic estimation and calculation, especially that involving written calculation, but they have not always emphasized the distinctions that can arise among different components of estimation itself. Arithmetic estimation appears to involve several components, not a single process. Sowder and Wheeler (1989) emphasized that arithmetic skills, concepts, and attitudes were all important in influencing estimation ability. The concepts that they proposed to be most relevant to estimation ability were (a) understanding of the role of approximate numbers in estimation, (b) understanding that estimation can involve multiple processes and have multiple answers, and (c) understanding that context can influence the appropriateness of an estimate. Consider, for example, estimating the sum of 23 + 59. Concept *a* could involve understanding 23 and 59 can be rounded to 20 or 25 and 60, respectively. Concept *b* could entail recognizing that all of the following might provide a reasonable estimate: "23 + 59 is about 20 + 60 or 80"; "23 + 59 is about 30 + 50 or 80"; and "23 + 59 is a bit less than 25 + 60 or 85." Concept *c* could include understanding both the importance of the size of the numbers in the task (e.g., an estimate that is 40 more than the exact answer would be rather unreasonable for 23 + 59, but reasonable for 230 + 590) and the importance of the practical context (e.g., it is usually prudent to underestimate the amount of money that one has available to spend and to overestimate one's likely expenses).

Case and Sowder (1990) and LeFevre et al. (1993) have emphasized the importance of coordinating different components of estimation. The former have proposed that this need to coordinate the different components places intrinsic cognitive limitations on children's estimation competence before the age of 11 or 12, however they are taught. Their argument was that estimation "requires the coordination of two qualitatively different sorts of component activities: (a) using nearness judgment to select appropriate substitutes for the addends and (b) mentally computing the sum of the substitute numbers" (p. 79). In the case of 23 +

59, this could mean coordinating the judgment that 23 is near to 20 and 59 is near to 60 with the computation that $20 + 60 = 80$. According to Case's theory of intellectual development, children are not able to achieve this sort of coordination until about 11 or 12 years.

LeFevre et al. (1993) also proposed a componential model but placed greater emphasis on the processes involved in estimation than had earlier researchers. They postulated the following three component processes: retrieval, calculation, and reformulation. Like Case and Sowder (1990), these researchers found a leap in estimation ability between Grade 4 (9 to 10 years of age) and Grade 6 (11- to 12-years-old) and further improvements beyond Grade 6. However, LeFevre et al. attributed the improvement to increased flexibility of strategy use, as well as to better coordination ability.

Individual Differences. The emphasis on development in many research reports may give the misleading impression that there is a final stage to the acquisition of estimation and that adults perform at a similar uniform level of competence. This is not so. There are wide individual differences in adult arithmetic-estimation ability (Dowker, 1992; Dowker et al., 1996; LeFevre et al., 1993; LeFevre, Smith-Chant, Hiscock, Daley, & Morris, chap. 7, this volume; Levine, 1982), and some adults perform very poorly. Strategy variability appears to differentiate adults of different ability levels, and at the extreme, professional mathematicians are very good arithmetic estimators and also extremely versatile in their strategy use (Dowker, 1992; Dowker et al., 1996).

Deriving New Knowledge. The study of estimation is not only important in itself but in what it reveals about arithmetic development and cognitive development more generally. In particular, in many areas of cognition, including arithmetic cognition, the ability to retrieve known facts and use known procedures is insufficient. It is necessary to be able to deal with imperfect and limited knowledge and to find ways of deriving unknown information from known information. This is important to cognition, in general, and especially to cognitive development, which involves building new structures from limited existing knowledge and concepts. Thus, the study of how children solve problems involving situations in which they have direct access to only some of the relevant knowledge can advance our understanding of both the nature of their existing knowledge and the developmental process.

Specifically as regards to arithmetic, there are a number of available techniques for studying children's strategies for deriving unknown information from known information. For example, children's use of arithmetic principles such as commutativity, associativity, and the inverse principle for precisely deriving unknown number combinations from known combinations has been investigated in several studies (Baroody, Ginsburg, & Waxman, 1983; Baroody, Wilkins, & Tiilikainen, chap. 4, this volume; Canobi, Reeve, & Patterson, 1998; Carpenter, 1980; Carraher, Carraher, & Schliemann, 1985; Cowan & Renton, 1989; Dowker, 1995, 1998; Dowker & Webb, 1995; Fuson & Burghardt, chap. 10, this volume; Ginsburg, 1977; Hope & Sherrill, 1987; Renton, 1992;

Russell & Ginsburg, 1982; Steinberg, 1985). However, estimation studies are more informative about how children derive unknown information either when a task is more open ended and a single exact answer is not required or does not exist or when a child's knowledge of the relevant domain is insufficient to achieve an exact answer, even by derived-fact strategies.

Associations and Disassociations Between Estimation and Mental Calculation. Some researchers and educators have proposed close links between estimation and mental calculation for two reasons (Reeve, 1936; Reys, 1984; Reys et al., 1982). One is that the two may involve similar processes (perceiving and using relations between numbers; using nonstandard calculation techniques; using front-end strategies to calculate from left to right, rather than the right-to-left strategies involved in most written calculation algorithms). The other is that computational estimation "increases [the] potential [of mental calculation]. Very often the complexity of numbers in a problem precludes mentally computing an exact answer, but the problem may be solved with computational estimation" (Reys, 1984, p. 551).

Numerous studies do indeed provide evidence for significant associations between computational estimation performance and calculation performance in young children (Dowker, 1997, 1998), older children (Rubenstein, 1985), and adults (Dowker, 1992; Dowker et al., 1996; Levine, 1982). For example, a study of adults with and without self-reported difficulties in arithmetic showed that measures of calculation and estimation were closely related in both groups.

Despite these strong associations, dissociations and discrepancies between computational estimation and calculation do occur both in the general population and among neuropsychological patients. Dowker (1994, 1998), for instance, reported a number of children who did show marked discrepancies between calculation and estimation; similar discrepancies were found among adults.

Macaruso and Sokol (1998) studied a group of young people with developmental dyslexia. Their participants ranged in age from 12 to 20 years and were regarded by their teachers as having basic weaknesses in mathematics. These researchers found that some individuals had difficulty with calculation but not with computational or quantitative estimation, whereas others showed the reverse pattern. Both Warrington (1982) and Dehaene and Cohen (1991) have reported neuropsychological patients with dyscalculia, who were nevertheless competent at estimation.

Such studies not only show discrepancies between estimation and calculation but between different aspects of estimation. Warrington's (1982) patient had a partial impairment in calculation, in which fact retrieval was far more impaired than procedural knowledge; estimation was essentially unimpaired. Dehaene and Cohen's (1991) patients had more severe calculation impairments but were unimpaired at particular aspects of estimation, namely those that involved the recognition and comparison of approximate magnitudes. One might expect such individuals to be unimpaired at the first of Case and Sowder's (1990) proposed components of estimation (using nearness judgments to carry out approximations). In fact, they were less competent at the second (adding the substituted numbers).

There is far less evidence for associations between arithmetic estimation and other forms of estimation than for associations between computational estimation and calculation. In a study of older secondary school pupils, Paull (1972) found no significant correlations between computational estimation, length estimation, and weight estimation. Hook (1992) and Dowker (1995) did not find significant correlations among computational estimation, length estimation, numerosity estimation, and real-world estimation. (The latter was gauged by such questions as: *About how tall is an average Englishwoman? About how far is it from London to Paris? About how old is the oldest person alive in Britain? About how many people can board a double-decker bus?*) Moreover, factors such as age and arithmetic calculation ability, both of which have been shown to affect computational estimation, do not always have the same influence on other forms of estimation. Although all studies (e.g., Case & Sowder, 1990; LeFevre et al., 1993; Sowder & Wheeler, 1989) comparing children of different ages have shown an improvement with age in computational estimation, Forrester, Latham, and Shire (1990) and Pike and Forrester (1998) found that age did not affect length or area estimation. Pike and Forrester also found that "number sense" tasks involving mental computation, derived fact-strategy use, and comparison of numerical magnitudes did not correlate significantly with length estimation, although they did correlate with estimation of area.

The Zone of Partial Knowledge and Understanding. Because estimation may involve responses to problems to which an individual cannot produce accurate answers, estimation must be considered with regard to an individual's knowledge and understanding *of a given type of problem*. A child who can, for example, add single-digit numbers but not multidigit numbers may not have to estimate if a task involves only the former but may need to do so if a task involves the latter. In other words, estimation is neither solely a feature of an individual nor that of a cognitive domain, but of the interaction between individual and domain.

Dowker (1989, 1997) has proposed that in order to describe the changes in responses with increasing computational difficulty, it may be useful to speak in terms of a zone of partial knowledge and understanding. This zone is related to Vygotsky's zone of proximal development, in that it reflects an extensive intermediate area, rather than a sharp cutoff point, between the level of difficulty at which children have complete independent mastery over items and the level at which they are unable to function at all. It is not, however, identical to Vygotsky's zone of proximal development. In particular, it is here considered over a wider range of difficulty and is not considered mainly from the educational point of view of assistance with learning.

Before children enter the zone of partial knowledge and understanding, they know sums or can readily calculate them by using well-learned procedures and prefer providing exact sums rather than estimates (though they may give the latter if the context does not require an exact answer). In this zone, there is some knowledge about numbers and arithmetic strategies, but it is incomplete. Arithmetic estimation may be regarded, especially in children and other non-experts, as a system or systems for dealing with varying degrees of partial arithmetic knowledge. In people with greater competence at calculation, the nature of estimation is slightly different. Although *capable* of calculating accurately, they may choose to save time and effort by making use of only some of their factual and procedural knowledge to determine an approximate answer.

A Study
of Young Children's Estimation

Dowker (1989, 1997) investigated the development of arithmetic estimation of 5- to 9-year-olds at a time when computational estimation was not explicitly taught in British primary schools. A key aspect of this study is the ways in which estimates change as addition items become more difficult with respect to an individual's knowledge. In the remaining portion of the chapter, I summarize previously reported results of this study, new findings regarding the strategies used by children and a comparison of addition novices' performance with symbolic and concrete addition, and the implications of both.

Participants

The study included 215 children from four Oxford primary schools and lasted for 3 years. Each child was seen individually for all parts of the testing. The ages of the children ranged from 4 years, 9 months (4-9) to 9-10. All of the children could read at least single numerals and could count at least to 10, with the exception of one boy of 6-10 who could not count reliably beyond 6. He was included in the study and did not show a markedly different pattern of performance from other children at the beginning-arithmetic level (see Table 9.1).

Procedure

In order to evaluate the children's competence in addition, a mental-calculation task was given to each child. This consisted of a series of addition items, graduated in difficulty from single-digit expressions (e.g., 4 + 5, 7 + 1) to three-digit ones (e.g., 235 + 349). These sums were simultaneously presented orally and visually in a horizontal format. The children's answers were oral and were recorded on a tape-recorder. The choice of the items and the decision as to the order of difficulty of sums were guided by current standard textbooks and standardized tests (e.g., the British Abilities Scales) and by observing a number of arithmetic classes in primary schools. Testing continued with each child until he or she had failed to give a correct response to six successive items.

Table 9.1: Levels of Mental Calculation Performance

Level	Item Just Within Range	Item Outside Range
Beginning arithmetic	Counts to 10	5 + 3
Addition to 10	5 + 3	8 + 6
Simple addition	8 + 6	23 + 44
Two-digit (no carry)	23 + 44	52 + 39
Two-digit (carry)	52 + 39	523 + 168

The children were then divided into five levels according to their perform-ance on the mental-calculation task. The criteria for assignment to the different levels are described in more detail elsewhere (Dowker, 1997, 1998). A brief summary of the levels and examples of the items that could and could not be answered at these levels are described in Table 9.1.

Four sets of estimation items were devised (see Dowker, 1997, for details). Each set contained nine items. The sets were designed to be progressively more difficult to solve. Set 1 consisted of sums between 5 and 10 (e.g., 5 + 4); Set 2, sums greater than 10 and less than 35 (e.g., 9 + 8); Set 3, two-digit sums between 35 and 100 (e.g., 18 + 59); and Set 4, mostly three-digit sums greater than 100 (e.g., 217 + 285). Each set was designed to correspond roughly to the base performance levels described earlier. Thus, Set 1 items were just beyond the capabilities of the beginning-arithmetic level; Set 2 items just beyond the capabilities of the addition-to-10 level; and so on. This *base correspondence* was designed such that children of each level would be given addition items that were just a little too difficult for them to solve directly by mental arith-metic. This approach was adopted in order to increase the likelihood that children would estimate answers rather than attempting direct solutions.

The task was introduced by giving the participants some examples of estimates made by imaginary children called "Tom and Mary," and inviting them to rate these estimates as "good" or "silly." After this introduction, the children were told, "Now I'm going to give you some sums, and I'd like you not to work them out, but to guess the answers like Tom and Mary did. See if you can think of some good guesses." The estimation set of the base correspondence was then given, this time with the children being asked to estimate the answers themselves, rather than to evaluate Tom and Mary's estimates.

The sums were shown to the children and were simultaneously presented orally. The children's responses were oral and were recorded on a tape-recorder. The order of presentation of items in each set was varied randomly among children. There was no time limit, but participants were encouraged to respond quickly.

One hundred eight participants were given higher sets (i.e., sets beyond their base-correspondence set). For instance, among these, 40 children of the beginning-arithmetic level were given Set 2, 29 of these 40 were given Set 3, and 20 of these 29 were also given Set 4. The number of sets beyond a participant's base-correspondence set was constrained by several practical factors, the most important of which was that many children left the schools to go to middle school.

Results

The number of participants given a set is listed in Table 9.2 by level. The medians and ranges of reaction times per item at for each of these entries are also given in the table. The three main results of this study are summarized next.

1. Children, at least from the time they can calculate sums of between 5 and 10, possess good intuitive estimation abilities. A majority of such children's estimates were *reasonable* estimates (defined as those that are within 30% of the correct answer and greater than the larger addend).

2. Estimation performance improves with calculation-performance level. Within the base correspondence, the proportion of estimates that were reasonable increased with calculation-performance level. The greatest difference was between children at the beginning-arithmetic level and those at higher levels.

3. For each performance level, estimation accuracy deteriorated as item difficulty increased. Both for groups and for individuals, there was a marked diminution in the proportion of reasonable estimates and a marked increase in unreasonable estimates (especially those less than the larger addend), as children moved further and further from their base correspondence.

Discussion

We consider the effects of calculation performance level and item difficulty on the *nature* of the estimates and the strategies used to obtain them. Although the term *strategies* is commonly used in this context, it may be slightly misleading in the case of such young children, as it carries a connotation of explicit

Table 9.2: Numbers, Ages, Reaction Times, and Responses of Children at Each Level-Set Correspondence

Level and Set	Number of Children	Age Range	Median Age	Range of Reaction Times	Median Reaction Time	Total Number of Responses	Exact Answers (excluded from most further analysis)	Number of Responses Included in Analysis
Beginning arithmetic								
Set 1	52	5-0 to 8-7	5-10	1 to 22 sec	2 sec	468	60 (13%)	408
Set 2	40	5-0 to 8-7	5-10	1 to 14 sec	2 sec	360	2 (1%)	358
Set 3	29	5-0 to 8-7	5-10	2 to 25 sec	3 sec	261	1 (0.5%)	260
Set 4	20	5-0 to 8-7	5-10	2 to 15 sec	2 sec	180	0	180
Addition								
Set 2	62	4-9 to 9-1	6-10	1 to 32 sec	3 sec	558	96 (17%)	462
Set 3	29	4-9 to 9-1	6-11	1 to 30 sec	3 sec	261	2 (1%)	259
Set 4	18	4-9 to 9-1	6-11	2 to 25 sec	2 sec	162	1 (0.5%)	161
Addition to 25								
Set 3	57	5-5 to 9-4	8-0	1 to 34 sec	4 sec	495	41 (9%)	454
Set 4	22	5-7 to 9-4	8-0	2 to 37 sec	3 sec	198	1 (0.5%)	197
Two-digit arithmetic (no carrying)								
Set 3	19	6-6 to 9-10	8-5	1 to 55 sec	4 sec	171	36 (21%)	135
Set 4	17	6-6 to 9-10	8-5	2 to 30 sec	4 sec	153	5 (3%)	148
Two-digit arithmetic (carrying)								
Set 4	27	6-10 to 9-7	8-7	2 to 50 sec	4 sec	243	42 (17%)	201

choice of a course of action. Most of these participants did not spontaneously describe estimation strategies, and attempts to elicit strategy descriptions during the pilot study period were unsuccessful. Children either said, "I just guessed," or interpreted the question as meaning that they had given a wrong answer and should change it. Nevertheless, many of their responses were highly consistent with previously described appropriate and inappropriate estimation strategies. To avoid both (a) the assumptions about explicit strategy choice and (b) the difficulties that arise from the lack of strategy description, the term "presumed implicit strategies" will be used here.

Presumed Implicit Strategies. Two broad types of presumed implicit strategies will be described here: *mechanical* strategies and *primitive front-end and rounding* strategies. The former are used inflexibly and produce easily identifiable systematic errors (e.g., stating an addend would result in answers of 3 or 5 for 3 + 5, 2 or 4 for 2 + 4, and 6 or 1 for 6 + 1) and can produce unreasonable or highly inaccurate answers (Baroody, 1989). Primitive front-end and rounding strategies are used more flexibly and consistently produce reasonable and even fairly accurate estimates.

1. *Mechanical strategies.* These strategies were used predominantly by children at the lower calculation-performance levels. Like the 5-year-olds studied by Baroody (1989), the children at the beginning-arithmetic level used mechanical strategies with some frequency. Novices used such strategies to manufacture some answer, even if implausible. More than one fourth (28%) of their responses to Set 1 and 18% of their responses to Set 2 involved the strategy of *adding one to an addend* (excluding the correct responses to the sums 1 + 6 and 9 + 1). Another 10% of their responses to Sets 1 and 2 involved *stating an addend* (usually the larger one). These strategies were rarely used by participants at higher levels or by participants at the beginning-arithmetic level responding to Sets 3 and 4.

Other mechanical strategies included *response biases and patterns*. To an even greater extent than the previously mentioned strategies, which at least work by manipulating a number or numbers within the item, response biases are mechanical: The answer to an item is predetermined without much regard to the combination itself. Extreme response biases, where a child gave the same response to every addition item, were very rare indeed (used by only three children within their base correspondence). However, children at the beginning-arithmetic level often showed mild response biases in the sense of giving the same answer to at least three items in the set. Response patterns involved responding with series of consecutive numbers (e.g., 10, 11, 12, 13), successive multiples of 10 (e.g., 10, 20, 30), and other rarer series (e.g., 66, 77, 88). These were rare, but were used by a few children at the beginning-arithmetic and facts-to-10 levels both in their base correspondence and for higher sets. In all, 50% of the protocols of children of the beginning-arithmetic level involved response biases or patterns, as did about one fourth of the protocols of 25% of children of the facts-to-10 level and 20% of those of the simple-addition level. Children at higher levels rarely gave response biases.

Increasing the difficulty of the items did not exert a consistent effect on the proportion of such responses at any level.

2. *Strategies specific to items containing two or more digits: Primitive front-end and rounding strategies.* Two strategies that were applicable only to two- or three-digit items are here discussed only in relation to Sets 3 and 4. Trafton (1978) called adding the left-hand-most digits the "front-end strategy." A still more accurate strategy is that of rounding the addends. Both these strategies can take a "nondecadal" form, where the resulting estimate is not a multiple of a power of 10 (e.g., 18 + 59 is about 83, 518 + 304 is about 837) or a "decadal" form, where the resulting estimate *is* a multiple of a power of 10 (e.g., 18 + 59 is about 60, 518 + 304 is about 800).

Primitive front-end and rounding strategies were typically used by children at higher performance levels. Such strategies were very rarely used by children at the two lower levels (where they were essentially only applicable to sets above the base correspondence). They were used with increasing frequency by participants at the three higher levels. Thus, 25% of simple-addition level responses, 43% of the two-digit-addition (no-carrying) level responses, and 48% of the two-digit-addition (carrying) level responses to relevant problems in the base correspondence were consistent with the use of a front-end strategy. Twenty-two percent of simple-addition level responses, 33% of 2-digit-addition (no-carrying) responses, and 40% of the two-digit-addition (carrying) level responses to relevant items in the base correspondence were consistent with the use of a rounding strategy.

Most instances of rounding and front-end strategies were nondecadal. This was one aspect of the general rarity of responses that were divisible by 10. Only 32% of estimates were divisible by 10, and a further 6% were divisible by 5. The frequency of responses divisible by 10 did *not* increase significantly with arithmetic performance level.

Can Children at the Beginning-Arithmetic Level Produce Better Estimates to Concrete Arithmetic Problems? At first sight, the study might appear to show that estimation ability of any sort is very limited in children of the lowest performance level. Although such children do use estimation strategies, these are often inappropriate and their estimates are more often than not unreasonable. However, children, in general, estimate less well as addition items become excessively difficult relative to their arithmetic knowledge. It could be that even the simplest estimation items in this study were too difficult *relative to these children's level of knowledge and understanding* to elicit their true estimation capacities. Indeed, as these children's arithmetic experience (at the verbal level) was so limited, *any* addition item might be too difficult *relative to their level of knowledge and understanding* to elicit their true estimation capacities. In other words, Set 1 might not be a "true" base-correspondence level for such children.

As young children perform better on tasks with concrete representations than on those with abstract ones (e.g., Hughes, 1986; Piaget, 1955), addition items presented in terms of concrete objects might reveal more computational estimation competence than those presented in terms of numerals. For this reason, 30 new children of the beginning-arithmetic level were presented with the Set 1 items using counters rather than numerals. In one item, six counters were shown to a child and then placed in an envelope; subsequently, three more counters were shown to the child and placed in the envelope. Next, the child was told, "First we put six counters in the envelope, and then we put three more counters in the envelope. Can you guess how many counters are in there now?" This was known as the Set 1 (counters) version.

Children did indeed perform better on this task than matched participants given the numerical version of Set 1. Table 9.3 shows that a higher proportion of the estimates to the concrete items was exact, and a higher proportion of the nonexact estimates to these items were reasonable. The concrete items were less likely to elicit the mechanical strategy of adding 1 to an addend. They were also somewhat less likely to elicit response biases (though the latter difference did not reach significance). Even on the concrete items, however, children were less accurate and more likely to use mechanical strategies than the more advanced participants given higher sets. Overall, the findings support the hypotheses that even children of the beginning-arithmetic level can produce reasonable estimates under some conditions. The results also provide further support for the need to take account of *both* calculation performance level *and* item difficulty.

Conclusions

Educational Implications

The existence of a zone of partial knowledge and understanding has educational implications for the teaching and learning of arithmetic and possibly of other subjects. On the one hand, giving children items that are a little "too difficult" for them (e.g., tapping the partial knowledge of the base correspondence or one set above) could be constructive, encouraging them to search for and invent strategies for solving them, with or without help. On the other hand, presenting them with items that are very far out of their range of understanding may disorient them severely and encourage random responding.

Vygotsky (1987) argued that "learning which is oriented toward developmental levels that have already been reached is ineffective from the point of view of a child's overall development" (p. 89). Similarly, Piaget (1955) suggested that children show most advancement when presented with tasks of moderate novelty with respect to their current knowledge state.

Implications for Cognitive Theory

The Componential Nature of Estimation. The results of the present study, together with those of Dowker's (1998) studies with older children and

Table 9.3: Performance by Children at the Beginning-Arithmetic Level on Set 1 Items Presented in Numerical and Concrete Formats

	Numerical (Standard) Format	Concrete (Counters) Format	Chi-square Comparisons Between Concrete and Numerical Formats
Accuracy:			
Percentage of exact responses	13	23	11.11**
Percentage of nonexact responses that were reasonable	27	37	8.8**
Strategies (percentages are of non-exact responses):			
Equal to addend	11	15	0.51
Equal to addend +1	28	17	12.66**
Percentage of protocols	53	38	2.25
Response guesses or patterns		25	

** $p < .01$.

adults, support the view that arithmetic estimation is itself a componential, not a unitary, phenomenon. Its componential nature becomes even more apparent if it is studied in its earliest emerging form when some of the components are still partially or completely absent. Relatively broad categories, such as approximation, translation, and compensation, are insufficient to define the essential components of estimation. Some essential components are listed in Table 9.4 in approximate order of their emergence. As can be seen from this table, most of these are relevant to other arithmetic abilities besides estimation.

It is interesting that LeFevre et al. (1993) found that an older sample of children used compensation and rounding but not the proximity principle. By contrast, the younger children in the present study appeared to use the proximi-

Table 9.4: Components of Estimation—Their Proposed Early Developmental Course

Calculation Performance Level	Typical Age	Item Difficulty Level	Concept/Skill
Beginning arithmetic	5 years	Any	The answer to a numerical problem is a number.
Beginning arithmetic (but not universal)	5 years	Any	The answers to sums of large addends are larger than those to sums of small addends.
Beginning arithmetic	5 years	Any	Use of numerical strategies *not* based on problem characteristics (e.g., response biases).
Beginning arithmetic	5 years	Sums not involving tens and units	Use of mechanical numerical strategies based on problem characteristics (e.g., adding 1 to an addend).
Beginning arithmetic	5 years	Concrete single-digit	Some clear signs of proximity principle: most responses exact or reasonable; nearly half of nonexact responses reasonable.
Addition to 10 and higher levels	6 years and older	Base correspondence	Clear signs of proximity principle: most responses exact or reasonable; most nonexact responses reasonable.
Simple addition and higher levels	6 years and older	Base correspondence	Some use of approximate front-end strategies.
Two-digit addition (no carrying) and higher level	7 years and older	Base correspondence and to some extent above	Frequent use of approximate front-end strategies; some of approximate rounding strategies.
Two-digit addition (carrying) and the next higher level	8 years and older	Base correspondence	Frequent use of approximate front-end and rounding strategies.
Advanced arithmetic (beyond ability range addressed in this study)	10 years and older		Frequent use of decadal front-end and rounding strategies. Appropriate and explicit use of strategies involving translation and compensation.

ty principle (in the sense of attempting, often successfully, to produce an estimate close to the exact answer) before they used rounding. Furthermore, they almost never used compensation. This suggests that, once certain estimation strategies are acquired, they may be applied rigidly and sometimes at the expense of known principles. Only later do they redevelop in a more advanced and accurate form and are again used flexibly.

This U-shaped relation between expertise and strategy use may, in part, depend on methods of instruction. However, educational experience may not be the main explanation, especially as this developmental pattern appears in a number of domains (Dowker et al., 1996). Novices may use a wide variety of strategies (appropriate and inappropriate) because they have not yet acquired a small set of well-learned strategies. People with extensive knowledge and ability may use a variety of strategies (mostly appropriate) because they have access both to a large number of strategies and to principles and relations that facilitate the invention of new strategies. People at an intermediate level of knowledge are more likely to have mastered and to rely on a limited number of strategies.

Individual Differences and Deriving New Knowledge. The main focus of this chapter has been the effects of arithmetic-performance level and item difficulty on the estimates that children produce. Nevertheless, even within a performance level, there are significant individual differences, both in the reasonableness of children's estimates (see also Dowker, 1997, 1998) and in the strategies that they use. No strategy is used consistently for any given set of addition items by children of any given performance level, reflecting both within-individual and between-individual variability. This study does not, however, permit strong conclusions about the sources of such individual differences or their relation to other components of arithmetic knowledge. Nevertheless, it should be noted that Dowker (1998) found that, even when arithmetic-performance level is taken into account, there is a strong independent relation between the production of reasonable addition estimates and the appropriate use of derived-fact strategies in arithmetic. This suggests that estimation is just one form of unknown-fact derivation through arithmetical reasoning. The latter includes estimation (approximate unknown-fact derivation) but also derived-fact strategy use (exact unknown fact derivation). Despite this generally strong association, however, there are some children who show strong discrepancies even between estimation and derived-fact strategy use (Dowker, 1995, 1998). Thus, although both arithmetic-performance level and appropriate derived-fact strategy use are associated with estimation performance, there must be additional sources and correlates of individual differences in estimation.

Relations Between Calculation and Estimation. Like accuracy (Dowker, 1997), estimation-strategy use improved with arithmetic competence. Protocols of children at the beginning-arithmetic level included a large number of mechanical strategies and response biases. Participants at three highest performance levels made increasingly frequent use of more appropriate strategies, including approximate (nondecadal) and occasionally mature (decadal) versions of front-end and rounding strategies. However, even at the highest levels, the strategies were frequently not used in an adult-like way. Most notably, children often seemed unaware of conventions concerning the number of significant figures appropriate to an estimate and often appeared to haphazardly choose a digit to add to the end.

Moreover, when children were presented with addition items *more than one level* above their base correspondence, the use of appropriate strategies, especially by children of the lower performance levels, declined with the level of item difficulty, as did the use of mechanical strategies, with one exception. The only type of mechanical strategy that did not decline with increasing item difficulty was the use of response biases and patterns (i.e., strategies that did not require consideration of the characteristics of the numbers in the problem).

Thus, the results of this study are consistent with those of some studies with adults (Dowker et al., 1996; Levine, 1982) in suggesting a fairly close association between calculation performance and estimation performance. Despite this association, computational estimation by children or adults is not merely one form of mental calculation, and the capacity of at least some forms of estimation is not dependent on a high level of arithmetic sophistication. Although the sophisticated use of computational-estimation strategies may, indeed, not emerge at least until early adolescence, as Case and Sowder (1990) suggest, some estimation capacities emerge very early indeed. By the second (addition-to-10) level, estimates are predominantly reasonable. At first sight, the study might appear to show that estimation ability of any sort is very limited in children of the beginning-arithmetic level because their strategies are often inappropriate and their estimates are more often than not unreasonable. However, such children performed considerably better (though still less well than children of higher levels) if they were presented with items in concrete rather than numerical formats. Thus, it seems quite likely that the poor estimation of the children of the lowest base-performance level in the standard condition reflected a lack of relevant knowledge of formal arithmetic, at least as much as a difficulty with estimation as such.

In sum, the evidence of this study indicates that, although calculation and arithmetic estimation do interact and support one another, they are distinct processes (or, better put, distinct groups of processes). This conclusion is further supported as the results of this experimental study converge with those emerging from neuropsychological studies of patients (Butterworth, 1999; Dehaene & Cohen, 1991; Warrington, 1982) and very recently from functional brain-imaging studies of healthy adults (Dehaene et al., 1999). See Delazer (chap. 14, this volume) for a detailed review and analysis of the neuropsychological evidence.

Implications for the Zone of Partial Knowledge and Understanding. The gradual decline of both the accuracy of estimates (Dowker, 1997) and the appropriateness of strategies as item difficulty increased relative to a child's knowledge supports the existence of a zone of partial knowledge and understanding. Near the beginning of the zone, children have insufficient knowledge to provide exact answers. Even so, this does not mean that they have no understanding of the arithmetic principles relating to the items presented. On the contrary, their knowledge and understanding, though falling short of the degree needed to obtain exact answers, are fairly extensive. Beyond the base correspondence, there is a progressive decline in both accuracy and the use of effective strategies.

Despite the finding of a progressive decline in performance as item difficulty increases, results of the present study indicate that knowledge and understanding do not diminish in a uniform way for all children, or in a monotonic way for any one child. One of the characteristics of this zone is its unevenness, with many oscillations within it. For instance, in spite of the very broadly predictable characteristics of the different groups, the same child commonly used different identifiable strategies for different sums in the same set. Indeed, it was uncommon for any one child, within or outside the base correspondence, to use a single strategy, even for all sums that were amenable to such a strategy. In fact, only 12 children appeared to use any one strategy *consistently* in responding to all sums amenable to such a strategy in a set.

Consider one typical example of inconsistency, Nicola (5-9, beginning-arithmetic level) responded to three Set 1 sums by stating an addend, to three by adding one to an addend, and to three by less identifiable strategies ($4 + 4 = 9; 9 + 1 = 3; 2 + 6 = 4$). Four of her estimates were reasonable. When given Set 2, she responded to three sums by adding one to an addend, to three by subtracting one from an addend, and to three by less identifiable strategies, one of which resulted in her one reasonable estimate to this set ($9 + 6 = 14$). The inconsistency of strategy use could not be attributed simply to a few specific sums eliciting particular strategies. Each of the more common strategies was used at times for each of the relevant sums. For instance, each of the sums in Set 1 and Set 2 sometimes elicited the strategy of stating an addend and the strategy of adding one to an addend.

The results of this study differ somewhat from those of Brown and Burton (1978) and VanLehn (1990), who reported that many (though not all) individual children demonstrated consistent "bugs" or error-producing strategies in written arithmetic calculation. The participants in the present study often dealt with partly or wholly unfamiliar material for which they had not yet been taught any specific strategy. The mostly older children studied by Brown and Burton and by VanLehn were incorrectly reproducing familiar but poorly understood arithmetic procedures that they had been taught. The differences may also reflect the fact that Brown and Burton and Van Lehn were dealing with written arithmetic, rather than mental arithmetic. The level and type of arithmetic experience are likely to be a more crucial factor here than the difference between oral and written calculation, as Hennessy (1992) found considerable use of variable, temporary, and sometimes conflicting strategies by children in the early stages of acquisition of the subtraction algorithm.

There are several possible reasons for the unevenness of the zone of partial knowledge and understanding. One of these must be the componential nature of estimation (and arithmetic) ability. Some components cease to function at a level of difficulty where others are preserved, and there may be individual differences as to which components disappear first. However, this reason, by itself, could not explain the extensive within-individual oscillations. Another reason for unevenness may be the human tendency to use different strategies for similar tasks or even the same task at different times.[1] Sometimes this variation reflects an adaptive response to specific properties of a task, but sometimes it occurs for no apparent reason. Parenthetically, strategy variability is by no means confined to novices or other children whose knowledge and understanding are partial. Additional reasons for the inconsistency of performance within the zone of partial knowledge and understanding may be that such understanding is unstable and fluctuates from time to time or that children's limited metacognitive ability restricts their access to known knowledge.

Extended zones of partial knowledge and understanding appear to occur in several domains. Studies by Siegler and his colleagues of the development of early calculation strategies for addition (Kerkman & Siegler, 1997; Siegler & Jenkins, 1989) and subtraction (Siegler, 1987) also indicate that "in young children's arithmetic, more- and less-advanced strategies co-exist and continue to compete over an extended period of time" (Siegler & Jenkins, 1989, p. 99). Although "the direction of change was always from less- to more-advanced strategies," their data did not support the "view that children progress from using Strategy A to using Strategy B to using Strategy C (or from Stage I to II to III"; pp. 99–100). Cowan and Renton (1989) obtained similar results.

There is evidence that arithmetic is not the only domain of children's development for which there is a zone of partial knowledge and understanding. For example, Kuhn and Phelps (1982) have suggested that the development of children's causal reasoning strategies involves "an extended period of highly variable performance in which valid and invalid strategies (are) used in conjunction with one another" (p. 39). Kuczaj (1977) and Marchman (1988) suggested such a process for children's acquisition of verb past tense verbs, also.

Evidence of zones of partial knowledge and understanding in several domains suggests that any adequate theory of knowledge or understanding must take into account both the extent and the fluctuating nature of intermediate states between complete knowledge of a domain and complete lack of such knowledge. This conclusion is consistent with Piaget's (1955) rejection of the notion of "structural unity" in either children or adults and his suggestion that "there are not general stages that permit fixed and verifiable correspondences in all domains, among all functions" (p. 818).

---

[1] Mathematicians (Dowker, 1992), and, to a somewhat lesser extent, other professional groups show great variability in the use of (mostly appropriate) estimation strategies (Dowker et al., 1996). LeFevre, Sadesky, and Bizanz (1996) even found considerable variability in adults' use of strategies for calculating single-digit addition combinations.

The oscillations and unevenness within this zone also imply that instructional techniques that assume a strict hierarchy of abilities, such that learners must master one skill thoroughly before they can progress to the next skill, maybe not only inefficient but sometimes impossible to implement. Using low-achieving 7-year-olds, Denvir and Brown (1986) investigated interrelations among different arithmetic skills with a view to establishing a hierarchy that might be applied to remedial teaching. They found that, although some skills were easier than others, and some skills seemed to depend on certain other skills, there was not a strict and universal hierarchy of skills that could be applied to all levels.

Newly invented derived-fact strategies may represent an area at the beginning of the zone of partial knowledge and understanding. This area of new knowledge falls between that of well-learned calculational routines and that of estimation-based answers.

Finally, consider estimation in terms of Hatano's (1988) distinction between routine expertise (skill in carrying out well-learned procedures) and adaptive expertise (ability to invent and apply a variety of procedures flexibly and appropriately) and Bryant's (1985) related distinction between "knowing when to do a sum and knowing how to do it." Effective estimation, such as the use of newly invented derived-fact strategies, can be seen as a set of strategies for predicting the results of numerical operations in situations where routine expertise is either unavailable or ignored in favor of more flexible, variable, and conceptually based strategies. Baroody with Coslick (1998) emphasized that "number sense permits flexibly switching among different representations of numbers and flexibly choosing among estimation or mental-computation strategies" (p. 7-4). Under favorable conditions, where the individual is not too far from the beginning of the zone of partial knowledge and understanding, or where he or she is highly adept at strategy selection, the estimation process will be highly successful. This was seen in the arithmetic-estimation strategies of mathematicians and to a somewhat lesser extent, accountants, who were outstanding examples of adaptive rather than routine expertise (Dowker, 1992; Dowker et al., 1996). Among children and other beginners, strategy variability in estimation and other arithmetic activities may be due more to the lack of a few well-learned strategies than to access to a wide variety of well-developed strategies. However, it still plays an extremely important part in exploring and mastering the domain of arithmetic and number.

Acknowledgments

I am very grateful for the help and cooperation of the staff and children of the following Oxford schools: St. Aloysius' First School, St. Barnabas' First School, St. Ebbes' First School, and St. Philip and St. James' First School. I would like to thank Dr. R. W. Hiorns of the Department of Statistics, University of Oxford, for valuable discussions about statistics. I am grateful to the British Academy and the Economic and Social Research Council for financial support.

References

Baroody, A. J. (1989). Kindergartners' mental addition with single-digit combinations. *Journal for Research in Mathematics Education, 20,* 159–172.

Baroody, A. J. (1992). The development of kindergartners' mental addition strategies. *Learning and Individual Differences, 4,* 215–235.

Baroody, A. J., with Coslick, R. T. (1998). *Fostering children's mathematical power: An investigative approach to K–8 mathematics instruction.* Mahwah, NJ: Lawrence Erlbaum Associates.

Baroody, A. J., Ginsburg, H. P., & Waxman, B. (1983). Children's use of mathematical structure. *Journal for Research in Mathematics Education, 14,* 156–168.

Brown, J. S., & Burton, R. R. (1978). Diagnostic models for procedural bugs in basic mathematical skills. *Cognitive Science, 2,* 155–192.

Bryant, P. E. (1985). The distinction between knowing when to do a sum and knowing how to do it. *Educational Psychology, 5,* 207–215.

Butterworth, B. (1999). *The mathematical brain.* London: Macmillan.

Canobi, K. H., Reeve, R. A., & Pattison, P. E. (1998). The role of conceptual understanding in children's addition problem solving. *Developmental Psychology, 34,* 882–891.

Carpenter, T. P. (1980, July). Heuristic strategies used to solve addition and subtraction problems. Paper presented at the 4th annual meeting of the International Group for the Psychology of Mathematics Education, Berkeley, California.

Carraher, T. N., Carraher, D. W., & Schliemann, A. D. (1985). Mathematics in the streets and in the schools. *British Journal of Developmental Psychology, 3,* 21–29.

Case, R., & Sowder, J. T. (1990). The development of computational estimation: A neo-Piagetian analysis. *Cognition and Instruction, 7,* 79–104.

Cockcroft, W. (1982). *Mathematics counts.* London: HMSO.

Cowan, R., & Renton, M. (1989, September). *Primary school children's strategies for addition.* Paper presented at the annual meeting of the British Psychological Society Developmental Psychology Section, University of Surrey.

Dehaene, S., & Cohen, S. (1991). Two mental calculation systems: A case study of severe acalculia with preserved approximation. *Neuropsychologia, 29,* 1045–1074.

Dehaene, S., Spelke, E., Pinel, P., Stanescu, R., & Tsivkin, S. (1999). Sources of mathematical thinking: Behavioural and brain-imaging evidence. *Science, 5416,* 970–974.

Denvir, B., & Brown, M. (1986). Understanding of number concepts in low-attaining 7- to 9-year-olds, Part I: Development of descriptive framework and diagnostic instrument. *Educational Studies in Mathematics, 17,* 15–36.

Department of Education and Science and the Welsh Office (1989). *Mathematics in the national curriculum: Non-statutory guidelines.* London: HMSO.

Dickey, J. W. (1934). The value of estimating answers to arithmetic problems and examples. *Elementary School Journal, 34,* 24–31.

Dowker, A. D. (1989, October). *Computational estimation by young children.* Paper presented at the meeting of the British Society for Research into Learning Mathematics, Brighton.

Dowker, A. D. (1992) Computational estimation strategies of professional mathematicians. *Journal for Research in Mathematics Education, 23,* 45–55.

Dowker, A. (1994, December). *Adults with mild specific calculation difficulties.* Paper presented at the meeting of the British Psychological Society, London.

Dowker, A. D. (1995). Children with specific calculation difficulties. *Links2, 2,* 7–13.

Dowker, A. D. (1997). Young children's addition estimates. *Mathematical Cognition, 3,* 141–154.

Dowker, A. D. (1998). Individual differences in normal arithmetic development. In C. Donlan (Ed.), *The development of mathematical skills* (pp. 275–302). Hove, East Sussex, England: Psychology Press.

Dowker, A. D., Flood, A., Griffiths, H., Harriss, L., & Hook, L. (1996). Estimation strategies of four groups. *Mathematical Cognition, 2,* 113–135.

Dowker, A. D. & Webb, S. (1995, December). *Young children's use of derived fact strategies in addition and subtraction.* Paper presented at the meeting of the British Psychological Society, London.

Edwards, A. (1984). Computational estimation for numeracy. *Educational Studies in Mathematics, 15,* 59–73.

Faulk, C. J. (1962). How well do pupils estimate answers? *Arithmetic Teacher, 9,* 436–440.

Forrester, M. A., Latham, J., & Shire, B. (1990). Exploring estimation in young primary school children. *Educational Psychology, 10,* 283–300

Forrester, M. A., & Pike, C. D. (1998). Learning to estimate in the mathematics classroom: A conversation-analytic approach. *Journal for Research in Mathematics Education, 29,* 334–356.

Ginsburg, H. P. (1977). *Children's arithmetic: The learning process.* New York: Van Nostrand.

Hatano, G. (1988). Social and motivational bases for mathematical understanding. In G. B. Saxe & M. Gearhart (Eds.), *Children's mathematics* (pp. 55–70). San Francisco: Jossey-Bass.

Hennessy, S. (1992). *The stability of children's mathematical behaviour: When is a bug really a bug?* Unpublished manuscript, Open University.

Hook, L. (1992). *Estimation strategies of psychology students.* Unpublished undergraduate research project, University of Oxford.

Hope, J. A., & Sherrill, J. M. (1987). Characteristics of skilled and unskilled mental calculators. *Journal for Research in Mathematics Education, 18,* 98–111.

Hughes, M. (1986). *Children and number.* Oxford: Blackwell.

Kerkman, D. D., & Siegler, R. S. (1997). Measuring individual differences in children's addition strategy choices. *Learning and Individual Differences, 9,* 1–18.

Kuczaj, S. (1977). The acquisition of regular and irregular verb past tense forms. *Journal of Verbal Learning and Verbal Behaviour, 16,* 589–600.

Kuhn, D., & Phelps, E. (1982). The development of problem-solving strategies. In H. Reese & L. Lipsitt (Eds.), *Advances in child development and behaviour, 7,* 2–44.

LeFevre, J. A., Greenham, S. L., & Waheed, N. (1993). The development of procedural and conceptual knowledge in computational estimation. *Cognition and Instruction, 11,* 95–132.

LeFevre, J. A., Sadesky, G. S., & Bisanz, J. (1996). Selection of procedures in mental addition: Assessing the problem-size effect in adults. *Journal of Experimental Psychology: Learning, Memory, and Cognition, 22,* 216–230.

Levine, D. R. (1982). Strategy use and estimation of college students. *Journal for Research in Mathematics Education, 13,* 350–359.

Macaruso, P., & Sokol, S. M. (1998). Cognitive neuropsychology and developmental dyscalculia. In C. Donlan (Ed.), *The development of mathematical skills* (pp. 201–225). Hove, East Sussex, England: Psychology Press.

Marchman, V. (1988). Rules and regularities in the acquisition of the English past tense. *Center for Research in Language Newsletter, 2.*

Paull, D. R. (1972). The ability to estimate in mathematics. (Doctoral dissertation, Columbia University, 1971). *Dissertation Abstracts International, 32,* 3567A.

Piaget, J. (1955). The stages of intellectual development in childhood and adolescence. (Reprinted in *The essential Piaget,* by H. E. Gruber & J. J. Voneche, Eds., 1977, pp. 814–819, London: Routledge and Kegan Paul).

Pike, C. D., & Forrester, M. A. (1998). The influence of number sense on children's ability to estimate measures. *Journal for Research in Mathematics Education, 29,* 334–356.

Reeve, W. D. (Ed.). (1936). *Approximate computation* (Twelfth yearbook of the National Council of Teachers of Mathematics). New York: Teachers' College Press.

Renton, M. (1992). *Primary school children's strategies for addition.* Unpublished doctoral dissertation, University of London Institute of Education.

Reys, R. E. (1984). Mental computation and estimation: Past, present and future. *Elementary School Journal, 84,* 547–557.

Reys, R. E., Reys, B. J., Nohda, N., Ishida, J., Yoshikawa, S., & Shimizu, K. (1991). Computational estimation performance and strategies used by fifth- and eighth-grade Japanese students. *Journal for Research in Mathematics Education, 22,* 39–58.

Reys, R. E., Rybolt, J. F., Bestgen, B. J., & Wyatt, J. W. (1982). Processes used by good computational estimators. *Journal for Research in Mathematics Education, 13,* 183–201.

Rubenstein, R. N. (1985). Computational estimation and related mathematical skills. *Journal for Research in Mathematics Education, 16*, 106–119.

Russell, R., & Ginsburg, H. P. (1984). Cognitive analysis of children's mathematical difficulties. *Cognition and Instruction, 1*, 217–244.

Sauble, I. (1955). Development of ability to estimate and to compute mentally. *Arithmetic Teacher, 2*(2), 33–39.

Siegler, R. S. (1987). Strategy choices in subtraction. In J. Sloboda & D. Rogers (Eds.), *Cognitive processes in mathematics* (pp. 81–106). Oxford: Oxford University Press.

Siegler, R. S., & Jenkins, E. (1989). *How children discover new strategies.* Hillsdale, NJ: Lawrence Erlbaum Associates.

Slater, I. (1990). *Children's estimating skills.* Unpublished dissertation, Wolverhampton Polytechnic.

Sowder, J. T. (1987). A report on the NCTM research agenda project. *Journal for Research in Mathematics Education, 18*, 325–329.

Sowder, J. T. (1992). Estimation and related topics. In D. A. Grouws (Ed.), *Handbook of research on teaching and learning* (pp. 371–389). New York: Macmillan.

Sowder, J. T., & Wheeler, M. M. (1989). The development of concepts and strategies use in computational estimation. *Journal for Research in Mathematics Education, 20*, 130–146.

Steinberg, R. (1985). Instruction in derived fact strategies in addition and subtraction. *Journal for Research in Mathematics Education, 16*, 337–255.

Trafton, P. R. (1978) Estimation and mental arithmetic: Important components of computation. In M. N. Suydam & R. E. Reys (Eds.), *Developing computational skills* (1978 yearbook, pp. 196–213). Reston, VA: National Council of Teachers of Mathematics.

VanLehn, K. (1990). *Mind bugs: The origin of procedural misconceptions.* Cambridge, MA: MIT Press.

Vygotsky, L. S. (1987). *The collected works of L. S. Vygotsky.* New York: Plenum.

Warrington, E. K. (1982). The fractionation of arithmetic skills: A single case study. *Quarterly Journal of Experimental Psychology, 34A*, 31–51.

CHAPTER 10

MULTIDIGIT ADDITION AND SUBTRACTION METHODS INVENTED IN SMALL GROUPS AND TEACHER SUPPORT OF PROBLEM SOLVING AND REFLECTION

Karen C. Fuson
Northwestern University

Birch H. Burghardt
Greenwood Education Consultants

A strong national effort is currently under way in the United States to reform school mathematics instruction, so that children become autonomous problem solvers (National Council of Teachers of Mathematics [NCTM], 1989, 1991, 2000). One recommended change is encouraging students to invent their own solution procedures for problems or calculation tasks. This is important for fostering their mathematical power or proficiency, which involves an understanding of mathematics, the thoughtful and fluent use of procedures, the capacity to engage in mathematical inquiry, and a positive disposition toward learning and applying mathematics. (For discussion of how, see Ambrose, Baek, & Carpenter, chap. 11, this volume; Baroody, chap. 1, this volume; Baroody, with Coslick, 1998.)

There is presently, however, an insufficient research base for understanding the range of solution procedures children can invent in a socially and cognitively supportive environment or of what supporting roles teachers should play in promoting such inventions. Most previous work on children's invented multidigit addition and subtraction procedures was limited to two-digit numbers (for reviews, see Beishuizen, Gravemeijer, & van Lieshout, 1997; Fuson, 1990; Fuson & Smith, 1997; Fuson, Wearne, et al., 1997; Labinowicz, 1985). Unfortunately, many of these procedures do not generalize well to larger numbers or depend on special solutions for the decades.

In this chapter, we report on an investigation into the mathematical thinking of high-achieving second graders as they worked in groups, learning to add and subtract horizontal four-digit symbolic expressions using base-ten blocks and written marks. Our focus is on conceptual learning of multidigit concepts and methods and on how to support it. We begin the chapter by describing the study. Next, we discuss the educational implications of its results. The most important is that children can invent efficient written procedures, some of which are conceptually or procedurally superior to the standard school-taught algorithms. We end the chapter with some general conclusions about the teaching and learning of multidigit addition and subtraction. Our key conclusions are: (a) Teaching tools such as using cooperative learning groups and manipulatives (e.g., base-ten blocks) must be used carefully and thoughtfully to promote conceptual learning. In regard to the former, teachers must actively help children learn how to use small-group discussions as a problem-solving resource. In regard to using manipulatives, it is particularly important that children be encouraged to consider each step in their concrete block procedure when inventing (or attempting to understand a written procedure) and connect each concrete step with the corresponding step in the written procedure. (b) In contrast to the rigid use of algorithms learned by rote, conceptual learning promotes adaptive expertise and flexibility.

The Study

In this section, we discuss, in turn, the theoretical perspective, methods, and results of the study.

THEORETICAL PERSPECTIVE

The theoretical perspective for this chapter is the analysis of children's conceptual structures for understanding English number words, multidigit written marks, and multidigit addition and subtraction described in Fuson (1990), extended in Fuson, Wearne, et al. (1997) and in Fuson, Smith, and Lo Cicero (1997), and summarized in Fig. 10.1. Children's construction of the connected network of conceptual structures identified in those studies was supported in the present study by the use of base-ten blocks, which can represent units of one, ten, hundred, and thousand that can be added, subtracted, and traded (units are represented by a "cube" 1 cm x 1 cm x 1 cm; tens, by a "long" 10 cm x 1 cm x 1 cm; hundreds, by a "flat" 10 cm x 10 cm x 1 cm; and thousands, by a "large cube" 10 cm x 10 cm x 10 cm).[1] These units can be described in block words and English number words and can be recorded as multidigit written marks. The term "written marks" is used to remind the reader that the meaning of multidigit numerals at any moment for any viewer of those numerals may differ from the meanings for those numerals used by the expert readers of this article.

Fuson (1990) identified two different unitary conceptions commonly used by children in the United States. One is a total unitary conception (e.g., viewing the numeral 26 as a pile of "twenty-six" units); the other, a concatenated single-digit conception (e.g., viewing 26 as a unitary 2 next to a unitary 6). A third common conception is a sequence-tens conception (e.g., viewing 26 as "ten, twenty, twenty-one, . . . twenty-six"). A productive meaning of multidigit numerals that is used less often by U.S. children is a multiunit conception in which each digit represents the number of ones, tens, hundreds, thousands, and so forth. Although many children can name these digit positions, only some use these quantities in their conceptions of multidigit numbers, and fewer yet apply them to their addition and subtraction methods. Base-ten blocks were found to be helpful in facilitating children's constructions of multiunit conceptions used in understanding traditional algorithms (Fuson, 1986a; Fuson & Briars, 1990). This study extended the use of base-ten blocks to supporting children's invention of multidigit addition and subtraction methods.

---

[1] Base-ten blocks are one useful manipulative for fostering grouping and place-value concepts and skills. A model that requires children to create (compose) their own group of ten from units or decompose a group of ten into units is somewhat more concrete than that with base-ten blocks, in which the units of the ten are already "glued" together. For a more complete discussion of grouping and place-value models, see Baroody (1990) or Baroody, with Coslick (1998).

Figure 10.1: Children's Conceptual Structures for Understanding English Number Words (Fuson, Smith, & Lo Cicero, 1997)

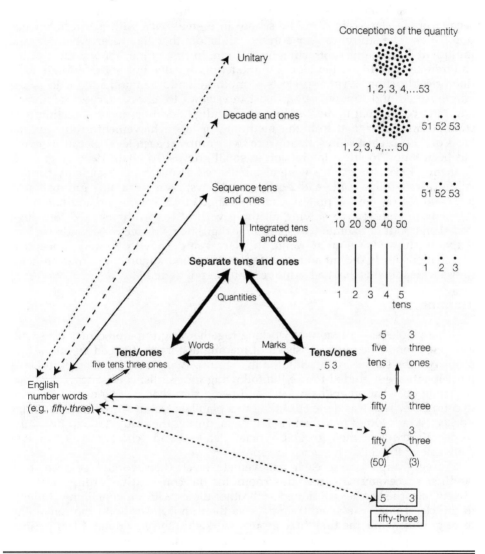

METHOD

Participants

The participants were the 26 students in the highest achieving class of three second-grade classes in a public school in a small city with a heterogeneous population. The study was done in the fall before they had received any formal multidigit addition or subtraction instruction. In first grade, about a third of the children had used base-ten blocks to model place value but not multidigit addition or subtraction. Written pretests of multidigit addition and subtraction were administered and followed by pretest interviews to assess place-value knowledge and conceptual understanding of multidigit addition and subtraction. The students were assigned to high-, medium-, or low-achievement groups on the basis of their pretest scores; there were two groups at each level. Because gender has been found to affect interaction in small groups (Kimball, 1989; Peterson & Fennema, 1985), the groups were also balanced as much as possible by gender. All but two groups contained 2 girls and 2 boys; both remaining groups had 2 boys and 3 girls. On the pretest, children ranged from solving no addition items correctly (6 children) to solving all three vertical (two-, three-, and four-digit items) and both horizontal (two- and four-digit) items correctly (4 children). Participants showed a similar range in place-value knowledge and conceptual explanations for two-digit and four-digit trading and alignment of uneven items (those with addends that had a different number of digits).

Training

One whole-class session on working together in groups preceded the small-group sessions. The latter consisted of reading a story that posed an interesting problem to be solved by the children in a group. While working on the problem, participants were guided to use the following four skills: conciseness, listening, reflecting on what others have said, and being sure that everyone gets a chance to contribute. This was done according to a plan laid out in "Epstein's Four Stage Rocket," a task found in Cohen (1984). Then, during the study, to help distribute students' power in their groups, official "leader" and "checker" roles rotated daily among the children in each group.

Three groups (one at each achievement level) then worked in large stair-landing spaces outside the classroom for 14 consecutive group sessions. Meanwhile, the teacher continued with other topics with the remaining students in the classroom. The same training was then undertaken with the remaining three groups, while the first three groups worked in the classroom. Class periods were 40 min in length, but effective learning time was only about 30 min because of set-up and clean-up time.

For each group, a supervising adult guided the initial 2- to 3-day experience with the base-ten blocks. This ensured the children chose names for each kind of block, knew the English names for the blocks, understood the relations between block arrays and the usual four-digit marks, and understood the ten-for-one trades for next larger blocks. Versions of the English words that regularized the words for the tens place (e.g., "four thousand five hundred *six ten* seven") were also used and practiced during this time. These words are modeled after the regular number words used in China, Japan, Korea, and Taiwan (e.g., Fuson & Kwon, 1992; Menninger, 1958/1969). These words potentially support children's construction of, and easy reference to, multiunit conceptual structures. The first three groups used digit cards to show their marks values for blocks and for addition and subtraction. These digit cards were index cards with a numeral written on each one; they were stored in a small box by numeral value. Because these were very time consuming to find and arrange (and because children often did not link blocks and digit cards), the second three groups wrote their block values and their addition and subtraction problems on a "magic pad." This was a large pad on which actions with the blocks had to be recorded as soon as the actions were done (children were to "beep" if such recordings were not done). Recording was done with a marker so that a permanent record could be obtained and analyzed. In both sessions, children also wrote on individual papers after the first several days of addition or subtraction.

In the addition phase, children were given horizontally written four-digit (and sometimes a three-digit plus four-digit) addition expressions to solve with the blocks and written multidigit marks. They were asked to link their block and mark solutions by recording everything they did with the blocks with the digit cards (first three groups) or the magic pad (second three groups). After a group had devised at least one correct addition method with the blocks and the marks, and most group members could carry out this method, that group moved on to subtraction. Subtraction was also presented as horizontally written four-digit (or three- and four-digit) numerical subtractions. The first additions required a trade from the thousands to the hundreds and a trade from the tens to the ones but not a trade from hundreds to tens. Later problems involved all three trades and various combinations of just two trades. The two high-achieving groups reached the last and most difficult task, subtractions with zeros in the top number. Groups spent from 5 to 8 days on addition and from 3 to 8 days on subtraction. The school allowed us only 14 sessions with each group. Therefore, the middle and low groups left addition before their lowest members fully understood it, and no group had sufficient time for every member to understand and be able to explain subtraction thoroughly, as judged by behavior in the group sessions.

An adult oversaw the videotaping of each group, took notes, and intervened when children's behavior became too rowdy or when the group became stuck on a mistaken procedure for a long time. (The criterion for a long time for the second three groups was one whole period; this time was sometimes longer for the first three groups.) Adults intervened minimally to provide children the opportunity to resolve conflicts and solve problems creatively and to approximate the environment of a real classroom in which a teacher would be able to observe and help any one group only a fraction of a period.

Data Collection

The videotapes of the group sessions were transcribed to provide verbatim records of mathematical statements made by children or adults, summaries of off-task discussions, descriptions of actions by the children, and descriptions of emotional states and interactions. Another transcriber checked each transcript.

Separate drawings keyed to the transcripts were made of all movement of blocks and writing of multidigit marks with digit cards, on magic pads, and on individual student papers (originals of the latter two were used for this summary).

RESULTS

In this section, the results regarding children's construction during the preaddition phase of relations among English number words, base-ten blocks, and written multidigit addition are briefly summarized to provide a context for the addition and subtraction results given next (for a full report, see Fuson, Fraivillig, & Burghardt, 1992). Next, the invention of multidigit addition with blocks and marks is briefly summarized across groups (for a fuller report of group interactions, see Burghardt, 1992, and Fuson & Burghardt, 1993). Incorrect addition methods and then correct ones are described and discussed. Subtraction is treated similarly (for a fuller report of subtraction group interactions, see Fuson & Burghardt, 1997). The supporting roles teachers played are mentioned where relevant throughout this section (and summarized in the next section on educational implications).

Summary of the Preaddition Phase

The names of the blocks chosen by each group related to perceptual features (mostly shape and size); food names were common. Children easily found the ten-for-one equivalencies between the little cubes and the longs, the longs and the flats, and the flats and the big cubes. They made few errors with respect to these equivalencies throughout the preaddition phase. Many verbal statements of the children about equivalencies were quite abbreviated and not very helpful to other group members ("ten of those"). Children were accurate in using English words and block words. They learned the regularized (East Asian based) tens words readily, though individuals varied in the extent to which they spontaneously used them in subsequent discussions. Adults did not support the use of these regularized tens words, because they were trying to intervene as little as possible. Children easily established relations among blocks, English words, and written marks. The need for zero arose in all groups and was successfully resolved. Some groups grappled with the issue of how to write block arrays that had more than 10 of one kind of block; the adult leader of other groups suggested that children only make block arrays with less than 10 of each kind of block. Some children regularized the English words even beyond the regular tens forms. They added the unit word *ones* so that every unit would be named. Such children also used zero with a multiunit or unit name, rather than omit that multiunit as English does (e.g., "three hundred zero tens four ones" instead of "three hundred four"). The rapidity of learning and low level of errors in this phase were partly due to the presence in most groups of a child who had used the blocks in first grade.

Addition

Overview of Block and Mark Multidigit Addition. In spite of the adults' initial instructions to link the blocks with written marks during addition, children in five of the six groups often functioned in two separate worlds—the blocks world and the written-marks world (see Thompson, 1992, for a similar result). Children quickly devised correct addition methods with the blocks (see Fuson et al., 1992, for more details). The collectible multiunits in the blocks were sufficient in most cases to direct correct block methods and constrain incorrect methods. These visually salient multiunits suggested solutions to the following two major components of multidigit addition: (a) what to add to what (the items were written horizontally and so did not cue adding like places) and (b) what to do when you have more than nine of a given unit. Every group immediately added like blocks to each other. They all eventually arranged the blocks for the second addend so that like blocks were below each other. Some groups pushed together blocks to make the answer, whereas other groups used extra blocks to make the answer in a third row below the two addends (simulating a procedure with written numbers). All groups added the blocks from left to right. Groups solved the second component (having more than nine of a given multiunit) in various ways. All, though, traded 10 of one kind of block for 1 of the next larger unit or put the 10 blocks in the next column to the left (often arranged spatially so that these blocks looked like one of the next larger block). Where and when they traded or put blocks varied, and the variations led to different written marks methods (described later). Children also often solved the single-digit addition of a unit mentally or with fingers rather than counting the blocks.

Necessary preaddition skills (counting blocks, copying the expression, writing digits) rarely caused difficulty, except that some magic-pad records were quite messy and difficult to read. However, children sometimes played with blocks from a model, thus changing the quantities added. Also, blocks used to represent addends occasionally merged with the bank of currently unused blocks. Such unintended block changes sometimes were responsible for long, unproductive digressions.

In the independent-marks world (marks methods not connected to blocks methods), different incorrect methods were used, some for several days. (Examples will be described next with the incorrect addition methods.) All but one of these methods involved a conception of written marks as concatenated single digits. In this conception, no multiunit values (e.g., tens, hundreds) were attached to the different marks' positions, so no information (other than, for some children, partial memory of two-digit addition instruction) was available to direct or constrain the placement of marks.

All of these incorrect block and mark methods were corrected by the groups when the adults insisted that the participants link the blocks and written marks. This linking enabled children to use the multiunit value of the blocks to identify erroneous methods and direct a correct trade.

Children's descriptions or explanations that used block words or multiunit names often facilitated correcting erroneous methods. Initially, though, participants ordinarily carried out addition with blocks or marks with little or no discussion or explanation. Consequently, it is likely that the different group members were not always aware of all of the important aspects of each other's activities. Furthermore, spontaneous descriptions or explanations often omitted block names or multiunit names. This frequently led to confused discourse (e.g., "ten," if said alone, could refer to one ten, ten ones, or ten of another multiunit) and to the arousal of concatenated single-digit conceptions in the listener. Imprecise language used to describe block actions also sometimes suggested wrong marks methods. Therefore, the adult leaders asked children to explain methods using block or multiunit names. This resulted in a more complete and accurate explanations by children and seemed to help the other members of a group.

Children rarely discussed issues of mathematical importance, even though they arose at least implicitly. For example, having more than nine of a given multiunit is only a problem when writing the answer in written marks. Specifically, if more than nine is written in a given column, this will make the whole multidigit number one digit too large. In contrast, noncanonical (more than nine of a given multiunit) block arrays or English number word forms are not ambiguous (we even say *fifteen hundred* as an acceptable alternative for *one thousand five hundred*). Only one group, however, said clearly why writing two digits in a given column is problematic. This group had wrestled with this issue in the preaddition phase when writing noncanonical block arrays. For example, when recording three flats, four longs, and 29 units as 3429, they said, "How come when Dh writes it on the magic pad it looks like *three thousand*?" (instead of three hundred . . .).

Consider a second example of the common failure to discuss mathematical issues. Several groups had controversies (some extended over days) about whether to add from the left or from the right. Without adult support, no group decided to compare these methods. Instead, the majority or a dominant member made an arbitrary decision. When the adult in one group suggested comparing the two methods and discussing them, the children did carry out both methods and engage in a good discussion. They decided that it was better to add from the right "because it was faster." (In that direction, they did not have to cross out their answers so often to increase them by the new traded multiunit.) Teacher support to identify and discuss such issues of mathematical importance seems to be necessary, at least until children are experienced in doing so.

The path of an individual group through multidigit addition was influenced by the extent to which the dominant and more socially skilled individuals in the group possessed and used conceptual multiunit knowledge they had learned before the study (see Fuson & Burghardt, 1993, and Fuson et al., 1992, for group-case studies of multidigit addition). Although the leader role was effective in that every child in the leader role talked more when being the leader than on preceding days, natural leaders, or at least dominant group members, also emerged for most groups. In some groups, a dominant group member imposed an incorrect method. In such cases, it was necessary for the adult to support less dominant group members by asking them to explain their view about these incorrect methods or about alternatives they were trying to propose. These children were unable or unwilling to confront the dominant member without such adult support.

Incorrect Addition Methods. Seven incorrect addition methods used with written marks are shown in Fig. 10.2. All of the methods are variations of the standard addition algorithm in the United States. In the standard U.S. method, one begins adding from the right, and any two-digit sum results in a small 1 being written above the next column to the left. Many students had been shown this multidigit addition procedure in first grade or by parents or siblings (facts

Figure 10.2: Incorrect Invented Multidigit Addition Methods

*A) When adding left to right, write 1 above next column to the right

```
  1  1
  2 8 3 4
+ 1 9 6 3
  3 7 0 8
```

B) Write all 1s above the far-left column

```
  1
  1
  1
  1 8 3 6
+ 3 5 9 7
  6 3 2 3
```

C) Write one 1 above far-left column; can't have more than one 1, so only write one 1

```
  1
  1 8 3 6
+ 3 5 9 7
  4 3 2 3
```

D) Write the 1 in the column that was added

```
  1 1 1
  1 8 3 6
+ 3 5 9 7
  3 3 2 3
```

E) Write 1 below the column, write right digit of the teen sum above the next column

```
  4   3
  1 5 2 7
+ 1 9 4 6
  6 1 9 1
```

F) Keep 9 (because "you can't have ten in a column"); write the rest above the next column to the left

```
              1
              1
              1
  4 6 4       1
  1 2 4 8     1 2 4 8
+ 2 5 7 5   + 2 5 7 5
  7 9 9 9           9
```

G) Each two-digit sum has tens and ones. Put the ten in the tens column and the ones in the ones column [or in its own column for hundreds]

```
    1                1 5              1
  3 9 6 7          3 9 6 7          1 5
+ 1 5 8 5   →    + 1 5 8 5   →    3 9 6 7
      2              1 2         + 1 5 8 5
                                  4 4 1 2
```

Note. All methods except those with an asterisk were done from right to left.

that emerged during the study). However, errors arose because they did not understand the standard algorithm and either misremembered this procedure (remembered it incompletely or inaccurately) or misgeneralized it. Sometimes versions of "teacher (or sister) rules" were used to justify a method.

The first five incorrect methods (Methods A to E in Fig. 10.2) involved writing the 1 somewhere other than above the next column to the left. Children's discourse about these methods involved concatenated single-digit language; they spoke about writing 1s someplace, not about adding multiunit quantities. The last two incorrect methods (Methods F and G) involved other types of invented procedures.

• *Method A.* This method involved adding left to right and writing 1 above the next column to the right. Method A arose in several groups because it modeled their left-to-right addition with blocks (which all groups did). However, because the addition with marks tended to be carried out independently from the addition with blocks, children did not use the block multiunit values to direct their mark trading. When adding 8 flats and 9 flats, for example, children always put 10 of the flats with the big cubes or traded them for a big cube, which was put with the existing big cubes. In both cases, they put the newly formed "group of a thousand" to the left of extant thousand blocks. In contrast, with no perceptual multiunits to direct the marks procedure, some children interpreted the standard procedure as "write the little one in the column *you are going to add next*" (the next column to the right), rather than as the column to the left (the column 10 times larger).

• *Methods B and C.* Both of these methods involved interpreting the standard two-digit algorithm as "write the 1 above the *far-left* column," rather than as "write the 1 above the *next* column to the left." Whereas Method B involved writing multiple 1s above the far-left column, Method C involved writing a single 1. Note that the latter also involved a second rule about adding ("You can't have more than one 1 in a column."). VanLehn (1986) considered a related subtraction error (always borrow left). As VanLehn discussed for the subtraction version of this error, when learned without multiunit quantity meanings, there is nothing about the standard two-digit addition algorithm that permits a child to distinguish these alternatives. From two-digit problems one cannot tell whether one puts the 1 above the next-left or far-left column. Similarly, with respect to Method A, one cannot tell from watching the standard algorithm being carried out whether the 1 is written above the next column you are adding or the column to the left. Methods B and C were used by several students until they were requested by the adult to link block and written mark methods. These incorrect procedures then immediately disappeared.

• *Method D.* This method involved writing the 1 above the column that was added. Unlike the common early multidigit error "vanishing the one" (Fuson & Briars, 1990), in which children do not know what to do with the 1 and so ignore it altogether (vanish it), Method D reflects some knowledge of the standard algorithm. Unfortunately, Method D results in the same answer as "vanishing the one" because the 1 is written above a column that has already been totaled and is, thus, never included in the sum.

• *Method E.* In this method, the places of writing the numbers in a two-digit partial sum are reversed. That is, the 1 in a partial sum such as 13 is written below the column, and the ones digit (the 3) is written above the next column to the left. This reversal error might occur more often if it were not for the fact that the addition of two numbers always results in a tens digit of 1. The pattern of seeing only 1s above a column is highly salient, and so many children may adopt this procedure even though they do not understand it. Methods D and E were infrequent.

• *Method F.* Imposed by a dominant girl, this method persisted for several days in one of the two groups in which it arose. The dominating girl quashed the frequent questions raised by all group members (including herself) by restating the following partially remembered teacher rules: "You can't have ten in a column" and "You can't have more than nine in a column." In one group, this rule came from an older sibling, as well as from a teacher. The restatements in both groups transformed this rule into "*you must have 9 (keep the 9)*" and then the rest were put above the next column to the left, an imitation of the standard algorithm. The amount over nine was written with a stack of 1s in one group to conform to the standard algorithm's writing of 1s. In one group the amount written or put above the next column to the left was sometimes the amount above 10, but 9 was still written below the column "because you can't write 10 there." In the group that most persistently used it, application of the method seemed to be facilitated or prompted, by the block-trading method and the language the girls in the group used to describe it. Everyone in this group almost always used concatenated single-digit language (no block or multiunit words). The girls, who were the leaders in this group, would find the sum of a given multiunit mentally or with fingers. For example, when adding pancakes/hundreds, they would say, "six plus seven is thirteen." They then counted 3 of these 13 pancakes to indicate the number of hundreds and, without comment, simply replaced the other 10 pancakes with a big cube. The girls not only failed to connect discarding 10 units (here, 10 pancakes) to adding a one new multiunit (here, a big cube), they described the carrying process as "take away" (e.g., taking three from the total 13 pancakes). As a result, for a long time, the boys did not realize 10 blocks were traded for a larger block. Indeed, the whole group continued to describe this trading as "take away x" (the number of ones in the teen sum).

• *Method G.* This method was invented and pushed by a dominant child who had strong understanding of two-digit numbers as tens and ones. However, for two-digit totals of tens and hundreds, he did not simultaneously consider the multiunit values (e.g., the sum of 1 plus 6 + 8 in the tens place was interpreted as 15, not 15 tens). His two-digit tens-and-ones conception of the written marks directed a modification of the standard algorithm in which the tens in any column sum were to be put with the tens, and the ones were to be put with the ones. Most of the children in the group found his basic argument to be sensible (put the tens with the tens and the ones with the ones), and their conceptions of two-digit numbers as tens and ones were strong enough to support this method. Other children in the group offered somewhat different variations of this procedure, and although the group spent several days using Method G or a similar method, the children seemed uncomfortable with these methods. In particular, when the sums of the hundreds or thousands columns were greater than 9, the ones digits for these columns were sometimes written in these columns to provide answers there, rather than in the ones place as their procedure demanded. The adult finally asked the group to link block and digit-card solutions and describe their methods in block words. The children immediately saw why their method did not work: "You have fifteen *long legs* or fifteen tens, not just fifteen, so it is one iceberg and five long legs [one hundred and five tens], not one long leg and five little guys [one ten and five ones]." Method G arose again, however, on the following day when they were using English words and not block words. The adult supported a child who objected to the group's return to this method but whose arguments were neither being accepted by the dominant member nor listened to by others. Once her arguments were heard, everyone, including its inventor, rejected Method G.

Correct Invented Addition Methods. The standard U.S. algorithm and the six correct methods invented by the groups are shown in Fig. 10.3. Because every group contained at least one member who knew the standard U.S. algorithm for two-digit numbers, this method strongly influenced the other correct methods used by the groups. The groups linked all of these correct methods to a parallel block solution. In each case, the written form captured what was done with the blocks. Methods I through N were each done by one to three groups.

Figure 10.3: Correct Invented Multidigit Addition Methods

H) Standard U.S. algorithm; add right to left; put the 1 above;

```
  1 1 1
  2 6 8 5
+ 1 9 6 7
---------
  4 6 5 2
```

I) Write 1 within total location

```
  2 6 8 5
+ 1 9 6 7
---------
  1 1 1
  4 6 5 2
```

J) Add 1 into top addend

```
  3 7 9
  2̶ 6̶ 8̶ 5
+ 1 9 6 7
---------
  4 6 5 2
```

*K) Mentally add in 1

```
  2 6 8 5
+ 1 9 6 7
---------
  4 6 5 2
```

*L) Add left to right; write 1 above and fix answers as go

```
  1 1 1
  2 6 8 5
+ 1 9 6 7
---------
  3̶ 3̶ 4̶ 2
  4 6 5
```

M) Add all multiunits first; fix total to standard numbers

```
  1 1 1
  2 6 8 5
+ 1 9 6 7
---------
  3 15 14 12
  4 5
  4 6 4
  4 6 5 2
```

or

```
  1 1 1
  3 15 14 12
  x  x  x
  4 6 5 2
```

N) Write problem in multiunit values

```
    1       1       1
   2000600805
+ 1000900607
-------------
   4000600502
```

Note. All methods except those with an asterisk were done from right to left. Method K was done in both direction.

• *Method H.* In the blocks version of the standard U.S. algorithm (Method H), whenever the total of a given kind of blocks was 10 or more, 10 of the blocks were traded for one of the next larger multiunit. This new block was then put above the blocks of that multiunit for the first addend, or 10 of the blocks were put there, often laid in the form of one of the new multiunit blocks. Thus, the blocks showed the meaning of the carried 1 in the standard algorithm as one of the next multiunit, which was made from 10 of the multiunit to the right. Children in all groups eventually described these block trades or block puts using block or multiunit names so that the trading involved was clear, though several groups did not do so spontaneously and needed the suggestion of the adult that they do so. In the traditional method, that 1 is mentally added to the top number, and then that number is added to the given second addend. One could, however, add the two given numbers in any order (e.g., add smaller to larger) and then add the 1 to that number. However, in several informal surveys (by the first author) of university students from all parts of the United States, almost all of them added in the right-to-left order as they were taught to do. Those who added in a different order said that they had invented their procedure. Such adding is quite difficult because you have to keep a new number in mind and add it even though it is not written there.

• *Methods I through N.* All of the invented methods (Methods I through N) are superior in some way to the standard algorithm, though some also have limitations that the standard method does not have. They all stemmed in some way from doing multidigit addition with the blocks. Some methods solved difficulties some children had with the standard algorithm, though none of them were direct responses to such difficulties.

Method I is superior to the standard U.S. algorithm conceptually and procedurally. In the standard algorithm, one adds part of the sum into the top addend (i.e., adds part of the answer back into the "problem"). By doing this, one continually changes the problem as one solves it. Some of the children in our study were confused when other children did this standard U.S. method with blocks (traded or put a block into a top addend pile of blocks), saying that people were changing the original problem. A couple of children also objected to this aspect of the standard written algorithm for the same reason. In Method I, each addend and the total have their own horizontal space; the total is always below the line. Thus, one is truly *regrouping the total* (moving part of it over to await adding it with that multiunit's total).

Method I is also procedurally easier than the standard U.S. method because it puts fewer demands on working memory, particularly for children who must compute single-digit sums. In adding the tens digits of 2,685 + 1,967, for instance, Method I involves adding 8 and 6 and then the resulting partial sum 14 and 1, whereas the standard algorithm involves adding 1 and 8 and then the partial sum 9 and 6. Note that, with the former, the addends of the more difficult computation (8 + 6) are visually present, whereas with the latter one addend (9) is not. Furthermore, if the more difficult computation must be redone (e.g., because of a perceived error) or is delayed (e.g., by a difficulty with the computational process or a distraction), children using Method I have a readily available record of the original item, whereas those who use the standard procedure must either compute 1 + 8 = 9 again or try to remember this partial sum. Note also that the more difficult computation in the case of the former (8 + 6) is slightly less difficult than that of the former (9 + 6). Perhaps more critically is when the more difficult computation in each case is done. For Method I, a child must store the partial sum for 8 + 6 (14) in working memory only briefly, because the next step is simply incrementing it by one, a relatively automatic process (Baroody, 1987). With the standard algorithm, a child must store the partial sum of 1 + 8 (9) in working memory and then tackle the more difficult computation of 9 + 6. Method I also makes it easier, particularly for developmentally less advanced children, to add two digits in any order (i.e., count- or add-on from larger) with less risk of forgetting to add the 1.

Method J is similar conceptually to the standard U.S. algorithm, but it makes the addition within a column easier. As with a blocks model, when the newly traded block is actually added into the pile, the traded 1 is added into the top digit, and this total is written above the original top digit. With Method J, children do not have to remember partial sums but simply add the two numbers they see. This method was taught to children in the Fuson (1986a) study to simplify the single-digit additions with base-ten blocks.

Children in two groups also added with blocks in a method related to Methods I and J. This method was never recorded in marks, so it is not listed in Fig. 10.3. In this method the traded block was put with the second addend blocks. This could be recorded by increasing the bottom number by one. This recording is as easy to add as is Method J. It might, however, be messier because there is not much room to write the increased number. Alternatively, the traded block could be written as a 1 below the second addend. Then, it would be close procedurally to the simple Method I (the two visible numbers would be added and the total increased by one), but not as robust conceptually because the trade is still being put into one of the addends.

Method K was used in two types of situations. In one group, it was a version of the standard U.S. algorithm in which the trades were not recorded. This method may have evolved in this group partly because the children would take away the blocks and the digit cards representing the addends and replace them with blocks and digit cards showing the answer. Although they did trades with blocks, they immediately took away the digit cards for that column and put in the answer card and never developed a method for recording their block trades with the digit cards. On individual papers, three of the four children did method K, adding right to left as in the standard algorithm and adding in the trade mentally. The fourth child used the standard algorithm, though he had not done so in the pretest.

Method K done with erasures also is a written version of the left-to-right blocks methods used in most groups. When a column addition required a "carry" to the previously computed column to the left, children erased the latter's original column total and then wrote the new total. Repeated use of this method might lead children to anticipate trades and record only the final sum for each column. This latter procedure is identical to the common European left-to-right look-ahead method: Add a column and then look ahead at the next-right column to decide if its sum is 10 or more; if so, the total of the first column is increased by 1 and recorded.

Method L was the other way in which children represented their left-to-right block method with marks. This method was similar to Method K, but using cross-outs instead of erasures and with the carried (traded or "put") 1 written above the appropriate column. Occasionally, children also wrote hybrids of these two methods, like Method K but using cross-outs instead of erasures or, like Method L, using erasures instead of cross-outs. When adding left to right, writing the small 1s above each column to show the traded or put block probably arose from children's exposure to the standard U.S. algorithm. Because the column was already totaled, increasing the total by one was simple, so there was really little need to record the 1 anywhere. In the standard algorithm, it is more important to record the 1 lest one forget while adding that column that a 1 had been traded or put from the previous column's sum. In Method L, it also would make more sense to record the block-trade or -put total (below the line) because the addends for a given column have already been used. As with Method I, this method is simpler than the standard U.S. method, because the 1 is added at the end (the column has been totaled and the ones digit in the total is written by the time you find out from the next-right column that a 1 is added). If the 1 were written with the total, Method L would be conceptually superior to the standard algorithm in the same way as Method I is. More important, both Methods K and L capture the strong tendency of children to move from left to right in adding the blocks and in other methods invented for two-digit addition (e.g., Kamii, 1985, 1989). Adding from the left is also beneficial because it supports children's competence with estimation by encouraging them to think about the largest digits first.

Method M was the result of an extended collaborative group effort in which a marks method arose from addition with the blocks without interference from the standard algorithm. This group worked well together, and they formed and used the social norms of including and explaining to all group members. They were the only group that continually linked block and marks methods. Their method separates multidigit addition into its two component processes. First, one adds like multiunits. The group did so by pushing the blocks of a particular size together and then recording them. Adding like multiunits can be done in any order, and these children did add and record the blocks addition in any order. The second component was to fix the answer into its standard written form. This was done by trading 10 of any block for one of the next-larger blocks and recording this trade. This also can be done in any order, and children did trade and fix in various orders. This method is conceptually robust, because it clearly shows the components of multidigit addition. It is also procedurally simple; one does only one kind of simple step (adding or trading/fixing) at a time and does not alternate between two kinds of steps. Writing unfixed answers and not fixing them is a common early error of children doing multidigit addition (e.g., Fuson & Briars, 1990). However, these children understood that writing two-digit sums was only the first step in their adding method and that they had to change the sum into a standard written form so that others could understand it. This group had had an extended discussion in the preaddition phase about how to "fix" noncanonical block arrays, so no one objected to their unfixed sums when they first made them (see Fuson et al., 1992).

The group did need adult support in order to move from the marks method as a way to record blocks addition to being able to use marks without adding blocks. First, they could not always reflect on their written fixing method, because their mark recordings were sometimes extremely messy, with the sums written all over the page. The adult asked them to make all future recordings neater and then showed them examples of their neat unfixed and fixed answers. Second, she asked them how they could fix a marks answer without doing the block trading. The children responded with many descriptions of block trades without doing such trades, so eventually everyone could fix the sum without actually trading blocks, if they thought about the individual block trades. In response to repeated requests to think of a way to fix the marks without thinking through all of the block trades, two children invented a method in which they wrote a small 1 above the right-hand digit to the left and wrote an x below that fixed 1 (see the answer to the right for Method M). After each 1 in the sum had an x below it (i.e., after all trades had been made), the sum could be fixed in one step by adding in the traded quantities. Both parts of this fixing method could be done from the left or from the right or in any order and were done in various orders. These 1s and xs were described clearly as ten-for-one block trades, so it is apparent that the children understood these marks as multiunit quantities.

Over the 2 days following this linking intervention, the adult supported a transition from block use by encouraging the children to use only the marks but to describe them in block words. The final two magic pad solutions related their own group method to the standard algorithm by writing both. On the final solution, one child also wrote little xs below the 1s in the unfixed sum to show this relation: "to show what I put up there when I carried." The combination of good group interactions, social norms for understanding, linked blocks and marks beginning from the blocks rather than the marks, and support of an adult to reflect on their invented method produced insightful and conceptually sound inventions by this group.

Place-value notation in itself does not explicitly show the multiunit values of numbers. Method N clarified what kind of multiunits were being added by writing each one out as standard marks, for example, writing two thousand as 2000, six hundred as 600, seventy as 70. Method N shows the adding of ones to ones, tens to tens, hundreds to hundreds, and thousands to thousands. Children learning to write multidigit numbers often make the errors of writing number as they sound. For instance, asked to record *fifty-three*, they may write 503 (write 50 to represent *fifty* and then 3 to represent *three*; see discussions in Baroody, 1987; Fuson, 1990; Ginsburg, 1977; Seron, Deloche, & Noel, 1992; Sinclair, Garin, & Tieche-Christinat, 1992). Method N was not such an error, however, but was invented by a girl in one of the high-achieving groups to show their blocks addition more clearly. Writing a problem like this for discussion might provide a memorable perceptual support for children having trouble constructing or using any meaning other than a concatenated single-digit conception of written marks. This form also permits discussion of the multiunit values of the 1s traded to the left. Because this method is also potentially misleading, however, it is important to discuss how it differs from normal place-value numbers. Such discussion emerged in the group that developed this method, when a boy exclaimed about a number written out this way, "It's seven billion!" Alternatively, numbers may be shown in expanded notation, which is just like Method N but includes a "+" between multiunits.

Subtraction

Overview of Block and Mark Multidigit Subtraction. The subtraction methods in most groups were dominated by the traditional U.S. subtraction algorithm, which moves from right to left, alternating "borrowing" (trading of the multiunits in the next-left column for 10 more of a unit) and then subtracting. One member of all but one group initially or eventually remembered borrowing (or *regrouping*, as it was called by some children) and suggested it as a marks method. None of the children already knew a block method of multidigit subtracting with or without borrowing; they had to figure these out. Children invented either a block-*trading* method (e.g., removing a pancake from the hundreds column and adding ten licorices to the tens column) or a block-*putting* method (just putting a pancake with the licorices in the tens column).

Because we were limited to 14 days and had only about 30 functional min a day, four groups did not have enough time to explore subtraction thoroughly. Two groups did not even have time to finish subtraction without zeros in the subtrahend. Thus, it is not clear how many of the difficulties would have been overcome with more time, more linking of numeric methods to the blocks, and more thorough explanations. These factors were effective in producing high levels of understanding of some method of addition. We outline the difficulties experienced by the children, because these need to be addressed in any subtraction learning experience. We observed the following three major types of difficulties: (a) failure to describe the full trading process in clear language (describing clearly both taking away 1 multiunit and adding its equivalent of 10 next-smaller units), (b) directionality of subtraction (the words used to describe it and the physical direction of taking away), and (c) the conceptual integrity of the horizontal multidigit numbers versus the functional separation into vertical column subunits when children wrote the expressions vertically.

During work with the blocks, most children who began with some notion of borrowing connected this conception to multiunit quantities and could describe trades in block or multiunit words. However, most children failed to describe or justify spontaneously what they were doing with the blocks or written marks. Even when adult leaders asked them to describe trading, they usually did not give adequate and complete descriptions. This was problematic because some children only saw half of the trade. For instance, children in several groups objected vehemently to block trading because it "was adding and we aren't adding" (seeing only the adding in of the new ten blocks to the right). These actions may have been more noticeable than the taking away from or moving of one block. In some groups, children acquiesced to trading only when both aspects of the trade were described in block language (e.g., "She took one licorice away, and she put on 10 teeth"). Some children used taking-away language for both aspects of the trade, thus creating confusions.

The use of two-digit tens-and-ones language without block or multiunit names and the double use of "ten" as the number of traded blocks and as a multiunit value led three boys in two of the groups to misunderstand trading as always giving *a ten* (e.g., a licorice block) to each column. This is similar to the incorrect addition Method G in which the 10 from each teen sum was given to the tens column.

Some aspects of the noncommutativity of subtraction and the resulting need to attend to the direction of subtraction caused difficulty. English terminology for subtraction is complex, with different words stating the same subtraction in opposite directions (eight take away two, take two from eight, eight minus two, two from eight, eight subtract two). For single-digit subtraction, one does not have to attend to the language order closely; on hearing two numbers one merely subtracts the smaller from the larger number. But for multidigit subtraction, direction is important. In all groups, the previously described subtraction language was used in all possible combinations of intent and accuracy. For example, a child might say and mean "eight take away two," say "two take away eight" but mean "eight take away two," and so forth. In some groups there were extended discussions about the correct way to say phrases and, in others, little or no such discussion.

Some groups established strong spatial top-to-bottom directionality for subtracting (all groups aligned blocks and written marks problems vertically). In these cases, everyone functioned from a shared perspective that they were subtracting the bottom number from the top number. Most children in these groups were not confused by, or did not notice, reversed subtraction statements. In the group that had the most prolonged discussion about the direction of phrases, everything about subtraction directionality was problematic. These students had questions about the direction of subtraction in the original horizontal problem (left–right subtraction direction) and in the vertical problem written by the children (up–down direction), as well as prolonged controversies about how to say various phrases correctly. Other groups did not have difficulty with any or all of these aspects of subtraction directionality.

The blocks themselves neither inhibited common incorrect methods nor directed correct methods in subtraction as powerfully as they had in addition. Children who carried their vertical perspective from addition into subtraction and who had not worked out strong overall problem directionality based on location (taking bottom blocks from top blocks) often subtracted the smaller number from the larger (e.g., for 342 – 185 got 143). Nothing in the blocks themselves helps to compose them into their two different multidigit numbers or makes the larger of the two multidigit numbers especially salient. This might have been increased by the tendency to show both numbers with the blocks (done by five of the six groups) and use a takeaway, rather than comparison, meaning of subtraction. Children using a comparison meaning in Fuson (1986a) did not make this error.

Within the groups, individuals took away in different ways. Some children subtracted mentally or with fingers using unit-based methods and then just took blocks away until only that answer remained. Some took away the bottom blocks first and then took that number of blocks from the top blocks. Some children took away blocks from those representing the top number first and then took away the bottom blocks. In groups where no blocks were taken away and new blocks were put in to show the answer, subtraction was done mentally or with fingers and the answer was then represented with blocks.

Incorrect Subtraction Methods. Incorrect subtraction methods that arose in the groups are illustrated in Fig. 10.4. They are arranged roughly, from most to

Figure 10.4: Incorrect Invented Multidigit Subtraction Methods

A) Subtract smaller from larger in each column

```
  4 6 5 2
- 1 9 6 8
  3 3 1 6
```

B) Take as many as you can down to zero

```
  5 2 8 6
- 1 6 2 9
  4 0 6 0
```

C) Add instead of subtract

```
  1 1 1
  4 6 5 2
- 1 9 6 8
  6 6 2 0
```

D) Left to right, put 1 digit above each column

```
  4 1 1 ¹6
  5̷ 2̷ 6̷ 6̷
- 1 6 2 9
```

E) Not cross out borrow; add top numbers then subtract

```
      4 13
  2 5 6 3
-   9 7 8
      3 5
```

F) Do not do a middle borrow; subtract smaller from larger[a]

```
  3 16  4 12
  4̷ 6̷ 5̷ 2̷
- 1 9 6 8
  2 7 2 4
```

G) Incomplete borrow, left column not decreased

```
  4 12    16
  5̷ 2 8 6̷
- 1 6 2 9
  4 6 6 7
```

H) Forget to reduce dot column answer by one

```
  .  .  .
  4 6 5 2
- 1 9 6 8
  3 6 8 4
```

I) All borrows mental; forget a borrowed-from decrease

```
  4 6 5 2
- 1 9 6 8
  2 6 9 4
```

J) Add one column, subtract others

```
  3  12  7 16
  4̷ 2̷ 8̷ 6̷
- 2 6 2 9
  5 6 5 7
```

K) Borrow tens to each column[b]

```
  1
  ↘
  3 10 10 10
  4̷ 0̷ 0̷ 0̷
- 1 7 3 5
```

L) Borrow a ten from thousands column

```
  3        10
  4̷ 0 0 0̷
- 1 7 3 5
```

M) Borrow 1 thousand for each column[b]

```
        1000
        2̶0̶0̶0̶
  3̶0̶0̶0̶ 1000 1000 1000
  4̷ 0̷ 0̷ 0̷
- 1 7 3 5
```

N) Borrow 1 thousand

```
  3        1000
  4̷ 0 0 0̷
- 1 7 3 5
```

O) Forget to reduce dot column answer by one; 0 thought of as a 10

```
  .  .  .
  4 0 0 0
- 1 7 3 5
  3 3 7 5
```

P) Bottom numbers ones and tens put on top, borrow as usual; several unclear steps (13, 3, 5)

```
              12
  3 13  3̷ 15
  4̷ 0̷ 0̷ 0̷
- 1 7 3̷5̷
  2 6 3 5
```

---
[a] Previous problem had only a thousand-to-hundreds and a ten-to-ones renaming.
[b] Blocks showed a "fatty" (a large or thousands cube) put in each top column.

least severe. As with addition, most of these (Errors D to P) were incorrect variations of the standard U.S. subtraction algorithm.

• *Methods A and B*. Children in the United States frequently make the first error (Method A in Figure 10.4; Fuson & Briars, 1990; VanLehn, 1986). Children look at a given column and subtract the smaller from the larger digit without considering the order of subtraction. This method was sometimes done only on a single column, especially on a middle borrow (Method F). Children in the United States make the second error (Method B) less frequently than the first; some Korean children also make this error (Fuson & Kwon, 1992). With Method B, the child preserves the order of subtraction and subtracts as much as possible down to zero. For example, for 6 − 9, six of the nine are taken to use up all of the top number, but the child does not know how to take the other three and so does nothing. The result of taking 6 − 6 = 0, so 0 is written as the answer. In two groups, a child mentioned negative numbers as a solution to combinations such as 6 − 9, but the group ignored this suggestion. These children needed the support of an adult to pursue this notion. Others have reported children inventing such negative number methods in which the negative numbers for given columns are then subtracted from the next larger position (Davis, 1986; Kamii, 1989).

• *Method C*. Error C, multidigit adding instead of subtracting, usually seemed to occur when children looked at the familiar multidigit layout, ignored the sign, and continued to use the method they had used for the past several days (addition). Children sometimes also added one column while subtracting the others (Method J). These errors were very infrequent.

• *Method D*. Error D arose from trying to adapt the traditional algorithm to a left-to-right method without linking it to the block left-to-right method used by the group. Error D seems to be a mixture of writing the traded 1 above the column to the right, writing the decreased number to the right, and making the far-right number look like the traditional algorithm (a teen number). This method was rare.

• *Methods E, G, H, and I*. Four different errors (Methods E, G, H, and I) arose from not crossing out the column from which 10 of that value were taken and then forgetting that the column had been diminished by one. Methods H and I were made by a Chinese-American girl, whose parents had taught her the traditional Chinese method of putting a small dot above a column from which a unit had been taken. The girl usually carried out this method correctly but, occasionally after a trade, forgot to decrease the left-hand column by one (the thousands column in Example H of Fig. 10.4). Method I included a similar lapse in one column, in problems where trading was done mentally.

• *Methods K through P*. Methods K through P arose on items with all zeros in the top number. Only the top two groups worked on these items. Both of these groups tried several incorrect methods before finding one that worked. The children recognized that the Methods K through P were incorrect, but they could not invent correct methods during the first day.

Correct Subtraction Methods. Correct subtraction methods that arose in the groups are shown in Fig. 10.5.

• *Methods Q, Ri, and S*. Method Q is the standard U.S. algorithm. This method arose primarily from children who knew at least the two-digit version.

Figure 10.5: Correct Invented Multidigit Subtraction Methods

Q) Right-to-left borrow, rewrite new value above top digit, and then subtract (standard U.S. algorithm)

$$
\begin{array}{r}
{}^{15}\ {}^{14}\\
{}^{3}\ \cancel{5}\ \cancel{4}\ {}_{12}\\
\cancel{4}\ \cancel{6}\ \cancel{5}\ \cancel{2}\\
-\ 1\ 9\ 6\ 8\\
\hline
2\ 6\ 8\ 4
\end{array}
$$

R) i) Alternate "one-step" trading and subtraction; ii) All trades first, then subtract

$$
\begin{array}{r}
3\ 15\ 14\ 12\\
\cancel{4}\ \cancel{6}\ \cancel{5}\ \cancel{2}\\
-\ 1\ 9\ 6\ 8\\
\hline
2\ 6\ 8\ 4
\end{array}
$$

S) Special features to facilitate keeping borrows clear[a]

$$
\begin{array}{r}
|\,4\,|\,13\,|\,6\,|\,16\,|\\
\cancel{3}\ \cancel{3}\ \cancel{7}\ \cancel{6}\\
-\ 1\ 6\ 2\ 9\\
\hline
3\ 7\ 4\ 7
\end{array}
$$

T) Draw dots to show the borrowed quantities and the top digits

$$
\begin{array}{r}
\vdots\ \vdots\ \vdots\\
5\ 3\ 7\ 6\\
-\ 1\ 6\ 2\ 9\\
\hline
3\ 7\ 4\ 7
\end{array}
$$

U) Fix all top digits first, left to right, then subtract each column

$$
\begin{array}{r}
{}^{15}\ {}^{14}\\
{}^{3}\ \cancel{4}\ \cancel{5}\ {}_{12}\\
\cancel{4}\ \cancel{6}\ \cancel{5}\ \cancel{2}\\
-\ 1\ 9\ 6\ 8\\
\hline
2\ 6\ 8\ 4
\end{array}
$$

V) Fix all top first, cross out but do top changes mentally before subtracting

$$
\begin{array}{r}
\cancel{4}\ \cancel{6}\ \cancel{5}\ \cancel{2}\\
-\ 1\ 9\ 6\ 8\\
\hline
2\ 6\ 8\ 4
\end{array}
$$

W) Decompose borrowed-from columns into the ten for the multiunit to the right and the remaining digit of that multiunit[b]

$$
\begin{array}{r}
\cdot\ \ \cdot\ \ \cdot\\
4\ 6\ 5\ 2\\
-\ 1\ 9\ 6\ 8\\
\hline
2\ 6\ 8\ 4
\end{array}
$$

X) Put a dot above a borrowed-from column, reduce its digit by 1, use teens in top digit when necessary

$$
\begin{array}{r}
{}^{6\cdot10}\ {}^{3\cdot10}\\
7\ 4\ 2\\
-\ 5\ 6\ 8\\
\hline
1\ 7\ 4
\end{array}
$$

Y) Just record the decreased borrowed-from part; do teens increase mentally

$$
\begin{array}{r}
{}^{4}\ \ \ {}^{6}\\
\cancel{5}\ 3\ \cancel{7}\ 6\\
-\ 1\ 6\ 2\ 9\\
\hline
3\ 7\ 4\ 7
\end{array}
$$

Z) Do borrows mentally: i) decrease top digit by 1; ii) subtract digits, then decrease answer by 1; or iii) increase bottom digits by 1, then subtract

$$
\begin{array}{r}
4\ 6\ 5\ 2\\
-\ 1\ 9\ 6\ 8\\
\hline
2\ 6\ 8\ 4
\end{array}
$$

AA) Add a 1 (signifying 10 or 100) to top digit and to bottom digit in next-left column

$$
\begin{array}{r}
4\ {}^{1}6\ {}^{1}5\ {}^{1}2\\
-\ {}^{1}1\ {}^{1}9\ {}^{1}6\ 8\\
\hline
2\ 6\ 8\ 4
\end{array}
$$

BB) Redistribute the 1 thousand as 9 hundreds 9 tens and ten[b]

$$
\begin{array}{r}
3\ 9\ 9\ 10\\
\cancel{4}\ \cancel{8}\ \cancel{8}\ \cancel{8}\\
-\ 1\ 7\ 3\ 5\\
\hline
2\ 2\ 6\ 5
\end{array}
$$

CC) Successive left to right gives to adjacent right column

$$
\begin{array}{r}
9\ \ 9\\
3\ \cancel{10}\ \cancel{10}\ 10\\
\cancel{4}\ \cancel{8}\ \cancel{8}\ \cancel{8}\\
-\ 1\ 7\ 3\ 5\\
\hline
2\ 2\ 6\ 5
\end{array}
$$

DD) A dot method like W, know middle 9s mentally

$$
\begin{array}{r}
\cdot\ \ \cdot\ \ \cdot\\
3\ 9\ 9\ 10\\
4\ 0\ 0\ 0\\
-\ 1\ 7\ 3\ 5\\
\hline
2\ 2\ 6\ 5
\end{array}
$$

EE) Give all tens, adjust for borrows, and subtract

$$
\begin{array}{r}
9\ \ 9\ 15\\
2\ \cancel{10}\ \cancel{10}\ \cancel{10}\\
\cancel{3}\ \cancel{8}\ \cancel{8}\ \cancel{8}\\
-\ 1\ 6\ 4\ 8\\
\hline
\end{array}
$$

[a] The magic-pad problem stimulating this method was extremely messy, with the columns of some borrowed digits not clear.
[b] Either a quantitative sharing or an anticipation and shortcut of Method CC.

Methods Ri and S are variations of this standard method. In both, after a column had been reduced by a trade, the new 1 ten coming from the left was written to the left of that number (to make a teen number), rather than that number being crossed out and the new teen number written above. Method S arose in response to a magic-pad problem with extremely messy writing so that the columns were not clear; children wrote the vertical lines to separate the columns in order to clarify the location of the traded two-digit numbers.

• *Methods U, Rii, and V.* Methods U, Rii, and V are all methods for fixing everything first in the top number so that borrowing occurs first in all applicable columns before subtraction begins. The fixing is done left to right in Method U and right to left in Rii (Ri and Rii look the same, but Ri alternates borrowing and subtracting). In Method V, the need for borrowing was noted in the top number at the start by crossing out all digits that would be changed by borrowing. These intended trades were then remembered as each column was subtracted, progressing from right to left. Method V arose after children had answered items with all zeros in the top number and thus had experienced fixing everything in the top number before beginning any subtraction. These methods are easier to carry out than alternating methods because the two major components of multidigit subtraction—trading to get more and subtracting—are each done all at once. Method U was taught successfully with base-ten blocks in Fuson (1986a) and Fuson and Briars (1990); it is less subject to occasional top-from-bottom errors.

• *Methods W and X.* Method W is the (correct) Chinese method of placing a dot above any column from which one has been given. Method X is the version that the children wrote the first time they used this method to show the meaning of the dot. This method is similar to the method presented in Korean textbooks, except that in that method the 10 is written above the next-right column (Fuson & Kwon, 1992). These methods that write a 10 support the take-from-ten method of single-digit subtraction taught in China, Japan, and Korea: for 14 − 8, take 8 from the 10 in 14, it is 2 that is then added to the 4 in 14 to get 6 as the difference.

• *Method Y.* Method Y is a clever abbreviation of the standard U.S. algorithm in which only the part that is difficult to remember is recorded. When borrowing, it is easy to remember the total in the increased column, because one is subtracting from it immediately. However, doing this subtraction may cause one to forget to decrease the next-left column by 1. The children who invented Method Y only showed this problematic part (the reduction of the left-hand digit in a trade); the rest was done mentally.

• *Methods Z and AA.* Example Z consists of three different methods done entirely mentally so that nothing extra is written. All three methods involve giving a block (or multiunit) to make 10 in the next right column, but they differ in the location from which that block is taken. Method Zii follows what happens with blocks when one subtracts from left to right; one subtracts within one block size (one column) and then gives one of the remaining blocks to the next-right column if it is needed. This subtraction procedure is analogous to the European left-to-right look-ahead method described previously for addition. Method Ziii users viewed it as an easy subtraction method, equivalent to subtracting one from the top number and then subtracting the bottom number. This method is easy if one is doing the subtraction by a forward method such as counting up from 7 to 15 (in the tens column, for example), because one can see the 5 (15) to which one is counting up. A version of this method (shown as Method AA) is common in Europe and in Latin America (Ron, 1998), but informal conversations indicate that it is rarely understood.

• *Methods BB through EE.* Methods BB through EE are alternative ways to show trading or putting for expressions with zeros in the top number. Both groups who got to such items needed some support from an adult to devise a method for getting more ones (Fuson & Burghardt, 1997). Each group unsuccessfully spent a whole lesson trying to solve this problem. Their multiunit knowledge was strong enough in each group that they discussed and rejected each incorrect zeros method shown in Fig. 10.4, but they needed a hint to devise a correct method. In one group, the experimenter asked the children, "Where do you usually put the thousands block?" This was sufficient for these children to invent a correct method using successive putting to the right (Method CC). In the other group, two children asked their parents how to solve such problems at home at night, and they brought in written marks methods from home. These methods (BB and CC) were then discussed, carried out with the blocks, and explained. Method BB was taught to one child by his father as looking at the first three digits (from the left) of 4000 as "four hundred," which needed to be reduced by one because one is given as ten to the ones column, leaving 399 (three hundred ninety-nine tens). Although the father's version did not say 400 tens or 399 tens, the children used this language with the blocks. Method BB was also developed as a shortcut to Method CC and as a solution to the erroneous method of giving 1000 to the ones column.

Educational Implications

In this section, we first discuss the result of our study in terms of the issues of adaptive expertise and flexibility and then describe general instructional guidelines.

FOSTERING ADAPTIVE EXPERTISE
AND FLEXIBILITY

Different conditions led to the invention and the use of correct and incorrect methods. Understanding these differences can illuminate how to support children's construction of adaptive expertise and flexible problem-solving strategies. In the present study, the problem to be solved was the invention of correct methods of four-digit addition and subtraction with blocks and with written marks. As discussed earlier, participants' use of incorrect methods was repeatedly stimulated by memories of some attributes of (usually two-digit) algorithms or "math rules" learned by rote from teachers, parents, or siblings. Children could not use this unconnected or meaningless knowledge adaptively or flexibly to direct the invention of correct methods or prevent that of incorrect ones. In contrast, the base-ten block environment simultaneously supported children's reasoning about grouping, place value, and multidigit addition (Baroody, 1990). When adults asked participants to link the blocks and written methods, they *self-corrected* their incorrect methods. The blocks-based instruction also enabled they to understand the standard U.S. algorithm, a procedure that—before the study began—they had known only by rote and could not explain. Almost all participants explained this method either during the study or on the posttest.

Working in a group created opportunities for developing adaptive expertise, because different methods, or different views of a given method, arose and needed to be resolved (Cobb & Bauersfeld, 1995). The explainers had to adapt their current knowledge to the issues raised by questioners, and the latter had to adapt to the explanations given. However, children did not spontaneously use clear referential language, which turned out to be crucial in helping everyone in a group understand each method. Such language involved clearly referring to all parts of the block actions, so that a listener could understand the "big picture" (the whole process). Either blocks language (i.e., the names of the different-sized blocks that each group had chosen) or place-value language (ones, tens, hundreds, thousands) was effective as long as the name of the position was used. The word "ten" had special potential for confusion, because it was sometimes a position name ("the tens [place]") and sometimes specified how many of some position ("ten of these"). Complete referential language, such as "ten tens," was helpful in directing attention to crucial features of a method and understanding them.

A striking result was that children's invented methods can be conceptually or procedurally superior to standard algorithms. Creating a learning environment that supports attention to and understanding of the crucial features of the domain can facilitate methods more adapted to the emerging expertise of children. For example, both addition Methods I and M are conceptually superior to the standard U.S. method. Both involve adding like units and then recording the total in a separate "total" space, rather than changing the "problem" by adding to the top addend as the solution proceeds. Changing the problem is difficult for some children to understand. Indeed, a number of participants objected to the standard method when members of their groups modeled it with blocks ("You're changing the problem"). Both Methods I and M can move from left to right as well as from right to left, thus accommodating the many children who prefer to move from left to right. (Note that the latter is consistent with how multidigit numerals and English text, for instance, are read. It is also consistent with the informal left-to-right mental multidigit procedures often used by children and experts; see Baroody & Tiilikainen, chap. 3, this volume.) Moving from left to right is messier than the standard U.S. method, requiring crossing out if you get a new traded multiunit. However, this step can eventually be eliminated with experience by moving to a look-ahead method discussed previously. Alternatively, children might decide to move to a right-to-left method, as did the one group who, as their adult leader suggested, compared such methods with left-to-right methods. Furthermore, for the reasons discussed in the previous section, single-digit addition within each column is also easier in addition Methods I, J, L, and M than in the standard U.S. method.

Some subtraction methods were also superior to the usual U.S. method that alternates borrowing and subtracting. The methods in which all of the fixing (borrowing, regrouping) was done first (in any direction) and all of the subtractions were done second were conceptually and procedurally better. The separation of the steps enabled these two crucial features to be more salient. They also eliminated subtract-top-from-bottom errors that often occur when children move right to left and alternate steps. Seeing a 2 and an 8 in some column automatically produces a 6. Unlike methods that do not alternate borrowing and subtracting, this automatic response must be inhibited when using the standard algorithm if the 2 is on the top.

Differences in the effectiveness of using blocks for addition and subtraction underscore the importance of a conceptual analysis of a domain. A visual or linguistic support is only as powerful as is its match to the underlying crucial features of the domain for which it is a potential support. Multidigit addition has the following two crucial features, both of which the blocks supported: (a) adding of like units (the blocks are very powerful here) and (b) fixing a unit when there is 10 or more of it by trading or putting 10 of the unit with the next unit to the left. The second feature also needs to be coordinated with knowledge of written place value, but the blocks helped greatly in understanding the conceptual shift from "10 ones" to "1 ten" (or "10 tens" to "1 hundred" and so forth) and the recording the new 1 (in various places).

Multidigit subtraction may be more challenging than multidigit addition in two ways. One is the noncommutativity of subtraction. That is, unlike addition, the order of subtracting terms does make a difference. The second is that the coherence of each multidigit number may be more obscured in the subtraction process than in the addition process. Because both the standard U.S. multidigit addition and subtraction algorithms focus attention on the digits of numbers one column at a time, many students do not view the top digits as one multidigit number and the bottom digits as another. By alternating the processes of borrowing and subtracting, the standard U.S. subtraction algorithm may reinforce children's focus on the columns of digits and exacerbate an incoherent view of multidigit addends.

There are several possible changes to our learning environment that might support these features of subtraction better. First, the integrity of each number might be supported by cardboard frames and by a discussion that subtracting can involve breaking apart a number into two smaller numbers. Second, only the number to be broken apart by subtraction need be represented with the blocks. Third, a comparative subtraction context might be used in which the larger number is actually split into a part that matches the other given number and the remaining part that represents the answer. This last method was used effectively in an earlier study (Fuson, 1986a) and has the advantage of encouraging children to count-up to solve the single-digit subtractions, which is easier and more accurate than is counting-down (Baroody, 1984; Fuson, 1984). However, counting-up can also be supported in a taking-away subtraction situation by taking away the entities representing the starting amount (Fuson, 1986b; Fuson & Willis, 1988).

Children had more trouble with subtraction than with addition in resolving how to get more of a unit and how to fix the situation when they had too many of a unit. Several kinds of experiences might help. The suggestions given previously might have helped children resolve the issues by enabling them to see multidigit numbers as wholes. Previous experience with simplifying noncanonical displays of more than 10 of a unit, as was the case for the most productive group, might be helpful. A teacher might raise this issue with the whole class, once a group encountered it. Helpful framing by the teacher could also be useful. Some of the groups needed suggestions from the adult leaders such as, "What else in the top number could you subtract eight little guys from?" or "In addition, when you had too many, you traded or put those over to the next column.

What if you traded or put that back now?" With such minimal help, all groups resolved this issue. Moving 1 unit to the next-right place seemed conceptually clearer than trading 1 unit for 10 of the next-smaller units. Such "putting" made it very clear that one was just moving part of the number from one column to the next. This was also not subject to the confusing "taking-away" language used by some groups to describe trading in subtraction or to noticing only the missing of half of the trade as some children did.

Yet another factor that might help account for the relative difficulty of multi-digit subtraction is that less time was spent on this operation, and so participants had less opportunity to construct an understanding of it. That is, the results are consistent with Hatano's observation in the Foreword that hurried instruction frequently does not enable children to effectively apply their learning.

Our discussion of the various correct methods in addition and subtraction and the advantages of some invented methods over the standard U.S. algorithms raises another crucial issue regarding adaptive expertise, namely "accessible algorithms." The superior algorithms were more accessible to children, because such procedures were more adapted to their knowledge. Such procedures facilitated understandings of crucial features of the domain, which, in turn, promoted adaptive expertise. These procedures were also accessible to children using less advanced (but still rapid and effective) single-digit methods and were readily explainable to them. Additionally, these methods were as general and as rapid to carry out as the standard methods. Environments that support children's learning of accessible methods, then, might facilitate adaptive expertise. Domain analyses and empirical work that identify and test accessible methods in various mathematical domains might enable many more children to build flexible adaptive expertise in those domains than at present with standard algorithms that have not been examined for their conceptual and procedural accessibility.

Some educators and researchers strenuously object to teaching any particular algorithms and argue that such teaching inevitably leads to the kind of rote, inflexible knowledge evidenced by some of the children in this study (particularly with subtraction). In our view, a social environment that supports sense making is more important than whether a particular method is or taught. That is, the focus should be on learning with understanding and setting expectations that all methods must be fully explained is central. Less advanced children can learn accessible methods from more advanced children, teachers, or a combination of the two.

INSTRUCTIONAL GUIDELINES

In this subsection, we discuss guidelines concerning the role of the teacher, group work, and manipulatives.

Tasks of the Teacher

An analysis was undertaken of the major teacher tasks assumed by the adults during the study and of those tasks that would have been helpful to assume. Teacher tasks that can support students' invention of calculation methods when working in small groups and using physical objects as pedagogical tools are summarized in Table 10.1.

These tasks may become intertwined when a group disagrees about which method to pursue. Some groups or children within a group may then need support so that the discussion is focused on mathematical issues, not on issues of power or use of rules from past authorities. ("My teacher last year" and "my sister" were both evoked as authorities in this study.) In this study, the pursuit of methods was more often resolved by dominance than by mathematical persuasion (Fuson & Burghardt, 1993). Of course, it is difficult in a brief intervention to create social norms different from those experienced in the regular classroom. Prolonged experience working in groups with the Social Norms 2Aa and 2Ab with an emphasis on using full quantity language to discuss mathematical issues should reduce the need for teacher support. In this study, most groups did adopt these social norms, at least part of the time, and the group inventing the innovative addition Method M conformed to them most of the time. Nevertheless, most groups would have worked better with more adult guidance in implementing these social norms.

As discussed before, most groups neglected to link block and written-mark methods, despite an adult's charge to do so. Children also rarely used block names or English multiunit values or fully described actions with the blocks. Groups needed persistent adult support for linking (Teacher Task 2Aa) and using quantity language (Task 2Ab). The blocks were powerful enough for addition that directing attention to crucial attributes (Task 2Ac) was not really needed. Quantity language, when used, also helped children see crucial attributes of a method and, thus, correct incorrect methods. For subtraction, directing attention (Task 2Ac) was needed for computations involving zero, and it might have been needed for groups where no one had experience with subtracting by taking from a larger multiunit.

Several of the groups were held back by the way they wrote their addition or subtraction solutions. These groups could have benefited from teacher guidance about how to record their work to facilitate reflection (Task 2Ae). The recordings of the socially effective group that invented addition Method M were often messy and all over the page, which led to considerable confusion. In subtraction, some groups completely blacked out numbers they were reducing by one, so it was hard to see what they had done afterward. One high-achieving group also sometimes made fancy curlicue numbers that even they then had trouble reading.

Adult support of a nondominant child (Task 2Ba), namely a suggestion that the group address her objections, was important for the second and final correction of incorrect addition Method G. An adult might also have focused attention on two interesting subtraction methods (getting negative numbers in a column and fixing all top numbers and then subtracting left to right) that were suggested by nondominant children but were not pursued. At the very least, the teacher could have encouraged the children to evaluate the procedure (e.g., explain why they thought it was wrong, checked whether it produced the correct answer).

Occasionally, when children made errors in counting or wrote a wrong number, no one in the group noticed the error, leading later to lengthy searches to recover from or find the error. In these situations, the other students were

---

**Table 10.1: Tasks of the Teacher to Facilitate Mathematically
Productive Small Groups**

---

1) Create social norms for children

 A) to understand and explain block and written-marks methods they use,
    not just get answers, and
 B) to help everyone in your group understand.

2) Monitor each group's interactions and, when necessary, provide support as
   specified by Points A and B.

 A) Support meaning building by

   a) helping children make the requisite links between the pedagogical
      objects (the blocks), written marks, and mathematical words;
   b) monitoring and helping children describe, argue, and explain using
      quantity language (here, block words and multiunit quantities);
   c) directing children's attention to crucial mathematical attributes by
      priming or eliciting helpful knowledge,
   d) encouraging children to count and write carefully and to check each
      other as they do these steps; and
   e) monitoring and helping children to record in ways that facilitate
      reflection.

 B) Support facilitative social interactions by

   a) providing social support to nondominant children to rescue good
      ideas;
   b) when necessary, directing attention to the task, ascertaining if there
      are current difficulties that are contributing to off-task behavior;
   c) encouraging discouraged children or groups.

3) Monitor group and individual progress and allow children sufficient time to
   construct the conceptual structures for the domain and function comfortably
   with them.

4) Encourage whole-class reflection on, comparisons of, and discussion of
   different solution methods.

passively observing, rather than actively monitoring, others' problem solving. The teacher's task here would be to encourage children in groups to count and write carefully and, especially, to check each other (Task 2Ad), that is, to share responsibility for producing a correct and reasonable solution.

Tasks 2Bb and 2Bc are related, though also independent. Individual children and whole groups sometimes engaged in sustained off-task behavior. At times, this occurred when children faced a problem they did not know how to resolve (e.g., subtraction with zeros), but it could also occur in response to distractions (e.g., a very hot day, an interesting event in the class just before, or an individual toothache). Some children also seemed to get discouraged at times and withdraw from the group (e.g., when their suggestions were ignored or when they did not understand). These clearly are also related to other teacher tasks (2Ac and 2Ae). We found that even a minimal hint may bring profound change to a discouraged group or child. In subtraction with zeros, a question ("Where did you usually put the ice cube?") was enough to create sustained engagement for the rest of the period by a boy who was easily discouraged and then was mean to other children. Indeed, while solving other problems involving zeros with blocks and marks, he even commented enthusiastically, "This is fun!"

It takes time for children to construct mathematically robust conceptions of a domain and use these conceptions to calculate in that domain. The groups in the present study spent from 5 to 8 days on addition and from 3 to 8 days on subtraction. Some children in four of the groups would have benefited from more time in addition, and all groups needed more time in subtraction. The appearance of multidigit numbers, easily seen as constantly seductive single digits, can be misleading and interfere with fledgling multiunit conceptions and suggest wrong methods. Furthermore, it takes a long time to solve a single four-digit addition or subtraction with blocks; our groups averaged about two such numeric problems per 30-min working session. Of course, they were slower in the beginning and faster at the end. If children are to describe, reflect on, and discuss an extended solution method with objects and written marks, they need quite a few examples before they begin to see and describe the overall pattern across the particularities of given numbers. This was particularly true for some group members, who initially did not understand all or part of the group's method. There were some such children in all groups, and they were supported to some extent by the adults' questions and directives. Such supporting also helped the faster members of the group to see and articulate overall solution methods rather than single steps.

Children with a more typical level of achievement and those with low achievement might have less initial knowledge and slower learning rates than members in the "low" group of our study, all of whom were in a class for students with above-average achievement. Average- and low-achieving children would need even longer to be able to carry out, understand, and explain a group's method. Both in this study, where base-ten blocks were used by children to invent methods, and in whole-class situations, where teachers are supporting a whole class to understanding and using a particular solution method (e.g., Fuson, 1986a; Fuson & Briars, 1990), children need weeks of time, not a single session, to learn. Using blocks for a single session results in little lasting conceptual gain (e.g., Resnick & Omanson, 1987; Thompson, 1992). However, if children have more time, use of Thompson's microworld (described in his 1992 report) can promote considerable learning. For example, in a case study of two children (Fraivillig, Fuson, & Thompson, 1993), one moved from a concatenated single-digit understanding of her correct addition algorithm to understanding and explaining it in quantity terms over days, and the other moved from no correct method to an invented and conceptual method over days. Hiebert and Wearne (1992) also reported that it took weeks for children to construct adequate two-digit addition and subtraction methods using base-ten blocks. All conceptual supports including manipulatives must connect with each child's existing knowledge. (This point has been made by many others; e.g., Baroody, 1989, and Clements & McMillen, 1996.) They must also help each child build new flexible readily used knowledge. These goals take time for such complex methods as multidigit calculation.

Insight, the rapid reorganization of conceptual structures that can result from making connections, might occur in one session, especially as children discuss and compare various methods. But insights assume that the child has already constructed the required multi-unit conceptions. Such construction seems to be for most children a slower process of pattern-making and connecting that leads to the gradual interiorization of mental images of the blocks that can be used to direct and correct thinking. An "instamatic camera" view of visual learning is not an adequate view of learning with visual supports.

We use "interiorization" because this word suggests retention of external characteristics, and children's expressions of internal representations suggested fairly direct perceptual adherences. Participants in our study who were asked by an adult on the final days of their groupwork on addition or on subtraction if they could describe their written marks method in terms of the blocks without using actual blocks. The children could use physical attributes of the blocks in describing or responding to questions about the method, so these attributes seem to have been interiorized and be accessible for use in constraining and directing-marks methods. Fuson (1986a) and Thompson (1992) also both reported such interiorization. Children in Fuson self-corrected errors when told to "think about the blocks." The best microworld student in Thompson reported that he thought about the blocks when he was "stumped or stopped" (p. 142).

This process of interiorization underscores two phases in the linking of physical pedagogical objects to the mathematical written marks and to the words whose meanings the objects are to support (see also Fuson et al., 1992). The first learning phase is the initial construction of meaning. In this phase, the mathematical marks record actions with the pedagogical objects (here, the base-ten blocks) and the words describe such actions. Gradually, these marks and words take on meanings derived from attributes of the pedagogical objects. The marks and words can then be used meaningfully, without the pedagogical objects. However, especially if alternative meanings for the marks or words already exist or can easily be constructed (e.g., treating multidigit numbers as concatenated single digits or the two-digit tens and ones conceptions), a second reverse-linking phase is helpful. In this phase, operations on the marks are occasionally described in terms of the pedagogical objects (here, actions on blocks). Such reverse linkings can serve to keep the correct meanings linked to the marks methods. If pedagogical objects are interiorized sufficiently by most children by the time small groups are ready for whole-class discussion, this discussion could take place quite rapidly in the reverse-linking block-word mode. Blocks themselves could be used when children are not following a particular argument or when a particularly difficult issue is discussed. But some children or groups may continue to benefit from carrying out particular alternative methods with blocks in order to understand them, or such methods could be drawn with block drawings (e.g., Fuson, Smith, et al., 1997).

Teacher Task 4 in Table 10.1 might have been helpful in this study. After students have worked on their group constructions for some time, it seems important for the teacher to encourage full-class reflection on and comparison of the groups' different solutions. This would enable important mathematical issues that arose only in one group to be reflected on by the whole class. Leading such reflective discussion would also provide an opportunity to carry out many of the other teacher tasks listed in Table 10.1 with the class as a whole (e.g., model and support full descriptions of methods). We could not implement Teacher Task 4 because of circumstances beyond our control (e.g., limited access to the participants and physical barriers, such as separation of groups by a stair landing).

Conditions for Learning in a Small Group

Working in a small group with the support of pedagogical objects does not necessarily lead to the construction of correct methods (for a full report on how children's interactions in small groups affect their invention of multidigit methods, see Burghardt, 1992; Fuson & Burghardt, 1993; Fuson et al., 1992). Knowledge, methods, and individual ideas can be socially destroyed (Tudge, 1992) or ignored, as well as socially constructed (Burghardt, 1992; Fuson & Burghardt, 1993; Fuson et al., 1992).

Small groups are stimulating "noisy" environments with multiple simultaneous visual, auditory, and kinesthetic stimuli, only some of which are mathematically relevant. The teacher tasks described in Table 10.1 focus on increasing the proportion of mathematically relevant stimuli and the ability of children to attend to them. In such a busy environment, a great deal is happening rapidly, and redundancy and salience are helpful. Thus, it might be beneficial for all children to verbally describe block or marks actions. Not all children are experienced in providing such descriptions. Helping students learn to ask whenever they do not understand a certain step is also important. When children in our groups did report lack of understanding, they were usually given help by their group (albeit not always with adequate explanations).

Knowledge under construction also can be quite ephemeral. One day a child may carry out a solution with blocks or marks, and the next day it may be gone or, at least, not accessible at that moment. A child in one group, who provided a full adult-like explanation of the group's subtraction method to a boy who had used the method himself the day before, commented on this phenomenon, "He understands one day, and then you have to explain it to him the next." The social conditions of the construction of individual knowledge have to allow for and support repeated opportunities for that construction and reconstruction in a particular domain.

There were at least four different sources of learning in the small group situation; examples of these types of learning are given in case studies of individual learners within the group context in Burghardt (1992). Most children learned by some combination of these sources. First, many children used features of the mathematical entities in the learning situation to direct and constrain their actions with those entities. Features of the blocks directed correct actions, and features of the written marks, sometimes combined with features of a rotely learned and dimly remembered standard algorithm, frequently directed incorrect actions. Second, some children learned some steps in a method, or a whole method, by observation and imitation of that method carried out by others in their group. Third, some children learned by receiving guidance of various kinds from another person, either a child in their group or the adult. This help sometimes was explicitly elicited and sometimes was given because the helper perceived a need for that help. This help ranged from physical actions to verbal directives, questions, and explanations and sometimes was a complex combination of most of these. Fourth, some children learned through cognitive conflict, demonstrated in discussion or argument. They disagreed about the accuracy of a method or some part of a method, and their verbal disagreement led them and sometimes others to change their view of the accuracy or inaccuracy of that part of the method. The first and fourth of these sources of learning are in keeping with Piaget's theories of learning (1965, 1970a, 1970b), whereas the second and third support Vygotsky's (1934/1962, 1934/1986, 1978) theories of learning. They all can contribute to an individual child's construction of knowledge. The balance among them also can be varied by the power of the pedagogical objects present in the situation, the knowledge and dominance relations across individual children, and the power of the social norms concerning helping, discussing, and explaining.

Pedagogical Objects as Sources of Learning

Pedagogical objects can support children's construction of correct meanings for mathematical words and written marks only to the extent such objects have salient features that suggest the correct meaning, do not possess misleading features, and are linked over a sustained period to the target mathematical words and written marks. We have seen that the different sizes of base-ten blocks are powerful in directing the two major components of multidigit addition: (a) adding like values and (b) when necessary, trading or putting 10 blocks of one size with the next larger blocks. In subtraction, the blocks do support subtracting like multiunits and can support understanding of taking from one of the next larger multiunit. However, the problems of directionality of subtraction and the lack of coherence of different kinds of blocks in making a single multidigit number are not addressed by features of the blocks. These require additional supports within the block context, as discussed earlier. The blocks also did not support a subtraction method using negative or minus numbers. One child wanting to try this method asked the adult if she had anything to make a minus four. Some kind of special mark on the blocks would be helpful to show any blocks considered as minus blocks. With such marks, the blocks could support the minus method sometimes invented by children in a supportive environment (e.g., Davis, 1984; Kamii, 1989). These examples indicate that an adequate learning environment might require both pedagogical objects and surrounding supports that together promote correct methods.

The surrounding supports we provided varied in their effectiveness. In the second session, we attempted to facilitate linking of the objects and written marks by asking children to write problems and solutions on a "magic pad" and to beep whenever a blocks action was not recorded on the magic pad. This fantasy-game approach was quite successful: Although unconnected to mathematics, it gave everyone an active role in monitoring the group action, seemed to help the linking considerably in some groups, and was fun and engaging, perhaps in part because it reminded children of video games. In contrast, the digit cards used in the first session often caused groups to splinter into pairs. It was natural for two children to use the cards (one to place and one to find the right card from the card box), leaving the other two children to focus on the blocks. These two pairs then would become separated in their actions and discussions.

Other possible outside supports include teacher directives concerning written marks. Thompson (1992), for example, had fourth graders circle the location of the answer in vertical addition and subtraction problems and calling this, "the place where you write the number of blocks of a place value after you add blocks having that value" (p. 126). Several children in both groups then invented a version of addition Method M, which Thompson termed "add within columns." In this version, each column was added (the 1 was written with the total, but slightly higher and smaller than the other digit) and then the answer was fixed to standard form. This method had been clearly suggested by Thompson's definition of the "answer place" in the introduction.

Any particular pedagogical object will support only certain meanings, though other meanings can sometimes also be supported by further additions to the learning environment. The salience of the separate multiunits in the base-ten blocks supported addition and subtraction methods of operating on separate like multiunits. In contrast, the hundreds board (a chart of numbers in sequence from 1 to 100, arranged in rows of ten) supports sequence methods, in which one begins adding or subtracting with one whole two-digit number and then counts up or down by ones or by ones and tens from that number. The hundreds board could support a sequence interpretation of the common European and Latin American subtraction Method K. For 62 − 34, for example, such a sequence method begins at 34 on the hundreds board, moves right 6 squares to 40, writes the small 1 by the 3 to show that one now is not at 30 but at 40, moves down two rows on the hundreds board to 60 (each vertical move of one square signifying an increase of one ten, from 40 to 50 to 60) and writes 2 in the tens column to show that increase of 20, and then counts up 2 more squares to get to 62, and writes 8 (the original 6 ones up to 40 plus the 2). Alternatively, all of the ones counting could be done at once. A similar sequence interpretation could be given for addition Method J. The 7 ones are added to the 85 to get 92; the 2 is recorded and the 8 is changed to a 9; the 60 is then added to the 92 to get 150; the 50 is recorded and the 600 is changed to 700; the 900 is added to the 700 to get 1600; the 600 is recorded and the 200 is changed to 3000; 3000 and 1000 make 4000. However, such sequence methods also require learning to count by tens, which must be supported somehow within the classroom or home environment. Children in our study did often count the base-ten blocks by tens when they were making block arrays or adding or subtracting blocks. Thus, the blocks can be used either with sequence methods or counting multiunit methods but are more likely to direct the latter without some outside suggestion for trying sequence methods of adding or subtracting.

Teachers do not necessarily understand the use of pedagogical objects to help children construct meanings linked to written marks and mathematical words. Hart (1987) reported that British teachers in the 1980s typically used base-ten blocks alone for an extended time and then moved abruptly to written marks with little (1 day) or no connections made between the blocks and the written marks. If pedagogical objects are well chosen, children do not need an extended time to operate with them. The objects will powerfully and quickly direct correct object methods. However, the meanings represented by the pedagogical objects will not become connected to the written marks or mathematical words, unless children have sufficient experience to overcome any misleading meanings stemming from the written marks (e.g., for multidigit numbers, concatenated single digit meanings) or words (e.g., two thirds, in fractions). Because written mathematical marks for multidigit numbers, rational numbers, and decimals, and the English words for these marks, all have misleading features (e.g., Fuson, 1992), this link may need to be sustained for a considerable time. We found in this study that children may require considerable prodding from their teacher to make this link between representations. In a study of a range of schools and a range of mathematical topics, Hart (1989) also found that the pattern of dissociation between pedagogical objects and written marks was pervasive; children usually operated in two different worlds and perceived these worlds as different. Her informal title for this study was a quote from one child in the study, "Blocks is blocks, and sums is sums" (Hart, 1989).

Conclusions

The results of the present study indicate that a meaningful and inquiry-based (an "investigative") approach to multidigit addition and subtraction instruction can foster children's adaptive expertise and flexibility (see also, e.g., Hiebert & Wearne, 1992; Pengelly, 1988). Specifically, with conceptual supports (e.g., teacher monitoring and feedback, pedagogical objects such as base-ten blocks, and the interaction of cooperative-learning groups), participants quickly devised correct addition methods with blocks. Furthermore, with adult prompting, they translated their concrete procedures into written procedures. Some of these invented written methods were conceptually or procedurally superior to the standard U.S. algorithm.

The results are also consistent with reservations about an "incidental-learning model" (Brownell, 1935) or a laissez faire problem-solving approach (see Baroody, with Coslick, 1998, and Baroody, chap. 1, this volume, for a detailed comparison of this approach, the investigative approach, and the traditional "skills" approach). Specifically, many incorrect written addition methods were invented because children did not link them to their block solutions. In such cases, adults had to insist that they connect their written solutions to their block solutions.

Block-trading methods for subtraction were considerably more difficult to develop than were those for addition. To a large extent, the participants' invention of both written and block subtraction methods followed a few students' memories of written methods. Children's use of imprecise language for blocks and written marks further contributed to difficulties in developing correct subtraction methods. Yet another key difficulty was that the participants did not have sufficient time to explore, analyze, discuss, and otherwise reflect on multidigit subtraction.

Children's invention of multiple methods of adding and subtracting are not just desirable because of the new mathematics learning goals (NCTM, 1989, 2000). The invention of multiple methods is inevitable. Whether with traditional instruction or with the investigative approach, children invent different methods, some correct and some incorrect. Correct inventions are typically directed by the child's conception of multiunit numbers and multiunit addition and subtraction.

Teachers in the United States and other English-speaking countries have a special responsibility to help children construct robust multiunit conceptions for two reasons. One is that English number words for two-digit numbers do not support such conceptions. Another is that few other conceptual supports are experienced outside the school. (See Miura & Okamoto, chap. 8, this volume, for a detailed discussion of both points.) The results of our study suggest that several specific teacher tasks are essential to support students' small-group invention of meaningful calculation methods. These tasks include creating an environment in which children can and do link concrete quantities to written methods; creating social norms in which understanding, explaining, and helping are integral; monitoring groups' interactions to help students to use clear quantitative language and to record their solutions; and supporting less dominant students or dispirited groups cognitively and socially.

This study further indicates that pedagogical objects, such as base-ten blocks, can provide a rich and powerful environment for student invention and learning. However, this is not something that happens automatically (Baroody, 1989; Clements & McMillen, 1996). The power of pedagogical objects is limited by their features and depends on the extent to which they are linked to a conceptual understanding of grouping and place-value concepts. Their power further depends on the extent to which they are linked to mathematical words and written marks and provide a bridge between these symbolic representations and conceptual understanding of grouping and place value.

This study also demonstrates that working in small groups can facilitate children's inventions of computational procedures and help them to deepen their arithmetic knowledge. Again, however, this does not happen automatically. Without the proper social and intellectual climate, working in a group can also hurt children and slow their learning. In a small-group setting with ambitious mathematical learning goals, therefore, a teacher's tasks are many and complex. As discussed earlier, teachers must lay the initial groundwork, constantly monitor the progress of each group, and otherwise support children's conceptual progress. Without such support, students may well invent unlinked and incorrect methods. With a positive climate and adult support, though, children can invent effective methods, some of which are better than the formal methods presently taught in the United States.

Acknowledgments

The research reported in this chapter was supported in part by the National Center for Research in Mathematical Sciences Education, which is funded by the Office of Educational Research and Improvement of the U.S. Department of Education under Grant No. R1 17G 10002, and in part by the National Science Foundation under Grant Nos. RED 935373 and REC 90806020. The opinions expressed in this chapter are those of the authors and do not necessarily reflect the views of OERI or of NSF. We thank Stacy Wolfe, Jennifer Wallace, and Linda Bastiani for their sensitive and intelligent work on this study and for their contributions to the data analysis.

References

Baroody, A. J. (1984). Children's difficulties in subtraction: Some causes and questions. *Journal for Research in Mathematics Education, 15*, 203–213.

Baroody, A. J. (1987). *Children's mathematical thinking: A developmental framework for preschool, primary, and special education teachers.* New York: Teachers College Press.

Baroody, A. J. (1989). Manipulatives don't come with guarantees. *Arithmetic Teacher, 37(2),* 4–5.

Baroody, A. J. (1990). How and when should place-value concepts and skills be taught? *Journal for Research in Mathematics Education, 21*, 281–286.

Baroody, A. J., with Coslick, R. T. (1998). Fostering children's mathematical power: An investigative approach to K–8 mathematics instruction. Mahwah, NJ: Lawrence Erlbaum Associates.

Beishuizen, M., Gravemeijer, K. P. E., & van Lieshout, E. C. D. M. (Eds.). (1997). *The role of contexts and models in the development of mathematical strategies and procedures.* Utrecht, Netherlands: Freudenthal Institute.

Brownell, W. A. (1935). Psychological considerations in the learning and the teaching of arithmetic. In D. W. Reeve (Ed.), *The teaching of arithmetic* (Tenth yearbook, National Council of Teachers of Mathematics, pp. 1–50). New York: Bureau of Publications, Teachers College, Columbia University.

Burghardt, B. H. (1992). *Analysis of individual children's learning of multidigit addition in small groups.* Unpublished doctoral dissertation, Northwestern University.

Clements, D. H., & McMillen, S. (1996). Rethinking "concrete" manipulatives. *Teaching Children Mathematics, 2(5),* 270–279.

Cobb, P., & Bauersfeld, H. (Eds.). (1995). *The emergence of mathematical thinking: Interaction in classroom cultures.* Hillsdale, NJ: Lawrence Erlbaum Associates.

Cohen, G. E. (1984). Talking and working together: Status, interaction, and learning. In P. L. Peterson, L. C. Wilkinson, and M. Hallinan (Eds.), *The social context of instruction: Group organization and group processes* (pp. 171–188). Orlando, FL: Academic Press.

Davis, R. B. (1984). *Learning mathematics: The cognitive science approach to mathematics education.* Norwood, NJ: Ablex.

Davis, R. B. (1986). Conceptual and procedural knowledge in mathematics: A summary analysis. In J. Hiebert (Ed.), *Conceptual and procedural knowledge: The case of mathematics* (pp. 265–300). Hillsdale, NJ: Lawrence Erlbaum Associates.

Fraivillig, J. L., Fuson, K. C., & Thompson, P. W. (1993). Microworld support of children's understanding of multidigit addition. In *Proceedings of the World Conference on Artificial Intelligence in Education* (pp. 161–168). (Conference held at Edinburgh, England.) Charlottesville, VA: Association for the Advancement of Computing Education.

Fuson, K. C. (1984). More complexities in subtraction. *Journal of Research in Mathematics Education, 15*, 214–225.

Fuson, K. C. (1986a). Roles of representation and verbalization in the teaching of multi-digit addition and subtraction. *European Journal of Psychology of Education, 1,* 35–56.

Fuson, K. C. (1986b). Teaching children to subtract by counting up. *Journal for Research in Mathematics Education, 17,* 172–189.

Fuson, K. C. (1990). Conceptual structures for multiunit numbers: Implications for learning and teaching multidigit addition, subtraction, and place value. *Cognition and Instruction, 7,* 343–403.

Fuson, K. C. (1992). Research on learning and teaching addition and subtraction of whole numbers. In G. Leinhardt, R. T. Putnam, & R. A. Hattrup (Eds.), *The analysis of arithmetic for mathematics teaching* (pp. 53–187). Hillsdale, NJ: Lawrence Erlbaum Associates.

Fuson, K. C., & Briars, D. J. (1990). Base-ten blocks as a first- and second-grade learning/teaching approach for multidigit addition and subtraction and place-value concepts. *Journal for Research in Mathematics Education, 21,* 180–206.

Fuson, K. C., & Burghardt, B. H. (1993). Group case studies of second graders inventing multidigit addition procedures for base-ten blocks and written marks. In J. R. Becker & B. J. Pence (Eds.), *Proceedings of the fifteenth annual meeting of the North American Chapter of the International Group for the Psychology of Mathematics Education* (pp. 240–246). San Jose, CA: The Center for Mathematics and Computer Science Education.

Fuson, K. C., & Burghardt, B. H. (1997). Group studies of second graders inventing multidigit subtraction methods. In J. A. Dossey, J. O. Swafford, M. Parmantie, & A. E. Dossey (Eds.), *Proceedings of the 19th Annual Meeting of the North American Chapter of the International Group for the Psychology of Mathematics Education, 1* (pp. 291–298). Columbus, OH: ERIC Clearinghouse for Science, Mathematics, and Environmental Education.

Fuson, K. C., Fraivillig, J. L., & Burghardt, B. H. (1992). Relationships children construct among English number words, multiunit base-ten blocks, and written multidigit addition. In J. Campbell (Ed.), *The nature and origins of mathematical skills* (pp. 39–112). North Holland: Elsevier Science.

Fuson, K. C., & Kwon, Y. (1992). Korean children's understanding of multidigit addition and subtraction. *Child Development, 63,* 491–506.

Fuson, K. C., & Smith, S. T. (1997). Supporting multiple 2-digit conceptual structures and calculation methods in the classroom. In M. Beishuizen, K. P. E. Gravemeijer, & E. C. D. M. van Lieshout (Eds.), *The role of contexts and models in the development of mathematical strategies and procedures* (pp. 163–198). Utretcht, Netherlands: Freudenthal Institute.

Fuson, K. C., Smith, S. T., & Lo Cicero, A. M. (1997). Supporting Latino first graders' ten-structured thinking in urban classrooms. *Journal for Research in Mathematics Education, 28,* 738–760.

Fuson, K. C., Wearne, D., Hiebert, J., Murray, H., Human, P., Olivier, A., Carpenter, T., & Fennema, E. (1997). Children's conceptual structures for multidigit numbers and methods of multidigit addition and subtraction. *Journal for Research in Mathematics Education, 28,* 130–162.

Fuson, K. C., & Willis, G. B. (1988). Subtracting by counting up: More evidence. *Journal for Research in Mathematics Education, 19,* 402–420.

Ginsburg, H. P. (1977). *Children's arithmetic.* New York: Van Nostrand.

Hart, K. M. (1987). Practical work and formalization, too great a gap. In J. C. Bergeron, N. Herscovics, & C. Kieran (Eds.), *Proceedings from the 11th international conference for the Psychology of Mathematics Education* (Vol. 2, pp. 408–415). Montreal.

Hart, K. M. (1989). There is little connection. In P. Ernest (Ed.), *Mathematics teaching: The state of the art* (pp. 138–142). London: Falmer Press.

Hiebert, J., & Wearne, D. (1992). Links between teaching and learning place value with understanding in first grade. *Journal for Research in Mathematics Education, 23*, 98–122.

Kamii, C. (1985). *Young children reinvent arithmetic: Implications of Piaget's theory.* New York: Teachers College Press.

Kamii, C. (1989). *Young children continue to reinvent arithmetic—2nd grade: Implications of Piaget's theory.* New York: Teachers College Press.

Kimball, M. M. (1989). A new perspective on women's math achievement. *Psychological Bulletin, 105,* 198–214.

Labinowicz, E. (1985). *Learning from students: New beginnings for teaching numerical thinking.* Menlo Park, CA: Addison-Wesley.

Menninger, K. (1969). *Number words and number symbols* (P. Broneer, Trans.). Cambridge: MIT Press. (Original work published 1958)

National Council of Teachers of Mathematics (1989). *Curriculum and evaluation standards for school mathematics.* Reston, VA: Author.

National Council of Teachers of Mathematics (1991). *Professional standards for teaching mathematics.* Reston, VA: Author.

National Council of Teachers of Mathematics (2000). *Principles and standards for school mathematics: Standards 2000.* Reston, VA: Author.

Pengelly, H. (1988, July-August). *Mathematical learning beyond the activity.* Paper presented at the International Conference on Mathematics Education (ICM, 6), Budapest.

Peterson, P. L., & Fennema, E. (1985). Effective teaching, student engagement in classroom activities, and sex-related differences in learning mathematics. *American Educational Research* Journal, *22,* 309–335.

Piaget, J. (1965). *The child's conception of number.* New York: Norton.

Piaget, J. (1970a). *Genetic epistemology.* New York: Columbia University Press.

Piaget, J. (1970b). *Science of education and the psychology of the child.* New York: Orion.

Resnick, L. B., & Omanson, S. F. (1987). Learning to understand arithmetic. In R. Glaser (Ed.), *Advances in instructional psychology* (Vol. 3, pp. 41–95). Hillsdale, NJ: Lawrence Erlbaum Associates.

Ron, P. (1998). My family taught me this way. In L. J. Morrow (Ed.), *Teaching and learning algorithms in school mathematics* (pp. 115-119). Reston, VA: National Council of Teachers of Mathematics.

Seron, X., Deloche, G., & Noel, M. P. (1992). Number transcribing by children: Writing Arabic numbers under dictation. In J. Bideaud, C. Meljac, & J. P. Fischer (Eds.), *Pathways to number* (pp. 245–265). Hillsdale, NJ: Lawrence Erlbaum Associates.

Sinclair, A., Garin, A., & Tieche-Christinat, C. (1992). Constructing an understanding of place value in numerical notation. Journal *of Psychology of Education, 7*(3), 1–29.

Thompson, P. W. (1992). Notations, conventions, and constraints: Contributions to effective uses of concrete materials in elementary mathematics. *Journal for Research in Mathematics Education, 23,* 123, 147.

Tudge, J. (1992). Processes and consequences of peer collaboration: A Vygotskiian analysis. *Child Development, 63,* 1364–1379.

VanLehn, K. (1986). Arithmetic procedures are induced from examples. In J. Hiebert (Ed.), *Conceptual and procedural knowledge: The case of mathematics* (pp. 133–179). Hillsdale, NJ: Lawrence Erlbaum Associates.

Vygotsky, L. S. (1962). *Thought and language.* (E. Haufmann & G. Vakar, Eds. & Trans.). Cambridge, MA.: MIT Press. (Original work published in 1934)

Vygotsky, L.S. (1986). *Thought and language.* (A. Kozulin, Ed. & Trans.). Cambridge, MA: MIT Press. (Original work published in 1934)

Vygotsky, L. S. (1978). *Mind in society: The development of higher psychological processes.* Cambridge, MA: Harvard University Press.

CHAPTER 11

CHILDREN'S INVENTION OF MULTIDIGIT MULTIPLICATION AND DIVISION ALGORITHMS

Rebecca Ambrose
San Diego State University

Jae-Meen Baek
Arizona State University

Thomas P. Carpenter[1]
University of Wisconsin-Madison

One of the significant achievements of recent research on children's mathematical learning has been the construction of detailed maps of their development of informal or intuitive concepts of arithmetic. Children's informal strategies for adding, subtracting, multiplying, and dividing have been clearly documented, and remarkably consistent and coherent portraits of their conceptual development of basic whole number operations have emerged (Baroody, 1996; Carpenter, 1985; Carpenter, Ansell, Franke, Fennema, & Weisbeck, 1993; Fuson, 1992; Gutstein & Romberg, 1996; Verschaffel & De Corte, 1993). This research characterizes the development of children's addition, subtraction, multiplication, and division concepts and skills in terms of the progressive abstraction of their informal strategies, a progression that is both predictable and largely principled.

In the 1970s and early 1980s, research focused on children's solutions of addition and subtraction problems involving relatively small whole numbers, problems that could be easily modeled with individual counters (Carpenter, 1985). More recently, researchers have turned their attention to problems that involve multidigit calculations, and significant progress has been made in characterizing the strategies that children construct to add and subtract multidigit numbers (Beishuizen, Gravemeijer, & van Lieshout, 1997; Hiebert et al., 1997). Fuson and her colleagues (Fuson & Burghardt, chap. 10, this volume; Fuson et al., 1997) have constructed a detailed taxonomy of the strategies that children construct for adding and subtracting multidigit numbers. Although a few researchers have documented that children also can invent strategies for multiplying and dividing multidigit numbers and have described some of the strategies they use (Heege, 1985; Kamii, 1994; Silver, Shapiro, & Deutsch, 1993; Weiland, 1985), little progress has been made in characterizing such inventions.

The goal of this chapter is to provide a more complete analysis of children's invented multidigit multiplication and division procedures and the concepts and skills that they depend on. We start by describing children's conceptions of multiplication and division operations and then describe the studies on which

---

[1] All three authors shared equally in the preparation of this paper. The authors are listed alphabetically.

our analyses of multidigit multiplication and division are based. The main sections of the chapter focus on recent research on the development of children's multidigit multiplication and division concepts and procedures. We end the chapter with a discussion of these findings in relation to related research and potential implications for mathematics instruction.

Constructing Meaning
for Multiplication and Division

In this section, we first consider how children construct meaning and strategies for multiplication and division operations in general. We then describe the types of problems used in our study, namely types of equal-grouping problems.

INFORMAL KNOWLEDGE AND STRATEGIES

By the age of 5 or 6, children can begin to construct meaning for multiplication and division operations by solving problems that involve grouping or partitioning collections of discrete objects (e.g., Carpenter et al., 1993, Greer, 1992; Hiebert & Tonnesen, 1978; Kouba, 1989). These problems are accessible because young children encounter these situations in their daily lives and can easily model the situations in the problems using physical tools. Consider, for example, the following ("groups-of") multiplication problem involving equal groups of discrete objects:

> Myrna gave her four friends three candies each. How many candies did she give her friends altogether?

Without instruction, children as early as first grade solve this problem by creating four groups of three items (blocks, rods, tallies, and so forth) and then counting all the items (Kouba, 1989). Consider also the following ("fair-sharing") division problem:

> Four sisters bought 12 cookies and shared them so that each sister got the same number of cookies. How many cookies did each sister get?

Children as young as 4 years old are capable of using informal procedures to solve such division problems (Pepper & Hunting, 1998). A common strategy for the problem above is to produce 12 items, distribute them into three equal piles, and then count the number of items in one of the piles.

There are a variety of situations that can be represented by multiplication and division that involve more abstract concepts including measure, rate, multiplicative comparison, rectangular area, and Cartesian products. (Carpenter, Fennema, Franke, Empson, & Levi, 1999; Greer, 1992). These more abstract problems were not used in the analysis presented in this chapter. Our analysis focuses on multiplication and division problems involving equal groups of discrete objects.

TYPES OF EQUAL-GROUPING PROBLEMS

Equal-groups problems, like those illustrated earlier and in Fig. 11.1, involve three quantities: (a) *the number of groups* (the 5 plates), (b) *the number of objects in each group* (7 cookies on each plate), and (c) *the total number of objects* (35 cookies altogether). Any of the three quantities can be missing in an equal-groups problem. Problems that involve finding the last quantity ($a \times b = ?$) can be called *groups-of multiplication*; the first quantity (? $\times b = c$ or $c \div b = ?$), *measurement division*; and the second quantity ($a \times ? = c$ or $c \div a = ?$), *partitive division*.

Groups-of Multiplication

Just as children do not initially change the order of the numbers when solving a "change-add-to" addition problem (see Baroody, Wilkins, & Tilikainen, chap. 4, this volume), they do not initially change the order of the numbers when solving a groups-of multiplication problem. Their thinking is guided by the situation described in the problem, rather than by an understanding of the mathematical property of commutativity (Carpenter et al., 1999; Kouba & Franklin, 1993). In the real world, 5 plates of 7 cookies each (Problem A in Fig. 11.1) is different from that of 7 plates of 5 cookies each. Thus, children may not recognize that the outcome of these two problems will be the same. As a result, they calculate the product of these two problems in different ways. For 5 groups of 7, young children generally make 5 groups of 7 blocks each; for 7 groups of 5, they generally make 7 groups of 5 blocks each. As we illustrate in the following sections, the distinction between multiplier and multiplicand continues to play a role in children's strategies for solving multidigit multiplication problems through at least the upper elementary grades. As Problem A in Fig. 11.1 illustrates, the multiplier represents the number of groups (5 plates) and the multiplicand represents the number of items per group (7 cookies per plate).

Measurement and Partitive Division

Because either the number of groups (the multiplier) or the number of objects in each group (the multiplicand) can be missing, it follows that there are two distinct types of related division problems. For *measurement*-division problems (also called *quotitive*-division problems), the total number of objects and the number of objects in each group are given, and the unknown is the number of groups. For the *partitive*-division problem, the total number of objects and the number of groups are given, and the unknown is the number of objects in each group.

Just as children distinguish between multiplier and multiplicand in multiplication problems, they treat measurement and partitive-division problems quite differently and do not immediately recognize that the same process can be used to solve both types of problems. Specifically, young children tend to solve measurement-division problems by using a measure-out procedure: counting out the total number of objects, making groups with the given number in each group, and counting the number of groups. They solve partitive-division problems by using a dealing-out procedure: counting out the total, dividing the total into a

Figure 11.1: Concept Map Illustrating the Connections Among Types of Equal-Groups Problems

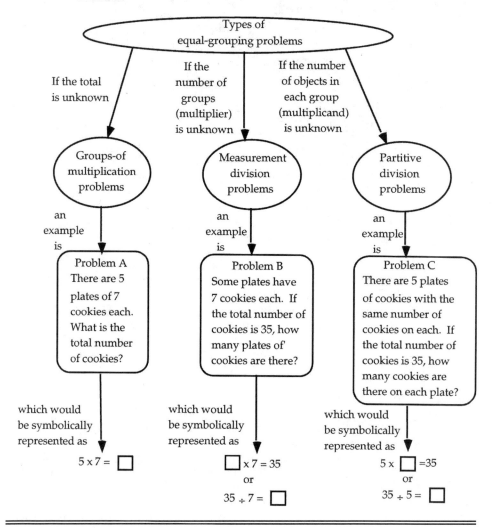

given number of groups so that there are the same number of objects in each group, and counting the number of objects in one of the groups. The distinction between measurement and partitive division continues to play out in children's strategies for solving multidigit division problems.

Our Studies of Multidigit Multiplication and Division

In this section, we briefly describe the studies on which our analyses of multidigit multiplication and division are based. Although children can and do construct their own procedures for adding, subtracting, multiplying, and dividing, their constructions do not take place in a vacuum. They are influenced by the contexts in which their problem-solving efforts takes place, including the nature of interactions with other children and adults, the tools available to represent and solve the problems, notational systems previously encountered or invented, and the like. Different programs of instruction provide different contexts for children's learning. As a result, different patterns of development of multidigit concepts and procedures have been observed. Some strategies may be more prevalent in some programs than in others. Notational systems used to represent the strategies may be different. Strategies dependent on the availability of a particular tool or notational system may not appear if the tool or notational system is not available (for a more complete discussion of some of these differences for addition and subtraction, see Beishuizen et al., 1997; Carpenter et al., 2000; or Hiebert et al., 1997). In spite of the differences, however, the research on addition and subtraction strategies suggests that there are underlying commonalities in the strategies children invent. That is, even with the diversity that is inevitable in different programs and classrooms, the basic multidigit strategies that children invent tend to fall into reasonably well-defined categories (Beishuizen et al., 1997; Fuson et al., 1997).

Our examples of children's invented multidigit multiplication and division strategies are derived from two primary data sources: a year-long field study in six elementary classrooms and a series of clinical interviews of students in three of the classrooms. One third-grade class, one fourth-grade class, one fifth-grade class, and three combination fourth- and fifth-grade classes were observed during mathematics instruction several times a week for an entire year. The classes were heterogeneous, representing a range of abilities and mathematical expertise. The children in the sample ranged in age from 8 to 11 years. The clinical interviews were conducted in the three combination fourth- and fifth-grade classes.

The class norms in all six classrooms focused on understanding mathematics (see Hiebert et al., 1997, for a detailed discussion of classrooms that focus on mathematical understanding). Each teacher expected the children to solve problems using strategies that they could explain to their classmates. In whole-group discussions, children were encouraged to analyze their peers' strategies and often were asked to compare and contrast strategies. Typically, four or five different solution strategies were discussed for a given problem, giving children the clear message that they could solve problems in any way that made sense to them. The teachers rarely introduced solution strategies. The standard algorithms were occasionally used by children who learned them at home. They were treated as viable options, only if the user could explain the steps with under-standing. Very few children adopted the standard algorithms as their favorite strategy.

With the emphasis on solving problems with understanding, there was a cor-responding de-emphasis on the acquisition of basic "number facts." The children were rarely drilled on the basic number combinations, and the teachers did not stress their acquisition as a central goal. Although the children occasionally had opportunities to test their knowledge of the multiplication tables, through games and exercises, most of the participants did not master all of the multiplication combinations.

In all of the classrooms, multidigit multiplication and division were covered in the first 3 months of school. Problems were typically given in story-problem contexts and interspersed with other mathematical topics. Multiplication prob-lems consisted of groups-of situations. Division problems involved either a measurement or a partitive situation. The teachers designed their own curricula and made their instructional decisions based on their knowledge of their stu-dents' thinking. Rather than treating multiplication as a prerequisite to the learning of division, division problems were given concurrently with multiplica-tion problems.

The examples of children's work in the next two sections illustrate the range of strategies that were observed. Although examples from individuals are used to illustrate a particular type of strategy, the strategies are representative in that a number of children were observed using each one.

The Development of Multidigit Multiplication Strategies

In this section, we discuss the types of multidigit multiplication procedures children invented, starting with the most concrete strategies and subsequently considering increasingly abstract strategies. We then discuss these strategies in terms of key aspects of their conceptual development.

TYPES OF STRATEGIES

Children's strategies for solving multidigit multiplication problems vary with their knowledge of addition, units, grouping by ten, place value, and prop-erties of the four basic operations. The most basic or concrete strategies entail the use of counters or base-ten materials to directly model problem situations. More abstract strategies build on children's knowledge of addition, doubling, and de-composition (e.g., $24 = 20 + 1 + 1 + 2$). Even more abstract strategies are based on knowledge of grouping by ten and place value.

Concrete Multiplication Strategies

Direct Modeling with No Partitioning of Factors. The most elementary strategies that children use to solve multidigit multiplication problems involve the use of individual counters to directly represent the problem. The most basic strategies are identical to those used with single-digit numbers. Consider the following groups-of problem: *Roberto made 6 plates of cookies. There were 23 cookies on each plate. How many cookies were there altogether?* Children might solve this problem by drawing 6 groups of 23 tally marks and then count the tallies one at a time. This solution requires little if any understanding of place-value concepts and is not fundamentally different from strategies that children use to solve single-digit problems.

Direct Modeling With Partitioning of the Multiplicand Into Tens and Ones. As children develop knowledge of base-ten number concepts, they begin to use base-ten materials rather than individual counters to model multidigit problems. For example, children might model the problem about Roberto's cookies by making six collections of base-ten blocks, each collection with 2 ten blocks and 3 ones blocks. They might then find the answer by counting the total by tens and ones.

As with addition and subtraction, this strategy can be abstracted to a procedure that is quite similar to the standard algorithm for multiplying by a one-digit multiplier. Without the blocks, children can conceive of the problem as six groups of 2 tens and six groups of 3 ones, or equivalently: 6 x 2 (tens) + 6 x 3 or 6 x 20 + 6 x 3. As with the standard algorithm, this solution depends on the distributive property and the ability to partition the multiplicand into its base-ten components. When children construct this procedure for themselves, they tend to use notation that is more transparent than the standard algorithm in illustrating both the distributive property and the base-ten number structure. They also tend to start at the left-most digit rather than starting at the right. Thus, operations with base-ten blocks may provide a concrete model that can be abstracted to a procedure for multiplying a multidigit number by a single-digit number that children carry out in their heads or with paper and pencil.

We call this kind of abstract strategy that does not involve manipulation of concrete materials an *invented algorithm*. In some articles we have referred to these strategies as *invented strategies* (Carpenter, Franke, Jacobs, & Fennema, 1998). We use the term *invented algorithm* because we do not want to imply that other more concrete strategies are not invented as well. It is important to recognize, however, that these invented algorithms lack the automatized quality that usually is associated with the term *algorithm*. Although invented algorithms may be automatized at some point, children tend to construct them anew to fit the problem at hand.

Limitations of Building on Concrete Strategies. Extrapolating from operations on physical materials is not so straightforward if the multiplier is a multidigit number. For example, a child might multiply 45 x 137 by making 45 sets of base-ten blocks representing 137. Not only would this process be extremely tedious, it would not provide a good model for abstracting procedures for multiplying by multidigit numbers. Efficient procedures for multiplying by multidigit numbers require some method of partitioning the multiplier, not just the multiplicand, and the solution described earlier does not do that. As a consequence, many of the procedures that children invent for multiplying multidigit numbers do not evolve directly from concrete models of groupings with base-ten materials.

Adding and Doubling Strategies

We next turn our attention to strategies that are not derived directly from abstractions of grouping base-ten blocks but are instead based on progressively more efficient techniques for adding. The most basic strategies also do not entail partitioning the multiplier, but increasingly efficient extensions of these strategies do provide a basis for doing so. The most basic abstract strategy entailed simply adding. For example, a child might solve the following problem by simply adding 34 seven times: *Aunt Sue bought 7 bags of candy for Halloween. Each bag had 34 pieces of candy. How many pieces of candy did Aunt Sue have?*

Doubling Strategy. Children soon learn to take advantage of the fact that the same number is being added to construct more efficient ways of calculating the sum. For example, Craig[2] wrote seven 34s vertically and then paired off 34s to generate three subtotals of 68. He continued pairing and generating subtotals to find his answer. Fig. 11.2 illustrates how each of the groups was represented as a numeral and doubling was used as a fast way to add the numbers. The doubling avoided the difficulty related to adding a long list of 4s and a long list of 3s (or 30s). Craig only had to add 34 and 34 once and then he knew his subtotal for the other two pairs. Doubling also utilized Craig's knowledge of addition combinations that were doubles. Doubles are combinations that children typically learn first (Carpenter, 1985). This grouping-by-two strategy is a natural step in using grouping to make calculation more efficient. The child creates a new iterable unit by clumping two of the multiplicands together. All of the subsequent strategies can be interpreted as more efficient versions of this primitive clumping procedure. In this particular solution the multiplicand was treated as a unit and was not decomposed. Often children partition the multiplicand and double the tens and ones places separately.

Complex-Doubling Strategies. Craig's strategy represents a relatively small step conceptually and by itself does not entail any notion that the multiplier can be partitioned. More powerful forms of doubling, however, are not only more efficient, they represent conceptual advances that pave the way for partitioning the multiplier. In complex-doubling strategies, children did not represent each of the multiplicands in the problem. For example, consider how Dana solved the following problem: *There are 47 children in a downhill ski club. A trip to Devil's Head costs 34 dollars for each child. How much does it cost to take everyone in the club on the trip?* Dana made the table shown in Fig. 11.3. She doubled both the number of children and the dollars until she would have exceeded the number of children going on the ski trip if she doubled again. She then added the number of dollars for 16 and 32 children to figure out the amount for 48 children (because 16 groups of 34 and 32 groups of 34 is equivalent to 48 groups of 34). Finally, she took away 34 dollars from this amount because the problem called for 47 groups of 34, not 48 groups. Note that Dana did not need to list each of the 47 children's 34-dollar skiing cost. Instead she kept doubling to create a new unit involving a given number of children and the associated cost for that number of children. Her notation allowed her to keep track of the number of children as well as the dollars associated with each as they were doubled and to make necessary adjust-

---

[2] All names are pseudonyms.

Figure 11.2: Craig's Invented Algorithm for 7 Groups of 34

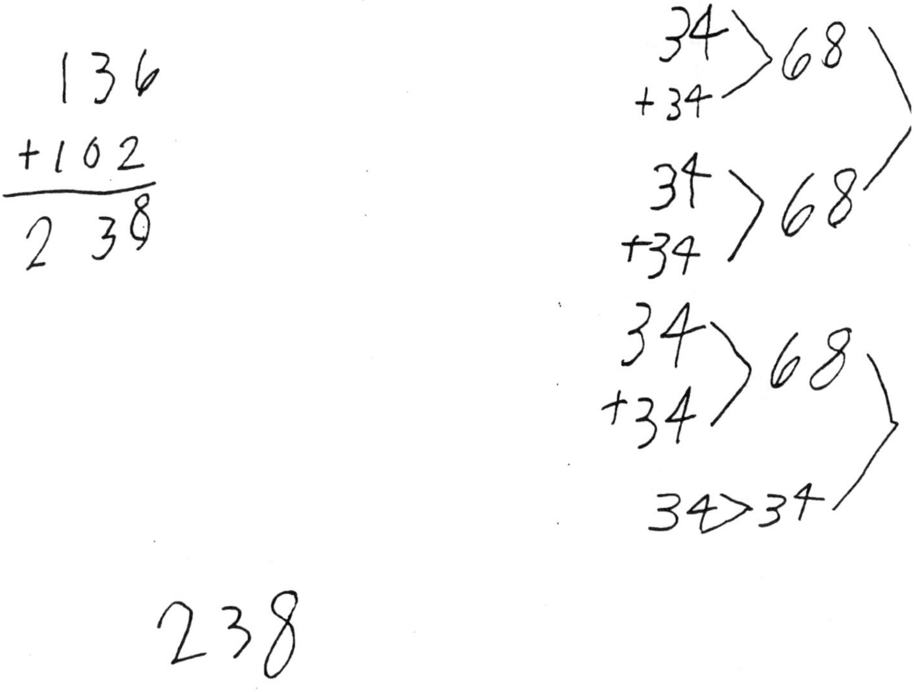

$$136$$
$$+102$$
$$\overline{2\ 38}$$

$$34 \rangle 68$$
$$+34$$

$$34 \rangle 68$$
$$+34$$

$$34 \rangle 68$$
$$+34$$

$$34 \rangle 34$$

$$238$$

Figure 11.3: Dana's Invented Algorithm for 47 Groups of 34

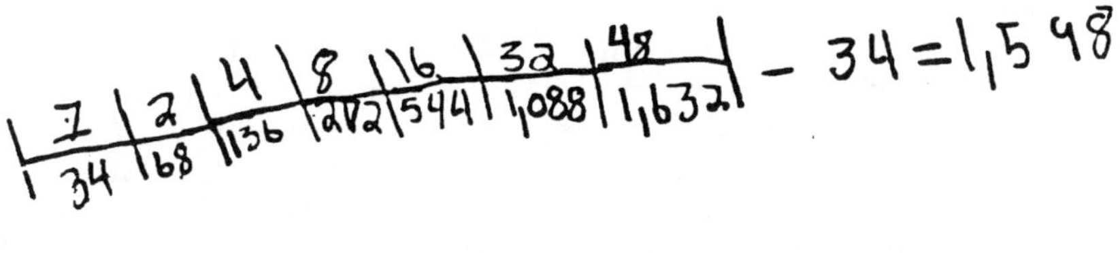

7	2	4	8	16	32	48
34	68	136	272	544	1,088	1,632

$$- 34 = 1,598$$

ments. Whereas Craig did not have to keep track of how many multiplicands he had added (because his first step involved writing all of the multiplicands), Dana's doubling strategy required this keeping-track process.

Although Dana's strategy did not utilize the base-ten structure of the multiplier, it did essentially entail partitioning the multiplier into units of 32, 16 and 1, and it made implicit use of the distributive and associative properties. Symbolically, Dana's doubling strategy could be represented as:

$$
\begin{aligned}
47 \times 34 &= (32 + 16 - 1) \times 34 \\
&= [(2 \times 2 \times 2 \times 2 \times 2) + (2 \times 2 \times 2 \times 2) - 1] \times 34 \\
&= (2 \times 2 \times 2 \times 2 \times 2) \times 34 + (2 \times 2 \times 2 \times 2) \times 34 - 1 \times 34 \\
&= 2(2(2(2(2 \times 34)))) + 2(2(2(2 \times 34))) - 34
\end{aligned}
$$

Although the doubling calculations are relatively easy, this notation illustrates the mathematical complexity of the strategy and makes explicit how Dana actually drew on the distributive and associative properties of multiplication as she created new units. We are not proposing that Dana had explicit understanding of the distributive and associative properties. It is doubtful that she did, but she did implicitly use them in appropriate ways.

Doubling came naturally to children. The teachers did not need to do much scaffolding with them as they worked through the doubling invented algorithms. Dana's invented algorithm can be seen as support for Confrey's (1994) assertion that splitting is a primitive notion that children develop alongside their notions of additive relations. Dana took advantage of the rapid nature of exponential growth as her multiplier and multiplicand doubled with each iteration, and in this sense she was using splitting notions, but her use of addition to create the iterations reflects additive notions.

Building Up by Other Factors. Doubling strategies can become quite automatic. Dana seemed to begin doubling both quantities without any significant planning. She began to reason about the multiplier only when she got to the point where repeated doubling would have exceeded the multiplier. Other invented algorithms involved planning from the start. In the following example, Bob considered how the multiplier might be built up in advance. He was solving the following problem: *An elementary school has 24 classes. If there are 32 children in each class, how many children are there at the school.* As Fig. 11.4 shows, he noticed that the 24 could be decomposed into 20 + 1 + 1 + 2 and further that 20 could be decomposed into 5 × 4. He first added up five 32s using the conventional column addition algorithm. Then he added four 160s to figure out the number of children in 20 classes. He added 32 to his running total and then added another 32 to figure out 22 classes. He then added two 32s at the side and added 64 to his running total to achieve his final answer. He explained: "I added this up. I added 5 up. That was 160. I did that 4 times and that would be 20 [classes]. After that, that was 640 [children]. I plused 32, that would be 21 classes. Plus one more class would be 22 classes. Plus two more classes would be 24. That would be 768 [children]." Bob's explanation shows how easily he could switch back and forth between the two dimensions in the problem. He was able to keep track of the number of classrooms he was working with without writing this down for each of his calculations.

Figure 11.4: Bob's Invented Algorithm for 24 Groups of 32

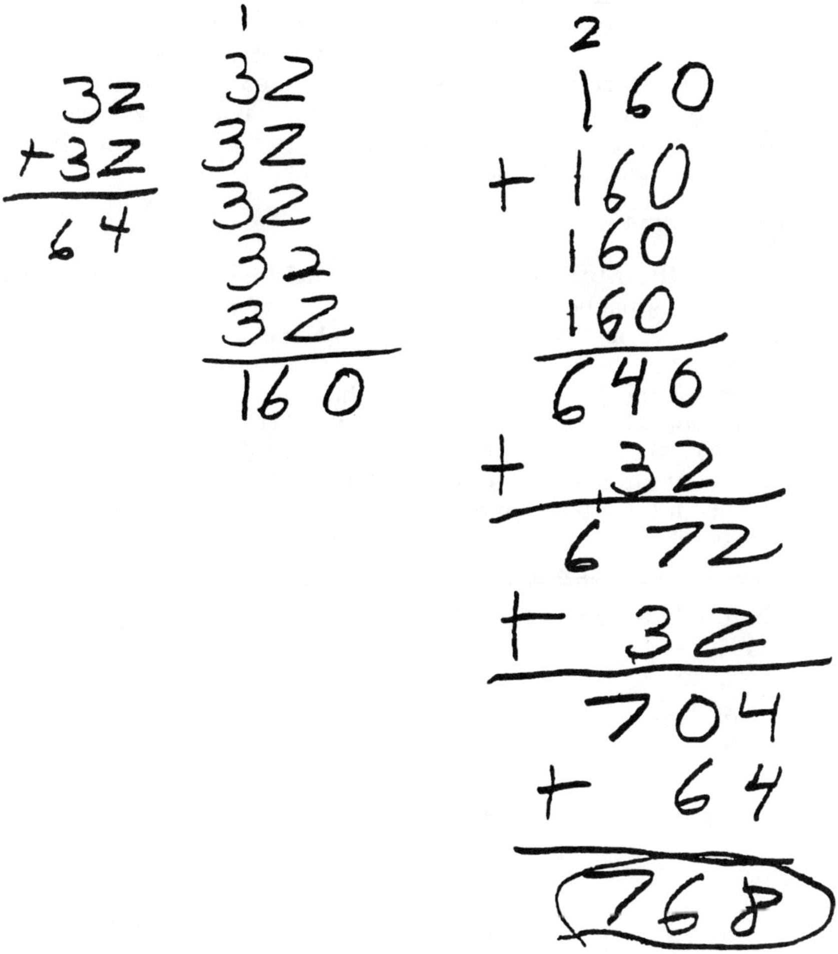

Symbolically, Bob's work consisted of the following:

$$
\begin{aligned}
24 \times 32 \;=\;& (20 + 1 + 1 + 2) \times 32 \\
=\;& [(4 \times 5) + 1 + 1 + 2] \times 32 \\
=\;& [(4 \times 5) \times 32] + (1 \times 32) + (1 \times 32) + (2 \times 32) \\
=\;& [4 \times (5 \times 32)] + 32 + 32 + (2 \times 32) \\
=\;& (4 \times 160) + 32 + 32 + 64
\end{aligned}
$$

The symbolic representation shows that Bob implicitly used the distributive and associative properties. Although the calculations he performed were fairly simple, the strategy involves some relatively sophisticated thinking.

Although the doubling and building-up strategies required number sense and understanding of number properties, we initially thought that doubling algorithms might be a dead end in that they did not appear to provide a direct path to developing strategies that would use base-ten principles. We came to realize that doubling strategies could provide a basis for developing strategies involving multiples of ten as the unit. The critical concept involved in the complex-doubling strategies is that the multiplier can be partitioned into units larger than one. Because of the unique properties of ten in our number system, partitioning the multiplier based on units of multiples of ten provides the most power. We turn next to invented algorithms that use ten as a unit.

Invented Algorithms Using Tens

Partitioning the Multiplier Into Tens and Ones. One of the least sophisticated strategies that begins to make use of groupings of ten is illustrated by the strategy John used to solve the following problem: *A card store has 43 boxes of cards for Thanksgiving Day. Each box has 24 cards. How many Thanksgiving Day cards does the card store have?* As Fig. 11.5 shows, John listed ten 24s and added them using the conventional column addition algorithm. This resulted in a new unit corresponding to 240 cards per 10 boxes. He then added 240 four times to determine the number of cards for 40 boxes. He added 24 three times to determine the number of cards in three boxes and added this sum to the running total to determine his answer.

Figure 11.5: John's Invented Algorithm for 43 Groups of 24

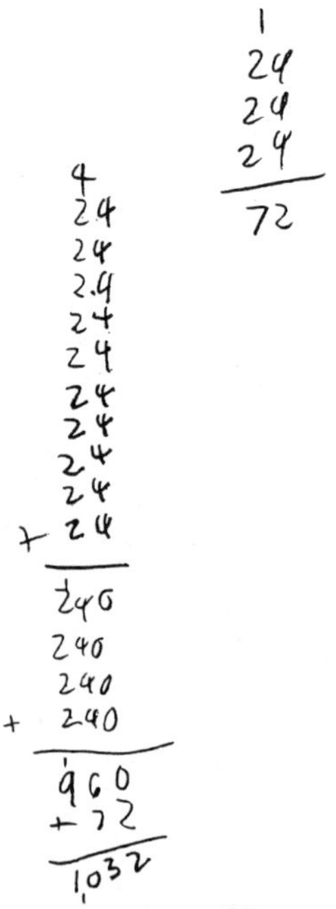

John was able to use base-ten thinking to decompose the multiplier of 43 into 40 and 3 and further into 4 x 10 + 3, but his knowledge of tens was limited in that he did not immediately recognize that ten 24s is 240.

Other children were capable of automatically computing ten 24s as Tim did for the same Thanksgiving card problem (Fig. 11.6). Neither John nor Tim explicitly noted the number of boxes involved in each of their subtotals but kept track of this in their head.

Partitioning Both Multiplier and Multiplicand. In the invented algorithms described thus far, the multiplicand has not been partitioned. More sophisticated invented algorithms decomposed both the multiplier and the multiplicand as illustrated by Sean's solution to the Thanksgiving card problem (Fig. 11.7). He set up a table with 4 and 3 on the top. He said that he kept 24 in his head and multiplied 20 by 40 and 20 by 3. Then he multiplied 4 (from 24) by 40 and by 3. Finally, he added the four partial products up and got his answer 1032. This invented algorithm differs from the others in that Sean used multiplication to calculate all four partial products. All of the other invented algorithms we

Figure 11.6: Tim's Invented Algorithm for 43 Groups of 24

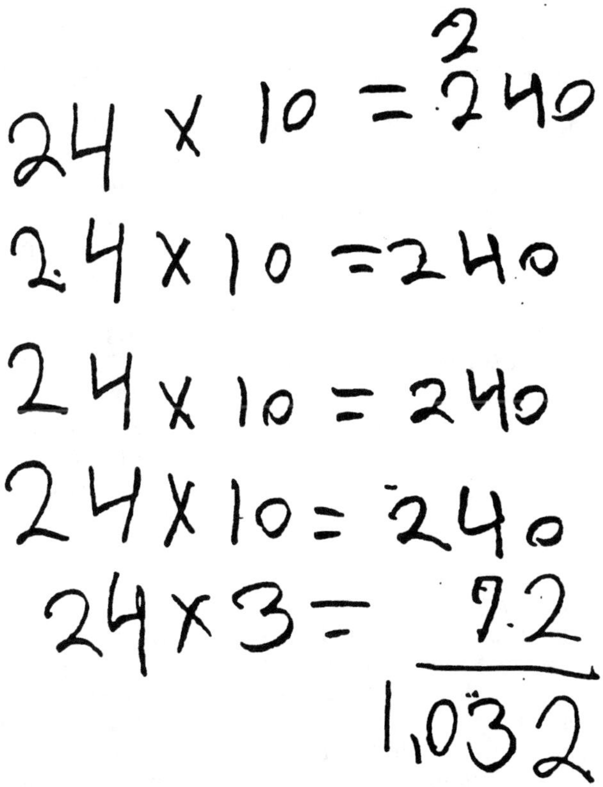

$$24 \times 10 = \overset{2}{2}40$$
$$24 \times 10 = 240$$
$$24 \times 10 = 240$$
$$24 \times 10 = 240$$
$$24 \times 3 = \underline{72}$$
$$1,032$$

Figure 11.7: Sean's Invented Algorithm for 43 Groups of 24

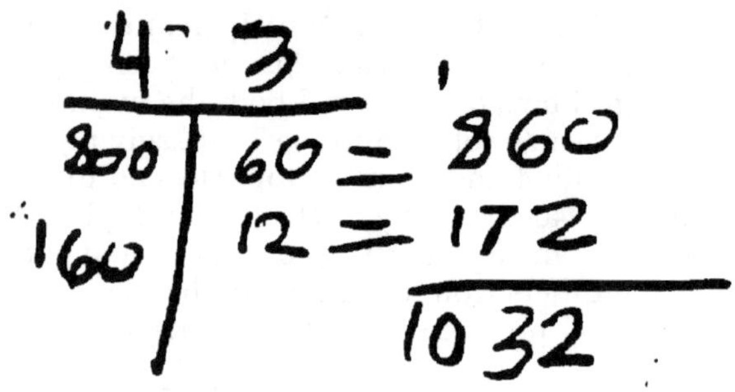

have described involved addition to do most of the calculations. The only direct multiplication that was used in previous invented algorithms was when Tim multiplied 24 by 10.

When Sean decomposed both numbers, it seems that he lifted the quantities out of the particular context of the problem and worked with them independently. Decomposing both quantities suggests a higher level of understanding of multidigit multiplication. Most of the invented algorithms we observed did not evidence this kind of abstraction and were more rooted in the particulars of the problem.

THE RELATION BETWEEN INVENTED MULTIPLICATION STRATEGIES AND TWO KEY CONCEPTS

In this subsection, we discuss how a failure to take into account an understanding of multiplicative commutativity and how an understanding of grouping (the creation of larger units) affected children's invented strategies.

Commutativity

For all types of strategies, word-problem contexts exerted a strong influence on children's decisions about what to do with the numbers in the problem. When problems described situations involving *a* groups with *b* objects in each group, many children in our study did not seem to recognize that they could reconceptualize the problem as *b* groups with *a* objects in each group. For example, one of the problems we observed children solve was *Mr. Party has 153 bags of balloons at his party-product store. Each bag has 37 balloons. How many balloons does Mr. Party have at his store?* Many children tended to think of this problem strictly in terms of 153 groups of 37 units. They were not inclined to use the commutative property to switch the numbers around, even though it might have made calculation easier. In brief, as discussed earlier for change-add-to situations (Baroody et al., chap. 4, this volume), the commutative property was not readily applied to problems because children's thinking was so tightly linked to the story-problem contexts.

The failure to capitalize on the commutative property stood out in the ways in which children dealt with units of ten. We found that children could easily calculate 24 times 10, for example, but did not use this knowledge to compute ten 24s. Consider the case of John. To determine the total of 10 boxes of 24 cards each, he laboriously added ten 24s instead of reformulating the problem as 24 tens, which he knew to be 240. In other words, when 10 was the multiplier, as in 10 groups of 24, many students repeatedly added the multiplicand. When 10 was the multiplicand, as in 24 groups of ten, children typically applied their base-ten understanding to automatically generate the product.

Why was the children's knowledge of 10 groups of n and n groups of ten so disconnected? It appears that the children knew that 24 groups of ten was 240 from the base-ten activities they had engaged in. These activities involve making groups of ten, not making 10 groups. The children did not see the connection between groups of ten and 10 groups. This difficulty seemed to limit the children's use of base-ten notions in their invented algorithms and might have influenced them to use doubling strategies.

It is striking that children made implicit use of associative and distributive properties but often failed to do so with the commutative property of multiplication, even when it could have made their calculation easier. The commutative property is typically considered easier for children to learn than the distributive property. From the strategies children used, it was clear that they could not utilize commutativity when solving problems in story contexts. They might be able to switch numbers around when dealing with symbols on paper but they do not readily make this switch when the numbers arise in a context.

As the children develop understanding of the commutative property, we would expect that they would begin transferring this understanding to their solution of story problems, allowing them greater flexibility in their problem solving. It is not clear that this understanding will evolve from demonstrations of the property using specific concrete or symbolic examples. Contexts involving arrays, area, or Cartesian products in which the role of the factors is not distinct could provide children with a basis for understanding and discussing commutativity. These problem types could be inserted into instruction along with the more common problems in which the roles of the factors are distinct so that children could integrate an understanding of commutativity into their understanding of their invented strategies. See Schliemann, Araujo, Cassundé, Macedo, and Nicéas (1998) for additional discussion of commutativity of multiplication in and out of school.

Creation of New Units

Many of the invented multidigit multiplication algorithms involved the creation of new units as the children built up to the final product. These new units were used to compute other units. For example, after determining that 5 classrooms of 32 students each had a total of 160 students, Bob treated 5 classrooms of 160 students as a unit that could be used to make further calculations. Dana's invented algorithm involved the creation of a new unit with each iteration of her solution. She used these various units to compose her final product. John created new units as he figured out that 10 boxes of 24 greeting cards would have 240 cards. All of these children used addition in order to create their new units.

The creation of new units from additive processes may provide a transition to the multiplicative reasoning that underlies proportional thinking among other things. Hiebert and Behr (1988) proposed that middle school mathematics (including emphasis on multiplicative and ratio thinking) represents a break in the fluid growth of additive conceptions, and that children have to think about numbers in new ways. Steffe (1988) proposed that children have to construct what he referred to as iterable units. He indicated that this was difficult for children. Dana's invented doubling algorithm, along with Bob's, Tim's, and John's invented algorithms all involved the creation of iterable units and in some cases multiple iterable units. It is notable that children could create these iterable units using addition. This calls into question whether the break that Hiebert and Behr proposed is as dramatic as they suggested. The invented algorithms we have outlined combine additive computation with work with iterable units. The children used their ability to add and incorporated it into mathematically complex invented algorithms that incorporated aspects of both the associative and distributive properties.

The Development
of Multidigit Division Strategies

In this section, we discuss the types of multidigit division procedures children invented, starting with the most concrete and subsequently consider increasingly abstract strategies. We then discuss the relation of these strategies to those invented for multidigit multiplication.

TYPES OF STRATEGIES

Just as distinctions between the role of multiplier and multiplicand played a critical role in children's multiplication strategies, differences between measurement- and partitive-division problems were manifest in distinctly different invented algorithms. At a very basic level, children as early as kindergarten can model both measurement- and partitive-division problems with concrete objects (Carpenter et al., 1993; Kouba, 1989; Kouba & Franklin, 1993). As with multiplication, they can also apply their knowledge of addition and subtraction to solve division problems. At the most basic level, addition or subtraction procedures apply most readily to measurement division situations.

Working With One Group at a Time

Repeated Subtraction or Addition for Measurement-Division Problems. Consider Joel's solution of the following measurement-division problem: *There were 180 peppers and they were sold in bundles of 6. How many bundles were there?* As Fig. 11.8 illustrates, Joel repeatedly took away 6, keeping track of his intermediate results. He continued to subtract until he arrived at 0 and then had to count how many subtractions he had made. For this same problem, some children began with 6 and repeatedly added 6 until they reached a total of 180. They talked about making bundles and keeping track of how many peppers they had used so far. These invented algorithms were rather long and there was potential for computational error. They are similar to the primitive multiplication invented algorithms in which children listed each of the multiplicands in the problem and then added them.

Figure 11.8: Joel's Invented Algorithm for 180 Divided Into Groups of 6

$$
\begin{array}{r}
180 \\
- \ 6 \\
\hline
174 \\
- \ 6 \\
\hline
168 \\
- \ 6 \\
\hline
162 \\
- \ 6 \\
\hline
156 \\
- \ 6 \\
\hline
150 \\
- \ 6 \\
\hline
144 \\
- \ 6 \\
\hline
138 \\
- \ 6 \\
\hline
132 \\
- \ 6 \\
\hline
126 \\
- \ 6 \\
\hline
120 \\
- \ 6 \\
\hline
114 \\
- \ 6 \\
\hline
\text{etc.}
\end{array}
$$

Distributive Strategy for Partitive-Division Problems. Repeated subtraction or addition is infrequently used for partitive-division problems because the number of elements in each set is the unknown and children do not know what number to subtract or add. Children could, however, begin to use base-ten concepts to solve partitive-division problems using visual representations as illustrated by Tiffany's solution of the following partitive-division problem: *Twelve children were sharing 228 M&Ms. How many should each child get?* As Fig. 11.9 shows, Tiffany performed the sharing articulated in the problem as she imagined distributing candies to children. Tiffany began by drawing the 12 boxes to represent the children and then wrote 10 in each box, counting by ten as she wrote, "10, 20, 30, . . . 120." Then she wrote 5 in each box as she counted on by fives, "125, 130, 135, . . . 180." Then she wrote a 2 in each box as she continued counting by twos, "182, 184, 186, . . . 204," and finally she wrote another 2 in each box as she counted on by twos, "204, 206, 208, . . . 228." Tiffany completed the problem by adding the numbers in one box to arrive at the answer of 19. Her verbal counts kept track of the running total that she was generating. She did not write these down, although with larger numbers she might lose track of her counts and have to recount.

Tiffany chose to use numbers she was comfortable with and organized her invented algorithm using skills she was confident in, counting by tens, fives and twos. In her written work she represented each of the 12 groups in the multiplier and wrote a number for each count that she made. Although Tiffany represented her solution with pictures and Joel did not, Tiffany's solution actually involved more conceptual knowledge about base-ten numbers that could provide a basis for developing more sophisticated invented algorithms.

More Advanced Abstract Strategies
That Do Not Involve Decomposition

Both Joel and Tiffany represented all of the groups into which items were partitioned, Joel by writing numbers representing each group and Tiffany by constructing a picture of each group and distributing units of 10, 5, and 2 into

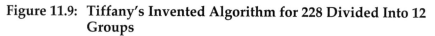

Figure 11.9: Tiffany's Invented Algorithm for 228 Divided Into 12 Groups

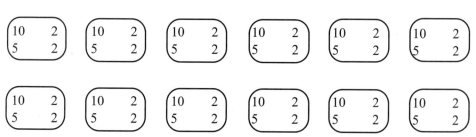

each of the groups. A major advance comes with children's ability to abstract the process so that they do not actually have to represent each of the groups. This advance parallels the complex-doubling strategy for multidigit multiplication that was illustrated by Dana's solution in Fig. 11.3. Children using these strategies recognize that any one group can serve as a representative of all the groups, because they all contain the same number of elements. This allows them to add or subtract multiples of the number of objects in each group to solve a measurement-division problem or to add or subtract multiples of the number of groups to solve a partitive-division problem. Tiffany was able to put multiple numbers of objects in each group, but she still needed to construct each group.

Although abstract modeling (not modeling each group) represents a major advance in children's thinking, their flexibility is still limited, and the distinction between partitive- and measurement-division problems continues to affect their solution strategies.

Using Tens in Partitive-Division Problems. Lynna's invented algorithm for the following partitive-division problem demonstrates the ease with which some children used tens in this kind of problem. *Hattie had 544 candies to share with her friends. She gave each of her 17 friends the same amount of candy. How many candies did each friend get?* As Fig. 11.10 illustrates, Lynna began with the dividend and subtracted 170 from it. It is important to note that Lynna conceived of this operation as subtracting 17 units of ten, not 10 units of 17. She knew the number of groups and was taking away 10 units from the total of 544 for each group. There are similarities between this strategy and Tiffany's. The difference is that Lynna was able to conceive of the 17 tens as a unit and did not have to construct each of the 17 groups as Tiffany did.

It appears that it was easy for Lynna to use units of ten, but she may have more difficulty taking larger units like 30. This choice required that she subtract 170 three times. For both multiplication and division, we saw children repeatedly multiplying by 10 rather than by multiples of ten. As one child reported in analyzing this invented algorithm, "If you know how to times with 10 then this

---

Figure 11.10: Lynna's Invented Algorithm for 544 Divided Into 17 Groups

544	
− 170	10 candies for each friend
374	
− 170	10 candies for each friend
204	
− 170	10 candies for each friend
34	
− 34	2 candies for each friend
0	32 candies for each friend

---

strategy is good for you." The child's perspective highlights that the skill that preceded utilizing this kind of strategy was a mechanism for multiplying, particularly multiplying by 10 or a power of 10.

This invented algorithm required some kind of keeping-track mechanism so the child would be able to go back through the problem to determine how many candies had been distributed. Some children explicitly noted what each subtraction represented, whereas others did this in their head. These solutions involved applying the distributive property. Symbolically the strategy involved the following:

$$544 - 17 \times 10 - 17 \times 10 - 17 \times 10 - 17 \times 2 = 544 - 17 \times (10 + 10 + 10 + 2) = 544 - 17 \times 32.$$

This invented algorithm bears some resemblance to the standard U.S. algorithm in that it involves alternating multiplication and subtraction. It departs from the standard distributive algorithm in that the child did not have to round the divisor and then estimate a quotient. In addition, the child treated the dividend as 544 rather than the abbreviated 54.

Using Tens in Measurement Division Problems.[3] Using a similar invented algorithm for measurement division requires that the child be able to think in terms of 10 groups of a given number of items in each group rather than a given number of groups of ten. This distinction is seen in the following two examples for the measurement-division problem: *The student council picked 896 apples and packaged them in bags with 35 apples in each bag. How many bags did they fill?* Aaron solved the problem by inventing the procedure illustrated in Fig. 11.11. His procedure is a measurement-division version of Lynne's invented algorithm for partitive-division illustrated in Fig. 11.10 and involves, in part, using 10 groups of 35. As we noted earlier, calculating 10 groups of 35 does not come as easily as calculating 35 groups of ten, and some children who could use groups of ten for partitive-division problems did not do so when they solved measurement-division problems. Rather, they used numbers they were more comfortable with, as exemplified by the invented algorithm in Fig. 11.12. In this much longer invented algorithm, the child worked with 1, 2, and then 3 groups of 35. He might have chosen to work with 3 groups of 35 because he was comfortable subtracting the number 105. The efficiency of working with 10 groups of 35 did not occur to him.

A Strategy That Involves Decomposing the Dividend

The invented algorithms discussed to this point dealt with the dividend as a composite quantity that children subtracted from. The invented algorithm discussed next involves decomposing the dividend. Although the U.S. standard division algorithm allows one to focus on parts of the dividend in performing each calculation, it essentially treats the dividend as a whole; additional parts of the

---

[3] The standard U.S. division algorithm refers to the traditional long-division algorithm, which involves starting with largest denomination in the dividend first and "pulling down" subsequent digits from the dividend. This procedure is sometimes identified as the "distributive algorithm." Note that invented procedure described in the text bears a strong resemblance to the less well-known subtractive or Greenwood algorithm.

Figure 11.11: Aaron's Invented Algorithm for 896 Divided Into Groups of 35

```
  896
 -350        10 bags
  546
 -350        10 bags
  196
 - 70         2 bags
  126
 - 70         2 bags
   56
 - 35         1 bag
   21
```

Figure 11.12: Another Invented Algorithm for 896 Divided Into Groups of 35

```
  896
 - 35         1
  861
 - 70         2
  791
 -105         3
  686
 -105         3
  581
 -105         3
  476
 -105         3
  371
 -105         3
  266
 -105         3
  161
 -105         3
   56
 - 35         1
   21        25
```

divisor are brought down as one subtracts successive multiples of the divisor. Standard U.S. addition, subtraction, and multiplication algorithms, on the other hand, partition each of the numbers for calculation purposes, and most addition and subtraction invented algorithms involve similar partitioning. We have seen that some invented multiplication and division algorithms leave one of the terms intact, but some children are inclined to generalize the notion of partitioning. Although it is not particularly efficient, one type of invented algorithm that we observed a number of children use involved breaking the dividend into component parts and then aggregating the results. For example, in solving the apple problem described previously, Robin began by looking at the dividend and broke it into ones, tens, and hundreds. As Fig. 11.13 shows, she partitioned 896 into 800, 90, and 6. She first divided 6 by 35 and got a quotient of 0 with 6 left over. Robin then divided 90 by 35 by adding two 35s and got 20 left over. She then worked on 800 ÷ 35 breaking 800 into 700 plus 100 and recognizing there are twenty 35s in 700 and two more 35s with 30 left over in 100. Robin added all the leftovers and realized that there was one more 35 in it. She added all of the quotients and figured out her answer, 25 groups of 35 with 21 left over.

Robin's invented algorithm was cumbersome to use because each of the three divisions generated remainders that had to be accumulated and then had to be accounted for. The invented algorithm required a great deal of keeping track and monitoring and involved several steps, leaving many opportunities for errors. Although the computation might have been unwieldy, the invented algorithm reflects an insightful use of the mathematical properties associated with division. She considered the total items that were to be divided up and made subproblems using parts of the dividend. In each subproblem she used various methods to derive the quotient. Robin demonstrated flexibility in adapting this algorithm to partitive or measurement situation.

Division as Building Up

Although division is often described as repeated subtraction, Kamii (1994) noted that children frequently solve division problems by adding up in some

---

Figure 11.13: Robin's Decomposing the Dividend for 896 Divided Into Groups of 35

$896 \div 35$

$6 \div 35 = 0$ with 6 left over

$90 \div 35 \rightarrow 35 + 35 = 70$; two 35s with 20 left over

$800 \div 35 \rightarrow 35 + 35 = 70$; $70 \times 10 = 700$; 20 35s with 100 left over;
two more 35s with 30 left over

$6 + 20 + 30 = 56$ leftovers, which will make one more group of 35 with 21 left over

$0 + 2 + 20 + 2 + 1 = 25$ groups of 35

way. Similarly, we found that participants used invented additive algorithms for both partitive- and measurement-division problems. Consider, for example, Hattie's candy problem (544 candies shared among 17 children). For this partitive-division problem, a majority of the children we studied invented the building-up algorithm illustrated in Fig. 11.14.

Essentially the invented additive division algorithms treat division as a multiplication problem with a missing factor. Every kind of multiplication invented algorithm that we have described was adapted for division problems. The difference was that instead of adding up the quantity a given number of times, the children kept adding until they reached the desired total. As with other invented algorithms, children had to keep track of what each addend represented, and then combine these quantities either as they were going along or at the end of their calculation. These invented division algorithms were analogous to the invented algorithms used by the children to solve join-change-unknown problems,[4] in that they built up to a target and kept track of how many steps they had made. Children were as facile with these division invented algorithms as they were with multiplication invented algorithms. The steps involved were no more complicated or difficult, and children became quite adept at using them.

Occasionally in building up to the dividend children would exceed it. As with the invented "overshoot and compensate" algorithm for join-change-unknown problems (Fuson et al., 1997), this typically did not bother them as they would make adjustments. For example, the strategy illustrated in Fig. 11.15 was used to solve the following problem: *There are 810 fifth graders at the District Olympics. They are placed in teams of 6. How many teams will there be?* Note that the depicted strategy involves overshooting the building-up process (resulting in an entry of 1,538 in the first column), (over)compensating by subtracting 384 twice, and compensating for this overcompensation by adding 24 and then three groups of 6. Although this invented algorithm may seem rather inefficient, the child who used it was able to discuss his work to show how he was able to keep track of his quantities, and he saw how he could adjust the invented algorithm to make it less cumbersome.

Figure 11.14: Building Up Invented Algorithm for 544 Divided Into 17 Groups

170	10 candies/friend
170	10 candies/friend
340	
170	10 candies/friend
510	
34	2 candies/friend
	32 candies/friend

---

[4] An example of a join-change-unknown problem is *Tess has 7 dollars. How much more money does she need to earn to buy a puppy that costs $11?* Children often solve this by counting on from *seven* to *eleven* and keeping track of the number of counts they make.

Figure 11.15: Overshoot and Compensate Invented Algorithm for 810 Divided Into Groups of 6

6	1
6	1
6	1
6	1
24	4
24	4
24	4
24	4
96	16
96	16
96	16
96	16
384	64
384	64
384	64
384	64
1536	256
− 384	− 64
1152	192
− 384	− 64
768	128
+ 24	+ 4
792	132
+ 6	+ 1
798	133
+ 6	+ 1
804	134
+ 6	+ 1
810	135

The invented building-up algorithms avoided one of the difficulties often associated with multidigit division, estimating a quotient. Rather than look at the dividend and think about how many divisors might fit into it, the children worked with quantities with which they were familiar as they built up to the dividend. By interpreting division problems as additive problems, children were able to use their doubling strategies. When children initiated division problems as subtraction they were less likely to use doubling strategies. For example, Margie solved the following partitive-division problem in two ways: *The geologists had 1548 rocks, which they put into 36 piles. How many rocks were in each pile?* (Fig. 11.16) The first way included taking away from the total quantity, which she did consistently with 10 in each group. When she executed the second invented algorithm, she started from 0 and worked up to the total. Rather than working with the same unit each time, her unit changed from 10 in each group, to 20 each group, to 40 in each group. To change units in this way for the subtractive invented algorithm would have required that she include an extra step of doubling her decrementing unit.

In the subtraction version of her invented division algorithm, Margie may have gotten so engaged in the work of subtracting the multidigit numbers and the borrowing involved that she did not look critically at her answer to decide if she might subtract a larger group of 36s. She would have had to disengage from her subtraction work to experiment with creating a larger group of 36s. In the second invented algorithm she could examine her total to decide if she wanted to continue adding 360s or to add larger chunks.

Discussion of Division Strategies

The children did not find division to be significantly different or more demanding than multiplication. They were able to adapt their invented multiplication algorithms to the division situations without much trouble. In fact, many of the invented division algorithms were essentially mirror images of corresponding invented multiplication algorithms. The technique of keeping the multiplicand intact, which was employed in most of the invented multiplication algorithms, was readily adapted to division problems. The standard U.S. multiplication algorithm, in which both of the factors are decomposed, look quite different from the standard U.S. division algorithm. Thus, it is arguable that children's invented algorithms for multiplication are better aligned with their division procedures than is the case for the standard multiplication and division al-

---

Figure 11.16: Margie's Invented Subtracting and Building-Up Algorithms for 1548 Divided Into 36 Groups

1548			360	
− 360	10		360	20
1188			720	
− 360	20		720	40
828			1440	
− 360	30		36	41
468			1476	
− 360	40		36	42
108			1512	
− 36	41		36	43
72				
− 36	42			
36				
−36	43			
00				

---

gorithms. Furthermore, by attempting division before they had fine-tuned their multiplication algorithms, children had opportunities to develop understanding of the links between the two operations.

Conclusions

ADAPTIVE EXPERTISE

Children's use of multiplication strategies to solve division problems exemplifies the adaptive expertise that grows out of understanding. The children were able to capitalize on their existing knowledge to tackle complicated problems. Their knowledge was so well connected that they could adapt and apply it to a variety of problems. In effect, this meant that they could develop one strategy to work through two kinds of problems, rather than learning a separate strategy for each type of problem. Their experiences inventing their own algorithms allowed them to build this adaptive expertise.

Another example of adaptive expertise is the way that the children employed their implicit understanding of the associative and distributive properties in their invented algorithms. Their implicit understanding of these properties allowed them to overcome their limited knowledge of multiplication combinations as they solved problems involving fairly large numbers. The complex-doubling strategy was a particularly efficient way to obtain an answer using simple processes. The children took the skills they had and applied them in creative and effective ways to a variety of problems, making the most of the skills that they had at their disposal.

COMPARING INVENTED
AND STANDARD ALGORITHMS

There are fundamental differences between invented and standard algorithms. Standard algorithms have evolved over centuries for efficient, accurate calculation, and for the most part are far removed from their conceptual underpinnings. Invented algorithms, on the other hand, are derived directly from underlying concepts of base-ten numbers, fundamental principles of multiplication and division, and relations among multiplication and division and other operations. The compact notation of standard algorithms tends to mask the underlying principles that make them work. For example, in the standard U.S. multiplication algorithm, single digits are multiplied without regard to values the digits represent or why it is possible to break multidigit numbers apart and multiply single digits. The place-value concepts and distributive and associative properties that underlie the operations are obscured by the notational efficiency of the algorithm. The principled basis of the standard U.S. division algorithm is even more difficult to unpack. For most invented algorithms, the underlying conceptual structure is more apparent. Because students construct invented algorithms based on their understanding of the situation, the principles that underlie the invented algorithms are closer to the surface.

The purpose of any algorithm is to reduce a complex calculation into a series of smaller calculations that can be performed using other well-established procedures or well-known number combinations. The standard multiplication and division algorithms break multidigit computations down into a series of calculations involving single-digit numbers so that mastered number combinations can be applied. Our examples illustrate that this is not uniformly the case with invented algorithms. Many of the invented algorithms that children construct do not involve breaking the problem down into single-digit multiplication problems. Rather, children often tend to keep at least one of the numbers in the calculation intact and simplify the calculation by multiplying by 10, doubling, or adding. This potentially reflects the fact that the children we studied were constructing the invented algorithms while they were still learning multiplication number combinations.

RELATION TO ADDITION AND SUBTRACTION INVENTED ALGORITHMS

With addition and subtraction, children frequently move directly from using base-ten materials to using invented algorithms, and these invented algorithms often represent abstractions of manipulations of physical operations on base-ten materials (Carpenter, 1997; Carpenter & Fennema, 1997; Fuson & Burghardt, chap. 10, this volume). The evolution of invented multiplication and division algorithms is more complex for two reasons. (a) Modeling multiplication or division operations involving large numbers is relatively tedious, particularly when the multiplier is a multidigit number. (b) By the time that children begin to work on multidigit multiplication and division, they can draw on a deeper and broader range of mathematical knowledge than was possible when they invented procedures to add and subtract. Consequently, many of the strategies that children construct represent extensions of their existing knowledge more than abstractions of manipulations of concrete representations.

There is some evidence that relying on addition and subtraction as a basis for developing multiplication and division concepts may cause difficulties when multiplying and dividing fractions and decimals, particularly when the multiplier is not a whole number (Bell, Greer, Grimison, & Mangan, 1989; Bell, Swan, & Taylor, 1981; Fischbein, Deri, Nello, & Marino, 1985). This has led Confrey (1994) to propose an alternative model for multiplication and division based on what she calls *splitting*. Splitting includes such operations as sharing, dividing, magnifying, and reducing. Although there are limits to conceptions of multiplication and division based entirely on addition and subtraction, there is a distinction between children's fundamental conceptions of multiplication and division and the procedures they employ in multidigit calculations. Clearly, children need rich conceptions of multiplication and division that generalize beyond whole-number operations and can capture the range of situations that can be modeled with multiplication and division operations. On the other hand, they also should understand the relations among the four operations and when these relations apply. Repeated addition is not an appropriate model for multiplication or division involving fraction or decimal multipliers, but there is a relation between addition and multiplication for whole-number operations that children should understand.

The participants in the studies of Bell, Fischbein, and their associates (Bell et al., 1981; Bell et al., 1989; Fischbein et al., 1985) had not acquired their limited conceptions of multiplication and division by inventing procedures for multiplying and dividing that drew on relations with addition and subtraction. There is no reason to expect that children will form narrow conceptions of multiplication and division by engaging in the kinds of meaning-making activities that are involved in constructing invented algorithms. We would argue that this kind of sense-making activity would mitigate against the kind of rule-based reasoning that multiplication always makes bigger and division always makes smaller found by Bell, Fischbein, and their associates.

THE ROLE OF INVENTED ALGORITHMS
IN THE CURRICULUM

Although invented algorithms are not always as efficient as standard algorithms, it is not clear that computational efficiency should be a high priority in these days of inexpensive calculating devices. From a purely computational perspective, invented algorithms have a number of advantages over standard algorithms. In many cases they break the calculation into more manageable steps that reduce the processing demands of the task. They are more user friendly in that the underlying concepts are closer to the surface. They generally are less prone to errors, such as leaving out zeros in quotients, errors that are common with standard algorithms. The invented algorithms we observed varied in the degree to which they utilized base-ten concepts. There are a variety of reasons that children should learn algorithms that use base-ten concepts, not the least of which is that such algorithms are a part of our culture, and children are expected to learn them. We are not proposing, however, that children must learn current versions of standard algorithms.

We have portrayed early examples of invented algorithms. As children use these over time, they should become more efficient and should begin to use organized and efficient notation. Teachers might help students to adopt notation so that it provides a reasonable extension such that the algorithm can be generalized. Many of the invented algorithms that we portray are not sufficient as a long-term goal of instruction, but some of the invented algorithms, with appropriate notation, are reasonably efficient and might be considered as alternatives for standard algorithms. For example, modified versions of Sean's strategy for multiplication (Fig. 11.7) and Margie's strategy for division (Fig. 11.16) would be appropriate culminating invented strategies for students to adopt. We would expect that Sean would develop a more efficient notation and that Margie would work with larger multipliers as their final revisions to these strategies. In the classrooms that we studied the teachers played a critical role in assisting students in developing efficient notations and encouraging them to use a variety of strategies, particularly those like Sean's and Margie's.

In considering the role of invented algorithms in the curriculum we need to consider not only the importance of students' developing techniques for multidigit multiplication and division, but also the concepts that students will study in future courses that depend on their knowledge of multidigit multiplication and division. We discuss converting fractions to decimals and polynomial division in algebra to show that the adaptive expertise that students develop through their work with invented algorithms will put them in a good position to understand these concepts when they encounter them.

Converting Fractions to Decimals. There are a variety of approaches that children can use to convert fractions to decimals, some of which are well suited to particular kinds of number combinations. We would hope that children's understanding of fractions and decimals would allow them to choose the approach that works best for the problem with which they are working. Students who have worked with invented algorithms have experience decomposing numbers. This experience decomposing multidigit numbers would allow students to decompose fractions and decimals in productive ways. For example, 3/8 can be converted to a decimal by decomposing 3/8 into 1/4 and 1/8 and recalling that 1/4 is equivalent to .25 and then taking half of .25 to determine a decimal equivalent for 1/8. Taking half of .25 can be done by decomposing it into .20 and .05 and then using the distributive property to take half of each of those quantities to find that half of .25 is .10 plus .025 or .125. Then .25 can be added to .125 to find the decimal equivalent for 3/8. We speculate that their work with invented multidigit multiplication and division would give students the disposition to adapt their technique to the numbers in the problem, the flexibility to decompose numbers in productive ways, and the ability to use the distributive property to attack converting fractions to decimals problems.

In addition to being able to use the distributive property to generate a variety of techniques for converting fractions to decimals, students will also need a general approach on which they could depend when their adaptive techniques do not work. Techniques like Aaron's (Fig. 11.11) and Margie's (Fig. 11.16) could be extended to handle the division required to convert a fraction to a decimal. Children could also use building-up techniques (see Fig. 11.14) to generate a decimal equivalent for any fraction. All of these techniques involve attention to equivalent fractions, a concept fundamental to converting fractions to decimals. When students use the standard division algorithm to convert fractions to decimals, this concept can be ignored. This brings us back to our argument in favor of making invented algorithms a central component of instruction. Invented algorithms utilize fundamental principles of arithmetic so that they are transparent to students rather than obscured.

Polynomial Multiplication and Division. Flexible use of the distributive property would put students in a good position to learn about polynomial multiplication and division. Students who use base-ten knowledge explicitly in their invented algorithms use the distributive property, which is key to multiplying polynomials. For example, Sean's strategy (Fig. 11.7) shows all of the partial products that result from decomposing the factors and applying the distributive property. For most students, the distributive property is not at all apparent in the standard multiplication algorithm. Students like Sean will have had informal experiences with the distributive property, experience that will support them in understanding this property when it is introduced in algebra (Schifter, 1999). Polynomial long division done in the traditional long division format requires an understanding of polynomial multiplication and subtraction, both of which should be understood by students experienced in using invented algorithms. Even though the students may not be familiar with focusing on the left end of the divisor as is done in both whole-number and polynomial long division, their adaptive expertise should enable them to transfer their understanding of the distributive property to this procedure.

Some may disagree with our stance that invented algorithms can serve as the basis for further learning in mathematics. Currently, either position on this issue is based more on value judgment than on empirical research. Whatever one's position, there is substantial evidence dating back to the early studies of Brownell (1945) and Van Engen and Gibb (1956) that algorithms should be learned with understanding (see also Hiebert, 1986; Hiebert & Carpenter, 1992). Invented algorithms provide a basis for linking algorithmic procedures with operations that children already understand in order to provide meaning for the procedures.

The elementary school mathematics curriculum has long focused on the algorithms for adding, subtracting, multiplying, and dividing whole numbers, fractions, and decimals. Recently, proponents of reform (e.g., National Council of Teachers of Mathematics, 1989, 2000) have recommended a reduced emphasis on traditional paper-and-pencil computational skills. Critics of reform consider this recommendation misguided and call for reinstating computation to its former place of prominence in the elementary mathematics curriculum (e.g., Loveless, 1997). The goal of the reform recommendations is not, however, to eliminate computation, but to enrich it so that it supports the development of number sense (Sowder, 1992) and provides a foundation for extending arithmetical concepts to algebra (Schifter, 1999). Giving children opportunity to invent algorithms can serve these goals.

Acknowledgments

The research and preparation of this paper was supported in part by grants from the National Science Foundation (MDR-8955346) and the Department of Education Office of Educational Research and Improvement of the National Center for Improving Student Learning and Achievement in Mathematics and Science (R305A60007-98). The opinions expressed in this paper do not necessarily reflect the position, policy, or endorsement of the National Science Foundation, the Department of Education, OERI, or the National Center.

References

Baroody, A. J. (1996). Self-invented addition strategies by children classified as mentally handicapped. *American Journal on Mental Retardation, 101,* 72–89.

Beishuizen, M., Gravemeijer, K. P. E., & van Lieshout, E. C. D. M. (1997). *The role of contexts and models in the development of mathematical strategies and processes.* Utrecht, The Netherlands: The Freudenthal Institute.

Bell, A., Greer, B., Grimison, L., & Mangan, C. (1989). Children's performance on multiplication word problems: Elements of a descriptive theory. *Journal for Research in Mathematics Education, 20,* 434–449.

Bell, A., Swan, M., & Taylor, G. (1981). Choice of operations in verbal problems with decimal numbers. *Educational Studies in Mathematics, 12,* 399–420.

Brownell, W. A. (1945). When is arithmetic meaningful? *Journal of Educational Research, 38,* 481–498.

Carpenter, T. P. (1985). Learning to add and subtract: An exercise in problem solving. In E. A. Silver (Ed.), *Teaching and learning mathematical problem solving: Multiple research perspectives* (pp. 17–40). Hillsdale, NJ: Lawrence Erlbaum Associates.

Carpenter, T. P. (1997). Models for reform in mathematics teaching. In M. Beishuizen, K. P. E. Gravemeijer, & E. C. D. M. van Lieshout (Eds.), *The role of contexts and models in the development of mathematical strategies and processes* (pp. 35–54). Utrecht, The Netherlands: The Freudenthal Institute.

Carpenter, T. P., Ansell, E., Franke, M. L., Fennema, E., & Weisbeck, L. (1993). Models of problem solving: A study of kindergarten children's problem-solving processes. *Journal for Research in Mathematics Education, 24,* 428–44.

Carpenter, T. P., & Fennema, E. (1997). A day in the life in one Cognitively Guided Instruction classroom. In J. Hiebert, T. P. Carpenter, E. Fennema, K. C. Fuson, P. Human, H. Murray, A. Olivier, & D. Wearne (Eds.), *Making sense: Teaching and learning mathematics with understanding* (pp. 101–114). Portsmouth, NH: Heinemann.

Carpenter, T. P., Fennema, E., Franke, M. L., Empson, S. B., & Levi, L. W. (1999). *Children's mathematics: Cognitively Guided Instruction.* Portsmouth, NH: Heinemann.

Carpenter, T. P., Fennema, E., Fuson, K. C., Hiebert, J., Human, P., Murray, H., Olivier, A., & Wearne, D. (2000). Teaching mathematics for learning with understanding in the primary grades. In E. Fennema & T. A. Romberg (Eds.), *Classrooms that promote mathematical understanding* (pp. 45–62). Mahwah, NJ: Lawrence Erlbaum Associates.

Carpenter, T. P., Franke, M. L., Jacobs, V., & Fennema, E. (1998). A longitudinal study of invention and understanding in children's multidigit addition and subtraction. *Journal for Research in Mathematics Education, 29,* 3–20.

Confrey, J. (1994). Splitting, similarity, and rate of change: A new approach to multiplication and exponential functions. In G. Harel & J. Confrey (Eds.), *The development of multiplicative reasoning* (pp. 293–332). Albany: State University of New York.

Fischbein, E., Deri, M., Nello, M. S., & Marino, M. S. (1985). The role of implicit models in solving verbal problems in multiplication and division. *Journal for Research in Mathematics Education, 16,* 3–17.

Fuson, K. C. (1992). Research on whole number addition and subtraction. In D. Grouws (Ed.), *Handbook of research on mathematics teaching and learning* (pp. 243–275). New York: Macmillan.

Fuson, K. C., Wearne, D., Hiebert, J., Human, P., Murray, H., Olivier, A., Carpenter, T. P., & Fennema, E. (1997). Children's conceptual structures for multidigit numbers and methods of multidigit addition and subtraction. *Journal for Research in Mathematics Education, 28,* 130–162.

Greer. B. (1992). Multiplication and division as models of situations. In D. Grouws (Ed.), *Handbook of research on mathematics teaching and learning* (pp. 65–97). New York: Macmillan.

Gutstein, E., & Romberg, T. A. (1996). Teaching children to add and subtract. *Journal of Mathematical Behavior, 14,* 283–324.

Heege, H. ter. (1985). The acquisition of basic multiplication skills. *Educational Studies in Mathematics, 16,* 375–388.

Hiebert, J. (Ed.). (1986). *Conceptual and procedural knowledge: The case of mathematics.* Hillsdale, NJ: Lawrence Erlbaum Associates.

Hiebert, J., & Behr, M. (Eds.). (1988). *Number concepts and operations in the middle grades: Vol. 2. Research agenda for mathematics education.* Reston, VA: National Council of Teachers of Mathematics.

Hiebert, J., & Carpenter, T. P. (1992). Learning mathematics with understanding. In D. Grouws (Ed.), *Handbook of research on mathematics teaching and learning* (pp. 65–97). New York: Macmillan.

Hiebert, J., Carpenter, T. P., Fennema, E., Fuson, K. C., Human, P., Murray, H., Olivier, A., & Wearne, D. (1997). *Making sense: Teaching and learning mathematics with understanding.* Portsmouth, NH: Heinemann.

Hiebert, J., & Tonnesen, L. H. (1978). Development of the fraction concept in two physical contexts: An exploratory investigation. *Journal for Research in Mathematics Education, 9,* 374–378.

Kamii, C. (1994). *Young children continue to reinvent arithmetic.* New York: Teachers College Press.

Kouba, V. L. (1989). Children's solution strategies for equivalent set multiplication and division word problems. *Journal for Research in Mathematics Education, 20,* 147–158.

Kouba, V. L., & Franklin, K. (1993). Multiplication and division: Sense making and meaning. In R. J. Jensen (Ed.), *Research ideas for the classroom: Early childhood mathematics* (pp. 103–126). New York: Macmillan.

Loveless, T. (1997, October 15). The second great math rebellion. *Education Week,* pp. 36–48.

National Council of Teachers of Mathematics. (1989). *Curriculum and evaluation standards for school mathematics.* Reston, VA: Author.

National Council of Teachers of Mathematics. (2000). *Principles and standards for school mathematics.* Reston, VA: Author.

Pepper, K. L., & Hunting, R. P. (1998). Preschoolers' counting and sharing. *Journal for Research in Mathematics Education, 29,* 164–183.

Schifter, D. (1999). Reasoning about operations: Early algebraic thinking in grades K–6. In L. V. Stiff & F. R. Curcio (Eds.), *Developing mathematical reasoning in grades K–12.* Reston, VA: National Council of Teachers of Mathematics.

Schliemann, A. D., Araujo, C., Cassundé, M. A., Macedo, S., & Nicéas, L. (1998). Use of multiplicative commutativity by school children and street sellers. *Journal for Research in Mathematics Education, 29,* 422–435.

Silver, E. A., Shapiro, L. J., & Deutsch, A. (1993). Sense making and the solutions of division problems involving remainders: An examination of middle school students' solution processes and their interpretations of solutions. *Journal for Research in Mathematics Education, 24,* 159–166.

Sowder, J. (1992). Estimation and number sense. In D. Grouws (Ed.), *Handbook of research on mathematics teaching and learning* (pp. 65–97). New York: Macmillan.

Steffe, L. P. (1988). Children's construction of number sequences and multiplying schemes. In J. Hiebert & M. Behr (Eds.), *Number concepts and operations in the middle grades: Vol. 2. Research agenda for mathematics education* (pp. 119–140). Reston, VA: Lawrence Erlbaum Associates; National Council of Teachers of Mathematics.

Van Engen, H., & Gibb, E. G. (1956). *General mental functions associated with division.* Cedar Falls, IA: Town State College.

Verschaffel, L., & De Corte, E. (1993). A decade of research on word-problem solving in Leuven: Theoretical, methodological, and practical outcomes. *Educational Psychology Review, 5,* 1–18.

Weiland, L. (1985). Matching instruction to children's thinking about division. *Arithmetic Teacher, 33,* 34–35.

CHAPTER 12

THE EARLY NUMERACY OF CHILDREN WITH SPECIFIC LANGUAGE IMPAIRMENTS

Chris Donlan
University College London

In this chapter, I examine the development of numeracy in children with specific language impairments (SLI), and offer an account of this development in terms of cognitive function. The studies cited offer a special perspective on a familiar theoretical question: What is the relation between language and thought? It is often suggested that mathematical thinking has a special abstractness and independence of operation. Wood (1988) quoted no less an authority than Einstein:

The words or the language, as they are written or spoken, do not seem to play any role in my mechanism of thought. . . . In thought are certain signs and more or less clear images which can be "voluntarily" reproduced and combined . . . the elements are, in my case, visual and some of muscular type . . . conventional signs and words have to be sought for laboriously only in a secondary stage. (p. 182)

This sort of introspection is not uncommon, but the opposite view is also familiar. Mathematical ability, or more precisely, numerical ability, is frequently considered to be language related or even language dependent. In an influential review of psychological research, Dehaene (1992) observed:

Calculation is the numerical activity par excellence. Calculation in turn rests on the ability to read, write, produce or comprehend numerals. Therefore number processing, in its fundamental form, seems intuitively linked to the ability to mentally manipulate sequences of words or symbols according to fixed . . . rules. (pp. 2–3)

According to such an account, Dehaene suggested, there is no need to postulate an autonomous "faculty of number" as a separate module of mind; the resources needed to support numerical processes may be those same resources that support language itself.

Theories of the relation between language and mathematical thinking have a special application with regard to children whose development is hampered by specific language difficulties. If numerical operations are not language dependent, then mathematics should offer these children an unhindered domain of learning. However, Hutt (1986), drawing on 25 years of teaching experience, explained:

> Whatever degree of difficulty is experienced by language-disordered children in the understanding and use of non-number language, that difficulty is magnified as they try to grasp the basic principles of number language. . . . Some young children with language disorders do not find it easy to generalize words for people, actions, colours and positional words. How much more difficult is their perception of the similarity between five trees, five boats, and five fingers. The fiveness of five is not as simple as it appears to those of us who cannot remember the time when we did not understand this concept. . . . Mathematical thinking must be even more precise than that required for the production of linguistic sequences. The responsibility for arriving at a series of logical conclusions via a series of logical procedures presents a constant challenge which some language-disordered children find daunting. (p. 124)

In this chapter, I examine the interaction between language and thought by studying the "natural experiment" of SLI in children. In particular, I explore the limitations imposed on numerical thinking by linguistic deficit. To provide background information about these issues, I begin with a two-part literature review. The first part brings together some contrasting perspectives drawn from current research on the development of numerical knowledge, emphasizing the role of language in the early stages of numerical processing up to the acquisition of simple arithmetic facts. The second part summarizes three different views regarding the causes of SLI in children, including the cognitive processes thought to underlie them. The main body of the chapter includes detailed accounts of current research into numeracy development in children with SLI. Finally, some conclusions are drawn concerning the extent of interdependence of language development and numeracy development in early and middle childhood.

Background

Language and Mathematical Development: Some Issues in Current Research

A body of recent research has suggested that numerical cognition precedes language acquisition in the human infant. Starkey, Spelke, and Gelman (1990) described an ingenious set of experiments with 6- to 9-month-old infants. First, they used a habituation paradigm to test discrimination of visual stimuli showing two or three familiar objects; participants showed a preference for numerically novel stimuli. The experimenters controlled novelty, spatial arrangement, brightness, color, density, and surface area. Starkey et al. then used an auditory–visual preference procedure. Pairs of displays of two or three items were shown while a sound accompaniment was played, presenting a single sequence of drumbeats corresponding in number to one of the visible displays. Looking time to the two displays was recorded for 10 sec after the onset of sound. Of the 16 participants (mean age 7 months), a significant number (12) looked longer at the numerically equivalent display. This effect was replicated with two more experimental trials.

Starkey et al.'s (1990) results suggest that infants as young as 6 months old are able to represent visually derived numerical information and subsequently compare it with an auditory stimulus. However, their results are inconsistent with those of two other studies (Mix, Levine, & Huttenlocher, 1997; Moore, Benenson, Reznick, Peterson, & Kagan, 1987). Furthermore, Mix, Huttenlocher, and Levine (1996) found no evidence of cross-modal transfer until after children had acquired conventional counting competence (about 4 years of age).

Wynn (1992) explored the arithmetic competence of infants. She concluded that 6-month-olds were capable of simple "addition and subtraction." Simon, Hespos, and Rochat (1995) replicated Wynn's findings but challenged her interpretation of the findings.

As this disagreement illustrates, it is not clear what the results of infant studies mean. To what are these babies responding? Is it number in any mathematical sense? One obstacle to interpretating the results of infant studies is the difficulty many of us experience in separating the notion of number from the spoken or written numerals used to represent it. We can be quite certain that 6-month-old infants do not have access to the meaning of these number symbols. Nevertheless, is there a way in which they might have some grasp of the underlying notion of number applied to sets of items or repeated events? The term *numerosity* may be preferred in description of numerical concepts that are not verbally specified. A key issue is the distinction between *numerosity* and *quantity,* where the former refers to a specified sum of separate entities, and the latter a more general measure of size or density, which might apply to single or combined entities. The experimental findings described here may not be conclusive in demonstrating awareness of numerosity in preverbal infants, but they do demonstrate that very young preverbal children are able to distinguish among stimuli, which older children and adults would identify as a number of objects or events.

How far can these early skills extend? There are at least two distinct viewpoints on this. Starkey et al. (1990) believed that their work, along with that of others,

> suggests that number is a natural domain of cognition, with foundations of its own. Infants do not appear to be endowed only with general, all-purpose abilities to sense and learn. They seem to have capacities to form and transform representations in particular domains of knowledge. . . . In each of these domains, children's knowledge will undergo development. Nevertheless, structures and principles of adult functioning are discernible near the

beginning of life, before the acquisition of language and the assimilation of culture. (pp. 126–127)

Although this view has wide support (see, e.g., Gallistel and Gelman, 1992; Wynn, 1998), there are strong counterarguments. Sophian (1998) offered a detailed commentary on the infant studies, considered in relation to the body of research that she and others have produced examining the development of counting skills in the *preschool* years. She argued that evidence for specific enumeration processes underlying the observed behaviors is lacking. Sophian further concluded that, from a developmental perspective, the move from infant number or quantity awareness to mastery of counting in the preschool years cannot be explained by the "natural-domain" hypothesis. For her, the key to early numeracy lies not in the unfolding of cognitive skill within children, but in their response to and interaction with their social context.

The origins of numerical cognition may well precede the acquisition of language, as has been argued (see Wynn, 1998, for a recent review). Nonetheless, it is clear that the linguistic context that supports the development of numerical skills is an influential factor from later infancy onward. Durkin, Shire, Riem, Crowther, and Rutter (1986) showed that number words constitute an important part of the lexicon shared between mothers and infants from at least the age of 9 months. The special set of lexical items that make up the spoken number sequence is, in developmental terms, a foundation element of lexical knowledge and appears to be a focus of shared attention and endeavour for all parents and children learning to communicate through language.

Fuson, Richards, and Briars (1982) offered a detailed account of the acquisition and elaboration of the number-word sequence in English. Although this research was carried out in the United States, there is no obvious reason to doubt its application to learners in the United Kingdom or to learners of languages other than English whose number systems are decade based. Fuson et al. characterized stages in the development of the number-word sequence as string (undifferentiated), unbreakable chain (differentiated but not separable), breakable chain, numerable chain, and bidirectional chain. In the initial string stage, the number words may be produced simply as a string of sounds not segmented into words and not appropriate for the establishment of 1:1 correspondence relations. In the second or breakable chain stage, children view each number word as distinct but cannot begin a count at any point other than *one*. In the third or breakable chain stage, they can count from any point in their known sequence. By the final or bidirectional stage, children can count up or down quickly from any point in the number sequence and use forward and backward counting to solve addition and subtraction problems.

Fuson et al. (1981) have provided important insights into number-sequence learning and its role in the development of arithmetic skills. Viewed from a linguistic perspective, their account also highlights the exceptional nature of the spoken number sequence as a set of lexical items. In most of the widely spoken Asian and European languages, at least, the phonological structure of items in the spoken number sequence and the syntactic rules for combining them map reasonably effectively onto the base-ten system of enumeration (see Miura & Okamoto, chap. 8, this volume, and Towse & Saxton, 1998, for a discussion of the important variations that occur). It is extraordinary that these systems readily allow the generation of new items without limit. Distinctive structural features include the systematic repetition of the first nine numerals to distinguish values at successive levels of magnitude. This economy of representation clearly facilitates rapid acquisition.

Furthermore, the rules governing the system operate so as to emphasize canonical order of occurrence for all items, while allowing independent occurrence of single items (e.g., use of single numerals to denote ages, house numbers), limited sequences of items (Fuson et al.'s, 1982, breakable chain), reversed sequences of items (backward counts), and even noncanonical strings (e.g., telephone numbers). No other set of lexical items operates in this way. A central feature is the canonical sequence and its systematic relation to phonological structure. This characteristic generally facilitates rapid acquisition, but as we shall see, it can operate as an obstacle to learning for some children.

In the early years of schooling, most children are required to become skilled in manipulating *written* number symbols that share some, but not all, characteristics with the spoken system. The set of written numeric symbols is soon accompanied by formal symbols for arithmetic. Intriguing recent research by Penny Munn (1994, 1995) in the United Kingdom has thrown some new light on this critical phase in numeracy development. Munn's longitudinal study tracked children's developing understanding and use of symbols during their attendance at preschool (ages 3 to 5 years). Previous work (Hughes, 1986) suggested a developmental progression from iconic symbol use (e.g., drawing four circles to represent four items) to conventional symbol use (using the appropriate written numeral). Munn's (1998) conclusions put a different emphasis on the developmental process. Based on longitudinal evidence from a novel experimental task, she reached two important conclusions. One is that the crucial change is children's understanding of the function of symbols, not the form of symbols they use. This characterization focuses on the conceptual framework within which the symbol is used. In the early stages of number writing, children may produce items that simply correspond with spoken numbers and have no further purpose. However, when children use a written symbol to represent the cardinal value of a set of items they demonstrate a fuller understanding of the function of the written symbol (see Bialystok, 1992). At this stage, Munn argued, the symbol becomes a cognitive tool, supporting more advanced numerical activity.

Munn's (1998) second important conclusion is that progress in symbolic function takes place across a range of activities including early aspects of literacy, as well as numeracy. She observed that children's developing understanding of the function of numeric symbols is closely associated with their understanding of the function of alphabetic symbols or print. To this extent, then, the crucial understanding that underpins symbolic function is not a domain-limited development specific to the acquisition of numerals, but rather a general understanding supporting the development of written language skills, as well as written number.

There is a widespread assumption that the development of arithmetic skills and the learning of number combinations, in particular, depend primarily on counting skill (e.g., Fuson, 1988; Ginsburg, 1977). In the influential model developed by Robert Siegler and colleagues (Siegler & Jenkins, 1989; Siegler & Shrager, 1984), successive implementations of counting-based strategies (e.g., the "*sum*" procedure of counting all, and later the "*min*" procedure of counting on from the larger addend) establish associations between addition items and their solutions in long-term memory. Repeated experience increases the strength of associations and thereby increases the probability that a solution may be directly (and rapidly) retrieved without recourse to counting. Viewed from this perspective, procedural skills in counting might be viewed as the central foundation of arithmetic.

However, other research has drawn attention to the importance of conceptual knowledge, as well as procedural knowledge. For example, there is strong evidence to suggest that children's understanding of arithmetic principles may be based on nonverbal calculation of the effects of transformation on small numbers of items. Huttenlocher, Jordan, and Levine (1994) have argued that children around 3 years of age compute exact sums based on nonverbal representations of numerosity. According to this account, the conceptual basis for later arithmetic development may not entail a verbal (counting-based) representation of numerical value but may draw on nonverbal symbolic processes that may be extensions of the nonverbal, nonsymbolic processes underlying number awareness in infants. However, Huttenlocher et al. acknowledged the likely importance of conventional skills in the subsequent development of arithmetic skills.

Various scholars (e.g., Baroody & Ginsburg, 1986; Baroody & Tiilikainer, chap. 3, this volume; Cowan, chap. 2, this volume; Fuson, 1988; Rittle-Johnson & Siegler, 1998) have drawn attention to the subtle interaction of conceptual and procedural knowledge that characterizes the development of mathematical skills of different sorts at different ages. As we have seen, this interaction maps, in part at least, onto the interaction of verbal and nonverbal processes in early numeracy. Conceptual frameworks, it is widely claimed, build on early emerging nonverbal processes; procedural skills are often associated with explicit verbal counting. Note, however, that this interaction is complex. Nunes and Bryant (1996), for example, suggested that the counting-on strategy developed as a result of a child's expanding representation of an addend, namely treating it as both a cardinal value and as the starting point of a count procedure (what Fuson, 1988, called the "embedded cardinal-sequence transition"). Baroody (1995) further suggested that this conceptual breakthrough is a result of computational experience. Specifically, children may discover that the sum of an $n + 1$ combination is simply the number after n in the counting sequence and recognize that adding more than one to a number must be several numbers after n in the counting sequence (see Baroody & Tiilikainen, chap. 3, this volume). The social context for learning that drives developments of this sort clearly depends on successful linguistic interaction (Nunes & Bryant, 1996).

Central to our concerns is children's success in developing a semantic system to represent the numerical meanings that underpin a wide variety of numerical activities. The semantics of number are the most intriguing aspects of the numerical system because they are both highly abstract (numbers need not be applied to concrete referents) and absolutely specific (numerical values are unequivocally determined). It may be reasonable to suppose, given the evidence reviewed here, that an efficient semantic system for number is built on a combination of verbal and nonverbal representations; an expanded representation, to use Nunes and Bryant's (1996) term, may entail just such a combination. Studies of numeracy in children whose speech and language development are specifically impaired offer the opportunity to gauge the involvement of verbal skills in developing number meanings. In particular, we may explore the extent to which children's knowledge of the spoken number system, and their linguistic skill in general, governs their ability to form accurate representations of numerical meaning.

Three Hypotheses About the Underlying Nature of SLI in Children

Children with SLI have selective impairment of language function not readily attributable to environmental deprivation, sensory impairment, motor disability, or any other cause (cf. Bishop, 1994, 1997). If it is the case that SLI is modular, so that affected children develop nonverbal skills appropriate to their age, then the pattern of acquisition of numeracy in children with SLI should help delineate the general involvement of verbal processes in numerical learning. Next, I discuss three different positions on this view.

Grammatical Deficit Hypothesis. Some researchers have specified theories of the underlying nature of SLI that are quite compatible with a modular account of the deficit. Gopnik and Crago (1991), for example, argued that SLI are caused by a dysfunction that is specific to language acquisition. Children with SLI, they proposed, fail to learn grammatical features of language in the normal way. According to Gopnik and Crago's theory, these children fail to identify and learn grammatical rules such as plural inflection. For instance, they may learn that the word *books* refers to more than one book, but they learn the word as a distinct lexical item, separate from its singular form. They are unable to learn the inflection rule and generalize its use. Gopnik and Crago's theory would make definite predictions about the development of numeracy in children with SLI. Problems with linguistic number marking (e.g., plural inflection) should be pervasive. The important interactions that occur between linguistic context and numerical activity (cf. Markman, 1979) may therefore cause confusion rather than foster development. However, proponents of this theory would not predict any effect on preverbal numerical representation, nor would they suggest problems in the acquisition of the early stages of the verbal number sequence itself (though acquisition of the grammatical framework for higher magnitude verbal numerals might be compromised).

General Symbolic Deficit Hypothesis. There is no universal acceptance that SLI is the highly specific linguistic disorder it may appear to be. Some theorists (e.g., Morehead & Ingram, 1976) have suggested that SLI entails an underlying representational deficit, affecting the processing of symbolic information generally, even where this information is not explicitly linguistic.

Johnston and Smith (1989) found that a group of children with deficits predominantly in expressive language performed significantly worse than age-matched controls on a reasoning task. A first experimenter made a selection from a collection of toys (e.g., a yellow *car*), and a second experimenter did the same from a somewhat different collection of toys (e.g., a blue *car*). A participant then had to pick a corresponding toy from his or her somewhat different collection of toys (e.g., a red *car*). In effect, a child had to induce the common property of the experimenters' choices and deduce which item in his or her collection matched it. Although children with SLI exhibited an understanding of the words used in this task on a preliminary verbal task (e.g., presenting a child with a collection of toys and saying, "Give me the red car"), they appeared unable to reason about them. Johnston and Smith concluded, "Language-impaired children are also thought-impaired" (p. 38).

Studies by Connell and Stone (1992) and Stone and Connell (1993) have gone on to suggest that children with SLI have not only a specific auditory-processing deficit, but also a general difficulty in processing symbolic information, whether auditorily or visually presented.

In a subsequent review, Johnston (1994) proposed that capacity limitations inhibit both verbal and nonverbal cognition in children with SLI. In support of her view, she cited specific difficulties with verbal counting and generally poor attainment in numeracy. For present purposes, we consider these hypotheses together as proposing a *general symbolic deficit*. The prediction here is that numeracy acquisition will be quite generally impaired in children with SLI. If their processing capacity for both verbal and nonverbal information is significantly limited, this should impose a general and cumulative deficit in the development of a semantic system for number.

Phonological Short-Term Memory Deficit Hypothesis. A third, and in some sense an intermediate, hypothesis accounts for SLI by proposing a memory deficit that is specific to the storage of phonological information. Gathercole and Baddeley (1990) suggested that children with SLI have "an impairment in the specialised storage of phonological information in working memory" (p. 357). This hypothesis has generated considerable debate and remains highly influential. Although Gathercole and Baddeley have acknowledged that their proposal lacks clarity in distinguishing between speech processing and memory processes, they have proceeded to amass a raft of findings relating deficits in phonological short-term memory (STM) to a range of indexes of language acquisition (see Gathercole, 1998, for a review). Their phonological STM hypothesis leads to distinctive predictions about numeracy acquisition. Most important, its proponents predict disruption in the acquisition of the number-word sequence, while sparing nonverbal processes in numeracy development.

Studies of Numeracy Among Children with SLI

In this section, I review evidence regarding numeracy development in children with SLI and consider the findings in relation to the theoretical predictions just outlined and summarized in Table 12.1.

Early Work

In a series of pioneering studies, Linda Siegel (1982) first investigated the impact of verbal processes on numerical concept formation in normally developing preschoolers. She used a nonverbal method for testing various concepts including numerical equivalence. Siegel used a procedure in which a sample array of two to nine dots was presented along with two possible match arrays within which density and length cues to equivalence were systematically varied. Participants were rewarded for choosing the correct alternative. Under these conditions Siegel found that 3-year-olds performed at chance level, showing no understanding of equivalence; 4-year-olds performed at a better than chance level, with the proportion of error responses varying according to array type.

Table 12.1: Predictions That Follow From Three Hypotheses About the Underlying Nature of SLI

Hypothesis	Effect on Preverbal Numerical Representation	Effect on Verbal Numerical Representation
Grammatical deficit	None	None (for early counting development)
General symbolic deficit	Significant	Significant
Phonological STM deficit	None	Significant

Siegel (1982) also explored the impact of linguistic concepts on performance and argued that the early stages of quantity concept formation may precede the acquisition of those relational terms used to describe them. In a further study, she and colleagues exploited the natural dissociation of verbal and nonverbal abilities in children with SLI in order to test the possible independence of verbal skills and numerical concepts (Siegel, Lees, Allan, & Bolton, 1981). Twenty-six preschoolers with normal nonverbal ability, as measured by standardized tests, but with specific deficits in verbal expression and comprehension were compared with 26 age-matched controls. Although the SLI group performed as well as controls when asked to make simple binary judgments (choosing the more numerous of two arrays), only 2 reached criterion in a match-to-sample equivalence test of the sort described previously, whereas 12 control participants did so. Siegel argued that verbal skills may be centrally involved in performance of the match-to-sample task through facilitation of place marking in a sequence and of information storage.

A Study of Conceptual and Procedural Skills in 6-Year-Olds With SLI

Rationale. For my doctoral thesis (Donlan, 1993), I replicated and extended some of the findings of Siegel et al. (1981) by including a contrast between performance of an equivalence task with smaller and larger set sizes. The possible distinction between quantification processes for smaller and larger set sizes has long been recognized. The process of nonverbal "subitizing" has been proposed to entail the rapid recognition of numerosity in small sets (e.g., Mandler & Shebo, 1982) by children as well as adults (e.g., Chi & Klahr, 1975). If nonverbal numerical processing is intact in children with SLI, then they should be able to establish equivalence (and demonstrate their conceptual knowledge of cardinality) when set sizes are small, through their impaired verbal skills may inhibit their performance with larger set sizes requiring counting and storage of counted totals.

Participants. Twenty 6-year-olds with SLI were recruited from both special schools with segregated placements and mainstream schools with integrated placements in different parts of England. Reliance was placed on clinicians' judgments. Specifically, teachers and speech therapists were asked to refer all children of appropriate age who were considered to have SLI and to exclude any children thought to have low nonverbal ability or whose language skills were not considered significantly impaired (e.g., children with a simple speech difficulty). In this way it was assumed that the sample would be broadly representative of the clinical population diagnosed as having SLI.

Three control groups were recruited from mainstream classes in schools in central Manchester. None of the control children was identified as having speech, language, or learning difficulties. The first control group was matched for age with the SLI group. This was done to establish the level of performance expected in children whose nonverbal ability approximates that of the SLI group, but whose verbal ability is superior. Two further control groups were recruited of 4-year-olds and 5-year-olds. In this way, a pattern of the development of skills could be built up to allow detailed comparisons between SLI performance and that of younger children with less advanced nonverbal abilities but broadly similar verbal skills. Details of age and gender of groups are given in Table 12.2.

Tasks. Donlan (1993) used a nonverbal match-to-sample task inspired by Siegel et al. (1981). Spatial arrangement of items was manipulated in order to distinguish matches based on numerosity from those based on simple perceptual comparison. The identity of items was also varied in order to provide a stringent test of participants' ability to represent numerosity at an abstract level. The three variations in the match-to-sample arrays were as follows: (a) identical shapes in identical canonical arrays (a *perceptual match*); (b) identical shapes with location change from match to sample (a *location change*); (c) canonically ordered shapes in the match array corresponded to randomly located pictures in the sample (an *object-plus-location change*). Manipulation of collection size introduced a further contrast. Low range included arrays containing two to five items. These could be processed using a nonverbal subitizing process. High range included arrays containing six to nine items. Examples of each type of array are shown in Fig. 12.1.

Table 12.2: Characteristics of Groups (Donlan, 1993)

	SLI	6-Year-Olds	5-Year-Olds	4-Year-Olds
Sample size	$n = 20$	$n = 19$	$n = 20$	$n = 20$
Mean age[a]	6–6	6–4	5–4	4–4
Age range[a]	5–10 to 7–2	5–10 to 6–9	5–2 to 5–6	4–2 to 4–8
Boys	17	10	11	12
Girls	3	10	9	7

[a] Ages reported in years and months.

Figure 12.1: Sample Stimuli From All Experimental Conditions in Donlan (1993)

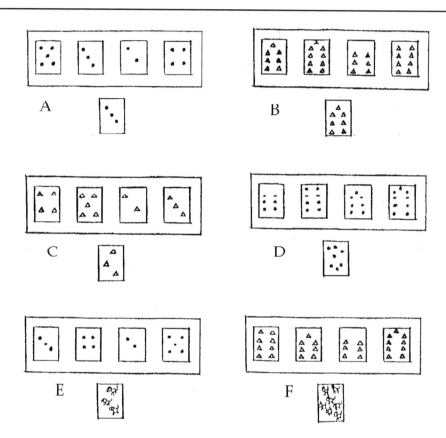

A= Perceptual Match, Low Range
B= Perceptual Match, High Range
C= Location Change, Low Range
D= Location Change, High Range
E= Object Plus Location Change, Low Range
F= Object Plus Location Change, High Range

All participants were given the following two standardized tests: (a) the Action Picture Test (APT; Renfrew, 1989), yielding scores for grammatical complexity and information content in expressive language; and (b) the Raven's Colored Progressive Matrices (Raven, 1985), which gauged nonverbal ability.

Results. The results of the two standardized tests are summarized in Table 12.3. APT grammar mean scores showed a substantial deficit in the SLI group (more than 2 standard deviations below the population mean); control scores fell short of the level expected for age but were still within the normal range. APT information scores also showed intergroup differences. SLI mean score fell more than 1 standard deviation below the population mean. Control means were close to those expected for their age. Nonverbal ability as measured by Raven's matrices showed all groups performing at a broadly comparable level, somewhat below that expected for their age, but still within the normal range.

On the nonverbal match-to-sample task, both SLI and 6-year-old controls (C6) performed close to ceiling level (five correct responses) in all conditions at the low number range, and the 4-year-old controls (C4) performed close to chance level (1.25 correct responses) in location-change and object-plus-location-change conditions at the high number range. These results restrict the interpretation of the experimental findings.

A 4 (groups) x 2 (number ranges) x 3 (displays) analysis of variance revealed a significant main effect for group and number range. Specifically, the SLI group significantly outperformed C4 and 5-year-old controls (C5; $p < .01$, Games-Howell post hoc comparison test) and performed on a par with C6. However, there is a possibility that the ceiling effect noted earlier may have obscured a real difference between SLI and C6. Low-range matches were far better performed than high-range matches ($p < .0001$). Comparison of means for the main effect of match type showed strong significant difference between perceptual matches and both other conditions ($p < .0001$), but not between location-change and object-plus-location-change conditions ($p = .55$). Superior performance in the perceptual condition was clearly established by these findings, but data for the comparison between location change and object plus location change may have been compressed by ceiling and floor effects. Similar reservations apply to

Table 12.3: Standardized Test Data from Donlan (1993)

	Action Picture Test (grammar) Mean Score (SD)	Action Picture Test (information) Mean Score (SD)	Raven's Colored Progressive Matrices Mean Score (SD)
SLI	61.5 (13.4)	83.1 (18.1)	87.9 (16.8)
6-year-old control	90.9 (13.2)	100.7 (12.4)	92.3 (10.9)
5-year-old control	92.4 (11.7)	99.7 (9.5)	93.4 (10.3)
4-year-old control	89.2 (15.3)	94.9 (18.7)	– [a]

[a] The standardization of this test does not include 4-year-olds.

interpretation of the significant interactions of match type with group and number range with group.

In view of the restrictions imposed on the analysis by ceiling and floor effects, it was thought useful to carry out further analyses excluding the restricted data. Two subsets of data were selected: The first included SLI and C6 responses for all match types at the high number range only; the second included C5 and C4 responses for all display types at the low number range only.

In the first reanalysis (SLI vs. C6 on high-range numbers), group membership was not a significant factor ($p = .101$). A strong effect of match type was found ($p < .0001$), with a significant interaction between group and match type ($p < .05$). Comparison of means for perceptual, location-change and object-plus-location-change conditions showed significant differences between the perceptual condition and each of the others ($p < .0001$), but not between location- and object-plus-location-change conditions ($p = .50$). The interaction of group and match type was such that the effect of match type varied significantly according to group, with location- and object-plus-location-change matches producing lower performance in the SLI group, and perceptual matches being managed equally well by both groups.

The second reanalysis (C5 vs. C4 on low-range numbers) showed that main effects of group and display were both highly significant ($p < .0001$), but no interaction was found between them ($p = .591$). Comparison of means for the different match types showed that perceptual matches were more successful than both other types ($p < .005$), and that location-change matches were significantly more successful than object-plus-location-change matches ($p < .05$). This final and important contrast differed from those of both other analyses.

The SLI group significantly outperformed both younger control groups, thereby demonstrating an overall performance level in advance of their language level. It was found that, in the high number range, children with SLI performed worse than similar-aged controls when matching in location- and object-plus-location-change conditions, but not in perceptual conditions. This finding was in line with predictions based on limitations in verbal processing, presumed to be strongly implicated in the counting and storage demands made in just those conditions in which the SLI group showed deficits.

However, no evidence was found that children with SLI showed poorer performance when matching in object-plus-location-change conditions than in location-change conditions. The ability of the SLI group to establish equivalence at a highly abstract level was clear. It is interesting to note in this regard that both younger control groups (C5 and C4) showed evidence of a difficulty in this area when working with lower numbers. Although the number-range difference obscures direct comparison of these findings, they are suggestive of age-appropriate conceptual ability in the SLI group.

Conclusions. What can we conclude from these findings? Clearly, to establish equivalence relations between sets distinguished by spatial arrangement and identity requires that cardinality be represented at an abstract level. This principle applies as clearly to low number sets as it does to high number sets. The present findings show no evidence that low number trials presented any difficulty to the SLI group, though the performance of younger control children was affected. To this extent the conceptual knowledge demonstrated by the SLI group appears to be both age appropriate and in advance of the group's language skills. In line with the proposal of Siegel et al. (1981) that children with SLI have special difficulty with tasks involving place holding in a sequence (e.g., counting and the storage of counted totals), the SLI group performed worse than age-matched controls when dealing with matches of high-number sets distinguished by spatial arrangement and identity of items. Thus, there appears to be a procedural deficit restricting performance by the SLI group in certain conditions. These apparently clear-cut conclusions are based on evidence that is suggestive rather than definitive; their strength will be evaluated in the light of evidence drawn from further studies.

Longitudinal Studies of the Mathematical Development in Children With SLI

Suppose we accept the suggestive evidence reported previously and extend it to make the general assertion that 6-year-olds with SLI have strong number concepts but weak procedural skills. How might this general picture change as children develop? How far might the procedural deficits of early childhood recover with time? To what extent might the conceptual strengths expand or diminish?

Fazio's Research. The questions posed previously have been addressed in an important series of studies carried out by Barbara Fazio in the United States. In her initial study (Fazio, 1994), she has examined the mathematical progress of children with SLI interviewed at ages 5, 7, and 9. Fazio found that most of the 5-year-olds could verbally count up to *six* or so. This performance was similar to the levels reached by younger controls matched for expressive language level and dramatically less than unimpaired age peers (most of whom were counting up to *twenty* and beyond). The accuracy of object counts was also poor in the SLI group. These procedural deficits, however, were not matched at a conceptual level. In striking agreement with the study by Donlan (1993), Fazio found that her SLI group showed relatively strong grasp of counting concepts, in general, and of the cardinality principle, in particular.

Fazio (1996) followed up her original preschool sample after a 2-year interval. Fourteen of the original 20 children with SLI were tested; these were children, now aged 6 or 7, who were still receiving speech and language therapy. Fifteen of the original age-matched controls and 16 of the younger language-matched controls were seen. The deficit in SLI children's verbal counting in comparison to controls was still severe. In comparison to age-matched controls, the level reached by the SLI group continued to shadow closely the level reached by the younger language-matched group.

By contrast, the SLI children's accuracy in object counting had improved relative to controls. High accuracy was achieved by both SLI and age controls in counting small (2 to 9) and large (10 to 30) sets of toys. Language-matched controls exhibited substantially poorer object counting.

SLI children also surpassed the performance level predicted by their language skills in an important new task, numeral reading. In the relatively demanding task of reading double-digit numerals, the SLI group performed similarly to age controls, far better than the younger language-matched group.

Across a range of simple arithmetic tasks, the SLI group performed worse than age controls but better than language controls. All children tended to use their fingers and count in these tasks, but the age controls used the counting-on strategy more often and the counting-all strategy less often than both other groups. These observations are especially important because the move to counting-on is a significant development in strategy use, one that appears to entail conceptual, as well as procedural, knowledge (Baroody, 1995; Fuson, 1988; Nunes & Bryant, 1996).

Around the age of 7, then, Fazio's (1996) SLI group showed some areas of strength. Despite persistent deficits in the efficiency of count procedures, they showed number-naming and basic arithmetical skills in advance of their language levels. However, Fazio's prediction, based on her hypothesis of underlying processes, was not so positive. She interpreted the pattern of SLI performance as supporting the "phonological STM deficit" hypothesis. She predicted that this restriction in verbal processing, so far affecting count efficiency but sparing conceptual knowledge, would have a cumulative effect on the development of arithmetical skills, especially inhibiting strategy development and the acquisition of arithmetic facts.

Work of Jordan and Colleagues. The results of Jordan, Levine, and Huttenlocher (1995, reported in Jordan, Hanich, & Uberti, chap. 13, this volume) are consistent with Fazio's (1996) prediction. These researchers found that although children SLI performed capably and in a comparable manner to same-age controls on a nonverbal arithmetic task, they performed significantly worse on analogous word problems, a task requiring verbal skill. Furthermore, these researchers found that when determining the answers of basic number facts, children with SLI relied on finger counting more than did same-age controls, who used a retrieval strategy more. Likewise, in a recent follow-up of her 1996 study, Fazio (1999) found that her SLI group had fallen increasingly far behind control levels in arithmetical skill, despite the fact that the control performance was low relative to age. The SLI group showed particular deficits in speeded arithmetic tasks and rapid retrieval of arithmetic facts.

Number System Knowledge in Children With SLI

If specific verbal-processing deficits produce cumulative deficits in arithmetical skill, how far do they restrict other aspects of numerical processing? Is knowledge of the number system liable to be globally impaired as children with SLI reach mid and late childhood? Our own studies have addressed this issue from a particular perspective. We have used Moyer and Landauer's (1967) magnitude-comparison task in which participants indicate by a key-press the greater of two numbers represented by computer-generated numerals. In this way, we have sought to explore the ability of children with SLI to interpret the relative-magnitude meaning of numerals and to access this meaning rapidly and accurately. The magnitude-comparison task lends itself this research aim in three ways. (a) It requires only a motor response and makes no explicit linguistic demands. (b) Accurate performance can only be achieved on the basis of sound knowledge of relative magnitude. (c) The pattern of latencies gives a strong indication of the cognitive resources involved in performance of the task.

Study by Donlan, Bishop, and Hitch. Donlan, Bishop, and Hitch (1998) investigated the single-digit knowledge of twelve 7-year-old children with SLI using a restricted number range (1 to 5), comparing performance on numeric and nonnumeric stimuli, and using a control group matched for receptive language skills. The former were, overall, not more accurate than latter. However, if the 2 children with SLI who did reach accuracy criterion are excluded, then the SLI group outperformed the language-matched peers on number comparison as well as nonnumeric comparison tasks. Furthermore, both of these groups showed the classic latency pattern first observed by Moyer and Landauer (1967), whereby response times are inversely related to the numerical "distance" between items. For example, it takes significantly longer to compare 8 with 9 than it takes to compare 1 with 9. This distinctive reaction-time function, the so-called symbolic distance effect, mirrors the effect seen in direct-perceptual judgment (e.g., of length, pitch, temperature) and has been found in normally developing children across a broad age range (Sekuler & Mierkiewicz, 1977). The findings of Donlan et al., taken alongside previous work, suggest that deriving meaning from Hindu-Arabic numerals is a task that draws primarily on nonverbal processes. Thus, it is tempting to assume that the important ability to judge the relative magnitude of numbers, which constitutes a basic lifeskill in contemporary society, should be as efficiently learned by SLI children as their normally developing peers.

Before drawing such strong conclusions from the study, however, we must acknowledge the following limitations:

1. The study is based on a relatively small sample; there is a risk that its findings may not generalize.

2. The range covered by each stimulus set is extremely small. The findings for the numerals 1 to 5 may not extend to the full range of single-digit numbers, or to multidigit numbers.

3. Even within the small sample studied, there were significant individual differences among the participants with SLI.

Study by Donlan and Gourlay. In an effort to address these issues, Donlan and Gourlay (1999) tested children's ability to judge the relative magnitude of all single-digit pairs of integers and a sample of two-digit pairs. The latter items included "reversals" (e.g., 39 vs. 93 and 18 vs. 81). Performance on these items can be taken as a direct indicator of an initial step toward understanding place value, namely that the order of digits in a multidigit numeral matters (elementary knowledge of positional notation).

Thirteen 8-year-olds with SLI were compared with thirteen 8-year-olds matched for age and nonverbal IQ (Age Control or AC group) and to 12 younger children matched for language-comprehension level (LC group). Accuracy for single-digit judgments was achieved by 100% of the AC group, 92% of the SLI group, and 69% of the LC group. Latencies were analyzed for all participants who reached the accuracy criterion. The group latencies showed a clear pattern (SLI = AC < LC) with uniform symbolic distance effects for all groups.

At the single-digit level, then, with the exception of 1 child, the number-system knowledge of the SLI group appears to be age appropriate. The second experiment examined two-digit judgments (range 10–99). Because the LC group had no formal school experience with two-digit numbers, only the AC and LC groups were tested. Three different judgment types were used. (a) Transparent trials involved simple decade comparisons (e.g., 70 vs. 50), comparisons in which a unit digit lower than either decade digit was shared by both numerals (e.g., 21 vs. 71), and comparisons in which both numerals contain repeated digits (e.g., 33 vs. 88). (b) Reversible pairs included 19 versus 91 and 12 versus 21. (c) Misleading pairs involved numerals in which the nontarget item contains a unit digit greater than the sum of digits in the target numeral (e.g., 18 vs. 21 and 32 vs. 29).

Sixty-one percent of the SLI group and 83% of the AC group achieved accuracy. Latency data were analyzed for all participants reaching the accuracy criterion. SLI and AC groups showed similar speed of response. Analysis of the effect of judgment types on response times showed that transparent trials were judged faster than both reversible and misleading pairs, and that this pattern was consistent across groups.

Another task testing comprehension of spoken two-digit numbers was presented using a printed 100 square. A participant was asked to point to 20 two-digit numbers spoken by the experimenter. The numbers were selected at random from those included in the judgment task. Again, 61% of the SLI group and 83% of the AC group reached the accuracy criterion.

If children can compare two-digit Hindu-Arabic numerals without comprehension of their spoken forms (Pattern 1), this is may be taken to indicate that elementary knowledge of positional notation does not require spoken number knowledge. If the reverse is found, and children fail to compare two-digit written numerals but succeed in comprehending spoken numbers (Pattern 2), then spoken number knowledge is not sufficient to support elementary knowledge of positional notation (but may still be a necessary precondition for it).

The performance of the control group was at ceiling. Although most these participants were successful on both tasks, two individuals showed Pattern 2. This pattern is consistent with the general principle that verbal number knowledge precedes knowledge of Hindu-Arabic numeral meanings (e.g., Bialystok, 1992; Ginsburg, 1977).

Within the SLI group, performance was more varied. Most (7) participants passed both tasks. Three failed both tasks, and 2 conformed to Pattern 2 (as did 2 AC participants). However, 1 participant with SLI showed Pattern 1, which suggests that spoken number knowledge is not a necessary prerequisite for elementary knowledge of positional notation.

First, as more than half of the SLI group was successful in comparing two-digit numbers, it is clear that specific language impairments in children do not necessarily preclude the acquisition of at least elementary knowledge of positional notation. The efficiency and processing strategies of these children were not distinguishable from those of the control group who were successful in the judgment task. One of the successful SLI participants was not able to match written numerals to spoken two-digit numbers satisfactorily. Taken together, these findings suggest that age-appropriate verbal skills may not be necessary for the development of place-value knowledge and that nonverbal representations underlie the acquisition of number knowledge.

Donlan and Gourlay's (1999) findings need careful interpretation. The individual differences in the group were substantial; one 8-year-old with SLI was unable to compare single-digit numbers, and 5 were unable to compare double-digit numbers. A full theoretical account of the developmental pattern must include an explanation of these differences, and we have yet to produce such a full account.

General Conclusions

I have reviewed a range of evidence to support the proposal that SLI do not necessarily present an obstacle to development of concepts of number. Studies by Donlan (1993) and Fazio (1994) have indicated that children with SLI at preschool and early school age possess concepts of cardinality superior to those of younger, normally developing controls matched for language level and approximating those of age-matched controls. However, there is clear evidence from the same studies that SLI children, at these ages at least, show substantial deficits in counting procedures. This dissociation between conceptual and procedural knowledge is important for understanding the general process of numeracy acquisition. It suggests that the role of nonverbal learning in conceptual development may be more substantial than has been acknowledged.

I have explored the unfolding nature of numeracy development in children with SLI through the longitudinal studies carried out by Fazio (1996). Her evidence suggests that the development of arithmetic skills may present an insurmountable obstacle to many children with SLI and that the procedural restrictions imposed by verbal-processing deficits may have cumulative effects, which, in time, restrict conceptual advances. It is plausible to suggest that poorly developed counting and STM skills may combine to limit strategy development in simple arithmetic, and that this limitation eventually constitutes a conceptual restriction (cf. Jordan et al., 1995, cited by Jordan et al., chap. 13, this volume; Rittle-Johnson & Siegler, 1998).

On the other hand, we have shown evidence that most 8-year-olds with SLI demonstrate elementary knowledge of positional notation an understanding that exceeds the knowledge level predicted by their language level (Donlan & Gourlay, 1999). This evidence again is consistent with an interpretation of conceptual knowledge as primarily nonverbal in nature.

As Rittle-Johnson and Siegler (1998) and others before them (e.g., Baroody & Ginsburg, 1986; Fuson, 1988) have suggested, the relation between procedural and conceptual knowledge shows subtle variation across tasks and developmental stages. Studies of children with SLI are starting to offer some insights into the relative contributions of verbal and nonverbal skills to this variation, but many of the underlying processes are still unclear. What are the nonverbal processes that appear to support representations of number meaning and of place value? Can these areas of knowledge really develop without verbal count skills? Does formal arithmetic skill, on the other hand, depend entirely on verbal processes? Are there ways in which nonverbal routes can bypass obstacles to fast retrieval? Research into numeracy and language development is in its infancy; we may hope for rapid progress in the next few years, progress that may cast some light on these important issues.

References

Baroody, A. J. (1995). The role of the number-after rule in the invention of computational short cuts. *Cognition and Instruction, 13,* 189–219.

Baroody, A. J., & Ginsburg, H. P. (1986). The relationship between initial meaningful and mechanical knowledge of arithmetic. In J. Hiebert (Ed.), *Conceptual and procedural knowledge: The case of mathematics* (pp. 75–112). Hillsdale, NJ: Laurence Erlbaum Associates.

Bialystok, E. (1992). Symbolic representation of letters and numbers. *Cognitive Development, 7,* 301–316.

Bishop, D. V. M. (1994). Developmental disorders of speech and language. In M. Rutter & L. Hersov (Eds.), *Child and adolescent psychiatry* (3rd ed., pp. 546–568) Oxford, England: Blackwell.

Bishop, D. V. M. (1997). *Uncommon understanding.* Hove, East Sussex, England: Psychology Press.

Chi, M., & Klahr, D. (1975). Span and rate of apprehension in children and adults. *Journal of Experimental Child Psychology, 19,* 434–439.

Connell, P. J., & Stone, C. A. (1992). Morpheme learning of children with specific language impairment under controlled instructional conditions. *Journal of Speech and Hearing Research, 35,* 844–885

Dehaene, S. (1992). Varieties of numerical abilities. *Cognition, 44,* 1–42.

Donlan, C. (1993). *The development of numeracy in children with specific language impairment.* Unpublished Ph.D. thesis, University of Manchester, England.

Donlan, C., Bishop, D. V. M., & Hitch, G. J. (1998). Magnitude comparisons by children with specific language impairments: Evidence against a general symbolic processing deficit. *International Journal of Language and Communication Disorders, 33,* 149–160.

Donlan, C., & Gourlay, S. (1999). The importance of nonverbal skills in the acquisition of place-value knowledge: Evidence from normally-developing and language-impaired children. *British Journal of Developmental Psychology, 17,* 1–19.

Durkin, K., Shire, B., Riem, R., Crowther, R. D., & Rutter, D. R. (1986) The social and linguistic context of early number word use. *British Journal of Developmental Psychology, 4*, 269–288.

Fazio, B. (1994). The counting abilities of children with specific language impairments: A comparison of oral and gestural tasks. *Journal of Speech and Hearing Disorders, 37*, 358–368.

Fazio, B. (1996). Mathematical abilities of children with specific language impairment: A follow-up study. *Journal of Speech and Hearing Research, 39*, 839–849.

Fazio, B. (1999). Arithmetic calculation, short term memory and language performance of children with specific language impairment: A five year follow-up. *Journal of Speech, Language, and Hearing Research, 42*, 420–431.

Fuson, K. C. (1988). *Children's counting and concepts of number*. New York: Springer-Verlag.

Fuson, K. C., Richards, J., & Briars, D. J. (1982). The acquisition and elaboration of the number word sequence. In C. J. Brainerd (Ed.), *Children's logical and mathematical cognition: Progress in cognitive development research* (pp. 33–92). New York: Springer-Verlag.

Gallistel, C. R., & Gelman, R. (1992). Preverbal and verbal counting and computation. *Cognition, 44*, 43–74.

Gathercole, S. (1998). The development of memory. *Journal of Child Psychology and Psychiatry, 39*, 3–27.

Gathercole, S., & Baddeley, A. (1990). Phonological working memory deficits in language-disordered children: Is there a causal connection? *Journal of Memory and Language, 29*, 336–360.

Ginsburg, H. P. (1977). *Children's arithmetic: The learning process*. New York: Van Nostrand.

Gopnik, M., & Crago, M. B. (1991). Familial aggregation of a developmental language disorder. *Cognition, 39*, 1–50.

Hughes, M. (1986). *Children and number*. Oxford, England: Blackwell.

Hutt, E. (1986). *Teaching language disordered children: A structured curriculum*. London: Edward Arnold.

Huttenlocher, J., Jordan, N. C., & Levine, S. C. (1994). A mental model for early arithmetic. *Journal of Experimental Psychology: General, 123*, 284–296.

Johnston, J. R. (1994). Cognitive abilities in children with language impairment. In R. Watkins & M. Rice (Eds.), *Specific language impairments in children* (pp. 107–122). Baltimore: Brookes.

Johnston, J. R., & Smith, L. B. (1989). Dimensional thinking in language impaired children. *Journal of Speech and Hearing Research, 32*, 33–38.

Mandler, G., & Shebo, B. J. (1982). Subitizing: An analysis of its component processes. *Journal of Experimental Psychology: General, 11*, 1–22.

Markman, E. (1979). Classes and collections: Conceptual organization and numerical abilities. *Cognitive Psychology, 11*, 395–411.

Mix, K. S., Huttenlocher, J., & Levine, S. C. (1996). Do preschool children recognize auditory-visual numerical correspondences? *Child Development, 67*, 1592–1608.

Mix, K. S., Levine, S. C., & Huttenlocher, J. (1997). Numerical abstraction by infants: Another look. *Developmental Psychology, 33*, 423–428.

Moore, D., Benenson, J., Reznick, J. S., Peterson, M., & Kagan, J. (1987). Effect of auditory numerical information on infants' looking behavior: Contradictory evidence. *Developmental Psychology, 23*, 665–670.

Morehead, D. M., & Ingram, D. (1976). The development of base syntax in normal and linguistically deviant children. In D. M. Morehead & A. E. Morehead (Eds.), *Normal and deficient child language* (pp. 209–238). Baltimore: University Park Press.

Moyer, R. S., & Landauer, T. (1967). Time required judgments of numerical inequality. *Nature, 215*, 1519–1520.

Munn, P. (1994). The early development of literacy and numeracy skills. *European Early Childhood Education Research Journal, 2*, 5–18.

Munn, P. (1995). The role of organised preschool learning environments in literacy and numeracy development. *Research Papers in Education, 10*, 217–252.

Munn, P. (1998). Number symbols and symbolic function in preschoolers. In C. Donlan (Ed.), *The development of mathematical skills* (pp. 47–71). Hove, East Sussex, England: Psychology Press.

Nunes, T., & Bryant, P. (1996). *Children doing mathematics*. Oxford, England: Blackwell.

Raven, J. C. (1985). *Coloured progressive matrices.* London: Lewis.

Renfrew, C. (1989). The Action Picture Test. (Available from the author at 2a Headington Place, Oxford, England).

Rittle-Johnson, B. R., & Siegler, R. (1998). The relation between conceptual and procedural knowledge in learning mathematics: A review. In C. Donlan (Ed.), *The development of mathematical skills* (pp. 75–110). Hove, East Sussex, England: Psychology Press.

Sekuler, R., & Mierkiewicz, D. (1977). Children's judgements of numerical inequality. *Child Development, 48,* 630–633.

Siegel, L. S. (1982). The development of quantity concepts: Perceptual and linguistic factors. In C. J. Brainerd (Ed.), *Children's logical and mathematical cognition. Progress in cognitive development research* (pp. 123–155). New York: Springer-Verlag.

Siegel, L. S., Lees, A., Allan, L., & Bolton, B. (1981). Nonverbal assessment of Piagetian concepts in preschool children with impaired language development. *Educational Psychology, 2,* 153–158.

Siegler, R. S., & Jenkins, E. (1989). *How children discover new strategies.* Hillsdale, NJ: Lawrence Erlbaum Associates.

Siegler, R. S., & Shrager, J. (1984). A model of strategy choice. In C. Sophian (Ed.), *Origins of cognitive skills* (pp. 229–293). Hillsdale, NJ: Lawrence Erlbaum Associates.

Simon, T. J., Hespos, S. J., & Rochat, P. (1995). Do infants understand simple arithmetic? A replication of Wynn (1992). *Cognitive Development, 10,* 253–269.

Sophian, C. (1998). A developmental perspective on children's counting. In C. Donlan (Ed.), *The development of mathematical skills* (pp. 27–46). Hove, East Sussex, England: Psychology Press.

Starkey, P., Spelke, E. S., & Gelman, R. (1990). Numerical abstraction by human infants. *Cognition, 36,* 97–127.

Stone, C. A., & Connell, P. J. (1993). Induction of a visual symbolic rule in children with specific language impairment. *Journal of Speech and Hearing Research, 36,* 599–608.

Towse, J., & Saxton, M. (1998). Mathematics across national boundaries. In C. Donlan (Ed.), *The development of mathematical skills* (pp. 129–150). Hove, East Sussex, England: Psychology Press.

Wood, D. (1988). *How children think and learn.* Oxford, England: Blackwell.

Wynn, K. (1992). Addition and subtraction by human infants. *Nature, 358,* 749–750.

Wynn, K. (1998). Foundations of numerical thought: Numerical cognition in infancy. In C. Donlan (Ed.), *The development of mathematical skills* (pp. 3–25). Hove, East Sussex, England: Psychology Press.

CHAPTER 13

MATHEMATICAL THINKING AND LEARNING DIFFICULTIES

Nancy C. Jordan, Laurie Blanteno Hanich, and Heather Z. Uberti
University of Delaware

Although mathematical learning difficulties are widespread among U.S. schoolchildren, they have been studied far less extensively than have reading difficulties. Reading ability, considered to be the hallmark achievement in elementary school, is frequently equated with a good education and high levels of intelligence. Children with reading disabilities are at risk for failure in all of the content areas and may be perceived as having a lifelong disability that limits their educational and vocational opportunities. It is not surprising that reading disabilities are the major source of referrals for special educational services in U.S. schools (Lyon, 1996). Mathematics disabilities in children, on the other hand, are often overlooked. Although most people feel ashamed to reveal that they are poor readers, it is not uncommon for individuals (even elementary school teachers) to admit readily that they are "bad" in math and to avoid mathematical activities (McLeod, 1992). In fact, our society's general reluctance to deal with mathematics may help explain why researchers have shied away from the study of mathematics disabilities (Ginsburg, 1997). Yet, many children in our schools are failing or seriously underachieving in mathematics and are ill prepared for higher level instruction in secondary school and college. Such difficulties are likely to be felt beyond the school years, as technological skills based on mathematical understanding become more important in the 21st century.

Studies on the normal development of mathematics skills have shown that most children, regardless of social class or cultural background, develop key elements of informal mathematical knowledge before they enter elementary school (e.g., Ginsburg & Russell, 1981; Jordan, Huttenlocher & Levine, 1992; Jordan, Levine, & Huttenlocher, 1995). For example, even babies appear to be sensitive to small numbers and number transformations (e.g., Antell & Keating, 1983; Sophian & Adams, 1987; Starkey & Cooper, 1980; Wynn, 1992). Young children acquire basic counting skills (e.g., Briars & Siegler, 1984; Fuson, 1988, 1992; Gelman & Gallistel, 1978; Gelman & Meck, 1983; Wynn, 1990) and can perform addition and subtraction calculations in a variety of contexts (e.g., Hughes, 1986; Huttenlocher, Jordan, & Levine, 1994; Levine, Jordan, & Huttenlocher, 1992; Mix, Levine, & Huttenlocher, 1999). Indeed, they use a wide variety of strategies to solve basic arithmetic problems (e.g., Baroody, 1984, 1987; Carpenter & Moser, 1982; Cowan, chap. 2, this volume; Fuson, 1982; Siegler, 1987, 1989, 1991), many of which are learned without explicit instruction by caregivers (Baroody & Tiilikainen, chap. 3, this volume; Groen & Resnick, 1977; Ilg & Ames, 1951; but cf. Cowan, chap. 2, this volume).

Research on normal mathematical development provides a framework for analyzing and understanding the performance of children who are having difficulties learning mathematics. In this chapter, we consider children's mathematics difficulties from a developmental-cognitive perspective. Our discussion focuses on young children, that is, through the primary grades. We begin by providing background information on domains of mathematical thinking underlying mathematics achievement in early elementary school. We next present the results of our research program on children's development of calculation abilities and discuss related work on children with mathematics difficulties (MD). We then present the findings of a preliminary study on the mathematical thinking of children with different types of learning problems. Finally, we delineate important research issues in the study of children with MD, with an eye toward future investigations.

Domains of Mathematical Thinking

To provide a framework for understanding MD in children, we first examine the course of normal development of mathematical thinking. We limit our discussion to single-digit (basic) number combinations, story problems, and place value and written calculation, all areas of mathematics that are emphasized in primary school.

Basic Number Combinations

Expert performance with number combinations requires two types of knowledge: (a) declarative knowledge and (b) procedural knowledge (Pellegrino & Goldman, 1987). Declarative knowledge involves the addition and subtraction combinations that are stored in a long-term memory (LTM) network, which is strengthened through experience and practice. Combinations with the strongest associations in the network are retrieved most rapidly. For example, addition combinations involving smaller sums are, in general, retrieved faster than are those involving larger sums. Procedural knowledge refers to the strategies a child uses to derive answers to problems that are not stored in the network (e.g., counting procedures). Both declarative and procedural knowledge are necessary for developing expertise in simple addition and subtraction.

Young children use a variety of strategies or procedures when generating answers to addition or subtraction combinations (see, e.g., Baroody & Tiilikainen, chap. 3, this volume; Cowan, chap. 2, this volume; Fuson, 1992; Ilg & Ames, 1951; Jordan, Huttenlocher, & Levine, 1994; Jordan et al., 1992; Levine et al., 1992; Siegler, 1987, 1989). To determine the sum of a simple expression, a child might: (a) represent each addend with his or her fingers and then count the union of the two sets (counting-all); (b) state the value of the first addend and then count upward the number of times of the second addend (counting-on from the first number); (c) state the value of the larger addend and then count upward the number of times of the smaller addend (counting-on from the larger number); (d) think of the answer to an easier number combination (e.g., a fact involving ties, such as 3 + 3) and then derive the answer by adding or subtracting; or (e) retrieve the answer directly from LTM.

On a subtraction problem, a child might: (a) represent the minuend (the initial amount) with his or her fingers and then fold down the number of fingers equal to the subtrahend (the amount taken away)—the answer is the remaining fingers (separating from); (b) match the number of fingers of the minuend to the number of fingers of the subtrahend and derive the answer by counting the unmatched fingers that remain (matching); (c) count upward from the subtrahend until he or she reaches the minuend—the answer is the number of words or fingers in the counting sequence (counting up); or (d) count backward from the minuend the number of times equal to the value of the subtrahend with the last number in the counting sequence being the answer (counting down). A child might also determine a difference by deriving an answer from a known number combination or by directly retrieving the answer from LTM.

Facility with addition and subtraction number combinations is acquired gradually during the primary grades (Carpenter & Moser, 1984; Jordan, Levine, & Huttenlocher, 1994; Levine et al., 1992; Siegler, 1991). In the beginning of kindergarten, a child might respond to addition or subtraction combinations by guessing or making rough estimates (see Dowker, chap. 9, this volume, for a more complete discussion). Gradually, children learn to calculate by counting with their fingers or other physical objects (i.e., counting-all in the case of addition and separating-from, adding-on, or matching in the case of subtraction). Kindergartners also might use direct retrieval to answer basic combinations with which they are familiar (e.g., those involving small numbers such as 2 + 1 or ties such as 1 + 1). In first and second grades, children develop faster and more efficient counting strategies (i.e., counting-on in the case of addition or counting-down and counting-up in the case of subtraction). Children also increase in their ability to derive answers from known number combinations during this period. By the end of the primary grades, most children can retrieve or reconstruct sums and differences automatically or semiautomatically, with minimal cognitive effort.

Arithmetic principles can also help children determine answers to number combinations (see, e.g., Baroody & Tiilikainen, chap. 3, this volume; Cowan, chap. 2, this volume; Dowker, 1995, 1998). For example, the commutativity principle (e.g., 2 + 4 = 6, so 4 + 2 = 6), the reciprocity principle (e.g., 5 + 2 = 7, so 7 − 2 = 5), and the complement principle (e.g., 8 − 2 = 6, so 8 − 6 = 2) all provide "shortcuts" to calculation (Russell & Ginsburg, 1984). Knowledge and application of these principles suggest a good understanding of the relations, including those between two operations.

Young children are both flexible and adaptive in their strategy choices when determining the answers to basic number combinations (Siegler, 1987,

1989, 1991; Siegler & Jenkins, 1989; Siegler & Robinson, 1982). When a child cannot retrieve an answer to a number combination, he or she frequently uses a "backup" strategy (i.e., any strategy other than direct retrieval) to increase the likelihood of reaching a correct solution. Thus, children may use direct retrieval on easier facts (e.g., 2 + 3) and backup strategies on harder ones (e.g., 4 + 5), allowing them to balance speed (direct retrieval is generally considered faster than the other strategies) and accuracy (backup strategies are more accurate than direct retrieval on harder problems). Recent studies of under-graduates (e.g., LeFevre et al., 1996) have shown that young adults are similar to children in their adaptability and flexibility on basic number combinations (see LeFevre, Smith-Chant, Hiscock, Daley, & Morris, chap. 7, this volume).

Story Problems

The ability to solve story problems involves comprehending the problem, selecting an appropriate operation (or appropriate operations), and executing the operation(s) to reach a solution (Lewis & Mayer, 1987). In addition to knowledge of number combinations and proficiency and flexibility with calcu-lation strategies, skilled performance on story problems involves understanding the language and the conceptual structure of a problem. Some children readily carry out addition and subtraction procedures when problems are presented as written expressions but cannot apply these procedures to solve story problems (Mayer & Hegarty, 1996).

Story problems involving basic addition and subtraction operations may differ significantly in terms of their conceptual and linguistic sophistication (Fuson, 1992; Riley, Greeno, & Heller, 1983). Moreover, the underlying semantic structure of the story problem affects children's solution strategies (De Corte & Verschaffel, 1987; Fuson, 1992; Ginsburg, Klein, & Starkey, 1997).

Many children can solve basic story problems before they enter first grade (e.g., Ginsburg et al., 1997; Jordan et al., 1992; Levine et al., 1992). For example, most kindergartners are successful with problems involving a simple change with an unknown result (e.g., *Meg had 4 pennies. Then Jim gave her 5 more pennies. How many pennies does Meg have now?* or *Meg had 9 pennies. Then she gave 4 pennies to Jim. How many pennies does Meg have now?*). In fact, before formal instruction, children are more successful on story problems, which are embedded in meaningful real-world contexts, than on number combinations, which are relatively free of context (Levine et al., 1992).

During first through third grades, children's story-problem skills become increasingly sophisticated (Riley & Greeno, 1988). Many first graders are successful on simple problems with an unknown change (e.g., *Jane had 3 pennies. Then Carl gave her some more pennies. Now Jane has 8 pennies. How many pennies did Carl give her?* or *Jane had 8 pennies. Then she gave some pennies to Carl. Now Jane has 3 pennies. How many pennies did she give to Carl?*). By second grade, most children can solve a variety of story problems involving a comparison (e.g., *Maria has 7 pennies. Ben has 3 pennies. How many pennies does Maria have more than Ben?* or *Maria has 7 pennies. Ben has 4 pennies. How many pennies does Ben have less than Maria?*). The calculation strategies available to children during this age period (e.g., counting-on or counting-down) are well suited to the situations described in these problems (Carpenter & Moser, 1984). By the end of third grade, most children show mastery of even more conceptually sophisticated story problems involving a comparison (e.g., *Jane has 7 pennies. She has 4 more pennies than Mike. How may pennies does Mike have?* or *Jane has 7 pennies. She has 4 pennies less than Mike. How many pennies does Mike have?*).

Place Value and Written Calculation

Skilled performance on multidigit addition and subtraction requires knowledge of several complex procedures (Pellegrino & Goldman, 1987). For example, when using the standard renaming algorithm taught in the United States to perform a multidigit subtraction problem, a child must process single columns from right to left, "borrow" when the bottom number is greater than the top number, and apply special rules if the top number is a zero. In addition to procedural skill, however, multidigit calculation is facilitated by mastery of number combinations and conceptual understanding of the place-value, base-ten number system.

Through formal instruction, children gradually learn conventional procedures for performing multidigit addition and subtraction problems. In a longitudinal study of first through third graders, Hiebert and Wearne (1996) found a close relation between children's understanding of multidigit numbers and their level of computational skill. For example, it was shown that children who developed the earliest understanding of place-value and base-ten concepts (i.e., in first grade) performed at the highest level on computational tasks at the end of third grade. This finding suggests that an early understanding of our number system leads to greater participation in learning mathematics throughout primary school.

Children's written calculation errors often reflect basic misunderstandings or "bugs" in their mathematical thinking (Brown & Burton, 1978; Brown & VanLehn, 1980; Ginsburg, 1996). Although many primary-school children are competent in following rules and procedures, they often follow the wrong ones. Memorizing a procedure without understanding its underlying principles can lead children to make consistent mistakes ("buggy procedures"). One common buggy procedure is regularly subtracting the smaller digit from the larger digit, whether or not the larger digit was on top or coming up with 10 instead of 11 when borrowing from a column whose top digit is 1. Resnick (1982) suggested that conceptual knowledge of the base-ten system helps prevent certain buggy procedures in young children's multidigit calculation.

In summary, children's competence with number combinations, story problems, and multidigit calculation increase significantly during early elementary school. Achieving mastery or fluency with these skills is complex, requiring declarative and procedural knowledge as well as flexibility, conceptual understanding, and linguistic abilities.

Development of Calculation Abilities in Young Children

In this section, we describe a series of studies on the development of calculation abilities in children conducted by the first author of this chapter and her collaborators, Janellen Huttenlocher and Susan Cohen Levine.

Rationale

During the preschool years, children acquire a number of quantitative abilities that are relevant to formal addition and subtraction calculation skills (e.g., Cooper, 1984; Gelman & Gallistel, 1978). However, they have limited success in performing verbally presented calculation problems such as simple story problems and number combinations (e.g., Ginsburg & Russell, 1981). Although this might indicate a lack of calculation skill, a number of other factors could limit children's ability to solve these kinds of problems. For example, the difficulty could be due to an inadequate understanding of the words and syntactic structure of a problem or to an inability to access mental representations of quantities when physical referents are not provided.

Nonverbal Arithmetic Task

We developed a "nonverbal" calculation task in the hope that these sources of difficulty might be eliminated (Levine et al., 1992). The task built on numerical transformation tasks previously described in the literature (e.g., Cooper, 1984; Gelman & Gallistel, 1978; Sophian & Adams, 1987) by requiring a child to arrive at an exact solution to a calculation problem rather than to make a judgment about the effects of the addition or subtraction transformation. On our nonverbal task, the child is shown a set of black disks (arranged in a horizontal line), which is then hidden under a box. In front of the child, the hidden set is transformed either by adding or subtracting disks through an opening in the side of the box. The child's task is to construct an array equivalent to what is hidden under the box.

Results

Our studies have produced three important results.

1. The Primacy of Nonverbal Calculation. *A child's ability to solve nonverbal calculation problems develops before his or her ability to solve conventional verbal calculation problems* (Levine et al., 1992). We found children as young as 4 years of age can solve nonverbal problems but have limited success on comparable story problems (e.g., *Mike had m balls. He got n more balls. How many balls did he have altogether?*) and number combinations (e.g., *How much is m and n?*) until they are 5 to 6 years of age. Participants performed best on nonverbal problems involving the use of concrete objects (i.e., disks) to represent numerosities, next best on story problems that refer to objects not physically present, and worst on number combinations that do not refer to objects (cf. Resnick's 1992 model described in Baroody, Wilkins, & Tiilikainen, chap. 4, this volume). These findings were statistically significant. Calculation items on all problem types involved sums or minuends of 6 or less. The mean percentage correct for each problem type and age in Levine et al.'s (1992) study are presented in Table 13.1.

2. The Universality of Nonverbal Calculation. The ability to solve verbal calculation problems varies significantly across social class, but the ability to solve nonverbal calculation problems does not (Jordan et al., 1992; Jordan, Huttenlocher, & Levine, 1994; Jordan, Levine, & Huttenlocher, 1994). We examined the performance of middle- and low-income kindergarten children on addition and subtraction calculations presented in nonverbal and verbal formats (Jordan et al., 1992). None of the participants had received formal instruction in arithmetic calculation in school. Children in the middle- and low-income groups performed at about the same level on nonverbal problems.

Table 13.1: Mean Percent Correct by Age Group and Problem Type in Levine et al.'s (1992) Study

Age	Nonverbal Problems	Story Problems	Number Combinations
4–0 to 4–5	43 (34)	18 (25)	12 (22)
4–6 to 4–11	57 (30)	32 (21)	15 (20)
5–0 to 5–5	55 (26)	32 (29)	24 (29)
5–6 to 5–11	74 (26)	61 (34)	46 (31)
6–0 to 6–5	82 (21)	74 (30)	68 (36)

Note. The numbers in parentheses are percentages that were calculated by dividing a standard deviation by a total number of items.

However, on verbal problems (i.e., both story problems and number combinations), the middle-income group performed significantly better than the low-income group. The mean percentage correct for each problem type and income level in Jordan et al. (1992) are presented in Table 13.2. Finger counting was associated with higher performance levels on the verbal calculation tasks; children in the middle-income group used their fingers to calculate on the verbal problems, whereas children in the low-income group did not. Middle-income children, however, still performed significantly better than low-income children on the verbal tasks when we adjusted for use of fingers in a subsequent analysis. When we adjusted for basic language abilities (based on a standardized measure of vocabulary and syntax), on the other hand, the income-group differences were eliminated on story problems and significantly reduced on number combinations.

Jordan et al.'s (1992) findings support our hypothesis that income-group differences on conventional calculation problems are associated with language and approaches to problem solving rather than with basic mathematical abilities. They also support Ginsburg & Russell's (1981) claim that calculation skills develop in a robust fashion despite environmental influences related to socioeconomic status.

One year later, we reassessed the calculation performance of the middle- and low-income groups (Jordan, Levine, & Huttenlocher, 1994) and found that after formal instruction in first grade, low-income children still performed as well as middle-income children on the nonverbal calculation task. Moreover, there no longer were income group differences on number combinations. The latter finding was associated with the development of more effective problem-solving strategies among the low-income first graders (i.e., finger counting). On story problems, however, the low-income group continued to perform significantly worse than the middle-income group. This result suggests that early

Table 13.2: Mean Percent Correct by Income Level and Problem Type in Jordan et al.'s (1992) Study

Income Level	Nonverbal Problems	Story Problems	Number Combinations
Low	59 (19)	35 (16)	23 (14)
Middle	64 (18)	55 (25)	49 (30)

Note. The numbers in parentheses are percentages that were calculated by dividing a standard deviation by a total number of items.

difficulties associated with language persist even after formal instruction in school.

3. The Robustness of Nonverbal Calculation. *Children's performance on verbal and nonverbal calculation tasks is differentially sensitive to variation in cognitive ability* (Jordan et al., 1995). In the studies described previously it was not clear whether the low-income children had specific language difficulties or more general cognitive weaknesses. Thus, we next compared the calculation performance of four kinds of kindergarten and first-grade children—those with low language but adequate spatial abilities (low language), those with low spatial but adequate language abilities (low spatial), those with low language and spatial abilities (delayed), and those with adequate language and spatial abilities (non-impaired).

As expected, participants in the low language group performed significantly worse than children in the nonimpaired group on story problems but not on nonverbal problems or number combinations, when a liberal criterion (correct answer regardless of strategy) was used. In contrast, children in the low spatial group did not differ from children in the nonimpaired group on any of the three problem types, although their overall performance was weaker. It is possible that children in the low spatial group used their relative strengths in language to compensate for their spatial weaknesses. Children in the delayed group performed worse than children in the nonimpaired group on nonverbal problems as well as on story problems, but not on number combinations. When we used a conservation criterion for the number-combinations task—one in which the use of backup strategies, such as using fingers was not allowed—the nonimpaired group outperformed the low language and delayed groups but not the low spatial group. Finger counting seems to serve as an important intermediate step for children with specific language and general delays. Our findings are supported by Fazio (1994, 1996), who also found "fact-retrieval" deficits among children with language difficulties (see Donlan, chap. 12, this volume, for a discussion of Fazio's and related research).

Discussion

To explain the findings from our group of studies, we proposed that although the ability to reliably solve nonverbal calculation problems may not require mastery of conventional symbols, it does involve some symbolic processes (or a mental model). That is, the young child might construct a mental version of the initial array of objects and then imagine the movement of items into or out of the array. The imagined mental array could then be used to produce an actual array of the proper numerosity. As the period between 2 and 3 years of age has been characterized as a time of change in symbolic capacity in many areas, we predicted that the ability to calculate should emerge when children are about 2 years of age and should be related to overall level of intellectual competence. We conducted three related experiments to test this prediction (Huttenlocher et al., 1994).

Our first two experiments showed that the ability to reliably obtain the correct answers on nonverbal problems emerges only after 2 years of age. In the third experiment, 3-year-olds who were in a special preschool program for children identified as having mild intellectual delays performed significantly worse than a group of matched controls on the nonverbal task. Overall, the results of three studies suggest that nonverbal calculation skills emerge after the approximation skills of infancy but before the conventional skills of school-age children. The development of this ability appears to be related to the underlying intellectual competence of the child but not to conventional training as reflected by such variables as social class (Jordan et al., 1992). The findings support the prediction that a mental or imagined model underlies the acquisition of basic calculation ability. They also indicate that the emergence of this ability does not depend on conventional symbols of arithmetic.

A subsequent study of individual differences among low-income preschoolers in Headstart programs (Jordan, Huttenlocher, & Levine, 1994) revealed that there are children who can respond correctly on nonverbal problems (involving small numbers), even though they are unable to count sets of objects (at least in a conventional sense) or to answer with a number word. This finding held when children were required to respond by putting out the correct number of disks as well as when they were given a choice of sets and asked to pick the "correct" one.

Conclusions

The programmatic body of research summarized in the Results section previously is consistent with the hypothesis that children between 2 and 3 years of age construct a mental model of addition and subtraction, if biology and the environment support the development of a general symbolic capacity. In contrast to conventional "symbolic schemes that are acquired from caregivers" and that only allow children to become "proficient on . . . corresponding story problems and number-fact problems" after 5 years of age, "such a model might, in principle, develop without input from caregivers. That is, a mental model for arithmetic . . . might involve only an ability to abstract numerically relevant information from situations. . . . The acquisition of verbal arithmetic skills [which involves an understanding of conventional skills, as well as an understanding of number transformations] might involve the mapping of conventional symbols onto a pre-existing mental model of number and number transformations" (Huttenlocher et al., 1994, p. 285).

Research on Children With MD

Based on developmental models of mathematical learning, Russell and Ginsburg (1984) examined different aspects of mathematics in fourth-grade children with MD as well as in control groups of third- and fourth-grade children without MD. They found that fourth-grade children with MD were not deficient in a variety of mathematics skills, including strategies for mental calculation, the ability to solve simple story problems, and the ability to solve written calculations. In these cases, the performance of children with MD was qualitatively similar to that of third-grade children without MD. Deficiencies, however, were reported in the following two areas: (a) facility with number combinations and (b) the ability to solve conceptually complex story problems involving basic operations.

Geary (1990) found that although first graders with MD used the same types of calculation strategies (e.g., direct retrieval, counting with fingers, verbal counting without fingers) as normally achieving children, they made more retrieval and computational errors and employed less mature calculation strategies. For example, first graders with MD relied on "counting-all" strategies whereas children without MD used more efficient "counting-on" procedures. A follow-up study in second grade (Geary, Brown, & Samaranayake, 1991) revealed that normally achieving children used direct retrieval more often than they did in the initial experiment and answered problems more accurately and with greater speed. In contrast, children with MD showed a pattern of strategy use that was similar to the one they used in first grade (i.e., they did not increase in use of direct retrieval and remained dependent on counting strategies) and made only minimal gains in retrieval accuracy. Additionally, the calculation procedures of children with MD in second grade were qualitatively similar to children without MD in first grade. More recent work by Ostad (1997, 1998) revealed that weaknesses in fact retrieval among children with MD persist throughout elementary school.

Cognitive analyses of mathematics skills in these studies suggest that mathematics difficulties are characterized by developmental lags in application of calculation strategies as well as by specific deficits in fact retrieval and the ability to solve complex story problems. However, it is not clear whether some children with MD have problems associated with one of these areas but not with others (e.g., difficulties in fact retrieval but not in understanding story problems). Moreover, in the aforementioned work (Geary, 1990; Geary et al., 1991; Ostad, 1997, 1998; Russell & Ginsburg, 1984), children with MD alone were not differentiated from children with both MD and reading difficulties. Geary's (1990) participants in the MD group had a low-average mean achievement score for both reading and mathematics. This suggests that these children had more pervasive academic weaknesses rather than specific difficulties in mathematics.

To examine whether children with specific MD perform differently from children with general academic delays, Jordan and Montani (1997) examined the calculation and problem-solving skills of two subgroups of third-grade children with MD, namely those with no reading difficulties and those with reading difficulties. A comparison group of normally achieving children was also examined. Each child was asked to generate answers to number combinations as well as story problems in conceptually simple and complex formats (Riley et al., 1983). Although they varied in terms of the semantic relations used to describe a situation, the simple and complex problems involved the same arithmetic operations, namely addition and subtraction. All of the problems were presented both in timed and untimed conditions. In the former, children were required to respond rapidly; in the latter, they were allowed to use more time-consuming strategies, such as verbal counting or counting with fingers.

Across complexity levels (simple and complex) and problem types (story problems and number combinations) the MD good readers group performed worse than the normal group in timed conditions but not in untimed conditions. The MD poor readers group, on the other hand, performed worse than the normal group, whether tasks were timed or not. An analysis of counting strategies in the untimed condition showed that children in all groups used similar types of counting strategies (e.g., counting-on from the largest addend in addition). Participants in the MD good readers group executed counting strategies very accurately, allowing them to achieve parity with children in the normal group when tasks were not timed. Children in the MD poor readers group, on the other hand, executed counting strategies less accurately and therefore lagged behind both the MD good readers group and the normal group in untimed conditions.

Jordan and Montani's (1997) findings indicate that children with more specific MD (i.e., MD good readers) have weaknesses associated primarily with number-combination facility, whereas children with pervasive academic delays (i.e., MD poor readers) have basic weaknesses associated with problem conceptualization and execution of calculation strategies. These findings are consistent with those of Dowker (1995, 1998) that children with a verbal and nonverbal IQ discrepancy (a population that may be similar to our MD good readers) perform better on tasks involving understanding and use of calculation principles than would be predicted by their basic calculation ability.

Because their data were based on observations made at only a single time point (middle of third grade), Jordan and Montani's (1997) findings did not provide information regarding how and when calculation and problem-solving skills develop. However, cross-sectional work by Ostad (1998) suggests that the performance of children with MD on story problems and number combinations remains relatively flat throughout elementary school. Jordan and Montani also did not provide information about higher level calculation and conceptual skills that are emphasized in the primary grades (i.e., multidigit computational skill and understanding of our base-ten place-value system) or about children's instructional programs.

An Investigation of Mathematical Thinking in Children With Different Types of Learning Difficulties

Based on a developmental framework, we developed a series of tasks to assess children's mathematical thinking in number combinations and story problems, as well as in place value and written calculation. We used the tasks to gather preliminary data on children with clinically diagnosed learning difficulties and are currently using them for a larger, long-term investigation. A summary of our investigation follows.

Participants

Fifteen children between 8 and 11 years of age were included in the study. All of the participants were drawn from the same school for children with learning difficulties and were diagnosed by a psychologist as having a learning disability. In each case, the diagnoses were based on low-achievement profiles. The population allowed us to examine children with clinically diagnosed learning difficulties rather than children with relative strengths and weaknesses in academic achievement. The 15 participants, all from middle-class backgrounds, were selected from a pool of approximately 40 children based on their patterns of achievement, determined by the Kaufman Test of Educational Achievement—Brief Form (KTEA; Kaufman & Kaufman, 1985).

Children were assigned to one of four ability groups. A standard reading or mathematics score of 85 or below on the KTEA (where the mean standard score is 100 and the standard deviation is 15) was considered to be low. The low math group consisted of 3 children who were low in mathematics but not in reading. The low math and reading group consisted of 4 children who were low both in mathematics and reading. The low reading group consisted of 4 children who were low in reading but not in mathematics, and the adequate achievement group consisted of 4 children who showed adequate performance both in reading and mathematics. The mean KTEA achievement standard scores, as well as the mean IQ scores (as assessed by the Wechsler Intelligence Scale for Children, Wechsler, 1991), by ability group are shown in Table 13.3.

Mathematics Tasks

Each child was given the following four mathematics tasks: (a) number combinations, (b) story problems, (c) use of principles, and (d) place value.

Number Combinations. The number-combinations task was adapted from research studies by Levine et al. (1992) and Jordan and Montani (1997). Twelve items involving a sum or minuend of 18 or less were read to each child. Half of the items involved addition (e.g., *How much is 7 and 6?*) and half, subtraction (e.g., *How much is 13 take away 6?*). Participants were told to use any method they wanted to figure out answers and were given a set of 20 disks. On each trial, the experimenter also made a record of children's calculation strategies, such as counting objects or verbal counting without concrete objects (Geary, 1990; Siegler, 1987, 1989).

Story Problems. Participants were asked to solve a set of 10 story problems ranging from conceptually simple to conceptually complex (Carpenter & Moser, 1984; Riley & Greeno, 1988; Riley et al., 1983). In particular, three types of story problems were used: change problems, combine problems, and compare

Table 13.3: Mean Achievement Standard Scores and IQ Scores by Ability Group

Group	Reading	Math	Verbal IQ	Performance IQ
Low math/ adequate reading (3 boys)	95	73	113	90
Low reading/ adequate math (3 boys, 1 girl)	83	108	98	99
Low reading/ low math (3 boys, 1 girl)	77	72	87	83
Adequate reading/ adequate math (4 boys)	110	96	94	90

problems. Problems were presented orally so problem-solving performance was not confounded with reading performance. However, a written version of the problem also was provided. Although the story problems varied in terms of the semantic relations used to describe a situation, they all involved addition and subtraction with one-digit numbers (i.e., sums or minuends of 9 or less). The story problems represented the most commonly occurring types of problems found in typical mathematics texts and, thus, the problems that children encounter as part of the mathematics curriculum.

Use of Principles. The use-of-principles task, adapted from Dowker (1995), tested children's knowledge of the commutativity, reciprocity, and complement principles. Participants were given three items corresponding to each principle. An example of each is *2 plus 4 equals 6, so how much is 4 plus 2?* (commutativity principle); *5 plus 2 equals 7, so how much is 7 minus 2?* (reciprocity principle); and *8 minus 2 equals 6, so how much is 8 minus 6?* (complement principle). The children were given credit only if they gave the correct answer automatically, within 3 sec.

Place Value. The place-value task was adapted from Kamii (1989) and Hiebert and Wearne (1996) and designed to assess children's *understanding* of the base-ten number system and place value as well as their *skill* in adding and subtracting multidigit numbers.

1. *Assessment of place-value and base-ten concepts (understanding).* The first two activities consisted of counting problems. In the first problem, three bundles of 10 popsicle sticks and 4 loose sticks were put in front of a child. The experimenter counted the sticks in one bundle with the child to show that there were 10 and then assured child that each bundle contained 10 sticks. The child was then asked how may sticks there were altogether. The second problem was more abstract. Four packs of lifesavers and 3 individual lifesavers were put in front of the child. The child was told that there were 10 lifesavers in each pack, but he or she could not see the individual candies. The child was then asked how many lifesavers there were altogether.

In the next activity, a child was asked to count a set of 17 chips and to read the number 17 written on a card. The experimenter then circled the 7 with the eraser of a pencil and asked the child to show what that part of the number means with the chips. The experimenter next circled the 1 and asked the child to show what that part of the number means with the chips (see Ross, 1989, for a more complete, description of the task and common difficulties with it). Finally, the child was given a story problem that could be solved easily using an understanding of place value and base-ten grouping (i.e., *There were 57 children playing outside at recess. They decided to make teams with 10 on each team. How many teams could they make?).* Based on Hiebert and Wearne's (1996) procedures, a child was considered successful on the "understanding" activity if he or she answered all of the items correctly.

2. *Skill assessment.* On the skill assessment activity, the child was given a sheet with 4 two-digit written computation problems—one addition and one subtraction problem that did not involve regrouping and one addition and one subtraction problem that involved regrouping. A child was considered successful on the "skill" activity if he or she answered all of the items correctly.

Findings and Discussion

A summary of our findings for each ability group is presented in Table 13.4. Participants in the Adequate Achievement group consistently showed what appears to be accurate and automatic production of number combinations. They also displayed good story-problem-solving skills, use of calculation principles, and understanding of place-value concepts. The single area of weakness for this group appeared to be in written calculation. Analysis of written calculation errors revealed that adequately achieving children sometimes used the wrong operation and made simple addition or subtraction mistakes, although their performance tended to be inconsistent. They showed some regrouping skills.

Table 13.4: Performance on Mathematics Tasks by Ability Group

	Arithmetic Combinations (12 items)			Story Problems (10 items) No. correct	Principles (9 items) No. correct	Place Value	
	No. correct	No. of trials, Objects Used	Mean Response Time in Seconds			Understanding	Skill
Adequate achievement							
1. Brad	12	0	2	8	7	yes	no
2. Mike	12	0	3	9	9	yes	no
3. Don	12	0	3	9	6	yes	no
4. Kurt	12	0	3	10	7	yes	no
Low math and reading							
1. Brian	9	11	7	6	7	no	no
2. Alice	9	11	6	7	6	no	no
3. Steve	9	8	29	3	7	no	no
4. Mark	2	0	3	0	0	no	no
Low math (adequate reading)							
1. Carl	11	0	8	3	4	no	no
2. Jim	12	0	4	9	8	yes	no
3. Tony	11	2	13	7	6	yes	no
Low reading (adequate math)							
1. Craig	9	10	20	4	1	no	yes
2. Kevin	12	0	1	10	9	no	yes
3. Carrie	12	11	21	7	4	no	no
4. Sam	12	10	6	7	8	yes	no

School records indicate that children in the adequate achievement group were diagnosed with attention deficits and fine-motor problems, weaknesses that may have affected their performance on written calculation.

Children in the low math and reading group showed weaknesses in number-combination accuracy, even though 3 of the 4 children used objects (i.e., fingers or disks) to aid calculation. Observations of counting strategies suggest that they were inaccurate with informal procedures, such as counting-on or counting-down. Story problem solving and place-value concepts and skills also were areas of weakness. Written calculation errors revealed weak regrouping skills (e.g., failing to borrow or carry) as well as poor facility with number combinations. Most children in the low math and reading group showed a basic grasp of calculation principles.

Children in the low math (adequate reading) group displayed accurate, but not automatic (i.e., within 3 sec), number-combination production. Instead, they relied on verbal counting or other backup strategies. Story problem solving, use of principles, and place-value understanding were adequate in 2 of the 3 children. Written multidigit calculation skills were generally problematic for the Low Math group. Written calculation errors were characterized by adding instead of subtracting, taking the smaller number away from the larger number regardless of its position, and borrowing incorrectly.

Children in the low reading group tended to use their fingers or disks on the number-combinations task, but their overall accuracy was high. Three of the 4 children performed adequately on story problems. Children showed mixed performance on the principles and place-value tasks. Analysis of calculation errors suggested some weaknesses in regrouping.

In sum, children in the adequate achievement group performed well on most tasks whereas children in the low math and reading group performed poorly. The weak performance of children in the low math and reading group appears to reflect pervasive cognitive delays. Participants in the discrepant achievement groups (i.e., low math group and low reading group) appeared to have particular difficulties with rapid (but not accurate) production of answers to basic addition and subtraction combinations, although variation within these groups was apparent. These findings support earlier work showing deficits in number-combination knowledge production among children with MD alone (Jordan & Montani, 1997), as well as in children with reading difficulties alone (Ackerman, Anhalt, & Dykman, 1986). The relation between specific component mathematical difficulties and specific component reading difficulties (e.g., decoding vs. comprehension) should be investigated further. Geary (1994) suggested that weaknesses in representation and or number-combination production are associated with dysfunction of the left hemisphere of the brain, a dysfunction that also could impair automatic word decoding (see Delazer, chap. 14, this volume, for a more detailed discussion).

Research Issues
in Mathematical Thinking
and Learning Difficulties

Our research, along with that of others, indicates that investigators must consider a number of issues when studying children with MD. These issues include examining (a) children's performance across different aspects of mathematical thinking, (b) identifying children with different patterns of difficulties, (c) assessing mathematical thinking within a longitudinal context, and (d) assessing mathematical thinking within a sociological context. A discussion of each issue follows.

Examining Performance Across
Different Aspects of Mathematical Thinking

Young children's thinking should be assessed on tasks that are directly related to the teaching of mathematics in elementary school and that provide information about their understanding of mathematics principles regarding counting, arithmetic, place value, and so forth (Baroody, 1996; Baroody & Ginsburg, 1991; Ginsburg et al., 1997). This should include testing of nonverbal number and arithmetic concepts that may provide a basis for formal mathematical knowledge. Studies should also examine children's problem-solving strategies and calculation errors as well as their level of accuracy. The extensive research on reading has likewise shown that assessment and teaching of specific reading and reading-related competencies is more effective in improving the achievement of children with reading difficulties than assessing and promoting general psychological processes, such as visual discrimination or short-term memory (Duffy & Geschwind, 1985; Roswell & Chall, 1994).

Much of the research on children with MD has narrowly focused on a single domain of mathematical behavior (e.g., number combinations). However, different aspects of mathematics require different cognitive skills (Carroll, 1996; Jordan et al., 1992) and mathematics difficulties may not be consistent across domains (Ginsburg, 1997). For example, when children produce the answer for an arithmetic expression, they may retrieve facts from memory or use appropriate calculation procedures. When solving story problems, children must understand complex language and solve problems presented in real-word contexts. Multidigit calculation problems require the ability to line up numbers and to interpret spatially represented numerical information as well as understanding of place-value and base-ten concepts (Geary, 1994). By looking at performance in several domains of mathematical thinking, we can determine whether children's skills develop differently in early elementary school and whether they have difficulties with some topics but not with others (Ginsburg, 1997).

Identifying Children With Different Achievement Profiles

In many investigations, children with MD are defined as a single group of low achievers in mathematics; children with MD alone are not differentiated from children with general academic weaknesses (i.e., children with both MD and reading difficulties). However, as we discussed in the previous section, recent work shows that children with MD who are good readers perform differently on mathematical thinking tasks from children with MD who are poor readers (Jordan & Montani, 1997). Thus, research on children with MD should include at least two MD subgroups (i.e., children with no reading difficulties and children with reading difficulties). For comparison, studies also should include a control group of grade-matched children with reading difficulties alone and a control group of children without MD or reading difficulties. Evidence suggests that certain reading difficulties coexist with MD (e.g., Geary, 1994; Rourke, 1993).

Group membership should be determined by performance on tests of mathematics and reading achievement with established reliability and validity, using investigator-defined selection criteria (e.g., a disability or weakness may be defined as scoring below the 25th percentile on the test). In the past, many studies relied on learning-difficulties identification criteria that were established by personnel in children's schools. Because these criteria often are subjective and may vary widely across schools, generalization across investigations is problematic (Lyon, 1994; Lyon & Moats, 1997).

Assessing Mathematical Thinking Within a Longitudinal Context

To date, few studies have examined mathematics difficulties from a longitudinal developmental perspective. Most investigations involve a "single-shot" approach, measuring performance individual children only at a single time point (Lyon, 1995). As a result, little is known about the pattern of growth in mathematical thinking and achievement over time and the predictors of individual differences in growth.

Comparisons with Children Who Outgrow Their Difficulties. Empirical studies of reading, however, indicate that only 28% of children with reading difficulties in first grade also had reading difficulties in third grade (Shaywitz, Escobar, Shaywitz, Fletcher, & Makuch, 1992). It has been suggested that a similar lack of stability exists for young children who are identified as having MD (Geary, 1990). If this is the case, it would be important to identify the cognitive characteristics of children who "outgrow" their difficulties as well as of those who "grow into" them (Ginsburg, 1997). Longitudinal (as opposed to cross-sectional) research on children with or at risk for MD is critical for addressing these issues.

Measuring Developmental Change. Growth-curve modeling, a state-of-the-art statistical procedure, holds great promise for the longitudinal assessment of children with learning difficulties, including those with MD. This technique is a special case of hierarchical linear modeling (Bryk & Raudenbush, 1992) and covariance structure modeling (Muthén, 1997). Growth-curve analysis allows an assessment of individual differences among children in initial levels of ability (e.g., in reading or mathematics achievement), as well as change in ability as a function of individual and group characteristics. An initial model is specified that allows each child to have his or her unique growth function. The individual differences in initial status and growth-rate parameters are then modeled as a function of characteristics that vary across individuals.

Growth-curve modeling has been successfully used to assess behavioral and academic change in children with reading difficulties (Francis, Shaywitz, Steubing, Shaywitz, & Fletcher, 1994; Shaywitz & Shaywitz, 1994). For example, this technique has been used to examine whether children with reading difficulties are characterized by developmental lags or by cognitive deficits (Shaywitz, Shaywitz, Fletcher, & Escobar, 1990) and to examine reading skill development in children who have received early interventions and later remediation (Foorman et al., 1997). Analogous analyses could be done with children with MD. Furthermore, growth-curve modeling of multiple mathematical domains simultaneously could help us to understand how the growth or decline in one domain is correlated with growth or decline in other domains (Willett & Sayer, 1996). For a full discussion of the applications of growth-curve analysis to the study of learning difficulties, see Francis et al. (1994).

Interpreting Mathematical Thinking Within a Sociological Context

With respect to disabilities research more generally, children's thinking should be interpreted within a sociological context. Lyon (1994), for example, noted, "No matter how reliable and valid a test has been shown to be with a standardization sample, the meaning of the test scores must be derived in relation to the specific child's cooperation, motivation, and adaptive behavior in the assessment setting, and in relation to the youngster's family, learning, and cultural background" (p. 8).

Most psychological studies on mathematics difficulties focus on deficiencies inside the child's mind, excluding outside factors that might be associated with poor achievement (Ginsburg et al., 1997). Thus, the impact of instructional variables on the development of children's mathematical thinking and achievement is not clear. For example, instruction that emphasizes "number-fact" learning over problem solving might influence children's skill development (Baroody, 1996). It is interesting that Carpenter, Fennema, Peterson, Chiang, and Loef (1989) found that students of teachers who focused on problem solving mastered more basic number combinations than those of teachers who focused on drill and practice. Research should examine whether this finding holds for children with different types of learning problems. Moreover, children who have received remedial services in school may outgrow their difficulties more readily than those who have not (Geary, 1990). Other relevant factors include children's class size, absentee rate, classroom teacher, prior-grade retention, beliefs and goals, motivation, socioeconomic status, and level of parental involvement. According to Lyon and Moats (1997), "A powerful way to disentangle the critical instructional conditions from the more nebulous historical and contextual conditions is to conduct longitudinal studies that allow for the measurement and prediction of change over time as a function of the total ecology" (p. 585).

In summary, future research should be aimed at expanding our knowledge of the nature and processes of mathematical thinking in children with learning difficulties. Data are needed that address the stability of early classifications of MD. Such information is important for making decisions about educational placements and programs for young children. Additionally, studies should assess children's performance on cognitive tasks that are directly applicable to mathematics education, that examine adaptive expertise and flexibility, and that provide a foundation for higher level mathematical learning. The data will provide an empirical basis for developing instructional and assessment activities that are aimed at improving instruction before children fall seriously behind in mathematics and before their difficulties are complicated by secondary factors such as math anxiety or math phobia. For example, if some children display good understanding and procedural knowledge but have specific deficits in remembering number combinations, they may require little more than implementation of bypass techniques in the classroom (e.g., providing increased time limits). In these cases, the use of a calculator or other computational aids might allow them to concentrate on their good problem-solving skills. In later grades, these children's difficulties with number combinations may disappear, or if the difficulties persist, they may be irrelevant to higher level mathematics (Ginsburg, 1997). Children who show more pervasive deficits in mathematical thinking, on the other hand, may need systematic intervention in problem conceptualization as well as in the development of effective computational strategies. Such weaknesses may continue throughout elementary school.

References

Ackerman, P. T., Anhalt, J. M., & Dykman, R. A. (1986). Arithmetic automatization failure in children with attention and reading disorders: Association and sequelae. *Journal of Learning Disabilities, 19,* 222–232.

Antell, S. E., & Keating, D. P. (1983). Perception of numerical invariance in neonates. *Child Development, 54,* 695–701.

Baroody, A. J. (1984). The case of Felicia: A young child's strategies for reducing memory demands during mental addition. *Cognition and Instruction, 1,* 109–116.

Baroody, A. J. (1987). The development of counting strategies for single-digit addition. *Journal for Research in Mathematics Education, 18,* 141–157.

Baroody, A. J. (1996). An investigative approach to teaching children labeled learning disabled. In D. K. Reid, W. P. Hresko, & H. L. Swanson (Eds.), *Cognitive approaches to learning disabilities* (3rd ed., pp. 545–615). Austin, TX: Pro-Ed.

Baroody, A. J., & Ginsburg, H. P. (1991). A cognitive approach to assessing the mathematical difficulties of children labeled "learning disabled." In H. L. Swanson (Ed.), *Handbook on the assessment of learning disabilities: Theory, research, and practice* (pp. 177–227). Austin, TX: Pro-Ed.

Briars, D., & Siegler, R. S. (1984). A featural analysis of preschoolers' counting knowledge. *Developmental Psychology, 28,* 607–618.

Brown, J. S., & Burton, R. R. (1978). Diagnostic procedural bugs in basic mathematical skills. *Cognitive Science, 2,* 155–192.

Brown, J. S., & VanLehn, K. (1980). Repair theory: A generative theory of bugs in procedural skills. *Cognitive Science, 4,* 379–426.

Bryk, A. S., & Raudenbush, S. W. (1992). *Hierarchical linear models: Applications and data analysis methods.* Newbury Park, CA: Sage.

Carpenter, T. P., Fennema, E., Peterson, P. L., Chiang, C. P., & Loef, M. (1989). Using knowledge of children's mathematical thinking in classroom teaching: An experimental study. *American Educational Research Journal, 26,* 499–531.

Carpenter, T. P., & Moser, J. M. (1982). The development of addition and subtraction problem-solving skills. In T. P. Carpenter, J. M. Moser, & T. A. Romberg (Eds.), *Addition and subtraction: A cognitive perspective* (pp. 9–24). Hillsdale, NJ: Lawrence Erlbaum Associates.

Carpenter, T. P., & Moser, J. M. (1984). The acquisition of addition and subtraction concepts in grades one through three. *Journal for Research in Mathematics Education, 15,* 179–202.

Carroll, J. B. (1996). Mathematical abilities: Some results from factor analysis. In R. S. Sternberg & T. Ben-Zee (Eds.), *The nature of mathematical thinking* (pp. 3–25). Mahwah, NJ: Lawrence Erlbaum Associates.

Cooper, R. G. (1984). Early number development: Discovering number space with addition and subtraction. In C. Sophian (Ed.), *Origins of cognitive skills* (pp. 157–192). Hillsdale, NJ: Lawrence Erlbaum Associates.

De Corte, E., & Verschaffel, L. (1987). The effect of semantic structure of first-graders' strategies for solving addition and subtraction word problems. *Journal for Research in Mathematics Education, 18,* 363–381.

Dowker, A. D. (1995). Children with specific calculation difficulties. *Links2, 2,* 7–11.

Dowker, A. D. (1998). Individual differences in normal arithmetical development. In C. Donlan (Ed.), *The Development of mathematical skills* (pp. 275–302). Hove, East Sussex, England: Psychology Press.

Duffy, F., & Geschwind, N. (1985). *Dyslexia: A neuroscientific approach to clinical evaluation.* Boston: Little, Brown.

Fazio, B. B. (1994). The counting abilities of children with specific language impairment: A comparison of oral and gestural tasks. *Journal of Speech and Hearing Research, 37,* 358–368.

Fazio, B. B. (1996). Mathematical abilities of children with specific language impairment: A two-year follow-up. *Journal of Speech and Hearing Research, 39,* 839–849.

Foorman, B. R., Francis, D. J., Winikates D., Mehta, P., Schatsschneider, C., & Fletcher, J. M. (1997). Early interventions for children with reading disabilities. *Scientific Studies in Reading, 1,* 255–276.

Francis, D. J., Shaywitz, S. E., Steubing, K. K., Shaywitz, B. A., & Fletcher, J. M. (1994). The measurement of change: Assessing behavior over time and within a developmental context. In G. R. Lyon (Ed.), *Frames of reference for the assessment of learning disabilities: New views on measurement* (pp. 29–58). Baltimore: Brookes.

Fuson, K. C. (1982). An analysis of the counting-on solution procedure in addition. In T. P. Carpenter, J. M. Moser, & T. A. Romberg (Eds.), *Addition and subtraction: A cognitive perspective* (pp. 67–82). Hillsdale, NJ: Lawrence Erlbaum Associates.

Fuson, K. C. (1988). *Children's counting and concepts of number.* New York: Springer-Verlag.

Fuson, K. C. (1992). Research on whole number addition and subtraction. In D. Grouws (Ed.), *Handbook of research on mathematics teaching and learning* (pp. 243–275). New York: Macmillan.

Geary, D. C. (1990). A componential analysis of an early learning deficit in mathematics. *Journal of Experimental Child Psychology, 49,* 363–383.

Geary, D. C. (1994). *Children's mathematical development.* Washington, DC: American Psychological Association.

Geary, D. C., Brown, S. C., & Samaranayake, V. A. (1991). Cognitive addition: A short longitudinal study of strategy choice and speed-of-processing differences in normal and mathematically-disabled children. *Developmental Psychology, 27,* 787–797.

Gelman, R., & Gallistel, C. R. (1978). *The child's understanding of number.* Cambridge, MA: Harvard University Press.

Gelman, R., & Meck, E. (1983). Preschoolers' counting: Principles before skill. *Cognition, 13,* 343–359.

Ginsburg, H. P. (1996). Toby's math. In R. S. Sternberg & T. Ben-Zeev (Eds.), *The nature of mathematical thinking* (pp. 175–202). Mahwah, NJ: Lawrence Erlbaum Associates.

Ginsburg, H. P. (1997). Mathematics learning disabilities: A view from developmental psychology. *Journal of Learning Disabilities, 30*(1), 20–33.

Ginsburg, H. P., Klein, A., & Starkey, P. (1997). The development of children's mathematical thinking: Connecting research with practice. In I. E. Sigel & K. A. Renninger (Eds.) *Handbook of child psychology: Vol. 4 Child psychology in practice* (5th ed., pp. 401–476). New York: Wiley.

Ginsburg, H. P., & Russell, R. L. (1981). Social class and racial influences on early mathematical thinking. *Monographs of the Society for Research in Child Development, 46*(6, Serial No. 193).

Groen, G., & Resnick, L. B. (1977). Can preschool children invent addition algorithms? *Journal of Educational Psychology, 69,* 645–652.

Hiebert, J., & Wearne, D. (1996). Instruction, understanding, and skill in multidigit addition and subtraction. *Cognition and Instruction, 14,* 251–283.

Hughes, M. (1986). *Children and number.* Oxford, England: Blackwell.

Huttenlocher, J., Jordan, N. C., & Levine, S. C. (1994). A mental model for early arithmetic. *Journal of Experimental Psychology: General, 123,* 284–296.

Ilg, F., & Ames, L. B. (1951). Developmental trends in arithmetic. *Journal of Genetic Psychology, 79,* 3–28.

Jordan, N. C., Huttenlocher, J., & Levine, S. C. (1992). Differential calculation abilities in young children from middle- and low-income families. *Developmental Psychology, 28,* 644–653.

Jordan, N. C., Huttenlocher, J., & Levine, S. C. (1994). Assessing early arithmetic abilities: Effects of verbal and nonverbal response types on the calculation performance of middle- and low-income children. *Learning and Individual Differences, 6,* 413–432.

Jordan, N. C., Levine, S. C., & Huttenlocher, J. (1994). Development of calculation abilities in middle- and low-income children after formal instruction in school. *Journal of Applied Developmental Psychology, 15,* 223–240.

Jordan, N. C., Levine, S. C., & Huttenlocher, J. (1995). Calculation abilities of young children with different patterns of cognitive functioning. *Journal of Learning Disabilities, 28,* 53–64.

Jordan, N. C., & Montani, T. O. (1997). Cognitive arithmetic and problem solving: A comparison of children with specific and general mathematics difficulties. *Journal of Learning Disabilities, 30,* 624–634, 684.

Kamii, C. (1989). *Young children continue to reinvent arithmetic.* New York: Teachers College Press.

Kaufman, A., & Kaufman, N. (1985). *Kaufman Test of Educational Achievement–Brief Form.* Circle Pines, MN: American Guidance Service.

LeFevre, J., Bisanz, J., Daley, K. E., Buffone, L., Greenham, S. L., & Sadesky, G. S. (1996). Multiple routes to solution of single-digit multiplication problems. *Journal of Experimental Psychology: General, 125,* 284–306.

Levine, S. C., Jordan, N. C., & Huttenlocher, J. (1992). Development of calculation abilities in young children. *Journal of Experimental Child Psychology, 53,* 72–103.

Lewis, A. B., & Mayer, R. E. (1987). Students' miscomprehension of relational statements in arithmetic word problems. *Journal of Educational Psychology, 79*, 363–371.

Lyon, G. R. (1994). Critical issues in the measurement of learning disabilities. In G. R. Lyon (Ed.), *Frames of reference for the assessment of learning disabilities: New views on measurement* (pp. 3–13). Baltimore: Brookes.

Lyon, G. R. (1995). Research initiatives in learning disabilities: Contributions from scientists supported by the National Institute of Child Health and Human Development. *Journal of Child Neurology, 10*, 120–126.

Lyon, G. R. (1996). Learning disabilities. *Future of Children, 6*(1), 54–76.

Lyon, G. R., & Moats, L. C. (1997). Critical conceptual and methodological considerations in reading intervention research. *Journal of Learning Disabilities, 30*, 578–588.

Mayer, R. E., & Hegarty, M. (1996). The process of understanding mathematical problems. In R. S. Sternberg & T. Ben-Zee (Eds.), *The nature of mathematical thinking* (pp. 29–53). Mahwah, NJ: Lawrence Erlbaum Associates.

McLeod, D. B. (1992). Research on affect in mathematics education: A reconceptualization. In D. Grouws (Ed.), *Handbook of research on mathematics teaching and learning* (pp. 575–596). New York: Macmillan.

Mix, K. S., Levine, S. C., & Huttenlocher, J. (1999). Early fraction calculation ability. *Developmental Psychology, 35*, 164–174.

Muthén, B. (1997). Latent growth modeling with multilevel data. In M. Berkane (Ed.), *Latent variable modeling and applications to causality* (pp. 149–161). New York: Springer-Verlag.

Ostad, S. A. (1997). Developmental differences in addition strategies: A comparison of mathematically disabled and mathematically normal children. *British Journal of Educational Psychology, 67*, 345–357.

Ostad, S. A. (1998). Developmental differences in solving simple arithmetic word problems and simple number-fact problems: A comparison of mathematically normal and mathematically disabled children. *Mathematical Cognition, 4*, 1–20.

Pellegrino, J. W., & Goldman, S. R. (1987). Information processing and elementary mathematics. *Journal of Learning Disabilities, 20*, 23–32.

Resnick, L. B. (1982). Syntax and semantics in learning to subtract. In T. P. Carpenter, J. M. Moser, & T. A. Romberg (Eds.), *Addition and subtraction: A cognitive perspective* (pp. 136–155). Hillsdale, NJ: Lawrence Erlbaum Associates.

Riley, M. S., & Greeno, J. G. (1988). Developmental analysis of understanding language about quantities and of solving problems. *Cognition and Instruction, 5*, 49–101.

Riley, M. S., Greeno, J. G., & Heller, J. I. (1983). Development of children's problem-solving ability in arithmetic. In H. P. Ginsburg (Ed.), *The development of mathematical thinking* (pp. 153–195). New York: Academic Press.

Ross, S. H. (1989). Part, wholes, and place value: A developmental review. *Arithmetic Teacher, 36*(6), 47–51.

Roswell, F. G., & Chall, J. S. (1994). *Creating successful readers: A practical guide to testing and teaching at all levels.* Chicago: Riverside.

Rourke, B. P. (1993). Arithmetic disabilities, specific and otherwise: A neuropsychological perspective. *Journal of Learning Disabilities, 26*, 214–226.

Russell, R. L., & Ginsburg, H. P. (1984). Cognitive analysis of children's mathematics difficulties. *Cognition and Instruction, 1*, 217–244.

Shaywitz, S. E., Escobar, M. D., Shaywitz, B. A., Fletcher, J. M., & Makuch, R. (1992). Evidence that dyslexia may represent the lower tail of a normal distribution of reading ability. *The New England Journal of Medicine, 236*, 145–150.

Shaywitz, B. A., & Shaywitz, S. E. (1994). Measuring and analyzing change. In G. R. Lyon (Ed.), *Frames of reference for the assessment of learning disabilities: New views on measurement* (pp. 59–69). Baltimore: Brookes.

Shaywitz, S. E., Shaywitz, B. A., Fletcher, J. M., & Escobar, M. D. (1990). Prevalence of reading disability in boys and girls: Results of the Connecticut longitudinal study. *Journal of the American Medical Association, 264*, 998–1002.

Siegler, R. S. (1987). The perils of averaging over strategies: An example from children's addition. *Journal of Experimental Psychology: General, 116*, 250–264.

Siegler, R. S. (1989). Hazards of mental chronometry: An example from children's subtraction. *Journal of Educational Psychology, 31*, 497–506.

Siegler, R. S. (1991). *Children's thinking.* Englewood Cliffs, NJ: Prentice Hall.

Siegler, R. S., & Jenkins, E. (1989). *How children discover new strategies*. Hillsdale, NJ: Lawrence Erlbaum Associates.

Siegler, R. S., & Robinson, M. (1982). The development of numerical understandings. In H. W. Reese & L. P. Lipsitt (Eds.), *Advances in child development and behavior* (pp. 241–312). New York: Academic Press.

Sophian, C., & Adams, N. (1987). Infants' understanding of numerical transformations. *British Journal of Developmental Psychology, 5*, 257–264.

Starkey, P., & Cooper, R. G. (1980). Perception of numbers by human infants. *Science, 210*, 1033–1035.

Wechsler, D. (1991). *Weschler Intelligence Scale for Children–III*. San Antonio, TX: Psychological Corporation.

Willett, J. B., & Sayer, A. S. (1996). Cross-domain analyses of change over time: Combining growth modeling and covariance structure modeling. In G. A. Marcoulides & R. E. Schumaker (Eds.), *Advanced structural equation modeling: Issues and techniques* (pp. 125–157). Mahwah, NJ: Lawrence Erlbaum Associates.

Wynn, K. (1990). Children's understanding of counting. *Cognition, 36*, 155–193.

Wynn, K. (1992). Addition and subtraction by human infants. *Nature, 27*, 749–750.

CHAPTER 14

NEUROPSYCHOLOGICAL FINDINGS ON CONCEPTUAL KNOWLEDGE OF ARITHMETIC

Margarete Delazer
Universitätsklinik für Neurologie, Innsbruck

In recent years, research has focused extensively on the learning, representation, and processing of mathematical knowledge, and neuropsychological investigations have played a crucial role in these efforts. It is now well established that mental arithmetic requires the activation of several different cognitive components (McCloskey, Caramazza, & Basili, 1985). Three components often discussed are (a) basic "arithmetic facts," such as $2 + 2 = 4$ or $3 - 1 = 2$, stored in and directly retrieved from long-term memory (LTM); (b) procedural knowledge, which guides the execution of procedures and algorithms; and (c) conceptual knowledge, which provides understanding of arithmetic operations and principles. The third component allows one to make inferences and to relate different aspects of arithmetic knowledge. Conceptual knowledge is flexible and can be adapted or applied to new tasks, whereas procedural knowledge learned by rote is relatively inflexible and can be applied to familiar tasks only. Thus, these two types of knowledge can differ considerably; the former may also be labeled adaptive expertise, whereas the latter can correspond to routine expertise (Hatano, 1988).

Our understanding of the multiple mechanisms involved in number processing is based on three different sources of evidence: experimental studies with healthy adults, developmental studies on the acquisition of numerical abilities, and neuropsychological analyses of the performance by patients with a brain lesion.[1] Although the disciplines of experimental psychology, developmental psychology, and clinical neuropsychology each use different methods of

---

[1] Acquired deficits in calculation or in number processing (e.g., number reading or writing) may arise from different neurological aetiologies, such as stroke, tumor, or head trauma. Since the beginning of the century it was known that brain lesions, particularly in the left posterior areas, could cause specific patterns of calculation disorders (Berger, 1926; Henschen, 1919, 1920; Lewandowsky & Stadelman, 1908; for a historical review see Boller & Grafman, 1983), a finding that has been consistently replicated (e.g., Grafman, Passafiume, Faglioni, & Boller, 1982; Hecaen, Angelergues, & Houllier, 1961). Dyscalculia may also occur together with agraphia (i.e., a deficit in writing), right–left disorientation and finger agnosia (i.e., the inability to identify fingers), as one of the symptoms that define the Gerstmann syndrome arising after left parietal lesions (Gerstmann, 1927, 1930, 1940; for critical views see Benton, 1987; Poeck & Orgass, 1966). Moreover, dyscalculia can also be observed in diffuse brain disease. In fact, calculation deficits have been described as an early sign of dementia (Deloche et al., 1995; Grafman, Kampen, Rosenberg, Salazar, & Boller, 1989; Parlato et al., 1992; Pesenti, Seron, & Van Der Linden, 1994).

investigation and draw inferences from different sources of data, they all aim to describe the same cognitive processes underlying numerical skills. Nowadays, it is becoming more and more evident that these approaches can greatly benefit from each other, and that combining them may be extremely productive. Developmental studies have provided insight into the acquisition process of numerical competence during childhood and, at the same time, increased our understanding of patients' difficulties. The development of detailed cognitive models has greatly facilitated the interpretation of acquired deficits in numerical abilities and helped to design rehabilitation programs. On the other hand, analyzing the patterns of impaired performance exhibited by patients with a brain lesion has been proven to be highly informative about the cognitive architecture and functioning of normal numerical abilities.

In neuropsychological research on numerical skills, major progress has been achieved in recent years. Most important, these efforts have led to systematic analyses of complex cognitive abilities and to the identification of individual processing components. As several examples (e.g., McCloskey et al., 1985; Warrington, 1982) show, the most fruitful approach in neuropsychological research in the last 20 years was the description of single cases (Caramazza, 1986; Caramazza & McCloskey, 1988). This approach is based on three fundamental assumptions. One is that impaired cognitive performance of a patient with a brain lesion reflects the functioning of a previously normal cognitive system with one or more components damaged (McCloskey, 1992). The first assumption is closely related to two further assumptions. Brain damage may determine selective deficits, leaving some cognitive components intact and disrupting others. Moreover, it is assumed that the cognitive system does not undergo a functional reorganization after brain damage; that is, the cognitive architecture does not critically change after brain damage. Given these assumptions, one may ask, "What must the normal cognitive system be like in order that damage to the system could result in just this performance pattern" (McCloskey, 1992, p. 108)? In this way, inferences about the general functional architecture of the cognitive system are drawn. Using the single-case approach, neuropsychological studies have contributed several important findings about number processing and arithmetic. Such research has revealed, for example, that number transcoding (e.g., numeral reading or writing) involves separate processing of lexical and syntactic information and that dissociation exists between fact knowledge (e.g., "fact retrieval") and procedural knowledge (e.g., general knowledge of arithmetic operations; McCloskey et al., 1985; Warrington, 1982).

In the past, neuropsychological research focused mainly on "fact-retrieval deficits" and, to a lesser extent, on procedural difficulties in acquired dyscalculia. Surprisingly few studies, however, were concerned with conceptual knowledge in dyscalculia and the relations among conceptual knowledge and other components of arithmetic processing (Hittmair-Delazer, Semenza, & Denes, 1994; Warrington, 1982). It is well known from developmental research that several types of knowledge closely interact in efficient calculation and that the different components of the calculation system (i.e., stored facts, procedural knowledge, and semantic/conceptual knowledge) benefit from their linking (Hiebert, 1986; Hiebert & Lefevre, 1986). Moreover, developmental studies have shown that the disconnection between stored schematic knowledge and conceptual understanding determines the occurrence of systematic errors in mathematics (Resnick, 1982; VanLehn, 1986, 1990). In contrast with the ample attention that developmental psychologists have directed to these issues, the role of conceptual knowledge in arithmetic performance has been only recently investigated in neuropsychological case studies (e.g., Girelli & Delazer, 1996). Clearly, future neuropsychological research should systematically investigate the role of conceptual knowledge in arithmetic and its relation with other types of knowledge.

In addition to its contribution to the field of psychology, such efforts should be crucial in neuropsychological rehabilitation. The preservation or restoration of conceptual knowledge underlying arithmetic performance clearly constitutes a critical factor in developing rehabilitative interventions of acquired deficits of numerical skills.

In the first section, I summarize how current cognitive models, which have been developed on the basis of neuropsychological data, depict the implementation of numerical skills, in general, and conceptual knowledge, in particular. In the next two sections, I review neuropsychological evidence regarding the relation between conceptual knowledge and (a) factual knowledge (namely, knowledge of basic number combinations) and (b) procedural knowledge of arithmetic.

Conceptual Knowledge in Neuropsychological Models of Calculation

In recent years, extensive neuropsychological data, as well as solid experimental evidence, have provided the basis for the development of cognitive models on number processing and calculation. These models outline both the functional architecture of the systems (i.e., functional components and pathways between them) and the internal structure and functioning of the various components. However, although some aspects of number processing have been extensively investigated and accounted for within different frameworks (e.g., Dehaene, 1992; McCloskey et al., 1985), others have received little attention and are poorly specified. Although the retrieval of overlearned arithmetic facts has been investigated in numerous studies, procedural knowledge has been poorly specified and conceptual knowledge has been almost totally neglected. Overall, proponents of cognitive models have emphasized the role of automatic processes in arithmetic, whereas they have underestimated the relevance of less routinized and more meaningful knowledge.

Warrington (1982) reported a case study, which had a major influence on cognitive models proposed later. The case involved a consultant physician DRC who, after suffering a left posterior intracerebral hematoma, was no longer able to add, subtract, or multiply without using laborious and time-consuming strategies. The patient himself noted that he had lost all automaticity in doing simple calculations. Despite these severe problems in "retrieving simple arithmetic facts from memory," DRC showed a performance comparable to matched controls in tasks that require approximate processing or understanding of arithmetic operations in general. It is interesting that he was able to estimate (a) the answer of basic arithmetic expressions (e.g., 5 + 7) and more complex calculations (e.g., 829 + 328), (b) the numerosity of visually presented quantities of dots (randomly arranged black dots, up to 100 dots), and (c) real-world measurements (e.g., the distance from London to New York). He could also provide accurate definitions of arithmetic operations. On the arithmetic subtest of the Wechsler Adult Intelligence Scale (WAIS), DRC achieved an age-scaled score of only 5. Given unlimited time, however, he answered 9 of 14 text problems correctly, including the 3 most difficult items. He had no difficulty explaining the appropriate sequences of arithmetic algorithms but showed marked difficulty in performing the actual computations.

The main result of this study was the clear-cut distinction between the knowledge of *arithmetic facts* (being impaired in DRC) and the *knowledge of arithmetic operations* (being preserved in DRC). Although the understanding of arithmetic principles was not tested explicitly, DRC's performance suggests that he preserved intact understanding of arithmetic (e.g., in answering text problems). An explicit distinction between accurate arithmetic computations and arithmetic processing, in general, has only recently been incorporated in all proposed neuropsychological models of calculation (Dehaene, 1992; McCloskey et al., 1985).

The McCloskey Model

McCloskey and colleagues (1985; McCloskey, 1992; see also McCloskey, Aliminosa, & Sokol, 1991; McCloskey, Sokol, & Goodman, 1986; Sokol & McCloskey, 1991; Sokol, McCloskey, & Cohen, 1989; Sokol, McCloskey, Cohen, & Aliminosa, 1991) suggested a cognitive model of calculation and number processing that strongly influenced the subsequent neuropsychological research on dyscalculia. The model draws a major distinction between the number-processing system, which includes the cognitive mechanisms mediating comprehension and production of Arabic and verbal numerals, and the calculation system.

Within the number-processing system, a further distinction is drawn between the numeral-comprehension systems and the numeral-production systems. The former translates numerical inputs into internal semantic representations of numbers; the latter converts these representations into written or spoken numerals. The semantic representations, which are assumed to specify the magnitude of the numbers (basic quantities of the number and their associated power of ten), are accessed in all cognitive operations dealing with numbers, such as reading Arabic numerals, calculation, counting, and so forth.

McCloskey et al. (1985) also proposed specific cognitive mechanisms devoted to calculation. More specifically, they posited the following three components: the comprehension of arithmetic signs, the retrieval of arithmetic facts, and, finally, the execution of calculation procedures. Moreover, the input and output of any calculation process are assumed to be in the form of abstract semantic representations. In support of these proposed distinctions, several single-case studies demonstrated the selective vulnerability of individual components of the calculation system. For example, Ferro and Botelho (1980) reported a selective deficit in the comprehension of written operation symbols (e.g., +, -). The selective impairment of arithmetic fact retrieval has been frequently reported. For example, Sokol et al. (1991) extensively studied a patient, PS, who consistently failed in retrieving basic multiplication facts, despite preserved knowledge of calculation procedures. It is interesting that presentation or response format did not influence the patient's performance in multiplication. Both the error rate and the error pattern were strikingly similar across different formats (nine combinations; dots, written verbal numerals, Arabic numerals). This result supports the assumption that arithmetic fact retrieval is mediated by representations that are independent from the format of input or output (McCloskey, 1992). For multiplication combinations, McCloskey and colleagues drew a further distinction. Combinations between 2×2 and 9×9 are considered to be stored individually, whereas multiplication combinations with a factor of 0 and 1 are thought to be answered by a stored rule. This subset of combinations typically yields uniform errors across different combinations (e.g., all $n \times 0$ items are answered with n).

The model of McCloskey et al. (1985) includes a number of components in the calculation system whose functioning is overlearned and more or less automatic. None of these components requires, in principle, even minimal understanding of what is done. Nevertheless, it seems unlikely that calculation is simply based on automatisms. In fact, although McCloskey and colleagues did not include conceptual knowledge in their model, they mention the contribution of conceptual understanding in some of their case reports. Sokol et al. (1989) defined conceptual knowledge in the following way: "By conceptual knowledge, we refer to an understanding of arithmetic operations and laws pertaining to these operations" (p. 584). Although McCloskey et al. did not study this phenomenon systematically, they gave some examples of preserved conceptual knowledge in two dyscalculic patients, namely MW (McCloskey et al., 1985; Sokol & McCloskey, 1991) and IE (Sokol et al., 1989; Sokol & McCloskey, 1991). These researchers argued that MW and IE featured a dissociation between arithmetic processing generally, as measured by the comprehension of arithmetic principles, and arithmetic computations, as measured by the retrieval of arithmetic facts. (Warrington, 1982, described such a dissociation previously.) It was claimed that MW showed preserved arithmetic understanding by using principled strategies to overcome his deficit. For example, unable to retrieve the result of 7×7 from memory, he responded to this expression by subtracting 7×3 from 7×10.

Similarly, IE was able to work out solutions she could not retrieve from memory. For example, she decomposed the combination $9 + 2$ into $9 + (1 + 1)$, then recomposed the outcome as $(9 + 1) + 1$, and finally answered correctly 11. Thus, she clearly applied (at least implicitly) the associative law of addition to reason out the sum of this basic combination. A further principle repeatedly applied was the commutative law; IE changed the operand order in addition when advantageous to her solution strategy (e.g., $2 + 9$ into $9 + 2$), minimizing the number of necessary computations. (For a discussion of this labor-saving device, see the following chapters in this volume: Baroody & Tiilikainen, chap. 3; Cowan, chap. 2; Baroody, Wilkins, & Tiilikainen, chap. 4). However, the understanding and application of these principles were not explicitly tested (e.g., $9 + 2 = 2 + 9$). From the analysis of the reported strategies it is not clear to what extent overlearned procedural knowledge was applied and to what extent conceptual understanding was involved.

Although their case descriptions indicate that McCloskey and colleagues (McCloskey et al., 1985; Sokol et al., 1989; Sokol & McCloskey, 1991) did not completely overlook the issue of conceptual knowledge, these researchers paid much greater attention to mechanisms involved in automatic fact retrieval and, to a lesser extent, to calculation procedures. However, the implementation of conceptual knowledge remains largely unspecified in this otherwise highly influential model.

Dehaene and Cohen's Model

An alternative to McCloskey's calculation- and number-processing model has been advanced by Dehaene and Cohen (1995, 1997; Dehaene, 1992).

Earlier Version. Dehaene (1992; Dehaene & Cohen, 1995) proposed a modular architecture based on three different codes, namely auditory-verbal code, visual-number form, and analog-magnitude representation. The auditory-verbal code operates on general-purpose language modules, the visual-Arabic-number form manipulates numbers in Arabic format, and the analog-magnitude code represents quantities as inherently variable distributions of activation over an oriented-analog number line (Dehaene).

In contrast with the McCloskey et al. (1985) model, the triple-code model does not assume any common amodal representations. It abandons the idea of a unique number concept and clusters numerical abilities in different groups according to the format in which numbers are manipulated (Dehaene). First, the auditory verbal code is dedicated to verbal input and output, counting, and to the retrieval of memorized addition and multiplication facts. In this view, addition and multiplication facts are considered part of a learned lexicon of verbal associations, such as other stored verbal information. Second, multidigit operations and parity judgments are performed on the Arabic code; that is, they require the mastery of the positional Arabic system. Finally, the abilities to compare and to approximate quantities rely on the analog magnitude code that represents the quantity of a numeral. As Dehaene stated, the analog magnitude code is the main, and perhaps the only, semantic representation of a number. Thus, in the early version of the model, semantic information was limited to the approximate representation of a number's magnitude, and no other types of semantic knowledge were considered.

Subsequent Version. Dehaene and Cohen (1997) subsequently modified their model with respect to the semantic-elaboration component. As already pointed out, they assumed that addition and multiplication combinations are translated into a verbal representation of the expression, which then is used to trigger completion of the verbal sequence. For instance, 2 x 4 is translated into *two times four*, which triggers the learned association *two times four is eight*. Dehaene and Cohen stressed that this direct route is blind to the meaning of the numbers it manipulates.

The direct route is not available for less overlearned operations (subtraction and division) or for complex computations. For basic subtraction and division combinations, a second, indirect route is employed, where meaningful manipulations are performed on internal quantity representations. Processing 5 – 2, for instance, involves starting from a mental representation of quantity 5 and decrementing this quantity twice—quantity 4 and then quantity 3 (Dehaene & Cohen, p. 222). Complex computations may also depend on an indirect route. More specifically, such computations may be decomposed into simpler ones (e.g., $9 + 7 = 9 + 1 + 7 - 1 = 10 + 6 = 16$). This decomposition process relies on the processing of approximate magnitudes (e.g., noticing that 9 is close to 10).

In their earlier studies, Dehaene and Cohen (1992; Dehaene, 1995) emphasized the role of approximate representation of number magnitudes as a dissociable information. For instance, the knowledge of approximate number magnitudes might be preserved in calculation and number-processing disorders, whereas the processing of exact number knowledge might be impaired. On the other hand, in their subsequent work, Dehaene and Cohen (1997) acknowledged that types of knowledge other than approximate number knowledge seem to be involved in the process of meaningful operations. In this framework, the semantic elaboration component includes exact categorical knowledge, such as exact distance knowledge on the number line, knowledge of arithmetic principles and arithmetic rules. In brief, in the previous version of their model, "understanding" consisted only of a mapping between numerals and approximate analog-magnitude representations; in the new version (1997), a wider definition of semantic elaboration was provided.

Dehaene and Cohen (1997) also speculated about the anatomical substrates of the two routes engaged in answering number combinations. In their view, bilateral inferior parietal areas hold semantic knowledge about numerical quantities and, thus, are relevant for the semantic route. A left hemispheric cortico-pallido-thalamic loop controls the production of rote verbal sequences of number words that represent the basic "arithmetic facts."

Neuropsychological Evidence

Arithmetic Facts, Conceptual Knowledge, and Backup Strategies

The knowledge of basic number combinations, such as $5 + 2 = 7$ or $3 \times 3 = 9$, is part of our common general knowledge. Such knowledge is generally thought to be stored in LTM and to be retrieved from there without further computational operations (McCloskey et al., 1985). Although individual differences in education, daily practice, or age must be considered, adults in our culture are assumed to access directly and even automatically retrieve simple arithmetic facts (LeFevre, Bisanz, & Mrkonjic, 1988; LeFevre & Kulak, 1994; see Ashcraft, 1995, for a review).

Other reports, however, have emphasized the importance of multiple routes even for basic expressions. In a detailed analysis of young adults' multiplication performance (LeFevre et al., 1996), fact retrieval was used in only 87.9.% of the trials (both factors being greater than 1 and smaller or equal to 9); that is, various nonretrieval strategies were employed in 12.1% of the trials. Derived-fact procedures involved the use of known arithmetic facts to derive solutions (e.g., for the expression 6×7, "I know that $6 \times 6 = 36$, so another 6 makes 42"). In repeated-addition procedures, one factor is added the appropriate number of times as indicated by the second factor, for example, adding $5 + 5$ to solve 5×2. Number-series solutions used memorized strings to produce an answer, for example, 5×7 by counting "5, 10, 15, 20, 25, 30, 35." For nine-times combinations, special nine rules were reported (LeFevre et al., 1996, p. 289; for a detailed review, see also LeFevre, Smith-Chant, Hiscock, Daley, & Morris, chap. 7, this volume).

The evidence that healthy adults use a variety of strategies to answer basic multiplication combinations is inconsistent with the conventional wisdom that they rely exclusively or almost exclusively on direct retrieval of arithmetic facts, as has been repeatedly argued by Baroody (1983, 1984, 1985, 1994; cf. Cowan, chap. 2, this volume). More germane to the current discussion, this evidence undermines the assumption underlying existing interpretations of dissociation data. For example, without establishing that IE (discussed earlier) used fact retrieval instead of a decomposing-recomposing strategy for $9 + n$ combinations before her brain injury, it is not clear whether the difference in her performance on conceptual- and factual-knowledge tasks is really the result of a brain injury, as Sokol and colleagues (1989; Sokol & McCloskey, 1991) argued. It is entirely possible that IE—like many of the adults in LeFevre et al.'s (1996) study—had always used a decomposition-recomposition strategy to reason out the sums of $9 + n$ combinations.

Although patterns of impaired performance with basic number-combination knowledge have been investigated extensively, few studies described the patients' use of backup strategies to overcome their deficits in combination facility (Warrington, 1982). This is surprising, given that the development of compensatory strategies may reveal preserved components of arithmetic processing (residual arithmetic facts, procedural algorithms, conceptual knowledge), as well as general processing resources (e.g., planning, monitoring, memory, attention, spatial alignment).

The most extensive analysis of backup strategies has been performed for patient BE (Hittmair-Delazer et al., 1994). This patient developed highly elaborate strategies to overcome his deficit with multiplication and division and showed excellent understanding of arithmetic principles. BE, a 45-year-old accountant, suffered a cerebral embolism affecting the left basal ganglia that left him with a right hemiparesis and a nonfluent aphasia.

BE's initial neuropsychological examination uncovered calculation deficits (as well as language difficulties). A more detailed follow-up examination revealed that this patient had lost facility with many multiplication combinations. Preserved combination facility involved, with few exceptions, mainly multiplication expressions with small factors, such as the table of 2 and some expressions with 3, 4, and 5 as factors. Rule-based multiplication (combinations involving 0 or 1 as a factor) was always answered correctly. It is interesting that division combinations showed a similar pattern. That is, facility with division combinations nearly always paralleled that of corresponding multiplication combinations (cf. the results of LeFevre & Morris, 1999, discussed in LeFevre et al., chap. 7, this volume).[2] On the other hand, addition and subtraction were both well preserved. Thus, BE, as in previous cases in the literature (e.g., McCloskey et al., 1985), showed a "fact-retrieval deficit" for multiplication and division combinations. When BE was repeatedly asked if he could think of a way to "solve the problems he could no longer retrieve from memory," he started to develop different and multiple strategies for each family of combinations. The algebraic equivalents of BE's strategies are given in Table 14.1. If the factor n was multiplied by the factor 4, BE could choose between strategies 4a and 4b. Because multiplication is commutative, BE could also choose among the strategies associated with each commuted counterpart. For the combination 5 x 8, for example, he could implement either the strategy for the factor 5 or one of the two strategies for the factor 8.

BE also developed strategies for division combinations, though he was slower and not always sure whether he could work out the correct result. As for multiplication combinations, the strategies were based on mathematical principles and were always mathematically correct. BE's division strategies varied from simple to complex.

---

[2] Division combinations may not be mastered by many people and could, therefore, lack their own representations in semantic memory. Division problems could be solved by strategies, using learned multiplication facts. Parallel deficits in division and multiplication are also consistent with the view that combinations of complementary operations (multiplication/division, addition/subtraction) may share the same data triplet (Baroody, 1985).

Table 14.1: BE's Backup Multiplication Strategies

Factor	Strategy Name	Strategy
3	3	$n \times 2 + n$
4	4a	$n \times 2 + n \times 2$
	4b	$10n \div 2 - n$
5	5	$10n \div 2$
6	6	$10n \div 2 + n$
7	7a	$10n - (2 \times n + n)$
	7b	$10n \div 2 + 2 \times n$
6 x 7 only	7c	$6 \times n + n$
8	8a	$10n - 2 \times n$
	8b	$10n \div 2 + 2 \times n + n$
9	9	$10n - n$

A simple strategy involved transforming a division combination into a fraction and reducing the latter by the factor of 2 or 3. If possible, the reduction was then repeated. For example, $28 \div 4 = 28/4 = 14/2 = 7$.

BE used a complex strategy for the combination $56 \div 7$. The divisor 7 was multiplied by 10, then the dividend was subtracted from the product 70, and the result 14 was divided by the divisor. The result of this last operation was subtracted from 10 to obtain the correct answer, 8. Although the strategy is logically valid for all cases[3], it is not convenient for all combinations of divi-

---

[3] If $70 \div 7 = 10$, then $(10 \times 7) - (8 \times 7) = 2 \cdot 7$. $70 - 56 = 14$. But 8 was unknown, so $(10 \times 7) - (a \times 7) = b \cdot 7$.
Step 1: $10 \times 7 = 70$
Step 2: $70 - 56 = 14$
Step 3: $b = 14 \div 7 = 2$
Step 4: $(10 \times 7) - (a \times 7) = 2 \times 7; 10 - a = 2; a = 10 - 2 = 8$

dend and divisor. It is useful only when 10 times the divisor is less than the dividend or 5 times the divisor is less than the dividend, which is less than 10 times the divisor (as shown in the previous example). In such cases, a relatively difficult division is circumvented (e.g., $56 \div 7 = ?$) by using an easily determined product (e.g., 10 x the divisor 7), a more familiar subtraction process (70 – the original dividend 56), a relatively easy division ($14 \div 2$ or 7), and another relatively familiar subtraction process (10 – 2).

It is interesting that BE always showed good intuition as to which of the possible strategies were useful and economic to reach a solution to the presented problem. He consistently chose strategies that simplified the solution process and, in most cases, he chose the most efficient strategy among several alternatives (i.e., he selected the strategy that required the minimal number of operational steps).

Thus, BE showed excellent conceptual knowledge of arithmetic despite his severe nonfluency with basic number combinations. He demonstrated an intact conceptual knowledge through his use of elaborate backup strategies based on mathematical principles. In fact, all strategies that he spontaneously developed could be expressed as mathematic equations where several underlying arithmetic principles could be identified (see Hittmair-Delazer et al., 1994). For instance, in multiplication, BE applied the same strategies for expressions and their commuted counterparts (e.g., the expression 6 x 9 was answered in the same manner as 9 x 6 (cf. Butterworth, Marschesini, & Girelli, chap. 6, this volume). As was the case for the associative and the distributive laws discussed earlier, BE appeared to have a clear understanding of the commutative law.

One may question whether BE's backup strategies are the same as the ones used by children. It might be hypothesized that they are a step "back" to algorithms learned earlier and represent overlearned procedural knowledge. In fact, multiplication is frequently taught as repeated addition in school (Siegler, 1988), and this strategy may, in principle, be performed without understanding the underlying concept. Also, the appropriate use of arithmetic principles does not prove understanding by itself. It is common to be taught the use of some principles without understanding them (Giaquinto, 1995). However, BE developed his strategies spontaneously, and they clearly differed from the ones used by children. It is reasonable to assume, then, that he did not previously use the backup strategies listed in Table 14.1, either in an automatic or semiautomatic fashion. If so, the case study of BE strongly suggests that conceptual knowledge and factual knowledge are mediated by separate cognitive mechanisms, and this case represents the first side of a double dissociation between the two components.

Further evidence for a dissociation between (impaired) factual knowledge and (intact) conceptual knowledge comes from the case study of patient DA (Hittmair-Delazer, Sailer, & Benke, 1995). DA was a 28-year-old man with excellent premorbid knowledge of mathematics because of his training and profession as an academically graduated chemist. Seven months after a bone marrow transplant, which he received as treatment for his chronic myelogenous leukemia, he developed right-sided hemiparesis and neuropsychological problems. Five months later a moderate weakness of his right arm and fingers was still present, and calculation difficulties remained as the only heavily disturbed domain of cognitive processing. DA performed well in a series of background tasks, assessing number processing (e.g., reading numerals), counting, subitizing, mental estimation, number knowledge (e.g., dates, measures), and procedural knowledge. In contrast to these well-preserved abilities, severe difficulties in simple calculation were found. Indeed, DA was unable to answer half of the basic addition, subtraction, multiplication, and division combinations. Despite this severe deficit in simple calculation, DA perfectly answered algebraic equations (performing above the level of matched controls) and gave adequate explanations and definitions of mathematical expressions. Moreover, he was also able to describe the necessary steps to solve arithmetic text problems, though he was unable to perform the actual computational steps themselves. This case provides further support for the view that the mental representation for understanding and using arithmetic principles is independent from that for stored fact knowledge. However, this does not mean that both types of knowledge, conceptual knowledge and fact knowledge, do not closely interact. Indeed, it seems likely that generating the answer of an arithmetic expression typically involves both types of knowledge.

The case study of DA also shows that basic number combinations (e.g., $3 + 2$, 5×4) are a separate subset of semantic memory, which may dissociate from other mathematical or numerical knowledge (such as mathematical formulae, dates, measures). In contrast to patient BE, DA never responded to a mental-arithmetic task by using backup strategies but always tried to use fact retrieval and, thereby, risked numerous errors. He thus preferred sophisticated guessing (Siegler, 1988) to safe strategies (e.g., counting), which were well within his conceptual or procedural capacities (individuals normally tend to choose more accurate strategies; Siegler, 1988). Evidently, patients may react differently to mental-arithmetic tasks.

The other side of the dissociation between knowledge of arithmetic fact and concepts (intact fact knowledge and impaired conceptual knowledge) has been only recently reported (Dehaene & Cohen, 1997; Delazer & Benke, 1997). JG, a 56-year-old, right-handed patient was operated on for a left-parietal glioblastoma (Delazer & Benke, 1997). After the surgery, JG clearly displayed the four deficits that define the Gerstmann Syndrome. Specifically, she was agraphic, had severe calculation deficits, had problems in right–left orientation, and had finger-recognition difficulties. Further tests, however, showed also apraxia and deficits in verbal learning. JG had severe deficits in answering basic addition, subtraction, and division items. It is surprising that she preserved the multiplication tables and answered within the range of normal subjects. JG was aware of her calculation deficits and repeatedly complained that she had lost her confidence with numbers. However, she never spontaneously used backup strategies to overcome her deficit. Although encouraged to work out the answers, she could not retrieve from memory by using paper and pencil, a written number line with numbers from 1 to 30, fingers, and tokens. JG was completely unable to apply overlearned procedural backup strategies or to develop new ones. She repeatedly stated that something inhibited her and that she was unable to grasp the meaning of arithmetic operations. It is surprising that JG also failed to represent multiplication combinations with any strategy, though she answered them without hesitation, retrieving the result from memory. Additional tasks adapted from Dowker (1995) confirmed that JG was unable to recognize and apply arithmetic principles. In multiplication, she was unable to apply the principle of commutativity (if 12 x 4 = 48, then 4 x 12 = 48) or to recognize the relation between multiplication and repeated addition of a factor (if 12 x 4 = 48, then 12 + 12 + 12 + 12 = 48). She neither recognized the relation between multiplication and division (if 12 x 4 = 48, then 48 ÷ 4 = 12), the 10 principle (if 12 x 4 = 48, then 120 x 40 = 4800), or the $a - 1$ principle for multiplication (if 12 x 4 = 48, then 11 x 4 = 48 − 4 or 44).

JG also had severe difficulties in composing a given sum by poker chips. For the number 52, for example, she commented: "I need two fifties." JG had a severe deficit in all tasks tapping conceptual knowledge of arithmetic, and she was unable to activate overlearned procedural knowledge in order to perform simple backup strategies. Yet, despite these difficulties, she preserved memorized multiplication tables.

It is worth emphasizing that different types of knowledge interact in the development and the execution of backup strategies. Besides general cognitive skills, such as planning, monitoring, attention, and memory, different components of mathematical knowledge are involved, including fact knowledge, procedural knowledge, and conceptual knowledge. These components may contribute to differences in developing backup strategies.

Indeed, the use of backup strategies may rely heavily on procedural knowledge and does not imply by itself conceptual understanding of arithmetic (Baroody, 1984, 1985). Consider, for example, the strategies of patient HH. This 25-year-old, right-handed man suffered a severe head trauma and had a resection of parts of his left temporal lobe. Two years after the onset of his illness, he was still severely aphasic and showed some calculational difficulties. He answered addition and subtraction combinations without hesitation but constantly used written backup strategies for multiplication and division. The response latencies for multiplication and division were usually longer than 1 min. Using his strategies, HH answered 61 of 64 multiplication items correctly. HH consistently added the first factor the number of times indicated by the second factor and never used other strategies than repeated addition (Fig 14.1). In division, HH always applied a corresponding strategy. He added the divisor until the sum matched the dividend and then counted the number of additions performed. HH's strategies were neither flexible nor economic. He never inverted multiplication factors in order to make the solution easier (e.g., inverting 3 x 9 into 9 x 3) and never used derived-fact procedures (e.g., subtracting 3 from 30 for 3 x 9). The rigid application of a single algorithm and the lack of

Figure 14.1: HH's Strategies for the Items 9 x 8, 4 x 4, 8 x 8, 32 ÷ 4, 7 x 5, 7 x 8[a]

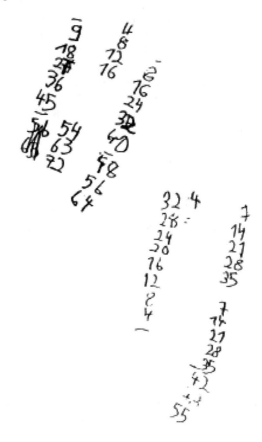

[a] An addition error occurred for this item.

flexibility may be taken as indication that HH's procedures were based merely on procedural knowledge.

Arithmetic Procedures and Conceptual Knowledge

Neuropsychologists uniformly agree that the retrieval of arithmetic facts and the execution of calculation procedures are supported by dissociable cognitive mechanisms. This assumption is supported by case reports of selective deficits concerning either basic fact retrieval (e.g., McCloskey et al., 1985; McCloskey et al., 1991), or complex written calculation (e.g., Girelli & Delazer, 1996; Grafman et al., 1989; Lucchelli & De Renzi, 1993; Semenza, Miceli, & Girelli, 1997). In contrast to the numerous studies on deficits in fact retrieval, only a few neuropsychological investigations were specifically concerned with complex calculation algorithms, and overall, findings on the cognitive organization of procedural knowledge in the human brain are rather scarce. Although arithmetic procedural knowledge has not attracted much interest in neuropsychological research, even less attention has been paid to the relation of procedural knowledge and underlying conceptual knowledge.

In developmental literature, the acquisition of arithmetic procedures and the difficulties typically encountered by young students have been extensively investigated (e.g., Fuson, 1990; Fuson & Kwon, 1992; VanLehn 1986, 1990). It has been reported repeatedly that most of children's errors in complex calculation arise from the use of incorrect algorithms rather than from difficulties in retrieving arithmetic facts. In fact, misconceptions in calculation algorithms frequently lead to systematic error patterns that characterize the performance of younger children (Brown & Burton, 1978; Resnick, 1982; Young & O'Shea, 1981).

Undoubtedly, conceptual knowledge and procedural knowledge closely interact in normal arithmetic performance. It should be noted, however, that the successful application of arithmetic procedures does not require conceptual understanding but can be done by schematic knowledge (VanLehn 1986, 1990). This issue has been addressed by Resnick (1982), who distinguished between syntax and semantics of a calculation algorithm. On the one hand, the syntax consists of a set of rules that specify how to proceed when solving a problem (e.g., start at the right-most column . . .). On the other hand, the semantics consists of the actual understanding of each step in the procedure. With some multidigit subtraction algorithms, the 1 inserted in front of a digit after "borrowing" really represents 10 of whatever units indicated by the digit's place value. Although the syntax reflects the underlying semantics, no explicit reference to semantics is needed to perform the algorithm successfully. Unquestionably, though, without conceptual understanding of an algorithm, systematic errors are far more likely (Resnick, 1982).

In neuropsychological studies, procedural errors have been rarely analyzed. In two recent studies (Girelli & Delazer, 1996; Semenza et al., 1997), a qualitative analysis of procedural errors has been performed, and two different types of procedural deficits have been identified. In the first type, procedural deficits are attributed to deficient monitoring mechanisms. In this case, patients typically have difficulties in ending the procedure, the number of errors increases as the procedure proceeds, and errors are unsystematic and inconsistent (Mantovan, Delazer, Ermani, & Denes, 1999; Semenza et al., 1997). In the second type, errors arise from difficulties in retrieving the correct calculation algorithm. That is, they stem from defective schematic knowledge. In this case, errors are typically consistent across trials and are comparable to the systematic calculation bugs observed in children.

Girelli and Delazer (1996) recently described an example of a procedural deficit of the second type. MT, a 55-year-old retailer, suffered a left-hemispheric stroke that left him severely aphasic. Though intensive speech therapy was performed, language deficits did not improve significantly over the course of 4 years. Apart from aphasic difficulties, problems emerged in number processing and calculation. MT's calculation deficit, however, was not attributable to comprehension or production difficulties. He performed error free on a test of basic addition and subtraction combinations, but not on a test for basic multiplication combinations. He also mastered complex written additions appropriately, although he systematically failed when presented with multi-digit subtraction problems. In a closer analysis, it was shown that the nature of his errors was highly systematic and consistent across trials. MT systematically subtracted the smaller digit from the larger, whether the latter was on top or bottom (see Fig. 14.2). The first example shows the typical "smaller-from-larger" bug. In the second example the same error appeared. However, in this example, and in all analogous items, the borrowing procedure was correctly applied.

MT's failure in subtraction procedures could be clearly attributed to inaccurate syntactic knowledge. The nature of errors was consistent across items and reflected the application of a faulty procedure, as frequently observed in children (Brown & Burton, 1978; Brown & VanLehn, 1980; Fuson, 1990; Fuson & Kwon, 1992; Resnick, 1982; VanLehn, 1986, 1990; Young & O'Shea, 1981). It is

Figure 14.2: Examples of Systematic Errors

"Smaller-from-larger bug "   "Smaller-from-larger bug" with borrowing

interesting that within the subtraction procedure, a dissociation between pre-served subprocedures and lost subprocedures was found. For instance, MT pre-served the subprocedure of borrowing, although he systematically failed to cor-rectly subtract larger digits from smaller ones.

The dissociation between preserved and lost subprocedures is of particular interest because it is revealing about the relation between procedural knowl-edge and underlying conceptual knowledge. For instance, MT's errors violate the noncommutative structure of subtraction and the constraint that the digits of the minuend and subtrahend cannot be handled separately (they are part of multidigit numerals and represent a power of ten). Despite such basic errors and misconceptions, MT preserved other subprocedures, such as the borrowing. How-ever, applying the borrowing procedure while disregarding the noncommuta-tive structure of subtraction is a meaningless operation. Apparently, MT's pre-served subprocedures, such as borrowing, were based on pure schematic (proce-dural) knowledge.

Thus, MT's case provides evidence that in acquired dyscalculia, knowledge of calculation algorithms and underlying conceptual knowledge are distinct components. The case confirms earlier observations of Sokol et al. (1991) and McCloskey et al. (1991), who already described intact procedural knowledge not supported by conceptual knowledge in complex calculations. Sokol et al. re-ported a series of patients who failed to answer basic multiplication items in-volving 0 (5 x 0 or 0 x 2) and consistently applied the wrong rule, answering n x 0 with n (5 x 0 = 5, 0 x 2 = 2). The same patients, however, correctly answered multidigit items involving 0 and applied 0 procedures in complex calculations. Indeed, these 0 procedures (special-case procedures in Sokol et al.'s terms) al-low one to bypass the retrieval of single-digit 0 items by skipping intermediate lines of the procedure (Sokol et al., 1991). The dissociation between single- and multidigit calculation involving 0 suggests that the "special case procedures" consist of pure schematic knowledge not supported by an understanding of the algorithm performed.

In summary, neuropsychological case studies are in line with observations in educational psychology in which intact procedural knowledge without un-derstanding the conceptual basis is a well-known phenomenon (VanLehn, 1990). Undoubtedly, however, efficient calculation should benefit from the linkage of procedural and conceptual knowledge, even in adults.

Discussion

The distinction between mathematical *skills* and mathematical *under-standing* has a long tradition in developmental and educational psychology (Gelman & Gallistel, 1978; Hiebert & Lefevre, 1986; Resnick, 1982; Thorndike, 1922), but it has rarely been considered in neuropsychology. Arithmetic skills are often considered to include arithmetic facts and arithmetic procedures, both components consisting of exactly defined and overlearned knowledge (Girelli &

Delazer, 1996; Lucchelli & De Renzi, 1993; McCloskey et al., 1985; Temple, 1991). Arithmetic understanding has, to date, been variously called *conceptual knowledge* (Hittmair-Delazer et al., 1994; Hittmair-Delazer et al., 1995; Sokol et al., 1989), *semantic knowledge* (Dehaene & Cohen, 1995; Resnick, 1982), and *teleologic knowledge* (VanLehn, 1990). Although these concepts are not completely overlapping, they all refer to a type of knowledge that most scholars view as clearly distinct from procedural and fact-based information.

Ashcraft (e.g., 1982, 1983, 1992) applied the distinction between declarative and procedural knowledge to arithmetic. The former corresponds to the overlearned number combinations (i.e., arithmetic facts); the latter consists of a variety of strategies for retrieving an answer (e.g., counting procedures; Ashcraft, 1982). According to Ashcraft (1982), the major developmental change in performing basic mental arithmetic consists of a shift from using procedural knowledge (such as counting) to declarative knowledge (i.e., to retrieving stored facts from memory). This view, however, has been criticized by Baroody (1983, 1984, 1985, 1994). In his alternative account, the key change in development involves a shift from using slow counting procedures to using a combination of stored data and principled (relational) knowledge (i.e., to fast declarative plus fast procedural knowledge; Baroody, 1994, p. 149). Over the learning process, rules, heuristics, and principles would become more familiar, more automatic and interconnected, and overall, procedural knowledge would provide an efficient method for answering number facts. Thus, if Ashcraft (1982) emphasized the role of declarative knowledge in the development of arithmetic skills, Baroody (1983, 1984) stressed the importance of efficient procedural knowledge in the performance of more expert subjects.

The declarative–procedural dichotomy, however, does not account entirely for the types of knowledge involved in mathematics. More specifically, rules, algorithms, and procedures required in calculation can be learned by rote and successfully applied without being fully understood (e.g., Resnick, 1982; VanLehn, 1986, 1990). Although it is surely appropriate to distinguish between stored factual knowledge, on the one hand, and multistep procedures and algorithms required in complex calculation, on the other, there is reason to believe that knowledge of procedures does not necessarily imply "knowledge about" or conceptual understanding of the procedures themselves. Thus, at least three different domains of arithmetic knowledge have been differentiated: (a) memorized factual knowledge (allowing the retrieval of arithmetic facts), (b) procedural knowledge (guiding the execution of calculation procedures), and (c) conceptual knowledge (mediating the understanding of arithmetic operations and laws pertaining to them). The neuropsychological implementation of the three components and, in particular, the mutual relations among them clearly deserve further research. However, some relevant findings have been provided in recent years, and evidence concerning the relations between arithmetic facts and procedures, arithmetic facts and concepts, and concepts and procedures are considered in turn.

The distinction between arithmetic facts and arithmetic procedures is contemplated in all neuropsychological models of calculation, and it is well supported by several case reports (e.g., Girelli & Delazer, 1996; Hittmair-Delazer et al., 1994; Lucchelli & De Renzi, 1993; McCloskey et al., 1985; Semenza et al., 1997). The dissociability of the two components is not surprising if we consider the cognitive mechanisms underlying fact retrieval and procedures, respectively: The retrieval of basic arithmetic facts from LTM is presumably a single-step process that does not require further computational operations. The execution of calculation procedures, on the other hand, is a multistep process that requires specific syntactic knowledge of the algorithms to be performed. Moreover, the execution of arithmetic procedures puts high demands on general cognitive resources, such as attention, spatial control, planning, and monitoring. Yet, although arithmetic facts and arithmetic procedures present separable cognitive components, they closely interact. Arithmetic facts can be retrieved while performing complex algorithms; similarly, procedural knowledge is employed in several backup strategies to answer basic combinations not stored in LTM or to compute the answer to more complex items.

Recent neuropsychological evidence also supports the functional independence of fact knowledge and conceptual knowledge. In fact, intact conceptual knowledge with impaired fact knowledge has been repeatedly described (Hittmair-Delazer et al., 1994; Hittmair-Delazer et al., 1995; Warrington, 1982). In few case studies, an intact conceptual knowledge has been demonstrated by appropriate understanding of arithmetic operations as well as by the use of elaborated backup strategies developed to compensate for defective fact knowledge. The second side of the double dissociation has been reported only recently. Patient JG showed excellent knowledge of multiplication tables, but completely lost understanding of arithmetic (Delazer & Benke, 1997). Dehaene and Cohen (1997) reported a similar double dissociation in their description of two acalculic patients. Although they use the phrase *quantitative number knowledge* instead of conceptual knowledge, the performance of one of the patients seemed to reflect difficulties in understanding arithmetic operations and principles.

Finally, the relation between procedural and conceptual knowledge is of particular interest. These two components are so strictly linked that it is frequently difficult to disentangle them. There is vast evidence from developmental research that the successful application of a procedural algorithm does not depend on the conceptual understanding, a finding that has been confirmed in neuropsychological case studies. In fact, it has been shown that the application of subprocedures (Girelli & Delazer, 1996) or of special-case procedures (Sokol et al., 1991) is not bound to the understanding of the procedural steps performed. Thus, procedural and conceptual knowledge may dissociate, as in the described cases where the former is preserved and the latter lost. Undoubtedly, though, procedures applied without conceptual basis are more error prone and frequently lead to systematic error patterns (Resnick, 1982; VanLehn, 1986, 1990). Moreover, procedures consisting of a rotely memorized sequence of operational steps are bound to the specific context where they are learned. An example is patient HH's backup multiplication strategies. Although his strategies usually led to the correct result, they were neither economic nor flexible.

Although the single dissociation between intact procedures and impaired conceptual knowledge received empirical support in dyscalculia (Girelli & Delazer, 1996; Sokol et al., 1991), the reverse dissociation (impaired procedural knowledge and intact conceptual knowledge) has not yet been reported. Theoretically, evidence for such a dissociation should consist of newly invented procedural algorithms to compensate for the loss of previously known calculation procedures.

A further issue of interest in the discussion on conceptual and procedural knowledge is the understanding and use of arithmetic principles. In fact, understanding and application of arithmetic principles should be distinguished carefully. As Giaquinto (1995) pointed out, pure knowledge of an arithmetic principle is not equivalent to knowledge that requires understanding. That is, a principle may be successfully applied without being understood and thus consists of procedural knowledge. As an example, Giaquinto stated that one may be taught that $(a + b)^2 = a^2 + 2ab + b^2$ without knowing why that should be true. Several other examples may be given, and it is certainly a common experience for primary-school children to apply principles without understanding their conceptual basis. Thus, the application of arithmetic principles, as well as the use of backup strategies or the execution of calculation algorithms, may be based merely on procedural knowledge. In many cases, then, it will hardly be possible to establish whether or to what extent conceptual knowledge is involved.

In conclusion, recent neuropsychological studies provided clear evidence that different types of knowledge are involved in arithmetic processing and that they are functionally independent and separately implemented in the human brain. Although the independence of fact knowledge from procedural knowledge, on the one hand, and from conceptual knowledge, on the other hand, is well supported by neuropsychological case studies, other aspects of arithmetic processing clearly deserve more attention in future research.

References

Ashcraft, M. H. (1982). The development of mental arithmetic: A chronometric approach. *Developmental Review, 2,* 213–236.

Ashcraft, M. H. (1983). Procedural knowledge versus fact retrieval in mental arithmetic: A reply to Baroody. *Developmental Review, 3,* 231–235.

Ashcraft, M. H. (1992). Cognitive arithmetic: A review of data and theory. *Cognition, 44,* 75–106.

Ashcraft, M. H. (1995). Cognitive psychology and simple arithmetic: A review and summary of new directions. *Mathematical Cognition, 1,* 3–34.

Baroody, A. J. (1983). The development of procedural knowledge: An alternative explanation for chronometric trends of mental arithmetic. *Developmental Review, 3,* 225–230.

Baroody, A. J. (1984). A re-examination of mental arithmetic models and data: A reply to Ashcraft. *Developmental Review, 4,* 148–156.

Baroody, A. J. (1985). Mastery of basic number combinations: Internalization of relationships or facts? *Journal for Research in Mathematics Education, 16*, 83–98.

Baroody, A. J. (1994). An evaluation of evidence supporting fact-retrieval models. *Learning and Individual Differences, 6*, 1–36.

Benton, A. L. (1987). Mathematical disability and the Gerstmann Syndrome. In G. Deloche & X. Seron (Eds.), *Mathematical disabilities: A cognitive neuropsychological perspective* (pp. 111–120). Hillsdale, NJ: Lawrence Erlbaum Associates.

Berger, H. (1926). Über Rechenstörungen bei Herderkrankungen des Großhirns. *Archiv für Psychiatrie und Nervenkrankheiten, 78*, 238–263.

Boller, F., & Grafman, J. (1983). Acalculia: Historical development and current significance. *Brain and Cognition, 2*, 205–223.

Brown, J. L., & Burton, R. R. (1978). Diagnostic models for procedural bugs in basic mathematical skills. *Cognitive Science, 2*, 155–192.

Brown, J. S., & Van Lehn, K. (1980). Repair theory: A generative theory of bugs in procedural skills. *Cognitive Science, 4*, 379–426.

Caramazza, A. (1986). On drawing inferences about the structure of normal cognitive systems from the analysis of patterns of impaired performance: The case for single-patient studies. *Brain and Cognition, 5*, 41–66.

Caramazza, A., & McCloskey, M. (1988). The case for single patient studies. *Cognitive Neuropsychology, 5*, 41–66.

Dehaene, S. (1992). Varieties of numerical abilities. *Cognition, 44*, 1–42

Dehaene, S., & Cohen, L. (1995). Towards an anatomical and functional model of number processing. *Mathematical Cognition, 1*, 83–120.

Dehaene, S., & Cohen, L. (1997). Cerebral pathways for calculation: Double dissociation between rote verbal and quantitative knowledge of arithmetic. *Cortex, 33*, 219–250.

Delazer, M., & Benke, T. (1997). Arithmetic facts without meaning. *Cortex, 3*, 697–710.

Deloche, G., Hannequin, D., Carlomagno, S., Angiel, A., Dordain, M., Pasquier, F., Pellat, J., Denis, P., Desi, M., Beauchamp, D., Metz-Lutz, M. N., Cesaro, P., & Seron, X. (1995). Calculation and number processing in mild Alzheimer's disease. *Journal of Clinical and Experimental Neuropsychology, 17*, 634–639.

Dowker, A. D. (1995). Children with specific calculation difficulties. *Links2, 2*, 8–13.

Ferro, J. M., & Botelho, M. H. (1980). Alexia for arithmetic signs: A cause for disturbed calculation. *Cortex, 16*, 175–180.

Fuson, K. C. (1990). Conceptual structures for multiunit numbers: Implications for learning and teaching multidigit addition, subtraction and place-value. *Cognition and Instruction, 4*, 343–403.

Fuson, K. C., & Kwon, Y. (1992). Korean children's understanding of multidigit addition and subtraction. *Child Development, 63*, 491–506.

Gelman, R., & Gallistel, C. R. (1978). *The child's understanding of number.* Cambridge, MA: Harvard University Press.

Gerstmann, J. (1927). Fingeragnosie und isolierte Agraphie: Ein neues Syndrom. *Zeitschrift der gesamten Neurologie und Psychiatrie, 108*, 152–177.

Gerstmann, J. (1930). Zur Symptomatologie der Hirnläsionen im Übergangsgebiet der unteren Parietal-und mittleren Occipitalwindung (das Syndrom Fingeragnosie, Recht-Links-Störung, Agraphie, Akalkulie). *Nervenarzt, 3*, 691–695.

Gerstmann, J. (1940). Syndrome of finger agnosia, disorientation for right and left, agraphia and acalculia. *Archives of Neurology and Psychiatry, 44*, 398–408.

Giaquinto, M. (1995). Concepts and calculation. *Mathematical Cognition, 1*, 61–82.

Girelli, L., & Delazer, M. (1996). Subtraction bugs in an acalculic patient. *Cortex, 32*, 547–555.

Grafman, J., Kampen, D., Rosenberg, J., Salazar, A. M., & Boller, F. (1989). The progressive breakdown of number processing and calculation ability: A case study. *Cortex, 25*, 121–133.

Grafman, J., Passafiume, D., Faglioni, P., & Boller, F. (1982). Calculation disturbances in adults with focal hemispheric damage. *Cortex, 18*, 37–50.

Hatano, G. (1988). Social and motivational bases for mathematical understanding. In G. B. Saxe & M. Gearhart (Eds.), *Children's mathematics* (pp. 55–70). San Francisco: Jossey-Bass.

406   Delazer

Hecaen, H., Angelergues, T., & Houiller, S. (1961). Les varietes cliniques des acalculies au cours des lesions retroronlandiques. *Revue Neurologique, 105,* 85–103.

Henschen, S. E. (1919). Über Sprach-, Musik-, und Rechenmechanismen und ihre Lokalisationen im Großhirn. *Zeitschrift für die gesamte Neurologie und Psychiatrie, 52,* 273–298.

Henschen, S. E. (1920). *Klinische und anatomische beiträge zur pathologie des gehirns* (Vol. 5). Stockholm: Nordiska Bokhandeln.

Hiebert, J. (Ed.). (1986). *Conceptual and procedural knowledge: The case of mathematics.* Hillsdale, NJ: Lawrence Erlbaum Associates.

Hiebert, J., & Lefevre, J. (1986). Conceptual and procedural knowledge in mathematics: An introductory analysis. In J. Hiebert (Ed.), *Procedural and conceptual knowledge: The case of mathematics* (pp. 1–23). Hillsdale, NJ: Lawrence Erlbaum Associates.

Hittmair-Delazer, M., Sailer, U., & Benke, T. (1995). Impaired arithmetic facts, but intact conceptual knowledge: A single case study of dyscalculia. *Cortex, 31,* 139–149.

Hittmair-Delazer, M., Semenza, C., & Denes, G. (1994). Concepts and facts in calculation. *Brain, 117,* 715–728.

LeFevre, J., Bisanz, J., Daley, K., Buffone, L., Greenham, S., & Sadesky, G. (1996). Multiple routes to solution of single-digit multiplication problems. *Journal of Experimental Psychology: General, 125,* 284–306.

LeFevre, J., Bisanz, J., & Mrkonjic, L. (1988). Cognitive arithmetic: Evidence for obligatory activation of arithmetic facts. *Memory and Cognition, 16,* 45–53.

LeFevre, J., & Kulak, A. G. (1994). Individual differences in the obligatory activation of addition facts. *Memory & Cognition, 22,* 188–200,

Lewandowsky, M., & Stadelman, E. (1908). Über einen bemerkenswerten Fall von Hirnblutung und über Rechenstörungen bei Herderkrankung des Gehirns. *Journal für Psychologie und Neurologie, 11,* 249–265.

Lucchelli, F., & De Renzi, E. (1993). Primary dyscalculia after a medial frontal lesion of the left hemisphere. *Journal of Neurology, Neurosurgery and Psychiatry, 56,* 304–307.

Mantovan, C., Delazer, M., Ermani, M., & Denes, G. (1999). The breakdown of calculation procedures in Alzheimer's disease. *Cortex, 35*(1), 21–38.

McCloskey, M. (1992). Cognitive mechanisms in numerical processing: Evidence from acquired dyscalculia. *Cognition, 44,* 107–157.

McCloskey, M., Aliminosa, D., & Sokol, S. M. (1991). Facts, rules, and procedures in normal calculation: Evidence from multiple single-patient studies of impaired arithmetic fact retrieval. *Brain and Cognition, 17,* 154–203.

McCloskey, M., Caramazza, A., & Basili, A. G. (1985). Cognitive mechanisms in number processing and calculation: Evidence from dyscalculia. *Brain and Cognition, 4,* 171–196.

McCloskey, M., Sokol, S. M., & Goodman, R. A. (1986). Cognitive processes in verbal-number production: Inferences from the performance of brain-damaged subjects. *Journal of Experimental Psychology: General, 115,* 307–330.

Parlato, V., Lopez, O. L., Panisset, M., Iavarone, A., Grafman, J., & Boller, F. (1992). Mental calculation in mild Alzheimer's disease: A pilot study. *International Journal of Geriatric Psychiatry, 7,* 599–602.

Pesenti, M., Seron, X., & Van Der Linden, M. (1994). Selective impairment as evidence for mental organization of arithmetic facts: BB, a case of preserved subtraction? *Cortex, 30,* 661–671.

Poeck, K., & Orgass, B. (1966). Gerstmann's Syndrome and aphasia. *Cortex, 2,* 421–437.

Resnick, L. B. (1982). Syntax and semantics in learning to subtract. In T. P. Carpenter, J. M. Moser, & T. Romberg (Eds.), *Addition and subtraction: A cognitive perspective* (pp. 136–155). Hillsdale, NJ: Lawrence Erlbaum Associates.

Semenza, C., Miceli, L., & Girelli, L. (1997). A deficit for arithmetical procedures: Lack of knowledge or lack of monitoring? *Cortex, 33,* 483–498.

Siegler, R. S. (1988). Strategy choice procedures and the development of multiplication skill. *Journal of Experimental Psychology: General, 117,* 258–275.

Sokol, S. M., & McCloskey, M. (1991). Cognitive mechanisms in calculation. In R. Sternberg & P. A. Frensch (Eds.), *Complex problem solving: Principles and mechanisms* (pp. 85–116). Hillsdale, NJ: Lawrence Erlbaum Associates.

Sokol, S. M., McCloskey, M., & Cohen, N. J. (1989). Cognitive representations of arithmetic knowledge: Evidence from acquired dyscalculia. In A. F. Bennett & K. M. McConkie (Eds.), *Cognition in individual and social contexts* (pp. 577–591). Amsterdam: Elsevier.

Sokol, S. M., McCloskey, M., Cohen, N. J., & Aliminosa, D. (1991). Cognitive representations and processes in arithmetic: Inferences from the performance of brain-damaged patients. *Journal of Experimental Psychology: Learning, Memory, and Cognition, 17,* 355–376.

Temple, C. (1991). Procedural dyscalculia and number fact dyscalculia: Double dissociation in developmental dyscalculia. *Cognitive Neuropsychology, 8,* 155–176.

Thorndike, E. L. (1922). *The psychology of arithmetic.* New York: Macmillan.

VanLehn, K. (1986). Arithmetic procedures are induced from examples. In J. Hiebert (Ed.), *Conceptual and procedural knowledge: The case of mathematics* (pp. 133–179). Hillsdale, NJ: Lawrence Erlbaum Associates.

VanLehn, K. (1990). *Mind bugs. The origin of arithmetical misconceptions.* Cambridge, MA: MIT Press.

Warrington, E. K. (1982). The fractionation of arithmetical skills: A single case study. *Journal of Experimental Psychology, 34,* 31–51.

Young, R. M., & O'Shea, T. (1981). Errors in children's subtractions. *Cognitive Science, 5,* 153–177.

CHAPTER 15

ARITHMETICAL SAVANTS

Lisa Heavey
Institute of Psychiatry, London

The phenomenon of the *idiot savant* represents an intriguing paradox. Such individuals function at a low level of general intellectual ability, yet they demonstrate outstanding talent in particular domains (Howe, 1989; Treffert, 1989). Individuals who exhibit this learning difficulty are now more commonly referred to as savants, even though this term fails to reflect both their superior skill and mental deficiency. Abilities observed among this population include calendar calculation (e.g., O'Connor & Hermelin, 1984), music (e.g., Miller, 1989), art (e.g., Selfe, 1977), and mnemonic proficiency (O'Connor & Hermelin, 1989). The classification of savant may also be extended to people with intelligence in the normal range and a neuropsychiatric diagnosis, most commonly autism. Such cases are characterized by the overdevelopment of skill within a restricted domain, an ability that contrasts markedly with their general level of cognitive and social functioning (e.g., Steel, Gorman, & Flexman, 1984). Savants are rare, estimated by Hill (1977) to represent only 0.06% of the mentally handicapped population, although the incidence rate may be higher (up to 10%) among individuals with autism (Rimland, 1978).

The study of savants has revealed surprising insights into this paradoxical phenomenon. This research also provides useful insights into learning and cognition in general. For example, it offers a unique opportunity to investigate the relations between general intelligence and specific abilities. Undoubtedly, our theoretical understanding of savant ability has benefited in recent years from a shift in research approach away from largely descriptive single case studies to more systematic experimental investigations aimed at elucidating the cognitive processes that underlie their skills.

In this chapter, I review and synthesize evidence from both descriptive and experimental studies regarding a very rare savant talent, namely arithmetic ability. Arithmetical savants possess outstanding numerical skills, performing mental calculations that are impressive in the speed, extent of computation, or both. Similar to savants in general, such feats in the numerical domain represent an islet of ability that contrasts with their lack of everyday cognitive, social, linguistic, and adaptive behavioral skills.

In reviewing the various cases of savant numerical ability, five key issues are addressed in turn. First, what are the numerical and arithmetic competencies that characterize this specific savant ability (i.e., what can arithmetical savants do)? Second, by what methods and strategies do such savants perform their feats of calculation (i.e., how do they do it)? Third, are there features and cognitive characteristics common to the various cases that aid our understanding of the development and execution of savant arithmetic skills? Fourth, what does an integrated account of the development and operation of savant arithmetic ability reveal about how they represent and apply their knowledge? That is, can the competence of arithmetical savants be better characterized as routine expertise and inflexible, or as adaptive expertise and flexible (Hatano, 1988)? Fifth, are savant arithmetic skills and calendar-calculation ability acquired in a similar manner, and is there a relation between these two skills?

In the conclusion of the chapter, I discuss the implications of the research on savant numerical ability for our general understanding of arithmetic cognition. In these rare cases, the relation between numerical competence and different aspects of intellectual ability is revealed. For example, the variability and range of savant arithmetic skills provides insight into the functional architecture of the arithmetic domain. The cognitive and affective predispositions that play a role in the acquisition of savant numerical skills may reflect more general factors influencing the development of arithmetic ability in nonsavants. Finally, the study of savant calculators, many of who have received little or no schooling, reveals how arithmetic skills may develop with minimal structured input and instruction.

The Components of Savant Arithmetical Ability: What Can Savants Do?

The savant cases reviewed in this section are summarized in Table 15.1.

Early Cases

The first documented example of savant arithmetic ability concerns the mental calculation feats of Jedediah Buxton, an illiterate farm laborer born in 1702. As noted by Smith (1983), it is probable that Buxton was somewhat retarded. "His perpetual application of figures has prevented even the smallest acquisition of any other knowledge, and his mind seems to have retained fewer ideas than that of a boy of ten years old, in the same class of life" ("Life," 1754, p. 251, cited in Smith, 1983). Buxton exhibited impressive, but slow calculational prowess, taking 2.5 months to square a 39-digit number. In response to a question regarding volume (*In a body whose three sides are 23,145,789 yards, 5,642,732 yards, and 54,965 yards, how many cubicle eighths of an inch exist?*), he supplied the (28-digit) answer (either forward or backward) 5 hours later. When required to give the number of barleycorns required to reach 8 miles, he computed 1,520,640, assuming 3 barleycorns to the inch. Asked to give the area of a field 423 by 383 yards, he answered, "162,009 square yards" in 2 min.

Another early case of savant calculation is that of Thomas Fuller, who was brought as a slave from Africa to Virginia in 1724. He was described as a lightning calculator "of such limited intelligence who could comprehend scarcely

Table 15.1: Cases of Savant Arithmetical Ability (in the order introduced in text)

Arithmetical Savant	Source	Arithmetical Skills
Jedediah Buxton	Scripture (1891); Smith (1983)	E.g., multiplication and division of large numbers, squaring a 39 digit number
Thomas Fuller	Scripture (1891)	E.g., multiplication and division of 9-digits numbers
Jungris	Brill (1940)	Rapid addition of columns of 6-digit numbers
L	Scheerer et al. (1945)	Rapid addition of 2-digit numbers
George	Nurcombe & Parker (1964)	Rapid addition of multidigit numbers
Obadiah	Phillips (1930)	Multiplication, division, simple fractions
Sabine	Brill (1940); Wizel (1904)	Rapid 2-digit multiplication and division
RH	Kelly et al. (1997)	Multiplication and division of multidigit numbers
Fleury	Tredgold (1929), Critchley (1979)	Multidigit multiplication, division, squared and cubed roots, algebra
DS	Steel et al. (1984)	Multiplication, division, algeb ra, calculus, geometry
Elly	Park & Youderian (1974); Bogyo & Ellis (1988)	Multiplication, facotrization, prime number identification
Michael	Hermelin & O'Connor (1986); Anderson et al. (1998)	Factorization, prime number identification
HP	Heavey (1997)	Multidigit multiplication, division, prime number identification
AC	Stevens & Moffitt (1988)	Multidigit multiplication, division, prime number identification, algebra, calculus
John and Michael	Sacks (1985)	Prime number identification

anything either theoretical or practical, more complex than counting" (Rush, cited in Scripture, 1891). At nearly 80 years old, Fuller's calculation skills were formally documented and presented by Dr. Benjamin Rush to the Pennsylvania Society for the Abolition of Slavery in 1789. When asked, *How many seconds has a man lived who is 70 years, 17 days, and 12 hours old?* Fuller took only 90 sec to respond with the correct answer of 2,210,500,800. He even adjusted his answer to allow for leap years. When asked, *Suppose a farmer has six sows and each sow has six female pigs the first year, and they all increase in the same proportion to the end of eight years, how many sows will the farmer then have?* Fuller gave the correct solution of 34,588,806 in 10 min. He was observed to have initially misunderstood the question, which may account for the lengthier calculation time when compared to the previous problem.

Addition

In the following cases, savant numerical ability appears to be confined to the operation of addition. Brill (1940) detailed the case of Jungreis, whom he first met as a 6-year-old in 1917. Although Jungreis was of an average intellectual level, a history of language delay, vocal peculiarities, and social impairment render him an interesting case. Although able to state instantly the totals of columns of four- to six-digit figures, Jungreis was reportedly unable to subtract or multiply. This specific facility for lightning addition was lost at the age of 9 years, which Brill noted occurred within weeks of his father's death.

Scheerer, Rothmann, and Goldstein (1945) discussed the case of L, an 11-year-old boy with an IQ of 50 who was "retarded in the mastery of many skills, commensurate to his age, and he was lacking in social awareness with a limited repertoire of social responses" (p. 59). These researchers further reported an impressive ability to add the total of 10 to 12 two-digit numbers as quickly as they could be read. Despite having received arithmetic tuition, however, L made errors in adding, multiplying, and subtracting larger numbers and was unable to acquire basic arithmetic principles (e.g., $17 + 8 - 8$ must equal 17).

Nurcombe and Parker (1964) presented the case of George, age 11 years, whose delayed speech, social isolation, and repetitive behaviors strongly suggested a diagnosis of autism. Testing revealed a full-scale IQ of 75 with a marked verbal-nonverbal IQ discrepancy (subscale IQs of 106 and 46, respectively). George's numerical ability was reported to be remarkable. For example, he was able to solve the following sum, $32560 + 8274 + 3819 + 4158$, in seconds after the figures were written down.

Multiplication, Division, and Beyond

Obadiah, a 6-year-old calculating prodigy, showed rapid computation skills involving multiplication, division, and simple fractions (Phillips, 1930). With an IQ of 92, he presented as undisciplined, echolalic, lacking in imagination, impaired in forming social relations, and completely unable to care for himself.

In contrast to most savant arithmetic calculators, Sabine represents a case in which numerical ability was acquired following severe typhoid infection and violent convulsions (Brill, 1940). Prior to her illness, Sabine had developed normally and mastered reading and arithmetic at the corresponding age level. Following her illness, she was reported to have never regained her former intellect. When examined by Wizel (1904) at the age of 22, she was labeled as an "imbecile" and her intelligence placed at the level of a 3-year-old. She was capable, however, of rapid two-digit multiplication and division. Numbers from 11 to 99 were squared in seconds (e.g., she took 10 sec to square 97).

In a more recent study, Kelly, Macaruso, and Sokol (1997) reported the case of RH, a 36-year-old male with autism. Ability testing revealed a low receptive vocabulary score on the Peabody Picture Vocabulary Test (below the 1st percentile based on age-related norms) and a high abstract visual reasoning score using Raven's Colored Progressive Matrices test (above the 90th percentile based on norms for adults with IQs < 80). RH could mentally calculate multidigit problems in all four arithmetic operations (e.g., the division of 1716 by 78). His arithmetic skills did not extend, however, to identifying prime numbers, reducing fractions, solving division problems with remainders, or solving problems with multiple operations (e.g., $[47 \times 91] + 88$).

The calculation skills of Louis Fleury, described by Critchley (1979) as a "blind, intractable, destructive imbecile" included multidigit multiplying and dividing, squaring, deriving square and cube roots, and performing algebra. For instance, in an average of 4 sec, he could give the square root of any number running into four figures and in only 6 sec the cube root of any number into six figures (Tredgold, 1929). When asked for the values of x and y in $x^3 + y = 707,353,209$, where x and y are integers and y has four digits, he found $891^3 + 5,238$ in 28 sec. When required to give 6,137 as the sum of four squares, he gave the first answer in 130 sec ($74^2 + 20^2 + 15^2 + 6^2$) and a second answer 10 sec later ($78^2 + 6^2 + 4^2 + 1^2$). Critchley noted the contrast between Fleury's algebraic competence and his inability to understand even the basics of geometry. Whether Fleury was indeed intellectually impaired is questioned by Smith (1983), although he noted a possible history of psychological and motor difficulties (from Tocquet, cited in Smith, 1983).

Steel et al. (1984) presented the case of DS, an adult male with autism. Despite a full-scale IQ of 91 and notable mathematical abilities, he demonstrated a low level of social and adaptive functioning (e.g., an inability to bathe himself). Mathematical testing revealed DS was able to identify and explain five of the six following mathematical symbols; $\bar{x}$, $|x|$, $\sum$ (sigma), $\int$ (integral), Δ (delta), d/dx. He took only 45 sec to add each consecutive number from 1 to 100 (i.e., $1 + 2 + 3 \ldots + 100$), giving the correct answer of 5,050, although his method of computation is not reported. He could calculate the derivatives of the following functions in seconds: x^2, x^{2e}, $(2x^2 - 2x + 2)$, and cosine x. DS is notable among the current savant cases in having received, from the age of 11, formal tuition in mathematics. At the age of 16, he gained high school qualifications in geometry and algebra.

Prime Numbers

In several other cases of savant arithmetic ability, multiplication and factorization skills extend to the identification of prime numbers (i.e., a number with no factors other than itself and 1). By the age of 13, Elly, diagnosed with autism, could list all the primes from 1 to 1,000 and beyond (Park & Youderian, 1974). She was reported to spend days listing all the ways of factoring a number. For integers up to 100, she had systematically calculated and learned the squares and cubes. Bogyo and Ellis (1988) noted the rapidity of her multiplication skills. When presented with 2 three-digit numbers for multiplication, she produced the six-figure answer at a speed comparable with their computer. Although Elly's language skills were very limited, her nonverbal abstract reasoning ability was outstanding; she tested above the 95th percentile on Raven's Advanced Progressive Matrices Test.

Impressive factorization and prime number skills have been documented in other cases of high-functioning autism and Asperger's syndrome. Michael, who had a nonverbal IQ equivalent on the Raven's Progressive Matrices Test of 128 but an unscorable test performance on the Peabody Picture Vocabulary Test, was able to factorize five-digit numbers (Anderson, O'Connor, & Hermelin, 1998; Hermelin & O'Connor, 1990). He was also able to generate and recognize five-digit primes, taking an average 11 sec to recognize and 50 sec to generate primes of this magnitude. On such problems, Michael was significantly faster than a mathematics graduate selected as a normal control. HP, a 31-year-old autistic male (full-scale IQ 96, verbal IQ 97, nonverbal IQ 95) was also able to identify five-digit primes with ease (Heavey, 1997).

Consider next the case of AC, a 34-year-old male with a full-scale IQ of 99, a verbal IQ of 114, a nonverbal IQ of 82, and a near-ceiling performance on the Raven's Colored Progressive Matrices (Stevens & Moffitt, 1988). In addition to adding, subtracting, multiplying, and dividing six-digit numbers with ease and speed, he exhibited extensive knowledge concerning divisors up to 10,000 and the factors of prime numbers. To determine the extent of AC's mathematical ability, researchers presented him with first-year university-level calculus problems. Although able to work out simple equations with one variable, he was largely unable to find first derivatives of simple functions.

In these cases of savant ability, skill with prime numbers was accompanied by general arithmetic competence. In contrast, Sacks (1985) presented the case of the twins, John and Michael, reported to be incapable of even the most basic addition or subtraction or the comprehension of multiplication and division, yet able to generate prime numbers of a high magnitude. With IQs of between 60 and 70, the twins had, at various times, been diagnosed as autistic, psychotic, and mentally handicapped. Sacks first discovered their ability when he observed the twins involved in a numerical interchange, a "game" in which they would verbally "throw" six-digit numbers at each other, figures that Sacks later realized were prime. By volunteering an eight-digit prime of his own, Sacks joined in the game. He noted their response:

They both turned towards me, then suddenly became still, with a look of intense concentration and perhaps wonder on their faces. There was a long pause—the longest I had ever known them to make, it must have lasted a half-minute or more—and then suddenly, simultaneously, they both broke out in smiles. (p. 193)

An hour later, the twins were exchanging 20-digit primes. However, the accuracy of these numbers was never verified because Sacks' reference list discontinued after 10-digit primes. He also credited a further numerical feat to the twins. When a box of matches was spilled on the floor in front of them, they both cried "111" simultaneously; one twin then muttered "37," which was echoed by the other twin and repeated by the first twin again. The twins had instantly enumerated the array of matches and then factored the number into component primes. No further examples of this impressive subitizing skill are given.

In brief, the special arithmetic ability of some savants is limited to the operation of addition and impressive solely in the speed at which mental calculation is performed. In other cases, it is far more extensive. In general, although most savants are proficient in all four operations, multiplication is the favored operation from which squaring, cubing, factorization, and prime number skills may derive. For a very small number of savants, knowledge encompasses an understanding of fractions, geometry, algebra, and even calculus. Although such feats appear impressive in comparison to savants' performance in other cognitive domains and to the arithmetic skills of others with similar intellect, their skills typically do not surpass, or even equal, those observed in mental calculators of an expert level (Smith, 1983). In terms of intellectual ability, there is considerable range in full-scale IQ (from 50 to 99), with additional variation in intellectual profiles. Superior verbal relative to nonverbal IQ was observed in some cases, whereas an even profile characterized the performance of other individuals. Assessment in several cases indicates poor performance on language measures; thus, arithmetic ability does not appear strongly dependent on linguistic competence. However, impressive performance on a visual-spatial abstraction task was observed in a number of cases, suggesting that such a facet of cognitive processing may relate to arithmetic ability.

Savant Calculation Strategies and Methods: How Do They Do It?

Counting and Grouping

Prior to receiving any arithmetic instruction, the numerical achievements of Obadiah appeared to derive from an initial facility for counting and grouping. When presented with a 36-hole pegboard arranged in 6 x 6 rows, he rapidly counted the holes as units of 3, then as units of 6. To the question *If one apple costs 5 cents, what will 5 apples cost?* he counted quickly by fives until he reached 25. When asked how many seconds in 140 minutes, he counted quickly in multiples of 60. Obadiah's primitive calculations became less laborious as, with practice, the size of grouping units was increased. His ability to count in halves, thirds, and quarters and solve simple fractions (e.g., 1/3 of 30) is believed to stem from his early interest in time; he would spontaneously divide hours from halves and quarters to half minutes and seconds (Parker, 1918).

A similar, albeit more idiosyncratic, facility for grouping was noted in the case of Sabine (Brill, 1940). At the age of 13, she became interested in coins and buttons, both of which she would continually sort and count. Specifically, she would arrange the items into groups of 16 and subsequently was able to give numbers of varying magnitudes in terms of how many multiples of 16 they contained. For example, when required to give the number of coins she had, Sabine responded "6 x 16 + 8 more." After providing the answer to 23 x 23 (529), she then added that it was the same as "33 x 16 + 1. " When multiplying 14 x 14, Sabine answered "196" and then volunteered that it was the same as "12 x 16 + 4." Her knowledge of the number system thus appeared to incorporate the representation of numbers as multiples of 16. Through Sabine's verbalizations, Wizel (1904) gained insight into her calculation methods. In order to simplify the multiplication of any 2 two-digit numbers, she first factored the numbers into single digits before multiplying (e.g., 17 x 35 = 17 x (7 x 5) = (17 x 7) x 5 = 119 x 5 = 595), suggesting knowledge of multiplicative associativity.

Left-to-Right Multiplication

Smith (1983) offered insight into the calculation processes of Jedediah Buton. This savant was noted to possess several of the characteristics of an auditory calculator; that is, he would "hear" rather than mentally "see" numbers. More specifically, (a) Buxton had never learned to read or write numbers, and (b) he used a left-to-right multiplication method. In contrast to the conventional right-to-left (written) procedure widely taught in schools, this method begins with the multiplication of the highest magnitude digits in each operand and continues by the multiplication of all possible digit pairs in a left-to-right direction. This explanation is best served by an example (see Fig. 15.1). By retaining only the intermediate total, the demands placed on short-term memory (STM) are minimized. This left-to-right multiplication method is used by high school mathematics students skilled in mental calculation (Hope & Sherrill, 1987) and was discovered independently and employed by many of the expert mental calculators (Smith, 1983). In addition to the use of this efficient strategy, Buxton also demonstrated some small-scale calculation peculiarities. For example, to multiply by 378, he would multiply consecutively by 5, 20, and 3 to obtain 300 times the number. Next, Buxton would multiply successively by 5 and 15 to obtain 75 times the number. He then would multiply by 3 to obtain 3 times the number. Finally, Buxton would add the partial products to get 378 times the number (the product).

Figure 15.1: Left-to-Right Multiplication Method Using 348 x 461 as an Example (Smith, 1983, p. 110)

300 x 400	=	120,000
300 x 60	=	18,000
Sum		138,000
300 x 1	=	300
Sum		138,300
40 x 400	=	16,000
Sum		154,300
40 x 60	=	2,400
Sum		156,700
40 x 1	=	40
Sum		156,740
8 x 400	=	3,200
Sum		159,940
8 x 60	=	480
Sum		160,420
8 x 1	=	8
Total	=	160,428

Following the presentation of a series of multidigit multiplication problems, an analysis of RH's speed of calculation also suggested the use of the left-to-right multiplication method (Kelly et al., 1997). In contrast to the control participants presented with the same problems, RH's mean correct response times were more highly correlated with the use of this strategy (based on the number of computational steps required to obtain the solution) than the conventional right-to-left method.

Just as Buxton was noted to be an auditory calculator, Fleury, who was born blind, was a "tactile" calculator. His fingers would move rapidly while he solved problems, mentally "feeling" under his fingers a form of numerical Braille, often on his jacket lapel (Smith, 1983).

Memorization of Numerical Equivalents

Like modestly skilled (Hope & Sherrill, 1987) and expert mental calculators (Hunter, 1962; Smith, 1983), it appears that savants may, for some problems, draw on their existing numerical knowledge to recall rather than calculate a product. AC was able to retrieve arithmetic combinations directly, reportedly having memorized all squares of integers for 1 to 2000, all cubes of numbers from 1 to 1000, and tables from published texts containing all the divisors up to 10,000 (Stevens & Moffitt, 1988). Similarly, having calculated all the squares and cubes of integers up to 100, Elly had committed these to memory and was able to access this information directly as part of her calculations (Bogyo & Ellis, 1988). Kelly et al. (1997) also offered an explanation based on direct memory retrieval, rather than calculation, for RH's fast response times to two-digit squares.

Mathematical Shortcuts and Rules

Kelly et al. (1997) concluded that RH did not rely on shortcut strategies in mentally calculating the product of multidigit multiplication items, including two- by two-digit and four- by one-digit items. These items were divided into three subsets: easy, moderately easy, and difficult to solve with a shortcut strategy. For example, the item 899 x 7 was considered easy to solve by implementing a rounding-up strategy (i.e., 899 x 7 = [900 – 1] x 7 = [900 x 7] – 7 = 6,300 – 7 = 6,293). In contrast, an item such as 344 x 7 includes a three-digit factor outside a convenient rounding range and was thus deemed difficult. An analysis of calculation times revealed that, for both RH and five controls, no significant differences were found between the "ease of strategy" categories, indicating that arithmetic shortcuts were not employed. In a second experiment, Kelly et al. investigated RH's ability to learn a new computational algorithm for converting temperatures from Celsius to Fahrenheit. RH required much support in learning the algorithm and practice resulted in little improvement. He worked through each step of the computation in a rigid, methodical fashion. Indeed, for several problems, RH failed to use a shortcut or an easy solution strategy involving the inversion of steps in the algorithm.

In contrast to RH, AC was observed to adapt mathematical formulas to aid his calculations (Stevens & Moffitt, 1988). Specifically, he applied a variation of the binomial theorem to square numbers greater than 2000. In addition, AC used a variety of mathematical shortcuts and rules (e.g., the sum of all consecutive odd numbers will always equal a perfect square; all squares end in the digits 0, 1, 4, 5, 6, 9).

Evidence suggests that some savants apply an algorithmic method in determining whether a number is prime. Discovered in the third century B.C. by the Greek astronomer and mathematician, Erastothenes, this procedure involves the division of the target number by all the primes less than, or equal to, the square root of this number. If the target is not divisible by any of these smaller numbers, then it is prime. In Hermelin and O'Connor's (1990) investigation of Michael, in which he was required to generate and recognize primes up to five digits in length, his error rates were found to be consistent with the use of this strategy. Both Michael and the control participant showed a similar pattern of errors, with mistakes made almost solely for the larger numbers that were not divisible by either 3 or 11.

An inventive follow-up study offered further support for these findings (Anderson et al., 1998). In the first experiment, Michael and a mathematics graduate control were presented with a series of numbers, all less than 1,000, and required to identify whether each number was prime. The nonprimes (composites) fell into three categories depending on their lowest prime factor: (a) easy nonprimes (those divisible by 2 and 5); (b) computable nonprimes divisible by 3, 7, and 11, and (c) difficult nonprimes divisible by 13, 17, and 19. Although Michael was faster and more accurate than the control participant; the former took an average 14 sec to respond correctly compared to the latter's mean response time of 53 sec. Both participants showed similar response patterns in line with Erastothenes' strategy use. Primes took longer to identify than nonprimes; response times increased as the magnitude of the primes increased; response times for nonprimes were largely determined by the size of the lowest prime divisor, with the most lengthy times recorded for numbers with 13, 17, and 19 as divisors. Indeed, following testing, the control reported having used Erastothenes' strategy. In the second experiment, skilled normal participants were required to divide a series of target numbers (those presented in Experiment 1) by the prime numbers from 2 to 19. Using these response times as parameters, computer simulations of Erastothenes' method were then generated. The same set of target numbers was divided sequentially by each of the primes from 2 upward; division with no remainder signaled a nonprime; failure to divide without remainder by all primes less than the square root indicated a prime. A further simulation based on a simple memorization strategy was also used for comparison. This model assumed a list of primes stored in memory, ordered in terms of increasing magnitude. The process of identifying primes required the sequential matching of the targets with the numbers on the list, with each individual match between numbers equating to one unit of time. The key finding here is that the simulations of Erastothenes' method, not the memory-based model, provided the best fit to both Michael's and the control's response time data.

The verbal accounts of HP also indicate the use of this calculation strategy in identifying primes (Heavey, 1997). After questioning over several testing sessions, HP became able to provide insight into his strategy. For example, he identified 8,009 as prime in 14 sec, reporting that "3 did not go into it," neither did 7 or 11. The number 8,889 was rejected as nonprime in 3 sec, with HP stating "3 will go into it." The number 9,589 was identified as prime in 11 seconds. HP gave the following account: "3 and 7 won't go into it . . . 11 won't go into 9,870 [9,870 represents the target number 9,859 + 11] . . . 13 won't go into 982, and 13 will go into 39 [39, which is a multiple of 13, is subtracted from the target number to leave 9,820, which cannot be divided by 13]." HP had thus attempted to divide the number by 3, 7, 11, and 13 before deciding it was prime. Finally, when asked to give a prime between 10,500 and 10,600, he offered the number 10,511 in 6 sec (although 10,511 is divisible by 23 and therefore nonprime). He explained that it was not divisible by 3 and 7. In reply to the question, "How do you know it can't be divided by 111 and by 13?" he replied, "Thirteen will go into 611, and 10,511 − 611 = 9,900, and that can't be divided by 13." The use of Erastothenes' method appears to be subserved by an ability to fragment the target number into component amounts, numbers for which HP is able to rapidly access the divisors. From these reports, it also appears that HP discontinued the strategy for prime divisors greater than 13; his fast response times are certainly consistent with this. It is probable, however, that this incomplete application of Erastothenes' method reflects HP's lack of motivation under such test conditions. Indeed, during testing sessions, HP was more interested in asking the researchers whether certain five-digit numbers are prime, numbers that the savant stated he had "calculated" at home. He was invariably correct with these suggested primes (Heavey & Elander, 1999).

Little is known about the methods of savants who are skilled in addition only, such as Jungreis. However, as noted by Smith (1983), the operation of addition does not lend itself readily to the use of shortcuts. The speed of computation reported in such cases may simply reflect the use of well-practiced subroutines within this restricted area of the arithmetic domain.

Prime Number Generation Without Numerical Calculation

For the prime number skills of the twins John and Michael, Sacks (1985) rejected an explanation based on a process of calculation. Rather, their numeric ability is proposed to be iconic; they see numbers as a vast natural scene. He suggested that they have access to "an immense mnemonic tapestry, a vast (or possibly infinite) landscape in which everything could be seen, either isolated or in relation" (p. 190). Sacks even speculated on the form of these visual representations, suggesting a "numerical vine, with all the number-leaves, number-tendrils and number-fruit that made it up" (p. 191). It is interesting that Seron, Pesenti, Noeel, Deloche, and Cornet (1992) reported that nonsavants have similar, although more limited, visuospatial representations of numbers. It is unclear, however, why such a vivid and extensive representation of numbers manifests itself in the generation of sizeable primes, yet does not encompass an appreciation of the smaller scale relations between numbers that would aid basic arithmetic understanding. This discrepancy in the numerical skills of the twins (able to generate large primes, yet incapable of basic arithmetic) has been the subject of considerable speculation (e.g., Welling, 1994; White, 1988). Yet, this appears to be an atypical case; most savants generate prime numbers using calculation-based strategies. It is interesting that an earlier study that examined the twins' calendar calculation skills offered a somewhat different report of their basic numerical ability: One of the twins was capable of adding and subtracting two-digit numbers (Horwitz, Deming, & Winter, 1969). Such a basic level of arithmetic competence would still, however, fail to account for their outstanding ability with prime numbers.

In conclusion, savant arithmetic proficiencies are subserved by a variety of methods and strategies and thus resemble both expert mental calculation ability (Smith, 1983) and more basic arithmetic performance in the general population (e.g., LeFevre, Sadesky, & Bisanz, 1996). The methods utilized by savants range from a basic counting and grouping procedure to the use of a relatively advanced cognitive strategy in identifying primes. A number of savants apparently simplify computations by breaking down the individual operands (if composite) into their component factors. Direct retrieval from memory of numerical facts also appears to play a role in the calculations of some savants. Finally, several calculators utilize the left-to-right multiplication method adopted by many skilled and expert mental calculators.

Commonalities Among Cases of Savant Arithmetical Ability

Memory

An impressive memory for numbers is reported in almost every case of savant arithmetic ability. This is evidenced as part of the mental-calculation process; the ability to solve a multidigit problem requires the retention of operands and intermediate results as computation proceeds. The inability of some savants to read and write numbers (Buxton, Fuller) and blindness, in the case of Fleury, underscores their reliance on memory in performing calculations. Indeed, both Buxton and Fuller were able to leave lengthy calculations half-finished, continuing the problems some months later from exactly where they left off (Scripture, 1891). Prodigious numerical memory has also been observed independently of the calculation process. The twins John and Michael could repeat a number of 3, 30, or 300 digits with equal ease (Sacks, 1985). Jungreis could remember the lists of numbers presented within addition problems some 45 min after completing the calculations. Numerical facts or equivalents, such as squares and cubes, appear to be extensively represented in long-term memory (LTM) for some savants (Elly, RH, AC). Indeed, AC had memorized vast amounts of numerical information, including published mathematical tables containing all the divisors up to 10,000. This process of memorization was reported to be neither effortful nor time consuming (Stevens & Moffitt, 1988).

Formal testing has, however, revealed less striking evidence of mnemonic superiority among these individuals. Assessments of STM capacity in the form of digit-span performance are available for a number of savants. In most cases, digit spans fall in the 7 ± 2 range. L was able to recall seven digits forward and six backward (Scheerer et al., 1945), and HP could recall eight digits forward and seven digits backward (Heavey, 1997). Wechsler scaled scores on the digit-span subtest of 11 for George (Nurcombe & Parker, 1964) and 16 for DS (Steel et al., 1984) indicate immediate memory spans in the normal range (note that scaled scores range from 1 to 19, with a mean of 10). Particularly impressive was AC, who was at ceiling on this task, indicating a forward digit span of at least nine and a backward span of at least eight (Stevens & Moffitt, 1988). In contrast, smaller visual digit spans of four forward and five backward were recorded for RH (Kelly et al., 1997). For DS and AC, further testing revealed good auditory verbal memory for nonnumerical stimuli (e.g., word list learning) with poorer performance on visual-spatial memory measures. It is notable, however, that verbal memory represents a neuropsychological asset for individuals with Asperger's syndrome, with which AC was diagnosed (Klin, Volkmar, Sparrow, Cicchetti, & Rourke, 1995).

To recap, there is variability in the memory performance of savant calculators as revealed by formal testing, but no overwhelming evidence of consistently exceptional general mnemonic ability. This is consistent with findings on expert mental calculators. For example, testing of Wim Klein showed that his general memory did not exceed the average and Jacques Inaudi's memory for information other than numbers was quite poor (Smith, 1983). Conversely, investigations have shown that, with extensive practice, novices can learn to memorize large amounts of numerical information to a level comparable with most calculating prodigies (Chase & Ericsson, 1982). These studies of skilled memory have shown how experts, including those with expertise in mental calculation (Staszewski, 1988), can extend their limited STM by making use of LTM. Information is encoded in relation to existing knowledge structures and, at the time of encoding, retrieval cues are incorporated in the memory trace, permitting the individual to retrieve the required information at recall (Chase & Ericsson, 1982).

Early Arithmetical Development

Arithmetic Training and Tuition. Savants appear to vary in terms of the amount of arithmetic schooling received. In several cases, the facility for calculation appears to have developed in the absence of arithmetic tuition (Buxton, Fuller, John and Michael, Obadiah, & Jungreis). It is probable that Sabine, Fleury, George, RH, and Michael had received limited instruction. As a child, Elly was taught basic arithmetic (including fractions) by her mother, and both

AC and DS gained a formal education in mathematics. Such variability in arithmetic instruction appears contingent on such factors as the availability of special educational resources (relating to the time in which the savant lived), the extent of behavioral disturbance, and the degree of intellectual impairment. Thus, for some savants, such as L who failed to acquire basic arithmetic principles, intellectual and attention factors may operate to constrain the benefit of structured input and lead to its disuse. On the other hand, savant calculators whose intelligence falls in the normal range may derive greater gains from such input and may actively seek out relevant information. For example, HP, who had not received a formal mathematical education, stated that he had read about perfect numbers from a reference book.

An Interest in Numbers. An early and persistent interest in counting of a repetitive, almost compulsive nature, is common to most accounts of savant numerical skill. Obadiah was observed to be perpetually counting (Brill, 1940). A visit to the theater was recalled by Buxton in terms of the number of steps taken as part of the dances, the number of words spoken by the actors, and the number of times they had entered and left the stage. After learning to count to 100, Fuller then proceeded to count the number of hairs in a cow's tail (2,872) and the number of grains in a bushel of wheat. As a child, George was interested in trains and would always count the number of carriages they pulled (Nurcombe & Parker, 1964). When seen for psychological evaluation, he insisted on counting the time in seconds for the duration of the session. As noted previously, Sabine would continuously count coins and buttons (Brill, 1940), and HP's mother observed that, as a child, he would fall to sleep at night while counting and reciting sequences of numbers. A propensity for counting is also accompanied, in many cases, by a general interest in numerical stimuli. For example, HP had a fascination with car number plates and newspaper circulation figures (Heavey, 1997).

A strong early interest in numbers and counting is also typical of many expert mental calculators (Smith, 1983) and is evident among children in the general population. For example, Ginsburg (1977) provided many instances of preschoolers' spontaneous counting activities, and Court (1920) described her son Paul's immense interest in numbers and marked enjoyment in counting, which emerged soon after he began to talk. Therefore, although savants may differ from other individuals in terms of the strength and exclusivity of their numerical preoccupation (see next section), a basic interest in numbers appears characteristic of both savant and nonsavant arithmetic development.

Autism

Autism, diagnosable in childhood, is a psychiatric disorder that is characterized by qualitative impairments in reciprocal social interaction and communication, together with restricted, repetitive, and stereotyped patterns of behavior and interests (World Health Organization, 1992). Some three fourths of people with autism are mentally handicapped (Lockyer & Rutter, 1970). Despite the fact that individuals with autism constitute only a relatively small proportion of the mentally handicapped population, most savants are autistic (O'Connor & Hermelin, 1988). Indeed, Rimland (1978) estimated that 1 in 10 children with autism has a savant talent. Consistent with these observations, autism is common to all recent examples of savant arithmetic ability. Elly, DS, HP, Michael, RH, George, and possibly the twins, John and Michael, all share this diagnosis. AC is regarded as having Asperger's syndrome, a related disorder. In several of the earlier cases, behavioral descriptions strongly suggest autism. Thus, there is a need to consider the significance of this diagnosis: What predisposes individuals with autism to develop exceptional levels of arithmetic ability? A number of factors may be relevant. Children and adults with autism often display a strong interest in numbers; they may be preoccupied with bus numbers, train timetables, times, people's birthdays, and calendars. Numbers may appeal to individuals with autism because they are nonsocial, literal entities that require no appreciation of underlying semantics or motivational intentions. Unlike the chaotic social world, there is predictable order and regularity among numbers. The overfocused attention and obsessional tendencies associated with the disorder would sustain the preoccupation with numbers to the exclusion of other pursuits. Furthermore, the cognitive-processing-style characteristic of autism may also contribute to the development of numerical calculation ability. Individuals with autism are suggested to process information predominantly in terms of local rather than global features (Frith, 1989; Frith & Happé, 1994). Support for this suggestion includes the superiority of autistic individuals over controls on an embedded figures test (Shah & Frith, 1983) and the Wechsler block design task. Shah and Frith (1993) attributed the former's advantage to an enhanced ability to mentally segment the designs into their component parts. Recent research suggests that such a "segmentational" processing style may contribute to the development of graphic skill by savant artists (Pring, Hermelin, & Heavey, 1995; see also Mottron & Belleville, 1993), absolute pitch by musical savants (Heaton, Hermelin, & Pring, 1998), and calendrical calculation ability (day–date pairing) by arithmetical savants (Heavey, Pring, & Hermelin, 1999).

From our review of savant calculators, there is evidence that a *decompositional* strategy may play a role in arithmetic processing. A facility for grouping numbers was reported in several cases (e.g., Sabine and Obadiah), the calculations of some savants proceeded by breaking down the operands into their respective factors (Sabine) or into smaller integers (Buxton) and by breaking down the target number in a prime-identification task (HP). In addition, the twins John and Michael instantly recognized 111 matches spilled on the floor as three groups of 37. It is notable that a field-independent processing style, which may be allied with the mental-segmentation skill outlined earlier, has been suggested as a correlate of mathematical ability in nonsavants (Benbow, 1988). Thus, to recap, predispositions associated with autism at both the cognitive and behavioral levels appear to play a role in the development of savant numerical ability.

Savants as Experts: Numerical Ability and Knowledge Representation

Having summarized across the single cases of savant numerical calculation, I now integrate the information pertaining to the components of the ability, the methods used, and the commonalities among cases to suggest the following tentative interpretations of this rare savant skill. In most cases, the ability appears to develop from an early fascination with numbers, with such a preoccupation often observed in autism. This is frequently manifest as a process of continuous counting, from which familiarity and practice with number sequencing is derived. Numerical knowledge may thus develop from constant exposure to, and practice with, these series of numbers. However, the nature and extent of numerical knowledge representation appears to differ across the various savant cases. For those individuals proficient in the operation of addition only, their limited knowledge may reflect the sequential format in which number series were first encoded (i.e., 1, 2, 3 . . . 48, 49, 50). Through the continued application of well-practiced routines involved in multidigit addition, individual number combinations may also be encoded in the knowledge base. However, the repeated addition of numbers does not appear to promote the organization of knowledge to reflect other numerical relations and associations, specifically, the inverse relation between addition and subtraction and the multiplicative structure of the number system. Thus, the limited arithmetic abilities of some savants, for whom the application of procedures appears highly constrained and inflexible (Hatano, 1988), suggests routine expertise—a lack of underlying conceptual knowledge and an impoverished network of number representations, indicative of rote, rather than meaningful, learning (Hiebert & Lefevre, 1986).

For other savants whose abilities extend to multiplication and beyond, a more elaborate, interconnected numerical knowledge base may be suggested. A strong interest in numbers and counting may foster the frequent manipulation of numerical series, involving the imposition and extraction of groupings within sequences. For example, counting from 3 in multiples of 3 (i.e., 3, 6, 9, 12) may lead to the association of such numbers within the knowledge base. Over time, numerical knowledge may thus develop and reformulate to reflect the rule-governed multiplicative structure of the number system. The suggestion that some savants are able to induce and construct number patterns and relations helps to account for the development of their skills in the absence of formal arithmetic tuition.

For some savants, the reformulation of knowledge to reflect the internal relations between numbers may support and promote arithmetic procedures, including the use of shortcuts and rules. Indeed, given that most cases of savant arithmetic ability appear to have developed with little or no formal instruction, at least some *self-discovered* procedures for manipulating numbers and solving arithmetic problems must be assumed. Mathematical regularities may be extracted by some savants, such as AC's identification of the rule that the sum of consecutive odd numbers is always equal to a perfect square (i.e., $1 + 3 = 4$; $1 + 3 + 5 = 9$; $1 + 3 + 5 + 7 = 16$; Stevens & Moffitt, 1988). Knowledge of multiplicative associativity may be utilized in simplifying multiplication procedures; operands may be broken down into their single-digit factors, as in the case of Sabine. For savants such as Michael and Elly, knowledge of the relation between numbers and their respective factors, together with practice in the identification of such factors, would reveal certain numbers to be prime. Over time, an efficient means of identifying primes may be formulated (Erastothenes' method), that does not involve the division of the target number by all possible composites, but rather utilizes divisors that themselves do not have factors (other than themselves and 1) and thus cannot be broken down further. In this way, a shortcut to identifying these anomalous numbers (primes) may be derived from a knowledge base characterized by multiplicative and factor-product relations, an associative network of knowledge that supports the acquisition of a more advanced procedure (Carpenter, 1986).

This process by which some cases of savant arithmetic ability are suggested to develop is, in some respects, similar to descriptions of arithmetic learning in preschoolers (Ginsburg, 1977). Through the process of counting, the child discovers basic patterns and rules in numbers, and uses these rules to generate new, larger numbers (although these rules may be used without awareness). Indeed, Ginsburg (1977) offered several examples of young children perceiving complex patterns and regularities between numbers. If a child can count, he or she is able to construct addition or multiplication tables, with rote memory playing a minimal role. Techniques, such as repeated addition, are suggested to develop spontaneously as shortcuts for counting. Such economical procedures are evident across cultures and do not appear dependent on schooling.

The view that savant arithmetic ability (which extends beyond addition and subtraction) may be subserved by a structured numerical knowledge base aligns with accounts of savant ability in other domains (White, 1988). For example, organized knowledge representations are suggested to underlie savant musical ability (e.g., Hermelin, O'Connor, Lee, & Treffert, 1989), memory feats (O'Connor & Hermelin, 1989), and calendar calculation (Heavey et al., 1999; see also next section). Given the proposal that some arithmetic savants have access to an interconnected store of basic arithmetic combinations, are their feats therefore indicative of adaptive expertise (Hatano, 1988)? A possible exception to such a characterization of savant ability is AC, whose numerical skills were judged to be based on routinized processing; he was unable to solve problems requiring reasoning from mathematical rules when tested on university-level calculus problems (Stevens & Moffitt, 1988). He did, however, make use of mathematical shortcuts to aid other calculations. Similarly, Kelly et al. (1997) concluded that RH did not employ computational shortcuts in multiplying multidigit numbers and had difficulty in learning and applying an algorithm for converting temperatures. Like the savants skilled in the operation of addition only, RH's lack of flexibility appears suggestive of routine expertise, rather than adaptive, expertise.

However, the following four caveats should be noted. (a) It is possible that RH used shortcuts that differed from those tested by Kelly et al. (1997). (b) In view of RH's general intellectual level, he may have needed more practice with the conversion algorithm to apply it flexibly. (c) RH was taught the algorithm by displaying it on an index card (cf. the purposeful, meaningful, and inquiry-based method recommended by Baroody, with Coslick, 1998). As this may have seem irrelevant or may have been incomprehensible to RH, he may have lacked motivation for the task. (d) Furthermore, although RH was not observed to use shortcut procedures, he appeared to be utilizing the left-to-right method of multiplication favored by many expert mental calculators. If self-taught, this suggests evidence of inventiveness in developing this efficient procedure.

A key issue when considering the nature of expertise in arithmetic savants concerns the extent to which interconnected numerical knowledge necessarily implies the *explicit* processing and understanding of arithmetic concepts and relations. For some, knowledge may be integrated according to associations detected between numbers, but at a level below conscious awareness. Thus, connections between numerical concepts may not be consciously extracted or explicitly recognized but may nevertheless characterize the knowledge base and subserve the operation of arithmetic procedures. This conceptualization of savant ability is comparable to that proposed for calendar calculation (Heavey et al., 1999; see next section) and shares similarities with the process of native language acquisition and grammar use (Smith, 1983; Treffert, 1989). Such a proposal may also account for the prime number skills of the twins, John and Michael (Sacks, 1985). Structured knowledge representations reflecting relations and regularities between numbers may be activated implicitly to yield a generative product, in this case primes.

However, conscious access to stored representations and insight into arithmetic procedures is evident in some cases of savant arithmetic ability. For example, HP is able to verbalize the associations between different numbers and his shortcuts in identifying primes (Heavey, 1997). Such conscious access by savants may possibly represent a genuine number sense and true numerical understanding. It may also be an important factor in facilitating the generalization of knowledge to new problem areas. Furthermore, savants' explicit processing of numerical relations, utilization of efficient procedures, and flexibility with which knowledge is applied probably vary with intelligence. General intellectual ability appears to play a role and may even constrain the acquisition and use of rule-based strategies and shortcuts (cf. Baroody, 1999); it is the more intellectually able savants who are reported to use such methods. For example, Michael's speed of processing, as measured by an inspection time (IT) task, was in the range expected of individuals with average to above average IQ. This was considered sufficient to sustain the cognitive routines involved in Erastothenes' method (Anderson, 1992; Anderson et al., 1998). Also, as outlined in the following section, one of the most intellectually able savants (HP) can apply his arithmetic skills to the task of calendar calculation. In contrast, in the case of Jedediah Buxton (who, to multiply by 300, would first multiply by 5, 20, and 3), general intellectual factors may have limited the development of more efficient and flexible strategies.

Another factor that may be relevant to the nature of savant expertise is the context in which arithmetic learning occurs. For most savants, the acquisition of knowledge is likely to have been a solitary experience and, with social or communicative difficulties and little or no arithmetic schooling, opportunities for verbal interaction and encountering novel types of problem would be limited. Such conditions are considered important in the acquisition of conceptual knowledge and the development of adaptive expertise (Hatano, 1988). Thus, for some savants, the absence of support and encouragement in discussing arithmetic procedures, which could serve to make numerical relations explicit, may contribute to the restricted nature of their arithmetic ability. Certainly, it is difficult to conceive of how proficiency in areas such as algebra and calculus would develop without exposure to relevant problem examples and some instructional guidance.

The suggestion that an organized knowledge base underlies many examples of savant arithmetic calculation is consistent with the prodigious feats of numerical memory reported in the various cases. For the savants, like expert mental calculators (e.g., Hunter, 1962), numbers may be rich in associations; they can be encoded in relation to a substantial amount of existing numerical knowledge. In some cases, numerical representations may be further elaborated within other rule-based systems. Elly developed an idiosyncratic but ordered system of association in which prime numbers were linked with 29 different kinds of weather and were also charged with positive and negative affect (Park & Youderian, 1974). For example, the number 7 was thought of as "good" and was associated with cloudless days. Furthermore, it may be suggested that numbers are more memorable for savants because they can be processed as unitary items rather than a series of single digits. The following quote from the great mental calculator, Wim Klein, illustrates these points on the memorability of numbers: "Numbers are friends for me, more or less. It doesn't mean the same for you, does it, 3,844? For you, it's just a three and an eight and a four and a four. But I say, 'Hi, 62 squared'" (Smith, 1983, p. 5).

In conclusion, although some feats of some savants appear to be the product of routinized expertise, conceptualizing all arithmetic abilities of all savants solely as knowledge learned by rote may not be appropriate. From exposure to numerical information, savants may implicitly or explicitly formulate, relations between numbers and represent them within a structured knowledge base. However, general intellectual ability and the quality and extent of arithmetic education may limit conscious access to numerical relations and the application of knowledge and procedures across mathematical domains (i.e., the capacity for adaptive expertise and flexibility). Given the largely descriptive nature of most studies in this area, and the lack of systematic experimental investigation, our interpretation of savant arithmetic ability remains speculative. Clearly, future areas for research should include the structure of savant numerical knowledge and the characteristics of numerical memory, the implicit or explicit processing of numerical relations, and the application of arithmetic knowledge to related and novel problem areas, with such tasks presented to savants under meaningful, readily understood conditions.

Savant Arithmetical Ability and Calendar Calculation

It is interesting that several of the reviewed cases of savant arithmetic ability were also able to calendar calculate (the twins John and Michael, HP, L, AC, and possibly Fuller). Calendar calculation refers to the ability to rapidly supply the day of the week of a given date, with some savants able to perform calculations spanning thousands of years (e.g. Horwitz et al., 1969). Most calendar calculators are autistic.

There are important similarities between savant date calculation and savant arithmetic calculation in both the acquisition and operation of the skills. Savant date-calculation skills appear to be subserved by an organized knowledge base (Heavey, 1997; Hermelin & O'Connor, 1986). The ability may develop from an early interest in numerical stimuli, specifically, the processing of individual, isolated dates (Heavey et al., 1999). Through continuous exposure to dates, savants are also exposed to calendar regularities and repetitions, and such experience may facilitate the recombination of knowledge to reflect the patterns that characterize date information. Over time, the knowledge base evolves to reflect the structure and relations inherent to the calendar (Heavey, 1997). Such structure may then promote the use of calculation rules (Hermelin & O'Connor, 1986), even though such rules may not be consciously extracted or processed. Finally, such calendrical rules and regularities would permit the knowledge base to generalize to new dates that may never have been explicitly processed or deliberately memorized by the savant. As in Norris' (1990) connectionist model of savant date calculation, learning is proposed to be instance based, derived from many examples of day–date pairings, with the reorganization of knowledge reflecting the structural patterns detected within incoming input. Within such an account, access to calendar knowledge need not be conscious, nor is arithmetic skill proposed to play a critical role. Indeed, some calendar savants have only limited arithmetic ability (Cowan, O'Connor, & Samella, 1998) and, as a group, do not differ significantly from IQ and diagnosis-matched controls in their general arithmetic competence (Heavey et al., 1999).

In elucidating the relation between savant numerical and date-calculation skills, HP's verbal reports again proved insightful (Heavey, 1997). They revealed detailed structural knowledge of a 28-year period of the calendar from 1972 to 2000. (HP reported first looking at calendars in 1974 but also studied calendars from previous years.) Using his additional knowledge of the 28-year and 400-year cyclical repetitions in the calendar, he could rapidly calculate multiples of 28 and 400 to bring the target year within his well-practiced 28-year span. For example, he was able to generate the weekday for April 3, 3090, in only 4 sec. He gave the following explanation: "1974 to 1890, add on 1,200." To expand on HP's answer; the difference between 1974 and 1890 is 84, which is divisible by 28. The difference between 1890 and 3090 is 1,200, which is divisible by 400. Thus, he was using his knowledge of more recent years together with the 28-year and 400-year cycles to generate the answer.

The conclusion that HP utilized his arithmetic skills to extend his date calculations beyond his memorized span is consistent with the findings of Cowan et al. (1998) indicating that savant date calculators with greater arithmetic skill can calculate over a wider range than calculators with more limited arithmetic competence. Thus, although general numerical proficiency does not appear essential to the development of savant date-calculation ability, arithmetic skills may play a role in extending calculation spans.

Conclusions

Despite the rarity of the phenomenon, the study of savant numerical calculation ability can contribute to our general understanding of arithmetic learning and cognition. In this last section, I discuss the implications of this research for the following three areas: (a) how arithmetic knowledge is represented and used, (b) the cognitive and affective bases for arithmetic expertise, and (c) self-directed learning of arithmetic.

The Nature of Arithmetic Expertise

The highly constrained nature of skill in the case of some savants suggests a separable rather than unified structure to the arithmetic domain. In such cases of limited ability (e.g., skill in addition only), arithmetic feats may be explicable in terms of rotely learned knowledge and routinized processing. However, savants capable of multiplication may have the capacity for processing and representing relations among numbers, implicitly or explicitly. This associative knowledge is proposed to underlie some calculation procedures and the prodigious numerical memory reported for many savants. Such an interpretation of savant ability shares similarities with young children's early experience of counting and arithmetic, first language acquisition and the use of grammatical rules, and the development of savant calendar-calculation ability. For savants, true insight and understanding of numerical relations and the flexible application of arithmetic knowledge may be constrained by general intelligence and access to arithmetic instruction and input (involving exposure to novel problem examples). Even so, like expert and more modestly skilled mental calculators, some savants utilize both retrieval and nonretrieval methods, comprising a variety of calculational strategies and shortcuts.

Possible Precursors

Savant arithmetic ability does not appear to depend on linguistic competence, although nonverbal abstract reasoning ability may represent a cognitive correlate (cf. Donlan, chap. 12, this volume; Miura & Okamoto, chap. 8, this volume). Possible precursors of both savant and nonsavant arithmetic skills include an early interest in numbers and counting and a cognitive style favoring analytical, finely detailed processing.

Self-Directed Learning

Finally, the feats of savant calculators illustrate how, through inherent motivation, arithmetic proficiency may develop in a largely self-taught capacity. In terms of implications for teaching, this shows the potential for a preoccupation with numbers to develop into a constructive area of skill in persons with learning disabilities. For such individuals, arithmetic learning would be suggested to benefit from an approach that encourages and extends the propensity for self-directed learning, yet provides structure and support in making explicit the key connections among numbers and highlighting the similarities and differences among problems. New arithmetic concepts and problems should be introduced only when they can be readily related to existing knowledge, and the presentation format of the problems (e.g., counting objects, written sums, auditory presentation) should follow from the individual's preferred mode of numerical exploration and discovery.

References

Anderson, M. (1992). *Intelligence and development: A cognitive theory.* Oxford, England: Blackwell.

Anderson, M., O'Connor, N., & Hermelin, B. (1998). A specific calculating ability. *Intelligence, 26,* 383–403.

Baroody, A. J. (1999). The development of basic counting, number, and arithmetic knowledge among children classified as mentally retarded. In L. M. Glidden (Ed.), *International review of research in mental retardation, Vol. 22* (pp. 51–103). New York: Academic Press.

Baroody, A. J., with Coslick, R. T. (1998). *Fostering children's mathematical power: An investigative approach to K–8 mathematics instruction.* Mahwah, NJ: Lawrence Erlbaum Associates.

Benbow, C. P. (1988). Neuropsychological perspectives on mathematical talent. In I. K. Obler & D. Fein (Eds.), *The exceptional brain: Neuropsychology of talent and special abilities* (pp. 48–69). New York: Guilford Press.

Bogyo, L., & Ellis, R. (1988). Elly: A study in contrasts. In I. K. Obler & D. Fein (Eds.), *The exceptional brain: Neuropsychology of talent and special abilities* (pp. 265–276). New York: Guilford Press.

Brill, A. A. (1940). Some peculiar manifestations of memory with special reference to lightning calculators. *Journal of Nervous and Mental Diseases, 92,* 709–726.

Carpenter, T. P. (1986). Conceptual knowledge as a foundation for procedural knowledge: Implications from research on the initial learning of arithmetic. In J. Hiebert (Ed.), *Conceptual and procedural knowledge: The case of mathematics* (pp. 113–132). Hillsdale, NJ: Lawrence Erlbaum Associates.

Chase, W. G., & Ericsson, K. A. (1982). Skill and working memory. In G. H. Bower (Ed.), *The psychology of learning and motivation: Advances in research and theory, Vol. 16* (pp. 1–58). Academic Press.

Court, S. R. A. (1920). Numbers, time and space in the five years of a child's life. *Pedagogical Seminary, 27*, 71–89.

Cowan, R., O'Connor, N., & Samella, K. (1998). *The arithmetic abilities of calendrical calculators.* Unpublished manuscript.

Critchley, M. (1979). *The divine banquet of the brain.* New York: Raven Press.

Frith, U. (1989). *Autism: Explaining the enigma.* Oxford, England: Blackwell.

Frith, U., & Happé, F. (1994). Autism: Beyond "theory of mind." *Cognition, 50*, 115–132.

Ginsburg, H. P. (1977). *Children's arithmetic: The learning process.* New York: Van Nostrand.

Hatano, G. (1988). Social and motivational bases for mathematical understanding. In G. B. Saxe & M. Gearhart (Eds.), *Children's mathematics* (pp. 55–70). San Francisco: Josey-Bass.

Heaton, P., Hermelin, B., & Pring, L. (1998). Autism and pitch processing: A precursor for savant musical ability? *Music Perception, 15*, 291–305.

Heavey, L. (1997). *Memory in the calendar calculating savant.* Unpublished doctoral thesis, University of London.

Heavey, L., & Elander, J. (1999, December). *Strategy and rule use by a savant numerical calculator.* Paper presented at the meeting of the British Psychological Society, London.

Heavey, L., Pring, L., & Hermelin, B. (1999). A date to remember: The nature of memory in calendar calculating savants. *Psychological Medicine, 29*, 145–160.

Hermelin, B., & O'Connor, N. (1986). Idiot savant calendrical calculators: Rules and regularities. *Psychological Medicine, 16*, 885–893.

Hermelin, B., & O'Connor, N. (1990). Factors and primes: A specific numerical ability. *Psychological Medicine, 20*, 163–169.

Hermelin, B., O'Connor, N., Lee, S., & Treffert, D. (1989). Intelligence and musical improvisation. *Psychological Medicine, 19*, 447–457.

Hiebert, J., & Lefevre, P. (1986). Conceptual and procedural knowledge in mathematics: An introductory analysis. In J. Hiebert (Ed.), *Conceptual and procedural knowledge: The case of mathematics* (pp. 1–27). Hillsdale, NJ: Lawrence Erlbaum Associates.

Hill, A. L. (1977). Idiot savants: Rate of incidence. *Perceptual and Motor Skills, 44*, 161–162.

Hope, J. A., & Sherrill, J. M. (1987). Characteristics of unskilled and skilled mental calculators. *Journal for Research in Mathematics Education, 18*, 98–111.

Horwitz, W. A., Deming, W. E., & Winter, R. F. (1969). A further account of the idiot savant, experts with the calendar. *American Journal of Psychiatry, 126*, 160–163.

Howe, M. T. A. (1989). *Fragments of genius: The strange feats of idiots savants.* London: Routledge and Kegan Paul.

Hunter, I. M. L. (1962). An exceptional talent for calculative thinking. *British Journal of Psychology, 53*, 243–258.

Kelly, S. J., Macaruso, F., & Sokol, S. M. (1997). Mental calculation in an autistic savant: A case study. *Journal of Clinical and Experimental Neuropsychology, 19*, 172–184.

Klin, A., Volkmar, F. R., Sparrow, S., Cicchetti, D. N., & Rourke, B. P. (1995). Validity and neuropsychological characterization of Asperger syndrome: Convergence with nonverbal learning disabilities syndrome. *Journal of Child Psychology and Psychiatry, 36*, 1127–1140.

LeFevre, J., Sadesky, G. S., & Bisanz, J. (1996). Selection of procedures in mental addition: Reassessing the problem size effect in adults. *Journal of Experimental Psychology: Learning, Memory, and Cognition, 22*, 216–230.

Lockyer, L., & Rutter, M. (1970). A five to fifteen year follow-up study of infantile psychosis: IV. Patterns of cognitive ability. *British Journal of Social and Clinical Psychology, 9*, 152–163.

Miller, L. K. (1989). *Musical savants: Exceptional skill in the mentally retarded.* Hillsdale, NJ: Lawrence Erlbaum Associates.

Mottron, L., & Belleville, S. (1993). A study of perceptual analysis in a high-level autistic subject with exceptional graphic abilities. *Brain and Cognition, 23*, 279–309.

Norris, D. (1990). How to build a connectionist idiot (savant). *Cognition, 35*, 277–291.

Nurcombe, M. D., & Parker, N. (1964). The idiot savant. *Journal of the American Academy of Child Psychiatry, 3,* 469–487.

O'Connor, N., & Hermelin, B. (1984). Idiot-savant calendar calculators: Maths or memory? *Psychological Medicine, 16,* 885–893.

O'Connor, N., & Hermelin, B. (1988). Low intelligence and special abilities. *Journal of Child Psychology and Psychiatry, 29,* 391–396.

O'Connor, N., & Hermelin, B. (1989). The memory structure of autistic idiot-savant mnemonists. *British Journal of Psychology, 80,* 97–111.

Park, D., & Youderian, P. (1974). Light and number: Ordering principles in the world of an autistic child. *Journal of Autism and Childhood Schizophrenia, 4,* 313–323.

Parker, S. W. (1918). Orthogenic cases: XIII. Obadia, a child with a numerical obsession. *Psychological Clinics, 12,* 105–131.

Phillips, A. (1930). Talented imbeciles. *Psychological Clinics, 18,* 246–255.

Pring, L., Hermelin, B., & Heavey, L. (1995). Savants, segments, art and autism. *Journal of Child Psychology and Psychiatry, 36,* 1065–1076.

Rimland, B. (1978). Savant capabilities of autistic children and their cognitive implications. In G. Serban (Ed.), *Cognitive deficits in the development of the mental illness* (pp. 43–65). New York: Brunner/Mazel.

Sacks, O. (1985). *The man who mistook his wife for a hat.* London: Duckworth.

Scheerer, M., Rothmann, E., & Goldstein, K. (1945). A case of "idiot savant": An experimental study of personality organization. *Psychological Monographs, 58* (No. 4).

Scripture, E. W. (1891). Arithmetical prodigies. *American Journal of Psychology, 4,* 1–59.

Selfe, L. (1977). *Nadia: A case of extraordinary drawing ability in an autistic child.* London: Academic Press.

Seron, X., Pesenti, M., Noeel, M. P., Deloche, G., & Cornet, J-A. (1992). Images of numbers or "when 98 is upper left and 6 is sky blue." *Cognition, 44,* 159–196.

Shah, A., & Frith, U. (1983). An islet of ability in autistic children: A research note. *Journal of Child Psychology and Psychiatry, 24,* 613–620.

Shah, A., & Frith, U. (1993). Why do autistic individuals show superior performance on the block design task? *Journal of Child Psychology and Psychiatry, 34,* 1351–1364.

Smith, S. B. (1983). *The great mental calculators.* New York: Columbia University Press.

Staszewski, J. T. (1988). Skilled memory and expert mental calculation. In M. T. H. Chi, R. Glaser, & M. T. Farr (Eds.), *The nature of expertise* (pp. 71–128). Hillsdale, NJ: Lawrence Erlbaum Associates.

Steel, J. G., Gorman, R., & Flexman, J. E. (1984). Neuropsychiatric testing in an autistic mathematical idiot savant. Evidence for nonverbal abstracting capacity. *Journal of the American Academy of Child Psychiatry, 23,* 704–707.

Stevens, D. E., & Moffitt, T. E. (1988). Neuropsychological profile of an Asperger's syndrome case with exceptional calculating ability. *The Clinical Neuropsychologist, 2,* 228–238.

Tredgold, A. F. (1929). *Mental deficiency (amentia)* (5th ed.) London: Bailliere.

Treffert, D. A. (1989). *Extraordinary people.* New York: Harper & Row.

Welling, H. (1994). Prime number identification in idiot-savants: Can they calculate them? *Journal of Autism and Developmental Disorders, 24,* 199–207.

White, P. A. (1988). The structured representation of information in long-term memory: A possible explanation for the accomplishments of "idiots savants." *New Ideas in Psychology, 6,* 3–14.

Wizel, D. A. (1904). Ein Fall von Phenomenalem, Rechentalent bei einen Imbecillen. *Archiv fur Psychiatrie und Nervenkrankheiten, 38,* 122–155.

World Health Organization. (1992). *The ICD-10 classification of mental and behavioral disorders: Clinical description and diagnostic guidelines.* Geneva, Switzerland: Author.

ARITHMETICAL DEVELOPMENT: COMMENTARY ON CHAPTERS 1 THROUGH 8 AND REFLECTIONS ON DIRECTIONS

Jeffrey Bisanz
University of Alberta

When asked to comment on the first eight chapters of this volume, I eagerly agreed. On further reflection, however, I was not at all sure that I could provide the diversity of opinion that readers of a commentary might want to see. Consequently, I decided to discharge much of this task to three friends whom I call my "critics." I must begrudgingly admit that, when it comes to critical analysis, they do a better job than I. Sometimes they are overly critical, however, which is why I find their company difficult for extended periods.

One of my critics is intensely theoretical in his orientation. I refer to this person as TP (Theoretical Person). TP is capable of calm discourse about the nature of developmental theory, but more frequently, he flies off the handle over perceived inadequacies in matters of theory. Another critic is EP (Educational Person). EP was a graduate student in developmental psychology, but she abandoned that course to pursue a career in elementary education so that she could work directly with children. She is very conversant with developmental research and theory, but she is not easily impressed with its utility for her everyday work. The last critic is called MP (Methodology Person). MP avoids theoretical discussions to the extent possible, and even then he usually sticks to theory in the context of measurement or operationalization. In our first exchange we discussed the premise of the book, and in our second exchange we discussed chapters 1–8. I conclude with some summary observations.

Premise of the Book

Prior to meeting with my three critics, I thought it might be useful to whet their appetites with a description of the editors' goals for the volume and, then, to obtain some initial reactions to the task before us. I decided to communicate with my critics initially via e-mail, so that unnecessary debate could be minimized.

JB. In their title, the editors of this book make clear that their intention is to address two related issues: the developmental relation between concepts and skills, and the development of *adaptive*, as opposed to *routine*, expertise. The connection between these two issues may not be immediately transparent.

Those who study the development of mathematical cognition normally distinguish between three types of knowledge: factual, procedural, and conceptual (Bisanz & LeFevre, 1990; Cowan, chap. 2, this volume; Greeno, Riley, & Gelman, 1985). *Factual* knowledge consists of number facts (e.g., $3 + 4 = 7$) that are, as far as can be determined, stored in memory and retrieved as necessary. The process of retrieving number facts is assumed to occur without deliberation and without special mnemonic devices, much as one retrieves one's own middle name. So, for example, if "$3 + 4 = ?$" is presented and "7" is retrieved quickly and without intervening steps, then we would judge $3 + 4 = 7$ to be part of factual knowledge. *Procedural* knowledge consists of the repertoire of mental activities that can be used to solve problems. *Conceptual* knowledge comprises understanding of the fundamental principles that underlie and, in a sense, define mathematics. In elementary arithmetic, for example, the list of principles that could be targeted for study includes additive composition, commutativity, associativity, and inversion (Baroody, Wilkins, & Tiilikainen, chap. 4, this volume; Cowan, chap. 2, this volume; Klein & Bisanz, 2000). In the past, the tendency was to study any one of these three types of knowledge as if it were relatively isolated from the others. It has become increasingly clear, however, that we must study the interactions among these types of knowledge if we want to understand mathematical cognition and, especially, its development. Thus, the first issue addressed in this volume—the developmental relation between concepts and skills—reflects this growing concern for understanding how factual, procedural, and conceptual knowledge interact in mathematical cognition.

The second issue—the development of *adaptive*, as opposed to *routine*, expertise—is based on a distinction borrowed from Hatano (1988; see also the Foreword in this volume). Routine expertise comprises knowledge and skill that can be used effectively with only a relatively narrow set of familiar tasks. In contrast, adaptive expertise is based on knowledge and skills that can be used in a wide variety of contexts, unfamiliar as well as familiar. In their Preface, the editors make explicit the connections between these two types of expertise: "Adaptive expertise depends on conceptual understanding (well-connected knowledge) and its integration with procedural knowledge" (Baroody & Dowker, Preface, this volume, p. *xvi*). Thus, the difference between routine and adaptive expertise is presumed to depend on the quality and accessibility of conceptual knowledge.

The themes covered in this book are very important and timely. I cannot see how we can make further progress in understanding the development of mathematical cognition without charting the interactions among factual, procedural, and conceptual knowledge. Combining this concern with the distinction between routine and adaptive expertise provides a context and rationale for examining a wide range of issues that should be important for developmental research and for instruction.

Given the editors' goals, what do you expect or hope to see in these eight chapters?

TP. Thank you for that rather lengthy statement of the obvious. Of course I hope to see well-detailed theories that seem to capture the richness of the interactions between procedural and conceptual knowledge, to the extent that those two domains can be separated conveniently. I will be looking to see whether the authors explore the appropriateness of their theoretical constructions beyond the particular area they are addressing at the moment, and to see whether the theories have any potential for generality. Of particular interest will be whether the theories that are put forward are limited to characterizing states of development along a continuum or whether they actually have something to say about *why* and *how* development occurs. What we do not need, from the point of good developmental theory, are more studies showing that older children do better than younger children. Recent developmental "theories" tend to be extraordinarily domain specific and limited. Aside from describing steps in a sequence or general improvements in age, they have little to say about transition mechanisms (for information processors), principles of development (for Wernerians), or influences arising from particular kinds of environments (for contextualists). I appreciate the need for and value of domain-specific theories, but at some point we must attend to what these theories tell us about development generally.

EP. I suppose I agree, to some extent, but a theory so general that it cannot be used to guide expectations in specific situations is not of much practical value. I would like to see an understanding emerge from these chapters that would help me recognize my students' learning skills and styles of thinking, anticipate their difficulties, design good ways of assessing their current level of functioning, and prepare instructional experiences for them. I continue to look for insights I can use in the classroom.

I also should mention that the difference between adaptive and routine expertise reminds me of the need for researchers to not only acknowledge but also incorporate individual differences in their work. It seems to me that the agenda set by the authors emphasizes individual differences. In particular, the implication is that at least two developmental paths exist: One leads to routine expertise and the other leads to adaptive expertise. Recognition of these two paths will come as no surprise to teachers, but it may present a challenge to developmental psychologists, who often seem inclined to ignore individual differences or to presume that one form is a degenerate or insufficiently developed version of the other.

MP. I will let you two worry about whether the insights that emerge from these chapters are theoretically powerful or practically useful. My concern is that they make sense, given the data and the likely sensitivity of the measurement tools. I will be looking to see how well the conclusions are supported by the evidence. Your introductory comments, JB, already raise concerns. Were you asleep at the switch? If the distinction between factual and procedural knowledge depends on whether retrieval or some more extended, multistep procedure is used, I wonder how well that distinction is tested empirically. When someone recalls an answer, how can we be sure whether it is actually retrieved in a single step? It sounds to me as if a pretty sophisticated method would be required, and one that is guided by a pretty powerful theory about what retrieval is and is not. I am prepared to bet that the same problem exists in distinguishing between procedural and conceptual knowledge. What about the distinction between "well-connected" and "unconnected" knowledge, which the editors see as being critical for understanding the difference between adaptive and routine expertise? If we want to study the role of connected and unconnected knowledge in developing expertise, then these constructs must be measured separately and compared. In general, I will be watching to see how well the authors operationalize and measure their constructs.

JB. Well, sure, of course those ideas crossed my mind in some form or another. Certainly there are many ways in which knowledge or understanding might be measured (e.g., Bisanz & LeFevre, 1992); the trick would be to operationalize "connected" knowledge. Given all of your comments, I suppose we also should be watching for (a) mechanisms or principles of development that have some generality within and beyond the domain of mathematical thinking, (b) insights that have practical value in education, (c) sensitivity to individual differences, (d) the degree to which conclusions are well supported by evidence, and (e) how well critical constructs are operationalized.

Discussion of Chapters 1 to 8

Following the exchange above via e-mail, the four of us met to discuss each of the chapters separately. I have recorded the resulting discussion as faithfully as possible, with only minor editorial concessions to the constraints of coherence and civility.

Chapter 1: Setting the Stage

JB. In chapter 1, Baroody describes a variety of issues related to the developmental relation between conceptual knowledge and solution procedures, and he critically reviews existing views in light of current evidence. His purpose is, in part, to provide a theoretical framework for the subsequent chapters. I found the historical perspective described in the first section to be quite informative. The author identifies a range of theoretical approaches and their historical roots (Fig. 1.1), describes current views on the relation between procedural and conceptual knowledge (Fig. 1.2), and tries to draw connections between past and present issues.

EP. Informative, yes, but not entirely satisfying. For example, there is a 50-year gap in the account, from the 1930s to the 1980s. So I could not really get any sense for how these different approaches evolved, whether or how conflicts were resolved, or why the proponents of the different approaches held the views that they did. The theorists described from the earlier period (Brownell, Dewey, and Thorndike) all had prescriptive insights for education that are correlated with practices and positions found today, of course, but I was unable to gain a sense of historical development between then and now. This section is more of a sketch than a serious historical account.

JB. It is brief, to be sure. Nevertheless, in the second section of the chapter the author does manage to raise a number of important issues that help to define the problems that researchers face today. For example, they point to the possibility that the distinction between conceptual and procedural knowledge may blur with development and that conceptual knowledge can play instigator (direct) as well as supportive (indirect) roles in problem solving. They outline various views of how skills and concepts might be related developmentally (i.e., whether skill precedes concepts, or concepts precede skill, or whether the two develop simultaneously or interactively), and then evaluate the evidence for these alternatives.

TP. I would be hard pressed to think of a more important theoretical issue than that of how skills and concepts interact over the course of development, but again the explication here is sketchy at best. These are core issues, but the reasons for their importance require some very careful theoretical elaboration. The views described seem more like vague hypotheses than compelling theoretical alternatives.

MP. Agreed. Moreover, the evaluation of the four competing alternatives was very sketchy; I would have liked to seen a more compelling case for the connection between evidence and conclusions.

JB. Okay, so "sketchy" seems to be the operative word here. Nevertheless, I think this part of the chapter is valuable. Researchers in the field need to appreciate the scope of the issues, and historical reviews can help to convey some sense of that scope. With only a few exceptions (e.g., Ginsburg, Klein, & Starkey, 1998; Resnick & Ford, 1981), serious attempts have not been made to highlight historically pervasive issues in research and practice about the development of mathematical thinking. Perhaps the author tried to pack too much into too little space, but I think his effort will help to reinforce the need for more elaborated analyses on the history of the field.

In the last section of the chapter, Baroody turns from discussing relatively pure theory to commenting on educational implications. Here he reviews different philosophical approaches to teaching mathematics, and he discusses present attempts to reform mathematics education. I thought this section was very helpful as an overview of instructional orientations and the complexities involved in changing curricula radically.

TP. I might add that the author's counterarguments to the attack on constructivism in mathematics education were right on target. I was also pleased to see some clear links between theory and education. I would hope that, if this chapter were to be revised in 10 years, the connections between theory and practice would be even much tighter than they are now.

MP. I wish the same could be said about theory and educational assessment. If we emphasize in our theories that there is more to learning mathematics than remembering arithmetic facts, then we will have to develop assessment methods that help to capture what it is that children should be—and are—learning. The relation between theory and assessment was barely touched on here.

EP. I am not surprised. Too much psychological work on the development of mathematical thinking is amazingly mute with respect to educational issues. At least the authors here made a serious and informative attempt to discuss psychological development in the context of curriculum issues.

JB. I thought it was very interesting that the authors underscored the need for teachers to understand cognitive development and the psychological underpinnings of mathematical thinking. Clearly, those of us doing research in this area have something to contribute to instruction and assessment.

EP. Just as clearly, to me, is the fact that teachers and students have something to contribute to developmental theories. Developmental researchers could benefit if they would spend more time learning about instruction in the real world, and about the interaction between teachers and learners in schools.

TP. Touché.

Chapters 2, 3, and 4: Issues and Approaches

JB. In the next three chapters by Cowan (chap. 2), Baroody and Tiilikainen (chap. 3), and Baroody et al. (chap. 4), the focus shifts from outlining a comprehensive framework to reviewing, evaluating, and synthesizing research on specific aspects of arithmetic development. Cowan begins with a intriguing, if brief, historical account of the relative emphasis on calculational skill versus mathematical understanding in English schools. This section complements American-centric accounts (including chap. 1 in this volume and Ginsburg et al., 1998) and, at the same time, highlights some striking similarities.

EP. Indeed, the crass, pay-for-results approach in England of the 1860s strikes me as being fairly similar to some equally mindless proposals in contemporary times.

JB. What follows is a solid, informative, and fairly comprehensive review of research on factual, procedural, and conceptual knowledge of addition, with special emphasis on the latter. The chapter ends with some very thoughtful insights on issues that need to be investigated and better understood.

TP. I think it is worth pointing out that Cowan's review and evaluation of the succession of models developed by Siegler and his colleagues provide a different perspective than the comments by Baroody and Tiilikainen in chapter 3. Readers should be encouraged to read both accounts to get a range of insights and informed opinions.

More generally, aside from the obvious breadth and scope of scholarship, a striking characteristic of this chapter is the sense of humility that is conveyed. In the context of surveying a broad range of hypotheses, results, and conclusions, Cowan points effectively to many important gaps in our understanding of the development of mathematical cognition. He notes, for example, that our understanding of children's knowledge of arithmetic principles is "fragmentary," that our understanding of the interactions between skill (procedures) and knowledge (concepts) is far from complete, and that we know very little about how experiential and cognitive variables influence development and individual differences in development. I find the humility refreshing. At this point, a little humility becomes the field.

EP. I also appreciated the honest humility reflected in this chapter. Three observations stood out for me. The first concerns the contrast between what we know about children in the early grades of school versus those who have not yet entered schools. Cowan documents the fact that school-aged children show considerable mathematical competence, but it is clear from his review that much less is known about the arithmetical knowledge and skill of preschool children. This relative ignorance needs to be remedied. Better knowledge about preschoolers presumably would enable teachers in the early elementary grades to better adapt their instructional practices to their students. Moreover, teachers and caregivers in day cares and nursery schools are called on increasingly to prepare children for school. Again, a more detailed understanding of how preschoolers approach mathematical tasks would provide a basis for optimizing instruction.

The second observation is that, despite the obvious prevalence and importance of individual differences for education, little is known about the factors that cause or maintain these differences. I am happy to see someone point to this area of ignorance and to suggest the kinds of questions—concerning cognitive and experiential variables, for example—that must be addressed if we are to establish instructional practices grounded on a sound theory of development.

The third observation is that, if Cowan is correct, we still know relatively little about the costs or benefits of emphasizing conceptual understanding versus calculational skill in instruction. Cowan's view on this point differs somewhat from that of Baroody in chapter 1, who argues that the major issue now is how to integrate calculational skills and conceptual understanding in instruction. On the surface, it is hard to understand how these issues could not have been addressed and fully resolved over the past 70 years. As a teacher, developmental research will have the potential to affect my practice when it can provide a clear answer to these instructional problems. Meanwhile, I do my best in the class-room.

MP. I suspect that the reason this last issue has not been addressed conclu-sively is that instructional practices are not so black and white as implied by the dichotomy between skill-oriented and concept-oriented approaches. Based on this chapter, I also see now that measurement of some of the outcomes to be tested, such as "conceptual understanding" of particular concepts, is not straight-forward. Cowan does a good job in describing some of the alternatives that are used to measure "understanding," and he notes that little is known about the relations among these various methods. Until these methodological issues are resolved in the research community, it is hard to see how sound theories and solid instructional implications will be forthcoming.

TP. These methodological issues are based in turn on theoretical and even philosophical issues about what constitutes mathematical understanding, as Baroody notes in chapter 1.

JB. Yes, in fact the issue of "understanding" has been quite difficult (Bisanz & LeFevre, 1992). A promising development is that researchers have begun to use and compare multiple measures (e.g., Canobi, Reeve, & Pattison, 1998; Dowker, 1998). To summarize, then, I think we can agree that Cowan's chapter is informative and thoughtful, that it shows good theoretical sensitivity to gaps in our knowledge, and that it shows good methodological sensitivity to shortcom-ings in our measurement tools. Yes, perhaps the humility is appropriate for the field, but vigorous pursuit of the research agenda outlined by Cowan certainly would go a long way toward reducing the appropriateness of that humility.

EP. If so, can arrogance be far ahead?

JB. Rather than respond, let's proceed. In chapter 3, Baroody and Tiilikainen set out to compare and evaluate two competing theories of how arithmetic skill and knowledge develop in children. One is the strategy choice and discovery simulation (SCADS) model (Shrager & Siegler, 1998), the most current version of strategy-choice models developed by Siegler and his colleagues. SCADS is implemented as a simulation that mimics some aspects of children's strategic behavior and development in arithmetic. The second is a schema-based view (e.g., Baroody & Ginsburg , 1986). Most of this section is devoted to a very detailed evaluation of SCADS in terms of its theoretical plausibility and the degree to which it accounts for empirical evidence.

MP. Indeed, it is very detailed and very critical, but let the chips fall where they may. Evaluating all of the authors' claims is beyond the scope of our present discussion, but we should note how important these criticisms appear to be. If valid, one must question not only about the adequacy of SCADS in its present state, but also whether any revised model built on the same frame could ever be satisfactory. Clearly the research community must respond to the challenges these criticisms represent. If we hope for theoretical advances in this area, it is important that this dispute not just sit unattended!

TP. I agree about the need for this discussion to continue in the research community. I would be concerned, however, about the nature of that discussion. For example, the authors argue that SCADS is oversimplified because it does not accommodate certain strategies, forms of reasoning, and reflection. No one, not even Siegler and his colleagues, would contend that SCADS is the complete and final model of how arithmetic thinking develops. To the extent that existing evidence requires something that is missing from SCADS, an important question is whether SCADS can be revised to incorporate any such missing elements. After all, JB, you have told us before that SCADS and its predecessors can simulate some aspects of children's behavior and development, it captures some useful insights about cognitive development that apply in domains other than arithmetic, and it has stimulated informative lines of research. To reject SCADS and its future progeny merely because, in its present form, it is incomplete may amount to throwing out the baby with the bath water.

JB. I don't think the authors are implying anything about future progeny; they just want to clarify why the products of this approach are not very satisfying at present.

MP. If the elements missing from SCADS are very important and cannot be incorporated in any way, shape, or form, then of course the approach should be abandoned. This decision can only be made by the research community on the basis of extended, public deliberation.

Like TP, I am concerned about the basis for rejecting specific hypotheses or entire models. The authors make many comparisons of SCADS with a schema-based view, and the latter apparently wins every time. The schema-based view is not described in great detail, however. For example, it features a "web of conceptual, procedural, and factual knowledge" that, when "unconnected," renders children's estimation efforts inaccurate and inflexible. Alas, it is difficult to determine what the structure of this "web" is, what being "unconnected" means, and how these constructs might be tested without presuming the outcomes they are used to explain. Some elaboration here would have helped the authors' argument. In general, though, when accounting for data, an underspecified model will always have an advantage over a relatively well-specified model, because the latter is constrained by its details. I am quite aware that implementing a computer simulation such as SCADS involves many relatively arbitrary decisions. Consequently, the programmer/theorist has many obscure degrees of freedom to play with in producing a program that will account for the data. In general, though, the use of underspecified verbal theories probably provides even more degrees of freedom to the theorist. In the present case, how SCADS works is relatively clear, compared with the schema-based view. Whereas the schema-based view *allows for* outcomes that the authors deem desirable, it is not at all clear how the theory would actually *produce* these outcomes. The comparison between a relatively well-specified theory, such as SCADS, and an underspecified theory, such as the schema-based theory, rarely is so straightforward as the authors imply. Of course, the better specified theory could be so narrowly defined or tested that it is less interesting and valuable. This possibility must be part of the evaluation of the theory and the general approach.

TP. Well said, especially for a self-proclaimed dust-bowl empiricist! The point about underspecification needs to be underscored. Concepts like "web of knowledge" have intuitive appeal, but they are much too vague to be considered as serious theoretical constructs, at least in their present form.

But maybe, MP, our criticisms might be misdirected to some extent. Whenever the issue of underspecification arises, we must be wary about the possibility that what appears to one person as hand waving might appear to another as a fully adequate explanation. The issue might not be underspecification as much as it is an honest metatheoretical difference in what constitutes an adequate explanation. The authors write as if there is a rigid distinction between information processing and constructivist theory, a dichotomy that will appear worn and inappropriate to many developmental information processors, including you, JB. So, it is easy to believe that discrepancies in metatheory are critical here. Perhaps the differences between the theoretical positions of Baroody and Tiilikainen and of Shrager and Siegler (1998) might be addressed best by laying out their differing assumptions about what constitutes "adequate" explanation first, before criticisms about models and analyses are hurled about.

JB. Perhaps so. Whatever the opponents might think of that idea, we must give Baroody and Tiilikainen full credit for arguing that conceptual knowledge must be embedded, somehow, in the structures and processes that underlie mathematical thinking. This point seems to be neglected, still, in many of the so-called better specified models.

EP. Two points about this section stand out to me. First, the authors work hard to discredit SCADS because, in part, it is so aconceptual, so associative, so like an automaton, so . . . mindless. To me, the authors' characterization of SCADS makes it seem like a reasonable instantiation of what Hatano (1988) referred to as routine expertise. Clearly, many children show the characteristics of routine, rather than adaptive, expertise in their arithmetic as they go through school. These are the very children who require so much of my attention in the classroom! Rather than castigate SCADS, perhaps the authors should recognize it as a possible candidate for how routine expertise may develop. Perhaps the differences between SCADS and an elaborated schema-based model will turn out, in the long run, to reflect individual differences in the course of development.

JB. Now that you've said it, the point seems obvious.

EP. Second, I think that Baroody and Tiilikainen make an exceptionally important point at the end of this section. They claim that the adaptive expertise they see in preschoolers is strikingly different from the routine expertise they see in many school-aged children. The difference might be hard to measure, but as a teacher I think the claim is very tenable. The authors go on to argue that the change from adaptive expertise to routine expertise reflects a changing environment and, more specifically, a change in the nature of social mediation of learning. Prior to school, the argument goes, children learn about mathematics in contexts that are meaningful and purposeful and, thus, engaging and enjoyable. Once in school, mathematics is learned in contexts where the material has no connection to a child's everyday life or interests and, thus, does not make sense or is uninspiring. No detailed evidence is provided for this speculation, but it may well be true. If so, then of course we need to study children's learning environments prior to or outside of school, as well as those in school. Does it not make sense that a strong theory of cognitive development in mathematics *must* include a careful description of the environmental contexts in which learning occurs, and of how children respond to and manipulate those environments?

JB. Whatever defensive reply I might make to that last comment would only sound like a protracted excuse. You're right, and your criticism is not limited to just the theories in this chapter. Fortunately, good work is being done on the diverse contexts of mathematical learning (see Guberman, 1999, and chaps. 5 and 8 in this volume). The influence of this body of work must grow if theories on the development of mathematical thinking are to encompass the obvious importance of learning environments.

Let's turn to the chapter by Baroody et al. In contrast to the broad exposition in chapter 2 and the comparative theoretical approach in chapter 3, Baroody et al. focus on the development of one concept, commutativity, and they do so in considerable detail. In many ways this chapter is a model of careful exposition. The authors describe a provocative theoretical account (Resnick, 1992), they carefully distinguish alternative interpretations of this account, they evaluate evidence, and they note discrepancies. They finish by generating a modified theory and by indicating the kinds of research that must be done to resolve remaining ambiguities. The systematic, methodical approach taken by the authors is exemplary. Moreover, their modified theory of the acquisition of commutativity has to be taken as a significant advance.

MP. The methodical approach, the sensitivity to theoretical nuance, and the commitment to linking evidence and theory are indeed exemplary. I am concerned, though, about the heavy reliance on constructs that are difficult to operationalize. One of the ways in which change is proposed to occur, for example, is reflection on computational outcomes and experience. As noted earlier, reflection can be slippery construct. Still, the coherence of the successive levels in the proposed model (Table 4.4) is compelling.

TP. Yes, compelling, and perhaps we should not require well-defined mechanisms of change in every model; clearly this one has other strengths. I should note, however, that the specificity of the model concerns me a bit. I wonder whether the theoretical terms used to describe the model lend themselves to any degree of generality to, for example, the development of other concepts, or whether they will prove to be specific just to commutativity. As I noted earlier, I am concerned about the prevailing specificity of developmental theories. I should have liked the authors to comment on the extent to which the principles of development inherent in their model are likely to apply in other domains of development.

EP. Before we get too abstract, I would like to comment on the educational value of this work. The authors did not attempt to explore instructional implications, and the theoretical analysis does not obviously provide me with a ready way to analyze and enhance other forms of conceptual development. I was intrigued, however, with the authors' attempts to link the emergence of math concepts with young children's everyday, nonquantitative experience. These speculations were not confirmed with evidence, of course, but they help to illustrate some of the ways in which everyday experience might facilitate mathematical development. I dearly hope that linking everyday experience and the development of early mathematical knowledge soon becomes an essential part of empirical inquiry, as opposed to the subject of informed hand waving.

JB. When we consider these three chapters together, then, we get a wide-ranging review in chapter 2, a detailed comparison of two competing theoretical approaches in chapter 3, and a tightly focused analysis and synthesis in chapter 4.

Chapters 6 and 7: Links With Factual Knowledge

JB. Factual knowledge receives some attention in the next two chapters. Butterworth, Marschesini, and Girelli (chap. 6) describe a study on the relation between conceptual understanding and the organization of factual knowledge in school-aged children, and LeFevre, Smith-Chant, Hiscock, Daley, and Morris (chap. 7) review research on the relation between procedural and factual knowledge in adults. In some ways, the latter chapter is more general in scope, so let's begin with it.

One striking contribution of the chapter by LeFevre et al. is that it provides an excellent, integrative, and informative review of how adults generate the answers for basic number combinations. Included is traditional cognitive and developmental research, some recent neuropsychological studies, and a few cross-cultural studies. The current evidence, according to these authors, is that adults show considerable flexibility and diversity in solving even single-digit combinations, contrary to what we might expect based on the memory-based models of arithmetic performance that have dominated the experimental literature.

EP. Especially appealing to me is the argument that considerable individual differences exist among adults even in these simple tasks, an argument well supported by evidence. I would expect the more difficult and complex the task, the more pronounced the differences among individuals. Surely if adults differ in how they respond to combinations such as 4 + 5, researchers will find it difficult to ignore individual differences on *any* mathematical task.

JB. Yes, I think that this point is now well established (e.g., Dowker, 1992, 1998).

MP. I think a major contribution of this chapter is that it highlights a number of important methodological lessons that have been learned over the last 15 years. Psychologists as diverse as B. F. Skinner and Herbert Simon have warned us about the potential problems inherent in averaging across individuals or across conditions. Siegler (1987, 1989) and Baroody (1999) have illustrated these problems in research on children, and now LeFevre et al. have done the same with adults. Eventually this lesson should sink in. The chapter also is useful for illustrating the advantage of using multiple methodological approaches (different experimental designs, varying instructions, using measures that vary from latencies to answers on questionnaires) to gain converging evidence on critical issues. Finally, the authors clearly demonstrate the value of using self-reports in research with adults, and at the same time they note a number of possible methodological problems that accompany the use of this method. In my mind, the jury is still in session regarding the validity of self-reports. I suspect that their validity will depend on task, subject, and situational variables that are not well understood yet (Robinson, 2001). By highlighting some of these issues, LeFevre et al. remind us that we cannot ignore, but do not yet fully understand, self-reports as a tool in cognitive research.

TP. To my mind, a notable contribution is the reminder that development, or at least behavioral and cognitive change, continues beyond the acquisition of concepts (cf. Towse & Hitch, 1996). My impression is that much of the research on the development of mathematical thinking is focused on when and how children acquire particular concepts. Once the concept is acquired, researchers tend to think that their job is done. LeFevre et al. suggest that changes in the use of solution procedures can continue well beyond childhood, and that flexibility and adaptability in adulthood certainly are worthy of investigation. Good on them.

I cannot help but notice, however, the discrepancy between what is described and what is explained. The authors make a good case for the position that adults use diverse procedures in answering basic number combinations, but recognition of this fact leads to the question of how to explain it. Little insight is provided about what the constraints of the cognitive architecture or processing might be that requires or enables the observed diversity to exist. The real challenge now is developing good theories that will account for the differences among combinations and individuals that LeFevre et al. document so well.

JB. I suppose that a related point is that, despite the title of their chapter, LeFevre et al. have relatively little to say about representation. In contrast, representation is critical in the chapter by Butterworth et al. In the literature on mental arithmetic, it is often assumed that the organization of arithmetic facts in memory is determined by variables that influence strength of association, such as frequency and order of exposure. Butterworth et al. report a study in which they sought to determine whether children reorganize the representation of basic multiplication combinations according to a conceptual principle, commutativity. The authors thus seek to determine whether children's underlying representation of these combinations is determined by what they call a "passive" strengthening of associations based on frequency of presentation, or whether conceptual knowledge can influence the organization of memory. They conclude that, indeed, children reorganize their memory for arithmetic facts based on their growing knowledge of arithmetic. Impressive, eh?

MP. The question and approach are certainly interesting. The results are not entirely compelling, however. Consider one problem. The authors surmised that if their participants learned $m \times N$ before $N \times m$ (where $N > m$) and simply represented combinations according to frequency and order of exposure, then they should consistently produce answers to $m \times N$ faster than to $N \times m$. If, however, they eventually produce answers to $N \times m$ faster, then reorganization based on commutativity is implicated. Indeed, children showed an $N \times m$ advantage, at least after Grade 3.

If the children used retrieval on all items, then the authors' logic and findings would be compelling. There are other possibilities, however. For example, if the children used string counting (e.g., solving 5×3 by "counting" along the "string" 5, 10, 15), then the $N \times m$ advantage would be expected (because m counts of N is fewer than N counts of m). Because the authors neither collected self-reports nor made observations about how children generated answers, we cannot discount the string-counting possibility. Their results are suggestive, but until the solution procedures used by the children have been identified, the conclusions are tentative at best.

EP. When the next study is done, it also would be a good idea to actually measure both the instruction given to children and their understanding of commutativity. In the present study assumptions were made in lieu of actual empirical evidence.

JB. So, we can say that the study reported by Butterworth et al. is not entirely compelling but that the issues raised are very important and worthy of additional research. In conducting that additional research, some of the methodological points made by LeFevre et al. need to be incorporated. These two chapters, then, provide a valuable picture of some of the issues related to studying the interface between factual and procedural knowledge, and Butterworth et al. highlight the potential influence of conceptual knowledge in this melange as well.

Chapters 5 and 8: Learning Environments

JB. The remaining chapters in the first half of this volume are both focused on the symbolic content of the environments in which children learn mathematics. Seo and Ginsburg (chap. 5) describe a single study on children's understanding of the equal sign (=) to illustrate the nature of the gap that can exist between the intended meaning of symbols and children's interpretations of those symbols. Miura and Okamoto (chapter 8) explore the relation between language and children's acquisition of mathematical skill and knowledge.

I found the Seo and Ginsburg study to be a remarkable piece of work. In one sense it may appear narrow in scope, focused as it is only on children's understanding of the meaning of the equal sign (=). Children in the early elementary grades are so consistent in their failure to understand the relational meaning of this symbol that a small but vital research program has arisen around the phenomenon (e.g., Alibali, 1999; Perry, 1991). Seo and Ginsburg contribute to this work significantly by studying (a) how the equal sign is presented in textbooks, (b) how it is presented in a classroom, and (c) how children interpret the symbol as a function of the context in which it appears. This chapter is rich in illustrations of the problems of conceptual development and instruction. We get a sense for the mismatch between children's everyday concept of equivalence and their misinterpretation of the "=" symbol, the resilience of children's misinterpretations in the face of what would otherwise appear to be effective instruction, and the unintended ways in which textbooks can support a misinterpretation that interferes with learning.

MP. As adverse as I normally am to clinical interviews as a source of data, it is hard to imagine any other method that could yield the insights obtained in this study. The between- and within-child inconsistencies, as revealed in the transcripts, were just stunning. To cram these responses onto a numerical scale or to average across cells would have been to mute the power of the data.

EP. I agree entirely, and I'm happy to hear a dust-bowl empiricist recognize this point! To discuss method a bit more broadly, Seo and Ginsburg demonstrate the richness of insight that can arise when researchers analyze not only the responses or interpretations of children but also the environments in which those children develop. In this case the analysis of textbooks and teacher behavior were essential to gaining insights that otherwise would have been regarded only as speculative. I would like to see more of this sort of sensitivity and thoroughness in the mainstream of developmental research.

I must say also that I was humbled by the authors' observations. The teacher's approach to teaching was very, very competent, in my judgment. Children's misunderstandings persisted despite the teacher's best intentions and her efforts to introduce the concept of equivalence in diverse contexts. The important lesson here is that children's concepts and interpretations, some of which may be acquired prior to or outside of school, can buffer children from otherwise beneficial instruction. The value of research like this lies, in part, in informing teachers about the interpretations children are likely to bring to the learning situation. Teachers then can work to detect, build on, or correct these interpretations, as required.

TP. I, too, found this chapter to be entirely engaging. The results of the study do not lead to a particularly well-defined theory, but they highlight the elements a strong theory must comprise. The relation between symbol and meaning, for example, is fairly well ignored in most of the other chapters we have discussed. I want to raise one issue, however. I wonder how important it is to correct a child's misunderstanding of, for example, the equals sign. Perhaps it is, but I am not entirely sure why. One could imagine that the cost of *not* correcting this interpretation is that misunderstandings such as this one could persist to the point at which children believe that math consists mostly of meaningless, memorized manipulation of arbitrary symbols—in short, a mindless enterprise that becomes devoid of motivation. Clearly, Baroody (chap. 1) voiced this concern. One could also imagine that the cost of spoon feeding concepts to children might be that they lose the opportunity to struggle with and resolve conceptually difficult issues. Perhaps children benefit from the effort they spend in resolving inconsistencies, as Miura and Okamoto note in chapter 8. My point is that it would be desirable to have a theory—and maybe even some data—that would enable judgments about when direct instruction is likely to be optimal and when the child should be left alone to figure things out.

EP. I do not disagree, although the teacher in me is inclined to provide direct instruction whenever in doubt. In fairness to Seo and Ginsburg, however, note that they never recommend spoon-feeding. Their instructional approach consists primarily of helping children detect inconsistencies in their own thinking, so that they can begin to resolve those conflicts.

MP. Of course you are right. TP was merely distorting the authors' content to heighten the contrast he wanted to make. The tactic is all too familiar. My only remaining point on this chapter is that because the method was distinctly nonexperimental, we must be careful about making inferences about the causes of children's misinterpretations. Personally, I would like to see parallel experimental work that could be useful in testing some of the possibilities raised with Seo and Ginsburg's clinical-interview method. The power of combining methods would far exceed that of any single approach.

JB. With that as a last word on the chapter by Seo and Ginsburg, let's turn to the chapter by Miura and Okamoto. Thanks to the compelling body of research generated by Harold Stevenson, Shin-Ying Lee, and many others (e.g., Stevenson, Chen, & Lee, 1993), nearly everyone is now aware of the generally superior performance of students in Asian countries, as compared to their counterparts in North America, on measures of mathematical achievement. These initial findings have instigated a wide range of probing studies on factors that could contribute to cross-national differences in achievement, including cultural differences in attitudes toward learning, parental variables, teacher education and support, classroom instructional approaches, homework practices, and socially defined goals for children and youth. Representing a complementary line of research, Miura and Okamoto take the position that the language of a culture directly supports learning related to mathematics and that some languages (e.g., Japanese, Korean, Chinese) are more effective for this purpose than others (e.g., English and various European languages). The authors neatly describe why we might expect Asian languages to facilitate learning about number representation, counting, place value, and fractions, and then they summarize data consistent with these expectations. Their analyses also lead them to predict how languages might differentially support the use of regrouping in arithmetic and highlight quantitative information in normal communication. I suspect that a more lucid and concise description of the hypotheses and data in this area of research would be hard to find.

MP. Lucid and interesting, yes, but I find the general approach to be lacking in one respect. The studies typically are designed, in effect, to reveal a correlation between language group and an outcome measure. Usually the correlation has but 1 degree of freedom (i.e., one mean for each of two language groups). Correlation does not necessarily imply causality, and so the fact that Asian-language children perform better on a given task than European-language children does not lead ineluctably to the conclusion that language is the causal factor. The difference could be due to cultural attitudes, homework practices, and any number of the variables on the list you just described. The highlighted linguistic differences could be incidental to whichever factor is (or factors are) causally related to performance.

What is needed, it seems to me, is research that tests for predicted *interactions* between language and performance. For example, differences between two languages might lead to the prediction that Chinese-speaking children would perform clearly better than English-speaking children on Task A, where the linguistic differences are relevant, but that this difference should be reduced or negligible on Task B, where the linguistic differences are less relevant. Finding this sort of interaction would provide a compelling basis for arguing that linguistically related differences, and not any of a dozen other cultural variables, account for the data. This approach would provide stronger evidence for the intimate relation between language and performance than merely finding that one group of children consistently performs better than another.

JB. I am sure the authors are aware of this point, and indeed the kinds of interactions you describe have been revealed in other research (e.g., Miller, Smith, Zhu, & Zhang, 1995). I agree with you entirely, though, that the importance of predicting and testing for interactions needs to be highlighted in these kinds of studies. Another approach that might be useful would be to examine performance in bilingual (e.g., Chinese-English) children to see whether proficiency in one language helps or hinders performance in the other. This sort of research might reveal whether the advantages conferred by the linguistic structure of one language are tied to performance in that language or whether they transfer, in some sense, to performance in the other language. In bilingual children presumably all the other, potentially confounding, variables, such as homework practices and attitudes are neatly controlled.

TP. Bilingual children as a natural experiment, eh? I am far less concerned with matters of design than with matters of substance. I agree with you two empiricists about the delightful clarity of this chapter and about the need to go beyond simple language and performance comparisons. What intrigued me most, however, was the idea that the real significance of language differences might lie not just in particular linguistic markers or structure but, rather, in the extent to which languages support the detection and resolution of incongruities, a process that Miura and Okamoto refer to as *"comprehension monitoring."* This hypothesis, if correct, would link the rather circumscribed effects described in this chapter to a more general process of development. It would allow us to explain the results of these studies not just by noting, rather vaguely, that one language "supports a better understanding" or "makes relations more clear," but rather by suggesting a process by which superior understanding and clarity develop. If I am not mistaken, the idea of comprehension monitoring has been around for a long time. My hope is that the authors and others in this area can develop ways to elucidate the role of comprehension monitoring in relating language to cognitive development in mathematics.

EP. Doing so certainly would have implications for teaching mathematics. My observation is that, for many children, any inherent comprehension-monitoring processes go dormant as soon as pages of math problems come into view. The similarities between chapters 5 and 8 are worth noting. Like Miura and Okamoto, Seo and Ginsburg underscore the importance of detecting incongruities. Also, Seo and Ginsburg show how the ways in which we introduce and explain symbols to children can confuse the meanings we try to convey; Miura and Okamoto show how characteristics of our language can support or interfere with learning. As a teacher, I need to be aware of the elements of the child's symbolic environment—didactic or linguistic—that might affect development of the concepts and skills I am trying to foster. These two chapters help to illustrate the kinds of knowledge that teachers need to have to optimize their work with students.

As valuable as these chapters are, I could not help but wonder about whether any long-term effects arise from the phenomena covered in these types of studies. English-speaking children might take months longer to learn to count to 50 as compared with Chinese-speaking children, but sooner or later virtually everyone can do it. The way we teach equivalence may confuse children for a while, but eventually they all get it. I am inclined to believe that learning well and early is a good thing in the long run, but why should it be so? Is there any evidence facilitating the developments described in these chapters would or should have any long-term effects on the level knowledge and skill a student ultimately attains? If there are such effects, why do they exist? Is the explanation purely cognitive, whatever "purely cognitive" means, or are the effects created and maintained at least in part by the kinds of attitudes children develop toward mathematics as a result of such mundane activities as learning to count and deciphering what "=" means? The thrust of these chapters is that the didactic and linguistic environments children encounter affect their learning, at least in the short run. But why should we assume that these short-run effects have any long-term consequences?

TP. These are marvelous questions! Please, you really must consider returning to graduate school so that we can explore the theoretical advances that we must develop to . . .

MP. . . . completely obliterate any chance of getting good answers. What you need to do is to learn how to operationalize these questions in ways that will . . .
TP. . . . trivialize them, in the finest tradition of dust-bowl empiricism. . . .

At this point the discussion deteriorated to a level that rendered coherent and civil representation completely impossible.

Epilogue

The opinions of my critics were somewhat more pointed than what usually appears in published commentaries, but of course their conversation was not constrained by the usual conventions. As a group they evaluated these chapters for advances on several fronts. They examined proposed theories for generality, as well as local coherence. At the same time, the critics looked for any practical implications of insights and conclusions. They highlighted cases in which authors were sensitive to the issues, both theoretical and methodological, posed by individual differences. Where possible, they evaluated the extent to which conclusions were supported by evidence, as well as whether questions and constructs were operationalized appropriately. I certainly do not agree with all their comments and even wonder, in some cases, about how closely they read the chapters. Nevertheless, I suspect the criteria they used constitute reasonable and valuable guidelines that the rest of us might adopt in evaluating advances in the development of mathematical cognition. Clearly the first eight chapters of this volume are extremely helpful for illustrating some of the problems and prospects in this area of inquiry. Although it may be impossible to get my three critics in the same room again for some time, if I were to do so, I am sure they all would agree that the quality of ideas described in these chapters bodes well for advances in research and theory in the immediate future.

Acknowledgments

The author is grateful to Gay Bisanz, Leslie Mackey, and Laurie Schnirer for their helpful comments on a previous draft.

References

Alibali, M. W. (1999). How children change their minds: Strategy change can be gradual or abrupt. *Developmental Psychology, 35,* 127–145.

Baroody, A. J. (1999). The roles of estimation and the commutativity principle in the development of third-graders' mental multiplication. *Journal of Experimental Child Psychology, 75,* 157–193.

Baroody, A. J., & Ginsburg, H. P. (1986). The relationship between initial meaningful and mechanical knowledge of arithmetic. In J. Hiebert (Ed.), *Conceptual and procedural knowledge: The case of mathematics* (pp. 75–112). Hillsdale, NJ: Lawrence Erlbaum Associates.

Bisanz, J., & LeFevre, J. (1990). Strategic and nonstrategic processing in the development of mathematical cognition. In D. F. Bjorklund (Ed.), *Children's strategies: Contemporary views of cognitive development* (pp. 213–244). Hillsdale, NJ: Lawrence Erlbaum Associates.

Bisanz, J., & LeFevre, J. (1992). Understanding elementary mathematics. In J. Campbell (Ed.), *The nature and origins of mathematical skills* (pp. 113–136). Amsterdam: North Holland, Elsevier Science.

Canobi, K. H., Reeve, R. A., & Pattison, P. E. (1998). The role of conceptual understanding in children's addition problem solving. *Developmental Psychology, 34*, 882–891.

Dowker, A. D. (1992). Computational estimation strategies of professional mathematicians. *Journal for Research in Mathematics Education, 23*, 45–55.

Dowker, A. D. (1998). Individual differences in normal arithmetical development. In C. Donlan (Ed.), *The development of mathematical skills* (pp. 275–302). Hove, East Sussex, England: Psychology Press.

Ginsburg, H. P., Klein, A., & Starkey, P. (1998). The development of children's mathematical thinking: Connecting research with practice. In W. Damon (Series Ed.), I. E. Siegel & K. A. Renninger (Vol. Eds.), *Handbook of child psychology: Vol. 4. Child psychology in practice* (5th ed., pp. 401–476). New York: Wiley.

Greeno, J. G., Riley, M., & Gelman, R. (1985). Conceptual competence and children's counting. *Cognitive Psychology, 16*, 94–134.

Guberman, S. R. (1999). Supportive environments for cognitive development: Illustrations from children's mathematical activities outside of school. In A. Goncu (Ed.), *Children's engagement in the world: Sociocultural perspectives* (pp. 202–227). New York: Cambridge University Press.

Hatano, G. (1988). Social and motivational bases for mathematical understanding. In G. B. Saxe & M. Gearhart (Eds.), *Children's mathematics* (pp. 55–70). San Francisco: Jossey-Bass.

Klein, J. S., & Bisanz, J. (2000). Preschoolers doing arithmetic: The concepts are willing but the working memory is weak. *Canadian Journal of Experimental Psychology, 54*, 105–115.

Miller, K. F., Smith, C. M., Zhu, J., & Zhang, H. (1995). Preschool origins of cross-national differences in mathematical competence: The role of number-naming systems. *Psychological Sciences, 6*, 56–60.

Perry, M. (1991). Learning and transfer: Instructional conditions and conceptual change. *Cognitive Development, 6*, 449–468.

Resnick, L. B. (1992). From protoquantities to operators: Building mathematical competence on a foundation of everyday knowledge. In G. Leinhardt, R. Putnam, & R. A. Hattrup (Eds.), *Analysis of arithmetic for mathematics teaching* (pp. 373–425). Hillsdale, NJ: Lawrence Erlbaum Associates.

Resnick, L. B., & Ford, W. W. (1981). *The psychology of mathematics for instruction.* Hillsdale, NJ: Lawrence Erlbaum Associates.

Robinson, K. (2001). The validity of verbal reports in children's subtraction. *Journal of Educational Psychology, 93,* 211–222.

Shrager, J., & Siegler, R. S. (1998). SCADS: A model of children's strategy choices and strategy discoveries. *Psychological Science, 9*, 405–410.

Siegler, R. S. (1987). The perils of averaging data over strategies: An example from children's addition. *Journal of Experimental Psychology: General, 116*, 250–264.

Siegler, R. S. (1989). Hazards of mental chronometry: An example from children's subtraction. *Journal of Educational Psychology, 81*, 497–506.

Stevenson, H. W., Chen, C., & Lee, S.-Y. (1993). Mathematics achievement of Chinese, Japanese, and American children: Ten years later. *Science, 259*, 53–58.

Towse, J. N., & Hitch, G. J. (1996). Performance demands in the selection of objects for counting. *Journal of Experimental Child Psychology, 61*, 67–79.

ARITHMETICAL DEVELOPMENT: COMMENTARY ON CHAPTERS 9 THROUGH 15 AND FUTURE DIRECTIONS

David C. Geary
University of Missouri at Columbia

The second half of this book focuses on the important issues of arithmetical instruction and arithmetical learning in special populations. The former represents an area of considerable debate in the United States, and the outcome of this debate could affect the mathematics education of millions of American children (Hirsch, 1996; Loveless, 2001). At one extreme in this debate are advocates of unguided discovery learning, whereby teachers provide materials and problems to solve and encourage students to discover for themselves the associated concepts and problem-solving procedures. At the other extreme are those who advocate direct instruction and drill, whereby teachers provide explicit instruction on basic skills (facts, definitions, and procedures) and children are required to practice these basic skills until memorized by rote. In the first section of my commentary, I briefly address this debate, as it relates to chapters 9, 10, and 11 (by Dowker; Fuson and Burghardt; and Ambrose, Baek, and Carpenter, respectively). Chapters 12 to 15 (by Donlan; Jordan, Hanich, and Uberti; Delazer; and Heavey, respectively) focus on the important issue of arithmetical learning in special populations, a topic that has been largely neglected, at least in relation to research on reading competencies in special populations. I discuss these chapters and related issues in the second section of my commentary. In the third, I briefly consider future directions.

Instructional Research (Chapters 9 to 11)

Constructivism is a theoretical perspective based on Piaget's developmental theories (e.g., Cobb, Yackel, & Wood, 1992). The premise of this perspective is that children are active learners and must construct (meaningful) knowledge. An instructional implication of this premise is that students should be provided a context within which they, for example, discover mathematics principles and invent procedures or algorithms. Cobb and colleagues (1992), for instance, have argued that, with appropriate social-mathematical contexts, "it is possible for students to construct for themselves the mathematical practices that, historically, took several thousand years to evolve" (p. 28; cf. Al-Uqlidisi, 1978). As with any philosophy, though, opinions about how a constuctivist philosophy applies to instruction vary. An extreme position is that the teacher provides appropriate materials and a social context within which the materials are explored and discussed but does not provide formal instruction (e.g., a lecture) or strongly guide students' exploration of the material. (Baroody, chapter 1 of this volume, labels such a position the "problem-solving approach." See Table 1.1

on pp. 18 to 20 and the text on pp. 21 and 22 for a more detailed description of this approach.) A more moderate application of constructivist principles is embodied in a guided-discovery approach or what Baroody calls the "investigative approach" (see Table 1.1 on pp. 18 to 20 and the text on pp. 22 and 23 for a more detailed description of this approach.)

I have argued elsewhere (Geary, 1995) that an extreme (problem-solving) approach may not be practical. Still, I am willing to grant that the value of encouraging students to rediscover concepts and to invent or reinvent procedures is an empirical issue. I am also willing to grant that more moderate applications of constructivism (as represented by the investigative approach) may prove to be a useful feature of the elementary-school curriculum. However, this too is an empirical issue.

The research described by Fuson and Burghardt in chapter 10 and Ambrose et al. in chapter 11 represent a more moderate, and potentially useful, application of the principles of constructivist philosophy to mathematics education (see Geary, 1994, 1995, for discussion of more extreme applications of constructivist philosophy). Ambrose et al. provide a nice summary of children's early strategies for using multiplication and division to address issues related to measurement and the distribution of resources. From there, they describe a clinical-interview study in which third- to fifth-grade elementary school children were asked to solve a series of arithmetical word problems involving multiplication and division. The children's instruction did not involve the teaching of standard algorithms or an emphasis on memorizing basic facts. As a result, the children were required to invent their own algorithms for solving these problems. Ambrose et al. found that many, presumably most, of these children were able to rely on their knowledge of addition, subtraction, measurement, and related concepts to invent their own multiplication and division algorithms. The finding that children used related knowledge to construct these algorithms is not surprising, given that the tendency to "fall back" on related knowledge and procedures when solving novel problems is found in many, if not all, cognitive domains (Geary, 1994; Siegler, 1983).

In any case, there are some features of this instructional technique that appear to have promise, when used judiciously, for facilitating children's understanding multiplication and division concepts. For instance, many of the children used their understanding of and associated algorithms for solving multiplication problems to solve related division problems. As noted by Ambrose et al., making such conceptual links between multiplication and division is important and often not achieved if students are only taught the standard algorithms for solving multiplication and division problems. It is also likely that the invented algorithms provided children with experiences, such as decomposing and recombining sets of numbers, which could facilitate their understanding of numbers and how algorithms can be used to manipulate numbers.

However, there are other aspects of this instructional strategy that appeared to have been less effective. First, many of the students did not apply the commutative property of multiplication (that, e.g., $3 \times 4 = 4 \times 3$), nor did many invent a base-ten strategy for solving these problems. Second, it was not clear from the Ambrose et al. chapter how many children were successful and how many were not successful in inventing effective algorithms. Third, as Fuson and

Burghardt's work (described next) suggests, a discovery approach will be difficult to implement, at least in some areas, with many children. Fourth is the issue of teaching the standard algorithms and other facets of direct instruction. This last issue will be addressed after the discussion of Fuson and Burghardt's study.

Fuson and Burghardt provided groups of high-achieving second graders with base-ten blocks and with materials to represent quantities with written marks and asked them to solve relatively complex addition and subtraction problems (e.g., 2834 + 1963). As with the Ambrose et al. study, Fuson and Burghardt's approach was based on the general principles of constructivism and was designed to foster children's invention of addition and subtraction algorithms. An especially useful feature of this work is the detailed analysis of the children's progress during the learning sessions, as well as a detailed analysis of their successes and their failures. As for the successes, some of the invented algorithms, especially for addition, were clever and a few were better than the standard algorithm taught in U.S. schools; Method I, for instance, results in fewer demands on working memory than does the standard algorithm (see Fig. 10.3 in chap. 10). As with the Ambrose et al. study, there are features of this approach that are likely to facilitate children's conceptual understanding of numbers and addition and subtraction. For instance, the use of base-ten blocks to concretely represent quantities and the addition of these quantities is an especially attractive feature of this approach (Fuson, 1990; Geary, 1994), although it was less effective for subtraction. As Fuson and Burghardt note, their approach has the advantage of building on what children already understand about number and arithmetic and their associated strategies. In this way, children's new learning is strongly tied to what they already know, which is not always the case with direct instruction.

At the same time, there were difficulties with this approach. The social context was not always conducive to mathematics learning—for instance, being dominated by one child—and the general approach was time consuming and apparently not effective for all children. Even many of these high-achieving children invented incorrect algorithms, and many did not have the time to work on subtraction algorithms. It is likely that many lower achieving children will have similar difficulties, that is, a lack of time and invention of incorrect algorithms. On the basis of these difficulties, Fuson and Burghardt suggest that some balance between constructivist and direct instruction will be needed. I agree with this suggestion, with the caveat that the determination of this balance must be based on empirical research, that is, controlled studies that assess the most effective approach to teaching concepts and procedures. However, I disagree with Ambrose et al.'s suggestion that basic procedural and computational skills do not need to be taught in school and that the use of constructivist or direct instruction is a matter of values, not just empirical research.

In a recent empirical study, we found that cross-national differences in computational skills, including skill at retrieving facts and executing procedures, appeared to contribute to cross-national differences on tests of arithmetical reasoning, as measured by the ability to solve multistep word problems (Geary et al. 1997; Geary, Liu, Chen, Saults, & Hoard, 1999). Here, the advantage of Chinese students over their American peers on arithmetical reasoning tests was moderately to substantively reduced (depending on the sample), but not eliminated, when national differences in computational skills were statistically controlled. These findings are in keeping with the position that the automaticity of computational skills (e.g., fast retrieval of facts) reduces working memory demands associated with problem solving and thereby allows these resources to be allocated to more important aspects of problem solving, such as translating statements into quantitative representations (Mayer, 1985).

Even without the cognitive advantages of automaticity and the associated need for some degree of direct instruction and practice, the constructivist approach used by Ambrose et al. and Fuson and Burghardt appears to have considerable opportunity costs. Even if the constructivist approach was fully effective with all children (which has not been proven), the time required to construct invented algorithms is time that cannot be spent on other mathematical topics. Of course this is why early mathematicians invested so much time in developing procedures and representational systems (e.g., the base-ten system) for number and arithmetic. These procedures, such as the standard algorithm taught in U.S. schools for solving complex multiplication problems, are simply an efficient way to solve problems, although not the only or the most efficient ones. The goal of teaching these algorithms is to circumvent the centuries it took to develop these procedures (e.g., Al-Uqlidisi, 952/1978) in favor of more important aspects of arithmetic, such as conceptually understanding the base-ten system.

These arguments are not to say that students should be taught procedures without understanding the associated concepts; students should be taught effective computational procedures—and practice them to the point of automaticity—and should know the associated concepts (see Geary, 1995, 2001). It is now clear that the learning of conceptual and procedural skills are inter-related. A solid conceptual understanding of the domain (e.g., base-ten system) is important for avoiding and correcting procedural errors (e.g., Sophian, 1997), and the practice of procedures provides a context for children to learn associated concepts and problem-solving strategies (Siegler & Stern, 1998). Nor does this mean that constructivist techniques cannot sometimes be useful in mathematics education. As noted earlier, there are features of this approach that appear to be very useful, as illustrated by some children's linking of multiplication and division found in the Ambrose et al. study. I am simply arguing for a judicious use of this approach and for research—as nicely demonstrated by Fuson and Burghardt—aimed at determining when this approach is useful and when it is not.

Although Dowker's study (chap. 9) is not directly related to the issues associated with direct instruction versus constructivism, it has clear educational implications and speaks to the importance of computational skills. Dowker begins by providing a nice review of the relation between computational abilities and estimation skills in children and the dissociation between these skills that is sometimes found with certain forms of brain injury. In short, computational and estimation skills interact in many contexts but appear to be supported by distinct cognitive and neural systems (see also Dehaene, Spelke, Pinel, Stanescu, & Tsivkin, 1999). An innovative and important aspect of Dowker's work is the focus on how these distinct competencies interact. Specifically, she proposes that arithmetical estimation interacts with and, in a sense, extends computational skills. For problems that have been mastered (e.g., facts have been memorized), there is less reason to use estimation. Estimation is, however, very useful in contexts in which an exact answer cannot or does not need to be calculated, but its usefulness is greatest in a zone of partial knowledge and understanding. The proposal that estimation is most important within this zone—a zone determined by the level of computational skill and number knowledge—is especially interesting and potentially important. The zone provides an important framework for studying the relation between computational skills and estimation and for determining when use of an estimation strategy is likely to be effective (i.e., providing a reasonable close approximation of the actual answer).

Her large-scale study of the development of arithmetical estimation skills in elementary-school children demonstrates the utility of this approach. Here, 215 children participated in a 3-year study of the relation between computational and estimation skills. The children were classified based on their computational skills and administered estimation problems of varying difficulty. As found by others (e.g., Baroody, 1992), even when 5 years old, these children were able to make reasonable estimates for simple problems. The most interesting finding was that the development of children's estimation skills was tied to the development of computational skills. As computational skills improved, so did their ability to make good estimates. More important, the children's estimation skills appeared to be best at the level just beyond their ability to do accurate computations. As predicted by Dowker's model, children could estimate on problems that were somewhat more difficult than the problems on which they could easily compute exact answers, but could not estimate for problems several levels of difficulty beyond this. Finally, Dowker's finding that children used a variety of approaches to estimate is interesting and extends the work of Siegler and his colleagues, who have demonstrated that variability in problem-solving approaches is found in many—probably all—cognitive and academic domains (Siegler, 1996)

Research in Special Populations
(Chapters 12 to 15)

As noted earlier, research on the arithmetical abilities and learning of individuals composing special populations, such as children with learning disabilities, has been scant in relation to research on reading abilities in these same populations. Given this, the work by Donlan, Jordan et al., Delazer, and Heavey (chaps. 12, 13, 14, and 15, respectively) is a much needed contribution to the literature. Donlan and Jordan et al's work focuses on the arithmetical development of children with learning disabilities and will be discussed first. Delazer's chapter adds to our understanding of the relation between brain injury and arithmetical competencies, which, in turn, also contributes to the understanding of learning disabilities (Geary, 1993). Heavey's chapter is a fascinating and unique description of arithmetical savants and is discussed following the commentary on Delazer's work.

Jordan et al. address several important topics. The first concerns their nonverbal calculation task and the accompanying results. Here, a child views an array of disks, which is then hidden. Next, disks are either added to the hidden array or removed from it. The child is then asked to represent the resulting number of hidden disks using other disks. The task is important in that it allows children to demonstrate their ability to add and subtract without the use of language (e.g., verbally counting the array). The finding that many children can perform basic addition and subtraction using these disks before they can solve more formal arithmetic problems is also important, and in keeping with other studies that have used a nonverbal procedure (Starkey, 1992). An unresolved issue is the source of this ability. Jordan et al. argue that the ability to perform these nonverbal calculations is the result of the development of general intellectual abilities, and not the operation of a specific arithmetical module (see also Huttenlocher, Jordan, & Levine, 1994). Other researchers, including myself, argue that the ability to perform these nonverbal calculations reflects the operation of an evolved system of number-counting-arithmetic abilities (Gallistel & Gelman, 1992; Geary, 1995). In any event, the discovery and ability to assess these preverbal arithmetical competencies is an important contribution, whatever the source of the abilities.

Jordan et al. and I are in closer agreement with respect to the deficits that define a mathematical disability (MD). Jordan et al.'s research, our own work, and that of others have consistently revealed that children with MD demonstrate grade-appropriate arithmetical and mathematical skills in some areas but persistent deficits in others (e.g., Bull & Johnston, 1997; Geary, Hamson, & Hoard, 2000; Geary, Hoard, & Hamson, 1999; Jordan & Montani, 1997). The most consistently found deficit in children with MD is in the ability to quickly and accurately retrieve basic arithmetic facts from long-term memory (LTM). These children retrieve fewer facts than their academically normal peers do, and they quickly forget many of the facts that they do learn. When they can retrieve facts from LTM, children with MD make many more retrieval errors and sometimes show unusual reaction time patterns, in relation to their academically normal peers (Geary, 1993). For many of these children, the retrieval deficit appears to reflect a persistent, perhaps lifelong, disability (e.g., Ostad, 1997). The source of this deficit is currently unknown, although there appear to be two contributing factors. Some of these children appear to have a fundamental deficit in the ability to represent and retrieve information from semantic memory, as discussed next. Other children appear to have difficulties inhibiting irrelevant associations during the retrieval process (Barrouillet, Fayol, & Lathulière, 1997; Geary et al., 2000). For instance, when asked to determine the sum of 3 + 6, many of these children appear to recall 4, 7, and 9; 4 and 7 are the numbers following 3 and 6 in the counting string. These three "answers" then compete for expression, which, in turn, disrupts reaction times and results in more retrieval errors (Geary et al., 2000).

The work of Jordan et al.'s also represents an essential next step in MD research, the identification and study of MD subtypes. The finding of different patterns of functions and deficits in groups of children with different patterns of reading and mathematics achievement scores mirrors our recent work and speaks to the usefulness of this approach (e.g., Geary, Hoard, et al., 1999). Our results compliment those of Jordan et al. and suggest that children with low mathematics achievement scores but average reading achievement scores have difficulty holding information in working memory while counting and show the retrieval-inhibition deficit described earlier. Although definitive conclusions cannot be reached at this time, the pattern suggests that these children may have a developmental delay or a more fundamental deficit in the prefrontal cortex and the associated executive functions (see also Barrouillet et al., 1997; Geary & Hoard, 2001). Children with poor reading scores but average mathematics scores also show the retrieval-inhibition deficit. However, they do not appear to have working-memory problems while counting. In keeping with Jordan et al.'s results, we have found that children with low achievement in both reading and math show more pervasive deficits than do other children with learning disabilities, even after controlling for IQ, although they have grade-appropriate skills in some areas (e.g., number recognition).

In his chapter, Donlan addresses the important, but not fully understood, link between language development and arithmetical development. The approach taken by Donlan is innovative and complements the work of Jordan et al. In this approach, children with specific language impairment (SLI) are contrasted with language-matched and age-matched children on a variety of number and arithmetic tasks. The basic question is whether SLI will be associated with delays in the acquisition of number and arithmetic skills generally or in language-dependent number and arithmetic skills only. These questions are important in their own right, but they also are relevant to the issue of the modularity of the early number-counting-arithmetic system. Although Donlan's study is not a definitive test, a correlation between SLI and pervasive number and arithmetic deficits would be consistent with the position that early quantitative skills emerge from general cognitive abilities (e.g., Huttenlocher et al., 1994). Although not the only interpretation (see, e.g., Jordan et al., chap. 13, this volume), an association between SLI and a more circumscribed number and arithmetic deficits would be consistent with the position that certain early quantitative abilities are modular (Gallistel & Gelman, 1992; Geary, 1995).

Generally in keeping with the latter position, Donlan found that young children with SLI had age-appropriate number and arithmetic skills in some areas (e.g., conceptual understanding of counting) and deficits in others. Moreover, the deficits largely involved numerical processes, such as the use of verbal counting procedures to count objects, that are dependent on the language system, in general, and the phonological loop, in particular. These results are consistent with Jordan et al.'s findings that children with learning disabilities show both strengths and weaknesses in basic number and arithmetic skills and are in keeping with the position that disruptions in the phonological system underlie language and reading disorders and certain forms of MD (Geary, 1993). Because children use counting procedures to initially solve verbal arithmetic problems and because the articulation of number words involves basic phonetic and language systems, the associations in LTM between problems and answers should be represented, at least in part, in the same phonetic and semantic memory systems that support word processing and word retrieval. Any neurodevelopmental disruptions in the functioning of these systems might then place the individual at risk for SLI and for difficulties in the arithmetical processes that are supported by the same systems, such as arithmetic-fact retrieval.

On the basis of these theoretical considerations and on the comorbidity of MD and dyslexia, I argued that these disorders co-occur "because of a common underlying neuropsychological deficit, perhaps involving the posterior regions of the left hemisphere. At the cognitive level, this deficit manifests itself as difficulties in the representation and retrieval of semantic information from LTM. This would include fact-retrieval difficulties in simple arithmetic and, for instance, word-recognition and phonological-awareness difficulties in reading" (Geary, 1993, p. 356). Although it now appears that fact-retrieval deficits are more varied than originally believed, as described earlier, recent results confirm that children with comorbid MD and dyslexia are slower at accessing number and word names from LTM than are their normal peers and show arithmetic fact retrieval deficits (Geary et al., 2000). In short, there is reason to believe that SLI and certain forms of MD will be related and the approach used by Donlan to address this relation represents a very useful methodological adjunct to the approach used by Jordan et al. and in our research.

Delazer provides an excellent overview of prominent neuropsychological models of number and arithmetic processing and makes an important contribution to this literature. The basic strategy in this area is to examine the performance of individuals with dyscalculia—number and arithmetic deficits associated with overt brain injury—on an array of number, counting, and arithmetic tasks and note systematic deficits as well as intact functions. As noted by Delazer, most of these studies have focused on arithmetic-fact retrieval and the ability to execute arithmetical and other procedures (e.g., borrowing). Many of these studies show a double dissociation between these two competencies, with some individual showing fact-retrieval deficits and age-appropriate pro- cedural competencies and others showing the opposite pattern (e.g., Temple, 1991). Delazer contributes to this literature, and to our general understanding of arithmetical and mathematical development, by demonstrating dissociations between conceptual knowledge in arithmetic and algebra and retrieval and procedural competencies. In other words, conceptual knowledge appears to be represented in different cognitive and neural systems than are arithmetic facts and procedural knowledge. Caution about this conclusion is warranted, because the interpretation of the dissociative data is confounded by potential schooling effects (see Baroody, chap. 1, this volume; Geary, 2000).

Delazer's research and that of other neuropsychologists also has the potential to inform research on MD and vice versa. Many of the cognitive deficits associated with dyscalculia appear to be the same as those found with children with MD (Geary, 1993; Geary & Hoard, 2001). Although these patterns do not necessarily indicate that children with MD have suffered from some form of overt brain injury, they do suggest subtle neurodevelopment abnormalities. Neuropsychological and neuroimaging research on individuals with dyscalculia thus provides a framework for future neuroimaging research with individuals with MD. For instance, neuropsychological studies suggest that the difficulty that some children with MD have in retrieving arithmetic facts and words from semantic memory might be the result of abnormalities in the posterior regions of the left hemisphere and some subcortical structures, such as the basal ganglia (Dehaene & Cohen, 1991). Difficulties in inhibiting irrelevant associations, in contrast, might result from abnormalities in the prefrontal cortex (Geary & Hoard, 2001). Neuroimaging studies of individuals with MD will enable a test of these hypotheses. At the same time, the tasks used to study normal arithmetical development and children with MD, such as the nonverbal calculation task described by Jordan et al., might be fruitfully used in future studies of dyscalculia.

Heavey's chapter provides an excellent overview of arithmetical savants, that is, individuals who show moderate to severe general cognitive or social deficits but show exceptional abilities in one or several areas of arithmetic or mathematics. These studies again demonstrate that many quantitative abilities are modular, that is, distinct from social (e.g., language) and general cognitive abilities. The studies are also consistent with the neuropsychological research in that dissociations between different arithmetical and mathematical competencies are common among savants, that is, they may show exceptional abilities in one area, such as algebra, and poor abilities in another, such as geometry. In other words, even if quantitative abilities are distinct from language and other abilities, submodules, so to speak, of quantitative competencies would be expected (Geary, 1995). In any case, the studies of arithmetical savants speak to the importance of memorizing many basic facts and procedures, as well as understanding numerical relations (cf. Baroody & Tiilikainen, chap. 3, this volume). They also speak to using this knowledge as a platform for solving related but novel problems, in much the same way that Dowker described for the relation between computational abilities and estimation.

The most intriguing of Heavey's findings is that many savants show an early obsession with counting and number. Of course, such an obsession is probably needed to memorize the facts and procedures and to understand the conceptual nature of numbers that support savant abilities. More important, this developmental pattern suggests an inherent interest in early quantitative features of the environment that is separate from language and other social interests. An early interest in quantitative features of the environment, in turn, is in keeping with the position that very basic number, counting, and arithmetic skills represent an evolved domain of mind (see Geary, 1995, 2001; Gelman, 1990). Some scholars propose that evolved cognitive abilities are initially skeletal in structure. That is, the basic cognitive and neural systems are inherent but these systems are fleshed out, as children play, explore the environment, and interact socially. In theory, these early experiences flesh out skeletal competencies so that they are adapted to the local ecology and social group. If there is a rudimentary but inherent number, counting, and arithmetic system, then children should naturally engage in counting and other quantitative activities, which, in turn, would flesh out this system. Perhaps this inherent system is intact in many arithmetical savants and provides, along with an obsession with numbers, the foundation for acquiring their exceptional but nonevolved (e.g., an understanding prime numbers) arithmetical competencies.

Future Directions

The previously described chapters highlight both the progress that has been made in recent years in understanding children's arithmetical development and the sources of variation in this development, and point to future directions for research in mathematics education and mathematical cognition (see also Ashcraft, 1995). Issues centered on children's mathematics education are especially controversial these days and will likely require many years of further research on children's mathematical learning and constructive dialog before we fully understand how to best teach mathematics to children. The Ambrose et al.

and Fuson and Burghardt chapters approach this issue from a constructivist position, whereas others, myself included, have advocated a greater emphasis on direct instruction and practice of basic skills (Geary, 1995, 2001). The emphasis on direct instruction and practice is based on an evolutionary approach to cognition and cognitive development. Specifically, the argument is that the mind and brain were not designed to learn much of modern arithmetic and mathematics. Thus, social discourse and other activities sufficient for the acquisition of evolved competencies, such as language, are not likely to be sufficient for learning non-evolved competencies, such the base-ten system. In any case, the resolution of these conflicting views will require theoretical advances in conceptualizing children's cognitive and academic development—as illustrated by Dowker's chapter—and empirical research to determine the most effective combination of approaches for teaching different aspects of mathematics.

Another area of future direction, and an area illustrated by all of the remaining chapters, involves research on individual and group differences in arithmetic development and competencies. One example is research on learning disabilities in mathematics, as described by Jordan et al., which has been largely ignored, in relation to the extensive research efforts devoted to reading disabilities (Lyon, Alexander, & Yaffe, 1997). The other chapters also touched on important topics for future research as well, including the relation between language disorders and MD (Donlan), the identification of the cognitive and neural systems underlying MD and dyscalculia (Delazer), and the development of arithmetic competencies in other special populations, such as autism (Heavey). Other directions for future work include the development of assessment techniques that go beyond identifying children with low achievement and provide information about the source of their poor achievement. That is, we need assessment tools that are sensitive to the specific deficits (e.g., fact retrieval) of children with MD. Furthermore, we need to develop remedial techniques for use with these children and individuals with dyscalculia.

Acknowledgments

The writing of this chapter was supported, in part, by a Summer Research Fellowship awarded to the author by the Research Council of the University of Missouri at Columbia.

References

Al-Uqlidisi, A. (1978). *The arithmetic of Al-Uqlidisi* (S. A. Saidan, Trans.). Boston, MA: D. Reidel. (Original work published 952 A.D.).

Ashcraft, M. H. (1995). Cognitive psychology and simple arithmetic: A review and summary of new directions. *Mathematical Cognition, 1*, 3–34.

Baroody, A. J. (1992). The development of kindergartners' mental-addition strategies. *Learning and Individual Differences, 4*, 215–235.

Barrouillet, P., Fayol, M., & Lathulière, E. (1997). Selecting between competitors in multiplication tasks: An explanation of the errors produced by adolescents with learning disabilities. *International Journal of Behavioral Development, 21*, 253–275.

Bull, R., & Johnston, R. S. (1997). Children's arithmetical difficulties: Contributions from processing speed, item identification, and short-term memory. *Journal of Experimental Child Psychology, 65*, 1–24.

Cobb, P., Yackel, E., & Wood, T. (1992). A constructivist alternative to the representational view of mind in mathematics education. *Journal for Research in Mathematics Education, 23*, 2–33.

Dehaene, S., & Cohen, L. (1991). Two mental calculation systems: A case study of severe acalculia with preserved approximation. *Neuropsychologia, 29*, 1045–1074.

Dehaene, S., Spelke, E., Pinel, P., Stanescu, R., & Tsivkin, S. (1999). Sources of mathematical thinking: Behavioral and brain-imaging evidence. *Science, 284*, 970–974.

Fuson, K. C. (1990). Conceptual structures for multiunit numbers: Implications for learning and teaching multidigit addition, subtraction, and place value. *Cognition and Instruction, 7*, 343–403.

Gallistel, C. R., & Gelman, R. (1992). Preverbal and verbal counting and computation. *Cognition, 44*, 43–74.

Geary, D. C. (1993). Mathematical disabilities: Cognitive, neuropsychological, and genetic components. *Psychological Bulletin, 114*, 345–362.

Geary, D. C. (1994). *Children's mathematical development: Research and practical applications.* Washington, DC: American Psychological Association.

Geary, D. C. (1995). Reflections of evolution and culture in children's cognition: Implications for mathematical development and instruction. *American Psychologist, 50*, 24–37.

Geary, D. C. (2000). From infancy to adulthood: The development of numerical abilities. *European Child & Adolescent Psychiatry, 9*, II11–II16.

Geary, D. C. (2001). Darwinism, schooling, and mathematics: How an understanding of evolution can inform instructional practices. In T. Loveless (Ed.), *Curriculum wars: Alternative approaches to reading and mathematics. The great curriculum debate: How should we teach reading and math?* (pp. 85–107). Washington, DC: Brookings Institute.

Geary, D. C., Hamson, C. O., Chen, G.-P., Liu, F., Hoard, M. K., & Salthouse, T. A. (1997). Computational and reasoning abilities in arithmetic: Cross-generational change in China and the United States. *Psychonomic Bulletin & Review, 4*, 425–430.

Geary, D. C., Hamson, C. O., & Hoard, M. K. (2000). Numerical and arithmetical cognition: A longitudinal study of process and concept deficits in learning disabled children. *Journal of Experimental Child Psychology, 77*, 236–263.

Geary, D. C., & Hoard, M. K. (2001). Numerical and arithmetical deficits in learning disabled children: Relation to dyscalculia and dyslexia. *Aphasiology, 15*, 635–647.

Geary, D. C., Hoard, M. K., & Hamson, C. O. (1999). Numerical and arithmetical cognition: Patterns of functions and deficits in children at risk for a mathematical disability. *Journal of Experimental Child Psychology, 74*, 213–239.

Geary, D. C., Liu, F., Chen, G.-P., Saults, S. J., & Hoard, M. K. (1999). Contributions of computational fluency to cross-national differences in arithmetical reasoning. *Journal of Educational Psychology, 91*, 716–719.

Gelman, R. (1990). First principles organize attention to and learning about relevant data: Number and animate-inanimate distinction as examples. *Cognitive Science, 14*, 79–106.

Hirsch, E. D., Jr. (1996). *The schools we need: Why we don't have them.* New York: Doubleday.

Huttenlocher, J., Jordan, N. C., & Levine, S. C. (1994). A mental model for early arithmetic. *Journal of Experimental Psychology: General, 123*, 284–296.

Jordan, N. C., & Montani, T. O. (1997). Cognitive arithmetic and problem solving: A comparison of children with specific and general mathematics difficulties. *Journal of Learning Disabilities, 30*, 624–634.

Loveless, T. (Ed.). (2001). *Curriculum wars: Alternative approaches to reading and mathematics.* Cambridge, MA: Harvard University Press. *The great curriculum debate: How should we teach reading and math?* Washington, DC: Brookings Institute.

Lyon, G. R., Alexander, D., & Yaffe, S. (1997). Progress and promise in research in learning disabilities. *Learning Disabilities, 8,* 1–6.

Mayer, R. E. (1985). Mathematical ability. In R. J. Sternberg (Ed.), *Human abilities: An information processing approach* (pp. 127–150). San Francisco: Freeman.

Ostad, S. A. (1997). Developmental differences in addition strategies: A comparison of mathematically disabled and mathematically normal children. *British Journal of Educational Psychology, 67,* 345–357.

Siegler, R. S. (1983). Five generalizations about cognitive development. *American Psychologist, 38,* 263–277.

Siegler, R. S. (1996). *Emerging minds: The process of change in children's thinking.* New York: Oxford University Press.

Siegler, R. S., & Stern, E. (1998). Conscious and unconscious strategy discoveries: A microgenetic analysis. *Journal of Experimental Psychology: General, 127,* 377–397.

Sophian, C. (1997). Beyond competence: The significance of performance for conceptual development. *Cognitive Development, 12,* 281–303.

Starkey, P. (1992). The early development of numerical reasoning. *Cognition, 43,* 93–126.

Temple, C. M. (1991). Procedural dyscalculia and number fact dyscalculia: Double dissociation in developmental dyscalculia. *Cognitive Neuropsychology, 8,* 155–176.

Glossary of Abbreviations

ASCM = Adaptive-strategy-choice model (the second simulation of addition development developed by Robert Siegler and colleagues).

CCA = Concrete counting-all (a counting-based addition strategy that involves direct modeling).

CCS = Concrete counting-all shortcut (involves the use of pattern recognition, including finger patterns, to short-cut direct modeling of addition situation).

CAF = Abstract counting-all beginning with the first addend (involves determining the sum by counting both addends in successions starting with "one" and, thus, requires a keeping-track process).

CAL = Abstract counting-all beginning with the larger addend (the same as CAF, except a child counts up to the cardinal value of the larger addend first and, thus, may reduce the keeping-track process).

COF = Abstract counting-on from the first addend (involves starting with the cardinal value of the first addend).

COL = Abstract counting-on from the larger addend (involves starting with the cardinal value of the larger addend).

DOAM = Distribution-of-associations model (the first simulation of addition development proposed by Siegler and colleagues).

fMRI = Functional magnetic resonance imaging.

LTM = Long-term memory.

MCAF = Abstract modified counting-all beginning with the first addend (like CAF except that a child uses fingers or other objects while counting both addends).

MCAL = Abstract modified counting-all beginning with the larger addend (like CAL, except that a child uses fingers or other objects while counting both addends).

MCOF = Abstract modified counting-on from the first addend (like COF, except that a child uses fingers or other objects to represent the first addend and while counting out the second addend).

MCOL = Abstract modified counting-on from the larger addend (like COL, except that a child uses fingers or other objects to represent the first addend while counting out the second addend).

MD = Mathematical difficulties (including children with low achievement or learning disabilities).

min = another name for COL derived from early chronometric studies because the reaction time required to implement the strategy correlated with the size of the minimum addend.

RT   =   Reaction time.

SCADS   =   Strategy choice and discovery simulation (the latest computer model of addition development proposed by Siegler and colleagues).

SLI   =   Specific language impairment.

STM   =   Short-term memory.

sum   =   Another name for abstract counting-all (CAF or CAL) derived from early chronometric studies because the reaction time required to implement the strategy correlated with size of the **sum** of the two addends.

Author Index

467

Subject Index

B

Babies, See Infants

Back-to-basics movement, 17, 26

Backup strategies, See also Counting-all,
Counting-on, Invented strategies
for single-digit arithmetic,
Reasoning strategies, 49–51, 102,
103, 203–228, 362, 367, 375, 387, 389,
391, 392–398

Balance scale, 184

Base-ten concept, See Grouping (-by-
ten) concept or structure

Base-ten blocks, 232–234, 267, 268,
270–301, 455

Basic (number) facts, See Basic number
combinations, Number facts,
Retrieval

Basic number combinations, See also
Mental calculation with single-digit
numbers, Mental representation,
Reasoning strategies, Retrieval,
xvi–xix, 6, 7, 9, 25, 38, 39, 41–44, 53,
55, 68, 76, 101–104, 106–110,
189–202, 203–228, 361–370, 375, 378,
379, 385, 391–398, 445, 446, 454,
458–460
addition, xviii, 7, 35, 38–43, 52–55,
59–61, 67, 68, 84, 85, 87, 97, 106, 109,
110, 389–391, 396
division, 212, 391, 396
multiplication, xvii, xviii, 102,
189–202, 212, 389–391, 396
subtraction, xviii, 7, 55, 59, 104, 106,
211, 212, 391, 396

Bilingualism, 449

Binary view (of addition), See also Part-
whole (addition) concept or
problems, 47, 62, 150–156

Borrowing, See Regrouping

Brain, See Brain damage or dysfunction,
Neuroimaging

Brain damage or dysfunction, See also
Dyslexia, Dyscalculia, xix, xx, 14,
54, 55, 107, 208, 209, 247, 259, 375,
385–407, 456, 457, 459, 460

Brain imaging, See Neuroimaging

Brian injury or lesions, See Brain
damage or dysfunction

C

Calculation, 9, 25, 35–56, 75, 104, 105,
109, 117, 212–221, 235, 236, 250, 251,
260, 271–292, 311–323, 330, 332,
359–363, 370, 371, 373, 385–434,
454–457, 461

California standards, 27, 28

Cardinal-count concept, 64, 81, 115, 181,
203, 207, 213, 340–342

Cardinality principle or rule, See Count-
cardinal concept

Carrying, See Regrouping

Change-add-to (addition) concept or
problems, See also Word problems,
45, 47, 59, 96, 97, 137, 144, 150-156,
164, 184, 307, 319, 327, 362, 363, 371

Children with mathematical learning
difficulties (MD) or low
mathematics achievement, xix, 9,
43, 44, 89–91, 262, 359–384, 457–460,
462

Children with neurological disorders,
375, 413, 460

Children with specific language
impairments (SLI), xix, 337–358,
459, 460

Chinese instruction, instructors, or
learners, 29, 59, 60, 105, 190, 207,
222, 232–235, 271, 449, 450, 445, 455,
456

484

E

Equal-grouping problems, See Groups-of (multiplication), Measurement division, Partitive division

Equal partitioning, 308–310

Equals
equals sign, xvii, 9, 161–186, 447, 450
operator meaning, 161–165, 172–176, 178–182, 184
relational meaning, 161–165, 169, 172–176, 179–185, 447

Error analysis, 41, 102, 103, 117, 197–201, 260, 373, 375, 389, 390, 400, 401

Estimation, xviii, 9, 41, 46, 58, 75, 91, 95, 98–101, 109, 140, 143, 243–266, 387, 390, 391, 396, 442, 456, 457, 461

Estimation strategies, xviii, 90, 100, 101, 251–255

Event-related potential (ERP), See also neuroimaging, 55

Everyday Mathematics, 23

F

Fact retrieval, See Basic number combinations, Factual knowledge, Number Facts, Retrieval

Factual knowledge, See also Basic number combinations, Declarative knowledge, Retrieval, 99, 101, 104, 107, 110, 189–202, 203–228, 386, 396, 397, 402–404, 435, 436, 442, 445–447, 454, 455, 460, 461

Fingers, See Counting, fingers

Flexibility, xi, xii, xvi–xx, 2–4, 15, 24, 31, 44, 45, 101, 103, 224, 233–244, 262, 267, 289–292, 300, 301, 360–362, 385, 397, 398, 426–430, 442, 445, 446

Fractions, xviii, 9, 21–23, 25, 28, 231, 236, 237, 241, 301, 332–334, 367, 394, 411–413, 415, 449

Functional magnetic resonance imaging, See also Neuroimaging (fMRI), 55

G

Generalization, See also Transfer, xvi, xvii, 7, 16, 44, 50, 52, 61, 77–79, 84, 88, 89, 94, 104, 109, 145, 146, 377, 427

Goal sketch, See also Metacognition, 52, 56, 79, 80, 82–86, 88–90, 94–96, 98

Grouping (-by-ten) concept or structure, See also Base-ten blocks, Multiunit concept of number, Place value, Regrouping, xviii, 59, 60, 84, 230–232, 234, 239, 268, 279, 283, 290, 301, 310, 311, 314, 316–319, 322, 330, 332, 333, 341, 363, 371, 373, 375, 376, 454, 456, 462

Groups-of (multiplication) concept or problems, See Word problems, xviii, 306–308, 310–319, 415, 416, 424

Growth-curve modeling, 378

H

History of mathematics education, xii, xv, xvi, 35–38, 244, 437, 439, 440

I

Illegal strategies, 16, 62, 78, 79, 86, 88–92, 94, 274–278, 284–286, 399–401, 455

Incidental-learning theory, See also Problem-solving approach, 5, 7, 8, 21, 22, 300

Incorrect strategies, See Illegal strategies

Individual differences, 43, 44, 51, 53, 58, 67, 68, 78, 93, 94, 193–201, 203, 211, 212, 219–222, 246, 258, 362–368, 370–373, 376–378, 437, 440, 445, 446, 451, 462

Infancy, 56–58, 95, 110, 127, 141, 143, 338–340, 359

number, Number lines; Number patterns; Number sense; Numeral reading, Numeral writing, Protoquantitative knowledge or thinking

Numeracy, See Computational fluency

Numeral reading, 341, 342, 353–355, 385, 387

Numeral writing, 59, 60, 273, 282, 293, 385, 387

O

Operations on numbers, See Arithmetic concepts or principles, Backup strategies, Basic number combinations, Computational fluency, Illegal strategies, Invented strategies for multidigit arithmetic, Invented strategies for single-digit arithmetic, Mental calculation with multidigit numbers, Mental calculation with single-digit numbers, Procedural knowledge, Written calculation with multidigit numbers, Written calculation with single-digit numbers

Operator meaning or view, See Equals, operator meaning

Overlapping strategies
    overlapping phases, 45, 100
    overlapping waves model, 76, 223

Other-names-for-a-number concept, 75, 148, 170

P

Part-whole (part-part-whole addition) concept or problems, See also Schema, part-whole, Relations, part-whole, Word problems, 47, 97, 129, 134, 143, 144, 146–156

Part-whole meaning of fractions, 235

Partitive division, See also Word problems, 307–310

Peer interaction or peer-peer dialogue, See Small-group work

Phonetic memory, See Memory

Place value, See also Base-ten blocks, Grouping (-by-ten) concept or structure, Multiunit concept of number, Regrouping, 229, 230, 232–234, 237, 239, 268, 270, 276, 277, 282, 289, 290, 299, 301, 310, 311, 330, 354–356, 360, 363, 370, 371, 373–376, 399, 449

Practice, xvii, xix, 6, 7, 9, 10, 17, 21, 25, 39–41, 53, 54, 77, 84, 86, 427, 453, 456

Privileged-domain hypothesis or view, 5, 10, 111, 117, 118, 339, 340

Problem-size effect, 39, 45, 47, 48, 139–141, 150, 153, 193–200, 204–207

Problem solving, See also Word problems, xi, xii, xix, 13, 14, 19–21, 23, 24, 27, 28, 88, 170, 271, 370, 378, 379, 438, 455, 456, 458, 459, 461

Problem-solving approach, See also Incidental-learning theory, 17–22, 24, 453, 454

Procedural knowledge, xi, xvi, 4, 10–16, 19, 24, 25, 56, 75, 76, 81, 87, 111, 116, 117, 208, 222, 267, 342, 346–351, 356, 360, 362, 374, 377–379, 385–387, 389, 395, 397–402, 404, 435, 436, 442, 447, 455, 456, 460, 461

Productive disposition, See also Attitudes, Mathematical proficiency, xix, 19, 26–29, 267

Protoquantitative knowledge or thinking, 62, 64, 128, 135, 137, 138, 143, 144, 146, 148, 151, 155